Also by Tom Hayden

REUNION

Random House · New York

Reunion
A Memoir

TOM HAYDEN

*Grateful acknowledgment is made to the following for permission to reprint previously
published material:*

COLUMBIA PICTURES PUBLICATIONS: Excerpt from the lyrics to "The City of New
Orleans" by Steve Goodman. Copyright © 1970, 1971 Buddah Music, Inc., and
Turnpike Tom Music. Rights assigned to SBK Catalogue Partnership. All rights
controlled and administered by SBK U Catalog, Inc. International copyright
secured. Made in USA. All rights reserved. Used by permission.

HARCOURT BRACE JOVANOVICH, INC.: Excerpt from "Little Gidding" in *Four Quartets* by
T. S. Eliot. Copyright 1943 by T. S. Eliot. Renewed 1971 by Esmé Valerie Eliot.
Reprinted by permission of Harcourt Brace Jovanovich, Inc., and Faber and Faber
Ltd.

HEREFORD MUSIC: Excerpts from the lyrics to "Oh America" by Holly Near.
Copyright © 1973 Hereford Music. Words and Music by Holly Near. From the
album *Hang in There* on Redwood Records.

PANTHEON BOOKS: Excerpts from *Memories, Dreams, Reflections* by C. G. Jung. Recorded
and edited by Richard and Clara Winston. Translation copyright © 1961, 1962, 1963
by Random House, Inc. Reprinted by permission of Pantheon Books, a division of
Random House, Inc.

THE NEW YORK REVIEW OF BOOKS: Excerpt from "The Occupation of Newark" by
Tom Hayden, which appeared in the August 24, 1967, issue of *The New York Review
of Books*. Copyright © 1967 Nyrev, Inc. Reprinted with permission from *The New
York Review of Books*.

Library of Congress Cataloging-in-Publication Data
Hayden, Tom.
    Reunion: a memoir.

    Includes index.
    1. Hayden, Tom. 2. Legislators—California—
Biography. 3. California. Legislature. House—
Biography. 4. United States—History—1961–1969.
5. United States—Social conditions—1960–1980.
I. Title.
F866.4.H39A3 1988 328.794′092′4 [B] 87-43224
ISBN 0-394-56533-9

Manufactured in the United States of America

23456789

First Edition

BOOK DESIGN BY LILLY LANGOTSKY

TO TROY, VANESSA,
AND THE CHILDREN
OF THE SIXTIES GENERATION

Good morning, America,
How are you?
Don't you know me?
I'm your native son.

—STEVE GOODMAN, "The City of New
Orleans," as sung by Arlo Guthrie

We are people of this generation, bred in at least modest comfort, housed now in universities, looking uncomfortably to the world we inherit. . . . We would replace power rooted in possession, privilege, or circumstances by power and uniqueness rooted in love, reflectiveness, reason and creativity. As a social system, we seek the establishment of a democracy of individual participation. . . . If we appear to seek the unattainable . . . then let it be known that we do so to avoid the unimaginable.

—*The Port Huron Statement*

He remembered how once, as a youth, he had compelled his father to let him go and join the ascetics, how he had taken leave of him, how he had gone and never returned. . . . Yes, that was how it was. Everything that was not suffered to the end and finally concluded, remained, and the same sorrows were undergone.

—HERMAN HESSE, *Siddhartha*

Yes, there was the sun and poverty. Then sports, from which I learned all I know about ethics. Next the war and the Resistance. And, as a result, the temptation of hatred. Seeing beloved friends and relatives killed is not a schooling in generosity. The temptation of hatred had to be overcome. And I did so.

—ALBERT CAMUS, "The Wager of Our Generation" from
Resistance, Rebellion and Death

When you have chosen your part, abide by it, and do not try to weakly reconcile yourself with the world. . . . Adhere to your own act, and congratulate yourself if you have done something strange and extravagant, and broken the monotony of a decorous age.

—EMERSON, *Essays: First Series,* "Heroism," passage underlined by Robert Kennedy

Acknowledgments

First, I want to thank my family for supporting my hermitlike behavior for several months in 1987. I sat locked in a study, listening hundreds of times to U-2 and Paul Simon tapes, reviewing wonderful books I hadn't read for twenty-five years, sinking deeply into an earlier phase of my life. I began to understand how my wife temporarily goes into a different character when she is acting. It was difficult to live in my past while carrying out my life and responsibilities in the present. I thank my family for their respect.

A book begins with inspiration but ends like a construction project. The invaluable overseer of construction was Mary Burbidge, who located my oldest friends, searched libraries for out-of-print books, and expertly typed several drafts at all hours of the night. Ivy Colbert and Julie Coren spent countless hours reading FBI files and collecting photographs.

Lynn Nesbit, my agent, and Peter Osnos, my editor at Random House, gave me confidence and direction at crucial points. Mitchell Ivers also did a skillful job of editing.

I depended on the judgment and memory of many friends along the way: Hal Adams, Joan Andersson, John Balzar, Elizabeth Becker, Unita Blackwell, Paul and Heather Booth, Connie Brown, Robert Coles, Andrea Cousins, Geoff Cowan, Paul Cowan, Rennie Davis, Shirley Davis, Eric Dey, Dick and Mickey Flacks, Jean Fritz, John Froines, Bruce Gilbert, Todd Gitlin, Richard Goodwin, Anne Grimm, Casey Hayden, Sam Hurst, Jim Jackson, Sharon Jeffrey, Mildred Jeffrey, Doris Kearns (Goodwin), Christopher Kennedy, Courtney Kennedy

(Ruhe), Ethel Kennedy, Joseph Kennedy, Kerry Kennedy, Robert Kennedy, Jr., Carol Kurtz, Jim Lau, Jim Lawson, John McAuliffe, Bob Moses, Bob Mulholland, Jack Newfield, Lana Pollack, Richie and Vivian Rothstein, Bob and Marion Ross, Mike Royko, Jerry Rubin, Betty Ryan, Havi Scheindlin, Bobby Seale, Marilyn Shallet, Dan Siegel, Attila Shabazz, Steve Smith, Mort Stavis, Studs Terkel, Maria Varela, Anne Weills, Lennie Weinglass, Leni Zeiger. Most of these people never achieved celebrity status from their commitments; in a sane society, they would deserve it.

I also want to thank Dick Flacks, Todd Gitlin, Mary King, and Jim Miller for the understanding I obtained from their recent books on the sixties.

I am also indebted to attorneys Marty Echter and Ira Lowe, who succeeded in obtaining seventeen thousand pages of FBI files under the Freedom of Information Act.

Contents

Introduction

It is twenty years since I battled on the streets of Chicago.

The sun is shining over Santa Monica, and I am playing my usual position, right field, and batting seventh for the Hollywood Stars. Although none of us are from Hollywood, and none of us stars, we keep the name alive to respect tradition. The old Hollywood Stars played in our parents' time in the legendary Pacific Coast League. At forty-seven, I am the oldest player on the oldest team. It is the fifth year since I started playing hardball again; the desire surged back when my son, Troy, who is now fourteen, entered the Little League. Tomorrow I will coach his team in Culver City, yelling to him, as my father did to me, "That's okay, son. That's the way. You can do it, son. You can do it. That's the way."

I am married to a real Hollywood star: a beautiful, intelligent, infinitely creative woman. For one who never counted on a stable future, I have been a lucky man these past fifteen years. Jane Fonda is many persons—actress, rebel, fitness expert—but I love her most as the mother of Troy and Vanessa, not to mention a budding network of godchildren. Like myself, she loves the fullness of a family life she never had. Our own parents gone, we are, at middle age, the oldest of our clans.

I am a California State assemblyman, preparing to seek a fourth term. The state's Republicans attack me as if the Chicago conspiracy trial had never ended, but I am reelected every two years. I chair the state Assembly's Labor Committee and its Subcommittee on Higher Education, bemused to be dealing with many of the issues that drew me to public service as a Michigan student thirty years ago.

This life has unfolded in surprising ways. I grew up in the Midwest, gave my first speech in favor of the Peace Corps, and had my first nationally circulated article published in *Mademoiselle*. Ten years later I was accused of violent conspiracy against the American government. I pondered a future of prison, exile, perhaps martyrdom. Then, suddenly, my accusers—Richard Nixon, John Mitchell, et al.—were driven from office under a public cloud of scandal. It took a long time for me to accept that far from becoming a police state, the system had worked. During this long odyssey I tried to make the world fit my idealistic American values and met discord, then rejection, from my parents as well as the state. I reacted in ways which compromised my best judgment, and I experienced what Albert Camus called "the temptation of hatred." In the end, I was fortunate to reach a point of return, of personal and political reintegration. My life, and my original values, resurfaced intact from the depths of alienation. I was damaged, but a survivor.

I never expected to be where I am today. I know that challenges, surprises, and perhaps tragedies still lie ahead, but mine has been a full life already. How did I come from the social and personal breakdowns that seemed the historic fate of the sixties to my lucky balance of the eighties? What was achieved, and what was lost, in those times? Have they become merely a nostalgic memory, or can we, with a new maturity, apply the positive visions of the early sixties to the future?

Deep somewhere in my mind, I have been writing a memoir of the sixties for more than a decade. Although writing usually comes easy to me, I kept finding that I couldn't express myself and continually set my notes aside.

I suppose I needed distance, a period of time for those turbulent experiences to settle, as a fisherman waits for a clear surface of water. I needed to look back on my extended youth from a new stage of life. My parents' deaths in 1982 and 1986 led to a personal reassessment, and when I realized that 1988 would mark two decades from the watershed year of my generation, I began writing without stop. The result is this narrative outpouring, partly personal, partly historical. I have tried to convey my reflections as an ancient storyteller would, not by philosophizing, but by recounting those times as they happened on personal levels, letting the reader participate through his or her own memory, searching with me for the meaning.

There is an ongoing struggle today to define the sixties. On one side are conservatives who agree with President Reagan that the Vietnam War was a "noble cause" and the sixties an ignoble decade. On the other are those old associates of mine (Abbie Hoffman comes to mind) who adamantly express no regrets about their activities in those years. In between are a majority of Americans, confused about what they went through and what it means now. There are large numbers for whom the sixties are only a televised graphic—of police clubs and rock music, napalm and candles, a mystery waiting to be unlocked.

My own view is that life is a journey in which we draw different conclusions about the truth at different vantage points. Faithfulness to one's values is important, but changing one's mind, regretting a past view, or feeling remorse are not betrayals if the goal is truth. In fact, not changing one's mind often means being frozen in the past.

My goal in this book is to tell the truth, as I felt it then and as I view it now. I have tried to reflect on history through the lens of personal experience and explore personal life in a social context. Because writing about oneself is inherently self-serving, I have tried to be harder on myself than others. My simple hope is that this book will stir a therapeutic chord in all those who lived through, or are still affected by, the unique trauma of the sixties.

Throughout, I have inserted official commentary by U.S. intelligence agencies, usually the Federal Bureau of Investigation, in the form of memos obtained through Freedom of Information Act suits in the mid-seventies. For fifty years, J. Edgar Hoover pursued alleged subversives through FBI counterintelligence programs. When blacks rioted in 1919, he declared that communists fomented them into being "openly, defiantly assertive" of their racial equality. In 1968, he sent the media evidence of what he called the "scurrilous and depraved nature" of the New Left. Hoover began his files on me before I became an activist, when in a fall 1960 editorial for the Michigan *Daily* I innocently criticized his equation of patriotism with right-wing causes as simplistic. I include Hoover's intelligence memos, whatever their factual distortions, to instill the sense of being personally hunted throughout the sixties by the very authority figures I was raised to respect.

Hoover was obsessed with three forces of the sixties that are central to this book: the New Left, Robert Kennedy, and Martin Luther King (and through King, the entire civil rights movement). It has become fashionable to consider Hoover, who died in 1972, an aberration in his mania to crush dissent. But I now wonder if Hoover didn't represent the subliminal impulses of my parents' generation, the dark underpinnings of an open society. He started from the basic assumption that everything American was good and that any significant troubles were caused by outside influences. This guaranteed that the sixties protests, which arose from authentic American roots, would be met by misunderstanding, mismanagement, and overreaction. I believe that positive personal and political behavior depends on constructive responsiveness to protest from respected authorities. When the official response is an uncaring rigidity, the healthy character of protest gives way to the aggressive impulses lurking in us all.

I look back on the sixties with a sense of idealism rusted by tragedy. Starting with moral quests for elementary civil rights, we were drawn into a whirlpool that revealed both the dizzying possibilities and the devastating limits of hope and reform. A generation that stood originally for life was haunted again and again by the furies of death. Our best national leaders were slain, denying us our natural expectations for reform and twice destroying the prospect of a progressive presidency. Martin Luther King changed my life when, as a student editor in 1960, I interviewed him on a picket line. John Kennedy lifted my hope when he spoke in Ann Arbor that same year of a Peace Corps. In tears of rage, I stood over Robert Kennedy's coffin only eight years later. It seemed a full lifetime had passed, and I was not yet thirty. My personal future would have been different had these men lived; so would the lives of most Americans. I feel the loss more poignantly as the passing years fill with the emptiness of missed possibilities.

We ourselves became infected with many of the diseases of the society we wished to erase. Thinking we could build a new world, we self-destructed in a decade. Claiming love as our motivation, we could not subdue hate. Questing for community, we met our egos. That burden of self-imposed failures weighs heavily too.

And yet, tragedy illuminates the "nobility of human existence," as Rollo May has written. Despite outer repression and inner absurdity, we of the sixties accomplished more than most generations in American history. We ended a century of racial segregation in the South. We created the most massive resistance to a war in the nation's history. We reformed universities, and politically enfranchised millions of young people. We created a consciousness of women's rights and environmentalism. We strengthened democracy with a powerful ethic of participation.

Though humbled, I remain an optimist and an enthusiast for my original ideals. I believe that the world would be far more tragic without the effort, however naïve, to improve life in the here and now for those who suffer, that there is no more important vocation than to be a reformer. Facing the fundamental arbitrariness of life, we all can choose between competing impulses: the illusion of immortality by the amassing of worldly power or the stumbling effort to improve the quality of life through stubborn love. We chose the latter path in the sixties, and it was the right choice.

Broken connections seem more common than reunion and resurrection in the human experience today. I hope that the ideals of the sixties, tempered by harsh experience, can have a second coming in our lifetime. That, I believe, is the common wish of those like myself who sought so desperately to change the wider world, who suffered agony amid achievement, and who devoutly wish a wiser consciousness to those who follow.

GROWING UP IN THE FIFTIES

Part One

Title: THOMAS EMMETT HAYDEN
Character: SECURITY MATTER—STUDENTS FOR A
            DEMOCRATIC SOCIETY (KEY ACTIVIST)

Background:

a. Birth Date
Records of the Detroit, Michigan, Department of Health, 2 Wood-
land Avenue, Detroit, reviewed by SA [Special Agent] ▮▮▮▮▮ ,*
on December 17, 1964, contained certificate of birth number
26198 pertaining to THOMAS EMMETT HAYDEN. This birth record indicates that THOMAS EMMETT HAYDEN was born on December 11, 1939, at Women's Hospital, Detroit. His father was
JOHN FRANCIS HAYDEN, 5826 Iriquois, Detroit, age 33, race
white, born Milwaukee, Wisconsin, and employed as an accountant at the Fort Shelby Hotel, Detroit. His mother was listed as
GENEVIEVE GARITY, age 32, race white, address 5826 Iriquois,
Detroit, occupation housewife, and born at Oconomowoc, Wisconsin.

b. Citizenship Status
Subject is a United States citizen by virtue of birth as set forth
above.

c. Education
High School
On January 21, 1965, ▮▮▮▮▮ , Dondero High School, 709 North
Washington, Royal Oak, Michigan, advised SA ▮▮▮▮▮ that the
subject had attended Dondero High School from September of
1954 until June of 1957, at which time he graduated. He was
enrolled in the college preparatory course and resided at 710
Catalpa, Royal Oak. On January 21, 1965, ▮▮▮▮▮ , Counselor,
Dondero High School, Royal Oak, Michigan advised SA ▮▮▮▮▮
that he recalled the subject during the time he had attended
school there. He advised that HAYDEN had been editor of the
high school paper and was a very intelligent student, but that
HAYDEN refused to recognize authority and to accept discipline
at the school, and was therefore a source of some trouble to the
school administrator. He advised, however, that he had no reason
to question the loyalty of the subject . . .

*Material deleted by the FBI.

1. "Stand By Me"

In 1987, I took my thirteen-year-old son to *Stand By Me*, a nostalgic film about young boys growing up in the fifties in a small American town surrounded by farmland with railroad tracks running through, building themselves a tightly knit inner world from which they explored the unknowns of life. The movie is an ode to the decade in which I grew up. As we were leaving the movie theater, holding hands, my son looked at me and said, "Gee, what a great time to grow up, Dad. You can't grow up like that anymore."

The fifties were indeed the best of times for the pursuit of the American dream: After the trauma of two decades—Depression and Holocaust, two wars, the atomic bomb—came a dawn of stability and peace, along with a rising living standard, low inflation and unemployment rates, and an explosion of single-family housing in the newly expanding suburbs. America seemed to be making progress on the still-nagging problem of racism through Supreme Court school desegregation orders. For a minority who cared, McCarthyism had wrecked the Left, but what need was there for radical dissent and doomsday talk in this time of middle-class prosperity? The Cold War was preferable to a hot one, the mere testing of atomic weapons far better than their use. Cuba was still a place for pleasures of the flesh and Vietnam an unknown word in the political vocabulary. For Americans who had come through the embattled thirties and forties, it was a time of respite, when one could finally sit back and enjoy the good things in life, and raise one's children well.

It was in this atmosphere of affluence and affirmation that we who were the future radicals of the sixties grew up. In little more than a decade, Richard Nixon and Spiro Agnew would appeal to our "middle-American" parents to abandon their children.

My father and mother, John Francis Hayden and Genevieve Isabelle Garity, were born at the end of the Victorian age, met each other in the Depression, and brought me into the world on December 11, 1939, while Hitler's armies were marching across Europe. Their forebears—seven of my great-grandparents—journeyed through history's mists from such barren places as county Monaghan in old Ulster, looking for a better life during the potato famines and British persecutions of the mid-nineteenth century. The "boat people" of their time, they settled the Wisconsin frontier, sent their sons to die in the Civil War, and became peaceful dairy farmers, small merchants and laborers in towns with the Indian names of Nashota and Oconomowoc.

My father's family, composed of Haydens and Foleys, migrated to Milwaukee, where they would eventually root themselves in the emerging Irish-American political structure. An ancient drawing of James Foley's General Store and Post Office, in a Wisconsin historical magazine, gives a vivid flavor of the community of immigrants. Construction workers resting on their picks and shovels, women holding children, and a small knot of men in conversation are mingled around the big wood porch. James Foley, with a white beard, garbed in a full-body apron, presides over the neighbors at the front door. Someone is pasting up a campaign poster promising PROSPERITY FOR ALL. Atop the store is the Foleys' house, with a porch where two women are hanging out laundry to dry. A man is sitting in a rocking chair reading the newspaper. A large overhanging tree provides a welcome shade for the goings-on.

My grandfather, Thomas Francis Hayden, was a founder and teacher at the Milwaukee Law School, a tax assessor in the city's 3rd Ward, a justice of the peace, and director of the Northwestern Building and Loan Association. His wife, Mary Ducey Hayden, died of a liver disease at forty-four, when my father was just seven years old, leaving three sons and a daughter who were raised by a series of housekeepers while my grandfather worked his long hours. Perhaps because he had little or no mother's love, my father grew up to be a young man who could not easily show emotion. He either kept his feelings to himself or expressed them through a cynical humor that became his popular trademark. Over six feet tall, slender, and prematurely balding, he dressed in conservative suits and narrow ties. My favorite photo of him shows a smiling outdoorsman in fishing boots.

Following his father's example, my father trained himself in accounting and fiscal management, attending college in Milwaukee for two years. In his political leanings, he was a populist conservative, reflecting his philosophy of self-reliance in a harsh world. He regarded Franklin Roosevelt, for example, as a "blue blood" who wanted to spend everyone *else's* money for his social programs. He believed the little man was always being cheated by larger forces. For my father, charity and generosity were essentially private acts, at the heart of friendship and personal character, not public policies to be trusted to government bureaucrats. A man of wit and charm, he lived inside a small and private world of good friends in Milwaukee, many of them friends for life.

My mother, a tiny bird of a woman, grew up in a family of eleven brothers and sisters in Oconomowoc, about thirty miles west of Milwaukee, a town that has grown from five thousand to ten thousand residents in the last generation. Unless and until it is swallowed in one single suburb running between Milwaukee and Madison, the town will remain one of those flashbacks to small-scale America that lie invisibly off our freeways. The big white house and barn that my mother grew up in, and where I spent my summers, still stands on the main street of Oconomowoc, though it is now a doctor's office. When I return for a visit, I cannot believe that twelve children could fit on top of each other in this two-story structure with its big front porch. But fit they did, and happily, mainly due to my grandmother Ethel, an imposing, blue-eyed, silver-haired woman who greatly influenced me with her combination of stern authority and laughing warmth.

Grandma Ethel, or Nannie, as I called her, raised the brood alone. Her husband, Emmett Garity, who had left dairy farming to work in the canneries, was killed in an industrial explosion at the Carnation plant when my own mother was thirteen. Nannie was provided with only $4,300 from Carnation for the emergency medical expenses incurred when my grandfather died. Nevertheless, she provided for her family all through the Depression, opening a local restaurant, earning income as a midwife, and organizing her kids to take assorted jobs. Difficult as it seems in retrospect, this family was a happy and productive one.

A change was occurring in the status of women, who had gained the vote in 1920. My mother was drawn by this tide of independence into the flapper era and the urban life-style of Milwaukee, where she found work at a newspaper as a secretary with a promising future. There she met my father and, after a couple of years of dating, married him in 1937. For employment reasons, they moved to Detroit, the center of the dynamic automobile industry, which was ushering in a new era of industrial growth. My father worked behind a desk at a downtown hotel until he was hired as an accountant by Chrysler, the corporation that employed him for the rest of his life.

Loyal and patriotic Americans, they lived in a world of big families, small communities, and permanent circles of friends. They seemed content with their place. Even today, for example, nearly all my parents' siblings, and their children and grandchildren, live within an hour's drive of Oconomowoc. They sought no greener grass nor new frontiers; as far as they were concerned, they were already home. They took the American dream as their goal and their working lifetimes as the means to achieve it. Their ambition centered not on themselves or on public service, but mainly on their children.

My father was an Eisenhower Republican and my mother a Democrat who loved Adlai Stevenson. By nature, they were populists who resented any elites who took advantage of ordinary people, but their feelings were expressed in no public form. Neither religion nor ethnicity were powerful forces to be transmitted to me; their Catholicism was more formal than fervent, and their Irish roots were little noted. They were completing their transition into the mainstream of America, where a middle-class identity was replacing previous immigrant qualities. The values they did impart were those they tried to live by: education, enterprise, fairness.

My young life was secure. Other than being born half-strangled by my own umbilical cord (which some might argue formed my paranoid view of the world), nothing interrupted the comfort and tranquillity of our family. In 1943, when I was four, my father was drafted into the marines and my parents decided not to tell me until the last moment. My earliest memory is seeing my father drive his Plymouth down the driveway on his way to the marine base in California, and then seeing the garage burn down. The events were in fact separate, but my memory has fused them as a single sequence: disappearance, fire, loss, war.

Perhaps I also learned then that happy appearances are not what they seem. In any event, I learned to adjust; my mother and I took a train across the continent to join my father at his base in San Diego.

I loved the marines. I could sing every verse of "From the Halls of Montezuma" without understanding a word of it. I collected scrap metal for the war effort. I kept the silhouettes of Japanese planes on my wall and watched for their rumored attack on the California coast. My nightmares were about Japanese suicide squads running wild through our cities, with me leaping out of bed, climbing fences, and running in terror as they chased behind, shrieking, "Banzai!" One day the news came that my favorite uncle, Cy Garity, the only member of our family to see combat, had been killed in the Pacific by the accidental firing of a .30 caliber machine gun. It scared me.

When I wasn't absorbed with the war, I played and ran wild in the great outdoors that the canyons of San Diego then provided. I experienced earthquakes and caught lizards. I loved trying to hide from my father when he came home from the base, and I was delighted when he always found me.

But something about the military life changed my father. When the war ended, my mother and I left by train for home while he chose to hitchhike back to Michigan, to be by himself and to see the country he had never explored. While he had not been sent overseas, the excitement and camaraderie of the war years was enough to break and replace the moorings of family which bound us together before. When he finally returned home, he became president of the American Legion post in Royal Oak, a flat and spreading suburb twelve miles north of Detroit, where we settled down in a tree-shaded, two-story, white wood-frame house. Spending more time at the Legion Hall socializing with other veterans seemed to allow my father to relive the war he missed. For many of them, life seemed to have peaked somewhere in the Pacific. Like many of them, my father began drinking heavily.

One night, my father came home from the Legion post very drunk. My mother had taken the precaution of locking the door to their bedroom; I'm not sure why. I heard, seemingly for an hour, my father violently banging a hammer on their door and shouting for it to be opened. I never was able to tell either of them what I heard, trembling under my sheets that night. But not long after, my father came into my room, whispered to me that he and Mom were getting divorced, kissed me for the first time I could remember, and quietly was gone. I was scared and in slight shock as I watched him drive away for one more time the next morning. My intuitive sense was that life was very much out of control.

But my mother was as stalwart as she was tiny. She took protective care of me for the next seven years, never even involving herself with another man, working as a film librarian in the local school system. She worked there for twenty years, never missing a single day even when she was sick. She wanted to prove that a single woman could support herself, make her house and car payments, and save for her son's future.

Despite their divorce, my parents cooperated in raising me, implicitly teaching me that deep personal divisions could be submerged for a larger purpose. I attended school and lived in Royal Oak with my mother, but took off to Detroit for baseball, football, and hockey games on weekends with my father, and we all shared a family dinner every weekend. In the summers I worked on a fishing boat in northern Michigan and traveled with my father on forays into the Canadian wilderness after trout, walleyed pike, and muskellunge. My father and I were never closer than when there wasn't much to say but a lot to do together.

I attended the Shrine of the Little Flower Church and parish school for eight years, virtually the only boy in my neighborhood to attend Catholic school. The shrine, whose magnificent carillon dominated the skyline of Woodward Avenue, was not the usual Catholic parish. The pastor was Father Charles Coughlin, one of the most influential and controversial Americans of my parents' generation. At three o'clock every Sunday afternoon in the Depression era, thirty million Americans turned on their radios to hear the poetic baritone commentaries of this Irish priest. Father Coughlin's mass following competed with those of President Roosevelt and Huey Long for American hearts and minds. A good friend of Joseph Kennedy's, Coughlin was an advocate of the social gospel and an early New Deal supporter on economic and labor issues, but his populist condemnations of "international finance" became stridently anti-Roosevelt and anti-Semitic in the late thirties, notably after he was exposed by Treasury Secretary Henry Morgenthau for secretly speculating in the silver markets himself. After Coughlin helped form a third party against Roosevelt in 1936, the president expressed a severe displeasure at Church interference in politics, even threatening to unleash the Internal Revenue Service on the financial books of the American archbishops. In 1940, bowing to the orders of Church superiors, Father Coughlin ended his broadcasts. Since this obvious muzzling of Royal Oak's most famous citizen was something of a local scandal, especially embarrassing to a proper person like my mother, the story was never told to me until I discovered it many years afterward.

Later in the sixties, many friends and observers seemed to find a revelatory meaning in my having worshiped at the altar of this pro-fascist priest. Perhaps it is true that his jeremiads against communism, or his adoring sermons about the Catholic charity efforts in Vietnam, later had some reverse effect on me, but I was a very young man and had little grasp of the concepts behind his mesmerizing Irish voice. I remember none of the substance of what he said. I do recall all of us crying at our desks one day when the school authorities chose to broadcast live General Douglas MacArthur's radio speech in which he said, "Old soldiers never die, they just fade away." MacArthur, who wanted to escalate the Korean bloodshed, was the melodramatic hero and President Truman the villain at the Shrine of the Little Flower.

But politics was over my head. More pressing were the questions of how much truth to tell the priests in the confessional (would you actually go to hell forever if you left anything out?) and how to endure the long wooden rods of corporal punishment when we broke the rules in class (for such venial sins as throwing ink at each other, or clapping when ordered to remain quiet). Thinking back, I recall more hours on my knees for punishment after school for fooling around in class than for acts of contrition in the pews of the shrine.

Like many young Catholics, I was bonded to the Church more

by a fear of hell than by a positive identification with its values or works, much like the trembling character in James Joyce's *A Portrait of the Artist as a Young Man*. When I switched (for geographic reasons) to Royal Oak's public high school in ninth grade, most of my new school friends were Protestants or Jews, and I found it personally hard to believe that they were bound for hell or that my salvation was promised by the accident of birth. At the local pizzeria, my friends and I would incessantly debate whether there was a heaven and hell and go home still unsettled and uncertain.

As the years passed, my growing sense of independence would dictate a break with the kind of Church hierarchy that had made me live in such anxiety for so long. Only after making that break, and only after exercising real freedom of choice, would I later be able to accept the moral and miraculous content of religious faith as demonstrated by ministers in the civil rights movement, farm-worker priests in California, Catholic draft resisters during Vietnam, martyred nuns in El Salvador, Solidarity priests in Warsaw, and Jewish *refuseniks* in the Soviet Union.

In the Royal Oak area there lived many families better off than ours. Some of my neighborhood friends were Protestants whose fathers were executives in Detroit or sons and daughters of Jewish professionals and businessmen living in the adjacent community of Huntington Woods. I was less self-assured than they were. My Catholic upbringing and a late puberty made me mildly uncomfortable around girls and at social occasions in general. Shyness combined with stern warnings from my mother made me reject smoking, which was then a teenage rite of passage. I was skinny and, to make matters worse, I developed acne.

Though I enjoyed all sports, baseball was my game. I kept (and still have) a letter from my grandfather Thomas when I was one year old, urging me to hurry and grow so I could "play baseball with the big boys." I tried to compensate for my scrawniness through an aggressive drive to make the big play and to win. I remember watching my father play American Legion ball. He was older than the other players, but he had quick wrists and could slap the ball hard. I went with him to Tiger games at Briggs Stadium, or I listened on the radio. Al Kaline was my Tiger hero, but my greatest thrill was seeing Satchel Paige throw two innings of scoreless relief. We visited the Baseball Hall of Fame in Cooperstown, New York, and spent summers visiting big-league ballparks, getting autographs from such greats as Stan Musial and Leo Durocher. When I was old enough, I joined the Little League and played for the Dunn's Camera Shop team. I usually played outfield, but I wanted to pitch. With my skinny left arm and long fingers, I could throw a roundhouse curve ball into a right-handed hitter's fists. One June evening in 1952, when I was twelve, the Dunn's Camera coach sent me to the mound. I remember being nervous and wild in the first inning, but after every pitch I could hear my father's voice urging me on from the dark stands behind home plate. "That's OK, son. That's the way. You can do it, son. You can do it. That's the way." He steadied me. I pitched a no-hitter.

LEFTY GETS MIDGETS 1ST NO-HITTER, the headline read the next day:

> Southpaw Tom Hayden has a fond memento of his very first pitching assignment in the Royal Oak midget baseball league. He fashioned a 7–2, no-hit victory for Dunn's Camera of Royal Oak Elks. He struck out 15 and walked four, facing 26 batters in the six-inning stint. It was the season's first no-hitter in the 12-and-under circuit which plays every weekday night at RO Memorial Park.

My baseball career had peaked, however; it was downhill from then on. There were a few more miracle moments, like hitting a bases-loaded single up the middle against the biggest kid on the block—Billy Freehan, who became an all-star catcher for Detroit, dominating the World Series in 1968. But I just didn't have the size and talent, and my parents preferred that I put down the ball and pick up the books.

As early as second grade, I was known as a brainy, advanced kid, winning spelling contests and reading aloud to enraptured nuns from St. Thomas Aquinas, my Catholic namesake. My mother, who always loved to tell stories about my childhood, would later inform anyone who asked, "Tommy always had his nose in a book."

I attended George A. Dondero High School, a red-brick, two-story structure enrolling over two thousand students in half-day sessions. Tennis courts, a football stadium and track, baseball fields, and a railroad line sprawled behind the school to the edge of the quiet residential neighborhood where I lived, three blocks away. I took classes in the mornings, engaged in school activities immediately afterward, and played baseball, football, and basketball in the streets until darkness. I traveled a creative and offbeat path in school, befriending a group of students who shared a sense of being different and a mood of independence. About a dozen of us soon became a tight-knit clique and would remain friends for many years. Some of our parents were professionals, but most were just entering the middle class: an owner of a tile store, the proprietor of a gun shop, a commercial artist for a department store. By religion, they were mainly Protestant, including one girl, Lynn Buri, whose family was fundamentalist (in college, I went to a Billy Graham crusade with her and interviewed the famed minister). A smaller number were Jewish, and I was one of the few Catholics.

We gravitated toward the interesting, less traditional, younger teachers at the school. I don't quite understand why, but we saw ourselves naturally as leaders, shaping the school's purposes. Years later, when I asked one of these friends, Jim Lau, for an explanation, he simply said, "We felt we could do things that needed doing and get attention. We didn't want to just cruise the drive-ins." Another, Shirley Davis, remembered: "It fit with our energy. There were kids in trouble, kids absorbed in sex, kids who cruised. I liked the cruising, but the student activities touched the intellectual energy in me. My father only went to fourth grade, but there was no doubt that I was going to college."

Some of us ran successfully for class offices, participated in the school plays, and produced our own variety shows. I became editor of the school paper, *The Acorn.* On the side, we edited an underground paper, *The Daily Smirker,* a takeoff on the *Daily Worker* but with the satirical content of *Mad* magazine. " 'Tis a bright day that brings forth the adder" was the logo on its masthead. I wrote a column that included comments such as "If the girls' necklines keep dropping and the hemlines keep going up, the next fad will be wide belts" and "Life started in a cell and a lot of them end there."

More seriously, we raised college scholarship money. "A free public education is America's first line of defense against its enemies," I noted in an editorial, advocating that every class raise funds through dances, parties, and passing the hat, "in

order that several deserving students could be
toward a college education each semester." W
cut, polished, and created an Oak Stump trop
of the football game with our crosstown rival
today. Lau and I even made and sold "mad
of papier-mâché and painted in Dondero's b
give a boost to the school spirit at Royal Oak
the hats that the local Royal Oak paper, the
the "mad hatters":

> These two boys have started a new fad at Ro
> of their ingenuity can be seen at any football
> been selling like wild fire and Tom says that
> out of business.

I had crushes on most of the girls in the
serious girlfriend was a Dondero junior, A
was, at sixteen, very sexy. Honey-haired a
she came from a more affluent corporate fan
side of town, who, for some reason, thought
the status ladder, and undeserving. My moth
were snobs. Sex for me in those days consiste
combined with desperate groping in the se
Nash Rambler (whose gear stick was hard
troubled relationship, not only because of
cause Anne was an independent, romantic
while I worked as a camp counselor in w
learned that she was involved with one of i
Collier, a coeditor of *The Smirker*. Throbb
drove angrily nonstop across the state, plan
in the direction of a hospital with my bas
when I arrived at his front door and confr
and embarrassment cooled me off. He apo
would forget it. Obviously, I never have;
became more wary of the world.

But as for political consciousness, I was st
letters at the school's door declared ENTEI
FORTH TO SERVE. Our senior class mott
Kennedy's inaugural address: "To do mor
the world does for you, that is success." T
embraced. I recall being impressed by idea

r than by ideology or party label. While I cried with my
-school classmates at MacArthur's farewell, I also felt
thing idealistic about Adlai Stevenson in the same year,
;h most of my friends were for Eisenhower. For years I was
ious to the social problems under my nose, so it has never
rised me that it takes a long time for someone to become
ically aware.

ie anticommunist hearings of Senator Joseph McCarthy
: in high gear when I was in seventh grade, but I was
ing baseball in the Little Leagues. I attended an all-white
school, watched black maids waiting for buses on street
ers in the morning and evening, but I had no sense of
m. I only later learned that we had moved out of downtown
oit because the blacks were moving in. The Little Rock
ol crisis and the Montgomery bus boycott both happened
ng high school; both went right by me.

lid have a sense of "in" and "out" based on class. The nearby
suburbs of Birmingham and Grosse Pointe produced young
and women who were too beautiful to touch, who drove
cars while I borrowed my mother's Rambler, and who
e immaculate white to tennis matches on clay courts while
)layed in mismatched outfits on cracked cement courts with
al nets. I knew those people were different—they didn't
1 seem to sweat.

ut for young people like myself, the world of the fifties was
ely a one-dimensional one, as Herbert Marcuse would define
ter, lacking in any real social conflict. There seemed to be
r one reality, one set of values: those of the comfortable
dle class. There being only that one reality, life was already
;rammed: You went to high school, then college, then got
ried and found a job. If you were talented or lucky, you
ht move from your hometown to a more exciting life on one
he coasts.

was the boring and prearranged nature of this existence
caused the first tiny irritations that would grow to rebellion
r. Among my circle of friends, there was little excitement or
llenge in the life given us, nothing much to dream about or
forward to. As we grew in creativity and independence, we
stifled by parents, schools, and church. We sneered at
ownnosers," those students who would do anything to
ise the teachers. It seemed as if everything important had to

be discussed in our cars or pizza parlors, not within the proper institutions. You couldn't discuss sex with your parents; you couldn't argue whether God existed with the nuns; you couldn't discuss how boring school was with your teachers. Instead, we had to memorize answers to everything, whether we agreed or not, and found we could be rewarded and advanced only in this way.

None of this subterranean searching developed into political awareness or a desire for action, but it did spawn a little clique of nonconformists. Our sense of life's absurdity was best captured by Alfred E. Newman, the grinning idiot on the cover of *Mad* magazine who was always asking "What, me worry?"—which could have been the motto of suburban America in the fifties.

As a farewell graduation prank, I wrote an editorial with a concealed message mocking the high school. The actual editorial was a sincere call for greater commitment to building the new scholarship fund. "Every concept which advocates change must undergo crucial stages on the pitted road to acceptance," I prophetically noted. But the initial letters of each paragraph, when read vertically, spelled *go to hell*. It was an impulsive gesture, very much in the consciousness of a *Mad* devotee. But I made the mistake of gleefully telling someone, who in turn passed the word to the school administration. The officials were shocked and overreacted. I was called into the principal's office and threatened with expulsion from school only a few days before graduation.

I was stunned, more by having to confess the deed to my parents than by the possibility of not graduating. For my mother and father, this incident probably initiated a dread feeling of "losing" their son and the American dream of advancement. But for the moment, they supported me even while finding my behavior incomprehensible. They put the blame on unidentified "influences" (which meant this would not have happened at Catholic school with its greater discipline and punishment) and devoted themselves to pleading with the principal for my cap and gown. I didn't know how to protest, picket, or boycott—and could only faintly explain what disturbed me about the school—so I too sheepishly begged for another chance.

Finally, a compromise was worked out: no cap and gown, no

honor pins, no participation in the graduation ceremony, just a straight diploma. And as a deterrent to future misbehavior on my part, the principal vowed to keep a record of the incident in the school files for five more years, promising to remove it only if I corrected my ways. I don't know if the file is still there, because I never went back.

Five years later, I was in jail in Georgia.

I graduated with good grades, if not a cap and gown. My parents always wanted me to go to college and, fulfilling their dreams for me, I applied to the University of Michigan in Ann Arbor and was admitted. Though my maverick instincts were emerging in high school, I still expected to receive a liberal education and pursue a career in journalism. Despite my detours into pranks and skepticism, I was still following the American dream. The inscriptions on the high school graduation pictures we gave each other capture the flavor of those intense, enjoyable, creative years and suggest a future filled with more of the same:

I hate to say what I would be like if I
had not met you. Probably normal. Now
I'm a damned pervert . . . thanks for
being such a good friend and blood brother.
Jim [Lau]

To the boy I pick as the most likely to
succeed. Of course, I never pick a winner
though. Seriously, I think you're a great
guy and who knows? Maybe this time I did
pick a winner!
Shirley [Davis]

I'd really hate to see you become one of
those damn college guys because individuality
looks good on you.
Jim [Collier]

You have been a real hit and have done a great
job for the Acorn and Smirker—every class
needs a good promoter.
Martha [Cavanaugh]

You are the exception, Tom. There is no
one I so despise at times and adore at
others. You are funny and yet sad, far away
and yet I feel like I know you so well.
You're the hardest person to say good-bye
to. I don't know why. I can't write how I
feel—do you understand, Tom? I can never
forget you.

Good-bye
Lynn [Buri]

There were several alternative cultural models beckoning to those of us who in a few years were to become activists: the fictional character Holden Caulfield, the actor James Dean, and the writer Jack Kerouac. The life crises they personified spawned not only political activism, but also the cultural revolution of rock and roll. Elvis Presley, it is said, watched James Dean in *Rebel Without a Cause* a dozen times. These characters, in their different ways, were responding to the human absurdity and emptiness of the secure material life parents of the fifties had built.

Holden Caulfield, the antihero of J. D. Salinger's 1951 novel, *The Catcher in the Rye*, is a young man who narrates his life from the mental institution in which he is confined. Unable to communicate with his parents and teachers, he is kicked out of Pencey Prep for a failure to adjust to what he considers the "phoniness" of the class and dormitory atmosphere. For Holden, school is "full of phonies, and all you do is study so that you can learn enough to be smart enough to be able to buy a goddam Cadillac someday, and you have to keep making believe you give a damn if the football team loses, and all you do is talk about girls and liquor and sex all day, and everybody sticks together in these dirty little goddam cliques."

But there is a caring side to Holden's character, especially toward underdogs and innocents. When confronted with whether there was any one person or thing he had ever liked, he singles out a "skinny little weak-looking guy" who jumped out a school window and killed himself after being humiliated by bullies. Holden would like to escape to the countryside, live by a brook, and, in his dream of dreams, be the "catcher in the rye," rescuing little kids as they run over "some crazy cliff." But it is precisely this attempt to be gentle and humane that makes Holden a loser in the "game" of life. Unable to be the kind of man required by prep schools and corporations, Holden can find no alternative to the reality he so deeply understands and goes over the "crazy cliff" himself.

The hospitalized Holden was the first image of middle-class youth growing up absurd; James Dean provided a visual image of living defiance. *Rebel Without a Cause* was a film about *pre*-political awareness, that of middle-class "juvenile delinquents." It begins with a drunken Jim Stark, played by Dean, lying in the street cuddling a toy monkey. When the police arrest him, he laughs as if being tickled. Like Holden Caulfield, part of him is still in the child's world of gentleness and play. And as with Holden's insanity, Jim Stark's delinquency is simply a reaction to the world of parents, teachers, and police who are themselves truly delinquent as models for youth. When Jim Stark is cut in a knife fight, he looks for support from his father and is told, "In ten years you'll look back on this and wish you were a kid, you'll laugh at yourself for thinking this is so important." His mother doesn't want her son to "get involved," even though he is a witness to the car-crash death of a friend in a "chicken" race.

The whole film abounds in cosmic metaphors, beginning with a scene in the school planetarium where stars are exploding into extinction "in bursts of gas and fire" (just as in the deadly chicken races). The teacher lectures that "man, existing alone, seems to be an episode of little consequences"—to which Plato (played by Sal Mineo) responds: "What does *he* know about man alone?" The lonely character of Judy (Natalie Wood) joins Plato and Stark as a counterfamily against an uncaring society. The climax of the film finds Dean trying to protect the innocent and neurotic Plato against his own internal demons, but failing as Plato runs straight into the bullets of paranoid policemen. At the end, aware that they have lived a delusion, Stark's parents painfully reconnect with their son.

Jack Kerouac's *On the Road* was published in 1957, the year I graduated from high school. In the coming three years, I too hitchhiked to every corner of America, sleeping in fields here, doorways there, cheap hotels everywhere, embracing a spirit of the open road without knowing where I wanted to go. Kerouac's fictional character Dean Moriarity was based on Neal Cassady, a real person who lived on the outer edges of cultural change

throughout the sixties, finally dying in February 1968 by a railroad track in Mexico, wasted from alcohol and sleeping pills. In
the late fifties, however, Cassady (or Moriarity) became a powerful rebel, a combined image of the cowboy/explorer corralled in
the new suburbia that now occupied the once-vast American
frontier.

The "new frontier" was on the road, not in the suburban life
that tamed the human spirit. The personal instinct to take risks
and journey into an emotional and intellectual wilderness had
to be expressed. The universities provided no answer. They
were "nothing but grooming schools for the middle-class nonen-
tity which usually finds its perfect expression . . . in rows of
well-to-do houses with lawns and television sets in each living
room with everybody looking to the same thing and thinking of
the same thing. . . ." Kerouac aroused a deep desire "to prowl
in the wilderness" among young readers like myself: "The only
people for me are the mad ones . . . the ones who are mad to live,
mad to talk, mad to be saved . . . the ones who never yawn or
say a commonplace thing, but burn, burn, burn like fabulous
roman candles exploding like spiders across the stars. . . ."

Traces of this same theme—the pressure to surrender youthful dreams in order to "grow up"—were present throughout a
short story I wrote titled "A Misty Kind of Perfect Thing," not
long after high school. When I look at the story today, it seems
to mirror the choices I saw between careerism and idealism;
there seemed to be no satisfaction in the first and no outlet for
the latter.

In my story, I was a successful forty-one-year-old foreign
correspondent who felt a deep sense of personal failure at not
having ever written a serious novel or play. The other main
character, Martha, was modeled after a friend in my high school
clique, Roberta Braman. She was a beautiful, pensive class
leader who developed an honest frustration over what do with
her life. In our real lives as well as in my short story, we acted
together in a stage version of *Lost Horizon,* which takes place in
the utopian world of comfort and harmony, Shangri-La. In the
play, the main character—Conway—leaves Shangri-La to seek
his own self-determination. Martha and I stayed behind, afraid
or incapable of going on this further journey. "He was leaving
high human achievement," I wrote, "and going on somewhere
still 'beyond.' "

In my story, Martha and the journalist pursued their careers separately after leaving school. He succeeded in a material way, but felt confused and incomplete. "What the hell, I figured, maybe higher commitments and searchers like Conway were things to leave behind in the schools with ivy walls and halls of books." He and Martha met two more times. Once, she was singing at a "mediocre" place in New Orleans. "We drank and laughed, and for a minute I thought it was college and high school dreaming again."

By their next contact, Martha was getting married to a show-business manipulator (I described him as a "swollen man") in order to advance her career. It hurt to see her wind up with this operator.

> Once when we were young, it might have been to both of us a misty kind of perfect thing to chase by moonlight. . . . Conway wasn't simply a person; he was a different, much larger entity. . . .
>
> I still felt myself a failure at creative work, although I sold two mediocre stories to American magazines. That was the extent of it. Forty-one years; two short stories. Forty-one years. One third of each day at work, one third in bed, hours lost in eating, weeks lost in projects, years lost growing up and growing old, in the petty drabberies of the everyday nonsense, leaving precious little time to write a poem or love a woman. I had done neither for many years.

My story ended with Martha killing herself with a pistol.

> Her last words on the way to the hospital, according to the papers, were something like "Connie . . . Connie . . ." Of course, I knew she meant "Conway" but . . . it wouldn't mean anything to those who have no feelings or blood or dreams. They couldn't comprehend the thing that hurt and killed her, and I can see it only dimly. She couldn't be better than the world of swollen men, and so she took her life. I alone can see it, that perfect misty state, and on a night like this I can almost reach for it again. I have not cried in years but perhaps I will this night. I have ridden over the bad spots before. I don't know, as she used to say. Maybe I'll start to write that play again.

Looking at this sentimental if sophomoric story thirty years later, it is obvious that I thought Shangri-La was Royal Oak and the United States of the fifties—a material paradise with all things provided, all choices made, everything laid out neatly. But it was designed, in my words, to promote "mediocrity." Anyone who was too different was classified as deviant or delinquent. Who would "stand by me"? Not the authorities. They had built a world barren of the sorts of challenges that one could truly aspire to. To make money, to obey the law, to say your prayers was not enough. Nothing met the need for enrichment and adventure. A fine, normal upbringing in America had left me anticipating a lifetime of unfulfilled expectations.

Eventually this resentment of the future that had been prepared for us would find its way into a desire for self-determination, and as I found that others shared the same condition, the personal feelings would lead in time into politics.

THE MOVEMENT BEGINS

Part Two

2. The Conversion: Ann Arbor, 1957-61

Ann Arbor is one of the classic college towns where the sixties generation first commingled, where it was inspired and then alienated, and where it formed its distinct identity. It was the birthplace of Students for a Democratic Society, the Peace Corps, and the Vietnam teach-ins. None of this could be anticipated on the morning in September 1957 when my father drove me there. The leaves were brilliantly changing colors as we passed over the Huron River, by the charming arboretum, and through the shaded old neighborhoods toward the towers of the university. I felt a nervous excitement at the prospect of my sudden independence. With its twenty thousand students trudging through its sprawling domain, the university was vastly more imposing than the cloistered culture of Royal Oak only fifty miles away. After dropping off my belongings, including one gray suit, a tennis racket, and my first shaving kit, and checking into the registrar's office, we shook hands and said good-bye, smoothing over the moment's magnitude, showing no emotion while promising to call each other regularly.

In those days, large research universities like Michigan were beginning to dominate the national academic scene. After the *Sputnik* launching in 1957, the federal government began pouring vast sums into scientific research, accelerating an emphasis on research, scholarly publications, and scientific method, even in the "softer" disciplines of sociology, psychology, and political science.

Providing a quality liberal arts education for undergraduates became distinctly secondary in the research university's priorities. At the same time, unprecedented numbers of my generation were enrolling in universities; total enrollments doubled from 3.7 million to 7.8 million by the end of the decade (and kept climbing to 9.6 million by 1973). Setting a tone which has continued to prevail, the universities adopted what Alexander Astin has called the "reputational" and "resources" definitions of excellence. Campus achievement was based on numbers of prestigious researchers, scholarly publications, PhDs, national security contracts, laboratory square footage, big-ten championships—everything but the best-quality education for the two thirds of the students who were undergraduates.

This shift was noted by Clark Kerr, president of the University of California, in a controversial book, *The Uses of the University*. His own university, Kerr pointed out, was the "world's largest purveyor of white mice" and would "soon have the world's largest primate colony"; in addition, it had one hundred thousand students, including thirty thousand at the graduate level, but spent "much less than one third of its expenditures directly on teaching." Labeling the new multipurpose educational conglomerate a *multi-versity*, Kerr was sensitive enough to see it was a "confusing place for the student" who "has problems of establishing his identity and sense of security within it . . . the casualty rate is high . . . the walking wounded are many." But he also, saw the multi-versity as inevitable and was optimistic at the end of the fifties that "employers are going to love this generation . . . they are going to be easy to handle. There aren't going to be any riots."

Kerr and others like him clearly underestimated the conflict for new students like myself between our heady expectations and the reality of student life. There was a kind of congested loneliness on the campus of Ann Arbor. Educational historian Frederick Rudolph said of the generation then entering college that we knew the "experience of being abandoned, but somehow the sensations of self-reliance never seemed to follow." Throngs of incoming freshmen like myself, leaving home for the first time, were required to live in massive, unimaginative dormitories that reminded us of urban public housing projects. Making us feel like dots on a grid, the dorms, called quadrangles, were divided into floors, corridors, and numbered cell-like rooms just large enough for two persons.

At Ann Arbor, there was North Quad, South Quad (where I lived), East Quad, and West Quad. Nearly thirteen hundred young men were cramped into my sterile quad, arbitrarily assigned to roommates, whether we preferred each other's company or not. An eleven P.M. curfew was imposed. The cafeteria food was processed and served with, it seemed, as little flavor or nutritional value as possible. After freshman year, students moved out and began to discover that the surrounding community was just as curiously lacking in adequate student services. Off-campus housing was hard to find; parking was scarce; even the libraries lacked enough seats.

The barracks culture, with its twin lacks of privacy and community and its sink-or-swim message, extended to the academic sector as well. Lecture classes typically involved a distant professor speaking from notes, three times weekly, to a jammed crowd of three hundred or more students. Smaller classes usually were led by teaching assistants (TAs), young graduate students who earned part-time income by teaching seminars where one could learn what was intended to be taught in the larger lectures. While many of these TAs were stimulating, they had no training as teachers (neither did the senior faculty). Instead, they were serving as apprentices to full professors, usually helping on research and writing projects for their bosses while trying to eke out their own doctoral thesis.

It soon became obvious to most freshmen that we were unwanted orphans in the educational hierarchy, an amorphous mass of bodies that might someday become academic sorcerer's apprentices. While their dollars subsidized the research-oriented university, our parents remained blissfully content that their children were obtaining the presumed status and educational benefits of the UM degree. Not surprisingly, about 40 percent of undergraduates never finished their four-year programs in this impersonal atmosphere, a dropout rate that remains the same today.

As in high school, I managed to find a creative handful of professors and classes. I briefly explored the fraternities, but found them absorbed in mindless partying and status comparisons. In a short time, I involved myself with the institution that would become my own fraternity, the Michigan *Daily*.

Located just behind the administration building in a digni-

fied, ivy-covered, two-story, red-brick building, the *Daily* was
the most important student institution on the campus and perhaps the most respected university paper in the United States
(competing each year with the *Harvard Crimson* and a few others
for national awards). It attracted not only would-be journalists
but, more important, many thoughtful student activists who
wanted to challenge the university to live up to its educational
ideals. The paper was professional; reporters and editors
worked every day from noon until late at night. It rolled off the
presses on the first floor at about three A.M. and circulated six
days a week among tens of thousands of university readers. It
was intensely competitive, with reporters rising from rookie
status to important news "beats," then to desk-editor positions,
until finally the outgoing senior editors proposed their succes-
sors to a university board of control. When I walked across its
massive, churchlike stone floors, I was impressed, even in awe
of the place. An older friend from Royal Oak, Joanie Katz,
introduced me around and made sure that I was provided interesting assignments. Within a year I was spending more of my
time at the *Daily* than in classrooms, eating take-out while editing copy there late at night, even falling asleep on the desks.

Through the *Daily*, I formed a picture of the university and
the world. I met and wrote about Governor G. Mennen "Soapy"
Williams, the liberal Democrat who later served in the Kennedy
administration. I covered regents' meetings, where I watched
conservative corporate leaders in action for the first time. I
followed the dismissal of an allegedly Marxist professor and
learned the history of the McCarthy period. I wrote about racial
discrimination in the fraternity system and learned what it was
to be attacked by outraged alumni. I covered a minor riot against
dormitory food and crusaded successfully to prevent the arbitrary expulsion of the two ringleaders. Along the way, I was
fortunate to find supportive professors in political science, philosophy, and journalism, who intellectually complemented my
work on the paper. I formed an idealistic conception of the
university as a "community of scholars" and, in a stream of
editorials, measured it critically against the impersonal bureaucratic atmosphere.

I rose in the *Daily*'s ranks, drawing the concerned interest of
administrators, the respect of some of the faculty, and a growing
following among many students. My parents were pleased at the

prospect of my becoming a professional journalist, and I imagined myself as a future foreign correspondent. But as in high school, my drive for success was tempered by a disquiet about the world around me. I rejected, for example, the campus honorary societies that automatically incorporated rising *Daily* editors along with fraternity and student government leaders in their exclusive ranks. After my freshman year, I took an apartment with a student named Tom Lamm (whose brother later became governor of Colorado), who resembled the James Dean character in *Rebel Without a Cause*, even down to the white T-shirt and red jacket he routinely wore to classes. We immersed ourselves in philosophy, kept our distance from the fraternity culture, rode motorcycles, and individually hitchhiked to all corners of America during vacation breaks. Gradually, I began going out with women who had the same searching qualities. All the while I managed getting good grades and promotions at the *Daily*, but that part of me still exploring the emotional and intellectual wilderness remained very strong.

There was yet another network of students who were attracting my curiosity, and I, without knowing it, was attracting theirs. They were the first core of student activists exploring a new politics on the threshold of the sixties. By 1959, the first signs of national campus activism were visible to a careful eye. In 1957, students in Berkeley formed a reform-minded campus political party called SLATE, the first of its kind. In 1958, ten thousand students joined a school-desegregation march in Washington, D.C., an event that startled me as I chose pictures and designed a front-page layout of the event for the *Daily*.

To the extent there were any organized student groups in the late fifties, however, they were small, fragmented, lineal descendants of left-wing groups that had last flourished in the thirties and flickered out by the McCarthy period. Whether socialist, communist, or anarchist in their political roots, they tended to be confined to students who were from Jewish, immigrant, New York backgrounds. One such group which had seen better days was the Student League for Industrial Democracy (SLID), an offshoot of the New York–based League for Industrial Democracy (LID), which in turn was an educational arm of the once-proud, now-musty trade unions like the International Ladies Garment Workers Union. The venerable SLID was formed in 1905, making it the first student organization in America and four years the senior of the National Association for the Advancement of Colored People (NAACP). In its robust years, its top ranks included such future leaders as Jack London, Walter Lippmann, Upton Sinclair, and John Dewey. But in recent times it had been virtually dormant, reflecting the exhaustion of the American Left by the fifties.

In 1959, however, the improbable was about to happen. In the unlikely setting of Ann Arbor, a visionary young man named Robert Alan Haber was planning to take over the New York–based SLID and convert it into Students for a Democratic Society (SDS). His apartment, above a hangout called the College Inn, was just behind the *Daily* building. Looking then as he would twenty-five years later, Al Haber was bald, smooth-skinned, bespectacled, of average height, trim in build. I judged him to be ten years older than I. It was never clear if he was enrolled as a student or graduate student or whether he was just dropping in on lecture courses. However, when I visited his one-room apartment, I was amazed that every wall, from floor to ceiling, was filled with books. They covered every subject, especially politics, history, and philosophy. Al built himself an amazingly large desk in the center. His bed was against the wall, and there were a few plants and a cat, which sat on Al's lap and licked itself. I had never seen anything like this apartment. Al was writing what he called a "tome." Like his other vagaries, it wasn't clear if he was writing an academic thesis, a book, or an open-ended notebook. He would only identify the chapter headings as "Art," "Science," "History," and the like.

But Al's eccentricities and nondescript appearance created a certain charisma. When he spoke, I felt an intense, intellectual focus, even when I didn't understand what he was talking about. Al's father, William Haber, was a senior university professor and official, a major figure in the Jewish community, and a prominent national Democrat whose deep ties went back to his own youthful, New Deal idealism thirty years before. Picking up the threads of his father's political past, Al wanted to weave them into a new fabric for the students of his time. Somehow intuition told him that a new student movement was around the corner. His practical instincts (he was also a carpenter) told him that he must attract and mold a nucleus of followers.

The main two he recruited, who would form SDS with him,

were also rooted in a radical history, though they were much younger than Al. Sharon Jeffrey, a sophomore who looked like a cheerleader with her blond hair, blue eyes, and quick smiles, was the daughter of Mildred Jeffrey, a top leader of the United Auto Workers, a close associate of Walter and Victor Reuther since the industrial strikes and sit-ins of the thirties, and a powerful woman in the Democratic party. Sharon was a born organizer with great talent. She also became Al's girlfriend. Bob Ross was a small and muscular native of the Bronx, raised one block from Yankee Stadium, who still spent his summers as a New York lifeguard. According to family lore, his grandparents met at a gathering of Russian revolutionaries on the Lower East Side—but on entering the university in Ann Arbor, his modes of disaffection tended toward jazz and the beat poets. Haber revived the young Ross's political interest, and Ross quickly proved to be precocious, articulate, and well versed in left doctrines.

Haber wanted to recruit me into his small conspiracy, but I was absorbed with work at the *Daily*. I liked him well enough, but he was too involved in what I considered theoretical abstractions at the time. The only campus group that drew my active interest was called Americans for World Responsibility, the creation of two graduate students, Al and Judy Guskin, who began a lobbying campaign for an international peace corps. It was before that group that I gave my first public speech, twenty double-spaced pages that took me forty-five minutes to read.

Haber's plan, already in the works, was to recruit a new cadre of student activists from around the country to the LID and gain the blessing of the LID elders for a revival of the student organization, now to be named SDS. In keeping with its tax-exempt educational character, Haber proposed holding a conference on "civil rights in the North" in Ann Arbor in the spring of 1960. Haber's intuition was prophetic. On February 1, 1960, the historic events of the decade unexpectedly began. Four unknown black students staged a sit-in at a segregated lunch counter in Greensboro, North Carolina, and started what was soon called "the movement." From that point until the August 1963 march on Washington, there commenced an era of unmatched idealism in America. The student civil rights movement took the moral leadership, showing how values could be translated into direct action. Students across the country became agents for social change on a larger scale than ever before. A new, more hopeful, presidency was in the making. In this brief moment of time, the sixties generation entered its age of innocence, overflowing with hope.

It was the moment Al Haber had waited for. In Ann Arbor, he, Jeffrey, and Ross joined the picket lines that began to form at the local Kresge chain store to create support and pressure on behalf of the students trying to desegregate lunch counters in the South. Their plans for the May civil rights conference blossomed. I watched the picket lines as a reporter and wrote supportive editorials. The marchers, a few students like Ross and Jeffrey combined with a number of longtime off-campus liberals and radicals, were singing old labor songs I didn't recognize. The singing was spirited; the songs were suddenly relevant. I felt an affinity with them for the first time, but still I remained an aspiring *Daily* writer, not yet thinking of myself as an activist. I enjoyed expressing myself in words, but I was not comfortable carrying a picket sign.

My attitude imperceptibly changed as spring 1960 wore on. As thousands of southern students were arrested, and many beaten, my respect and identification with their courage and conviction deepened. The SDS civil rights conference was a surprising success. Sharon's mother arranged a ten-thousand-dollar UAW grant that could employ Haber as a full-time organizer. The presidential primary campaign of John Kennedy, which invoked a return to government activism after eight quiet years, was also fanning the early fire of my political passion.

But that spring I primarily focused on the grueling competition to become the *Daily* editor in chief for the coming 1960–61 year. The paper was proudly autonomous within the university community, but ultimately it was controlled by a board that reflected administration, faculty, and private interests. So far as I knew, the board had never interfered with the paper's internal freedom, but this year was different. My fledgling activism, frequent criticisms of the university, and partisan coverage of the civil rights movement were worrying the campus administration. Privately, they were not sure they wanted a strident advocate controlling the editorial pulpit—neither were some of the outgoing senior editors, who held more conservative political views than mine. I felt as if I were on trial without quite knowing the accusations or how to defend myself. I wanted the job badly.

Weeks of impasse followed, while I waited nervously. The question broadened from my qualifications to whether the judgment of the outgoing editors—who had decided to recommend me—would be respected or overturned by the board. Finally, in a late-night meeting, the board named me the new editor. Much relieved, I committed the paper to greater editorial coverage of the new movement of students "seeking a voice in the decisions affecting our lives." I was beginning to think of myself as an oracle for this student awakening.

It was June 1960. Haber, Ross, and Jeffrey went to the New York City SDS convention. Promising to invigorate the organization, their leadership was approved by the twenty-nine voting delegates present. I, on the other hand, decided to hitchhike to Berkeley and the Bay Area, already known as the mecca of student activism. I planned to learn about the new activists firsthand, cover the Democratic National Convention in Los Angeles for the *Daily*, then end the summer by attending the National Student Association (NSA) congress in Minneapolis before settling into my senior year.

The Bay Area was radiating with a utopian spirit. Support for the sit-ins was intense. Locally, there was an electric effect when many students were arrested and physically hosed down on the marble steps of San Francisco City Hall for protesting the House Un-American Activities Committee. On the Berkeley campus, the student leaders of SLATE were demanding the right of student government to debate and take action on "off-campus" issues, a practice forbidden by the UC administration as too "political." I was dropped on Telegraph Avenue, the main street running directly south of campus, where coffeehouses, bookstores, and cramped apartment dwellings throbbed with energy.

I had a cup of coffee and crossed the street to Sproul Plaza. Leafleteers were rallying support for the students arrested in the anti-HUAC protest. As a woman handed me a leaflet, I politely introduced myself and asked her if she knew anyplace I could stay for a few weeks. Somewhat to my surprise, she gave me a phone number of one of the campus political leaders. Within a few hours, I moved into a brown-shingled, two-story house south of the campus on Hillegass Street. My hosts were an experienced group of student activists who, knowing I was the incoming *Daily* editor, wanted to give me a complete orientation to the movement. The room they assigned me belonged to Michael Tigar, a law student away for the summer; later in the decade, he would be helping with our legal appeals in the Chicago conspiracy trial.

In the weeks ahead, they took me to see the Livermore Laboratories, where most of America's nuclear weapons development still takes place under the auspices of the University of California. There I secured an interview with Dr. Edward Teller, a prototype for the *Dr. Strangelove* movie character. Teller patiently described how nuclear war could be survived and, in any event, why it was "better to be dead than red." After hearing his arguments, I signed a statement supporting an August 6 pro-disarmament rally commemorating the atomic bombing of Hiroshima and Nagasaki.

Acting Assistant Attorney General
Criminal Division
1-13-75

(re wiretaps)

Plaintiff	**Date**	**Location**
Hayden	8-3-60	San Francisco

Information concerning this overhearing as well as other information was furnished to this Bureau in a teletype communication dated August 4, 1960. The last page of this teletype contains a handwritten note as follows: "Substance given orally to ████████* Atomic Energy Commission Hqter [headquarters] 8-5-60 by ████████.

Detroit T-2, who has furnished reliable information in the past, advised in August 1960 that Thomas Hayden, editor of the Michigan "Daily," was national coordinator of a non-violence movement in connection with Hiroshima and Nagasaki Day activities August 6 and 9 at San Francisco, California. . . . [Hayden] had indicated that there was no official organization connected with this demonstration, but it was a radical theme, "No More Hiroshima—Youth Wants Peace." . . .

The same Berkeley activists took me to the Delano, California, fields where Mexican farm workers labored twelve hours daily in the hot sun for miserable wages, and they introduced me to

*Material deleted by the FBI.

organizers who claimed that one day they would achieve a union.

I was soon convinced that student activists had to be organized into campus political organizations, which would have to be linked together into a single, unified student organization. I eagerly looked forward to the coming NSA congress as the first chance for many of the new student leaders across the country to meet each other face to face. But my Berkeley friends mysteriously warned me that the NSA leadership was not to be trusted. The NSA hierarchy, a permanent elite of former student leaders, were said to be more interested in channeling the new activists into safe political directions than in building an independent student movement. Overwhelmed by everything I was hearing and experiencing, I simply logged this advice in my growing notebooks. Meanwhile, I wrote several full-page articles for the *Daily* proclaiming a "new student movement." These provoked the worst fears of the administrators back in Ann Arbor, who warned that I was "creating a self-fulfilling prophecy."

I flew to Los Angeles and the Democratic convention in a state of innocent wonderment at the scale of the city. Even its airport overwhelmed me. I quickly adjusted and plunged into the convention events, brashly introducing myself to Robert Kennedy one morning while he was buying newspapers and mints in the hotel lobby. My chief impression was how young he seemed to be (he was thirty-nine) in contrast to my image of politicians. So was his older brother, the nominee, whose New Frontier speech, delivered at sunset in the open-air Memorial Coliseum, stirred me deeply (despite the warnings of my radical friends that Kennedy was a phony liberal). Kennedy's implicit point was that the spirit of youth was affecting even the political process, a message that gave further legitimacy to the new awakening among students.

Marching outside the convention arena were blacks and whites in support of the demands of the southern civil rights movement. My most significant encounter during the convention week was there on the picket line: I interviewed Dr. Martin Luther King, Jr. "Ultimately, you have to take a stand with your life," he told me gently. I felt odd writing the words in my journalist's notebook. As I left the line, and later as I left Los Angeles, I asked myself why I should be only observing and chronicling this movement instead of participating in it. King was saying that each of us had to be more than neutral and objective, that we had to make a difference. That was something I realized I always wanted to do. Now the way was becoming clearer.

From California, I headed toward the National Student Association conference, the final experience of my summer-long transformation and my formal introduction to the world of serious student politics. Over one thousand student leaders gathered at the University of Minnesota. Editors and student government leaders from major campuses across the country were present in a mood of anticipation. The fifties had been uneventful years for the National Student Association, and this congress represented a fresh energy. I did not know it at the time, but the NSA, which was formed in the first years of the Cold War, was funded primarily by the CIA and State Department for the purpose of combating communism abroad. The Soviet bloc sponsored or encouraged student movements in many countries, especially in the Third World, as well as annual Youth Festivals where anti-imperalist, anti-American themes were commonplace. Not wanting these large gatherings of future political leaders to go unchallenged, the CIA decided to covertly fund the NSA to represent the "free world." That explained a curious contradiction which became apparent when I came in contact with the organization: Its participants ranged from students like myself to conservatives from small Catholic colleges, while its national and international officers were often ten years older, more sophisticated, and deeply involved in distant international intrigues—they were actually gathering intelligence on foreign student leaders for the U.S. government.

To make matters more complicated, these older NSA leaders, despite their ties to U.S. government agencies, tended to be quite liberal, a response to the revolutions of rising expectations they saw everywhere in the world. The most famous of these NSA founders in the early fifties was Allard Lowenstein, who later denied any knowledge of the CIA funding and who played a major role in the politics of the decade. Lowenstein, an elder statesman of NSA by the time I arrived, welcomed the student civil rights movement in the South, as did most NSA leaders. But the older NSA leaders also felt a need to keep control of their organization and shroud its sources of money. Their secrecy eventually led to suspicion as the spirit of democratic decision making among students emerged. In a few years the organization began to fade in relevance, finally self-destructing completely when its CIA connection was made public in 1967.

At the time, however, the NSA was the only national forum for students. It took strong stands in favor of the issues I most believed in, provided for an exchange of views and experiences, and was almost an apprenticeship for future American political leaders. Among those active in 1960 were Barney Frank, future congressman from Massachusetts; Steve Roberts, now a Washington correspondent for *The New York Times;* and Ed Garvey, who founded and represented the players' union in the National Football League.

There also was a woman who interviewed potential applicants, including myself, to participate in an international youth festival, where her task force was planning to offset communist influence. It was tempting, partly because the travel to Europe was paid for by her committee, and partly because I was curious to meet her. This miniskirted woman kept coming up in conversation among eager young men; her name was Gloria Steinem, later the editor of *Ms.* magazine and perhaps America's best-known feminist

We talked twice in her office, where she explained how an American delegation including outspoken liberals like myself could defend the United States against Soviet-sponsored delegations to the 1962 Helsinki youth festival eager to exploit American racism. She was sophisticated and appealing, and only a scheduling problem kept me from taking her offer.

CIA MEMORANDUM

TO: Director
    Federal Bureau of Investigation
    Attention:

FROM: Deputy Director (Plans)

SUBJECT: Eighth World Youth Festival—U.S. Participation

    1. In its efforts to counter the effect of Communist propaganda directed against free-world participants at the Eighth World Youth Festival, this Agency ▮▮▮▮▮▮ **.***

*Material deleted by the CIA.

 has encouraged politically articulate Americans to participate in the Festival. By their participation in "official" Festival activity, those Americans will gain access to key delegates from the developing areas and engage such delegates in personal discussions in order to point out the fallacies of Communist propaganda and express the genuine interest of the free world in the problems and aspirations of underdeveloped countries.

2. ███
███
███

3. The individuals listed in the attachment ████████. The fact that their names appear on this list does not indicate endorsement of their reliability by this Agency. We will, however, subsequently identify for your information those persons who cooperate consistently and fully.

4. This Agency has found past reporting by the Bureau in connection with U.S. Festival activity most useful. We would appreciate receiving information on individuals listed in the attachment which indicates questionable reliability.

5. We have particular and continuing need for information concerning USFC plans for maintaining tactical control of the U.S. "delegation" at the Festival or which clearly link the USFC with the Communist Party of the United States or reveals control of the USFC by the international Communist movement. Subject was one of the individuals cooperating with the ████████ in connection with the EIGHTH WORLD YOUTH FESTIVAL.

ADDENDUM: DOMESTIC INTELLIGENCE DIVISION

Central Intelligence Agency has advised that they have never had an operational interest in Hayden. They did state that in view of the fact that subject was scheduled to attend the Eighth World Youth Festival, he was considered as "a potential target" but no further action was taken.

Still emerging was a basic question of whether, as *Daily* editor, I should be working through the NSA establishment or dedicating myself to a fully independent movement on the model of the southern students. Haber was already decided on building SDS. He attended the NSA congress to recruit more student leaders, skillfully organizing the Liberal Study Group to introduce and bring together the more progressive students attending the congress.

My pragmatic side told me that if I could become editor of the *Daily*, it was equally possible that students with my politics could successfully take the leadership of NSA. My more romantic instincts sided with the new and independent pulse of action among the student activists all around me. What really interested and excited me was how the new political atmosphere on the campuses was spilling into the congress proceedings. To be sure, there were cautious and careerist student representatives who didn't want to see any boats rocked, and even some vocal right-wingers who wanted to invade Cuba (this group became Young Americans for Freedom, an anti–New Left conservative group whose members eventually created much of the New Right in the eighties).

There were extraordinarily bright and eloquent student leaders, like Timothy Jenkins of Howard University, a black who was elected vice president for national affairs, in charge of civil rights work. After a dramatic debate, the congress voted overwhelmingly in favor of a Haber resolution which not only put NSA on record in favor of the southern sit-in movement, but virtually declared a new era of student social action and responsibility.

But the focal point of the Congress, and a key to my own transformation, was the presence of about twenty-five representatives of the Student Nonviolent Coordinating Committee (SNCC), the students fresh from beatings and jail, gathered for a foundation-funded retreat that paralleled the larger meeting. Here were the people I'd been writing about, from SNCC chairman Charles McDew, a black Jew who recited the Talmud, to Bob Zellner, white and all-American with a deep southern drawl, ready to be arrested anywhere. They were in many ways like myself—young, politically innocent, driven by moral values, impatient with their elders, finding authentic purpose through risking their "lives, their fortune, and their sacred honor"—in short, a genuinely revolutionary leadership. In their heated intellectual discussions at the seminar, values were never separate from analysis. For direction, they quoted not Marx but the Talmud, not Mao but Camus: "A man can't cure and know at the same time. So let's cure as quickly as we can. That's the more urgent job."

They lived on a fuller level of feeling than any people I'd ever seen, partly because they were making modern history in a very personal way, and partly because by risking death they came to know the value of living each moment to the fullest. Looking back, this was a key turning point, the moment my political identity began to take shape. The student culture, exemplified by conformist fraternities and impersonal lecture halls back in Ann Arbor, had left me searching for more. The *Daily* was engaged in the real world, but "objectivity" stunted my desire to make a commitment. Haber and the SDS were to be respected, but they were too cerebral. Here were the models of charismatic commitment I was seeking—I wanted to live like them.

One of them in particular drew my attention. A philosophy graduate student at the University of Texas and a leader of the sit-ins in Austin, her name was Sandra Cason, but everybody called her Casey. She was beautiful, tall and blond with deep questioning eyes, and she held a position of great authority within the group because of her ability to think morally, express herself poetically, and have practical effects. A teaching assistant in English literature and a counselor at one of the huge dormitories on the Texas campus, she decided to move into something called the Christian Faith and Life Community, where approximately fifty people studied, lived, worshiped together in what was called an "intentional community." They looked for their mission in the world, debating theologians Paul Tillich and Reinhold Niebuhr and the existentialists. It was, at the time, *the* liberated spot on the silent campus, the only integrated housing around. From such beginnings came an activist force central to the sit-ins when they began that year in Austin. In addition, Casey and her roommate, divinity student Dorothy Dawson, were close to campus editor Robb Burlage and the muckraking writers for *The Texas Observer* Ronnie Dugger and Willie Morris. Together they were among the most eloquent white voices of the new southern upheaval.

I fell under Casey's spell at once, as did most other men I knew, and followed her wherever she appeared at the congress. The most memorable moment of the whole week was the debate on whether to endorse civil disobedience against southern segregation, and Casey's speech moved the convention:

> An ethical question is always both utterly simple and confusingly complex. On this particular question I only hope we do not lose

its essential simplicity in the complexity. I would touch on the first point first—its simplicity. When an individual human being is not allowed by the legal system and the social mores of his community to *be* a human being, does he have the right to peaceably protest? . . . Perhaps in this situation protest is the only way to maintain his humanity. . . .

Should fear of violence keep a person from nonviolent protest of an injustice? Should a person who does not strike back be blamed because he is struck? I simply fail to understand why, if the presence of Negro students sitting quietly or white and Negro students sitting together is so infuriating to a mob that they resort to violence, the students should be blamed for the sickness of the mob. . . .

I feel some pity for the segregationist and realize it will be difficult for him to accept the changes that *must come.* But I am not free as long as he keeps me from going where I please with whom I please, and I do not think that fear of him should keep me and others from trying to right the wrong for which he stands. . . .

As I see it, a person suffering under an unjust law has several choices: He can do nothing; we have never advocated this in a democracy. He can use legal means; this has been done and will be done. However, if he sees the slowness of the legal means and realizes he is a human being *now* and the law is unjust *now,* he has other choices: He can revolt—I think we should all be proud and glad that this has not been the course of the southern Negro—or he can protest actively, as southern students have chosen to do, and he must take the consequences. I do not see the law as immutable, but rather as an agreed-upon pattern for relations between people. If the pattern is unjust or a person does not agree with the relations, a person must at times choose to do the right rather than the legal. I do not consider this anarchy, but responsibility.

I cannot say to a person who suffers injustice, "Wait." Perhaps you can. I can't. And having decided that I cannot urge caution, I must stand with him. If I had known that not a single lunch counter would open as a result of my action, I could not have done differently than I did. If I had known violence would result, I could not have done differently than I did. I am thankful for the sit-ins if for no other reason than that they provided me with an opportunity for making a slogan into a reality, by making a decision into an action. It seems to me that this is what life is all about. While I would hope that the NSA congress will pass a strong sit-in resolution, I am more concerned that all of us, Negro and white, realize the possibility of becoming less inhuman humans through commitment and action, with all their frightening complexities.

When Thoreau was jailed for refusing to pay taxes to a government which supported slavery, Emerson went to visit him. "Henry David," said Emerson, "what are you doing in there?" Thoreau looked at him and replied, "Ralph Waldo, what are *you* doing out *there?*"

What are *you* doing out there?

I was struck as much by the speech as the speaker. She put into words the transformation I was undergoing, from would-be journalist (a profession where "consciousness of complexity" seemed foremost) to activist (where "consciousness of simplicity" and commitment are primary). I quoted Casey's speech extensively in my report to the *Daily*. We met for only a few minutes at the congress, but I idolized her. I returned to Ann Arbor surging with a crusader's definition of myself and a memory of her in my mind.

September 1960 marked the beginning of my final year at Michigan. My studies turned heavily toward political science and philosophy, reflecting a need to anchor my newfound spirit of activism in a greater intellectual grounding. I read the Greek classics. I studied the historians of the Holocaust and totalitarianism. Casey sent me James Agee and Walker Percy's *Let Us Now Praise Famous Men*, which I read urgently. I sent her *Siddhartha*, Herman Hesse's story of a young man's quest for meaning. I struggled with Sartre's *Being and Nothingness* and found myself preferring Camus. The polemical attacks of sociologist C. Wright Mills on "establishment intellectuals" created a model of a new kind of committed intellectual. A philosophy course taught by Professor Arnold Kaufman introduced me to the concept of "participatory democracy." What I was discovering was that ideas are most "relevant," and therefore exciting, when they illuminate and clarify a situation one is already involved in. The search for the meaning of life was now enriched by the discovery of meaning in the movement.

Then there was the *Daily:* Though hardly militant by later standards, my editorials kept up such a constant drumbeat for university reform and restructuring (a greater role for students and faculty), for civil rights and peace (front-page coverage of the sit-ins), and for sheer *involvement*, that the Ann Arbor administration was increasingly disturbed. One day the vice president for student affairs, an affable and disarming fellow with a strictly managerial bent, invited me for coffee in the Student Union. As he chewed on his pipe, he politely warned me that my editorials were "demagogic" and that such incitement could lead to the excesses of Nazism and Stalinism. Of course, he said, the university had no intention of interfering with the paper, but thought I should know his concerns.

Especially troubling to the university that fall was the formation, at my initiative, of VOICE, the first independent student political party on the campus, modeled after SLATE in Berkeley and dedicated to a greater "student voice in the decisions affecting our lives." The organization drew together most of the campus activists and eventually became the Ann Arbor affiliate of SDS. At the same time, Al Haber and others continued to solicit my greater involvement as they spread their SDS organizing network to other campuses. Though still primarily committed to the *Daily,* I now lent them a willing hand by traveling and speaking outside of Ann Arbor. I began to see the building of a national student movement through SDS as a possible, even likely, project beyond college graduation.

My most serious longings, however, were pointed south to the civil rights movement, and though I didn't admit it, toward Casey. I was pulled toward romance within action, or perhaps action within romance. That October, I flew south to an Atlanta conference of SNCC, the first southwide meeting since the sit-ins began eight months earlier. It was a remarkable experience, once again, in its level of fervor and uncommon bravery. Since February, thousands had been jailed across the South, and many were victims of violence, including beatings, bombings, shootings and, in the case of one young man in Texas, the carving of the initials *KKK* in his chest with a knife. Despite their obvious patriotism, the activists had been accused of "communist leanings" by former President Truman, had stunned and paralyzed the white liberal establishment in the South, and challenged and divided the older generation of black leadership as well. The presidential campaign between Kennedy and Nixon, then in its final throes, would be heavily influenced by the movement as well, with Democrats wanting a heavy black turnout but fearing a southern white backlash.

In the eye of this storm, SNCC met to turn itself into a more organized network than before. Even at this initial stage, the key organizational ideas of the sixties were debated into the night.

On the one hand, the movement needed coordination, communication, an ability to make decisions across local and state lines, and money for bail. On the other, spontaneity and local initiative were invested with such mystical significance that any sign of bureaucracy, or delegating of authority to older groups, was profoundly suspect. After all, the movement began with the spontaneous act of four students, not with a decision of the NAACP national office, not even by Dr. King's Southern Christian Leadership Conference (SCLC). Dr. King's organization, which might have seemed the closest in spirit and methods, evoked the greatest paranoia within the SNCC core; the students feared that their individuality and flexibility (and egos) would be swallowed under the personal mantle of Dr. King. Instead of becoming a "youth branch" of the SCLC, they chose to form an independent organization. Instead of a single charismatic leader, they chose a model of decentralized leadership through the example of direct action. In this course, they were strongly influenced by a remarkable forty-year-old black woman named Ella Baker. The elegant Miss Baker (as she was called) organized NAACP chapters in the dangerous South of the fifties and worked with SCLC until the formation of SNCC. With her encouragement, SNCC chose a new chairman, Marion Barry of Fisk University (later to be mayor of the nation's capital), authorized a one-room office in Atlanta, formed a coordinating committee with delegates from each southern state, and set out to build positive but independent relationships with other civil rights groups.

I advocated this form of "anti-leader" organization and saw the debate repeated several times in the course of the many movements of the sixties. Such decentralized and essentially voluntary forms are inevitable whenever movements erupt with the seemingly endless energy they did during that decade. Wherever one looked there seemed to be new and unexpected movements: blacks, peace people, students, women, environmentalists, Gray Panthers, gays, and on and on. Each of these applied to themselves the concept of having a voice, *their* voice, in decisions affecting their lives, and each derived tremendous vitality from their grass-roots origins. Perhaps they were not meant to be permanent, only to serve a purpose. But in retrospect, most—and perhaps all—suffered from serious problems associated within this antibureaucratic model. There was a chronic competition and rivalry over status and power that few leaders survived, as if beneath the egalitarian rhetoric there was a resentment of anyone with significant authority and a dire fear of formalizing it, even if that authority was based on achievement or could be useful for communicating through the media. Equally troubling was the near impossibility of giving such spontaneous movements a competent administrative framework, which resulted in a lack of stability and permanence. The inability of SNCC or other movement-based organizations to find solutions to these problems sealed their future demise and assured the continuance of the very bureaucratic organizations and parties that the movements originally belittled as being irrelevant, even obsolete. It may be that being on the cutting edge of change and making high-risk personal commitments are ultimately incompatible with the requirements of building lasting reformist organizations; or perhaps, the two approaches to social change uncomfortably depend on a lasting tension with each other.

The contradictions in my own nature were far from settled. In less than two weeks, I would be swept up yet again, this time late on a dark, rainy night in Ann Arbor when candidate John F. Kennedy first endorsed the proposed Peace Corps to a cheering crowd of students. The occasion of a national leader calling on students to play an idealistic role was clearly another turning point for our generation, and I was excited as anyone on the rain-swept Student Union steps that night. I stood next to Kennedy, taking notes and was permitted a short interview on the elevator taking him upstairs to his room. I do not remember what he said, only the glow of his warm and welcoming personality.

But I was convinced that while the nation, and my generation, needed Kennedy as president, the effort undertaken by SNCC would be the real catalyst to change. We could only benefit from a responsive president, but the president would be responsive only if there was a movement already toppling the century-old walls of segregation in the South. Morally and politically, I was sure I had found the place to be, but another level of personal fascination was drawing me into this whirlpool of history: my infatuation with Casey, who I knew would be present at the Atlanta meeting in October. She remained, perhaps because of the historic moment as well as her personal qualities, the most interesting woman I'd ever met. To my relief, she was indeed there in Atlanta and, to my surprise, I discovered late one night that she felt her own attraction toward me.

I went back to Ann Arbor in a state of joy. The SNCC workshop was inspirational. I felt I was falling in love and called or corresponded with Casey several times a week. The watershed presidential race, ending in a Kennedy victory by less than a point, ushered in a profound change. Now there was a chance to be in the very center of history, touching and being touched by people whose everyday actions made headlines and rippled out to alter the national mainstream.

Shortly after the Kennedy inauguration, in February 1961, while I was still *Daily* editor, there were alarming news reports of the plight of black sharecroppers in rural Fayette County, Tennessee, who were living in tents, having been evicted from their homes for registering to vote. I helped fill a station wagon full of canned food and warm clothing and drove to Tennessee with several Ann Arbor friends. Casey drove from Austin to meet us. On arrival at the tent city, we were warmly received by the poor people and by Jim Forman, a black activist from Chicago who became SNCC's executive director. Though Fayette's population was mostly black, no blacks had been registered in the county since Reconstruction. Here, on a chilly February night, local people were living in a starlit field in what they called a freedom town. I was deeply impressed.

While we were unloading the foodstuffs from the car, the bright searchlight of a county sheriff's vehicle appeared out of the darkness. The doors swung open, and two uniformed officers strode toward me. I was so nervous that my right leg buckled, and I lost my balance. When they queried us about our business, I told them I was writing an article for the *Daily* and asked for directions to the local newspaper office. They complained that I should be reporting about the racial problems where I came from, but gave me directions and, apparently satisfied, soon departed.

We drove into a tiny town and found the newspaper office, where I obtained permission to phone my lengthy story to the *Daily*. All seemed to be going well when, suddenly, one of my friends pulled me off the phone to observe that a little mob was gathering outside on the sidewalk. There were a dozen or more white men, most of them carrying clubs, looking through the window at us and muttering unheard obscenities. I told the *Daily* in Ann Arbor that we were surrounded and asked them to phone the Justice Department. I called the local police (who were just down the street) and asked for immediate assistance. In a minute or two, one of the sheriffs we'd seen earlier appeared outside, mingling with the menacing crowd. Everybody seemed to be on first-name terms except us. I finally decided that we should leave the newspaper office, walk swiftly across the sidewalk to our car, and drive straight north, which we did, surprising the crowd momentarily. We locked the doors, gunned the engine, and roared down the street, followed by a carload of locals at ninety miles an hour to the county line. Finally, we were safe, but I never forgot my introduction to the rural South.

My *Daily* articles on Fayette County were widely read on campus. In general, the *Daily* was having more and more effect as Ann Arbor students began to awaken. Soon the national debate over civil rights and students' rights became concentrated on a local practice of the university. I investigated the charges of several women students that the office of the dean of women was spying on their dating and social habits. Some white women reported that the dean was informing their parents that they were seen dating black men. They were frightened, had trouble studying, and one woman dropped out of school. I turned over my interviews to a Faculty Senate Committee and finally exposed the story on the *Daily*'s front page, actions which led the university to remove the dean and promise reconsideration of her controversial policies. The episode climaxed near the end of my days at the *Daily*, and I was surprised at the university's quick and surgical response. They appeared to be scapegoating the dean to avoid an embarrassing situation, without necessarily changing their fundamental paternalism. Pleased as I was with the faculty response, it did not change my cynicism toward the institutional rigidity of the university. My final editorial, written on May 30, 1961, was headlined LIVING THE KEPT PLEDGE and concluded, "My deepest fear about the university is that we are adrift intellectually and humanly."

I was chafing to graduate; the South was beckoning. The Freedom Riders were risking their lives trying to desegregate interstate travel all across the Deep South. SNCC also was embarking on voter registration drives in areas of the historic Black

Belt where blacks were forcefully and utterly disenfranchised. The Kennedy administration was struggling between the moral and legal claims of the civil rights activists on the one hand and its political alliances with southern Democratic politicians on the other. Students across America were responding enthusiastically to the message of involvement.

Not only did I want to go south after graduation, but I wanted to be there with Casey. The times were right for us. By letter, phone, and occasional visits, we kept integrating into each other's lives. Before the winter of 1960–61 was over, we were thinking of marriage. As I recall, this was primarily my idea in the beginning. My experience with women was less than mature, limited to a flurry of brief and superficial relationships throughout my Ann Arbor years. It was conventional that I wanted to be married after falling in love. Perhaps insecurity made me possessive as well. She, on the other hand, was nearly two years older and considerably less certain than I. Like myself, Casey came from a background of divorce. Her father, whom she rarely saw, was a Texas labor organizer and an alcoholic. Her stepfather was abusive. She told me she was more unstable than I knew and openly wondered if marriage could work. We were alike, however, in our sense of moral adventure, our existential sensibility, our love of poetic action, and our feeling of romantic involvement. We were in love with each other, and equally, with the times. She agreed to live with me in Ann Arbor during the summer of 1961, after which we would transplant ourselves to Atlanta, where she had been offered a YWCA job doing campus "human relations" under the direct supervision of Ella Baker.

I had a conflict. Approaching the end of my tenure at the university and the *Daily*, I was divided over what to do. The editor of *The Detroit News* offered me a job in the paper's Washington, D.C., bureau, which I turned down (to my father's consternation). I did not want to report on the world; I wanted to change it. But how?

As I saw my options, they were to pursue reform through the NSA by running for one of its national offices or to join Haber in creating the still-undefined SDS. In either case, I decided that my short-term focus would be the South, my task the building of northern student support for the southern movement. Finally, graduation came but with a decision no nearer. Casey and

I moved to New York for the summer months, where we could be closer to both the SDS and NSA offices and then get married in the fall. NSA, then headquartered in Philadelphia, asked me to draft a major pamphlet on the civil rights movement for international distribution. Haber had decided to start building SDS with the financing, and within the organizational shell, of the venerable but (I thought) senile LID. This was not my preference, but it was the only way, Haber reasoned, to find funding, a national office, and links to the liberal and labor communities whose support we would need.

Casey and I said good-bye to my parents on a summer day in Royal Oak. They bought us a car for my graduation, a green Corvair station wagon (it was two years before Ralph Nader would burst on the scene with *Unsafe at Any Speed*). I believe they took some comfort in the fact that we planned to marry and that Casey appeared to be a normal, indeed all-American, woman. But it was difficult for them to absorb the reality that their only son—in whom they had invested their savings from years of tiring work, their son who was a successful student and whom they imagined as a top reporter or editor—was instead driving off in their Corvair straight for the center of social violence in America, for the purpose of helping . . . Negroes. Though he never tried to dissuade us, my father was convinced that something was deeply wrong, and I recall my mother shaking her head and saying, "I don't know *what* you're doing." Whatever demon had possessed me during my years away from home, they seemed to feel, could no longer be exorcised by them. I certainly did not know how to explain my yearnings in terms they could understand. At least they were decent about the departure.

When one is young, or at least when I was young, there always seems to be a vast expanse of future time in which to reconnect with uncomprehending parents. I didn't see that, from their perspective, time was rapidly passing by. Their failed marriage, and now the threat of failed parenting, must have haunted them as the Corvair pulled away.

The New York summer was dismal, except perhaps as an experience in growing up. When we arrived in the Bronx late at night to stay at a friend's house, I left our suitcases in the car; the next morning, we were without possessions. Never mind, I thought, we can scavenge, as I often had in Ann Arbor. Clothes, as few as necessary, could be obtained from secondhand stores, cinder blocks and boards for the bookcase from construction sites. One bright day in an affluent part of Manhattan, I spied a beautiful mattress on the curb in front of a brownstone. Immediately, I transported it to our apartment, a prize possession. The next morning, I discovered why even rich people throw mattresses away: bedbugs. Through such episodes the summer proceeded, interspersed with constant debate over SDS versus NSA.

The SDS option was clear: Haber proposed to deploy me as a field secretary in Atlanta, where I would participate in the civil rights movement but also travel and write for northern campus audiences, thus building support for an eventual national organization—SDS—out of the healthy response of students who were committed to ending southern racism and applying the principles of democracy to their own lives as well. My concern with this approach was a distrust of New York–based politics and a sense of the problems inherent in building an independent student organization with no resources save those of the inbred and old-fashioned New York circles whose time-bound and overly ideological institutions were alien to my student experiences.

At the end of a difficult summer, Casey and I drove to Madison, Wisconsin, for the NSA congress that would be decisive in my choice. I remained reluctant to embrace Haber's vision of laying a new organizational foundation and reluctant to work again in New York. Despite my experience with NSA over the summer, which had been negative, my preference was to work through NSA to the fullest extent possible and only break away to build a new organization if conservative forces blocked NSA's reform. They had been reluctant to publish the pamphlet I had written, without quite explaining their reasons. More important, they had interviewed me for membership in an exclusive two-week international-relations seminar and rejected me on the strange grounds that I already was sufficiently knowledgeable about foreign policy. I was angered at the decision, since participation in the seminar was widely viewed as a crucial step toward proving one's acceptability for national office in the organization. Moreover, I believed that their real reason for rejecting my application was a fear that I could not be controlled by those I considered their old guard, not suspecting their CIA affiliation at the time.

However, the NSA elite did induct one of the campus leaders involved with me in exploring the development of SDS, my friend Paul Potter from Oberlin College. Paul, along with his roommate, Rennie Davis, was one of the many gifted student leaders around the country actively sought by Haber to make his SDS dream a reality. Tall and lanky with sunken piercing eyes, Paul was the intellectual of the duo; short and athletic, Rennie was the spark plug on campus. Both were from farm backgrounds; together, they founded the Progressive Student Alliance at Oberlin, a campus party like SLATE and VOICE.

The congress, held at the Madison campus of the University of Wisconsin that year, was testimony to the rapid changes that were taking place among conscious students around the country. There was little disagreement over the need to bring students into the campus decision-making structure, to accelerate support for the civil rights movement, and to bring about a new national climate conducive to initiatives for peace. There was an underlying tension, however, over whether change could be brought about through the existing system of student movements, liberal foundations, and the Democratic administration in Washington or whether more radical departures, like those pioneered by SNCC, were indeed necessary. As the congress unfolded, I actively explored running for the office of vice president for national affairs, a post where I would have been the bridge to SNCC and civil rights efforts. However, in a few days it was clear that my espousal of direct action was antagonizing as many delegates as I was mobilizing. The NSA old guard busily spread rumors that I was too militant. I realized finally that I was likely to lose, blamed it on the secretive NSA elite in an angry speech, and withdrew in favor of Paul, who had a less threatening manner and more respectable credentials. In the end, Paul won by a very close vote.

On the last night of the Congress, a yellow notepad was obtained from the office of the NSA president. It was an organizational chart of the convention's political forces. On one side was a box inscribed *Hayden-Haber*, on the other a box labeled *YAF* (Young Americans for Freedom). Lines were drawn upward from the two boxes to a circle at the top of the chart which was marked *Control Group*. It was a diagram for preventing the election of a "militant" like myself, drawn by someone skilled in manipulating student movements abroad, now bringing his or her talents home.

Haber was delighted at my withdrawal, ignoring my hurt. Casey, I think, was simply happy to put the frustrating North behind us and head again for Atlanta. The segregated South seemed more engaging than the politics of the North for her. I healed from the loss and felt relief at finally having a clear personal agenda. I would be the SDS field secretary operating out of the South.

My search for a vocation had been a troubled one. I had wanted in high school to be a foreign correspondent, and in my short story, to be a novelist or poet—aspirations which mixed idealism with impact. In the university I had found both through the *Daily*. Now, agonizingly but intently, I found a new outlet, through writing and speaking about a movement I would also participate in, at the price of a conventional career and, perhaps, parental affection and solidarity. All discussion being over and having decided that no choice was comparable in challenge to this one, I plunged toward the bleeding front lines of the South with Casey as if all my life I had been waiting, in Camus's terms, "to love or die together."

We were married that fall in Austin, by the Reverend Joe Matthews of Casey's Faith and Life Community, in a ceremony that juxtaposed Ecclesiastes ("All is vanity . . . there is no new thing under the sun") with Camus ("I, on the other hand, choose justice in order to remain faithful to the world"). Before the service, the minister tried to counsel us about the seriousness of the commitment we were undertaking. Casey wondered aloud how we, so young and free, could take a vow of permanent sexual fidelity; unresolved, we left it out. Neither could we agree on why a formal institution like marriage should be embraced, but we went ahead, laughingly accepting the absurd in the context of our love, marrying each other in a circle that included Casey's mother and friends, and Al Haber. Neither of my parents attended.

At the reception after the wedding, I remember philosophizing very knowingly about not having babies under the shadow of nuclear weapons. It was mistaken to bring children into the world, I opined, since the new megaweapons threatened any future except what we created through risk and struggle. Casey sat next to me, silent, as I recall, but I think she nodded.

No one at the gathering was willing to disagree.

3. Never Turn Back:
The South, 1960-62

The movement began making its push into the Black Belt, the heart of the old Confederacy, as Casey and I arrived, newlyweds, in Atlanta in the fall of 1961. She became immediately employed as the YWCA's liaison to SNCC, and I became SDS's first field secretary, at a salary of sixty-two dollars per week. Though not a typical young American couple, we were very happy. We rented a pleasant, white two-story cottage behind someone's home in the northeast section of the city, about ten minutes' drive from the headquarters of SNCC, SCLC, and Dr. King's Ebenezer Baptist Church on Auburn Avenue in the heart of the black community. Our landlords thought of us as a young journalist and a church worker, a description we didn't mind.

The news from the front lines was grim: From the southwest Georgia town of Albany (near Plains, the home of Jimmy Carter), to a central Alabama county called Lowndes, to southern Mississippi towns named Liberty and McComb, SNCC workers were engaged in desperate efforts to secure a niche for organizing and voter registration. Barely after arriving in Atlanta, I was quickly drawn into efforts to protect a SNCC project by exposing Mississippi to the conscience of America.

Mississippi: the heart of darkness, the undying core of racist resistance, where even the bravest protestors sucked in fear with every breath. The vast Mississippi Delta, home of sprawling

cotton plantations and the birthplace of the blues, had a deserved reputation as the poorest, most repressive area in America. Statewide, blacks were 43 percent of the population, but
only 5 percent of the registered voters in 1960. In the Delta there
were even more blacks and fewer registered. Their median income was $1,100, one third that of whites. Two thirds of black
families had no bathtubs, no showers, and one half of those
families had no running water at all. Many lived in tar-paper
shacks on the edge of the cotton fields they worked.

In the three counties targeted for SNCC voter registration
drives—Pike, Amite, and Walthall, all in the rural south of the
state—virtually no blacks dared to vote. In Pike, where blacks
totalled 38 percent of the twenty thousand residents of voting
age, only two hundred cast ballots in 1960. In Amite, with blacks
47 percent of the eligible, only one individual voted. In Walthall,
not a single one of the eligible blacks voted. No one could recall
civil rights organizers in these three rural counties except
briefly in the fifties. According to reliable legend, the first of
them was shot and killed in 1952, and a second shot and run out
of state shortly after.

And yet SNCC was ready to take the challenge. Thinking
back, I am still not sure where their courage came from. How
are seemingly ordinary people capable of extraordinary feats?
Perhaps like soldiers who know their cause is worth dying for,
they were simply and bravely carrying out their acknowledged
duty. Perhaps the civil rights movement had reached sufficient
scale that they knew an individual sacrifice would not be forgotten or in vain. We were imbued with very idealistic American
values: a belief in racial integration, not just as a future ideal, but
as an ideal to be practiced in the here and now; a belief that
places like Mississippi were not part of the American dream, but
nightmares that America would awaken from; a belief, finally,
that the Constitution, the president, and the American people
were really on our side. Our example would mobilize them. One
local movement leader in 1961 stated these feelings simply and
clearly: "My sole reason for demonstrating was to reach the
better people—who hadn't thought about injustice before.
. . . We were depending on the white community. We had faith."

These motives were often conveyed with effect. One television commentator at the time described black demonstrators as
"deeply moving . . . American citizens rising up with devastating orderliness and good manners to demand their constitu-

tional rights." Of course, these attitudes were not shared by all, but as underlying assumptions they help explain how one could confront the back roads of Mississippi alone, and they are a clue to the angry turn to "black power" and violence a few short years later when the American promise delivered too little, too late.

At the time, I didn't recognize how thoroughly *American* were the SNCC sentiments; I was more struck by how challenging and revolutionary they were in contrast to those of the white northern students searching for meaning through abstract ideas alone. I traveled to Mississippi for the Freedom Rider trials in mid-September. The trials of two hundred Freedom Riders took place in a segregated Jackson courthouse. I took notes to send back north to SNCC supporters:

> The trials average about 40 minutes each. The judge has ruled that the terms "race," "Freedom Rider," "white," "Negro" and "CORE" are not to be used in court as they are irrelevant to the question of breach of peace. The hypocrisy is beyond description. No mention of the only essential issue: equal rights or no equal rights. No Negroes on the jury. A segregated courtroom. Use of the law as a mummery . . .

After attending a SNCC strategy meeting, where plans were mapped out for taking the voter registration drive into the heart of the Mississippi Delta, my reaction was akin to a religious conversion:

> Most important is the crazy new sentiment that this is not just a movement but a revolution. . . . In our future dealings, we should realize that they have changed down here, and we should speak their revolutionary language without mocking it for it is not lip service, nor is it the ego fulfillment of a rising Negro class, but it is in truth the fact of life in the South this minute, and unless the North or the government or nuclear war intervenes, we are going to be down here soon ourselves in jail, or fighting, or writing, or being lynched in the struggle. It is a good, pure struggle . . . a struggle that we have every reason to begin in a revolutionary way across the country, in every place of discrimination that exists. There is no reason for us to be hesitant anymore. There is no reason for us to think we can do something more important out of jail.

Two years ago we in effect falsified this movement to claim it was an event with which we identified. We didn't really. We saw it as something we should extend, that . . . could provide a cutting edge for more reforms through the society. Well, now the southern movement has turned itself into that revolution we hoped for, and we didn't have much to do with its turning at all. . . . Now they are miles ahead of us, looking back, chuckling knowingly about the sterility of liberals, tightening grimly against the potency of the racists. In the rural South, they will be shouting from the bottom of their guts for justice or else. We had better be there.

A remarkable SNCC organizer named Bob Moses had settled in Mississippi shortly after the bloody Freedom Rides of May 1961. A twenty-five-year-old teacher at the Horace Mann School in New York City, Moses was moved by the faces of the black students he saw leading demonstrations on television. "They were kids my age, and I knew this had something to do with my own life," he said.

People who came in contact with the quiet, shy, bespectacled Moses knew they were in the presence of a special leader. Rather than preach and arouse people, rather than make himself the visible leader, Bob instead set an example through practice, gained loyalty by listening, helped individuals empower themselves. He created the pattern of non-leadership that affected many of us for years.

Traveling through Mississippi looking for contacts, Moses met a longtime NAACP member, Aimzie Moore, who convinced him to leave New York for good and establish a new voter project in the state. Moses's contacts led him finally to a farmer named E. W. Steptoe in Pike County. A civil rights pioneer in the area, Steptoe was a small, proud man possessed of ancient wisdom, innumerable stories to tell, and a shotgun behind his living room door. He tried to register to vote in 1953 but was failed by the registrar. After the Supreme Court decision of 1954, he tried to organize an NAACP chapter only to have it broken up by the Ku Klux Klan. "My uncle," he recalled to Moses, "was run into the woods and stayed for weeks, living on raw food. Then he finally came out, and he left the county." Now Steptoe was ready again, to give shelter, contacts, and advice to Moses and other SNCC organizers filtering into the back country. At first Bob couldn't find a place to meet in McComb, a city of eight thousand in the heart of Pike County.

Eventually, however, he was helped by the local dry cleaner, Ernest Noble, and Mrs. Ilene Quinn, proprietor of a small restaurant called South of the Border.

A handful of people soon registered by themselves, successfully, but one was fired upon shortly after. On August 15, Moses took three people to register in Liberty, where they were allowed to fill out the voter forms, a minor victory in itself. Moses was arrested and held in jail for two days. On August 28, he was beaten very badly by Billy Jack Caston, cousin of the sheriff and son-in-law of state representative Eugene Hurst. Moses needed eight stitches in his scalp. At first he tried to hide both his injury and his bloody shirt to keep the local people from being frightened, but since he couldn't conceal his blood, he decided the next day to do the unprecedented and brought a suit against his white assailant for assault and battery. At the trial on August 31, about one hundred angry whites showed up, and Moses had to be taken out of the chambers by police, his suit dismissed.

Bob set up a Freedom School in McComb that same August. The school drew about twenty people, half under twenty-one years of age, who studied the complicated registration form used to exclude blacks. Some black history was added as well to compensate for the official school texts, which described the Civil War as the War of Northern Aggression, praised the role of the Klan, and pointed out certain merits of slavery.

The violence rose. In the first week of September, as Casey and I arrived in Atlanta, two more SNCC workers were beaten for attempting to register people. Bob Moses could feel the tide of fear overcoming the desire to vote among the local people. Fewer and fewer were willing to go down to the courthouse. On September 25, an Amite County NAACP member, Herbert Lee, was shot and killed in broad daylight by Eugene Hurst, the elected official whose son-in-law had assaulted Moses. Shot in the brain with a .38, Herbert Lee's body was left in the gutter for two hours. For the next three nights, Moses traveled the back roads, sleepless, awakening frightened sharecroppers, looking for possible witnesses to the murder. He failed to find anyone willing to come forward. In late October, a federal grand jury considered indicting Eugene Hurst. A black sharecropper named Louis Allen said he could testify as an eyewitness if protection was given. None was. Word got around that Allen might talk. He was killed by a shotgun blast two years later.

Incidents like these raised questions about the commitment of the Kennedy administration. Moses once said that from America, Mississippi seemed unreal, and from Mississippi, America seemed unreal. One's first reflex in trying to understand the slow pace of federal action is to blame it on ignorance, the lack of understanding in the administration of the real depth of rigid entrenchment of segregation in the Deep South. But this comforting explanation seems without merit in retrospect, since the FBI and Justice Department received a regular stream of reports, phone calls, and eyewitness accounts of the mayhem in Mississippi.

The Kennedy administration was caught in the contradiction of the whole Democratic party between its civil rights rhetoric and its political alliances with Dixiecrat segregationists. Having contradictory coalitions was not new to the Democratic party. The difference was that New Deal economic populism and rhetoric against "plutocrats" was able to unite the northern and southern wings of the Democratic party during the Depression, but the new populism of the sixties, based on racial equality, challenged the Dixiecrats. The administration could not please both the civil rights forces and the old South.

At the very beginning of the New Frontier there emerged a pattern of timidity and tokenism on the part of the Kennedys, an attitude that planted seeds of skepticism and anger in the civil rights workers as it tested the limits of conservative and southern support for the administration. Eventually John and especially Robert Kennedy would see from personal experience that their human and political destiny lay with the civil rights movement, but not before SNCC concluded that the liberal administration had to be seriously pressured for even moderate reform. The administration, in the person of Attorney General Robert Kennedy, urged SNCC to channel its militance into voter registration and helped secure significant private foundation support, but it took little or no action against those intimidating or preventing southern blacks from exercising the franchise. The administration relied for law enforcement mainly on an FBI headed by J. Edgar Hoover who, we now know, believed Martin Luther King was both a communist tool and an evil man. King's estimate of the FBI, which was shared throughout the movement, was that the FBI agents were "white Southerners who have been influenced by the mores of their community. . . . To maintain their status, they have to be friendly with the local police and people who are promoting segregation." These agents, unfortunately, were the chief intelligence and enforcement arm of the Kennedy administration in the South.

Kennedy also yielded to the prerogatives of entrenched southern segregationist senators in the appointment of federal judges to the courts in their region. One of these Kennedy-appointed judges, in Georgia, said, "I don't want these pinks, radicals and black voters to outvote those who are trying to preserve our segregationist laws and other traditions." Another, from Mississippi, said, "I am not interested in whether the registrar is going to give a registration test to a bunch of niggers on a voter drive."

A pattern of slow and token official reform achieved at the price of blood and frustration began to characterize the time. The antidiscrimination executive order in federally assisted housing, promised in 1960, finally came twenty-two months later and was narrower in scope than its original promise. The decision by the Interstate Commerce Commission, which banned bias in interstate travel as requested by the administration, came only after the bloody Freedom Rides battered through the doors of southern bus terminals. The sending of courageous federal marshals to protect James Meredith's 1962 enrollment at the University of Mississippi was similarly in response to a violent confrontation with international repercussions. The administration's clear and meaningful support for the August 1963 march on Washington would be memorable, but it came only after President Kennedy tried to persuade black leaders not to hold the march.

These administration initiatives and decisions would be recorded in history as important acts, but from a grass-roots, frontline perspective they were isolated and reactive interventions in a relentless daily process of racial conflict that eventually would grind down the goodwill of the most dedicated and aware civil rights workers. In places like McComb, Mississippi, there was not much sign of the New Frontier.

On the night in 1961 before Herbert Lee was killed, for example, Moses and E. W. Steptoe met with one of the most sincere of Justice Department officials, John Doar. Then in charge of the Civil Rights Division, Doar later endured the violence of James Meredith's entry into the University of Mississippi, and in 1973 became the staff director for the congressional Watergate proceedings against Richard Nixon. On that fateful night in 1961, Moses and Steptoe tried to convince Doar that Herbert Lee was going to be killed unless he received federal protection. Lee, a neighbor of Steptoe, was enrolled in Moses's voter school and was the first to try to register to vote since the assaults on SNCC workers. A Pike County judge had declared at a recent trial of SNCC workers, "Every effort you make to stir up violence in this community will be met. Some of you are local residents; some are outsiders. Those of you who are local residents are like sheep being led to the slaughter. If you continue to follow the advice of outside agitators, you will be like sheep and be slaughtered."

So far as I know, John Doar did not act.

The Mississippi crisis had reached this point when I first began working in Atlanta. Phone calls were coming into the Atlanta SNCC office from organizers in McComb hiding in the back of the dry cleaning store owned by the courageous Ernest Noble, while police and white vigilantes roamed the streets outside. It seemed certain that some of my new friends were going to be killed in a matter of days. Paul Potter, now an NSA official, and I volunteered to go to Mississippi to investigate, report to federal officials, and seek media interest.

We took an overnight flight from Atlanta to Jackson. Bob Moses was also aboard the plane, but we agreed to travel apart. In the early dawn we rented two separate cars and drove south from Jackson three hours to rural McComb.

Agreeing to meet Moses later, Paul and I checked into a McComb motel, two white men with northern accents driving a conspicuous car. Russian agents couldn't have been much more obvious, and that's how we were soon regarded. Our plan was to use our skin color and journalistic credentials to move around both sides of town and form impressions before our presence was widely noted.

Black students at segregated Burgland High School were planning a demonstration two days hence. Their protests had begun a few weeks before with a sit-in at the local bus station. As a result, two students were expelled from school and one of them, Brenda Travis, was now confined at the "Colored Girls Industrial School," a reformatory in remote Oakley, Mississippi. The Burgland students were demanding Brenda's release and protesting the murder of Herbert Lee. We planned to stay through the march after spending some time interviewing figures in the white community.

The next morning we left the motel room for the short ride to downtown McComb, where we encountered a spectrum of segregationists ranging from moderate to extreme. The first, a newspaper editor named Oliver Emmerich, was viewed as the town liberal for having editorialized against the police whipping of an arrested black youth in the fifties. For this editorial, Emmerich himself was beaten by a mob of his angry readers. Despite this, Emmerich—a rotund, educated, slightly pompous man accustomed to speaking for *all* McComb—opposed any form of desegregation. He did allow that blacks had reached a "more civilized state" since the days "back when you couldn't have them in your living room," but he was certain that the high school protests were "manufactured" and lectured us on the ills being visited on the South by hypocritical northern liberals like ourselves.

Finding no sympathy from the most "progressive" force in town, we decided next to discover what the police chief, George Guy, might have in store for SNCC. The classic central-casting stereotype of a redneck sheriff, Guy left no doubt as to his intentions. Blacks, he declared right off, are "better treated down here than anyplace in the world. We pay 'em, support their schools with taxes, work 'em. But they know they're niggers. They know their place." From his desk he pulled out several photos of SNCC organizers, conveniently supplied by Emmerich's newspaper. About Bob Zellner, a white activist whose drawl was as deep as his Alabama roots, Guy said, "They'll kill that one if he comes back down here. We can't keep him protected. We don't go for that mixing stuff."

I suddenly felt less camouflaged in my white skin. I wondered what the chief would think if he knew I was a close friend of Zellner's—or if he knew already and was not saying. I wondered if the chief's choice of words meant there were people loose in town more violent than he, and whether he would look the other way if a lynch mob showed up. Maybe the chief knew more than either of us college-educated "white boys" realized. We would soon find out.

Using pay phones, we arranged to meet the SNCC organizers after dark. We drove the rented car to a closed gas station at an agreed hour. There we left ours to get into a vehicle parked in the garage shadows, apparently empty. When we opened the door we found Charles McDew of SNCC grinning in the back seat. "Welcome to McComb, the Camellia City of America," he drawled, and we moved forward into the street.

McDew was the chairman of SNCC. A former Massillon, Ohio, football player, a combination of intellectual, jock, and playboy, McDew was an instant positive force in any situation. His ear-to-ear grin, white teeth on black face, and absolutely arrogant fearlessness, drove the segregationists crazy. He laughed at people who wanted to lynch him and goaded the timid into action, quoting Hillel the Elder: "If I am not for myself, who will be for me? If I am only for myself, what am I? If not now, when?"

McDew steered us to a darkened house not far from the gas station. We went through a back door into the basement. Lights were on, and Bob Moses looked up from his desk with a placid smile. Blankets were hung over the windows around the room.

We stayed up late discussing SNCC's vision and plans. Moses viewed Mississippi as a focal point. By bringing local and ultimately national pressure to bear on this most rigid stronghold of segregation, the whole South could be cracked in time. But the breakthrough would require organizers getting enough local people to overcome their fear of voting. The national press and Justice Department would be forced to react only if there was violent suppression of the right to vote. The project was beginning here in these southern counties, Moses said, because this was the first place he'd found local people ready to support a registration drive. He was clearly struck with the moral strength of the rural blacks, whose family structures were tight and supportive, who lived close to the land, and whose values were relatively untainted by the consumer society. These were the people Moses was depending on. He spoke of Mr. Steptoe, of the dead Herbert Lee, of others he'd met, sharecropper women like Unita Blackwell and Fannie Lou Hamer in Mississippi's northwestern Delta. These people only needed encouragement to believe they were qualified to vote and act as citizens, and that would have to come from organizers willing to accept the danger.

We ended our talk late at night and returned dead tired to our motel room, planning to meet the following morning at the

Freedom School Moses and McDew had opened, and from there go to observe the high school students' demonstration.

When we arrived at the Freedom School the next morning, I saw McDew nonchalantly sauntering up the street to the church. Along the sidewalk were a dozen whites yelling curses at him. For the first time in my life, I heard people threatening openly and loudly to kill someone on the spot. McDew flipped them the finger, as if they were just another morning nuisance, and walked safely into church.

I couldn't get used to the fear growing in me. Terror is the disappearance of any line between what is probable and what is only possible. I couldn't tell if the screaming segregationists were going to open fire, or if a car coming down the street was going to swerve and try to run me over. I didn't know how to cope with raving psychopaths only a few feet away from me. Give them the finger too and swagger into the church? Chuckle and pretend to agree with them? Show them my press card and ask for an interview?

Now that McDew was gone they were yelling toward the church: "We oughta cut off your nuts, put 'em in a bag and throw 'em in the river." Then they turned to me and asked "what the fuck" I was doing. I replied as steadily as possible, "Just reporting," and moved casually toward the car. Once inside, I locked all the doors and drove with Paul over to the school where the march would begin.

At the high school, the kids were already lining up outside— one of the youngest group of demonstrators yet to join the civil rights movement. Paul and I stood alongside them, taking notes. Chief Guy appeared suddenly, his mood less civil than the day before. I walked over and politely asked him if he knew what the students were planning to do and when. "Don't ask me," he answered coldly. "Get McDew to tell you." He knew who we were.

The students were ready to march. A flyer proclaimed their stand:

> In the schools we are taught democracy, but the rights of democracy have been denied us by our oppressors; we have not had a balanced school system; we have not had an opportunity to participate in any of the branches of our local, state and federal government; however, we are children of God, who makes our fellow

men to love rather than hate, to build rather than tear down, to bind our nation with love and justice without regard to race, color or creed.

We, the Negro youth of Pike County, feel that Brenda Travis and Ike Lewis should not be barred from acquiring an education for protesting an injustice. We feel that as members of Burgland High School, they have fought this battle for us. To prove that we appreciate their having done this, we will suffer any punishment we have to take with them.

As they started to move, we got in our car to follow and observe. A police officer came over to inquire about our identity, although we'd introduced ourselves twice to Chief Guy. We said we were observers gathering information.

"You sure aren't gathering much information sitting around with your windows rolled up," he said, opening and unlocking the driver's door. "We can't protect everyone around here, 'specially outsiders like yourselves." He ordered us to drive to the police station for further identification.

We began driving, slowly, alongside the march, one police car escorting us. The students were moving along the dusty road of the ghetto toward the viaduct and railroad tracks, where they would enter the paved, white section of town. They were carrying American flags and signs. I watched them briefly before noticing that the police car was turning right, away from the route downtown. I smiled and nodded to the students marching by.

As we stopped for a traffic light, the right passenger door—which we thought was locked—came ripping open, and two very muscular white arms yanked Paul out on the ground. Though it took only seconds, it seemed like a slow-motion nightmare watching Paul roll into a ball under someone's stomping boots. Then the same hands were yanking me from the car, tearing my hair as I fell into a crouch of nonviolence. Punches and kicks started landing from every direction.

I remember being on my feet, still claiming ridiculously that I was a reporter, being pushed around by a little knot of screaming men while a sheriff slowly separated us. One of the witnesses told the officers that Paul and I were riding in the car and fell out on our heads. But in the confusion, a miraculous thing happened: A white photographer from Emmerich's paper whispered that he had taken pictures and hidden them. He told us we should get out of town because, he said, "They are coming to take you" from the motel that night. We were arrested and ordered to City Hall.

A big crowd was waiting for us on City Hall steps, yelling more threats. We went inside, were booked, and were taken into a small room where suddenly there appeared a tall, well-dressed gentlemen with an executive bearing who identified himself as a representative of the Mississippi State Sovereignty Commission. That body, in our understanding, was the respectable political front for the Ku Klux Klan, White Citizens Council, and other segregationist organizations. This man had an investigator's badge, asked a lot of questions about our backgrounds and purposes, and several times suggested that we would be charged with "vagrancy."

We were resigned to spending an indefinite time in jail, and hoping only to avoid further beatings, when he declared we had to leave town immediately. Faced with that or jail, we asked for our car keys. In a few minutes, we were racing north to Jackson, the blood on our clothes and swellings on our heads the only reminders of our stay in the Camellia City.

At the Atlanta airport, we were met by two FBI agents who wanted to interview us. The agency had been mobilized by repeated phone calls and telegrams from the SNCC office condemning the beatings and threats to our lives. We told them our story, specifically claiming that Chief Guy knew that we were going to be attacked and that the police waited until the beating was over before intervening. We also emphasized that by Chief Guy's own admission the lives of civil rights workers were in danger, a threat which required protection from the FBI.

FBI MEMORANDUM   **10/12/61**
File # 44-1211

THOMAS EMMETT HAYDEN, legal residence 560 Moreland Ave., NW, Atlanta appeared at the Atlanta office of the Federal Bureau of Investigation, at which time he typed the following statement:

> **". . . It was clear that they knew about our every action in the two days. It was clear that the beating was not accidental . . . How were we recognized by a man I had never seen? How did he know we were driving towards**

City Hall? Where did the police go? When did the Sov.
official appear? . . . And how did the photographer know
we were staying at the Lake Motel, if he had not heard
something from the police?"

Investigation indicates assault was by Carl Hayes, a local electrician, who was later arrested for assault and battery. No indication police were involved. Potter and Hayden interviewed in
Atlanta and did not allege any mistreatment by police.

The next morning we flew to Washington to tell our story to
Justice Department officials and call for stronger federal action
to protect civil rights workers. We met in what seemed the very
spacious office of Burke Marshall, the assistant attorney general
in charge of civil rights. Marshall, a sympathetic though legalis-
tic aide to Robert Kennedy, was destined to be in the thick of
every civil rights crisis involving the administration in those
years. He listened gravely to our recounting of the previous
day's events and showed his keen awareness of the denial of
voting rights in rural Mississippi. I therefore was stunned when
he came to his main suggestion for us:

"I think Bob Moses and those others down there are going to
be killed. There is no way we can protect them. Can you help
us persuade them to leave those areas?" he asked, peering quite
sincerely over his glasses.

"Is the Constitution not in effect in Mississippi?" I responded.
"Are you really saying that there are parts of the country where
violent racism is stronger than the federal government can control, that these lynch mobs are outside the reach of the law?"

He seemed unflappable and replied again, very evenly, "I'm
afraid they'll be killed if they stay down there."

Marshall was, of course, trying to be decent and helpful
within his own framework. But from that point on I began to
feel that we had been officially abandoned.

While SNCC continued its voter registration efforts in the
Mississippi Delta, a new crisis was prompting a return to nonviolent direct action in Georgia, where a handful of SNCC workers began setting up operations in the fall of 1961. The area,
described by W.E.B. DuBois in *The Souls of Black Folk*, was as
forbidding as any part of Mississippi:

For a radius of a hundred miles about Albany stretched a great
fertile land, luxuriant with forests of pine, oak, ash, hickory and

poplar, hot with the sun and damp with the rich black swamp-
land, and here the cornerstone of the Cotton Kingdom was laid.

Albany was a city of sixty thousand, about one third black, the
only semiurban locale in this vast area of the Black Belt. Nearby
was the hamlet of Plains, where a farmer named Jimmy Carter
was active in local business and political affairs. At Albany High
School, the student body president was Hamilton Jordan, later
to become chief of staff in Carter's White House. To the east
stretched Terrell County, among the most violent and segregated in the South. In 1958, the U.S. Justice Department chose
Terrell to file the first suit claiming voting rights violations
under the Civil Rights Act passed the previous year. Only 48 of
5,036 eligible black voters were on the rolls in a county where
70 percent of the potential voters were black. In 1959, *The Washington Post* chronicled the conditions facing blacks who attempted to vote there. Almost thirty years later, I found the
article in an old folder, torn out and yellowed, its contents still
stunning:

> A Negro was beaten severely in his front yard by police. He was
> hauled senseless into court and died from a crushed skull five days
> later. Another Negro was shot to death in his backyard by police.
> A third Negro was shot in the buttocks by police when they
> investigated a disturbance call at a juke joint. A Negro mother was
> slapped in jail when she went to visit her son there. Two dozen
> Negroes tried to vote. Many were teachers. All failed.

"Well, Cap," the *Post* quoted the sheriff,

> "I believe we ought to be strict about who votes. There isn't a
> nigger in Georgia who wouldn't take over if he could. They want
> all the power. The nigger has progressed under our system and
> we sure wouldn't progress under his. Isn't that right? I tell you
> this, Cap, all this agitation is the work of communists. . . .
> "A man who knows the nigger can tell when dissatisfaction is
> brewing. Niggers up late at night are suspicious. You know, Cap,
> there's nothing like fear to keep niggers in line. I'm talking about
> outlaw niggers."

I visited Albany in late November, less than a month after the
Interstate Commerce Commission (ICC), on a request of Robert
Kennedy, banned all discrimination of facilities used for inter-

state travel. The Freedom Rides had opened the way for the ruling; now the question was what would happen to black or integrated groups who used the bus and train terminals of the Deep South. Just before my arrival, five students were arrested while attempting to use the Trailways restaurant facilities. Two of them were indefinitely suspended from all-black Albany State College, and five hundred people gathered to protest at City Hall, an unprecedented number.

I drove into Albany on November 29, planning to gather details and generate telegrams and calls of support from northern campuses. In a letter to SDS, I described conditions in the local SNCC office:

> The new office is located in a run-down pocket of the S. Jackson street Negro community. Leaving the car and crossing the side-walkless dirt space to the office, one can read the lettered signs on its old door:
> Wake up Tom and Vote
> Want Paved Roads? Then Vote
> A Voteless People is a Voiceless People
> Inside are two rooms alive with action. A tape recorder is going with SNCC people singing freedom songs. The volume is way up. The rhythm of the mimeograph provides a counterpoint to the intense "We Shall Overcome."
> On the shelves are pages of the "Student Voice," waiting for recruits who will staple them. Lists of the names and addresses of the Negro community hang from the walls, checkmarks noting those who have registered to vote so far. The ringing of the phone momentarily cuts off the singing and the mimeo's rattle. "Good evening, Student Nonviolent Coordinating Committee . . ."
> There is no reply, and everyone's face shows they already know the party at the other end of the line. There is a steady, repeated beeping sound. The tapping sound is tape recorded; Charles Jones also records the time of day and the date; the beeping suddenly ceases.

I went to dinner that night at the home of a local family who were unafraid to welcome civil rights workers. We talked of the recent local Albany election, which had resulted in a victory for a "moderate" white, Asa Kelley. My host thought the voter registration drive was already forcing whites like the new mayor into greater moderation. Unlike rural Mississippi,

Albany had a rising new class of young black professionals whom she hoped the white establishment would recognize and accept. As we ate, a phone call came from the police station, from a SNCC worker just arrested back at the office for "trespassing" on the grounds of Albany State. Warrants were out for the SNCC workers who were sitting around the dinner table as well. After hanging up, we sang three verses of "We Shall Overcome" in the living room. My friends prepared for being arrested. I called New York to dictate telegrams of support to be sent to the students in jail and to the Justice Department.

The Albany Movement was beginning; history would later record that "never in the nation's history had so many people been imprisoned in one city for exercising the right of protest." Not knowing the shape of things to come, SNCC decided that a Freedom Ride from Atlanta to Albany was necessary to challenge the segregationist defiance of the new ICC order. Casey and I were among the eight tapped to take the train to Albany on Sunday morning, December 10. We worried briefly whether the railroad would even let us sit in an integrated group as we boarded in Atlanta. When the conductor asked us not to sit in the "white" car, we refused. To my relief, he shrugged and walked off. We had integrated a passenger car, and we sat back to enjoy the experience. Not until we neared Albany a few hours later did my anxieties return.

Our plan was to enter the railroad terminal in Albany and test whether Police Chief Laurie Pritchett and local officials would let us integrate the terminal or continue their policy of noncompliance with the ICC order. When the train finally drew into the station, there was an eerie anticlimactic quiet. We disembarked and strolled into the terminal's empty waiting room, where, through the windows, I began to see a large crowd of blacks watching with eager interest across the street. We were welcomed by two local SNCC leaders, who started to discuss taking us to a church rally, when suddenly Chief Pritchett appeared from where he had been waiting and observing. Pritchett ordered his officers to arrest us for "blocking the sidewalk" and "obstructing traffic." In a swirling maneuver, all of us were quickly grasped and forcibly escorted to police wagons for the ride to jail.

Our jailers separated us into cells for blacks and whites, men and women. Mine was the dingiest I'd ever seen, a drunk tank that already held four men in its darkness.

"This one here is a nigger lover, boys," the jailer drawled as he slammed the metal door. "Take good care of him for us."

As my eyes adjusted, I could see there was one man for each of the four metal cots. The only space was on the floor between them, where I noticed a puddle of urine and the pathways of cockroaches. My first worry was how to fend off any or all of my cellmates. Fortunately for me, none of them looked to be in very good shape. They were there to sleep off their drunkenness, not to fight a second Civil War. I lay on the wet floor and assembled my wits.

It was my twenty-second birthday. I borrowed a pencil and piece of paper from a civil rights lawyer who was allowed a brief visit, and I began to compose a letter:

> The cell from which I write is perhaps seven feet high and no more than ten feet long. The only light penetrates from a single bulb beyond the bars down the hall. My human cellmates are sleeping, but the cockroaches are up and around quite early. . . .

To those who did not pass through the southern civil rights experience, willfully going to jail may seem like a career-threatening act of despair. It was not. It was both a necessary moral act and a rite of passage into serious commitment. For individuals to break through the veil of fear that held people back from directly confronting the wall of segregation itself required raw courage and philosophical commitment. The possibility of violence, even death, was omnipresent. Entering jail meant achieving a personal freedom from fear. Once there, a spirit of intense solidarity, concern for others, singing and storytelling, and deep reflection bonded people into a stronger community. As the catacombs were to the early Christians, the jails were the places where a new faith was fortified. One could not be in the civil rights movement without wanting to be in jail.

The hours passed, and then suddenly late in the second day, we were bailed out. A few minutes later, we walked into a church packed with black people who welcomed us as heroes. Their singing, which became a special feature of the Albany movement, was more inspired than I'd ever heard. A group of young people, who became known as the Freedom Singers, were leading the throng in my favorite song. It sounded like a dirge, then rose in a powerful force:

We've been 'buked and we've been scorned,
We've been talked about sure as you're born,
But we'll never turn back.
No, we'll never turn back.
Until we've all been freed,
And we have equality.

We have walked through the shadows of death.
We've had to walk all by ourselves.
We have hung our heads and cried,
Cried for those like Lee who died.
Died for you and he died for me,
Died for the cause of equality . . .

A very powerful mass movement, the first on such a scale since the 1956 Birmingham bus boycott, was born in Albany that week. Albany's mayor later said that our arrests were his "biggest mistake. We never should have arrested those Freedom Riders." Two days later, 267 more students were arrested at our arraignment, and the next day two hundred more. "We can't tolerate the NAACP or the SNCC or any other nigger organization to take over this town with mass demonstrations," declared Chief Pritchett. The National Guard was mobilized a day later. The jails were filling, and Martin Luther King agreed to commit time and personal leadership to seeing the Albany struggle succeed. Meanwhile, the Albany mayor and Georgia's governor assured Robert Kennedy by phone that the entire crisis was provoked by outside agitators.

The Albany battle unexpectedly went on for months, the movement rising then ebbing, unifying then factionalizing, and the city's white leadership unwilling to yield any fundamental ground—even with the president of the United States urging negotiations. Occasional violence and arrests continued, with bail costs constantly mounting. Our trial for the original Freedom Ride finally was held on a clear spring morning, and Casey and I chose to sit on the black side of the segregated and jammed Albany courtroom. The gesture ended the trial before it began. My last recollection of Albany justice came as I was dragged across the courthouse floor and yanked like a rubber pretzel through the revolving doors. The trial was not rescheduled.

The importance of Albany to us all, as time dragged on with few results, was a new sense of doubt among both activists and black followers toward the practice of nonviolence itself. The complete rigidity of local officials and the lack of decisive help from Washington undermined the belief in "loving one's enemy." The movement's nonviolent strategy presupposed a conscience, somewhere, that could be aroused. But here it was dormant or nonexistent. At one march, blacks hurled rocks at police for the first time in the movement's turbulent history, an act which so shocked Dr. King that he called for a day of penance. But in a vicious circle, the more that Dr. King demonstrated nonviolence, the more resistant was the power structure and the more prolonged exposure there was to the apparent failure of the movement. The minister who earlier had hoped to "reach the better people" was later quoted as saying, "The white church, and the white community, let us down. The white community was without a heart, without a conscience."

Pat Watters, author of one of the best histories of the southern movement, detected a sense of "final despair" from the prolonged impasse of the Albany conflict, and a turn toward a time when "nonviolence became only a tactic for influence, not a matter of personal ethics." Religious appeals to immoral power seemed increasingly irrelevant. It was clear that a "cost" factor had to be inflicted on the oppressors. If they lacked souls, they did not lack self-interest. Their power, economic and political, would have to be challenged by our creation of some form of *new* power. If this was the dawn of a new realism, it was also a rip in the moral umbilical cord linking us to American society.

We had not lost our vision or moral fervor, but we began to suspect that our parent society had.

4. | Port Huron: June 1962

From the Albany jail in December 1961, I composed a letter to my friends in SDS. We were to meet in Ann Arbor in two weeks to decide the fate of the organization. Now, in my tired isolation, I understood the question that had been troubling me for months. Simply put, it was whether SDS was going to get its act together and become a national organization, a counterpart to SNCC in the rest of the country.

I didn't want to go from beating to beating, jail to jail, a lone field representative for an organization that was little more than a mailing list. SDS was still mainly an idea nurtured in the minds of a few dozen activists. While I traveled the South, Al Haber was making phone calls, sending out mailings, and paying personal visits to the bright new activists he seemed to scent all over the country. Now was the moment to see if SDS was an idea whose time had come.

SNCC could not go on alone. There was an entire generation to arouse, primarily about civil rights but also about the larger issues that SNCC itself had begun to raise. Casey and I had written an analysis of a tension "between the continuing need to maintain the spiritual source of the movement and the newer need, faced by all organizations, for expertise and comprehension of the whole process of social change."

Haber had called the Ann Arbor meeting of key activists to

decide, once and for all, whether to launch a call for our new national organization. Sitting in jail, I composed a letter that was to be sent out prior to the meeting. To those invited, I posed three questions on the sheet of paper provided me:

- What direction do we want to give SDS?
- How much does each of us want to share in its shaping?
- What are we personally prepared to contribute?

Without recognizing it, I was beginning to acknowledge that my role in the South was limited. SNCC didn't need me in their well-filled ranks. Where I could be more useful was in galvanizing students nationally to confront the system and change it.

About a week after leaving the church meeting in Albany, I found myself in the snows of Ann Arbor, huddled with forty or so activists who, it turned out, were eager to commit their lives to building a national student movement together. But how? After three days of searching discussion, we decided to draft a "manifesto of hope" that we could propose as an "agenda for a generation." We believed that the new values directing us away from conventional careers to unexpected commitments had to be expressed. We felt a need to declare our aspirations to the generation of young people we were trying to awaken, in hopes that the larger society would listen in time. I was put in charge of the first draft. So began the writing of what became *The Port Huron Statement*, the formative declaration of SDS.

I still don't know where this messianic sense, this belief in being right, this confidence that we could speak for a generation came from. But the time was ripe, vibrating with potential. Students like ourselves were struggling for something more than a twenty-five-cent hamburger in the South. We needed to put our goals into words. Many of us were student leaders who were conditioned to believe that if you spoke out, you would get a hearing from the Kennedy administration. In the phrase of the novelist Doris Lessing, we possessed "the power to create through naïveté."

At that point, the organization consisted of myself, reporting from southern battlefronts; Al Haber, using a phone and mimeograph in New York; a few functioning chapters in such places as Ann Arbor, Oberlin, and Swarthmore; eight hundred dues-paying members (at one dollar a year); and two thousand scattered activists on mailing lists. Despite this skeletal structure, we were convinced that we were riding the beginning of a great wave of student action. As the mood of expectation grew, Haber began looking for a site for our founding convention.

Casey and I were still living in Atlanta in the spring of 1962, still fully involved with each other and the civil rights movement. We organized a workshop in Chapel Hill, North Carolina, bringing together SNCC and SDS activists for the first time. The attempt was to connect the issues of race, poverty, and political disenfranchisement into a comprehensive strategy, but the meeting faltered on a difference of outlooks. Many of the northern SDS activists, articulate in a bookish sense, came with theoretical blueprints for realigning the Democratic party, linking organized labor with civil rights organizations, repealing right-to-work laws in the South, and the like. The SNCC activists on the other hand, articulate in a poetic sense, approached issues from the spiritual perspective that enabled them to cope with daily persecution. Finding a shared purpose, a linkage between moral witness and electoral politics was difficult. Casey shared SNCC's impatience with the "intellectualizing" of the northerners. I felt split, convinced that the movement needed a more political direction than perpetual civil disobedience, but agreeing with Casey that the primary question was changing the values of society, not just modifying government structures. I argued that *moral* realignment had to precede political realignment, a view that became central to the manifesto on which I continued to work.

Shortly after the conference, Casey moved to New York with me, where I could be surrounded with books, documents, and files, scrambling to finish the draft so that Haber could mimeo and mail it out before the SDS convention. I sent a long reading list to our members, reflecting the thirty-odd texts I was consulting in preparation of the document, ranging from John Dewey to Fyodor Dostoyevsky to the Democratic party platform of 1960. I was not looking for a political line, but for inspiration. "Are there any prophets," I asked in a letter, "who can make luminous the inner self that burns for understanding?" If there was an intellectual assumption most in SDS shared, it was that politics should flow from experience, not from preconceived dogmas or ideologies. The lesson of our experience was that the civil rights and student movements had taken all political intellectuals by surprise. We were making a chapter of history no one had predicted. In formulating our vision and ideas, therefore, it was most important to draw lessons from that same experience instead of relying on the textbooks of others. We were not anti-intellectuals, but we were determined to study all philosophies through the lens of our own experience, accepting the relevant and pruning the irrelevant, searching for a language and vision all our own.

The two writers who had the most powerful influence on us were Albert Camus and C. Wright Mills, both of whom died in the early sixties.

Casey introduced me to Camus's essays shortly after we met, and I began referring to them in *Daily* editorials not long after. A Frenchman born in colonial Algeria, Camus experienced both the Nazi occupation of Paris and the agonies of the French-Algerian and Indochinese wars. Beginning with the ultimate existential question—"Judging whether life is or is not worth living amounts to answering the fundamental question in philosophy"—Camus developed a reasoned and dramatic defense of individual moral action against hopeless and "absurd" odds.

Many, if not all, SDS and SNCC founders immersed themselves in Camus's writings. We thought that, like the fictional citizens in Camus's *The Plague*, Americans were going about business as usual while denying the existence of pervasive and threatening evils. It was our task to awaken the nation to these evils and face them ourselves through daily personal acts like registering voters in the South. Camus's hero, a doctor who treated plague victims and organized sanitation teams (while in the process losing his wife and a friend), expressed the philosophy that I was searching for: "All I maintain is that on this earth there are pestilences and there are victims, and it's up to us, so far as possible, not to join forces with the pestilences."

In passages that seemed to foreshadow our own future, Camus warned of a "desperate weariness" that came from long struggles against such evils; of the "blind endurance that had ousted love from all our hearts," since love "asks something of the future, and nothing was left us but a series of present moments." He wrote that the plague swallowed up everything and everyone, causing a "sense of exile and deprivation, with all the crosscurrents of revolt and fear. . . . There are times . . . when the only feeling I have is one of mad revolt."

He juxtaposed such "mad revolt" against the genuine rebellion that consisted of standing against injustice even if life is "absurd," without apparent meaning. This act of rebellion by itself asserted a human nature worth preserving from extermination and drew the individual from solitude to solidarity: "I rebel—therefore we exist."

I took not just consolation but inspiration from these reflections. If Auschwitz, Hiroshima, and Nuremburg were the "birth pangs" of our generation and middle-class apathy our inheritance ("A single sentence will suffice for modern man: he fornicated and read the papers"), Camus taught us how to confront our legacy. It was not necessary, he said, to know pragmatic outcomes before deciding to take ethical action: "I understand why the doctrines that explain everything to me also debilitate me at the same time. They relieve me of the weight of my own life, and yet I must carry it alone."

The path of taking action without certainty of the effects, I believed, represented a confidence that the individual mattered in history, that nothing was entirely determined, that action created an evidence of its own. Why else take your life in your hands in Mississippi? Why else plunge into an effort to change the world?

I also realized there was a limit to rebellion for its own sake. None of us wanted to be Sisyphus, pushing the boulder up the hill over and over. I wanted to win. Was there an ideology that could translate our values and channel our energy effectively toward success? And, if so, was the task to connect ourselves with an existing ideology—pacifism or socialism, for example—or would it be necessary to invent a blueprint of our own?

Here I fell under the powerful influence of the heretic sociologist C. Wright Mills, whom I began to read at the suggestion of Dick and Mickey Flacks while I was editor of the *Daily*. Descendants of the radical Jewish culture of New York City, they rode in their baby carriages in peace marches and grew up in the traditions of the Left. The Rosenbergs were their teenage martyrs, Paul Robeson and Pete Seeger their cultural heroes, but Khrushchev's undeniable revelations in 1956 about Stalin's reign of terror had disillusioned and depoliticized them, as it had thousands of other believers. Dick and Mickey married shortly after high school and, while retaining their youthful ideals, decided to pursue professional careers and family life.

Having seen too many of their parents' generation give their entire lives to political movements only to be destroyed or disenchanted, the Flacks were searching for balance and stability. They were committed to family, career, and long-term radical change. Mickey was an administrative assistant in an academic research center, and Dick a diligent graduate student of social psychology. The student activism of the early sixties surprised and interested them, and my quixotic editorials rejuvenated Dick's interest in politics. He was fascinated that I was a home-grown idealist with a Catholic, midwestern background; a similar fascination drew him to C. Wright Mills.

A Columbia University professor with the same Texas populist roots as Casey, C. Wright Mills defied the drabness of academic life and quickly became the oracle of the New Left, combining the rebel life-style of James Dean and the moral passion of Albert Camus, with the comprehensive portrayal of the American condition we were all looking for. Mills died in his early forties of a heart attack during the very spring I was drafting *The Port Huron Statement,* before any of us had a chance to meet him, making him forever a martyr to the movement.

I was influenced deeply by *The Power Elite,* which Mills wrote in the mid-fifties. In my own introspection, I was torn between rival beliefs about power in American society. I was certain that power was held undemocratically, but I also believed that power could be transferred through the democratic process. What theory, I asked, could reconcile these apparently contrasting notions? Liberalism, it seemed, refused to embrace the concept of undemocratic power; instead, it asserted that there existed a rough pluralism between contending interest groups like labor and management, or between the two major political parties. In the liberal view, disparities of power could be corrected through the political system of lobbying and elections. My experiences as a student and in the South taught me to suspect this model. To start with, southern blacks and students like ourselves— together fifteen million people—were not allowed to vote, the very simplest precondition for being an "interest group" in liberal theory. Efforts to reform the system on the elementary level of voting rights, which meant taking American ideals seriously, were met with racist violence and official tokenism. In addition, I was already predisposed to assume that there was an "establishment" with permanent power running the country without being elected or even known to the average citizen. But at the same time, the Marxist theory of a ruling class, with its power based on controlling the means of production, seemed mechanical and dogmatic, its conclusions as dreary as liberalism's were rosy. I could not accept the traditional Marxist view of government as the "executive committee of the ruling class," merely an instrument of the business agenda. Such a view threatened the premise for which we were risking our lives: that we could register people to vote as a step toward their becoming free and equal human beings, that we could gain recognition within the existing decision-making process for those who were currently excluded. The Marxist model asked me to believe that this was an illusion, that real power lay elsewhere, or that inclusion in a bankrupt system was not worth dying for. As a corollary to dismissing reform, it held out its own myth—that of distant revolution.

In *The Power Elite*, Mills suggested the notion of a broad elite, rather than an economic class, drawn from the upper circles of the corporate, political, and military worlds, whose power, he claimed, rested on a bureaucratic convergence of their interests, not on a conscious and coordinated conspiracy. The immediate glue holding together the power elite, Mills felt, was the Cold War, the division of the world into two camps, good and evil, American and Russian, and the permanent nuclear arms race and military-based economy that this view demanded. Although President Eisenhower had warned of a military-industrial complex, and President Kennedy called for visions "beyond the Cold War," American society in the fifties and early sixties was still deeply in the grip of Cold War thinking, a mentality that led the country into places like Vietnam, which were seen as Soviet proxies. Mills linked this mentality to the rise of apathy and the decline of dissent. The assumption of an evil and threatening foreign enemy justified a growing centralization of power in the hands of the Pentagon, a lessening of attention to domestic issues, and it created, in Mills's apt phrase, a "state of acquiescent dread" among the public at large. What most interested me was Mills's exploration of the factors that made people uninterested and apathetic in the face of Camus's plague. Mills feared the emergence of the "cheerful robot," an individual in mass society having only an illusion of reason and freedom, existing in an isolated personal context divorced from the larger structures where his or her destiny was being determined. Thus cut off, the individual took life's problems to be the workings of a mysterious fate, not the responsibility and doing of bureaucratic elites. It struck me that Mills was describing the world of my father, especially in *White Collar,* a book about the new middle class typified by accountants and clerks: "Between the little man's consciousness and the issues of our time, there seems to be a veil of indifference. His will seems numb; his spirit meager." As I pored through Mills, I saw an image of my father, proud in his starched white collar, occupying his accountant's niche above the union work force and below the real decision makers, penciling in numbers by day, drinking in front of the television at night, muttering about the world to no one in particular.

If the thirties had been a political age with clear economic issues and choices, Mills wrote, the new era was one of "unease" and "indifference," signifying the loss of individual moorings in a sea of bureaucratic expansion. If the task in the thirties had been to demand jobs for the unemployed, the task in the fifties was more complicated: Put simply, it was to prevent the coming of the cheerful robot by transforming these drifting individuals into self-aware citizens, the amorphous masses into an educated public.

The concept of a "self-cultivating public" was rooted for Mills in the period between the American Revolution and the Jacksonian era. In those times, Mills believed, Americans showed they could become self-governing individuals, reading aloud from Tom Paine, arguing on street corners, attending town meetings, creating real grass-roots democracy. That is what Mills yearned for, and what SDS set forth to carry out. He seemed to be speaking to us directly when he declared in his famous "Letter to the New Left" that all over the world young radical intellectuals were breaking the old molds, leading the way out of apathy. He rejected the classic leftist model in which the working class was the key agency of change. Instead, he identified ourselves, the young and the intellectuals, as the new vanguard. It was a heady mandate, and Flacks and I felt validated personally. Mills became so influential for Dick and Mickey that they named their first son, born in 1966, after him. Mills's fatal heart attack, which I read of in *The New York Times* while I was preparing the SDS manifesto, deeply jarred me. It was as if he was broken by the attempt to wake up America. My fascination continued; two years later, I wrote a master's thesis on him, titled *Radical Nomad.*

Mills's analysis validated us not only personally, but as a generation and as activist-organizers, the political identity we were beginning to adopt. We tried as organizers to penetrate what Mills called the private "milieu" of those we were trying to reach, whether southern blacks or the students next door to us. Such people often felt helpless, or blamed themselves for their fate, too isolated to identify and blame larger institutions. Organizers in SNCC and SDS talked to people not only about specific issues, but about their lives and feelings. We attempted to show that the power elites were to blame for seemingly individual troubles, and communicated that they had to take back power and responsibility over their lives. Mills shed intellectual light on this therapeutic process.

In a speech I gave in Ann Arbor in March 1962, while working on the proposed SDS manifesto, I cited a survey which showed that only 3 percent of all students in the fifties gave high priority to "being active in national affairs or being useful." Five times as many believed that the university's function was to teach "getting along with people" as opposed to "citizen participation." A Gallup survey concluded that youth would "settle for low success and won't risk high failure"—exactly the opposite of my orientation. An attack on apathy was an even higher priority for me than talking of issues such as racism and war. My speech, which became a widely distributed SDS pamphlet called simply *Student Social Action,* echoed Mills in saying that behind apathy exists

> the decomposition of democracy in this country. People are becoming more remote from the possibility of a civic life that maximizes personal influence over public affairs. There is a deep alienation of the student from the decision-making institutions of society . . . fewer and fewer individuals are able to perceive truly beyond their immediate and limited circles, their mileus. . . . A sense of powerlessness evolves. . . . To the extent that these powerless participate in public affairs, they participate with impotency. . . . They seek to conform their actions to what the Top People like, they just try and get by, feeling pretty content most of the time, enjoying the university's benevolent laxity about drinking regulations, building up their exam files, playing it cool.

I described the main character in Camus's *The Stranger* as the "paradigm of the man lacking relatedness to anything at all" in whom I saw the profile of a drifting generation whose "public lives were undeveloped" and private lives restricted to a "privately constructed universe," a place of systematic study schedules, two nights a week for a beer, a steady girl, early marriage—all programmed and under control.

The opposite of apathy was personal independence, which I believed was the university's responsibility to encourage:

> The main concern of the university should not be with the publishing of books, getting money from legislators, lobbying for federal aid, wooing the rich, producing bombs and deadly bacteria. . . . The main and transcending concern of the university must be the unfolding and refinement of the moral, aesthetic and logical capacities in a manner that creates genuine independence.

In defining this independence, I stressed the development of whole human beings as more important than simply recruiting people to an issue or an *-ism* of any kind. I defined what I meant by personal independence and why it was of such crucial value:

> —a concern not with image or popularity, but with finding a moral meaning in life that is direct and authentic for the self.

> —a quality of mind that is not compulsively driven by a sense of powerlessness, nor one which unthinkingly adopts values of the Top People, nor one which represses threats to its habits, but one which has full, spontaneous access to present and past experience, one which openly faces problems which are troubling and unresolved.

> —an intuitive alertness to that which is capable of occurring, to that which is not yet realized, and passion for continuous unfolding of human potential.

This was literally a first draft of the manifesto I was preparing for Haber and the upcoming SDS convention. These were the qualities, I was certain, that were needed before a genuine, lasting, and effective political movement could be built. With these weapons, I said, we "might unravel the heavy cape of impotence . . . and bring once more the will and the ability to exert real influence over events as citizens." In the first reference to the central theme of *The Port Huron Statement*, I asserted that "democracy, real *participative democracy*, rests on the independence of the ordinary people."

My concluding advice was directly personal rather than political and programmatic:

> All over the world the young intellectuals are breaking out of the old, stultified order. Before you call them "communist" or "extremist" or "immature," stop a moment, let yourselves be a little more insecure, so that you can listen to what they are saying and perhaps feel the pulse of their challenge.
>
> Their challenge politically takes many forms, with which we may agree or disagree; but the essential challenge is far deeper. It is to quit the acquiescence to political fate, cut the confidence in business-as-usual futures, and realize that in a time of mass organization, government by expertise, success through technical specialization, manipulation by the balancing of official secrets with the soft sell, the incomprehensible destructiveness of the two world wars and the third which may be imminent, and the Cold War which has chilled man's relation to man, the time has come for a reassertion of the personal.

The speech was well received, and I knew it was the right public appeal for SDS to make. It became a prelude to the manifesto I was writing. I kept struggling with the lengthening draft of the convention document, not finishing until May. Originally conceived as a twenty-page statement, the draft was now seventy-five pages long. Even worse, Haber could not find a site for the convention. Tempers and frustrations rose. At the last possible moment, Sharon Jeffrey's mother, Millie, secured a retreat site belonging to the Michigan AFL-CIO near the small town of Port Huron, ninety minutes' drive north of Detroit on Lake Huron's shores. We sent out maps along with copies of the seventy-five-page draft to waiting chapter leaders around the country, reaching their mailboxes just before they began driving to the convention. Haber and I were better on dreams than details.

My father and I had gone perch fishing out of Port Huron many times when I was a boy. Using two and sometimes three hooks, we usually caught a large stringful of the small, hard-fighting fish. On one trip in 1957, we took my high school girlfriend, Anne Grimm. Struggling to be a good sport on the rolling waves, she got sick all over the boat. It embarrassed her, but we laughed over the episode for a long time.

As I returned five years later, Port Huron remained a small community, unaffected by the changes beginning in America. Driving north of town for fifteen minutes, we found the AFL-CIO camp right on the lake's spacious and beautiful shoreline. Built by labor movement women in the thirties, it consisted of a central hall and a cluster of cabins, all made of sturdy oak, with screened-in porches on all sides. There was a shining beach at our doorstep, and soft, sandy trails through glens of tall trees all around.

The sixty people who came to Port Huron were enchanted with the surroundings and expectant about the days ahead. Who were these people? Some were from backgrounds that I have termed political. Besides Haber, Ross, Jeffrey, and the Flackses, there was Paul Booth, a Swarthmore College student leader who came from a social-democratic family heritage, a nuts-and-bolts political reformer. There was Steve Max, whose father was a former editor of the *The Daily Worker* (I joked with Max that I was the former editor of *The Daily Smirker,* an "important voice of bourgeois youth"). Max was a caricature of the New York political man, always in search of a new party to join or a leaflet to circulate, never tiring of meetings, debates, and demonstrations, arguing every tactic from an ideological perspective. In fact, Max was extremely funny and humane, as well as shy, but he viewed movements and politics in impersonal terms, even in the language he employed, for example, when he advocated "political realignment" of the Democratic party, as if it were essentially a vehicle whose axles needed adjustment.

There were others, like Casey, whose political beliefs arose from religious or spiritual roots: a Protestant seminarian named Jim Monsonis, who became the SDS national secretary, and Mary Varela, who had a Catholic college past. They came prepared to debate the importance of vision and morality in politics, seeking a balance between their religious and secular experiences, striving for a community more than a party, but a community with strategy. Still others were student leaders like myself: Robb Burlage, editor of the University of Texas paper; Gary Weissman, student body president at the University of Wisconsin; Betty Garman and Becky Adams, from Skidmore and Swarthmore, respectively. We were already more achievement-oriented than the others, given our campus backgrounds. By nature we wanted to succeed, not simply serve as a marginal conscience of society; but we did not want success at the expense of broad principles.

While Dick Flacks came to write about Port Huron for a small left-wing weekly, most of us came self-confidently to found a movement. Steve Max came to propose another political line; we came to declare a crossroads in history. "We may be the last generation in the experiment with living," declared one apocalyptic section of the draft. Where others might have felt isolated from mainstream America, we believed its familiar apathy could be lifted. However difficult the odds ahead, our backgrounds of achievement made us feel charmed.

In the spirit of the times, we tended to adapt to, and learn from, the differences between the various backgrounds of those who came to Port Huron. A sense of radical history, a focus on values, and a desire for relevance, taken together, could enrich and reinforce the strength of our common understanding.

As people arrived from all over the country, many of them tired or exhausted, they began complaining that the draft manifesto was too long and had arrived too late for their examination. I was in some trouble. We held a long impromptu meeting at which I begged them not to reject the draft, however awkward and lengthy it was. The organization needed a statement of its vision, and the convention would flounder or collapse without adopting a document of some kind. Finally, reluctantly, a creative compromise was proposed. We would consider the statement a "living document," rather than try to make it formal and binding, which would have been impossible. No one would have to answer for every point, paragraph, or phrase.

To expedite the process of considering a seventy-five-page draft, a further procedure was suggested by the ever-inventive Paul Booth. Issues which the whole group considered to be major would be termed "bones" and given a hour's plenary debate. Relatively important matters, or "widgets," were given thirty minutes, and minor issues, or "gizmos," were to be dispensed of within five minutes. The group was not to concern itself with language; that would be the job of a postconvention drafting committee. There was one exception: My opening section was considered less than exciting as an "agenda for a generation." It began, "Every generation inherits from the past a set of problems—and a dominant set of insights and perspectives by which the problems are to be understood and, hopefully, managed. . . ." I was told to rewrite it in a more sweeping and visionary manner and bring it back to the full meeting for approval.

We designed small democratic groups—something like those which C. Wright Mills had imagined—to sit around tables, or under trees, drinking coffee, taking notes, arguing animatedly, over eight separate sections of the draft: themes and values, the role of students, American politics, the economic system, racism, communism, foreign policy, and the nuclear issue.

Just before we began, however, there was an ugly moment that hinted at trouble to come. Despite our own arrogance, we had gone to some lengths to build good relations with the older liberal-left community, particularly the LID. Not only were we dependent on the AFL-CIO for our site, but we invited several leading intellectuals to join us and provide input, including Arnold Kaufman, the Michigan theorist of "participatory democracy" and Harold Taylor, president of Sarah Lawrence University, an important influence on me since the days I was a student editor. We knew that as we attempted to break new ground it would be important to have sympathetic and established friends who could defend and interpret us in the existing political world.

Michael Harrington was another such friend. At age thirty-two he described himself as the "world's oldest young socialist." The author of *The Other America,* a work on poverty that became a classic when President Kennedy praised it, Harrington was easily the most charismatic of the political intellectuals we listened to. I met him first marching outside the Democratic National Convention in Los Angeles, then again several times in New York, and I admired his extraordinary debating talents and writing style. He was a personal friend and had attended our wedding. An Irish Catholic from St. Louis, he had become a fervent democratic socialist and was widely whispered to be the next Norman Thomas. Harrington was brilliant at polemics, particularly among the combative and sectarian denizens of the New York intellectual Left. Now he was representing the LID.

Sectarianism, the incestuous infighting among left-wing groups and intellectuals over doctrine, has roots going back to the beginning of the Left itself. The early manuscripts of the young Marx were notable in their humanism. At some point, however, his writing became a bible for atheists in search of a new and total belief system; Marx became Marxism. Then, with the revolution in the Soviet Union, Leninism entered the Left's vocabulary as the model of a centralized, disciplined, secretive party. Leninism in time splintered into the rival dogmas of the communists, social democrats, Trotskyists, and so on, divisions which were sealed in blood in the Stalinist slaying of the exiled Leon Trotsky in Mexico in 1947. Martyrdom now fused with dogma, and a small group of Trotsky's former followers gathered in New York (Trotsky himself had lived on the Lower East Side) under the guidance of Max Schachtman, Trotsky's personal secretary of many years, who himself had broken with Trotsky in the late thirties. Swiftly becoming known as Schachtmanites, defining themselves principally as anti-Stalinists, or socialists without a country, in opposition to communist parties everywhere, they attracted a small but serious network of intellectuals, including the young Michael Harrington, into their debates. Those of us entering SDS from nonpolitical backgrounds found this atmosphere amusing, obscure, and irrelevant, like fervent religious sects poring over catechism or the Torah. I could not understand how seemingly serious people could get so enmeshed in such endlessly divisive hairsplitting debates. Surely there was no lesson in their experience for us.

In addition to its doctrinal warfare, there was an organizational spirit to sectarianism that was at opposite poles to what our New Left was about. Like the communists they hated, the Schachtmanites were obsessed with organizational intriguing and "boring from within" larger and more respectable organizations. They were most successful in the AFL-CIO. In a curious twist of history, Schachtmanite anti-Stalinism converged with the Cold War interests of the CIA, which covertly funded many AFL-CIO programs abroad. The average workingman in Detroit had no idea that his union dues were subsidizing the intrigues of former Troskyists who were weeding suspected communists out of American trade unions and carrying out CIA-funded programs in the Third World.

The same Schachtmanites also bored from within the Democratic party toward political realignment, the making of a more liberal party through the purging of southern racists (a goal we tended to share, though for simpler reasons). Their youth group, the Young People's Socialist League (YPSL—pronounced YIP-sal), was pursuing a similar strategy of boring from within the fledgling SDS, which they thought would be a more respectable and nonsocialist front group for working on single-issue projects while recruiting future YPSL cadre one by one.

Two of their number, Tom Kahn and Rachelle Horowitz, worked in the LID office keeping an eye on Haber. Kahn, then in his mid-twenties, was the author of an impressive pamphlet on political realignment. He was slender, sallow, and the first gay man I'd met. From the perspective of my primitive prejudices, that made him a wimp. More startling was the fact that he enjoyed a personal relationship with Bayard Rustin, the striking, silver-haired, black elder statesman of the movement who had shaped the Montgomery bus boycott in 1956. I had a phobia against attending meetings at their apartment, which I remember as being filled with innumerable clocks. The other leader of the YPSL cabal, Rachelle Horowitz, as imposingly plump as Kahn was thin, maintained an incessant office chatter about the latest intrigues on the New York Left. Communists, including former ones like Steve Max, were, in her lexicon, all "Stalinists"; anyone not sharing her ideological hatred of the Soviet Union was a "Stalinoid" or an "anti-anticommunist" (Haber and I were suspected of these latter leanings). Harrington was their most popular public voice, an Irish Catholic mid-westerner like myself, for whom the texts of Marxism seemed to be new scriptures. (If so much history of an obscure cluster of YPSLs seems odd, consider this: Kahn became chief speechwriter for AFL-CIO president George Meany, who was an extremely conservative Cold Warrior; Rustin organized the 1963 march on Washington and later urged the civil rights leadership to support Hubert Humphrey and avoid the Vietnam issue; Horowitz became a top leader of the American Federation of Teachers and married Tom Donohue, secretary-treasurer of the AFL-CIO, labor's second most powerful position. The cabal had nothing if not staying power in its strategy of boring from within. The doctrinal fight that was about to occur over Port Huron would have long-term consequences in splitting labor's form of liberalism from that of the New Left.) At the time, all the intellectual infighting and plotting was too much for my innocent midwestern mind to fathom, but I didn't want anything to do with this nest of YPSL political incest.

Harrington went to Port Huron as the key LID liaison and observer of what SDS was up to and, as he read my draft of *The Port Huron Statement,* became incensed at my deviations from the LID correct line. First, he found the section on the Soviet Union, always the first doctrinal litmus test, insufficiently hard line. I had simply questioned whether the Soviet Union was *inherently* expansionist, aggressive, and bent on taking over the world by military means, or whether it was becoming a defensive and paranoid status quo power. It was an important question, one which I did not fully resolve but one which reopened a debate that Harrington's group thought had been settled twenty-five years before. I then went on to question whether American military policies had been truly effective in deterring communist-led revolutions or whether they had imposed right-wing, antidemocratic military dictatorships, which were themselves spawning the conditions of communist revolt. I wrote that "to support dictators like Diem [in South Vietnam] while trying to destroy ones like Castro will only enforce international cynicism about America's 'principle.' We should end the distinction between communist hunger and anticommunist hunger." Harrington was offended by the statement that "an unreasoning anticommunism has become a major social problem for those who want to construct a more democratic America." I specifically singled out members of the Left for throwing "unreasoning epithets" at each other.

The section on organized labor was even more upsetting to Harrington, Horowitz, and Don Slaiman, another AFL-CIO leader present. While criticizing business for its attacks on labor and supporting new organizing drives among the unorganized, I wrote that "labor has succumbed to institutionalization, its social idealism waning under the tendencies of bureaucracy, materialism, business ethics. . . . The successes of the last generation perhaps have braked, rather than accelerated, labor's zeal for change."

While those were the only criticisms of the AFL-CIO in a document calling labor the "most liberal of the mainstream institutions" and declaring that "a new politics must include a revitalized labor movement," they were enough to bring Harrington and his allies into the Port Huron setting full of defensive anger.

The tension exploded on the first evening in an impromptu debate that began with some critical remarks by Harrington and lasted into the night. Most of us, myself certainly, were not prepared for, and were antagonized by, the pontificating style of sectarian debate. In an insightful comment years later, Steve Max described those of us who were new to this tradition as "kids [who] came from households where nobody raised their voice. They had never heard anybody shout about politics. . . . In the tradition I was used to, you sharpened the differences, you had a knock-down, drag-out fight, winners and losers." By contrast, we looked for consensus, points of agreement, ideas that could lead to joint action. We found divisions painful to address and winning debates by a close margin no victory at all. To make matters worse, this open and nonconfrontational ethos had allowed us to seat as a nonvoting observer one Jim Hawley, an eighteen-year-old representative of something called the Progressive Youth Organizing Committee (PYOC), a front group for the Communist party. He left the next day, but not before Harrington and Slaiman relived their ideological wars with communism.

Behind the arguments over communism, Harrington and Slaiman were much too invested in defending the American labor movement. They were true believers in the "labor metaphysic" Mills had described, the sacrosanct doctrine that organized labor was the only genuine agency of change and could not be faulted, least of all by a bunch of neophyte students. No one had a right to question labor's leadership on every social issue of the time. And none of us had a right to question the anticommunist priority that had been axiomatic in the liberal-labor community for the past generation. Our two sides were talking completely past each other, however; the question of what to do with a centralized and secretive Communist party in the midst of larger movements, which certainly was a question from the thirties to the forties, was totally irrelevant by the sixties. Because of McCarthyism as well as its own doctrinal problems, the American Communist party was simply no longer a force. Moreover, we were utterly confident that organizations like SNCC and SDS could not be "taken over" by secret groups and that our visiting critics were paternalistic and paranoid.

The fallout from that night was long-lasting. In the short run, after the Port Huron convention, Haber and I were suspended from our LID posts. It was the second time for Al. The year before, the LID fired him for two months simply because he proposed turning SDS into an "action" as opposed to an "educational" organization, a change affecting their tax status. This time, we were called to defend ourselves before the LID board with Harrington as the accuser.

Within months, however, our positions were restored through the intervention of principled individuals like Harold Taylor and, surprisingly, Norman Thomas, who chastised the LID for their rigid behavior. Never again, though, would we feel attached to the LID or its tradition, and three years later SDS divorced itself altogether. Meanwhile, Mike Harrington was transformed in our minds from an important role model to a negative one. He later regretted his behavior, realizing that he was not fighting some newly reincarnated Stalinists but only admiring protégés who wanted to make their own independent decisions. Having been drawn into official Washington's atmosphere of power and status because of his book on poverty, only to experience a simultaneous rejection by the young radicals whose respect he badly desired, was too much for him. He went through an identity crisis and later wrote of experiencing a nervous breakdown before finally righting himself and resuming the role of a respected social critic.

The political damage to those of us in SDS was severe. As a formative experience, we learned a distrust and hostility toward the very people we were closest to historically, the representatives of the liberal and labor organizations who had once been young radicals themselves. We who had enough trouble gaining acceptance from our real parents were now rejected by our political father figures. What was at stake was not ideology, but basic trust from one generation to the next. From our perspective, it was we, not they, who were risking lives and careers to achieve democratic social change in America. They were pointing fingers and missiles at the Soviet Union without doing enough to advance freedom in Mississippi and southwest Georgia. They were discrediting any reasonable merits of anticommunism by demanding a form of loyalty oath from the young to the old.

Here lay the larger importance of what might seem a minor, though bitter, dispute in the history of the times. Mike Harrington, the LID, the AFL-CIO, even Walter Reuther, who was a financial supporter of SDS, eventually took their militant anticommunism to such a dogmatic extreme that they supported U.S. military intervention in Vietnam. Harrington, to his credit, was the first to defect from the consensus, but not until the mid-sixties. Reuther followed later in the decade. Others did only when the Republicans took the White House in 1969, while some never changed their hawkish views. Since they essentially represented the liberal-left wing of the Democratic party, they legitimized the pro-war positions of a spectrum of Democrats extending all the way to the White House. Without their initial support for the Vietnam War, debate within the Democratic party would have begun much earlier. Instead, the dissent of the New Left necessarily focused on the follies of the Democratic party and was forced outside the party into increasingly unconventional forms, including protests in the streets.

In retrospect, I regret that the extreme overreaction to SDS by its elders left me numb to potentially valuable lessons of their experience. If our elders could see us only through the distorting lens of the past, it was true as well that my infatuation with "the new" made it difficult to sift out what made sense in their paranoid critique.

Whether to the crimes of communism described in Orwell or Kafka, or to Camus's injunction that heinous acts could be rationalized by cultivated intellectuals, or to the repeated warnings that revolutionary leaders become ruling Frankenstein's monsters, I reacted with one feeling: These horrors won't happen to us; we are too good.

The absurdity of the LID overreaction to the SDS was shown in the new language that Dick Flacks, himself a weary veteran of the wars of the Left, inserted in *The Port Huron Statement* to further clarify our positions on communism:

> As democrats we are in basic opposition to the Soviet Union. Communism, as a system, rests on the total suppression of organized opposition . . . The communist movement has failed, in every sense, to achieve its stated intention of leading a worldwide movement for human emancipation.

It was hard to believe after the night of arguing with Harrington and Slaiman that the actual convention discussion of the draft statement had yet to begin. With the communism question out of the way, however, we could return to the harder task of drafting a generational appeal. Harrington and Slaiman went back to New York, and we went to work on the real mission before us. I don't remember getting much sleep that week or missing it. As the hours blended into days, I kept getting renewed energy from the intensity of the group process. We debated and put on paper the deepest values that had carried us this far. I was so exhausted late one night that I actually slept on the floor at the entrance to the breakfast line so that I would be awakened in the morning.

Finally, I crafted a new introduction that won approval:

> We are people of this generation, bred in at least modest comfort, housed now in universities, looking uncomfortably at the world we inherit. . . .

This was clearly a generational appeal directed in particular to the middle class, a call to the comfortable to get involved. As we grew up, I noted, "our comfort was penetrated by events too troubling to dismiss": racial bigotry and the nuclear arms race. Then there came "paradoxes" (the choice of words still interests me—the old Left would have said *contradictions,* but *paradox* was an intellectual discovery, not an objective conflict): the paradox between the Declaration of Independence and racism; the paradox between official professions of peaceful intent and a galloping military budget; between automation and idleness; affluence and undernourishment; growth and the environment; the need for new ideas versus national stalemate; and one other, embarrassing in retrospect, between the prospective beneficial use of nuclear power—which we hailed as a decentralized energy source—and the greater likelihood of nuclear destruction.

Standing between us and social change was the hard fact of apathy, the "felt powerlessness of ordinary people," which rested on a sense of hopelessness and perhaps the most outstanding paradox: "We ourselves are imbued with urgency, yet the message of our society is that there is no viable alternative to the present." The new introduction continued:

> Beneath the reassuring tones of the politicians, beneath the common opinion that America will "muddle through," beneath the stagnation of those who have closed their minds to the future, is

the pervading feeling that there simply are no alternatives, that our times have witnessed the exhaustion not only of utopias, but of any new departures as well.

Feeling the press of complexity upon the emptiness of life, people are fearful of the thought that at any moment things might be thrust out of control. They fear change itself, since change might smash whatever invisible framework seems to hold back chaos for them now. For most Americans, all crusades are suspect, threatening. The fact that each individual sees apathy in his fellows perpetuates the common reluctance to organize for change. The dominant institutions are complex enough to blunt the minds of their potential critics and entrenched enough to dissipate swiftly or repel entirely the energies of protest and reform, thus limiting human expectancies. Then, too, we are a materially improved society, and by our own improvements we seem to have weakened the case for further reform.

This formidable list of obstacles was only meant to make our task more necessary and daring. Beneath the glaze of contented apathy, I asserted, were deeply felt anxieties and a "yearning to believe there is an alternative to the present," a yearning to which we would appeal.

The audacity of the introduction continued as we plunged into the section on values, the heart of *The Port Huron Statement*. While most political groups and some of the participants might start by describing their goals in a programmatic sense, it was our consensus that if a movement were built around a consciousness of new values, a program and tactics would naturally follow. The discussions of our values, both in small-group and plenary sessions, were the most intense and liberating of the convention. Plato once wrote of values, in a passage that influenced me in college, that "in everything that exists, there is at work an imaginative force, which is determined by ideals." The values discussions at Port Huron were our trips to Plato's cave, to ask the question, Why are we doing what we are doing? It was a question much on everyone's mind, given the unusual and unexpected turns our lives had taken, but Port Huron was one of the only opportunities to explore it with each other.

There seemed to be two perspectives for us to consider: One was associated with the theologian Reinhold Niebuhr, who was convinced by the experiences of the thirties—the emerging

Holocaust and Stalinism—to adopt a stark view of the soul, becoming what we called a Cold War liberal, closely associated with Hubert Humphrey and the Americans for Democratic Action. Borrowing from Luke (16:8), he argued that the cynics of the thirties, the "children of darkness," were "in their generation wiser" than the "foolish children of light," the pacifists and idealists of the time. We considered ourselves the new "children of light" and his pessimism seemed to deny that our current hopes could be realized. His philosophical defense of democracy incorporated this anti-utopian despair. "Man's capacity for justice makes democracy possible," he wrote. "But man's inclination to injustice makes democracy necessary." We were clearly not ready to accept such gloom.

The second perspective was linked to the Enlightenment, to Marxism, to the liberalism of John Stuart Mill and John Dewey, to humanistic psychologists, and in some ways to C. Wright Mills, and it held a more optimistic view of human possibilities, akin to ours. According to the enlightened tradition, humankind was "infinitely perfectible" if supported by open, educative, and liberating institutions. Essentially, this was also the belief of those who embraced nonviolence as a philosophy, not simply as a tactic. While most of our experience in seeing oppressed and forgotten people struggle with courage for their rights made us confident and utopian, we also had encountered enough evil to doubt that love alone was the cure. Finally, after much introspection and debate, we examined a third option, closer to our understanding of Camus, that asserted the necessity of struggling for a better world as the only way to live. Human greatness, Camus had written, lies in man's "decision to be stronger than his condition." Since the case for neither hope nor despair could finally be proven, it was left to human beings to attempt to live according to moral values and to create institutions that would advance the process.

Mary Varela, a fair-complexioned Mexican-American with deep brown eyes, was a student body president at Alverno College, a small value-centered institution near Milwaukee. For seven dollars a week, she was a national traveler for something called Young Christian Students. She believed that a "religious spirit" came to earth in 1960 to "move in the world," and that faith was fueling revolution in the South and in Latin America. More religious than political, Mary was silent during most of

Port Huron. "The political ideology was over my head," she said. "I never observed factions before. I met my first communist, Steve Max, and I was his first Catholic!" During the intense values discussions, Mary pulled out her copy of Pope John XXIII's *Pacem in Terris* encyclical and read a section that declared that human beings were "infinitely precious" rather than "infinitely perfectible," with "unfulfilled capacities" for good, not "unlimited" ones. We accepted the pope's formulation and included it verbatim in the document without any citation.

In describing our values, we used the word *man* to refer to both men and women throughout *The Port Huron Statement*, reflecting a blindness toward the blatant discrimination against women that afflicted society. The women's movement of the era had not begun. Only a few of us read Simone de Beauvoir's *The Second Sex*. Doris Lessing's *The Golden Notebook*, which had a major effect on the early SDS, was just being published. Mickey Flacks demanded that I read Betty Friedan's *The Feminine Mystique* when it appeared in 1963. The National Organization for Women (NOW) was not formed until 1966. Yet twenty-five years later, despite the male-centered language, the values expressed in *The Port Huron Statement* seem carefully thought through and universally applicable:

> We regard men as infinitely precious and possessed of unfulfilled capacities for reason, freedom and love. . . . We oppose the depersonalization that reduces human beings to the status of things—if anything, the brutalities of the twentieth century teach that means and ends are intimately related, that vague appeals to "posterity" cannot justify the mutilations of the present.
>
> The goal of man and society should be human independence. [These words came from my earlier speech on "Student Social Action."] But this kind of independence does not mean egotistic individualism—the object is not to have one's way so much as to have a way of one's own. Nor do we deify man, we merely have faith in his potential.
>
> Loneliness, estrangement, and isolation describe the vast distance between man and man today. These dominant tendencies cannot be overcome by better personal management, nor by improved gadgets, but only when a love of man overcomes the idolatrous worship of things by man. As the individualism we affirm is not egoism, the selflessness we affirm is not self-elimination. On the contrary, we believe in a generosity of a kind that imprints one's unique individual qualities in the relation to other men, and to all human activity.

When we turned to the question of what *system* would make these strivings most possible to realize, we arrived at the heart of the matter, the advocacy of a "participatory democracy" governed by two central aims:

> . . . that the individual share in those social decisions determining the quality and direction of his life;

> that society be organized to encourage independence in men and provide the media for their common participation.

Political life, in a participatory democracy, would be based on several root principles:

> that decision-making of basic social consequence be carried on by public groupings;

> that politics be seen positively, as the art of collectively creating an acceptable pattern of social relations;

> that politics has the function of bringing people out of isolation and into community, thus being a necessary, though not sufficient, means of finding meaning in personal life;

> that the political order should serve to clarify problems in a way instrumental to their solution; it should provide outlets for the expression of personal grievance and aspiration; opposing views should be organized so as to illuminate choices and facilitate the attainment of goals.

As for the economic sphere, participatory democracy would mean three things:

> that work should involve incentives worthier than survival. It should be educative, not stultifying; creative, not mechanical . . . encouraging independence, a respect for others, a sense of dignity, and willingness to accept social responsibility, since it is this experience that has crucial influence on habits, perceptions and individual ethics;

> that the economic experience is so personally decisive that the individual must share in its full determination;

> that the economy itself is of such social importance that its major resources and means of production should be open to democratic participation and subject to democratic social regulation.

This latter clause was added to satisfy the criticism that the document was more "new" than "left." In the draft I had written that "private enterprise is not inherently immoral or undemocratic—indeed, it may at times contribute to offset elitist tendencies." The words were struck.

There was one other value included in this basic statement, seemingly as an afterthought to the long discussion of participatory democracy. A paragraph was inserted that declared "violence to be abhorrent because it requires generally the transformation of the target, be it a human being or a community of people, into a depersonalized object of hate." This was taken for granted and provoked no discussion.

It was an ambitious and sweeping statement of values, all the more so in the context of the times. We were rejecting the limited concept of democracy that had come to prevail, one in which expertise, specialization, and bureaucracy had come to count for more than popular will. We fought for voting rights, but what we singularly wanted was *participation*—not new representatives, but new constituencies acting in the historical process. In part, our democratic idealism flowed from a populist root, the belief that an informed public would make "better" decisions about its own interests than anyone else. But what stands out more boldly in retrospect was that we were envisioning a new and alternative process that involved people as independent and creative human beings, expressing a new force outside of existing institutions, a society apart from the state, rehabilitating itself from apathy and thus dissolving the immediate structures of its oppression.

We did not anticipate that the oppressed in whose name we spoke would want to enter the middle-class world we were rejecting—which is largely what happened as blacks achieved the right to participate. Nor did we anticipate that the nihilistic side of human nature we acknowledged could surface in ourselves when democracy failed or was too slow in responding—which happened to SDS in only seven years. At the time, we were having a transcendent experience, the kind that happens perhaps once in a lifetime. When we saw the aurora borealis at night, or finished work at sunrise, we blessed our luck at being alive and together. We were truly in love with each other; as Casey wrote later, "it was a holy time."

The programmatic sections of *The Port Huron Statement* made

for an idealistic and sometimes curious litany slightly to the left
of the Democratic party in its content. We railed at an economy
dominated by "remote control" according to priorities of the
military-industrial complex and envisioned the new and humane possibilities of automation if introduced in the service of
human ends. We condemned the perpetuation of the Cold War
at the nuclear brink and called for joint steps to replace the arms
race with an alternative race toward disarmament, economic
development, and industrialization. We identified racism as a
"steadfast pillar in the culture and custom of this country" and
targeted the congressional coalition of Republicans and Dixiecrats for demise. There were planks calling for a more decentralized public sector, an antipoverty program, economic
development in depressed regions, cities having more local control and "access to nature," public health and mental health
programs, more teachers and smaller classes in an "internation-
alized" education system, more money for a "decent prison environment," help for small farmers, and a major science
initiative ("the International Geophysical Year is a model for
continuous further cooperation between science communities
of all nations," we for some reason declared).

Then we asked a final set of questions:

> What are the social forces that exist, or that must exist, if we are
> to be at all successful? And what role have we ourselves to play
> as a social force?

The answer began with an analysis of the civil rights movement, contending that for all its victories it had reached an
impasse that could be broken only by organizing for political
power, in order to change the "quality of southern leadership
from low demagoguery to decent statesmanship." This, we believed, would deal a blow to the entire reactionary coalition that
held its power through the grip of racist southerners in the
congressional seniority system.

Second, we noted that "the broadest movement for peace in
several years emerged in 1961–62, including several peace can-
didacies for Congress and a widespread intellectual interest in
a nuclear test ban and disarmament talks." But so far, we noted,
the peace cause remained tied to an emotional single issue ("ban
the bomb"), and the activists operated only on the peripheries

of mainstream institutions. The peace movement, like the much larger civil rights movement, would have to enter the political process and make the case for new priorities to other constituencies slighted by the military budget, such as labor and educators. In the meantime, we argued, peace activists should begin studying the key question of conversion from military to peacetime production and make the abstract issue of war and peace "relevant to everyday life, by relating it to the backyard [shelters], the baby [fallout], and the job [military contracts]."

Next came the critical analysis of organized labor, which already so bothered our AFL-CIO hosts. We added a paragraph on the need for middle-class students to overcome their "ignorance, and even vague hostility" toward labor bureaucrats by working together with labor on educational programs, local political campaigns, and union organizing drives on campus.

Additionally, there was an endorsement of a "new spirit of Democratic party reform," which we felt was beginning to grow at local levels throughout the country. We noted that "pillars of the liberal community" such as *The New Republic* magazine and Americans for Democratic Action (whose student coordinator was an ally of ours) were lately critical of the president. We concluded that a resurgent Democratic party liberalism could not be effective, however, without new linkages between the various movements for civil rights, peace, labor, and student interests. No one could go it alone successfully. All these disinherited groups needed a "political party responsible to their interests," and the Democrats could not be that party so long as they tolerated the "perverse unity" between national Democrats and southern segregationists. Without using the slogan of "political realignment," we concluded that all the movements should "demand a Democratic party responsible to their interests." This represented a sincere concession to the Max Harrington–realignment position, combined with an instinctive hesitancy toward concluding that our vision could be realized simply by the decline of the Dixiecrats. We wanted more than a Democratic party of pragmatic northern liberals.

This was the political side of SDS asserting itself toward goals that today seem noncontroversial and in some ways have been achieved. But then we veered back to the key question of who would be the catalyst, the "agency of change," that would inspire and shape this vast joining of forces. The answer was ourselves, through a new role for students in the university communities across America.

The university, we asserted, was now central to the new information-based society that America was fast becoming. Therefore, we said, "no matter how dull the teaching, how paternalistic the rules, how irrelevant the research that goes on," the new social use of university resources—symbolized in the New Frontier's reliance on Harvard and prophesied in several books about "postindustrial" society—demonstrates the "unchangeable reliance by men of power on the men and storehouses of knowledge." The fact that the university was becoming "functionally tied to society in new ways" meant that, for ourselves, there were "new potentialities" and "new levers for change" making the university a "potential base and agency in the movement for social change."

We inventoried the features of the university community that were important to our effort: the "need for real intellectual skills," a base of people in "significant social roles" across the country, a constituency of "younger people who matured in the post-war world," a place for honest debate between people of both liberal and more radical perspectives, and a capacity to tolerate controversy about new ideas. Returning home to C. Wright Mills, we wrote that

> a new left must transform modern complexity into issues that can be understood and felt close-up by every human being. It must give form to the feelings of helplessness and indifference, so that people may see the political, social and economic sources of their private troubles and organize to change society. In a time of supposed prosperity, moral complacency and political manipulation, a new left cannot rely on only aching stomachs to be the engine for social reform. The case for change, for alternatives that will involve uncomfortable personal efforts, must be argued as never before.

We quickly added—I think at Bob Ross's suggestion—a recognition that we had no illusions about the university system completing "a movement of ordinary people making demands for a better life"; nor did we ignore the vital need for university reform. But we did maintain that from universities across the nation "a new left might awaken its allies, and by beginning the process towards peace, civil rights and labor struggles, reinsert theory and idealism where too often reign confusion and political barter.

"As students for a democratic society," we ended,

> we are committed to stimulating this kind of social movement, this kind of vision and program in campus and community across the country. If we appear to seek the unattainable, then let it be known that we do so to avoid the unimaginable.

Now it was over. Five days had passed. In the beginning we had offended some allies; in the end it didn't seem to matter. We were fused by the power of imagination, transformed into seeing ourselves as some sort of a wandering tribe that had found its lost identity and spoken its first authentic words to a wider world. We had asserted our role in the coming history of our times. Those who do so are usually prophetic or mad. We would find out soon enough which we were, or whether we were both.

We printed up twenty thousand copies of *The Port Huron Statement*, with a price tag of thirty-five cents. In time, it became the most widely read pamphlet of the sixties generation.

Immediately after the Port Huron convention, Al Haber and I drove to Washington to take our statement to the White House. We met there for an hour with Arthur Schlesinger, the resident liberal historian, and he agreed to bring our views to the attention of the president.

For the occasion, I wore a tie.

5. Triumphs. Transitions. Tragedies: 1962–64

The euphoric peak of the early sixties—the civil rights march on Washington—preceded the abyss of John Kennedy's death by fewer than one hundred days. Such were the times—triumph and tragedy began to shadow each other. The potential of the Kennedy administration, and an era, were slain on a Dallas afternoon. Our personal lives were strained and fragmented. Just as we reached for it, the promising vision of Port Huron foundered, and the age of innocence was ended.

After the Port Huron convention in 1962, my plan as the new SDS president was to establish a headquarters in Ann Arbor while attending graduate school. The New York office would remain the administrative center, but many of the organization's political leaders came to be concentrated in Ann Arbor; by 1963, they included the Flackses, Bob Ross, Rennie Davis, Paul Potter, Mary Varela, and Carol McEldowney. It was an exciting core.

I drove to Ann Arbor ahead of Casey, to look for housing and work. About a mile from the central campus, near Yost Field-house, I rented a convenient single-family house at 715 Arch Street. It had nondescript gray shingles, a breezy front porch, and a large basement I could turn into an SDS office. For income, we had my graduate student's stipend, but finding a job for Casey was not as easy. Finally, through church contacts, I lined up a secretarial position at Ann Arbor's Presbyterian church. Meanwhile, I enrolled and found part-time employment at a research institute. Looking back, I was not aware that these new arrangements primarily benefited myself. Casey was leaving a full and challenging life in her native South to become a graduate student's traditional wife in a distant northern town. We planned the time in Ann Arbor to be brief, however. The purpose was not to pursue an academic career, but to build a national campus profile for SDS. In a year or so, we expected to define long-term roles for ourselves in the movement and settle in somewhere.

The Arch Street basement became a storm center of protest activity right below our kitchen floor. There was a side door people could use, and the flow of activist traffic was constant. The pace of political activity in Ann Arbor was escalating. There were regular meetings of SDS leaders to discuss and plan general strategy for the organization. Phone calls from the South brought pleas for bail. I was in perpetual motion, trying to keep up regular contact with the New York office, follow daily dramas in the South, speak on college campuses in the East and Midwest, and generally fan the flames of organization.

We were jolted by the Cuban missile crisis in mid-October. The unfolding confrontation was kept secret from the American public for nearly a week. When the bare facts became known, they appeared to contain the most real threat of nuclear war in our lifetime. Around the country, thousands felt the same way. The Arch Street phone lines burned with calls stimulating local demonstrations in favor of a negotiated resolution, including several protests in Ann Arbor, where the school board rejected a civil defense proposal to create fallout shelters in schools.

These were the first truly visible signs of a grass-roots peace movement in the sixties. But to what avail? Ending a futile week, Casey and I drove to Washington with the Flackses and many others. We were convinced that we were driving into the bull's-eye where Russian missiles would soon hit. I remember prominent muckraking writer I. F. Stone, like an Old Testament figure, giving an apocalyptic speech in a Washington church. The announced deadlines for a negotiated U.S.-Soviet settlement had passed. Stone was talking about the beginning of World War III. I couldn't take it anymore. Feeling utterly powerless, the four of us went to a restaurant, and waited. Nothing happened. At that moment, Robert Kennedy was talking in deadly earnest with Soviet Ambassador Anatoly Dobrynin. Early the next morning, Nikita Khrushchev began withdrawing Soviet missiles from Cuba. The crisis had passed.

We were deeply concerned, however. For the second time since coming to office, the administration had marshaled military force over the threat of Cuba. Clearly JFK's sense of crisis management involved playing the nuclear "card," an option we found unthinkable. In our White House conversation with Schlesinger only three months before, Haber and I could not understand the administration's depth of obsession about the Castro revolution. In fact, much later histories revealed that the Kennedys were relative moderates compared to most of their advisers during the missile crisis and were prepared, if necessary, to pursue diplomatic alternatives to nuclear conflict. The Joint Chiefs of Staff, Dean Acheson, Maxwell Taylor, and many others were pushing for an immediate air strike on Cuba, a course that would have resulted in massive civilian casualties and likely retaliation from either Cuba or the Soviet Union. With the 1962 congressional elections three weeks away, Republicans were waiting to exploit any sign of Kennedy's weakness. The experience had been a startling reminder of the fragility of our lives.

Flacks and I wrote a mimeographed memo to SDS members expressing shock over how close we came to nuclear disaster at the hands of those in Washington we called the "war party." With "desperate optimism," we concluded that the "priority today, as never before, is to build a base of power." Citing the widespread local protests during the missile crisis, we proposed that the peace activists, together with the civil rights movement, concentrate more energy on congressional politics in 1964. "Congress is a keystone of the warfare state," we wrote. "But of all the institutions supporting the Cold War, it is the most crucial one which can be affected by the advocates of peace." There had to be pressure built on the Kennedys from the so-called doves, we argued, to offset the entrenched voices of the militarists. Since these reactionaries were also segregationists in many cases, there was a natural connection, we wrote, between strategies for peace and those for civil rights. The common aim, we said, should be to shift the congressional balance in favor of "new priorities." Despite our shaken assumption that the world was relatively safe from nuclear war, it remained our confident axiom that the Kennedy administration was pragmatic and movable in our direction. They would be reelected, we were sure, but only with a strong push by liberal constituencies. Despite the shock of October, we still believed that we could master the future.

That Ann Arbor winter was a depressing one for other reasons: SDS remained mostly an intense subculture of discussion. Underlying the strategy issues was the more personal question of where to locate ourselves, what to do with our lives. Shouldn't everyone be living and organizing outside of institutions? we asked. Shouldn't there be a northern version of SNCC? The Flackses seemed committed to a professional niche, and even that was the subject of serious debate. I suggested that Flacks become a new I. F. Stone, or that he and I explore working at the Institute for Policy Studies, a new liberal-to-radical think tank in Washington. But he and Mickey remained committed to the stability symbolized by pursuing a Ph.D., having children, expressing themselves through teaching and local activism. Some SDS leaders like Sharon Jeffrey, tired of the endless discussion, simply went off to organize tutorials in Harlem under the banner of the Northern Student Movement, a spin-off of SNCC and a forerunner of the domestic Peace Corps. For others, the debate continued; we were on the nervous threshold of new commitments.

In my political intensity at the time, I failed to invest enough in my marriage. In Doris Lessing's *The Golden Notebook*, the character Anna is furious with her lover, a political man who is driven primarily by his own needs, not hers. "None of you [men] ask for anything—except everything, but just for so long as you need it," she fumes. "It's the times we live in," he lamely explains. I had asked almost the impossible of Casey. After six months in Ann Arbor, Casey moved from her secretarial job to another in a survey research office, little more than compiling information and pushing paper, while her comrades in the South continued to struggle with life-and-death issues daily. Her roots were cut, her identity undermined. "I just couldn't connect," she told me later, "and it was cold up North. I couldn't get into the style of intellectualism in Ann Arbor." She missed the "spiritual and action elements of the southern experience." Once, during a particularly rambling discussion, she broke in to say, "I seriously believe y'all are discussing bullshit," then drifted away to bed.

Had I been more supportive, I might have enrolled in a university in Atlanta, where Casey could have continued the struggle, but I was too self-centered, my SDS involvement too intense, to have imagined such an alternative. In addition, both Casey and I both were from family backgrounds where it was common, when faced with confusion, to shut down emotionally. Several years later, she was among the first to note the ignored condition of women within the struggle for civil rights and coauthored one of the first calls for women's liberation.

At the time we were married, I was twenty-one years old, the product of a single-parent home, entering into a decade in which the average length of marriages was six years, and divorce rates rising by 33 percent. I hardly received a mature education about women as friends or lovers from my Michigan upbringing. In Catholic tradition, Eve was both dependent on Adam and his temptress; she soothed his loneliness yet caused his fall. A man's purpose was to enjoy, but not be basically distracted by, relationships with women. Around this time, my important friend and mentor, Harold Taylor, president of Sarah Lawrence College, advised me never to build my life plans around a woman, but around a career—then, if a woman fit in, so much the better. The university experience added the exploration of sexual relationships—a parallel to the free marketplace of ideas—absorbing more energy and emotion than academic life itself. This new sexual freedom, however, only tended to legitimize promiscuity. Women could freely take multiple boyfriends, but not as freely escape their image as passive objects. For male students like myself, the new climate simply meant that more women were openly "available," but it told us nothing about the souls and needs of those women.

The early movement of the sixties inherited and deepened the climate of male-dominated permissiveness. I remember being startled at a student editors' conference in New York in 1960 when one of my colleagues, a young radical from Queens College, leered and said, "The first thing you have to understand is that the movement revolves around the end of a prick." The movement was a chauvinist's paradise, the positions of power were dominated primarily by men, and the opportunities for unequal sexual liaisons were legion. Writers like Simone de Beauvoir were interpreted to advocate these "free relationships" and to condemn monogamy and marriage as being deadening.

In short, I wasn't prepared for a responsible marriage. In the South, Casey had represented the image of a sought-after "goddess," through whom I could achieve a higher sense of worth and calling. In my immaturity, I was infatuated with that idealized image. I acted traditionally by marrying her right after college, but it was a time when both of us were questioning all traditional arrangements. Then we planted ourselves directly in the center of a social revolution that was assaulting every institution. It was an incestuous time, when everyone in the center of the movement was involved with everyone else, and there was no permanence. Casey, I believe, understood the stakes better than I did, if only because she was two years older. Because she came from a more alienated childhood, she lacked my conventional confidence in marriage. She had learned from childhood, she later said, to "fragment relationships in order to handle uncontrollable emotional situations." So when she felt trapped and drying up in Ann Arbor, she became dead to me, and I reacted by retreating from what I didn't understand. The breakup when it came, therefore, was understood not so much as a personal failure but yet another example of how society dehumanized and atomized us all.

I practiced the curious male stoicism that consists of withdrawing from someone else's pain. Like Camus's alienated narrator in *The Fall*, I was "in love principally with myself," taking refuge among women, as if they were "natural harbors."

Soon I became romantically interested in another movement woman, Andrea Cousins, a sensitive, brown-eyed, olive-skinned Sarah Lawrence student. She had spent a summer studying in Guinea with Sharon Jeffrey and was full of compassionate attachment to the poor of the world. Sharon introduced us at an NSA meeting in fall 1962 and after a long night of talking, we felt uncomfortably like soulmates. Like myself, she was involved with someone else. We did not expect, and could not control, the feelings we were experiencing. When the conference was over, Andrea left for New York. Sharon, sensing what was occurring, was increasingly upset. Close to Casey and myself, she also was to become Andrea's roommate in New York, where the two of them were going to work for the Harlem Education Project, a tutorial and social services program.

Andrea was the daughter of Norman Cousins, the liberal editor of the *Saturday Review*. As an undergraduate editor, I had admired Cousins as a model of committed journalism. Now, as an evolving young radical, I was critical of his belief that disarmament could be achieved without basic economic and structural change. In that period, he was deeply involved in the internal diplomacy leading toward the 1963 nuclear test ban treaty. But, like many parents of the time, he had a far less liberal attitude toward his daughter's freedom to pursue relationships. He sensed, I think, that I represented not only a different political viewpoint but a threat to his parental controls. One weekend he discovered the two of us staying at the Cousinses' Connecticut home and reacted with a frightening rage. In retrospect, I can understand his patriarchal response; all fathers have it to some degree. But at the time I felt like a target in the center of a daughter's struggle for independence from her father. In turn, Andrea was trapped in the middle of my disintegrating marriage. It seemed impossible to solidify our turbulent emotions or know what we wanted from each other. Most of all, everything seemed out of control, as if sexual transmission lines ran through my heart while being powered and switched from somewhere else.

Casey and I were becoming strangers. "I didn't want to leave," she wrote me afterward. "It was the only thing to do at the time." Hurt and jealous, she left in the middle of a peace meeting in Boston. I thought we were ready to return to Ann Arbor, but she had developed other plans. While I drove away in a cold daze, she stayed in Boston with Robb Burlage, the former editor of the University of Texas paper and the former husband of Casey's Austin roommate, Dorothy Dawson. Not long after, Casey left Boston alone and returned South to rejoin SNCC, where again she became a key organizer in the Atlanta office.

I went back to Ann Arbor, divided and directionless. Andrea was still in New York, but I didn't know if she was any more than a distant beacon. After a few months, I agreed with Casey to fly to Atlanta and try to explore what feelings remained between us. She was living with Mary King, a SNCC worker who was later prominent in the Carter administration, in an apartment that I remember as sparse, with madras-covered beds on the floor and freedom posters on the walls. Casey had buried herself in long hours of work and was just beginning to emerge from her protective shell into a new sense of self-confidence. Whether it was enough for us to reconnect again was the unknown. But on my second day there, she received a phone call at her apartment from Norman Cousins in New York, who somehow had obtained her number. "Mrs. Hayden," he solemnly intoned, "your husband has been sleeping with my daughter, who is a young and innocent girl. I think you should know that this is going on and that you should do something about his irresponsibility."

"I see," was all that Casey could say into the receiver. She hung up, devastated more by the call than by the information—which she already knew. Both of us were so upset that our time together was effectively cut short. "I'm sorry it happened," I said of Cousins's bizarre call. "So am I," Casey answered, far away again. Once again, there was nothing to do but leave.

Not long after, I saw Andrea again. Desperate for something to "work," I sat on a lawn with her and asked if she "needed" me. Quite predictably, she resisted, frightened at the idea of a man who wanted her to need him. What I really needed, looking back, was a maturity that no one could give me.

A pall fell over Ann Arbor, where Casey's and my marriage had been a bright hope to our little circle of friends. When it unexpectedly fell apart, so did some measure of confidence in ourselves. Mickey Flacks thought I was, plain and simple, an "asshole." Others walked around in silent pain. "It was very upsetting to all of us," Sharon Jeffrey said later, "because we were really committed to the integrity of relationships." Bob Ross told me, "Your political involvement, your organizational intensity produced an intolerable situation. I found it hard. I was still very young and the child of divorced parents. You were the first sibling in my new 'family' to get divorced. It meant that our seamless, loving, and romantic community was breaking up."

Indeed it was: Bob and Sharon, who began a relationship after Al and Sharon broke up, were now breaking up themselves; after Mary Varela left Paul for Rennie, Paul and Sharon formed a relationship. We "practised love carelessly," as Bertolt Brecht once and forever described radicals in their youth.

Yet history still seemed to be on our side. Absorbing my pain, I continued exploring for a new and larger mission beyond the way station of Ann Arbor. Increasingly, SDS activists were involving themselves in community civil rights movements near campuses such as Swarthmore with promising results or joining urban tutorial projects as Sharon Jeffrey had. Despite the momentary madness of the Cuban missile crisis, the direction of the Kennedy administration still left a window of hope for the struggles for civil rights, peace, and an end to poverty.

In June 1963, the president began a visible turn toward peace, or at least, in the measured words of David Halberstam, "the beginning of an end to a particularly rigid era of the Cold War." Addressing students at American University on June 10, he rejected the collision course with communist governments he had pursued at the Bay of Pigs in 1961. "If we cannot end our differences [with communist countries]," the president declared, "at least we can help make the world safe for diversity. For in the final analysis, our most basic link is that we all inhabit this small planet." A month later, Kennedy signed a nuclear weapons treaty banning tests in the atmosphere, in space, and beneath the sea.

Even more dramatic was the course of the southern civil rights movement and the pressure it was building for a new commitment from the Kennedy administration. Mississippi authorities had forced the administration into a bloody confrontation over desegregating the University of Mississippi in September 1962. Two bystanders were killed, and a U.S. marshal was shot. That winter, Greenwood, Mississippi, became the scene of more bloodshed. Bob Moses, Jimmy Travis, and Randolph Blackwell of SNCC were shot and wounded in February 1963, and their office was burned to the ground. Vigilantes shot up the home of another civil rights worker's parents. Then the focus shifted dramatically, to Birmingham, Alabama, where demonstrations for desegregation and jobs had begun in April.

Birmingham was a turning point, receiving greater national and global attention than any previous showdown. It revealed the pathological hatred underlying segregation as well as the potential for black violence and made the civil rights issue synonymous with the Kennedys. The nemesis of the movement was T. Eugene "Bull" Connor, the city's director of public safety, whose provocative language and deeds were publicized throughout the world. In mid-April, he arrested Dr. King, and Birmingham blacks responded with greater fervor. King's bail arrangements were made through the intercession of Robert

Kennedy. On May 2, Connor turned hoses on children and, for the first time, the jails of an American city were clogged to overflowing. A moderating agreement was negotiated with Kennedy aide Burke Marshall's assistance, but then bombs ripped apart the home of a local black leader and Dr. King's motel room. Blacks spontaneously took to the streets, and unprecedented burning and looting took place. Over the next two months, there were nearly eight hundred demonstrations and fourteen thousand civil rights arrests in seventy-five southern cities. On June 11, the president sent new civil rights legislation to Congress and declared on national television:

> We face a moral crisis in this country and as a people. It cannot be met by repressive police action. It cannot be left to increased demonstrations in the streets. It cannot be quieted by token moves or talk. It is time to act in Congress, in your state and local legislative bodies, and above all, in our daily lives.

On that same historic date, there was a violent confrontation at the University of Alabama when two black students were enrolled. Three hours after the president's speech came a reply from white Mississippi: NAACP leader Medgar Evers was shot in the back as he walked up the steps to his home, the first recognized civil rights leader assassinated in the sixties.

By this time, the combined national civil rights leadership had decided on a march on Washington stressing "jobs and freedom" and calling for federal action to stem the anarchy developing in the South. At first Kennedy opposed the idea as counterproductive, but wisely he chose to cooperate with the planners of the event.

At four A.M. on August 28, Andrea and I boarded a bus in Harlem bound for the march on Washington. It was a climactic moment of integration and goodwill as marchers climbed aboard buses all over the country that dawn. Arriving in Washington several hours later amid a sea of people, I missed seeing Casey. She was somewhere in the throngs around the Washington Monument with a SNCC delegation from Atlanta. Their attitude was cynical, even bitter, toward the Kennedy administration's policies in the South, and the attempt by march organizers like Bayard Rustin to tone down the prepared remarks of SNCC chairman John Lewis. SNCC wanted to criticize the administration's tokenism in the South, but the march leaders had agreed not to attack the Kennedy policies. Sharing the SNCC feeling, I nonetheless sensed that day a turning point, an opportunity for the movement to sweep the country. It was true that the president's cooperation had moderated the tone, deflected pressure away from himself and Democratic leadership, and caused a significant censoring of John Lewis's speech, but if there are ever times when the power of idealism can create a new consensus, this was one of them. It was clear that the country was ready for a broader movement to deal with civil rights and poverty, with Mississippi instead of Vietnam, with racism rather than an arms race.

That there still would be cataclysmic violence in this process, however, was underscored only a few days after the March with the bombing of a black desegregation lawyer's home in Birmingham. Then, five days after the integration of twenty black children into the local schools, there came the bombing and killing of four young black girls at the Sixteenth Street Baptist Church. These insane events, which included the killing of two more blacks in subsequent street violence, seemed to intensify the nation's and the president's commitment to a new order in the South. But at the Birmingham funeral, author John Killens offered a different ominous message: "Negroes must be prepared to protect themselves with guns," he said.

After the first death, there is no other. —DYLAN THOMAS

The final omen that tragedy could overwhelm hope came on November 22. I was aboard a flight from Chicago to Minneapolis, where I was speaking to a conference of foreign student leaders studying democracy on U.S. government fellowships. As the plane pulled up to the gate in Minneapolis, the choked voice of the pilot came on:

"Ladies and gentlemen, we have reports that the president . . . President Kennedy . . . has just been shot . . . and that he is . . . dead. . . . The president is dead in Dallas. . . . I'm sorry we don't have more information."

Behind me a young man wearing a GOLDWATER FOR PRESIDENT button smiled in glee and started to stand, then sat down again.

I looked at the other passengers. They all seemed stunned, drawn into themselves, alone. We deboarded silently, and I had the sensation of floating as I walked into the airport. Some people inside were starting to cry, but most kept moving mechanically forward. The pay phones were all in use, with lines forming behind each one. A group of African students met me just inside the gate and respectfully extended their condolences. The speech, I agreed, should be called off. I turned around and looked for the first flight back to Chicago and on to Ann Arbor.

By my arrival at Chicago's O'Hare Airport, the news was spreading that Lee Harvey Oswald had been arrested for the assassination and that he was a "radical leftist." Oh, God, I thought, looking for the first phone to call the SDS office in New York. We had no Oswalds on our mailing lists. The next news bulletin announced that he was a member of Fair Play for Cuba, a small and dedicated pro-Castro group. The premonition nagged me that the New Left was somehow going to be blamed for this new madness. And there was another thought: This was a setup.

In Ann Arbor, I spent the next three days in front of the Flackses' television set. We followed the breaking news, watched the murder of Oswald over and over, and let the event etch its way like a toxic acid into our consciousness. This was the most unexpected happening of my life, having been raised in the climate of a stable American presidency—that of Franklin Roosevelt—in an unstable and warring world.

C. Wright Mills had described American society as fundamentally stable, a mass society in the hands of a powerful elite with shared interests. But the "lone assassin" Oswald had singlehandedly shattered this stability and determined the presidency with a single bullet. Dick Flacks and I thought and wrote of him as a "lurker," a member of a floating "lurking class" dissociated from bureaucratic rationality, capable of turning hallucinations into history. But if he was not alone, if he was, in his own words, a "patsy," then we were dealing with a violent conspiracy perhaps reaching into the power elite itself. Either notion was enough to unsettle my world. The scent of evil and the cloud of tragedy, forces beyond knowing or control, were now present in my life in a more personal way than ever before. I cried for John Kennedy's small, saluting son, for his family, for myself.

The tragic consciousness of the sixties generation began here, and would continue and grow. Deepening that consciousness in the next weeks was my sense that the truth of the assassination was being covered up, that it might never be disclosed or agreed upon, and that we would be left to make whatever image of this national patricide our own fantasies or fears, hopes or illusions required. To conclude, as I did, that a conspiracy of more than Oswald was involved, meant living with the certainty that John Kennedy's killers were still among us.

I now believe that at the time of his death John Kennedy was embracing the necessity of greater association with the civil rights movement. Frederick Douglass's perspective on Abraham Lincoln seemed to fit John Kennedy: "From the genuine Abolitionist view, Mr. Lincoln seemed tardy, cold, dull and indifferent, but measuring by the sentiment of his country—a sentiment he was bound as a statesman to consult—he was swift, zealous, radical and determined." I also think that the president was moving toward disengagement of U.S. military forces in Vietnam, beginning with the withdrawal of one thousand of seventeen thousand advisers by the end of 1963. Further, he was quietly opening a dialogue with Castro's Cuba, backing away from the Cuban exiles he had supported at the Bay of Pigs, and was pursuing a policy toward the Soviets which would, a decade later, come to be known as détente. He was accumulating, in short, a long list of enemies who might seek the survival of their interests in his death. Whether any of them played a role in his murder remains unknown, but in his dying their fantasies and projects were resurrected. Just two days after the president's death, Lyndon Johnson signed a national security memorandum that restated the U.S. goal in Vietnam was helping the Saigon government to a military "victory." The dialogue toward global détente was chilled. Johnson projected a strong military image to neutralize the Goldwater electoral threat that lay ahead and deepened a political alliance with southern Democrats to ensure his reelection. In the new president's unlimited vision, these contradictions could be managed along with a grandiose "war on poverty." The vision was wrong.

Like most of my friends in SDS and SNCC, I soon reverted to the preassassination belief that America's gradual turn away from Cold War militarism and toward domestic priorities would continue, especially if we kept sufficient pressure on Johnson. SNCC had organized a freedom vote in Mississippi in early November, with the help of Allard Lowenstein and a group of northern students. An astounding number of blacks—eighty thousand—were willing to cast freedom ballots to indicate their desire to vote. Out of the freedom vote experience came the seed of a more far-reaching idea for the coming summer of 1964.

I suggested to Bob Moses that SNCC organize a challenge to the seating of the racist Mississippi Democratic party at the coming Democratic convention. His response was to create a "freedom summer," bringing hundreds of white, middle-class students to live in Mississippi, register black voters, help in educational and service projects, and build toward a challenge of the incumbent party. At first, the plan was rejected by the local SNCC staff, who worried about being overwhelmed by a core of ignorant, naïve, and privileged college students. But the idea took hold: Only when America's middle-class children were taking life-threatening risks would their parents at last listen and react against the treatment that had gone on against blacks for decades. The further goal, based on the successful 1963 freedom vote, was to organize an officially integrated (though mostly black) Democratic party in Mississippi to challenge the credentials of the segregated party.

A Freedom Democratic Party: The very idea stirred the imagination of activists nationwide as well as dirt farmers in the smallest Mississippi communities. Here was the concrete possibility of realigning the Democratic party that we in SDS had dreamed about. Thus the plan for a "Mississippi summer" came to pass.

High hopes, however, ended in death and betrayal. I attended part of the early summer training session for the Mississippi volunteers at a small women's college in Oxford, Ohio. There was already plenty of worry about violence. On June 21, even before the final group of volunteers had left for Mississippi, we learned that three volunteers were missing near the small town of Philadelphia, Mississippi. One was a black Mississippi native, James Chaney, who was on the CORE staff; two others were civil rights workers from New York, Michael Schwerner and Andrew Goodman. Andrew, a twenty-one-year-old Queens College student, had only just arrived in Mississippi. Though we assumed immediately that they were dead, their mutilated bodies were not found until August 4, buried under an earthen dam outside Philadelphia in northeast Neshoba County. (Philadelphia, Mississippi, is the same town where Ronald Reagan launched his 1980 presidential campaign with a speech defending states' rights.)

In a speech to the Ohio gathering, Bob Moses had drawn on Camus to point out that the "country isn't willing yet to admit it has the plague, but it pervades the whole society." At the August funeral for Chaney, Schwerner, and Goodman, Moses noted that the United States government was attacking Vietnam even though it was unable to protect freedom in Mississippi. The funeral was the day after the Tonkin Gulf incident in which U.S. planes first bombed North Vietnam. Moses's speech indelibly joined the issues of civil rights and Vietnam in our emotional core.

That summer Casey was playing a central role in the upcoming challenge the Freedom Democrats would mount at the Democratic convention. When she learned I was coming to the Atlantic City convention, she wrote me a letter, reflecting the pressure of the times.

> Tom:
> . . . Work is most of my day. Nights sometimes are good but mostly lonely. Am seeing a good person and am I suppose in love which is strange and hard because it can't be conducted with any kind of security or safety or continuity. But is opening me up a little more, I suppose.
>
> I am tense and pretty high strung lately, find myself being really grumpy, which I hate. Work from 8 to 10 or 9 to 12 on the convention challenge—enclosed is booklet about it all.
>
> It is hot.
>
> I feel little poetry anymore, but love the trees, which remind me of poetry sometimes.
>
> Let me know about the car. Just realized I have no home address. Hope this reaches you.
>
> C.

> Are you happy? I can't really analyze me anymore—am sorry for the brevity and distance of this note. Forgive it.
> Love,,,,
> c

I drove down the Jersey shore to Atlantic City to witness the outcome of the challenge of the Mississippi Freedom Democrats to the seating of the racist delegation at the Democratic National Convention. The Mississippi Summer had been effective in focusing the nation's concern, and SNCC had accomplished its most phenomenal political organizing in the development of the Freedom Democratic Party (FDP). Only three years after I had seen and documented violent repression against individual blacks trying to vote, the FDP held a political convention in Jackson of eight hundred delegates, mostly the rural people who were the heart and soul of the movement from the earlier days. Now, with SNCC's aid, they had researched the rules of the game and chosen a delegation of sixty-eight citizens, including four whites, to travel to Atlantic City, where they would make a well-documented claim to be the legitimate Democratic party of Mississippi. The excitement around this organizing project was phenomenal.

One summer volunteer later published a letter that captured the excitement:

> This is the stuff democracy is made of. All of us are pretty emotional about the names of the counties of Mississippi. Amite and Sunflower and Tallahatchie have always meant where this one was shot, where this one was beaten, where civil rights workers feared for their lives the minute they arrived. But on Thursday, Amite and Tallahatchie and Sunflower and Neshoba didn't mean another man's gone. They meant people are voting from there; people who work fourteen hours a day from sun-up to sun-down picking cotton and living in homes with no plumbing and no paint were casting ballots to send a delegation to Atlantic City. As the keynote speaker said, it was not a political convention, it was a demonstration that the people of Mississippi want to be let into America.

What happened was a turning point in political history and a thoroughly embittering experience for the movement. When I arrived as an observer, Casey and others were organizing a sophisticated presentation before the credentials committee with at least a marginal hope of seating the Mississippi people. As she recalled it later, "I never thought we would be seated. It was a long shot at best. I never was heavy into hope. It was more a question of ethical necessity than winning. But I was a minority, I'm sure." While receiving support from a growing number of individual Democratic delegates, they were being resisted forcefully by many of the most prominent liberal and labor leaders in the party, including Walter Reuther, attorney Joseph Rauh (who had served as the Freedom Democrats' legal counsel), Walter Mondale (then chairman of the credentials committee), and Allard Lowenstein (who originally helped inspire the 1963 freedom vote).

The liberal agenda clearly was to promote the vice-presidential candidacy of Hubert Humphrey, who seemingly needed to prove his team loyalty to Lyndon Johnson by beating back the Mississippi challenge. It came down to a bitter conflict between two generations of civil rights forces, the elder more established and influential within the existing system, the younger more insurgent and definitely outside ("the stone the builders rejected," Bob Moses called them). The elders lived mainly in a world of hotel meetings and negotiations, the younger generation in a modern underground railroad. The elders viewed themselves as pragmatic, distrusting the younger generation as purist, while SNCC and FDP defined themselves as the only force upholding the professed ideals of America and the Democratic party. In the first view, the main threat came from the Goldwater Right; to them, replacing the Dixiecrat segregationists was a long, piecemeal process. In the newer view, the main danger was that of northern liberals accommodating the racist South and leaving black people no political outlet for their aspirations.

Casey called the liberals "finks." "It never occurred to us that we would be turned down," wrote Mary King, one of Casey's more hopeful friends, in a later account. They were. The Humphrey offer to FDP was a classic political compromise: two "at large" seats for the FDP, to be chosen by him and seated alongside the segregationist delegation. There would also be a promise that the regular Mississippi party would not be credentialed as an all-white party in future conventions. This meant only a symbolic victory for the FDP, since it allowed the segregated party to choose a token handful of black participants in time for 1968 without any change in the repressive system that prevented black registration and voting in Mississippi. The pressure to accept the Humphrey compromise intensified with the lobbying of NAACP leader Roy Wilkins and even Dr. Martin Luther King.

From a later perspective, I can understand the "logic" of both positions: The realism of the liberals was shortsighted; the pure idealism of SNCC would lead to isolation. What was needed from the liberals was not an expedient compromise formula, as if they were dealing with mere self-interest, but a *moral* and *emotional* recognition of the essential rightness of FDP and SNCC's position. Failing that, the same gulf that separated the moderates from the activist forces in the South, the same distance that had opened between traditional liberalism and the New Left, was deepened and gorged with hostility. In the end, it was the instinct of the blacks from the Mississippi Delta, strong and outspoken women like Fannie Lou Hamer from Ruleville and Unita Blackwell from Mayersville, to refuse the compromise. They could judge the proposal only by one very real standard: whether it would tangibly improve the harrowing lives of people in the Delta. They were not ready for the world of political compromise. As one of the Mississippi people lamented, "We didn't come all this way for no two seats, since *all* of us is tired."

The Mississippi challenge was over, but its legacy would spread like a cancer. No longer would it be possible to believe or assert that national officials did not "know" what was happening in the rural South. No longer was it possible in SNCC or related organizations to argue for strategies of appealing to the "conscience" of national leaders. The seeds of a strategy based on power, *black* power, rather than on love and integration, were planted in Atlantic City.

Though I was only a peripheral participant in the concentrated events of those few days, I too left in a totally stunned mood. Driving toward Newark under a full moon, I ran straight into two deer and killed them instantly.

AMONG THE POOR

Part Three

6. Newark: 1964-67

On a sweltering day in July 1964—a few weeks before the Democratic convention—I stepped out of a car after an all-night drive from Ann Arbor and found myself looking for the first time at the black ghetto of Newark: Scores of furniture stores, foul-smelling markets, and cheap record shops lined the baking streets of tar. Young people carrying school books in one hand and holding radios to their ears with the other crossed the street. Mothers carried large bags of groceries while trying to keep trailing children out of the traffic. A few men stood outside a bar in animated argument. A police car slowly cruised by, the officers glancing at me, the only white who was clearly not a merchant. Off this commercial street ran several red-brick streets into a residential community of fifty-year-old wood-frame houses with dirt front yards that had been a white district only ten years before.

The sight of the neighborhood, which would be my home for the next four years, left me unbalanced. None of my reading or class work prepared me to know the ghetto, or know concrete economic realities, or know the real operation of political machines. And here I was to organize, as if I knew something that those living here didn't know. I was twenty-four years old and preparing to lead the poor in an assault on the downtown power structure. But first I had to get a street map, then an apartment, and some savvy—quick.

I had arrived on this Newark street corner as part of a new and unprecedented event in the history of American students: the migration of hundreds, and ultimately thousands, into organizing projects in impoverished communities from Harlem to Appalachia. Instead of choosing conventional careers and the benefits of middle-class life, students were settling in ramshackle houses in the Mississippi Black Belt, or apartments in Chicago's Uptown, in attempts to organize society's outcasts. The spirit of this effort, which would soon see a pale and token reflection in the federal government's VISTA and antipoverty programs, was one of transformation, from book-carrying students to American *kibbutzniks* dedicated to organizing the poor for power. We who bore witness to squalor in the midst of affluence would ultimately be ignored. This failure would come to be a *missed opportunity*, a road tragically not taken, as American society flirted briefly with a "war on poverty" only to consume its generosity in a war on Vietnam. Had the nation been able to focus on its internal agenda, students might have triumphed as catalysts to channel the frustrations of poverty into constructive reform. Instead the cities, and soon the campuses, were lit by what James Baldwin forecast as "the fire next time."

During the critical juncture of 1963–64 the early SDS leaders decided to organize the poor. There are nineteen people in a black-and-white group photo of that early SDS leadership taken at the end of a September 1963 national meeting in Bloomington, Indiana. The men are dressed mostly in the short-sleeved, button-down shirts of the time. Rennie Davis and Robb Burlage have briefcases, and Todd Gitlin wears a sports jacket with a Harvard insignia. Our hair is uniformly close-clipped. The women are wearing dresses or skirts, with one exception in tight-fitting khaki slacks. I am standing to one side with my shirt hanging over my pants, more disheveled than the others. All of us, however, are raising clenched fists.

It was at this meeting, shortly after the march on Washington, that we finalized our plans for developing a northern parallel to SNCC, sending student organizers into slums to organize the poor. Evolving independently from SDS, which would still organize the campuses, we called ourselves the Economic Research and Action (ERAP Project—"EE-rap"). Knowing of SNCC's emerging plan for a Mississippi Summer, we decided to recruit and send hundreds of young people into urban areas at the same time, though for longer than a summer, in an attempt to organize the white as well as the black poor. The program was ambitious. Walter Reuther, thanks again to Mildred Jeffrey, sent a five-thousand-dollar check to help us get started in 1963. Rennie Davis, one of our best organizational minds, was chosen to direct the national ERAP office in Ann Arbor. A young student named Joe Chabot was dispatched to Chicago to get a "feel" for unemployed youth. SDS chapter leaders scouted possibilities for storefront projects in cities across the country. Our confidence was fueled by President Johnson's announcement in January 1964 of an "unconditional war on poverty in America." We knew that the ultimate official effort would be a token in comparison with the real needs. Instead of calling for the more radical "participatory democracy," for example, the government's programs set as its goal "maximum feasible participation" of the poor in self-help programs, leaving the practical control in the hands of local authorities. But to us, it seemed that our movements were again setting the agenda—as we had in civil rights—and the government was responding, giving us legitimacy and a sense of effectiveness.

Not everyone in our circle shared this enthusiasm. In our first serious difference, Al Haber strongly opposed the ERAP and what he called its "cult of action." He felt it was still more important to intellectually define a "radical agenda" and prepare people to be radicals in their professional careers. To me, he represented an inconclusive intellectualism that was frustrating the birth of SDS as an active force. The ERAP concept was far from a leap into "mindless activism," as he bitterly charged. If anything, ERAP was a product of intense thinking about the intertwined issues of race and poverty and how to bring them to center stage in a nation consumed by the Cold War. Todd Gitlin, the new SDS president, and I helped draft a statement on the "triple revolution" of nuclear weapons, industrial automation, and civil rights at Princeton University in early 1964. Key sponsors of the "triple revolution" statement included Robert Oppenheimer, Gunnar Myrdal, and economist Robert Theobald, as well as United Auto Workers officials. We exuberantly felt we were heading in the right direction, intellectually as well as personally. Nuclear weapons made warfare increasingly obsolete, the Cold War was receding, and the combination of new technologies with rising expectations dictated the necessity of a new focus on jobs and economic issues.

By spring 1964, there were plans for organizing ERAP projects in cities as diverse as Chicago, Cleveland, Newark, Boston, New Haven, Philadelphia, Oakland, Baltimore, Louisville, and Hazard, Kentucky (deep in Appalachia). While finishing my graduate work in Ann Arbor and trying to decide where to go after June, I was impressed with Carl Wittman, one of the moving forces behind ERAP, who already had formed an effective project in the Chester, Pennsylvania, ghetto near the Swarthmore campus. Together, we wrote an ERAP strategy paper entitled *Toward an Interracial Movement of the Poor?*, a cumbersome document arguing the imperative of organizing across racial lines to win the support of a majority of Americans. We still believed in the integrationist philosophy of SNCC and Dr. King, but both of us were impressed by the deep appeal of Malcolm X in the northern ghettos. Carl, Vernon Grizzard, Connie Brown, and other Swarthmore students encountered Malcolm in the Philadelphia area and felt the urgency to prove that at least some whites were not "devils." I had a brief but similar experience in Ann Arbor when the Muslim leader lectured to an overflow crowd. Afterward, I attended a private dialogue that turned into an intense argument. I found myself liking Malcolm for his dignity, passion, and intelligence, and I thought as a young and opinionated journalist that he enjoyed sparring with me. The argument became vociferous over whether whites are racist at birth or merely conditioned to their prejudice. Like Carl, I wanted to prove in action that an integrationist perspective stressing common economic interests could still work. So when Carl suggested that I join the budding Newark ERAP project, I was interested. I'd never been to Newark before, but I'd heard an airplane stewardess describe it as the "armpit of the world." That was good enough for me.

When I told my parents of this new mission, they politely suggested I was throwing my life away. My father had just remarried (his new wife, Esther, was also a Chrysler employee) and become a father again in late 1963. I visited Detroit in early 1964 to meet my one-year-old sister, Mary, who was curlyhaired, playful, and adorable. As she posed for photos on my lap, I tried to explain my decision to go to Newark. My father was already disturbed that I had passed up a journalism career to go south. The breakup with Casey added to his sense of my instability; now came Newark. "I don't know, Tom, how you got involved in these things," he said, keeping his temper but shaking his head. "It certainly wasn't the way we raised you."

My mother, still living in Royal Oak, already accepted the fact that I was following my own lights, but she felt hurt as well. My sojourn to the South had seemed dangerous but at least temporary. There was still time for me to return to journalism or law school, she believed. The commitment to Newark seemed to give away the third decade of my life and promised to fill their middle years with trauma, confusion, and a foreboding sense of parental failure. My father was beginning to assume that he'd lost a son to bizarre radical influences; my mother was more trusting, but nonetheless baffled at my behavior.

When I arrived, Newark was the only major American city with a black majority. Viewed from a national political perspective, the city was defined as a liberal Democratic stronghold. Its officeholders, led by Mayor Hugh J. Addonizio, were for voting rights, social welfare, and all the "good things" the Dixiecrat wing of the party opposed. Over a half century, as many as 100,000 black families had migrated from the South in search of those "good things" in this northern city. But on arrival, they found a different reality than the image of the liberal North. The city's elected government included only one black official, an aging, patronage-oriented councilman named Irvine Turner. White or black, city officials were widely perceived as corrupt. Construction costs on city contracts were higher than anywhere in the United States. Gambling was the city's biggest business, and the narcotics trade flourished. Anthony "Tony Bananas" Caponigro and Anthony "Tony Boy" Boiardo were among the Mayor's biggest campaign contributors. Ordinary people were the casualties. With a total population of 400,000 people, Newark ranked highest in the country in crime, maternal and infant mortality, tuberculosis, and venereal disease. Unemployment citywide was 15 percent, and much higher in the black community. One third of the city's children dropped out of school, and less than 10 percent achieved normal reading levels. In 1960, 32.5 percent (41,430) of its housing units were officially substandard. Nearly 30,000 of those dwellings lacked internal heating systems, and 7,000 had no flush toilets. There were 5,000 totally abandoned units and 13,000 public housing units—more per capita than any American city.

The thirteen of us who signed up for Newark were a cross section of the activist generation, coming primarily from middle-class homes and major campuses like Michigan, Swarthmore, Amherst, and Howard. Only one of us was black, a highly talented organizer named Marv Holloway, though we were soon joined by two others, Junius Williams and Phil Hutchings, later a SNCC chairman. Faulty preparation misled us into believing that the Clinton Hill neighborhood was racially integrated in makeup. Carl Wittman had received a misleading picture from the white liberals in the Clinton Hill neighborhood who had agreed to sponsor our presence. In fact, the whites tended to be middle class and lived on the avenues high on the hill, while the blacks were poor and lived at the bottom. The city's poor whites lived in the East Ward; we were in the South. We decided to stay in Clinton Hill, regardless of our being mainly white, and made long-range plans to target the East Ward, plans which were ultimately carried out in the late sixties. These were the years before "black power," the years when television carried regular news of white civil rights workers in the black South; there was still some degree of black identification with young white activists. One young black girl told her parents that I looked like one of the Beatles (a flattering if far-fetched observation). At any rate, we believed—correctly, it turned out—that we would recruit new staff out of the black community.

The ERAP spirit was one of voluntary poverty and simple living. We believed you could not organize poor people without living on their economic level in their neighborhood. Sharing shelter and meals was also the only way to pay for a large project on a small budget. ERAP projects in different cities would enthusiastically compete for the lowest food budget; for a time, the Newark staff was eating for fifty cents a meal per person. We could not subsist on guilt, however, and soon the expenditure rose, though never beyond poverty levels.

We rented two or three apartments in the ghetto; each apartment housed as many as eight or ten of us. We dressed casually, usually a khaki verson of the SNCC jeans "uniform." There was little privacy—as time went by only a few of the permanent people, or an occasional couple, were allocated rooms of their own. Even then, the bed, study table, and chairs were crammed into a tiny space. Others, less fortunate because their status was transitory, slept on couches or floors—often for weeks. One person even built a bed in a closet to achieve a little privacy.

There was not a lot of monogamy in this self-sacrificing community. It was a time of questioning for all traditional relationships, placing collective needs above personal ones and exploring new ways to relate in an open atmosphere. Couples tended to be respected, but were not even given special dispensations like taking meals together.

In the fall of 1964, Casey arrived in Newark for a two-week stay. The Atlantic City convention had been exhausting. SNCC was beginning to feel a serious tension over whether educated and qualified whites were unconsciously interfering with the leadership development of local blacks. A power struggle was casting shadows on the community of love, with advocates of greater structure and discipline arrayed against decentralists like Bob Moses. For Casey, after the failure of the huge FDP effort, there seemed nothing to do. She came to Newark to explore ERAP and, less explicitly, to see what remained of our marriage. There was nothing there but the awkward friendliness that besets former lovers. She stayed in my room off the kitchen, but we couldn't re-create our former intimacy, and she soon began going into Manhattan to see Willie Morris. Finally, she returned to Mississippi to live in a freedom house in Jackson with Mary King.

I visited a Mississippi SNCC retreat as winter began and found the participants wearied, tense, and searching for direction, totally unlike the intense élan of only three years before. Blacks were withdrawing from whites, who were reacting with painful defensiveness, and the memory of Atlantic City—as well as the shadow of Vietnam—hung over the future menacingly.

As SNCC fell into these internal divisions, Casey and others increasingly became stoned. Not long after we formally divorced, represented by an Atlanta civil rights lawyer who had defended us during the sit-ins. It cost sixty-three dollars and seemed logical.

After nearly a year in Newark, I became involved with another staff organizer. A diminutive, shy, and quiet Swarthmore graduate, Connie Brown seemed out of place in the ghetto streets. But her soul was caring, her sense of individual psychology acute, and she became an excellent organizer, forming a welfare rights organization.

Connie and I came together one gray day in February 1965, returning in a bus from the National Poor People's Conference in Cleveland. A radio announced the news of Malcolm X's murder in Harlem. Both of us had encountered Malcolm, she in the

Chester, Pennsylvania, organizing project, and we had followed with enthusiasm his recent evolution away from diatribes against "white devils." He had been a hopeful bridge between the efforts of SNCC and ERAP. Now he was dead, at the hands of his former Muslim brothers.

As the news sank in, Connie and I leaned against each other on the backseat of the bus, filled with fifty somber blacks and a few whites, as it rolled along the freezing interstate. Discovering intimacy, we stayed together after that. It was almost impossible to live as a couple amid the stress generated by ten organizers. In search of privacy, we tried living in a single-room abandoned tool shop. The cement structure was just behind the two-story, wood-frame house the staff rented at 227 Jelliff Avenue. Our "home" lacked a bathroom and heat, and the Newark winters were freezing. I went to absurd lengths to make the place warm, installing a potbelly stove and scaffolds of blankets for insulation. We were alone at last, but unable to survive the winter without an indoor toilet, we gave up and moved back into a single room of the chaotic front house.

Amid the bedlam of the time, there were relatively few liaisons between staff and community people. They were not allowed as a matter of principle (unless they were deemed "serious" and "responsible"). This wall of separation, erected for organizational reasons, only intensified the need for what affection and intimacy was possible among ourselves. There even appeared, very discreetly, a few gay and lesbian relationships—a phenomenon I still did not understand. When I learned that a woman I'd slept with was lesbian, I was shocked. Upon discovering that Carl Wittman was gay (I don't recall the term used then), I noticed a tendency in myself to withdraw from him. It was all very unspoken. When Carl decided to move to Hoboken to begin a project of his own, we never discussed his real feelings, nor mine.

Our spartan life-style offended some white liberals and even certain blacks who thought we were "slumming," and in the end it was too demanding of people, but I am convinced that we affected most of the people we were trying to reach with our willingness to sacrifice. Our acts separated us clearly from any other would-be organizers, missionaries, or social workers these poor had ever seen. Instead of looking down on them, we tried to apply our skills in a process of "looking up," searching for answers from their experience instead of from experts.

The goal of our organizing plan was for people to overcome their fears and self-doubts and go on eventually to become their own community organizers and leaders. Every morning about nine-thirty we held a staff meeting. Between ten and twelve, and again in the afternoon, we went out in two-person teams to what we called "the blocks." The neighborhood was divided by streets, each to be organized door by door into block associations. We went to each house asking people their grievances and talking up the need to form an organization. About one out of every ten or fifteen people would be interested; at that rate, you had to talk with 150 people to get a house meeting of fifteen or twenty people, the minimum size we defined as a real group. The common grievances were dilapidated housing, high rents or property taxes (for the few on each street who were home-owners), lack of streetlights and effective garbage collection, welfare, and police abuse. This neighborhood process did not lend itself to organizing around jobs issues. We tried, with only limited results, to organize hospital workers into a union by recruiting workers to attend house meetings, but it was difficult to unify them.

Petty, emotional differences often kept people from working together: parental hostility toward the life-style of young people, for example, or a homeowners' tendency to blame welfare mothers for their problems. There was a pervasive pattern of blaming individual weakness as the cause of social ill. Most people lived inside the narrow "personal milieu" C. Wright Mills had described; our task was to penetrate that isolated web and replace it with a *social* one. To accomplish this, we found a process that worked quite naturally. We would encourage one person after another at meetings to talk about specific problems until they were all shaking their heads in agreement and a *system* of collective abuse had become apparent. Thus, the first step was in transferring blame from oneself to institutions. In addition, through the therapeutic experience of speaking out after so many years of voicelessness, a sense of pride and ability could begin to grow. Our work was to encourage this process, through which the people we had organized became organizers themselves. Our leadership had to be transformed into theirs.

It was hard but rewarding work. Hard because we were rejected nine out of ten times at the door, often by people who needed help the most. But it was rewarding, because that 10 percent could develop into a large number of committed people—and did. In a few weeks, we had 250 people meeting in about fifteen block groups. We began knitting them into a neighborhood-wide organization so that people from each block would see their common problems in larger perspective. We held weekly meetings of the block leaders, which led to a neighborhood leadership body. We opened a storefront office on a seven-day basis. Soon our mimeos were pouring out leaflets announcing meetings and demonstrations or outlining in simple terms such subjects as tenants' rights and where to get legal aid. We encountered friction with some of the white liberals who had helped invite us to Newark and were now becoming threatened by the emergence of a grass-roots organization of black poor people they couldn't control. From that rift, so similar to the conflicts between SDS and the LID old guard, we concluded that we would have to form an organization of our own rather than joining a coalition with more traditional forces in the city. We named ourselves the Newark Community Union Project (NCUP, pronounced EN-cup) embodying the idea that people in communities controlled by outside and downtown interests had to form unions just as they did in the workplace to contend with the front office.

One day I received an invitation to Washington from the Peace Corps, which was then headed by Frank Mankiewicz. They asked me to "explore" working together on a common project, but wouldn't give more details. Curious, I flew from Newark Airport to hear what they had in mind. Ever the organizer, I think I was wearing a red-and-black wool jacket on top of the usual khakis. I met with Mankiewicz after a long preliminary meeting with an aide and was startled to hear him ask if I would be interested in training Peace Corps volunteers in Latin America. The Andes could be mine, he said, laughing. I said, no, I didn't think so, but made a counteroffer that NCUP train VISTA volunteers in American slums, barrios, and hollows. VISTA was the federal government's response to SDS and SNCC organizing, providing an opportunity for volunteer service in poverty areas. While the VISTA volunteers were more moderate and conventional in approach than, say, NCUP organizers, many of them were motivated by strong idealism and compatible objectives. My proposal was serious, and we agreed on an informal training arrangement. After a few more meetings, the idea lapsed; but ironically, the Campaign for Economic

Democracy (CED), which I formed twelve years later in California, did train VISTA workers on a grant from the Carter administration.

Official recognition of poverty had been triggered by Mike Harrington's *The Other America,* but the real impetus for federal action was the threat of violence and radicalism in the cities. The federal troubleshooter assigned to Newark, Father Theodore Gibson, acknowledged as much in an interview with the local paper when he said he was "convinced that the antipoverty program was the key to racial peace in Newark this summer." Even members of the most militant groups, he said, "were so busy working on antipoverty projects that they had little time to stir up dissension."

Instead of trying to contain these ghetto energies, I believed it was necessary to release the potential of people who were bottled up by the system. Contrary to the image of unstable and dangerous ghetto culture, I was impressed by how many people responded quickly and enthusiastically to positive incentives and how many were personally well-organized and responsible individuals in spite of the pressures of being made marginal. I found countless people in Newark who truly were "the salt of the earth," living decent and caring lives in spite of a system that minimized their potential.

Over the course of a few days in 1965, I kept a journal, excerpts from which were published in the Fall 1965 *Partisan Review.* The journal conveys an accurate sense of how we lived, worked, and thought in those times:

> MONDAY: Staff meeting at 10:00. Mike was supposed to have found bail money for this afternoon in case we have trouble. He didn't. Connie said she'd call her sister's boyfriend and see if she could get money pledged by afternoon. I was worried because among the community members of NCUP, the organizer is expected to be "competent" (know the law, get bail money, etc.). Behind the expectation are two things: (1) the people feel the seriousness of the stakes and they want proof that we also are serious; (2) some are afraid, a natural thing when it's the first demonstration for many of them, and they have to lead it themselves.

NOON: Tied up with phone calls to Episcopalian civil rights committee in New York; fund-raising for the National Poor People's Conference in Newark, August 27–29.

Finally got to Eighteenth Avenue at 2:00. Told Mrs. Queen, who lives in a two-room place with no toilet or closet, about the demonstration demanding a traffic light. Said she'd be there. Wondered whether she said it because she wants to "please" me: today would be a test. She's always drinking and tough to understand. Says "her baby" was run over in the street, but no one else remembers the incident. Then she seems more agitated about "the Jew" (her landlord) who won't give her a toilet or a closet, and who she says will evict her if she complains. She uses the commode next door, and hangs all her clothes on a big peg.

Miller was home from work (drives a truck for the county) at 3:00, so I caught him before he got in the house where I knew he would take a nap. In the first few discussions I had with him, he was what we call "strong." From Georgia, he confidently supports a family and holds down a job, has been stepped on by white people all his life, is "very fond" of me but says I can't understand the race problem because I'm white. He is hard on Lyndon Johnson. "That man can pick up the phone and drop that ole bomb! Now why can't he pick up the phone and help us, you tell me that!" It is the same question most people here ask, only Miller is perhaps angrier and more informed. His brother Willie, nineteen, is also tough. Sitting on the porch with us, he said he'd like to "rack up" some white people like they did in Los Angeles. Everybody seems either to favor or to absolve what the people did out there [the Watts riots in Los Angeles, summer 1965].

I began talking with Miller about the need for the traffic light. When I first got here a month ago, the people thought the traffic problem was a good issue to organize around. I used to think such issues were "superficial," they didn't deal with root problems, etc., but I've felt my thinking shift bit by bit this year. I had to learn that *real* children are killed, all the time. What the city fails to do about such "minor" ills, which are within its ability to correct, is a clear measure of the callousness of the officials. That the people accommodate, by their silence at least, to the city's failure on such small matters, is a measure of how deeply they feel the futility of ever changing anything. Most people I talked to see the traffic problem, not on the basis of narrow self-interest, but as part of a system so abrasive that it cannot even implement its own stated goals without militant pressure.

The twenty people I'm working with see the demand for a traffic light as a departure point for a community movement and a way to wrest something real from City Hall. They started with a petition, not because most people believe in "channels" as such, but because "we should give them a chance." A little apprehension too, over doing something "wild" that "other colored people" might not understand. So Sampson and I collected two hundred names one Saturday morning, and the following week Miller's sister Rosalie took them down to the mayor's office. (She was afraid, because of Welfare, but she did it anyway. Afterward I took her to see a CORE person who works at Welfare. We reassured her about her political rights, but told her to call him if anyone bothered her about her benefits.)

Since then, two weeks ago, some of the people have favored "giving the city enough time," and others were in favor of "protesting the runaround we're getting." Last week we held a meeting with people on Avon Avenue, four blocks away, who also want a traffic light, and the agreement was we'd back each other up if there was no action by today.

Miller had been missing meetings, because he had the flu just after his wife and father were sick, and today he was taking the more cautious position: "Got to give them time. Some things they stall on, but some things, you know, takes time." Miller's feeling reflected his experience with a militancy that went nowhere and his interest in finding tactics which would get the traffic light as well as organize people. I told him we would have to go over to the other block and see what people wanted to do; if they wanted to go ahead and demonstrate, Miller said he would accept it. His brother went with several of us to the other block meeting.

FOUR O'CLOCK: The people on the other block, Avon Avenue, were in a different situation. They had seen someone, apparently from the Traffic Division, out surveying the street on Friday. This made them feel it might be sensible to wait and see what the city would conclude about the petition, which they too had signed and sent in to City Hall. However, since the people I was with from Eighteenth Avenue had received *no* word from the city, the Avon folk said they were willing to go with us to demonstrate. I thought they were a little nervous and maybe caught in the trap of following "official procedure"—but I checked my feeling, because I'm usually much too suspicious or impatient. I said, finally, "OK, then let's go over to Eighteenth and demonstrate." About ten people—most of those there—came with me, Sampson, and Willie. Walking over to Eighteenth, I was a little nervous, partly because I never tried before to stop busy traffic, but mainly because I didn't know what the people from Avon Avenue would think if only a few from our block came or if we were all arrested and banged around.

When we got there, an early skirmish of what I expect to be a major political war for control of the Central Ward had begun. About six Negro men were trying to prevent us from demonstrating by cornering people and telling them not to be fooled by the "whites and outside agitators." They represented the organization of Irvine Turner, an old-fashioned Central Ward Democratic councilman. His men were pushing us around a little, but our people told them very sharply to "get out of the way of right." People were refusing to go along with their "leaders."

We finally went into the street. The first time across, we just slowed traffic, then came back to the corner to see whether the police were going to do anything. There was a squad car one block away, parked, the patrolmen motionless. So we went out again, this time to block the traffic. Some of the people driving cars were actually cooperative and turned off their car engines. After about fifteen minutes, one policeman walked up to us, saying something cordially to Sampson. You could tell they were terrified of another Los Angeles riot. The cop surprised us by agreeing to clear the street of traffic, and he went off to create a detour two blocks around us. Then a Public Service bus tried to slip through our line as it was scattering, but Fred Douglas stopped it by running out in its path. The two hundred of us cheered him, and everyone began to feel we were flexing a set of muscles the community had not felt before.

The captain from the Fourth Precinct finally came by. He took several people to a pay phone and called the deputy mayor, Paul Reilly, who said that he'd provide us with stop signs and a traffic cop in forty-eight hours, meet with us in the morning, and commence an immediate "traffic study" to determine if a light is needed. They came back, and we had a street meeting to hear the official promises. Many of the people were dissatisfied, but no one wanted to stay out in the street after dark. So it ended with everyone very pleased. I was especially happy because every person I'd been working with came down and joined the picket line. Some people from Avon Avenue were there too, and they started planning a meeting to decide what to do for themselves.

ELEVEN O'CLOCK: Came back to apartment after eating with Sampson, who was jubilant. I read the papers, some of Sartre's *Nausea*, told a few staff people what happened, and finally relaxed enough to fall asleep around 2:00. New fan in the room created cool air; some people in Trenton gave it to us.

TUESDAY: Had to be up at 8:00, everyone else asleep, littered around on couches and the floor. J.C., a staff guy from the neighborhood, was asleep on the stairs because he came back late and the door was locked. I walked over to Vera's on Hunterdon, where Junius sleeps, and woke him up for the car keys. Got to Eighteenth Avenue about 9:00, and drove downtown along with the second carload. Let everyone off at City Hall, while I parked. Wanted to get in late, personally, so the officials wouldn't be able to deal with me as the "leader." When I got upstairs, all nine people were sitting around the desk of Deputy Mayor Reilly. His hair looked drowned by pomade; he tried to talk, and gesture with his hand, like John Kennedy, but it came off awkwardly. We first ran into Reilly during last summer's riot scare, when he came down to our office to persuade us against demonstrating. People made him wait outside the door for forty-five minutes, then spurned his pleas. We had several other encounters with him at his office, mostly so that people would get experience in carrying their problems to City Hall. He always kept his charm, except for one time when a woman threatened to hit him with his own ashtray.

This morning Reilly was cordial, surrounded by a half-dozen aides, including the chiefs of Sanitation, Traffic and Signals and the Fourth Police Precinct. The people were telling him off in relatively polite terms, no one acting as spokesman. One elderly lady told about all the traffic accidents that had happened during the many years she was a registered Democrat; Reilly thanked her for registering and reporting the accidents. A young guy said Newark was a "powder keg"; Reilly said the whole administration was worried but felt that "communication" was better in Newark than other cities with racial tension. Sampson kept saying we would demonstrate again if a light wasn't put up; Reilly said he needed time to do things within the law. He said a survey was needed before the city could decide on a light, but he would take "immediate" precautions for children in the area. We left, giving him as little sense of what we would do next as he had conveyed to us.

We had a short meeting back on the street. Sampson and his brother, Fred Douglas, decided to make a leaflet telling the neighborhood what happened. Otherwise, we decided to wait a couple of days to see what the city would do.

I felt sick from not enough food and sleep, so I went over to Louise Patterson's and tried to rest on her couch. But staff people kept coming in, asking Louise for money (she's the NCUP "banker").

I went back to Eighteenth Avenue and spent the late afternoon sitting with some friends on their front porch.

EIGHT O'CLOCK: Stopped by at the Program Committee (weekly decision-making meeting in the Clinton Hill project) to tell them what had happened at Reilly's office. About twenty-five people were there, half of them regular activists and half newcomers. They are tied up especially in War on Poverty politics, since NCUP people recently elected the officers to the official local board. Since then they developed a proposal for a community-run recreation program. Already they are fighting with the police over who should run the summer "play streets." The police are the official sponsors, but NCUP people make up much of the paid street staff. The battle will really develop over the question of whether the city administration will permit local people to set up a recreation program, which would strengthen the role of NCUP and independent poor people working in the antipoverty program. About twenty-five people went down to Washington during the "Assembly of Unrepresented Peoples" and talked to the Office of Economic Opportunity about pressuring Newark's City Hall to respect the "maximum feasible participation" of the poor as officially required in the War on Poverty. Like the Justice Department's "protection" of Negro voting rights against hostile southern officials, our people feel Sargent Shriver's office should protect the poor in the official poverty program against City Hall. Results of the meeting were vague; but at least an investigation is going on, and people now see the national character of the problem much more concretely.

It was difficult and important to spend time at the Program Committee and at the same time feel separate from it. When I decided to move out of Clinton Hill, the original project area, and into the "bottom" of the Central Ward ghetto, it felt like I was tearing out all kinds of anchors that kept me secure. My other feeling was semi-panic about the possibility that things I'd been working on would collapse, based on an unrealized lack of confidence in other people. Getting over these feelings took time. We're all more or less conditioned to be at the "center of things" and around familiar people; this is reinforced when, as strangers in a ghetto isolated from much of the established order, we develop all kinds of stakes in our basic community, the project. One of the strains of organizing, therefore, is that it propels you to move out of situations you've created on toward strange new people and problems. The drain is serious.

NINE O'CLOCK: Dropped by meeting of United Freedom Ticket, an independent "party" of Negroes and whites running for state, county, and city offices.

Background: It began two years ago when the Essex County Democratic machine split with one of its Negro assemblymen, George Richardson. He then organized the "New Frontier Democrats" with no support except from a few old friends and ran an all Negro–Puerto Rican ticket for state and county seats. The machine and others dismissed him as a crank, but his ten thousand votes were enough to allow several Republicans to defeat Democrats. Since then, Richardson has remained the leader of the anti-machine civil rights forces in the city. This year he's widened his coalition to include whites. He's getting increased support from some Negro clergy, and a little support from white religious and neighborhood leaders (some of whom think NCUP is far too extreme). He's getting no support, however, from the AFL-CIO or liberal whites who make up the county power structure of the Democratic party. Questions:

1. Leadership: We've felt that fixed leaders are a danger because they tend to monopolize knowledge, contacts, and decisions; they can reduce a movement to a body of dependent followers; they are shaped into "bargainers" who adapt to the styles of the powerful. Would a Richardson campaign carry us directly toward this trap?

2. Middle-class programs: Most political reform movements seek to make change *for* people instead of *through* people. The problem is that the "solutions" are imposed administratively on people, life patterns are disrupted willy-nilly, and new problems are created. Such programs cannot reverse the dynamics of "welfare oppression" because they do not make the promotion of democracy their key value. Would Richardson offer only this kind of program?

3. Orthodox political campaigning: Reformers and reactionaries alike tend to see people as objects to be "lined up" in support of their campaigns. The goal is to "win," so *any* tactic that creates votes is allowed. This can leave a *shell organization* after the campaign; the politician is safely cut off from organized and independent people, and he takes a seat at the bargaining tables remote from the ghetto. The shell, when lubricated, becomes a patronage machine geared to winning the next election, thus repeating the cycle. Not only are the voters merely used, but a great number of people are never mobilized at all. They do not register, or they register and ignore voting. Their so-called apathy is rooted in a realistic view of the quality of politics and the possibilities for change. Would the dynamics of the campaign undermine NCUP's attempt to organize the really "alienated" people?

4. The coalition: The Freedom Ticket, as Richardson conceives it, would include persons and groups of very different interests based on values, race, class, experience, and personality. He hammers at the theme that each group should respect the validity of other approaches. Richardson's ticket in fact includes certain people who seem to think our activity is unacceptable. Some further questions:

Do poor people need to be organized into groups of *their own* in order to gain confidence, identity, and the power to genuinely bargain with other groups?

How can we work with "leaders," such as the more conservative clergy, and also work with the people in their congregations to lead themselves?

What kind of people, styles, and rules of structure can satisfy so many competing interests?

In spite of these unanswered questions, I've been guardedly hopeful about the Freedom Ticket. A lot of it rests on an impression of Richardson himself. Since first meeting him, I've sensed a lot of courage there, as well as an uneasy radicalism. He's one of those tough people who resisted the pressures inflicted on Negro men in the North. He's been in the rat race, and outside of it, and feels effective in both situations. He's easy for people to talk to. He knows that the ghetto respects racial pride and strength; he's willing to push back the Turner people if they get rough. There is no "pragmatic" political reason that I can see for him to endorse us publicly; on the contrary, our alleged radicalism would impose a real strain on his coalition. In addition, his is a relatively open organization, one which might become more democratic because of popular pressure. Then, too, unless we join him in some way, we may be isolated from a political campaign, which most community people are interested in, in our area. The Freedom Ticket will campaign in the areas we've organized, and our possible differences with Richardson would seem pretty incomprehensible to most people. Finally, we probably can run a council candidate of our own, in a way of our own choosing, on his ticket this time and in the spring election.

The question is not whether we need political power, but how to create *people's* political power. How can it be achieved through electoral politics without sapping the roots of the movement here? We may be able to run an NCUP member on Richardson's slate whose own character, as a poor Negro, cannot be fit into the system's routines. The campaign might take shape around the ideas of (1) representation of the black poor and (2) a program determined and advanced by the people affected.

We must decide soon. But how to do it without splitting NCUP? There seem to be three tendencies: (1) Some people want to work with Richardson somehow; (2) others need time to decide;

(3) some people would rather continue regular community organizing. A major problem is finding an organizational formula that allows these different interests to exist without conflict. A second problem is that of the "timetable." In the Richardson campaign, and in the official antipoverty and urban renewal programs as well, there are pressures demanding that you meet the system's timetable or else "miss out." It creates a motive for quick, elitist decisions, followed by a selling campaign among those who were not in on the decision making. The point is that we need *time*, if new orientations are going to root and grow in people. Just possibly, we're far enough along so that people may force decisions to include them. Perhaps Richardson can't get our "manpower" without opening up his organization to people's voices, demands and energy. Maybe. Otherwise, where do we go?

WEDNESDAY: Nine o'clock. New reality on Eighteenth Avenue. A traffic cop, four "Watch For Children" signs, and a stop sign at the cross street. People taking notice, talking about it, surprised and a little proud.

NOON: Downtown to buy back issues of the *Newark News*. Stopped to see Morton Stavis, a Newark attorney who is a counsel to the Mississippi Freedom Democratic Party, and who always helps out NCUP. He'd been thinking about the Los Angeles thing. He was leaning to the view that the only long-run "solution" lies in reconstructing the Negro family by a planned and complex program of jobs, changes in the welfare structure, education, and other attacks on the generational "cycle" of poverty.

We had a long discussion. I had no "constructive" alternative to propose, but wondered just whose "family structure" such advocates wanted Negroes to follow? Not mine, I hoped. It seemed a case of blaming black family structures but not the structure of unemployment.

Mort and I talked about two different extremes toward which American society might tend in the next few years. He wants to take a view of gradual progress, racial assimilation, fairer economic distribution. When I hear this I picture an expanded "welfare state" in which plenty of inequalities remain, but with more cushions and comforts for all. At its best, this would mean some kind of new legitimacy for those currently causing "disorders."

But then I wondered: This country has mobilized its various interest groups only around foreign wars. Could it mobilize as much on domestic problems such as civil rights or poverty? We know that many top government officials and business leaders understand the need for a crusade against racism and poverty, if only to preserve the country's image and reduce disorder. But others at the top disagree, and still others don't care because they do not feel the problem directly. Then, too, the federal or pluralist system itself puts up countless roadblocks against a mobilization directed from Washington.

Should the Great Society fall, the country might move toward the other model: the Watts riot. Perhaps economic and racial divisions are too deep to be healed by Lyndon Johnson even with all his allies. Perhaps even the community organizers, even those in SNCC and SDS, are too "reformist" for the angriest people in this country. Perhaps the only form of action appropriate to angry people is violence. Some days when I feel the violence everywhere, or watch City Hall step on someone pointlessly, or see how little support there is for the kind of work we're doing, I expect the Los Angeles example to happen everywhere, and I wonder, deep down, where will I be then?

Stavis and I sat for a minute, he with his thirty years' experience and me with my five years of the movement. Then he got a phone call and went back into his practice. I returned to the Central Ward, and had a long soda at Bernice's Restaurant on Eighteenth Avenue.

FIVE O'CLOCK: John Barnes, an old Turner associate connected with the Mayor's Human Relations Commission, sauntered down Eighteenth Avenue until he saw me sitting on a porch. Smiling a lot, he said he'd been with the mayor (he called him by the last name to indicate his independence) that morning, and it was agreed we'd get our traffic light. He was especially worried about what we might do next and feared conflict between ourselves and the Turner people. The man I was with said we would "take Newark apart" unless we got the light, which made Barnes shudder. When Barnes went off, I asked my friend what he thought. "He's a stool pigeon, you can sure tell that," said the man.

Later that night, Sampson called to say that the head of the Human Relations Commission had come right up to his apartment to assure us about the traffic light and find out what we were going to do next. With him, Sampson went on, he brought a young, white married couple, dressed just like "SDS people," but representing the government's antipoverty program, VISTA. They asked Sampson and his brother to call a meeting of their neighbors and said they would be working in the neighborhood for a while to "help people improve themselves." Sampson and his brother politely said no.

I was over at another Avon Avenue meeting where people decided to demonstrate in the street on Monday if the city took no action about their traffic problem. When I came back, I bought some hamburger meat and went to a friend's house to cook it. Then Carl Wittman came in from a long trip of visiting organizing projects around the country. He went especially to see what shape organizing in white communities was in. He said it was "bad," and that he'd decided to "keep up his slow work among whites in Hoboken." "Out of enthusiasm, or from doggedness?" I asked. "Doggedness, for sure," he said, and then he drove me back to the apartment.

In 1965–66, as the Vietnam War escalated, I could steadily feel time running out for building an effective movement against discrimination and poverty. Nevertheless, I kept knocking on doors.

The first door I knocked on in Newark was 61 Hillside Avenue, a single-family, brown-shingle house in Clinton Hill. It was not the heart of the ghetto, but a once-white area that was steadily deteriorating. The woman who came to the screen door was attractive, perhaps forty years old, light-skinned, with a wide, smiling face. Her name was Bessie Smith: like the famous singer, she said, laughing shyly. With an open attitude that I found very common in those years, she invited me into her kitchen for a glass of water, then a cup of coffee. Her two little kids, Michael and Connie, stared amusedly from their bedroom door. On their black-and-white television a soap opera droned on behind our conversation.

In approaching Bessie Smith, I followed the formal rules of organizing, which are simple enough: when the door opens, smile, speak politely and quickly, saying something like, "Hello, I'm Tom Hayden, from the Newark Community Union Project. We're knocking on doors trying to get people together to do something about [high rents, rats and roaches, the lack of garbage collection, streetlights, etc]. Do you mind if I ask you some questions about how you feel about these issues, and whether you would like to join us in doing something about them?"

After that, the format became less rigid. An organizer could become more conversational and try to enter the life of the other person deeply enough to understand his or her interests and values, and then make a judgment about what to ask. The latter approach, I always found, would allow me to find potential leaders as well as make strong personal relationships with them.

Bessie Smith was such a leader. While fixing dinner at her stove, she described a life of happiness with her husband and two children, but nonetheless a life of blocked potential. She had charisma, intelligence, charm, and had never found a public way to use her gifts. She was one of the few registered Republicans I met in the black community, a choice she made "just to be different than everybody else."

When her husband, Thurman, arrived home from work at his camera shop, he didn't seem to think anything was strange about a young white man sitting in the kitchen talking to his wife. In fact, he laughed with delight, a deep throaty laugh. "You're here? Goo-o-o-d, I've been hearing about you *militants*. City Hall, boy, they don't like you at all. That's goo-o-o-d, you must be doing something." He laughed again. Thurman was slightly older than Bessie and walked with a slumped posture that made me realize that he commuted long hours to his job each day and that he wanted to relax in his favorite living room chair as soon as he was home. Like Bessie, Thurman was a natural, even outspoken leader by personality. In his youth, he said, he supported the "unemployment councils" someone tried to organize, but since nothing seemed to come of efforts at change, he remained on the sidelines. Both he and Bessie were critical of traditional black leadership, which participated mainly in patronage politics at City Hall, and they thought something new needed to happen. Imbued with a certain optimism from watching events in the South, they gladly volunteered to help create a block club on Hillside Avenue. Thurman preferred to work behind the scenes, but he urged Bessie to take an active, visible role, which she did.

Over the next year, Bessie Smith was one of perhaps twenty-five very talented people who led the organizing of the Newark Community Union Project. Many were women like herself with children, who could use their phones during the day. Some were mothers on welfare. The men were typically employed in the private sector, where they were free of political pressure. Many of the young men were unemployed or school dropouts. Our organization extended even into the world of street hustlers, but it was mainly composed of mothers and the working poor. We had our share of unbalanced people, alcoholics, and egomaniacs, but I doubt whether it was a higher percentage than in society at large. It is a fact that none of our white organizers, male or female, was ever the victim of a criminal assault during the four years I lived in Newark.

The official poverty program didn't seem to see these large numbers of people who were more than ready to participate as responsible citizens in a system providing them with adequate jobs, housing, and avenues of political expression. Instead, the "war on poverty" funneled money from Washington straight into the City Hall machinery that most black people distrusted. To make matters worse, the same program offered a range of paternalistic remedies based on the idea that the poor were to blame for most of their own problems. Psychological counselors opened offices in the ghetto while hundreds of teenagers were relocated to Job Corps camps to acquire "discipline." The poor would learn "work habits" and "job-interview skills" (for jobs which everyone agreed were nonexistent). As for "community action," its role was very limited. Usually VISTA volunteers would process individual grievances to the proper authorities, or engage in self-help projects like cleaning up vacant lots. Participation was limited mainly to this client status for the poor, with occasional opportunities to sit on handpicked "advisory committees."

Nevertheless, people like Bessie Smith tried to make the poverty program work for the poor. The entire NCUP staff and leadership made a decision that we would take the limited idea of "maximum feasible participation" seriously and expand it. Staying out of the Newark antipoverty program meant we would have no access to tangible resources, and a new elite would soon be competing with us in speaking for the poor. Involving ourselves meant risking our independent identity, but there was little choice if we wanted to have an impact on daily lives and stay in the forefront of defining solutions. It so happened that the Newark OEO program, run by Cyril Tyson, a very effective proponent of self-help, had evolved a relatively open structure in which groups like ourselves could participate. The city program was divided into seven geographic areas, the services in each to be operated by area boards which would be elected from the community at large.

The difference between NCUP and the area boards was the

difference between a supportive community and a bureaucracy, between participatory democracy and administrative management, between power for poor people and services for poor clients. In Bessie's words,

> NCUP means that people *can* get together. The fact that they can get together with other people and they don't have to feel inferior or ashamed because maybe they don't know how to speak well, and they won't be outwitted, so to say, with parliamentary procedure. People don't feel that they are looked down upon.

Another of our NCUP members, Mrs. Dora Holder, described her first Area Board meeting as a baffling maze:

> Confusing! Lots of people jumping up and shouting, "You're out of order!" My mother had something she wanted to say, and I kept punching her to say it. But she said, "No, I'm not going to stand up." She felt it wouldn't do any good, because the only people that were talking were people on the board or committees, or something like that. Every time you looked, they were talking.
> This one got up and started hollering at people. He said he was there to help the meetings run smoothly. But to me, it was running pretty smoothly until every time you turned around, someone would say "you're out of order." We didn't know when to say the right thing at the right time! When is the right time? You don't know so you don't say anything. You don't go back because what's the use of sitting there at a meeting, if you want to say something, but you're afraid to say it because it may be out of order?

But just as the Freedom Democrats studied the rules of the Democratic party, we studied the rules of the area boards until we understood them better than anyone. We organized the members of NCUP block clubs to attend their local area board meetings as they would a political convention. At one early meeting, we caused an uproar by passing a motion that a majority of the members of the governing board of an area board must be poor themselves—defined as unemployed, on welfare, or living on an income of less than four thousand dollars for a family of four. At subsequent meetings, we elected candidates to the boards and lobbied successfully for a community-based service center where, for example, attorneys could represent tenants against landlords. We involved professional urban planners and economists to suggest job-creating development programs. Along with our involvement in independent local politics, we were becoming a highly visible threat to the status quo by working within the system. A local Catholic priest who worked too closely with us was removed to another parish. Our local City Council representative complained that we had our "fangs" in the program. The mayor and City Council at one point cut funding for the program from $800,000 to $200,000 for fear that we would exercise too much influence.

Bessie Smith was our star, our most persuasive and effective leader, a potential candidate for future office. Thurman and her kids were proud of her, unthreatened by the many hours she trudged off to meetings or studied bureaucratic reports. Finally, our organizing efforts succeeded in electing her as one of the *citywide* trustees of the antipoverty program, an unexpected triumph that sent ripples of fear and respect through the city's leaders.

On the night of her election, Bessie Smith died in her sleep. Thurman said she lay down, sighed, closed her eyes, and never moved again. I nearly lost my bearings over her death. Though everyone, including her competitors, spoke movingly of Bessie's leadership achievements, I felt a personal guilt. I had entered her life, and that of her family, and possibly changed it in ways that brought pressure, stress, and death. I stayed on Thurman's front couch for two weeks after Bessie's death, helping with the kids and mostly clinging to the place where we had spent so many hours together.

NCUP's work was far from over, and other leaders surfaced to fill the vacuum Bessie left. One of them, Jessie Allen, was from somewhere down South and could barely speak understandable English. When I first met him, he wanted to go on a rent strike against his landlord. A Korean War veteran and former boxer, he had a metal plate inside his head and drank heavily to kill the various pains in his life. He became an NCUP staff organizer, a prominent leader in the antipoverty program, and was eventually elected councilman from the Central Ward, the hard-core ghetto of Newark replacing the machine of Irvine Turner. He, too, died suddenly, of a heart attack. The Bessie Smiths and Jessie Allens deeply affected me. They, and many like them, lived in the world of the unqualified and ignored, and yet they were as qualified and, more important, as decent human beings as I would ever meet. If they had been welcomed, instead of systematically rejected, by the establishment, there might have been a saving period of grace and goodwill before the breakdown that was coming.

With progressive government policies and enlightened business attitudes, a profound and positive transformation was possible in 1965–66. Indeed, the War on Poverty and the 1965 Voting Rights Act appeared outwardly to represent just such enlightened approaches. But neither reform addressed poverty and basic economic issues in a full sense. If they had, with effective job creation and better education, the emerging leadership in the ghetto might have created a black community with hopeful expectations, self-determining but not separatist. Instead, the official policies promoted opportunities for a new stratum of middle-class blacks, political brokers, middle managers, and professionals increasingly removed from the vast and permanent underclass of people outside the scope of the antipoverty program. But if the new middle stratum were drawn from the ghetto into token positions in the government and business worlds, who would be left behind to fill the vacuum?

The poverty program's achievements resulted in greater social isolation of the underclass. Although the underclass was mainly perpetuated through the desperate children of the ghetto, it was also expanded in the late sixties by the forced migration of poor, uneducated southern blacks pushed off the land by agricultural automation, the very blacks whose living conditions in the Black Belt SNCC sought to stabilize and improve.

In a prophetic speech I didn't grasp completely at the time, Bob Moses once described the southern movement as engaged in a race between voting rights and automation. The more that the sharecropper economy was challenged by the movement, the greater the white plantation owner's incentive to displace workers with cotton-harvesting machines, thus forcing tens of thousands northward. In addition, the southern Dixiecrats pushing for an expanded Vietnam War were benefiting from the export of newly enfranchised blacks from South to North. The failure of reform nationwide, therefore, steadily led to family crisis, rising violence, eventual separatism, and a polarized and overheated policy climate in which it became virtually impossible to speak of ghetto pathologies, as Daniel Patrick Moynihan did, without being attacked as racist. And so those very pathologies began to explode: In 1959, 15 percent of black births were out of wedlock, growing to 57 percent in 1982; black-on-black violence rose until over 40 percent of all murder victims in the 1980s were black; drug addiction, teenage motherhood, and welfare dependency rates all spiraled.

My old friend, attorney Morton Stavis, was not wrong in 1965 when he stressed proposals that would strengthen black families; neither was Moynihan. But at the time, such ideas inevitably seemed like "blaming the victim" when they failed to place sufficient evidence on the government's responsibility. The ERAP analysis, in retrospect, was even more on target: We accepted the existence of pathology (the term first came to my attention in Kenneth Clark's influential *Dark Ghetto*), and we tried to cure it by building self-esteem and power. In addition, we believed that inner scarring could not begin to heal without drastic external improvements in jobs, education, and housing. Effective training and real jobs for young black males, instead of the draft for Vietnam, would have accomplished more than anything else to defuse poverty and strengthen community life. Instead, the government guaranteed welfare for mothers and warfare for sons, leaving work opportunities to the chance of a marketplace that was fast being automated.

While time was running out in those crucial middle years of the decade, all our efforts failed to turn the antipoverty program around. The more we used its flexible provisions to advance our cause, the more its hierarchy changed the rules of the game. The most we could achieve—and it was something—was the control of certain services flowing into our neighborhoods. Although this absorbed several of our best people, providing Band-Aids instead of political organizing, we continued to grow.

We tried everything in those few short years: petitions, demonstrations, electoral politics, rules skirmishes within the War on Poverty. We established a living alternative, a community of individuals who acted differently, who stood up with backs straight, who spoke out in unwavering voices, for the previously silent poor. We asserted, in the lyrics of Paul Simon, that "the words of the prophets are written on subway walls, tenement halls."

But no one in officialdom was listening to these sounds of silence.

By July 1967, it was too late.

FBI MEMORANDUM   **8/19/67**

Hayden, head of the Newark Community Union Project, is a trained agitator . . . based on . . . the fact that Hayden has directed the movement and placement of demonstrators during several recent demonstrations in Newark. Hayden appears to him to have been trained in such matters, but ██████* has no actual knowledge of any training received by Hayden.

TO: Director, FBI
FROM: Newark

RECOMMENDATION: In view of the fact that Hayden is an effective speaker who appeals to intellectual groups and has also worked with and supported the Negro people in their program in Newark, it is recommended that he be placed on the Rabble Rouser Index.

---

*Material deleted by the FBI.

7. *The Fire Next Time:*
July 1967

When the Newark riot began on July 12, 1967, I was playing football.

This minor fact turned out to be quite important in saving me from a conspiracy indictment. The police were sure that an outside mastermind had to be manipulating events that week. They tried for weeks to blame me for the riot, but were stopped cold when a secretary, herself the wife of a policeman, confirmed that I indeed was playing football. She knew because her employer, attorney Leonard Weinglass, was throwing passes to me in front of his office.

Besides football, my friend Len liked his human-scale law practice, teaching property law to Rutgers students, and his memories of Yale Law School and air force service in Greenland. We first met inside a Newark tenement building. A close friend of his, a VISTA volunteer who knew me slightly, brought us together in what became a long friendship. I persuaded him to take some court cases involving rent strikers and welfare mothers. He was a few years older than I was, balding and affable, a character out of a Philip Roth novel. His strong sense of morality, even guilt, combined with his sincerity and intelligence, made him a very effective courtroom advocate for unpopular clients. He might have made an excellent candidate for office, but he was never much for politics. He was good company. When downtown, I would often drop by his office—across the street from Rutgers Law School—for conversation, a break, some football in the street, as I did on that particularly hot night in July.

While I kept trying to catch passes over my head by streetlight, a phone call came to Len's office indicating that "trouble" was starting in the Central Ward. We jumped in his car and drove ten minutes to the lower economic pits of Newark's ghetto.

We parked amid the tall housing projects, which looked like a ghostly gathering of prisons, and walked quickly toward the Fourth Police Precinct, an aging brick building, where hundreds of people were milling around. It looked like the Bastille during the French Revolution.

Moments after we arrived, a Molotov cocktail hit the wall of the police station and broke into a long spiraling column of flame. The people cheered. Len gasped, half smiling in awe. It was the opening shot in a rebellion which, along with the one in Detroit the following week, would be the largest of those violent years. In five days, twenty-six people were killed, a thousand injured, fourteen hundred arrested and sixteen million dollars' worth of damage done to property, as nearly six thousand police, state troopers, and national guardsmen tried to restore order.

The roots of the violence lay tangled in years of blind neglect by the authorities. Newark's officials were confident that their city was immune to the wave of urban riots occurring throughout America. In May, a city official told *The New York Times* that only a "few agitators" wanted any violence; in June, Mayor Hugh J. Addonizio declared that his "open-door" administration had the confidence of the black community. It was not the first time I would hear pompous proclamations from high officials blindly on the brink of their political graves.

The immediate cause of friction was the behavior of Newark's virtually all-white police department. The police force reflected the white ethnic groupings—mainly Italian and Irish—that dominated Newark's government in the generation before transition to a black majority. Seeing themselves as defenders of a way of life on the decline, many of the officers were overflowing with resentment. Their hostility and defensiveness was expressed in a five-day, five-thousand-strong demonstration in 1965 in response to local civil rights marches against police brutality.

While fiercely opposing a civilian review board, the Newark police offered no convincing alternative for dealing with widespread citizen complaints against their officers. An in-house complaint-referral system lacked the confidence of the community and, when occasionally used, didn't deter irresponsible behavior. Of a meager sixty complaints lodged against police in the six years before July 1967, the police investigators substantiated the claim of brutality only twice, meting out only minor discipline in both cases. Under increasing community pressure in 1965, the mayor agreed to forward certain complaints to the FBI; but of seven cases reported by July 1967, no action was taken by the federal authorities either.

The explosion was set off by a routine incident on the night of July 12. Two policemen arrested a black cab driver for tailgating and driving the wrong way on a one-way street. The cab driver, John Smith, was badly beaten in the course of the arrest, leaving him with broken ribs and a split scalp. Community people saw Smith being dragged into the Fourth Precinct. The rumor spread that the police had beaten the cab driver, and angry people began to assemble on the streets. Civil rights leaders, hearing of the beating, arrived at the police station in time to see Smith's condition and lodge complaints of unnecessary force. But this night would not end with a mere exchange of words on a picket line. The "moment" had arrived, the Molotovs flew, and in an hour the looting of nearby white-owned stores was under way.

There were thousands of people on the streets taking advantage of the temporary police paralysis, ripping iron bars off storefronts, smashing windows, and loading their arms with tape recorders, toasters, televisions, clothing, and bottles of liquor. There were well-dressed middle-class couples, no doubt on their way to a party or movie, shirtless young street people, hustlers, groups of neighbors, even people driving trucks up to the inviting windows. There was exhilaration and no sense of guilt; after all, it was felt, the store owners had been ripping off the ghetto for years. Most interesting, there was an order of sorts within this "breakdown of law and order." As I wandered through the stores and streets for two hours, I saw no one injured, trampled, or cut by flying glass, no one fighting over property, no one criticizing the events. There were a very few people totally crazed by the excitement, starting fires in certain stores, throwing Molotovs onto factory roofs, and taunting the police.

The patrolman questioned Hayden as to why he was not attacked by the mob, the patrolman not knowing who Hayden was, why Hayden had stopped there to talk with him and he talked to them. ... It should be pointed out that this was at the height of the riot and the rioters were particularly anti-white, and here was a white man, Thomas Hayden, able to move among them without any difficulty whatsoever.

I didn't even find the rioters to be especially anti-white. They seemed surprised to see me and other whites from NCUP in the streets, but there was no open hostility that first night. The rebellion was against racism, against the system, against indifferent politicians, but it was strangely color-blind on a personal level. Looked at from the inside, this apparently irrational explosion was a classic case of a "festival of the oppressed." I began to understand that beneath the image of disorder, and beyond the traditional debates over nonviolence, there was another dimension here: The riot was a rite of passage from feelings of servitude to the proud psychic independence of "black power."

When Governor Richard Hughes rolled into Newark after the second night with four thousand virtually all-white National Guardsmen and five hundred state troopers to relieve Newark's thirteen hundred police, a grim weekend of military occupation and terror began. Until that point, despite the widespread looting, no one was dead. Now, however, an eerie tension settled on the streets, as people backed into their homes or stores and watched the circling convoys of police cars, jeeps, and military trucks patrolling the ghetto. Bayonets were attached to the guard's M-1 rifles or .30 caliber carbines, which they carried in addition to .45 caliber pistols. Armored personnel carriers weighing eleven tons, as well as trucks with mounted machine guns, joined the patrol by Friday afternoon. By that night, the police or military had killed ten blacks, and wounded one hundred with gunshot; another five hundred were treated at City Hospital for various injuries. By the end of the weekend, another ten were dead, at least fifty wounded, and over five hundred arrested. I spent most of my time with NCUP staff, poverty program attorneys, and news reporters trying to piece together the stories of the killings. I sensed an indiscriminate violence against innocent people—several of them mothers looking out their windows—as I interviewed shaken witnesses in their homes and cross-checked details with other investigators.

For instance, nineteen-year-old James Rutledge was killed on Sunday afternoon. According to police, he was caught in a looted tavern, pulled a knife, and had to be shot. The body of James Rutledge had forty-two holes in the head and upper torso.

Rose Abraham, a domestic worker, was shot by police as she searched for one of her six children in the streets. She was not operated on for six hours after her husband brought her to the city hospital.

Ted Bell, twenty-eight, an employee in a looted bar, told people not to run if police started shooting. A moment later a police bullet killed him. There was Leroy Boyd, with six .38 caliber bullets in his body and a bashed-in head; Rebecca Brown, a mother of four, killed when the military fired into her apartment building while she attempted to snatch her two-year-old away from a window; William Furr, thirty-five, shot in the back in broad daylight for carrying a six-pack of beer down the street, as a *Life* magazine photographer clicked off the sequence; Hattie Gainer, killed by a police bullet fired into her apartment as her three grandchildren watched; Richard Taliaferro, twenty-five, wounded and then "finished off," according to eyewitnesses, one week before his induction into the U.S. Army.

In the course of this mayhem, one policeman and one fireman were also killed by bullets that could have been fired by blacks but just as possibly by guardsmen. Though *Life* magazine sensationally reported a "secret meeting with the snipers," I believed they were being set up, and one account later noted that the journalists paid money for the interview. Months later, Newark's police chief told an investigating commission that "it was so bad that guardsmen were firing on police and police were firing back at them. I think a lot of the reports of snipers were due to the, I hate to use the word, trigger-happy guardsmen, who were firing at noises and firing indiscriminately."

"Where are you going, nigger?" "Kill that nigger bitch." "Get moving or I'll take that camera and wrap it around your head." "You son of a bitch, I'll fix you so you don't drive any more cabs." "Where do you think you're going, you black bastard?" "Kennedy's not with you now." These were typical of the hundreds of verbal police attacks our investigators recorded. The police additionally smashed approximately one hundred black-owned stores that had been spared by looters. They simply shot into the windows marked SOUL BROTHER or broke in with rifle butts.

The jails were overflowing by Sunday. Over fourteen hundred blacks were detained, on bail ranging from $1,000 to $10,-000. Most were charged with looting, only three with attempted arson, and none for shooting and bombing. Except for 150 juveniles, no one arrested was fed until Saturday, many not until Sunday.

While white suburbanites read of looting, arson, and snipers, the truth was that the looting was essentially dying down *before* the massive military buildup began. Arson, while frequently reported, was actually limited to twenty-five cases, nearly all before Saturday. The troops were not protecting the downtown business district or the white suburbs by patrolling the inner city. From a pure crowd-control standpoint, had the black areas been cordoned off, they would have cooled down by the weekend. Instead, the troops were provoking and intimidating people.

Governor Hughes declared that the "line between the jungle and law and order might as well be drawn here as anyplace in America," adding for good measure that blacks "had better choose sides" because "the side of law and order has joined this to the finish." Perhaps carried away as commander in chief, he also announced a "thrill of pride in the way state police and the national guard have conducted themselves." His words sounded more like those of a Rhodesian military governor than a liberal Democratic politician. To the black community, the governor's purpose seemed not to restore order in the most efficient way, but to teach a lesson: that anarchic rebellion, even against years of empty promises, would be forcibly punished and that white authorities would kill human beings for stealing property.

In this grim setting, we at NCUP had long discussions about what to do. Once the military occupation began, we were in serious danger, like everyone else, if we went out on the streets at night, even to our office. We watched the endless military patrols racing down the street with automatic weapons pointed at the houses. We observed the daily confrontations between poorly trained National Guardsmen and unpredictable swarms of black teenagers taunting them at bayonet point. We tried to collect as much food and medical supplies as possible from outside the community, having great difficulty with the logistics. (One of the shipments came from a community store in New York run by a zany, passionate former civil rights worker named Abbie Hoffman—the first time our paths crossed.) I worked relentlessly on collecting the detailed eyewitness complaints.

One night as I worked at the Legal Services office, a phone call came from Furman Templeton, a young black governor's aide who had attended Newark Law School. His message was that Governor Hughes was finally beginning to search for an alternative to the military occupation, but that serious debates were still raging between "hawks" and "doves" within his circles. Templeton asked if I would come, as an eyewitness, to make a presentation. Also invited was a close friend of mine, Bob Curvin of CORE. I immediately agreed. It would be weird to meet the man whose decisions were leading to all the grief I was documenting on my desk, but I would do anything to help end the madness.

Shortly, a state troopers' car pulled up outside the Legal Services office. As I got inside, four troopers were standing outside the vehicle at military attention with automatic weapons drawn. We were going only a short way to the Federal Building, but for security reasons the troopers drove in a long, whipping circle around the outside of the city to get there. Most troopers came from conservative downstate New Jersey towns, and at the time all but five of twelve hundred were white. Sitting between these uniformed musclemen in the back seat, racing through the dark streets with lights low and weapons drawn, listening to the hysterical chatter of the radio system, seeing fire engines, armored cars, flashing lights, all reinforced by the original mindset which the men themselves brought to the ghetto, I could see how they believed themselves to be at war. They had no human contact. Each group of blacks turning the corner might be the enemy. None could be talked to or trusted. It was an urban Vietnam. These men, I realized, were the governor's official point of contact with the community during the crisis.

The vehicle slowed cautiously at the Federal Building, and the troopers leaped out and pointed their weapons at the rooftops. I was escorted inside the building and entered a suite of offices which seemed to be used as a headquarters or crisis center for officials. I saw a bewildered Bob Curvin immediately, then the other figures began taking shape, until I at last saw the governor, a strangely cheery, curly-haired, ruddy man who motioned us to be comfortable. The doves present included Furman Templeton as well as an "urban specialist" from the Ford Foundation, Paul Ylvisaker. The hawks were mainly the police, trooper, and National Guard officials sitting grim-faced along one side of a mahogany table.

I didn't feel comfortable in the isolated "war room," sitting there red-eyed, wearing a faded shirt and Levi's, talking about the mechanized terror in the streets. I had no exact idea of why we had been called, but I assumed that our task was to convince the governor to withdraw his troops. As with Vietnam, he was worried about a possible "bloodbath" if they withdrew and also about a political backlash if the rioting then continued.

"Governor," I began, "there is a massacre going on outside in the streets, and it is caused primarily by the presence of the troops. In the first two nights people rioted and looted, yes, but the violence did not get directed against people until you brought the troops here. Now there has been so much brutality against so many innocent people that you have radicalized the whole community into a hatred. If you don't get the troops out, some people might really start firing on them. If you don't get them out, you could have twice as many dead in two days, and no end in sight. You should leave the people alone, let them bury their dead, heal the injured, take back the prisoners, let the normal fabric of life be restored. Nothing is likely to happen if you withdraw, but if you stay it will only get worse." Bob Curvin said much the same thing, containing his anger and concentrating on the need for a solution.

The hawks at the table complained that their men were being fired on and had to fire back for protection, that a withdrawal would be followed by more ransacking and bloodletting. The doves, in their turn, wanted steps toward peace through negotiations. The governor asked what we thought of an enclave theory—the withdrawal of troops from one neighborhood and, if no violence followed, more withdrawals later. Bob and I looked at each other, then I said, "It's not necessary to test the water. You should just withdraw. But if it would give you greater security, you should begin in our neighborhood, Clinton Hill. Let it begin there, and the rest will follow."

I didn't expect much. Here we were, sitting in a command post, telling the governor that the reality in the heads of his military advisers was either crackpot or fabricated. In moments we would return to the streets, where the patrols roamed like sharks and the sounds of confrontation continued. We ended the meeting feeling pointless, confused by the governor's charming manner. He shook our hands firmly as we left and asked if there was anything he could do for us. I remember Bob Curvin blinking and requesting, with irony, protection from the Newark police. The governor laughed, reached for his card, and scribbled a note on the back. Mine was inscribed *To Tom, Good Luck, Dick Hughes.*

To my surprise the governor announced a complete troop withdrawal the next morning. Peace returned.

Dazed from the week's violence, we tried to pick up the pieces. I threw myself into writing about what had happened. Some very accurate articles appeared in *The Washington Post* by Leroy Aarons and Hollie West, two reporters with whom I had collaborated. My own study was published by *The New York Review of Books* and later by Random House. It included, for each of the murdered people, a reconstruction of the circumstances of their deaths according to the eyewitnesses I could find.

One day, state investigators showed up at Len Weinglass's office looking for me. I reluctantly came from the ghetto, suspecting that they were not investigating the brutality of the police. I met a man named Andrew Zazzoli, who was charged with presenting evidence on the Newark violence to a special grand jury. With hostility, he quizzed me about each of the killings I had cited. He seemed intent on either disproving each of my charges or finding ways to sue me for defamation of the policemen. I was later called before the grand jury, for three hours, to testify not on what I knew about the murders, but on who my sources were. I refused to give them any names beyond what I had written.

Nothing came of the nine-month grand jury investigation, not a single indictment for any of the killings. The grand jury did, however, condemn my *Rebellion in Newark*. A local writer, Ron Parambo, wrote a detailed book two years later, titled *No Cause for Indictment,* making essentially the same charges as mine. Again, there was no response. Instead of addressing the real causes of violence, Newark officials went to Washington,

D.C., claiming that NCUP was to blame. Zazzoli testified before the U.S. Senate that the account given in *Rebellion in Newark* was false. At the same Senate investigation, Captain Kinney of the Newark police accused NCUP of "infiltration and actual seizure of control" of the antipoverty program. Following that "revolutionary" step, he testified, we conspired to "replace the leadership of the Newark police department" and from there "to replace the system of government under which we live." In the same breath, he testified that "economic conditions in Newark are probably better than in most cities in the United States," and that "employment opportunities are ample."

Even more startling was an opportunistic chorus of blame against NCUP by LeRoi Jones, the well-known black nationalist poet, and Anthony Imperiale, an organizer of fifteen hundred armed white vigilantes with armored cars named "jungle bunnies." They later appeared together on a radio program with Police Captain Kinney to blame "so-called radical groups" for Newark's crisis. A week later, both were featured in a Newark police proposal for $750,000 to fund "local patrols" in their respective ethnic communities.

But a state fact-finding commission convened after the July violence interviewed over seven hundred witnesses during five months and concluded that "excessive and unjustified force" was to blame in Newark, "a pattern of police action for which there is no possible justification." Though it failed to do a case-by-case investigation of the deaths, the commission recommended a probe of official "corruption" in Newark. In July 1968, Newark's police chief was indicted on gambling-related charges; a local jury acquitted him. At the same time, the city councilman from Clinton Hill, the nemesis of NCUP, was recalled by the voters. Late the following year, Mayor Addonzio, Councilman Turner, and two other council members were tried, convicted, and sent to jail for some sixty-five counts of conspiracy to commit extortion.

Richard Hughes remained governor of New Jersey until 1970, then became chief justice of the state's Supreme Court from 1973 to 1979. In 1982, when I was running for political office, I received a letter of support from him:

> You recommended the withdrawal of heavy armor and most of the National Guard and State Police. You predicted that the riot

would run its course and end if the inflammatory military and police presence was removed. After you left the meeting and after much discussion, I ordered the removal of these elements and to my knowledge no further shooting nor injuries occurred. Your prediction was correct and the riot was soon over.

The explosive days of July exhausted the dreams of the early sixties and climaxed the period of NCUP's vitality. Traditional arrangements in the city were nullified by the upheaval. The new period would be symbolized by the cry of "black power." This rising nationalism, already stirring before the events of July, took on irreversible strength after the bloodshed. The crisis had revealed a nearly universal white apathy to black fate. The days were winding down when credible blacks would be able to work closely with whites as partners in common cause. A resurgence of separatism, always present in black history, was becoming the foreboding alternative to interracial alliances. The exact political content of black power could vary—from the simple ethnic politics already practiced by Jews, Irish, and Italians, to exotic cultural (African) nationalism, to Muslim withdrawal, to the militancy of revolutionary vanguards. Only one thing was clear: Black people would now primarily rely on themselves for choosing their destiny.

NCUP started making adjustments: The organization slowly wound down for another year, most of its members ultimately flowing into mayoral and City Council campaigns, as well as holding their positions in the antipoverty program. Phil Hutchings, convinced by Stokely Carmichael's message, became the chairman of SNCC in its final days. Another staff member, who had been a bright Howard University law student and a survivor of racist bombings against SNCC in McComb, turned urban guerrilla after Newark, then Muslim, before a nervous breakdown incapacitated him. Some of the white staff moved into the East Ward, a polyglot enclave of some dozen European nationalities, and spent several years in further organizing. Among other achievements, they developed an alternative school for white dropouts. Some of them still remain in the Newark-Hoboken area twenty years later, leading fights for better schools. Several others moved to New York, taking their time to reflect about next choices. One joined the "psychedelic revolution" in California. Carl Wittman was reborn as a gay rights activist, traveling to California, Oregon, and finally back to North Carolina, where in 1986 he died from an AIDS-related illness.

As always, we were embodying larger patterns in our local behavior. The rise of black power to replace the civil rights movement first surfaced in the cauldron of the South, in the wake of the rejection of the Mississippi Freedom Democrats. The failure in Atlantic City led to profound internal questioning, dissension and friction within SNCC. Was realigning the Democratic party a real possibility or, as Atlantic City suggested, a futile hope? Was there a white community to be counted on, or were blacks on their own? If integration was rejected by society, weren't a new black identity, pride, power, and separatism justified? Could that consciousness be developed in organizations that included whites in key roles? These questions bore down on SNCC activists immediately after the Mississippi Summer. Their circle of love could not take the strain. Friends became strangers, and the circle broke into factions. Whites like Casey suddenly lost their legitimacy and their roots in SNCC. Ideologically, they could not disagree with the demand for black control, but the personal consequences were shattering. The community, which was their total source of friendship, income, and personal efficacy, was disintegrating. In time, they began to see new identities for themselves, in the fledgling consciousness of women's rights, or the antiwar movement, where new barricades of oppression needed breaking. These gaps widened beneath the surface of the still-ongoing civil rights movement between 1964 and 1965 and broke to the surface in 1967.

Sometimes an era culminates, like fireworks, in a shower of energy that appears overpowering while actually receding. The era that began with the sit-ins had reached such an ending with the great Selma, Alabama, march of February 1965. In one final spasm, the integrated civil rights movement met in bloody trial with the violent state power of Alabama. Nuns and rabbis marched alongside Dr. King and SNCC leaders. After still more deaths and unbelievable brutality, the president and Congress were obliged finally to pass the Voting Rights Act of 1965. Lyndon Johnson, who earlier in the year planned to reduce the emphasis on civil rights, declared, "We shall overcome." The original demand of the movement—for the end of legal and political segregation—was largely achieved in the relatively short span of five years. But by now it was not enough to quench the thirst of blacks across the nation. In places like Newark, where they already had the right to vote, they still remained second-class citizens; in the South, poverty remained to be conquered.

At the same time, the dynamic of the early sixties was ending: Hope surrendered to cynicism. While the blood flowed in Alabama, the president sent 150,000 combat troops over to Vietnam. Blacks saw that their sons were second class in the employment office, but stood disproportionately tall in the front lines of war. Boxer Cassius Clay refused the draft, saying, "No Vietcong ever called me nigger," and as part of his new consciousness, he became Muhammad Ali. Malcolm X rose to prominence, was gunned down, and most of SNCC attended his funeral. And when James Meredith was shot in 1966, and the last of the traditional marches made its way through Mississippi, Stokely Carmichael and SNCC called for black power. Independent political power became the goal of a local party Stokely formed in Lowndes County, Alabama. Its name and symbol: the black panther. After twenty-seven arrests in the South, Stokely, a graduate of the Bronx High School of Science and Howard University who moved as easily among whites as blacks, was becoming a transformed, radicalized, and messianic figure.

As late as 1966, while he was twenty-four years old and still an idealist in Lowndes County, Stokely wrote *The New Republic:*

> I have hope for this nation. . . . Excluded people must acquire the opportunity to redefine what the Great Society is, and then it may have meaning. I place my hope for the United States in the growth of belief among the unqualified that they are in fact qualified: they can articulate and be responsible and hold power.

But by 1967, a racist social order had penetrated his soul and psyche. Hate would now contest with love, violence would compete with legalism, martyrdom with failure, and the Third World with America as his home. In a few years, he abandoned the United States for Ghana. In spring 1967, H. Rap Brown was elected SNCC chairman; little known then, he shortly made famous the saying "Violence is as American as apple pie." In December 1967, the inevitable happened with an odd formality:

Whites were expelled from SNCC by a vote of nineteen to eighteen, with twenty-four abstaining. Though the decision was by secret ballot, it is clear that whites themselves provided the critical votes to guarantee their own departure. What happened in SNCC reverberated in SDS and in ERAP and wherever organizers gathered to chart their futures.

I did not see then, as I sadly do now, that there was a pathology involved in this painful transition. The combined experience of racism, brutality, and official expediency had rusted SNCC's idealism until it gave way to the volcanic hatred and aggression that swells in the lower depths of the human personality. The politics of separatism and violent rhetoric were neither realistic nor humanistic. But they provided a psychic revenge against a society's rejection and hypocrisy and a way to turn that rejection into strength by instilling fear into white society. The search for a revolutionary answer amid the failure of reform was a political illusion; after all, if nonviolent and moralistic appeals to the Constitution were met with force and scorn, a violent rejection of America would surely hold even less possibility of success. And if idealism was abandoned, what passion could replace it but malevolence? At the time, however, it seemed once again that the movement was growing and responding to experience, that there was an inner logic, an objective destiny driving people toward the changes that were taking place.

In *The Wretched of the Earth*, Frantz Fanon, a black psychiatrist from Martinique who had served in a French hospital in Algeria while secretly helping the Algerian revolutionaries, opposed nonviolence and endorsed violent struggle. He spoke not only in political terms but, more strikingly, as if violence was an inevitable expression of the human nature of the oppressed:

> At the level of individuals, violence is a cleansing force. It frees the native from his inferiority complex and from his despair and inaction; it makes him fearless and restores his self-respect. . . . The colonized man finds his freedom in and through violence.

Even more explosive, however, was Jean-Paul Sartre's introduction to Fanon's book. Referring to Indochina and Algeria, but striking a chord from our own experience, Sartre seemed to capture the era: "We are living at the moment when the match is put to the fuse." The "irrepressible violence" of the colonized, he argued, was not an expression of "savage instincts," as I had also sensed in Newark, but a case of "man re-creating himself. . . . The native cures himself of colonial neurosis by thrusting out the settler (in himself) by force of arms." Sartre condemned sympathetic, armchair progressives for a "racist humanism," for being "accomplices of colonialism," and, citing Fanon approvingly, for filling the "fat, pale continent" of Europe with "narcissism."

There is no way to explain the power of Fanon's explosive message at the time, however, except by fully understanding the vulnerability of the SNCC/SDS generation after the apparent failure of the liberal and nonviolent strategies. To those of us for whom turning back was unthinkable, Fanon and Sartre seemed to prefigure the next stage that lay ahead, the stage that C. Wright Mills had hinted at in his book on Cuba, and we studied extraordinary words like these with awed attraction:

> The new man begins his life as a man at the end of it; he considers himself a potential corpse . . . But this weariness of the heart is the root of an unbelievable courage. We find our humanity on this side of death and despair; he finds it beyond torture and death. We have sown the wind; he is the whirlwind . . . We were men at his expense, he makes himself man at ours: a different man, of higher quality.

I had been fascinated by the simplicity and power of the Molotov cocktail during those days in Newark. There could be no military defense against such an easily constructed missile. Nor were its possibilities for asserting a systematically denied manhood lost on me. I provided a napkin drawing of such a missile to writer Andrew Kopkind, whose editors at *The New York Review of Books,* apparently sensing the potent appeal even to their intellectual audience, printed a David Levine version of the drawing on their cover a month after the upheaval.

I groped for a new position of my own. The Newark experience taught that violence, however dubious in its moral and political implications, could not be ignored as an option, if for no other reason than that it was now part of reality.

In an article for *The New York Review,* I informed my readership that "the role of organized violence is now being carefully considered" by a new breed of black activists. While recognizing that "tactics of disorder will be defined by the authorities as criminal anarchy," I ventured that "it may be that disruption will create possibilities of meaningful change." But I concluded that social change would ultimately depend on whether strong organizations of poor people could be built:

> Violence can contribute to shattering the status quo, but only politics and organization can transform it. . . . The ghetto still needs the power to decide its destiny on such matters as urban renewal and housing, social services, policing and taxation. . . . In order to build a more decent community while resisting racist power, more than violence is required. People need to create self-government. *We are at a point where democracy—the idea and practice of people controlling their lives—is a revolutionary issue in the United States.*

These writings about Newark apparently attracted and concerned a wide audience. The *New York Review* article caused an intellectual stir, marking the first time that a legitimate and established journal lent its imprimatur to such incendiary speculation. At the same time, my *Rebellion in Newark*, I learned, became required reading in many police academies and Special Forces training centers.

The only politician who expressed an interest in what I was doing was Robert Kennedy. A few months before the Newark violence, I received a call from Jack Newfield, a close friend and a reporter for *The Village Voice* who had written an early and sympathetic book on the New Left, communicating an invitation for a meeting with Senator Kennedy. A few days later I visited the senator's New York City apartment with Newfield and Staughton Lynd, a friend from my days in Atlanta and Mississippi who was by now active in the peace movement. Our agenda focused mostly on Vietnam, but our talk began with Newark, the condition of black America, student radicalism, and what could be done by those in power. Kennedy, I surmised, was pondering a presidential campaign. Over his long and painful journey through the sixties, he was approaching the vision I had taken to Newark in 1964, one of uniting blacks and whites around an economic populism, finding a strategy of reform for the alienated through localized participatory democracy. He mentioned in particular his commitment to creating a more self-sufficient and independent black community through an economic development project in Bedford-Stuyvesant. He had a remarkable notion of what the president should do: cajole the television networks to do a two-hour documentary on ghetto life, in order that all Americans could "experience what it means to live in the most affluent society in history without hope." He would make poverty statistics public by city, then call in local leaders to argue and negotiate over real solutions.

I instinctively liked Bobby Kennedy, though I had already moved to a harder, more skeptical, vision of the world by the time we met. One small example of his sensitivity stays with me. At the beginning of our conversation, Kennedy asked Staughton's ten-year-old son accompanying us if he wanted anything to drink. The boy shyly said that he would like a 7-Up. A few moments later, Kennedy returned from his kitchen with a large glass, which the nervous youngster promptly dropped on the thick, gray carpet. The senator leaned over and in a half-solemn voice said, "That's all right, the dog likes it better on the rug."

Despite his humanism and evident curiosity, however, I was convinced that Robert Kennedy was still only searching for an answer to the racial crisis and was limited in his search by the conservative parameters of presidential politics. If he had a hopeful approach, it lay in the still-possible resurrection of goodwill between black and white Americans that he might generate in his prospective campaign. He was the only candidate who could win votes from ghetto blacks and Irish hard hats, the two conflicting poles of a potential populist coalition. In the months ahead, I would visit Kennedy again at his Hickory Hill residence outside Washington and talk with his aides several times about possible strategies for winning a majority in a presidential campaign and also helping the besieged black community through public policy. I still believed it was morally and politically necessary for an independent movement to focus on issues rather than on the personalities of candidates. I thought such a movement would help Robert Kennedy, and the deepest part of me wished him well because he renewed a hope that I had almost buried but secretly wished to keep alive: that after the torments of the early sixties, a new administration in Washington would understand that a redistribution of power, not simply the legislating of civil rights, was now at stake.

But most of our subsequent discussion—on that day and thereafter—concerned the issue that had come to overshadow, as well as deepen, the race crisis: the Vietnam War. President Johnson was justifying the escalating conflict by claiming that he was only continuing policies begun by John Kennedy. I could sense that Robert Kennedy was deeply angered at the invocation of his brother's name in defense of a war without purpose. He also knew it was impossible to concentrate on the ghettos of Newark or Bedford-Stuyvesant while worrying about 400,000 Americans in rice paddies in the Mekong Delta. Civil rights and antipoverty efforts were being sacrificed to a war with poor and nonwhite people thirteen thousand miles away.

And so the fate of NCUP was inevitably bound to the national absorption in war. Our legacy is hard to isolate from the very different times that crushed it like a vise. If there had been a national concentration on problems of race and poverty instead of on Vietnam, the outcome might have been different. Instead there was a missed opportunity. So much for our innocent belief in controlling our own destinies. To accept the weight of historical forces was a defeat of our original idealism. Yet we did prove that, with sufficient commitment and skill, a movement of poor people could be built and taken seriously in a major city. If that could be done in Newark—a Mississippi of the North in terms of poverty levels and inbred racial hostility—it could be done anywhere in affluent America. We developed a deserved reputation as the city's most dedicated and aggressive organization, taking up countless small but effective struggles against slumlords, city inspectors, the welfare office, judges, police, and City Council members. Those we opposed as corrupt were eventually drummed out of office. We helped pave the way for the election of Kenneth Gibson as the first black mayor of Newark.

Yet there was no permanent redistribution of power to the poor. Staying out of the system entirely would have left our people powerless, unable to exploit the small but real possibilities of such programs as the war on poverty. Going into the maze of programs, on the other hand, meant being swallowed up in tedious services lacking any political edge. Permanent organizers, the only force capable of working both inside and outside the structures, were hard to find and harder to keep. The white organizers left largely because of black power, but also

because of other issues such as Vietnam. Other organizers, recruited from the community, could not withstand forever the
pressures of low incomes and long hours. They were gradually
hired by social agencies, manpower programs, or consulting
firms, draining the community of its only possibility of independent leadership.

The poor remained poor—after NCUP, after black power,
after the black mayor. I don't think they ever got that traffic
light we fought for; instead, the neighborhood was redeveloped
out of existence.

Throughout the Newark experience, I continued to pursue
two paths: the practical (what is to be done?) and the philosophical (what is the meaning of life?). A *New Republic* article I wrote
in 1966 gave a straightforward answer to the first question: "Real
accomplishments are possible . . . modest gains, which mean
something to individuals and neighborhoods: rent control, play
streets, apartment repairs, higher welfare payments, jobs." But
it anguished at length over the philosophical issue:

> It means, at this time, working with little belief in progress. There
> simply is no active agency of radical change—no race, class, or
> nation—in which radicals can invest high hopes as they have in
> previous times. Nor is there much possibility in the here and now
> from which to gather strength. That "the people" often are bril-
> liant and resourceful should not blind us to their faults. . . . If
> radicalism is unable to bank fully on history or morality, what is
> available? This problem, however it is stated, is wearing down the
> strength of many people in the new movements. . . .
>
> Is the only value in rebellion itself, in the countless momentary
> times when people transcend their pettiness to commit them-
> selves to great purposes? If so, then radicalism is doomed to be
> extraordinary, erupting only during those rare times of crisis and
> upsurge which American elites seem able to ride.
>
> The alternative, if there is one, might be for radicalism to make
> itself ordinary, patiently taking up work that has only the virtue
> of facing and becoming part of the realities which are society's
> secret and its disgrace. . . . Radicalism then would give itself to,
> and become part of, the energy that is kept restless and active
> under the clamps of a paralyzed imperial society. Radicalism then
> would go beyond the concepts of optimism and pessimism as
> guides to work, finding itself in working despite odds. Its realism

and sanity would be grounded in nothing more than the ability
to face whatever comes.

Looking back, I still find myself drawn to this rationale for
working despite odds. Right action, and right livelihood, are
good in themselves. They cannot be sought through withdrawal, only through engagement in the world. The desire for
success is a necessary and fundamental part of that engagement,
but success, however empowering, remains inherently temporary and leads forward to new problems.

There is a certain satisfaction I feel about those times. Though
we lived in an urban hell, I loved the souls that were cast into
its lower depths. Our relationships were rich, our politics principled, our message pure and prophetic. We transformed the
silent and humiliated outcasts into a proud force to be reckoned
with. Though the city would remain poor, it would never be the
same.

In October 1983, I returned to Newark to receive an award
from the United Community Corporation, the official name of
the antipoverty program, almost twenty years after its incep-
tion. Most of my old friends were still there, still turning their
shoulders to the rock, still soldiers of Camus. There was a Bessie
Smith Community Center, and Thurman still carried on, the
director of a minority contractor's program, approaching retire-
ment age. (He died of cancer in 1987.)

Though continuing to gripe about City Hall, now it was at
least *their* City Hall, where they were as welcome as anyone else.
If a new establishment had arisen on the ashes of the old, they
could be a thorn in its side with a telephone call instead of a
Molotov cocktail. If too many of their children were suffering
from drugs and unemployment, if homelessness and schizophre-
nia were greater problems than ever, it was also true that many
people were living richer and more constructive lives because of
the inspiration of the young men and women who had knocked
on their doors long ago.

If they and I had achieved less than our dreams, we had also
created a way station for future generations on a longer road to
justice than the Tom Haydens of the sixties had expected. If I now
served as an elected official in a faraway state, my heart knew
that I would always represent a certain few precincts in Newark.

TO: DIRECTOR, FBI (100-438281)   DATE: 2/14/68

FROM: SAC, NEWARK (100-48095)

SUBJECT: THOMAS EMMETT HAYDEN
          SM-SDS (KEY ACTIVIST)

. . . Concerning his residences 227 Jelliff Avenue, Newark, and 631 Hunterdon Street, Newark, New Jersey, it is to be noted that both of these neighborhoods are almost entirely Negro and are in the ghetto area of Newark, which was the scene of Newark riot of July, 1967. Prolonged surveillance of his present residence is not feasible, and at the most only spot checks at various hours is all that can be discreetly and safely conducted.

HAYDEN, because of his past activities as a leader of a community project among the poor in this area, is especially well known, and it is logical that any prolonged surveillance could come to his attention. With his access to the media of press, radio, and television, it is possible he might use any such surveillance to the embarrassment of the Bureau.

The Newark Police Department in their investigation of the causes leading up to, and the results of the Newark riot of July, 1967, have expressed their interest in TOM HAYDEN since they consider him to be an associate of, and acquainted with many individuals whom they know to have been active participants in protests in Newark prior to the Newark riot of July, 1967 . . . According to the Newark Police Department, the leaders in these demonstrations at city meetings were all friendly with TOM HAYDEN, and the Police Department considers him part of the overall group that aroused the Negro people on these issues.

Because of the above, the Newark Police attempt to cover the activities of HAYDEN whenever possible. They, too, have related that any attempt to run full, discreet surveillances in this area would prove fruitless because of the suspicions that residents of this area have of any outsiders.

Newark will await the results of recommendations of the New York Office concerning technical coverage [wiretapping] in "Liberation" magazine which would serve as a means of covering HAYDEN'S activities and plans in connection with the peace movement and possible disruption of the National Convention to be held in Chicago, Illinois. Further, Newark will continue its efforts to locate a bank account for HAYDEN in New Jersey to possibly establish his source of funds. Newark will also augment the coverage supplied by the neighborhood source with spot fisurs [field surveillances] in the neighborhood. Newark will also maintain a close liaison with the Newark Police, in view of their continuing interest in HAYDEN, to determine any information they might have on his activities, plans, or travel.

Newark is contemplating the possible use of counterintelligence methods against HAYDEN in order to neutralize his effectiveness. It is understood that no such measures would be taken until such recommendations are submitted in full to the Bureau and authorization received.

VIETNAM

Part Four

8. The Other Side: Hanoi, 1965

In November 1965, while still immersed in Newark, my life suddenly took another direction. As the shadow of the Vietnam War cast its darkness over my hopes, I was drawn toward the shadow's mysterious source. I became one of the first of the few hundred Americans to visit and have contact with North Vietnam during the war. What began as an exercise in amateur diplomacy taught me more than I could imagine about war and revolution and inflicted unhealed scars, not to mention political baggage, that I still carry today.

It began with a phone call from Staughton Lynd. He and his wife, Alice, were among the few remaining advocates of nonviolence as a way of life whom I knew well. Quakers by faith, they were drawn to the South to contribute to the civil rights movement; Staughton had directed the freedom schools in Mississippi in 1964. About a decade older than I, he looked trim and professional in his white shirts and ties, and his manner was caring and gentle. His parents, Robert and Helen Lynd, were pioneering sociologists who had authored *Middletown*, a well-known study of community power structures of Muncie, Indiana. Robert Lynd had also written *Knowledge for What?*, a study which had influenced C. Wright Mills and younger sociologists like Dick Flacks. In the fall of 1965, when many whites left SNCC, Staughton took a history department appointment at Yale. Increasingly, he was absorbed with the agony of Vietnam and was a major speaker at rallies and teach-ins. "Brother Tom," he asked, when I answered the phone, "how would you like to go to Hanoi?"

I was stunned.

Barely able to control his emotion, Staughton explained that Herbert Aptheker, a Marxist historian, had been in Eastern Europe at a conference attended by several North Vietnamese, who invited him to visit their country and asked if he would bring with him two noncommunist Americans concerned with peace. Aptheker invited Staughton; as a Quaker, Staughton saw himself as a potential peacemaker, and was hopeful of finding a negotiating bridge between our government and Hanoi. He was worried about the public image of traveling with a communist, but there was no other practical possibility. In addition, he asked me, how could he call for peace with a communist government but be unwilling to travel there with a communist? He had insisted on one condition from Herbert: that he select the third person.

Staughton's first choice was Bob Moses, who was beginning to connect the civil rights and peace issues, but Bob couldn't or wouldn't go, perhaps reasoning that it would be too much additional pressure for SNCC to bear. Staughton turned to me.

I also worried about the smear campaign that would surely be aimed at NCUP and SDS from the trip. I took the startling proposal back to a staff meeting in Newark and several days of soul-searching followed. We sat around the floor of the apartment trying to develop a rational approach to an issue that was almost beyond our understanding. Few, if any of us, had ever traveled outside the United States. Our involvement with the Vietnam issue was confined to reading what we could and bringing several carloads of Newark people to demonstrations in Washington.

But in the end, the possibility of turning a corner of history outweighed the dangers. I applied for a passport for the first time in my life, and raised two thousand dollars for the trip from several liberal supporters of NCUP. There was virtually no time, but I started to read and consult heavily. I knew the most sensitive question would be, Wasn't I supporting the enemy against our boys? Being for peace was one thing, but traveling to Hanoi was quite another. Was I an American or a traitor? In my innocence of American political history, I thought that, in fact, the proposed trip was a very American thing to do and that the best way to support American soldiers was to end the killing.

The fledgling antiwar movement was already becoming a serious problem for the government, and talk of repression of "unpatriotic" elements was in the air. The cause of national division, as I saw it, was that the president, who promised in 1964 not to "send any American boys nine or ten thousand miles away from home to do what Asian boys ought to do for themselves," was doing just that. In 1964, the Democratic party process had failed on two counts: It had rejected the Mississippi Freedom Democrats' credentials challenge and reneged on Johnson's pledge of "no wider war" in Vietnam. As a result, the turnout for the spring 1965 SDS march on Washington had been unexpectedly large. I was deeply impressed that day with three speakers: Bob Moses of SNCC, who said that Vietnam was a "mirror of America," Paul Potter, now SDS president, who said that the war was a "sharp razor" that would force us to "name the system" that was causing it, and Staughton Lynd himself, who compared the Vietnamese to figures being crucified. The huge march was followed a month later by massive and innovative teach-ins on college campuses and then in October by nationwide demonstrations involving over 100,000 people in nearly a thousand cities.

Draft boards were reclassifying certain protestors from II-S, which was a student deferment, to I-A. I vacillated between conscientious objection, although I didn't know whether I was an absolute pacifist, and the II-S deferment, although I didn't approve of the student privilege. When my number finally came up, I went to the induction center at Whitehall Street in lower Manhattan. I remember a great many very young and nervous men standing in naked embarrassment, a concentration-camp image that has never left my mind. I was classified I-Y, officially because of allergy problems, but I suppose in reality because the military wasn't taking any "maladjusted" protestors at the time. Shortly after, David Miller, a young Catholic pacifist, became the first person to burn his draft card, and the draft resistance movement began spreading.

Reading Kirkpatrick Sale's important 1973 book on SDS, I was reminded of how fiercely we were then opposed by Mississippi Senator John Stennis, chairman of the Armed Services Committee. Our segregationist foe was calling for the administration to "immediately move to jerk this movement up by the roots and grind it to bits before it has the opportunity to spread further." More important and crucial to understanding the New Left was the fact that liberal Democrats were ardent believers. Vice President Humphrey charged that the "international communist movement" had "organized and masterminded" the antidraft campaign. Senators who would later become doves, like Mike Mansfield and William Proxmire, were critical as well. James Reston of *The New York Times* attacked the peace movement for "not promoting peace but postponing it." Attorney General Nicholas Katzenbach declared that antidraft activity "begins to move in the direction of treason." The tone was set by President Johnson, who was convinced that a Soviet web of influence lay behind the emerging peace movement. Doris Kearns, a young, liberal White House intern who became a distinguished historian, later described him as raving about "communist conspiracies" threatening his administration.

What became known as the generation gap stemmed from the very different world views of those of my father's era and my own. My father's generation believed—correctly—that they had defended democracy against *foreign* despotism; we believed we were defending democracy from its enemies at home. Chuck McDew, the first SNCC chairman, summarized the difference: Our parents wanted to "make the world safe for democracy"; we felt impelled to "make democracy safe for the world." Second, our parents had seen a case of clear aggression across national boundaries by Nazi Germany in the late thirties, and it was met in the United States by calls for isolationism, peace pledges, negotiations, and worst of all, silent indifference, until it was too late for many victims. "Never again" was not only the postwar cry of the Jewish community, but also an instinctive response for Americans like my parents. In the wake of the world war, Soviet tanks rolled into Eastern Europe, and five years later the Korean War added new fears about foreign aggression, this time from the Chinese. It was predictable that my parents' generation would accept the official view that a "free" South Vietnam was being invaded by a northern aggressor with six hundred million Chinese waiting in the background. They were prepared to believe the logic of Lyndon Johnson that "the battle against Communism must be joined in Southeast Asia . . . or the

United States must inevitably surrender the Pacific and pull out our defenses back to San Francisco." Or as *The New York Times* editorialized in 1950 "Indochina is critical—if it falls, all of Southeast Asia will be in mortal peril."

In retrospect, there is even something idealistic in my parents' generation's willingness to support a war against such unbelievable odds. Experience had taken them prisoner, and they failed to see Vietnam as a popular and nationalist struggle, with elements of a civil war, against the new foreigners, who happened to be Americans. In my generation's world view, the most apparent and unwanted invaders were our own armed forces— "white boots marchin' in a yellow land," as Phil Ochs sang—the very opposite of the dynamics of World War II.

Sadly, I had no chance to debate these diverging lessons of experience with my father. Perhaps I might have convinced him that the situation was not the same as in the days when I watched the San Diego skies for Japanese attackers. Perhaps not; for marine private Jack Hayden, *Semper fidelis* was an important commandment. My 1964 visit to my new sister was the last for a long time. As my life became more unconventional, and my image more notorious, my father stopped answering my letters. Our relationship descended into a complete break.

My relationship with my mother was different but no less troubled. Her loyalty was to her son, not to the U.S. Marines or any other institution, and she found the war incomprehensible. Years later, she would say *Indonesia* when referring to Indochina. But she made it painfully clear that my behavior caused her boundless embarrassment in her midwestern small-town circles. To maintain a relationship with me, she felt she had to cut her ties to her inquisitive neighbors.

I decided to go to Hanoi. I needed to know who this supposed enemy was. If my parents were wrong, the United States was making a disastrous mistake. If they were right, what did the U.S. government want to keep from the media and the American public by making travel to North Vietnam illegal by administrative directive? We were committing our human and economic resources to the discretion of a president who, in 1964, had pledged "not to send a single American boy." Was North Vietnam really invading South Vietnam, or was the United States itself intervening in an internal conflict? Was our government really only bombing "steel and concrete" military targets, as the president swore, or was the civilian population itself being assaulted? Was peace through military escalation just around the corner, or were conventional American military tactics futile against a popular guerrilla war? Was there really no hope for a negotiated settlement or was the United States escalating the war in a vain effort to impose a settlement from a position of strength? The journey would be a fact-finding mission. The war was too serious to let the facts be defined and monopolized by Lyndon Johnson and the Pentagon.

I also hoped that I could bring back an image of the Vietnamese as human beings. I was deeply disturbed by stereotypes of the "faceless Vietcong." Whether it was Lyndon Johnson as a congressman orating against being "bullied by any Oriental with a knife," or more sophisticated claims about Asian indifference to individual life, Americans were dehumanizing the enemy to make killing thousands of them easier.

Finally, there was an ethical imperative, the same one which Thoreau had argued with Emerson during the Mexican-American War (and which Casey had cited in the speech that affected me so deeply five years before): Jailed for refusing to pay taxes in support of a war against Mexico, Thoreau spoke of the need to be "citizens of the world." In our time, C. Wright Mills had called for a "separate peace" between humanists in both Cold War blocs. We wanted to let the Vietnamese people know that napalm was not the monolithic message of American society, that there was "another America" that was not at war with them, and that there were Americans supportive of negotiations and a political settlement.

In preparation, I read *Man's Fate*, Andre Malraux's classic 1933 novel of revolutionary Asia, and was amazed to discover the history of anticolonialist Westerners in Indochina. In the 1920s, Malraux had been associated with the earliest Vietnamese revolutionaries and had even edited an anticolonialist paper in Saigon until it was shut down by the French government. On the way to Hanoi I read Malraux's novel, underlining the famous passage in which a police officer, about to put a young revolutionary to death, asks, "What do you call dignity? It doesn't mean anything." The doomed revolutionary replies, "The opposite of humiliation."

. . .

On December 21, 1965—four years after being jailed in Georgia and conceiving *The Port Huron Statement* and ten days after my twenty-sixth birthday—our two-engine Chinese passenger plane entered the airspace over North Vietnam. We had careened from plane to plane across the communist world, stopping in Prague, Moscow, and Peking, where we were the first American travelers in many years. My quick impression from these first stops was that there was hardly a unified international communist "conspiracy" behind the Vietnamese. In fact, our brief discussions with Soviet and Chinese spokesmen showed they had national interests of their own in the Vietnam crisis. The Russians wanted nothing to interfere with a developing coexistence with the United States, and Herbert Aptheker echoed their view. But in Peking, we found leaders on the verge of Mao's Great Cultural Revolution who were eager to reject the "coexistence" thesis on behalf of a doctrine of permanent "people's war." In this view, any negotiations with the United States were a betrayal of the Vietnamese revolution, which the Chinese felt should continue to "total victory"—or the last drop of Vietnamese blood. These dialogues only increased my interest in whether Vietnam, as a small country, could find any independence in a world of such powerful blocs.

Now we were over the place itself; below was "enemy territory." The skies were thick with billowing clouds, and through them I could see green rice fields, carefully sustained by dikes and levees, a countryside nurtured through monsoons for four thousand years. The capital itself appeared lazily, a sprawling maze of low-scale yellowed buildings left behind by the French, surrounded by dense residential districts about five miles in diameter. There was occasionally a tiny hamlet or road crossing, but no signs of the "steel and concrete" the president claimed to be bombing, unless it was the lone railroad track rolling south of Hanoi. That narrow two-lane road next to the tracks—a country lane by our standards—was indeed "Highway One," I was told.

According to U.S. State Department regulations, it was not "valid" to use a passport for travel to North Vietnam (or China, Cuba, Albania, or North Korea). Since this seemed to us to be an administrative tactic to interfere in freedom of travel, we decided upon a counter technique: instead of using our passports, we traveled on visas issued by our hosts. A North Vietnamese soldier in olive-drab uniform came aboard the plane and waved us toward the terminal, a one-story, pale-green structure containing perhaps three rooms (it was bombed to rubble several years later). As I stepped to the ground, a Vietnamese man with a finely chiseled face, dressed in a suit and tie with a dark sweater, smiled and asked in a British accent, "Tom Hayden? Welcome to Vietnam."

He was Do Xuan Oanh, a representative of our host group, something called the Peace Committee. As with many things Vietnamese, the construction of his name was the exact reverse of ours, a cultural fact that I was struggling to understand. It meant that his last name (which was pronounced *weng*) was his first, or familiar name, and his first name was actually his last. While I was deciding which to address him by, Oanh kept unbalancing me with his formal British tone of speaking, which he had developed through listening to the BBC.

We drove on a rough road in two powerful black Russian-built Volgas, vehicles which look something like the limousines of American gangsters of the 1930s. Out the window I watched dozens of water buffalo guided by men, women, and children through the deep mud of freshly irrigated fields. The people wore conical straw hats, faded old shirts, and rolled-up pants. Many were without shoes, while others wore "Ho Chi Minh sandals" made from scrap rubber. Children were everywhere, the little ones often carried on the hips of the slightly older. They held hands and clustered by the roadside to peer into our cars. I wondered who on earth they thought we were. If they were the quaking targets of the U.S. Air Force, it did not show. They seemed to be gossiping about us and would occasionally shout things that seemed to be funny.

The inner city was a visual flashback to French colonialism. The Vietnamese had seized it from the French in August 1945 when they declared an independent state, using quotes from the American Declaration of Independence. Aside from keeping the streets immaculately clean, it didn't look as if the former servants had spent much time refurbishing the previous master's buildings. The walls were invariably a faded plaster, the structures spacious and high-ceilinged with long, narrow windows opening out on little balconies.

We finally stopped at a several-story building, the former colonial Hôtel Métropole, now renamed the Thong Nhat, or

Reunification Hotel. Inside there was a lobby with pillars along the sides and overhead fans, leading to an elegant little bar which was a historic watering hole for journalists and diplomats in this and previous wars. After a ritual glass of sweet rice wine, we were led to our upstairs rooms, each of which seemed large enough for a family, complete with four-poster beds covered with mosquito netting, little tables brimming with fruit, candy, tea leaves, and thermos bottles of hot water. I was exhausted but couldn't rest.

Shortly, after taking my first walk in the streets of the city, I rushed to set my impressions down in notes. Cars were almost completely absent, leaving a calm silence broken by an occasional trolley and the whirling, clicking sounds of thousands of bicycles. Often couples rode together, the woman or child seated sideways above the rear fender. Now and then a water buffalo tugging a cart of wood came plodding around a corner. Some people walked along with long bamboo poles suspended across their shoulders, on which hung baskets of bricks and belongings. Though many children had been evacuated to the countryside, a few played games in the street that resembled hopscotch and jump rope, eagerly tempting us to join. Some of the adults would show exasperation as bicycles plied through the streets, veering dangerously close to each other, but the overall impression was of patience and harmony. There were no armed police visible anywhere, though I was sure they could be summoned. I saw no beggars.

In Hanoi's center was the Lake of the Restored Sword, referring to a legendary tale of national resistance. It was surrounded by a park and the trolley line. As I looked more closely at the streets, I was startled to see hundreds of individual bomb shelters, which looked exactly like manholes with covers, just large enough for an adult and an infant, or perhaps two cramped adults. On some of the park benches by the shelters, couples sat talking intimately, while on others people read or slept. Some children played in and around a larger bomb shelter, which looked like the outdoor restroom in an American park.

First impressions are very important to me, and the dawning sense I had that day in Hanoi was of fearlessness, calm determination, pride, even serenity. If the buildings were drab, the people's faces were not. They showed curiosity, sentimentalism, directness, gentleness, dignity. They were not faces I associated with a communist city. In later years, I would walk through East Berlin, for example; its surface seemed depressed in comparison with what I saw on my first strolls through Hanoi. Though I was fast succumbing to a romantic conception of the Vietnamese I met, my views of revolution and violence were still forming. In notes at the time, I rejected the stereotype of the Vietcong guerrilla as a "mean little man, living like a beast off berries in the jungle, occasionally disemboweling a villager to terrify others, so feebly endowed with personal values that he can be the torturer or the tortured without flinching." I was seeing with my own eyes that these were human beings before me, many of them inspired (and inspiring) because of their revolutionary experience. On the other hand, I wrote, "The Vietnamese revolution has not been pure; innocent people have been killed; decent men have been purged." But this revolution was also a fact, an objective force which could not be reversed by American violence, only hardened. Staughton and I concluded that "we believe in identifying with the revolutionary process and finding ways within one's limits to make it as humane as possible."

Most of my memories of the Vietnamese experience are collective ones, a whole society more than specific individuals. The language barrier and cultural modesty kept most of the individual Vietnamese we met from projecting any trademarks or idiosyncrasies. Perhaps it was Do Xuan Oanh I came to know best. Then forty-three years old, he was born aboard a fishing boat on the magical Halong Bay in the Gulf of Tonkin. As a youth, Oanh worked in the French coal mines; in spare hours, he studied music. In the war against the French, he joined the Vietminh army in the jungles. His wife had been seized and tortured by the French in Hanoi; because she still felt the effects of the cold, damp weather, we met the shy, smiling mother of two only briefly.

After the 1954 Geneva Accords, Oanh joined the Peace Committee, which, I learned, was a mechanism frequently used by communist governments to develop "fraternal" relations with peace movements or nongovernmental visitors from other countries. In 1965, we were the committee's first American guests, a fact which kept Oanh and his friends continually anxious. I was intrigued at his dual task, which was not only to guide us through North Vietnam, but to educate his own country favorably about America. It was Oanh's intent to point out a "progressive" and "democratic" side of American life to the Vietnamese, who were under daily siege. As I was beginning to lose faith in precisely the American virtues that Oanh was determined to idealize, our relationship became one of intense discussion. When I first asked him why he was so interested in putting a positive face on the United States, Oanh remarked simply, "To reduce hatred." There were strategic reasons as well: North Vietnam wanted to affect American public opinion. That is why, I assumed, nearly every Vietnamese we met quickly and mechanically drew a distinction between the American government's policy and that of the "progressive and democratic American people."

But Oanh, in addition, seemed to be a genuine romantic. We discovered that he had recently published a song about Norman Morrison, an American Quaker friend of Staughton's who had burned himself on the steps of the Pentagon two months before. While the American press dismissed the suicide as that of a disturbed and demented individual, Oanh was fascinated that Morrison, an American, had chosen an Asian, and Buddhist, form of death. Oanh's widely published poem, which said that "Morrison's flame will enlighten life," made the Quaker protestor known to thousands in North Vietnam.

There was one thing that seemed even more touching than Oanh's focus on Morrison; we learned that Oanh had laboriously translated *The Adventures of Huckleberry Finn* into Vietnamese. Shortly before we arrived in the country Hanoi newspapers had reported that a copy of Oanh's translation was found on the body of a schoolgirl killed by American bombs. Though obviously trusted to represent the Hanoi government faithfully, his personality ranged far beyond most bureaucratic boundaries. After so many years of hearing about faceless communist apparatchiks, his openness and Western ways were deeply disarming.

I also was impressed with the historic antiquity of revolutionary nationalism in Vietnam and how little even "informed" Americans like myself knew of it. I understood the long resistance war against the French and the legendary military triumph at Dien Bien Phu reasonably well, but not the depth of betrayal the Vietnamese felt over the 1954 Geneva Accords, which were supposed to have been followed by internationally supervised, secret-ballot national elections two years later, elections which were never held. The United States opted to support the new Republic of South Vietnam, rather than risk the overwhelming likelihood that Ho Chi Minh would prevail at the ballot box. But the fact that *national* elections were agreed to—by all negotiating parties, including the French—meant that Vietnam was recognized as one country divided into two temporary zones, not two separate countries, as our government subsequently attempted to stress.

The Geneva Conference was only "yesterday" in the span of Vietnamese national history. As I visited one museum after another and interviewed several Vietnamese historians, the weight of a thousand years of resistance wars settled on me. There was the "people's war" of the thirteenth century, when the Vietnamese resisted 500,000 troops of Kublai Khan, culminating in a surprise sinking of the Mongol ships in the Bach Dang River in 1288. There was the Tay Son peasant revolt at the time of the American Revolution, an insurgency that climaxed in a Tet offensive in 1789. Little bronze arrows said to be a thousand years old were given to us by a museum director who had fought at Dien Bien Phu. He cried when he said good-bye to us; many of these supposedly "stoic Orientals" shed tears during the course of our conversations.

At night I carefully studied *The Tale of Kieu,* a long narrative poem by Nguyen Du. It was urged on me by a Vietnamese writer as a key to the Vietnamese identity. Written in the eighteenth century, it was the epic story of a young woman, Kieu, who was separated from her lover and who experienced constant degradation, betrayal, and attempts on her life until she met him once again. Kieu's search, my friend was trying to tell me, was that of every Vietnamese for unification. Her willingness (and theirs) to sacrifice everything for principle was set down in lines known to most Vietnamese: "It matters little if a flower falls if the tree can keep its leaves green."

What drew my attention equally was another poem by the same author about the fate reserved for the long series of rulers who tried to vanquish Kieu's Vietnam on behalf of their own imperial ambitions. It appeared that the Vietnamese had seen and survived all forms of foreign vanity:

> *There were those who pursued power and glory,*
> *Who dreamt of conquest and power . . .*

Their golden palaces crumbled,
And they envied a humble man's lot.
Power and riches make many enemies . . .

There were those who lived in curtained palaces,
Priding themselves on their wealth and beauty.
Then the storm came and thrones changed hands . . .
Broken are the hairpins and the flower vases,
Gone the animated voices and the laughter . . .

There were those who wielded great power,
Whose red-ink characters decided men's fates,
Who were fountains of knowledge and experience.
But prosperity and power engender hatred.

There were those who pursued riches,
Who lost appetite and sleep
With no children or relations to inherit
*   their fortunes,*
With no one to hear their last words.
Riches dissipate like passing clouds.
Living, they had their hands full of gold.
Departing from this world, they could take
*   not a single coin . . .*

There were those at the head of proud armies
Who sacked palaces and overturned thrones.
In a display of might like storm and thunder,
Thousands were killed for the glory of one man.
Then came defeat, and the battlefield was
*   strewn with corpses.*
The unclaimed bones are lying somewhere in a
*   far-away land.*
The rain is lashing down and the wind howling,
Who will now evoke their memory?

As I tried to absorb all this history, I began to feel that we Americans—especially those fighting these people—were like the characters in Joseph Conrad's *Heart of Darkness*, losing their moorings by wandering ever more deeply into an alien and bottomless cultural quagmire. "Whom the gods would destroy, they first make mad": to which I would add, Whom they would make mad, they first make ignorant.

Looking back, there were dimensions of Vietnamese history that our hosts neglected to mention. I wish I had known, for example, of their centuries of imperial expansion southward into the kingdoms of Champa and Cambodia. Between 1650 and 1750, the whole Mekong Delta was wrested from the Khmer people, a historic root of the tragic and incomprehensible war between Vietnam and Cambodia in the late 1970s. These vital omissions aside, what the Vietnamese told us was essentially true, a history hidden from American minds like mine.

I encountered more of my ignorance by the day. We toured a factory that produced agricultural implements, for example, but the factory had been decentralized into small shops underground for protection against bombing. It was built over the site of a former French prison and named after a Vietnamese leader who fought against Genghis Khan. Of course, I thought, why not? With a tape recorder, I asked the workers what difference the Hanoi government had made in their lives; over and over the answer was concrete: literacy, education, a better standard of living. One told me he supported the Vietminh (the organized resistance against the French) by "following the factory to the forest," where it was reassembled and production resumed. This had been his "normal" life for most of twenty-five years.

When we visited Phu Dien cooperative near Hanoi, it was the same oral history: stories of fighting to preserve real gains of the past. In this six-acre village of one thousand people, we were told that 137 people starved to death in 1945 (which, again, was like yesterday for many of these people), part of a nationwide famine just prior to the coming to power of the Vietminh. Another forty-five were killed in the French reconquest effort of 1946. There was mass illiteracy at that time, along with a host of uncontrolled diseases; everyone, they said, carried bamboo poles on their shoulders. But now, they continued, 75 percent of the households had bicycles, flasks of boiled water, and mosquito nets. Half their land was plowed by tractors, not buffalo; 85 percent of the homes were brick; fewer shoulders were burdened, and everyone was attending school at least part-time.

When I asked these villagers about communism, however, there was a tendency to rhetoric, but only in the way that some Americans attribute all good things to free enterprise. I asked two young women, carrying rifles as many did, what they thought of the American argument that their regime was a dictatorship under Chinese influence. They were peasants as well as members of a local self-defense group; two nights weekly they studied history, literature, and chemistry. They smiled demurely and scoffed at my question: "We love the party and socialism because thanks to the party our country has been liberated," they replied. "As women, we are conscious of our duties, and that is why we do what we do, not because of orders from the party, or from our government, or from China. We do things ourselves, by our own consciousness, not relying on any-one else." I found something wooden in their answers, and didn't think it was simply the translation. But on the other hand, theirs were simple patriotic statements, not different from the replies most Americans might give to similar questions. Did they feel free to speak up directly to their government? "Yes, of course, if you have something to say to the government, you should say it directly."

Certainly in my later experiences in places like Moscow or Warsaw, such questions would provoke comments of a more cynical nature, even cause people to lower their voices and look over their shoulders before speaking. But not here.

As dusk came to the village, someone placed a lantern on the table around which these villagers and I had gathered, and they began questioning me with a destabilizing simplicity. "Do the American people know that their government is escalating the war?" "Do they know the reality of our country?" "What do *you* think, now that you have visited our village, because your government says we are not free and we live in slavery?" It gradually struck me that while these people lived under a one-party state with a government-controlled press, they were not easily deceived on the life-and-death issues. Many of them had seen it before, and all of them could measure the bombs and rockets falling, the number of young men leaving the village for war, the casualties, the increasing economic burdens. They knew more about their reality than we did in democratic America.

I found it hard to answer them, trying to be truthful and sensitive. I said that although Americans valued the family, hard work, and patriotism, just as these villagers did, the American people, in ignorance of Vietnam, might believe the president and support a further escalation of the war. The faces in the candlelight were somber and interested as the translator ex-plained my words.

A bell called people to school, breaking our dialogue. One of the village leaders took my hand and said, "We would like to extend our thanks for your calling on us, and we wish you to convey to the American people, particularly the laboring people, our best wishes." Oh, sure, I thought. Mom and Dad will be real pleased, and so will the folks at Chrysler.

During our ten-day visit, we rushed to the large bomb shelter in the lower quarters of the Thong Nhat several times, but U.S. planes never attacked. We sensed that the wheels of diplomacy were turning, though we had no idea whether peace negotiations were near.

One afternoon we left Hanoi in two jeeps heavily camouflaged with branches and leaves. As the sun set two hours later, we slowly bumped around a bombed-out bridge across a narrow river and entered Nam Dinh, a major textile center about a hundred miles south of the capital. With a population of ninety thousand, including a majority of Catholics, Nam Dinh had been bombed repeatedly. So for security reasons, night became day: People reversed their normal schedules and, as darkness came, moved around with flashlights to do their shopping in dimly lit stores. Their tiny beams also lit the way for countless bicycles and knots of pedestrians. Many people gathered in little circles, enjoying the cool of the evening for a cigarette and conversation. We drove out to the edge of town where a nursery school had been devastated by bombs and rockets. Walking through the rubble, I could read a slogan on a shattered wall: LET US BRING UP HEALTHY CHILDREN, LET US EDUCATE GOOD CHILDREN.

A short distance away was a bombed pagoda. Great holes in its high walls and roof allowed the light of stars to shine through. Searching the floor, I found some fragments of religious statues and put them in my pocket to take home. A monk in saffron robes told us that plans were already made to rebuild the structure.

Finally, we visited a textile factory, or rather, that twenty-by-thirty-foot section of a factory which had not yet been removed to the forests. All was dark except for the beams right in front of the women working at the weaving looms. Rifles hung on the ends of the looms. They barely looked up to notice us with our notepads, cameras, and tape recorders. I sensed they were either not in much of a mood for American visitors or simply tired and strained.

Our interpreter broke into this surreal scene. "In order to ensure your safety, we have to leave now," he evenly said. An

American bomber was prowling nearby, and we were under instruction to leave the city. We quickly said good-bye to those hosts who had briefly emerged from Nam Dinh's shadows to help us understand their world, then began the blackened drive back to Hanoi. Though we were on the slender road that the United States attacked most frequently, I felt overprotected compared to the people we left behind. But, I said to an interpreter, they seemed to be calm. "They have no other way to be than calm," he replied. As we bounced along the road, we heard the muffled thunder of bombs in the distance for the first time. Before the war was over, Nam Dinh would be completely destroyed—several times.

At the same time as our visit, the Johnson administration launched a "peace offensive," an international effort to create an image of willingness to talk rather than bomb. Of Johnson's effort, columnist Joseph Alsop wrote that "domestic political considerations were the prime motives of the vast international vaudeville which the President staged." But in Hanoi, Staughton Lynd took the ray of hope seriously and endeavored to discover as much as possible about North Vietnam's bargaining position. We met with officials like Ha Van Lau and Nguyen Minh Vy; unknown to us at the time, they would play prominent roles in the negotiations with the United States a decade later. Then on January 5, the day before our departure, we went to meet Prime Minister Pham Van Dong, one of the legendary leaders of the Vietnamese revolution from its infancy.

We drove to the former residence of the French governor-general, where the prime minister held official meetings, a lovely executive mansion surrounded by an expanse of gardens and lawns. As we stopped at the base of a high stone staircase, Pham Van Dong appeared at the top step and walked down alone. Perhaps it was his historic aura, but he was among the most striking world leaders I have ever seen. He was taller than most Vietnamese, and the features of his face seemed somehow like an American Indian's. His skin was reddish brown, his lips thick, cheekbones wide and prominent, and above a high forehead was a dramatic shock of silver hair. He wore a gray Oriental suit with a high collar buttoned at his throat, circled by a scarf. At sixty years, his eyes carried both the sparkle of youth and the depth of age.

Unfortunately, our meeting was too formal. It was, I believe, the first time that a top Hanoi official had met with Americans in any capacity. Pham Van Dong's staff asked us to submit diplomatic questions in advance, which we did. Our discussion was largely confined to a cordial exchange of views. Even so, Pham Van Dong's emotions and sentiments—which I came to know better through several meetings in subsequent years—came through clearly enough in this forty-five-minute talk. Steering away from diplomatic detail, he spoke in broad strokes:

> The Vietnamese people feel that they are fighting for a just cause against barbarous aggression. That is the central reality. The same thing happened when you fought against the British. . . . The liberation movement in South Vietnam has become stronger than we here [in Hanoi] expected. I personally could not have imagined it. I was very anxious and concerned about what would happen when 200,000 American troops came. . . . When we say that we will fight ten or twenty years longer, these are not the words of rhetoric. . . .
>
> The world is one. It is becoming smaller and smaller. History makes us closer to each other. That is a tendency which nothing can prevent. . . . The great truth of our time is that we must be brothers, fraternal toward each other. The highest sentiment is fraternity. This is the age of that sentiment. That is a noble ideology. If you have the opportunity to meet President Johnson, will you please ask him: Why is he fighting against us? There is no reason for it. . . .

At the end of a cordial discussion along these lines, an aide presented us with Pham Van Dong's written answers to diplomatic questions we had submitted. These were formulated in the more cryptic language of diplomatic negotiators. Pham Van Dong was not a dreamy sentimentalist; he also had been the chief Vietminh negotiator at Geneva. In this statement, he denied that North Vietnamese troops were in the South, a statement we believed with difficulty. Staughton's guess was that several thousand Vietminh troops, regrouped northward as part of the Geneva Accords, had returned to the South. He later felt that our hosts, in attempting to justify the rebellion, which was indigenous to the South, had not told us the whole truth. He was right. There was of course a Ho Chi Minh Trail, and North Vietnamese soldiers traveled it. Most visitors to Hanoi were similarly misled.

Pham Van Dong called for the creation of a "broad national democratic coalition administration" in South Vietnam, including the NLF (National Liberation Front), but neutral and nonaligned. Most important to Staughton, the North Vietnamese were not intransigently demanding an American military withdrawal *before* talks with the United States could begin, as the Johnson administration claimed. We were told that a withdrawal of some "newly arrived [American] units," coupled with some sign of recognition of the NLF, would be enough to begin a process of negotiations.

We thanked Pham Van Dong for consenting to see us and returned to our hotel for our last evening in Hanoi. Staughton was excited by the diplomatic discussions and went off to type up his notes. Too overwhelmed by the entire trip to sit in my room, I went down to the Thong Nhat bar to watch the waitress, whose name was Minh Tinh. After two glasses of rice wine, I decided she was the most beautiful woman in Vietnam, a judgment I might have reached soberly. She wore a white jacket over black silk pants and wooden shoes that clicked on the tiled floor. Knowing that I could not understand her, she sang and talked to me with a teasing smile (as one might with a pet, I thought). Minh Tinh was also the leader of the hotel's antiaircraft militia, a medal-winning marksman and a national Ping-Pong champion. Irresistible and incomprehensible, romantic yet hardened, close but untouchable—like Vietnam. If I could only really know her . . . But it was time to go home.

Nothing came of our diplomatic "clarifications." Staughton spent several hours with State Department experts going over our notes, in which they saw nothing new. At the same time, the media was full of right-wing calls for our prosecution under the Logan Act, which prohibits "unauthorized persons" from engaging in diplomacy on their own, or under U.S. codes regarding "misuse" of passports. After three weeks, the United States resumed its bombing. Two days later, on February 2, the State Department temporarily withdrew our passports, declaring that we had acted in a manner "prejudicial to the orderly conduct of foreign relations" (a federal court later reversed the department's action).

We did manage to persuade Hanoi to admit an American correspondent for the first time, Harrison Salisbury of *The New*

York Times. Later that year, he caused a public sensation with fourteen front-page articles charging that civilian casualties in North Vietnam were massive.

The Hanoi visit definitely deepened my sense of isolation from an America at war. The effect on my family was severe. When the news of our trip broke, the Michigan papers ran articles spotlighting both my parents. The *Royal Oak Tribune* news lead described my trip as "controversial and illegal" and myself as "one of those people that nobody really knows well." It then went on to describe my parents as divorced for a decade and printed their separate addresses. "The father," the *Tribune* went on,

> "surprised" by his son's unauthorized trip into the world's current No. 1 trouble spot, has had only minimal contact with Thomas in recent years. . . .
>
> "Tom was never in the service," he said in answer to a reporter's question, "but I don't know why."
>
> Hayden said his son's interest in such fields as civil rights and anti-U.S. foreign policy movements hadn't begun to bud while the family was living together. "I think he picked all that up in college," the father speculated.
>
> The mother, Mrs. Gene L. Hayden, 1217 East Fourth, Royal Oak, probably knows more about her only child than anyone in the area. But she has skillfully evaded reporters since news of the Hanoi trip broke Tuesday.
>
> Mrs. Hayden, a film librarian, talked only briefly with reporters, saying she hopes her son returns safely and "brings back some useful information." Mrs. Hayden said she had heard "many fine things" about Lynd.
>
> Then she locked herself in her office at Martin Road School, 2500 Martin, Ferndale. Janitors barred reporters from entering the building. She left the school in her car, accompanied by a pet poodle, Tuesday afternoon, and has not been located since. A neighbor said Mrs. Hayden has "left town."

In fact, my mother moved into a motel and didn't leave for a week. A few friends came by her house, knocked on the door without success, and left little notes which she saved and I found many years later:

> Gene dear,
> I've tried to call you—many times—so please, when you can, call me. I just wanted to tell you how much we're all thinking of

you—and if we can do anything at all, let us know . . . We've been friends for so long—18 years!—and I'd like to help if I can, when you must be distressed and worried. Herb is sick, with a strep throat, but the rest of us are well. Bruce is enjoying his Christmas presents so much. The living room is impossible! My thoughts are with you constantly . . .

Much love,
Jane

Came by to "hold your hand" and set a spell—call me when you have a chance.

Gladys

Dear Gene,
We called to no avail, and I can't blame you for not answering your phone! Hank and I wanted to offer you a "refuge" from the mob in case you were in need of a place. My prayers and Masses have been with you and Tommy all week. Thank God there are still a few people left in this world with the courage of their own convictions.

Katie

I first saw the war as America invading and dividing Vietnam. Now it was Vietnam, like a malignant tumor, invading and dividing us.

FBI MEMORANDUM   **1/3/66**

. . . inquiry was made this morning of Department Attorney James Welden to determine whether the Department is actively considering prosecution when Aptheker, Lynd and Hayden return to the United States.

Welden said that the Department is extremely interested in prosecution.

FBI MEMORANDUM   **2/11/66**

The attached article, which appeared in the "New York Times," indicates that the Administration is deliberately refraining from immediate prosecutive action against Aptheker, Lynd or Hayden "for fear of upsetting its current peace offensive." The article states that both the Justice and State departments, "apparently acting on orders from the White House," have decided to go slow in taking any legal action on the case.

At approximately 3:40 pm, 1/11/66, Yeagley called and said he had talked to the Attorney General and the Attorney General was concerned that the investigation might cause a "furor." Yeagley said in view of this, we should restrict our investigation to interviewing members of the press media who were known to be at the airport when Aptheker, Lynd and Hayden returned to the United States.

TO: DIRECTOR, FBI   3-10-66
FROM: SAC, Newark

In planning the future course of this investigation, consideration has been given to requesting Bureau authority to interview the subject.

Several factors indicate that this would be the next logical step. These factors include: statements made by Herbert Aptheker that he considers the subject to be mildly anticommunist, lack of any statements or activities of the subject prior to his trip to Hanoi indicating any disloyalty to the United States, possible intelligence information possessed by the subject as a result of his trip to Hanoi.

It is also felt that subject's trip to Hanoi and his statements since his return may qualify him for the Security Index . . . Prior to recommending subject's inclusion on the Security Index on this basis, an interview of the subject to explore his present attitude seems desirable.

(referred to CIA)

To: SAC, Newark   4-1-66
FROM: DIRECTOR, FBI

THOMAS EMMETT HAYDEN

(referred to CIA)

With regard to your consideration that subject be interviewed, it is pointed out to you that the matter of subject's recent trip to Hanoi is still under prosecutive consideration by the Department of Justice and, therefore, no interview of the subject should be contemplated at this time.

You should submit your recommendations as to whether or not the subject should be included on either the Security Index or the Reserve Index.

FBI   **SECRET**

TO: DIRECTOR, FBI
FROM: SAC, Newark   4-19-66

THOMAS EMMETT HAYDEN

RECOMMENDATION:

In view of subject's recent unauthorized trip to North Vietnam
with Aptheker and Lynd, it is being recommended that he be
placed on the Security Index of the Newark office.

ADDENDUM DOMESTIC INTELLIGENCE DIVISION   5-6-66

Central Intelligence Agency has advised that they have never
had an operational interest in Hayden.

---

9.   The War Comes
Home: 1966–67

Picasso's grotesque painting of bombing victims in Guérnica during the Spanish Civil War depicted an incident in which eighty civilians were killed. In Vietnam, there were Guérnicas everywhere. The American government rained fifteen million tons of bombs, rockets, and shells on Indochina, at least seven million from the skies. In comparison, the United States dropped two million tons of bombs in all of World War II, and one million during Korea. Twenty million bomb craters were left behind in Indochina, three million from B-52s, which cut them forty-five feet wide and thirty feet deep. Over one million Indochinese were killed, two million wounded, and over nine million people turned into refugees. These statistics are now lost in history.

In response to this growing destruction, American society began to polarize in the mid-sixties. An antiwar movement grew to a larger scale than at any previous time in American history; loose coalitions could mass upward of 250,000 for rallies. Martin Luther King linked Vietnam with racism; he declared, accurately and controversially, that our government was the "chief purveyor of violence in the world today." Draft resistance, including exiles in Canada and Sweden, was spreading among thousands of young men; an estimated 500,000 violated the draft laws, compared with 1.6 million of the 13 million Vietnam-era veterans who actually saw combat during the Vietnam decade.

Discontent was surfacing even among GIs on an unprecedented scale; it was a handful of veterans, for example, who first
shocked my future wife, Jane Fonda, then living in France, with
stories of war atrocities. With the Democrats in power escalating the war and the Republicans even more hawkish, the prospect of reform dimmed. "From protest to resistance" became a
movement cry. Disruption and civil disobedience were becoming more frequent.

I continued organizing in Newark, living on a contract for a
book coauthored with Staughton Lynd about our Vietnam trip,
and trying to speak as often as possible on campuses.

FBI MEMORANDUM   **3/2/66**

Detroit, Michigan

Re: Thomas Emmett Hayden

On February 25, a source, who has furnished reliable information
in the past, furnished a flyer, a xerox copy of which is attached,
advertising the appearance of Thomas Hayden . . .

On March 1, a second source, who has furnished reliable information in the past, advised that Thomas Hayden did make an appearance on February 26. According to this second source, at
approximately 4 p.m., Hayden was interviewed by several local
television and news media.

The second source further advised that Hayden was the featured
speaker on February 26 at the DeRoy Auditorium, Wayne State
University.

Hayden said the United States was wrong in being there, but
should not withdraw immediately. He said they should stop
bombing North Vietnam and gradually withdraw their troops
over a period of time after they have assured the Hanoi government that they will be willing to sit down to negotiations and to
an eventual supervised free election.

According to this second source, there were approximately 240
people present at this affair. . . .

NK T-3 advised that the "National Guardian" sponsored a forum
on politics and policy at the Riverside Plaza Hotel, 253 West 73rd
Street, New York City, on February 24, 1966. NK T-6 advised of
Hayden's appearance . . . and noted that in his talk, Hayden stated
that he saw a need for a great mass movement against the economic problems in the United States. Hayden stated that he saw
the community action programs within the antipoverty program
as the basis for mass action.

. . .

SDS MEETING, UNIVERSITY OF CHICAGO, MARCH 1, 1966:

NK T-9 advised on March 10, 1966 that Hayden, in his talk at this rally, managed to follow the theme of the meeting, which was for the United States to get out of Vietnam. Hayden attempted to paint a picture of the Northern Vietnamese being a cultural, peace loving people forced to tear up their flower gardens and build bomb shelters because of the United States.

CHINA TEACH-IN, UNIVERSITY OF MICHIGAN, APRIL 3, 1966:

NK T-11 advised on April 7, 1966, that Hayden participated in one of the seminars which took place at this China teach-in. Some of the comments made by Hayden during this seminar are as follows:

". . . There is no morality left in this society, everyone is sinking and decaying."

As to the subject of possible action, Hayden said there was a great need to come to terms on what we were willing to die for. He advocated that steps be taken to oppose the draft; that Americans should not be expected to die for US foreign policy or for the "empire" idea . . . He said that unless Americans, particularly religious leaders, are shocked into action to change US foreign policy, we will be forced to do much more. He suggested that students consider refusal to take the 2-S Selective Service System Deferment Classification and refuse to take Selective Service educational tests. He suggested that professors in grading a student are signing "death certificates" for such students.

ALLERTON FORUM MEETING, APRIL 23, 1966:

NK T-13 advised that a meeting sponsored by the Allerton Forum at the Allerton Community Center, Allerton Avenue and White Plains Road, Bronx, New York, took place . . . The speaker for the evening was Tom Hayden, identified as past president of the SDS. . . . The US Congress moves too slowly to offset and stop the efforts of the National Security Establishment, he said. What is needed, he said, is the election of officials who understand the threat of the National Security Establishment and who will fight to defeat it.

SIT-IN AT CITY COLLEGE OF NEW YORK, MAY 13, 1966:

NK T-14 advised that a sit-in demonstration was held at the office of the President of City College of New York, on May 13. The issue opposed by those sitting in was this school's compliance with Selective Service laws. The students sought a promise from school officials that no grades or class standings will be forwarded to local draft boards, nor would the school be used for the administering of any draft test. The demonstration at City College of New York was addressed by Tom Hayden, who urged opposition to the Selective Service System.

NK T-16 made available a copy of a booklet entitled "Student Social Action" by Tom Hayden . . . the booklet was a translation of the talk given by Hayden at the University of Michigan in 1962.

SDS, which could have led a focused movement against the war, instead was becoming more radicalized. As the first generation of SDS leaders migrated into community organizing, they were replaced by a younger leadership, who knew only the bitterness of the mid-sixties, not the intellectual excitement and political hope of the decade's beginning. The early spirit of pragmatism and experimentation was steadily replaced by the adoption of more radical, abstract, and ultimately paralyzing ideology. Instead of Camus, there came Sartre, Fanon, and then Herbert Marcuse, whose *One Dimensional Man* suggested that the system could not only absorb and muffle voices of reform but even exploit them to create the illusion of democratic possibilities.

Breaking away from this system of fraudulence became the agenda; for the first time, classical Marxist doctrines were legitimized in debate. Some were excited by the example of the Chinese Cultural Revolution and a pamphlet by Lin Piao, *Long Live the People's War,* which evoked a dream of rural masses encircling and strangling opulent urban capitals—the SNCC experience distorted and projected on a feverish global scale. Many, including myself, were inspired by the romantic guerrilla adventures of Che Guevara in Latin America. Still others searched for a Marxist explanation of the role of students. A small, doctrinaire, and intensely factional group called Progressive Labor (PL)— the types we had felt would never bother SDS—burrowed their way into the fringes of the organization and began a sectarian advocacy of a "student-worker alliance." Others, from a New York chapter, composed *The Port Authority Statement,* which asserted that students were a "new class" of intellectual workers who had a legitimate right to rebel themselves, not simply to serve as supporters of blacks or the poor. There was a subtle turning point in the way SDS saw itself. The language and style of the Old Left were beginning to seep into the New as the politics of Port Huron were rejected as "liberal" and "reformist." Still, SDS remained the symbol and activist vanguard of the antiwar generation.

Meanwhile, the once small and coherent movement of the early sixties had exploded in several directions. The free-speech movement at Berkeley began when the university banned student tables containing political literature from Sproul Plaza: "These are not necessary for the intellectual development of students. If that were so, why teach history?" commented Chancellor Clark Kerr. Soon there was a nationwide rebellion by students seeking reform of the universities, demanding a student role in decision making, the abolition of *in loco parentis*, and a curriculum more relevant to the urgent issues of the day. At the same time the women's movement began, at first in reaction to the paternalism festering in SDS and SNCC, but rapidly through small "consciousness-raising" groups and the founding of the National Organization for Women in 1966. In spite of these widening challenges to its priorities from many of its natural constituencies, the Johnson administration remained stubbornly committed to its course.

By mid-1967, even some leading members of Johnson's own party were preparing to take on the president. Allard Lowenstein started the Dump Johnson movement, a coalition of grassroots Democrats searching for a 1968 presidential candidate. He first sought out Robert Kennedy but floated the concept with others, including Senator Eugene McCarthy. There was even talk of a Martin Luther King presidential campaign. Partly in response to Johnson's policies, partly because of the growth of radicalism, there was a surge of energy among reformers in whom we had all but lost hope.

Dismissing the establishment as absurd, disaffected young people adopted a life-style eventually labeled the "counterculture." This was, in its way, an outgrowth of the earlier fascination with James Dean, Jack Kerouac, the blues culture, and the experimentation with mind-altering drugs by Aldous Huxley's disciples. As society's problems began to appear deeper, and conventional protest more futile, "dropping out," a denial of loyalty and conformity, took on massive proportions. In the years 1960–64, an occasional person would talk about Dr. Timothy Leary's LSD experiments at Harvard and in Mexico. But with the Sergeant Pepper generation, led by the Beatles and "just a passing phase," acccording to Billy Graham, came a fascination with Eastern religion, an increased use of marijuana and other drugs in search of "connectedness," and a general style that mocked the cold repressiveness of society. One of the best descriptions of the mood compared the counterculture to

> Indian tribes who turned to the Ghost Dance religion in their despair over the violence of the white man, believing there must be a time when the whole human race could come to a state of freedom from death, disease and misery by discarding all things warlike and practicing peace, honesty and good will.

By 1967, the "beatniks" had been given a new name—*hippies*—and their cultural withdrawal was evolving into a form of politics. Clashes with police during the Summer of Love in San Francisco's Haight-Ashbury district and the Sunset Strip of Los Angeles, the organizing of "be-ins" around the country, the appearance of scores of "underground" papers, and the success of *Rolling Stone* magazine gave a rebellious identity to the new youth culture. Where five years before, we had thought of ourselves as student catalysts of moribund adult institutions, the new vision was of *alternatives* to institutions now considered hopelessly decadent. Former civil rights workers like Abbie Hoffman and antiwar organizers like Jerry Rubin, both of whom I knew slightly, set out to politicize youth culture by forming the Youth International Party, the Yippies. Television, untried as a means of transmitting messages at the time SDS was founded, was seen by Abbie and Jerry as the way to project alternative values through a visual image. Instead of a weighty manifesto like *The Port Huron Statement*, a radical message was communicated by appearance, not by new ideas but by a seemingly new species, the "freak," who would first alienate, then challenge, and ultimately dispel the repressive attitudes of the majority culture.

I could no more be a hippie in 1967 than I could be a beatnik in the fifties. I loved the music of the times, but strictly as a background to my life. I went to few concerts, owned hardly any albums, rarely danced, and was privately frightened by the loss of control that drug advocates celebrated. On one of the few occasions when I tried marijuana, I found myself on the floor laughing hysterically during a supposedly serious meeting; another time, I became very angry at having lost all train of thought in the midst of an important conversation. All during the "cultural revolution" I remained the straight man, chastised by the Yippies for being dangerously uptight, power-driven, even—organizational! Still, I defended the "cultural revolution" as a response of my generation to our parents' world, and I saw the Yippies as challenging bourgeois values. Unfortunately I was not critical enough of the so-called new values they offered and often let myself become an ally of absurdity masquerading as revolutionary politics.

By the summer of 1967, a cross section of all these groups—from pacifists to New Leftists to Yippies—were forming an improbable plan to "confront the warmakers" at the heart of the military-industrial complex—the Pentagon itself—in an action that became one of the most memorable of the sixties. Much of the leadership for the march came from traditional pacifist leaders like Dave Dellinger, a lifetime war resister about twenty years our senior, and a calm, experienced negotiator of inter-organizational tensions. Dave was a hardy, red-cheeked, balding bear of a man with New England roots who came from the traditions of Protestant religious moralism that had long fired lonesome dissenters in America. A devoted disciple of Gandhi as well as a pragmatic coalition builder, he envisioned nonviolent civil disobedience outside the Pentagon. To his "left" were SDS and political radicals who sought "resistance," a term which loosely meant street fighting with the police until arrested. Bay Area activist Marvin Garson, a leader of the Stop the Draft Week confrontations that preceded the Pentagon protest, described this new militancy as more "street theater" than "insurrection." The point, he argued, was that "if you need conscription to have an army, then you will need an army to have conscription. The moral of our play is that you cannot have imperialistic war abroad and social peace at home." If this was not complicated enough, the Yippies arrived on the scene with plans to "levitate" the Pentagon, combining their sense of street theater with more bizarre religious plans for "exorcising" the evil spirits from the building. Their goal was to delegitimize Pentagon authority by mocking and unmasking it. This was clearly the most confrontational and threatening drama to yet develop in the growing war at home.

The degenerating Summer of Love was a summer of death in the ghettos. After Newark came the conflagration in Detroit in which forty-three people were killed and U.S. soldiers back from Vietnam were used for the first time on the streets of an American city. When we spoke of the war "coming home," it meant that there was a connection between the burning of villages and the burning of cities; between the impersonal automated air war and the students who said "do not fold, spindle, or mutilate" to their multiversities; between the horrors of macho violence and the rise of feminism; between the appearance of the "cheerful robot" and the songs of the long-haired poets.

While around me the currents of protest seemed to be passing through a particle accelerator, it was difficult to keep a personal focus. The trend toward black power made it impossible to work effectively in Newark after July 1967. No longer being a student, I had little interest in perpetual campus speaking tours. The Dump Johnson forces were too exclusively involved in Democratic party politics. The new youth culture was too anarchic and antipolitical. The SDS now lived for long-term revolutionary doctrines and denounced any efforts for immediate reforms. The traditional antiwar coalitions were infested with bureaucratic infighting.

My mind was on Vietnam as the central issue, the metaphor and mirror of our times, the moral and murderous experience that would mark our identity for the future. Just as it was necessary to discover our resolve in the segregated South, I thought it crucial to commit "our lives, our fortunes, and our sacred honor" (as Staughton Lynd once paraphrased the Declaration of Independence) against this slaughter of a distant people. In my mind, the task ahead took on the proportions of the American Revolution and the Civil War. I was looking for a plan to bring this crisis to a head, to lance the tumor that Vietnam was in our lives. Because of my visit to Hanoi, the war was not merely a bizarre dinnertime television spectacle, but a personal reality. I didn't know if comfortable Americans like ourselves could feel a solidarity with remote human suffering, but slowly a plan began taking shape. I have some faded notes from a speech I gave at the time which indicate the course I was contemplating, a course that led directly, although I didn't know it then, to Chicago and 1968:

1. Discontent is growing. The cost in taxes, blood, and bitterness—for a war that seems senseless—is too high for the average American.
2. There doesn't seem to be an effective political vehicle to express the sentiment. The United States doesn't have a parliamentary system like France in which the National Assembly could honorably vote "no confidence" in the prime minister. Our presidents are rarely defeated if they attempt reelection. *Only a massive rejection of Johnson in opinion polls and primary elections will force the Democratic Party to look for another candidate and policy.*
3. The trend is toward more disruptive forms of protest now that Johnson has shown he won't listen to 500,000 marchers, leading senators, religious and intellectual figures. Moderates think they can "dump" Johnson—doubtful because of party machinery. The movement can only have one goal in 1968 politics: *to make it impossible for the next president to be elected without first agreeing to end the war.* We can't predict, only struggle and take what comes.

An invitation from North Vietnam had come to myself and Dave Dellinger, suggesting a seminar-style meeting between antiwar Americans and delegations from Hanoi and the NLF. This would be the first opportunity for a person-to-person dialogue between so many citizens of the two countries. The Vietnamese had hoped the French government would host the meeting, but finally they proposed a retreat center in the more remote city of Bratislava, Czechoslovakia. I sensed the Vietnamese might use the occasion for a diplomatic initiative, perhaps the announcement of a release of some American POWs, which several of us had suggested by letter.

On a stopover in Paris, I met with Etienne Manac'h, the French foreign ministry officer dealing with Indochina, a diplomat with experience extending back to the French intervention. I knew that he had met privately with Bobby Kennedy a few months before, during the senator's European tour, and that Kennedy was reassessing his position on Vietnam. There was an apparent quickening of diplomacy on all sides. The NLF had just released a new program spelling out their vision of a coalition government in a neutralized South Vietnam, offering secret-ballot elections for the first time. The United States still refused to recognize the existence of the NLF, however. As far as Vice President Humphrey was concerned, they were an "illegitimate band of wandering minstrels."

Manac'h was depressed by American unwillingness to pursue the negotiated compromise he thought possible, in three stages which he outlined for me. In the first, stage, he advised, the United States would stop bombing in exchange for talks beginning. In the next, the United States could expect the right to ask "reciprocity" for the bombing halt. The NLF should de-escalate militarily. "But then to achieve a real cease-fire, the United States must talk to the NLF. That is the difficult heart of the matter." It was clear that he was speaking with confident knowledge of the Vietnamese terms. "The other side cannot, like you, push a button to turn the war on or off. It is impossible to stop the military subversion in the South without a political solution of the problem."

What struck me most was his analysis of the South and his understanding of the differences between the North and the NLF, differences dictated by over twenty years of Western influence in the South during which Hanoi was building a separate socialist state of its own.

"When the United States talks with the NLF," he said,

> there must be an equilibrium between what the United States will give [ultimate withdrawal] and guarantees concerning the South from the other side. The [NLF] southerners want a firm South, different from the North, with a role for the Buddhists, Catholics, the bourgeoisie or middle classes that are not major forces in the North. They say the North has a firm socialism now, and the problem of reunification will not be ripe for a solution for five to fifteen years. Immediate reunification is not in their interest, nor in yours, because it would be under communism. There would have to be a period of a coalition government and an effort to stabilize neutralism in the South. The West could use this period to advantage by giving immediate economic assistance.

He was convinced that this was the best of the limited options before the United States, offering the possibility of a neutralized South, political protections for the noncommunist nationalists, and if nothing else, a decent way for the United States to withdraw from an unwinnable war. The alternative, he prophetically argued, was deeper American involvement in the quagmire, military collapse of the corrupt Saigon regime, and reunification in the form of a seizure of power by Hanoi. He did not seem to think such a catastrophe was far away. I asked what Senator Kennedy's reaction had been to his analysis.

"I found Kennedy to be very open-minded," he answered, "not a man of illusions. I hope he will be as aware of the reality in Vietnam as he surely is about reality in America." When I offered the belief that he would be, Manac'h simply responded, "*Bien.* It required Dien Bien Phu for our nation to learn realism. I cannot be as hopeful as you."

The Bratislava meeting was a confusing success. The Vietnamese brought sophisticated delegations, including top officials who would later be the negotiators with our government. The American side was a motley cross section of the peace movement, ranging from poor people to ministers, from Dick Flacks to academicians like Christopher Jencks, from *New Republic* editor Andrew Kopkind to long-haired oracles of the underground press. For five days, with the aid of simultaneous translation, there was an exhausting, sometimes inspiring, often awkward dialogue about every dimension of the Vietnam crisis. While the Americans were deeply touched and educated by the experience, I was never certain about the Vietnamese agenda. They were silent about their military strategy; the Tet Offensive was less than six months away. They outlined a broader, more detailed program for a future coalition government in South Vietnam, but it included nothing that would attract Washington's interest. At the end they said that several Americans could visit the North and hinted that a POW release might be a possibility.

DEPARTMENT OF STATE   TELEGRAM   CONFIDENTIAL

SEPTEMBER 19, 1967

SUBJECT: US-NORTH VIETNAM MEETING IN BRATISLAVA

A. US SIDE DISAPPOINTED TO FIND BOTH DRV AND NLF REPRESENTATIVES INTRANSIGENT ON DEMAND US CEASE BOMBING BEFORE POSSIBILITY FOR NEGOTIATIONS COULD BE RAISED SERIOUSLY.

B. . . . SMALL MIXED PANEL GROUPS ALSO FUNCTIONED FOR A DAY OR TWO, BUT NOTHING CAME OUT OF THEM.

C. ATMOSPHERE IMPERSONAL DESPITE EVIDENT INTENTION OF US AND VIET-
NAMESE SPONSORS TO DEVELOP PERSONAL CONTACTS AND DEEPEN RELA-
TIONSHIPS. AMERICANS UNABLE PERSUADE VIETNAMESE TO SOCIALIZE AND
BUILD DESIRED CAMARADERIE.

████████*JOURNALIST TOLD DCM SEPTEMBER 18 IMPRESSIONS EXISTED IN
PRAGUE THAT MEETING WAS IN FACT OFFICIAL CONTACT AND THAT NEW
LEFT AMERICAN PARTICIPANTS WERE ACTUALLY SMOKESCREEN VEILING
THIS.

During a week of preparations for the conference, I became personally interested in Czechoslovakia, particularly after befriending a young woman receptionist at the hostel where I stayed in Prague. I was lonely; she was beautiful. Her name was Anna Sevcikova, a university student from Bratislava, blond and blue eyed, whose innocent purity was a relief from the tension and intrigue I was going through. Most of the Czechs I dealt with were bureaucrats, polite black-suited characters from the pages of Kafka. Sober, they were boring apparatchiks; after two or three drinks they became boorish clowns, pawing after women in our American delegation. Anna, however, loved to take me by the arm on nightly strolls into the free and fascinating youth culture of Prague and Bratislava. Her friends gathered in basement clubs, where they listened to rock and roll, danced, and engaged in lively political discussion. It was like Berkeley in 1960. As an American, I was a symbol of the freedom they longed for, and we talked of our dreams far into the night. One point they found hard to understand: Why would an American protest America? When I tried to convince them that the Vietnam War was wrong, that there were race and generational problems in America, they responded with disbelief. Their media and bureaucracy were such a joke, so servile to Soviet propaganda, that the students assumed anything said critically of America was the opposite of the truth. Kafka lived on in their consciousness. If the papers said the Vietnam War was American imperialism, Anna laughingly said, she and her friends assumed that the Russians were invading Saigon.

And yet Anna's spirit was lifting. There was a more open climate in the Czech universities than anyone could remember, a consequence of a call for reform from an unexpected source,

*Material deleted by the Department of State.

Communist leader Alexander Dubček. The energy among Anna and her friends was palpable, the sign that a utopian moment could be approaching. How amazingly alike were the young people around the world, and how romantic are the times, I thought, thrilled. Though we'd known each other only a week, Anna and I felt totally familiar with each other. It was very hard for me to leave Prague for the journey to Hanoi. Filled by Anna's sweetness and her friends' buoyant cheer, I was swept by sadness when we said good-bye. I hugged her for a long time under the pillars of her university, then walked alone across a vast square. In the months to come, we wrote each other sentimental letters several times, promising to meet again. But seven months later, just before the Chicago convention riot, Russian tanks occupied the same square where we said good-bye. I wrote Anna afterward, but I never heard from her again.

From the Bratislava conference, I recruited a delegation of New Left activists for the Hanoi journey. There were several ERAP-generation organizers: Carol McEldowney, an SDS founder with whom I had traveled to Fayette, Tennessee in 1961; Vivian Rothstein, a community organizer in Chicago; and Norman Fruchter, a novelist and organizer with the Newark project. We were joined by the black journalist Robert Brown, and an Episcopal priest with the same surname, John "Jock" Brown. Most important in terms of the future, I persuaded Rennie Davis to come.

While traveling, we first heard the news that the 1968 Democratic National Convention would be held in Chicago, Rennie and Vivian's city. We guessed instinctively that the convention would be the scene of a showdown and wanted to lay plans for being there.

In those days (perhaps now as well) I tended to be an unpredictable risk taker who needed the corrective balance of an administrator able to turn my raw visions into concrete achievements. To be most effective, the administrator would have to be a trusted friend. Rennie was both. He had come from Virginia through Oberlin College to SDS, inspired by its ambitious agenda. His father, John C. Davis, was chief of staff to President Truman's Council of Economic Advisers. Rennie was an all-American boy, a 4-H champion, a star basketball guard in high school, and an excellent student at Oberlin, where he was rooming with Paul Potter when Al Haber and I tried to recruit them to SDS. Of average size and well coordinated, usually dressed in conservative style, his brown hair cropped neatly, Rennie peered at you from behind thick glasses with a winning, almost excessive smile, his bright white teeth gleaming even more than his blue eyes. After Oberlin, he spent a year doing graduate work at the University of Illinois and took a scholarship to Ann Arbor for 1963–64, where he found himself in the center of the national SDS group. He and Paul roomed together again in Ann Arbor, where both of them fell in love, successively, with Mary Varela. With his Appalachian roots, Rennie was persuaded to join the ERAP experiment, where he served as a central administrator before he finally immersed himself in the hillbilly culture of Chicago's Uptown.

Rennie knew instinctively what I was slow to admit—that it would be impossible to devote significant energy both to the ERAP projects and to ending the Vietnam War. Since I had been largely responsible for persuading him to join ERAP, my strong feelings about the importance of my Hanoi experience and the struggle to end the war left him confused as to my priorities. But we depended on each other for balance, and he listened carefully. The war's escalation persuaded him even more, and in 1967 he was ready to travel to Hanoi.

While Rennie was getting ready to leave, his father was working on a computer modeling project in the Pentagon about the effects of a nuclear attack on Washington. Under a covert U.S. plan, in the event of a nuclear war, his father was slated to be secretary of Labor in a government installation deep in the mountains of West Virginia. Rennie and his father had their first serious falling-out over this project and were not able to resolve it before we left. To make matters worse, Rennie was unable to call his father at the Pentagon from Europe to explain where he was going.

Rennie was not the only one of us feeling personal tension. All but Jock were under thirty and lacking in international experience, unless one counted my visit to Hanoi when I was twenty-six. The youngest was Vivian Leburg Rothstein, then only twenty-one. With short, curly dark hair and shining blue eyes, she looked even younger and perfectly innocent. As an intensely moral and humanistic Berkeley undergraduate, she had been arrested in civil rights demonstrations, participated in the free-speech movement, learned community organizing in rural Mississippi, and came back in 1965 to enter an ERAP project. In Berkeley she met the man she would marry, Richie Rothstein, who was promoting the SDS "Build, Not Burn" alternative to the draft, a proposal for ERAP-style community service among the poor instead of the draft and Vietnam. Richie, then twenty-two, was a former student at Harvard and the London School of Economics whom I first met in the Liberal Study Group at the National Student Association congress in 1961. Stunned by the 1964 murders in Mississippi, he returned from London and came to Newark, where I suggested he throw himself into the Chicago ERAP project. One of the few married couples in SDS, Vivian and Richie represented a search for roots and long-term stability in political commitments, despite their relative youth. I wanted Vivian to join our delegation to Hanoi and become more involved in the antiwar movement, but her sensitivity and her youth made her worry frantically as we traveled across the world. A diary she kept on the trip reflected, honestly and painfully, the dangers all of us felt at the time:

> I am beginning to feel very scared and upset about the trip. I feel as if when we land in Beirut I would like to get a ticket straight to NY and forget about the whole crazy adventure. I'm afraid it's a bigger step politically than I realize. That my passport will be invalid, that I will not be able to get a job such as Hull House which helps organizing in certain areas. That in a sense I won't be able to lead anymore a "normal life."
>
> Life, when committed to working with the movement, is hard anyway. You don't allow yourself many luxuries. You work hard and get few rewards. You constantly challenge your work, your ideas and your abilities. And there is limited time for loving and relaxing together.
>
> I am also scared about the bombing. I don't know if I will be able to take the strain. I am just about to get my period now, so my strength is low and my emotional instability is high.
>
> Going to Mississippi was a strain, and involved fear and a political decision which was hard to erase. But this even more involves a change which is irreversible.
>
> I am also worried about my mother. She will be so terribly upset about this. I am endangering my whole life and future, and she knows it and is afraid I am acting in the haste of youth. Perhaps she is right. I feel right now that she is, and I am afraid.

For Vivian's life at least these fears were not realized. Twenty years later she is still married to Richie, a mother of two, a Santa

Monica director of a social agency sheltering the homeless. Her eighty-year-old mother, Margot Leburg, lives nearby and is a staunch volunteer in many community movements. But Vivian's anxieties were pervasive among young people taking risks in those days—and not unfounded.

We landed in Hanoi at night. The city lights were turned down to a faint glow. The bridge over the Red River had been bombed again and again. While the Vietnamese continually worked on its repair, they channeled people over the quarter-mile river in makeshift ferries built of boards lashed to long metal pontoons, pushed along by small motorboats. We waited nearly an hour for the ferry in a crowd of perhaps seventy-five people. It was an opportunity to observe the Vietnamese with their guard down. I saw many very tired faces, but no indication of low morale or discontent. A uniformed ferry officer jokingly warned people as their turn came, "Don't rush to get on the boat or you will be hospitalized."

On the bumpy ride across, I stood squeezed against a young mother who kissed and played with her tiny baby. I kept imagining U.S. jets streaking in low against the bridge repair crews as we bobbed slowly along. Rennie stood next to the rail and watched, holding some flowers against his chest. He had entered another reality.

During the two weeks we traveled through the country, the U.S. bombing was much heavier than it had been in 1965. While the attacking planes forced us into the ditch only once, the air raid sirens were frequent, and the population was heavily protected. Bomb shelters were always nearby. Children were almost never without their wide-brimmed, thickly woven straw hats, their defense against pellet bombs. We were told to wear or carry helmets everywhere.

One day in the countryside, an air raid siren went off, and our jeep suddenly pulled over. We scrambled into a ditch, where I covered my head with my hands, trying to peer at the sky. Still good at seeing the silhouettes of planes, I saw an American F-105 streaking overhead, then another, and I heard the rumble and crack of bombs and antiaircraft fire. We had spent the previous night in the hotel's bomb shelter, which was more comfortable than this ditch. There we had thick cement walls, chairs to sit on, companions to break the tension, and a feeling of protection from the rolling thunder and wailing sirens outside. But here in the ditch, we had no protection, like being naked in an electrical storm. I wondered if the F-105s were dropping their "guavas" and "pineapples," little cylindrical bombs that exploded into thousands of flesh-piercing pellets over the size of a football field. The pellets, like tips of porcupine quills, couldn't be removed without major surgery, and this wasn't Beverly Hills. I thought absently about my death, as if I were already outside my body. What would my poor, disturbed parents think, their only son killed by the bombs of his countrymen? No gold star for them. Who would ship me home, and where would I be buried? And the guys flying the U.S. plane above me, for whom I was "just another gook blip," what would they think and say if they knew that an American their age, from Royal Oak, Michigan, was in their radar screen? Would they shout "Holy shit!" Would they even blink or think twice before they dumped their pineapples and guavas all over my ass? The fighter bombers passed over us and turned toward the balmy South China Sea and their carriers.

Rennie was particularly struck by the magnitude of the destruction; so we were invited to a place called the Museum of Weapons, where the Vietnamese displayed every sort of American weapon they had so far recovered. We met with a Vietnamese chemist, a scientist researching the human impact of incendiary weapons, and an expert on the legality of the various gadgets of death. For all of us, the place was something like a carnival horror show. We snapped photos and took copious notes as we listened to our guides carefully describe their collection.

I noticed containers of CS gas, which I had seen used by Birmingham police against blacks.* I knew that a whiff of the stuff made one cough, cry, and usually experience nausea. The canisters were being discharged into narrow tunnels in South Vietnam where guerrillas—as well as peasants taking refuge from bombs—were lodged. Next I came to the several types of

---

*According to U.S. Army training manuals of the time, CS (o-chlorobenzal-malononitrile) was the Army's most powerful tear gas. The manual stated, "the physiological effects include extreme burning of the eyes, accompanied by copious flow of tears, coughing, difficulty in breathing and chest tightness, involuntary closing of the eyes, stinging sensations on moist skin, running nose and dizziness or swimming of the head. Heavy concentrations will cause nausea and vomiting in addition to the above effects" (*The New York Times*, May 20, 1969).

napalm at our government's disposal; Rennie shook his head in wonder at the variety. I had seen this evil substance only in the form of glistening, silvery containers in Redwood City, California, when Senator Wayne Morse, a staunch foe of the war, rallied citizens against its use. What I didn't realize is that the Redwood City napalm had already been surpassed by a new, improved form. Our Vietnamese experts toured us past the early napalm to what they called super napalm, which was introduced in 1967 and contained thermite, magnesium and phosphorous—to generate more burning power. Finally, they introduced us to napalm B, which incorporated a polystyrene designed to cling to the human skin even underwater. A total of 338,000 tons of napalm were used during the war.

As I tried to shake off images of peasants or VC cadre boiling in rice paddies and fish ponds, we moved on to see the really big bombs. They were lying on the museum floor, unexploded as the Vietnamese found them, like several sizes of gray-green sharks. There was the little two hundred and fifty pounder; the five hundred pounder designed for hitting flat on the earth's surface from a diving plane; the Navy's own thousand-pound monster; and a few two-thousand- and three-thousand-pound giants, which could rip open a hundred-foot-deep crater.

What affected me most were the fragmentation bombs, a scientific breakthrough of modern war. The day before, we had visited a makeshift hospital where children and adults stared at us in stoic pain as we observed X rays showing the pellets in their bodies. Now I fingered the bomb in my hand, like a green hardball. A pod-shaped "mother bomb," built to hold 640 of the smaller spheres, lay at my feet. When the individual bombs exploded, they released hundreds of pellets, which came at first in the smooth, round shape of a BB. Now, thanks to modern science, the pellets were shaped in a jagged way that made them difficult to remove surgically. The Pentagon termed them flak-suppression weapons, and it was true, I supposed, that they could do some damage if dropped on top of an antiaircraft crew. But such positions were well fortified in the areas of North Vietnam we visited, and the Vietnamese told us that the pellets could not penetrate wood. How then could they pierce military targets? I thought of the children with their outsized thatched hats, and the possibility entered my mind that this weapon was especially, and perhaps only, useful in a war against a civilian population. Years later, Michael Krepon, a member of the U.S. Arms Control and Disarmament Agency staff, confirmed that these bombs were "*the* weapon for area denial . . . the most indiscriminate and lethal area denial weapon developed for the Vietnam War."

I tried to concentrate on the words of our guide, who squinted through his glasses at sheaves of notes, seeking to be precise and unemotional as he reported the details of each raid, each death, each injury, the damage to houses, pagodas, factories, schools, even water buffalo and livestock, throughout the country, down to the exact time of the raid and the numbers and types of weapons used, as if someone in the world would care. Norm Fruchter, my fellow organizer from Newark, described the Vietnamese we met as "the last rationalists," a people who believed there was a sympathetic world opinion that would hear their case. But, as Rennie pointed out, they were far from naïve; there was a mystique to them that he and I were determined to penetrate.

To begin with, we asked, why don't they hate us? If we were among American blacks, or native Americans, we would be resented and made to feel guilty for our whiteness, for our lack of sufficient understanding, for our comfortable privilege, and we would find it hard to disagree. Why were these Vietnamese acquaintances, and not simply the English-speaking guides but the soldiers and victims, so seemingly without resentment? We, for instance, had met a province official during the bombing of his own city, who said, chuckling, "They can't stop us from having tea together." There were the street children in one town who led us to where American bombs had fallen that very day, who said, "Thank you for coming, American aunts and uncles." Would I show some foreign visitors the bombs dropped on my country, the damage done to my children, and then sit down to have tea and discuss the details? These were indeed the "wretched of the earth," but unlike the oppressed of Fanon's journals, they did not seem to need the therapy of counterviolence and reverse humiliation that led to the discovery of their souls through the denial of ours. Why?

Part of their response was courtesy toward invited guests, part an attitude of cultural reserve about showing grief to foreigners, and part of it a Marxism that mechanically categorized the American working class as peace-loving no matter how many of its sons were shedding Vietnamese blood. But there was something more, a strange combination of romanticism and a political world view, perhaps even an image of human nature, that gave these Vietnamese their confidence that many Americans were "progressive" and could be counted on to oppose the killing.

I asked as many Vietnamese as possible about the sources of this optimism. A diplomat of southern origins with forty years of experience spanning two wars laughed and confided that "at first we were taken aback by your youth." Seeing pictures of long-haired hippies in peace marches reminded him of the "corruption of our own youth under the French and in Saigon today." But he said, "We like your spirit and your easygoing manner, your lack of titles." He was reminded of a poem from his youth, which he repeated, laughing:

No need to eat,
No need to wear luxurious clothing,
No need to play,
In order to cast iron,
Or move mountains,
Or fill up the sea.
Let our blood boil against the insult of slavery.
Only that way will we become new people.

I received a more intellectual explanation from an interpreter and diplomat, Pham Van Chuong, who had been stationed in Eastern Europe, where he read the Western press in precise detail. Chuong had been separated from his family in South Vietnam, though he was in a buoyant mood after returning briefly to the "liberated zone" to marry his longtime fiancée. Thin and bespectacled, Chuong looked much more like a library-centered graduate student than a card-carrying red menace.

"Why do we show so much interest in opinion in the States?" he asked rhetorically. It was not that they expected to win the war on American television: "When you fight Muhammad Ali, you must concentrate on him, not hope he gets an upset stomach." Then he went on to answer my query:

There is a historical background. Centuries ago, with the Chinese, we found that their soldiers—as opposed to their generals—did not want to fight us so much. The same with the French, and today with the American soldiers in the South. The same with your people back home. Not that we think that all of them, or even most of them, are opposed to the war. But there are objective facts you cannot overlook. Many French people supported the government, but only from a lack of information or misunderstanding, not because their own interest coincided with the government's interest.

Chuong had referred me to the Confucianist writings of a Vietnamese official who served under the French in the 1920s. In the key passage, he wrote that the "overwhelming majority of people, who are called middle or average people, become good or bad according to the education or customs they acquire." Chuong pointed to the parallels between this Confucian teaching and one of the prison poems of Ho Chi Minh, called "Midnight," written in the early forties:

Faces all have an honest look in sleep.
Only when they wake
Does good or evil show in them.
Good or evil are not qualities born in man.
More often than not, they arise from our education.

"You see," Chuong continued, "when the facts become clearer, it is our experience that the American people will oppose this war." Again he elaborated:

We don't believe any people are motivated by narrow economic interests alone. They are also motivated by values. There are universal values we can appeal to. Moral values are common to honest, goodwilled people in any country.

There is such a thing as honor. It is part of our outlook. There is a common tendency in the world to judge actions by their practical effect alone. But we don't judge things simply that way. Perhaps it is out of romanticism. History is so full of heroic people who rise up; they may know their action will be futile, but they need to express indignation. Of course, when you are organizing a movement you must try to be practical, to succeed. We do not, for example, encourage the Buddhist monks to immolate themselves. But where the individual is concerned, it is very different from building a movement. For instance, when a student in Saigon stands before a gun, the probability is that he will die, and he knows that nothing will happen as a result. But he must show the rulers that they are opposed, and also set an example of courage for others. We remember these examples forever.

Let me tell you one story, about one of our leaders in Haiphong under the French. He was waiting in prison to be executed. Outside, his comrades sent in a peach as a gift. He gave out slices to his companions in prison rather than taking any for himself, and he buried the core in the dirt floor to grow a young peach tree. Then he was executed. The peach tree later grew up in the prison courtyard. After liberation in 1945, it became a memorial. We call it Tô Hieu's peach tree. Today an orchard is there.

We have a tradition of many such stories. We are technically backward, we have no computers, so maybe we can lead a more spiritual life. Anyhow, the history of our struggle is that no patriotic action is entirely futile. No action for justice goes unheard, and no crime goes unavenged.

What was remarkable about Chuong's outlook was how much we shared in common. Rennie was deeply affected by our meetings. He took notes on everything said by our hosts, asked careful questions, cried in makeshift hospitals, grinned in awe at the Vietnamese durability, and grew in moral courage. Rennie and I had always believed that our common project was to change the world. Here he saw people more audacious, more committed, more "real," than ourselves, and they affected him deeply. Toward the end of our stay, he became edgy about whether the international air schedules would permit him to get back to the United States to participate in the march on the Pentagon scheduled for October 21.

Even more than myself, Rennie had long searched for some sort of moral agency, whether an organization or class of people, who could redeem the world. For a time it had been our generation, then the dispossessed of Appalachia, now he was pulled to the Vietnamese, whose suffering and dedication surpassed his understanding.

A few days after our visit to the Museum of Weapons, Rennie went back and asked for one of the small green fragmentation bombs. He wanted to take it home, return it to its Pentagon origin, show it to the antiwar marchers, the media, whoever would see and listen, and reveal to them the truth that he had discovered on the other side of the world.

He flew home, with the bomb in his pocket.

10. *Prisoners: 1967*

Ⅰn Hanoi an emissary of the National Liberation Front passed me a welcome message: The NLF was ready to release several American prisoners held in the South as a "gesture of goodwill to the American people." This, however, was not so simple.

"We do not want to hand over the prisoners to the American government, which doesn't recognize us," Nguyen Thi Binh had already told me in Bratislava. She was the de facto foreign minister of the NLF. To me, she looked like a Vietnamese Mona Lisa. U.S. negotiators at the Paris peace talks, where she signed the peace accords next to Henry Kissinger, later called her a "harpie."

"We would like to release the prisoners in your hands, to Americans who stand for peace," she had said in her low-keyed voice. "It could be arranged through Cambodia."

I felt uncomfortable with the whole subject of American prisoners, having met twice with captured pilots in Hanoi. When Staughton Lynd, Herbert Aptheker, and I met a single POW in December 1965, it was only after anguished debate. I felt, according to my 1965 notes, that "decency compelled us to leave the man in peace and not humiliate him further." Staughton argued persuasively that it was humanitarian to see the prisoner, while not publicly announcing his name, and pass a message to his family. The Vietnamese, on the other hand, regarded the captured pilots as marauders who were attacking and killing their people; shooting them down was a matter of deep national pride. But they sought to show that they treated the pilots "humanely." I felt it was remarkable that the Americans were not killed immediately by villagers when they were parachuted into the areas they had so recently bombed. (Imagine the fate of a MIG pilot captured in Times Square after bombing Manhattan.)

But how could one define "humane treatment," and how could one communicate honestly through an interview under the eyes of guards? The Vietnamese wanted to seat the American prisoner on a chair lower than ours and film the meeting, conditions which we successfully opposed. Finally, in spite of extreme reservations, we went ahead and spent an hour with the American. The discussion with him began nervously, but we eventually relaxed and felt that a humanitarian purpose was served. The pilot had been in captivity for four months, having been shot down on his first mission, he said. We talked about our families, and he expressed a terrible loneliness for his children, who were just at the age, he said, "when they are forming opinions." He said that he knew little about the war and regretted not having paid more attention. While he told us that his treatment was better than he expected, he noted it was "no bed of roses," using American jargon. We couldn't tell if he was passing us a message with this phrase. At any rate, we were successful in later communicating to his wife and children that he was alive, which they did not know. We agreed not to publish his name.

On this trip five years later, our delegation had met with Douglas Hegdahl, a hapless twenty-one-year-old sailor from South Dakota who apparently fell off his ship and was rescued/captured by North Vietnamese crews in April 1967. An American youth about Vivian's age, Hegdahl was considered more a pawn than a pirate by the Vietnamese, and he claimed to have no opinions about the war. As far as we could tell, Hegdahl was treated adequately, and we were given a short tape recording to send home to his wife. Of greater concern were two other POWs we met, Elmo Baker, a badly injured, thirty-five-year-old Air Force major, and his cellmate, Captain Lawrence Carrigan, both shot down in August, about three months before our arrival. We met them across a green-and-maize table, under the unexpected lights of Japanese television, in what might have been the camp known later as the Hanoi Hilton, a worn compound within the capital proper. We were extremely nervous about meeting Americans under these auspices, a feeling that was reinforced by the cast on Baker's rib cage and his severely broken thigh. He could stand stood only with the help of a crutch. "Don't say anything to upset him," our friend Oanh said, on the advice of a Vietnamese doctor. Baker, a Missouri native, seemed anxious, but asked us to tell his family that he was alive, which we did. Carrigan caused us the greatest confusion. We chatted a little about the World Series and the like, and then he asked us why we opposed the war. Vivian, as I recall, responded that the Saigon government was corrupt and unrepresentative, that it was a brutal war, and that America had no right to be involved.

Carrigan, to our surprise, said he agreed. "You should go home and, not being belligerent, try to talk to the American people about the Geneva Accords," he advised us and continued, almost in a stream of consciousness:

I was just flying a plane, kind of a glorified truck driver. I used to argue with guys in the squadron about the war. But you understand, as long as you're in the service, you take orders from the guy that outranks you.

Sure, we knew. At flight school, there were two guys from Berkeley who told us about the antiwar demonstrations. We figured it was something to do on Saturday afternoon: get together and paint a sign. I remember econ class at Tempe [Arizona] State, the guy who used to sit next to me, all of a sudden he wasn't there, he got drafted. You look at this guy's notes, then he isn't there, it starts you thinking: Demonstrations are great, but do you really think they do you any good?

Being shot down was the biggest thing that ever happened to me except my wedding night. There we were coming down max fast from eighteen thousand feet in pod formation. I looked up following my lead and saw this cylinder SAM hit the lead, and the same one hit me. The kid in back said, begging your pardon, "Oh, shit." I decided I had it and punched off the canopy. "Things worked out as advertised. I don't know if the kid in back got out. I landed in the jungle and was there over three days, one vine after another. I got max tired. When I came to, there were about thirty people around me. I tried to escape and evade, but you can't with thirty people.

I don't know what the military will say, but do I seem brain-washed? After you've talked about your cellmate's wife, kids, base-ball scores, you run out of things to say. So we asked for something to read. They didn't give the stuff to us. We asked for it. They gave us books, magazines, all slanted. But before I had only our side. They never asked me to say anything about our government. But when I go home as a civilian, I'll tell people about the Geneva Accords. If three hundred other POWs are saying the same thing, what can they say?

I suddenly had the feeling that Carrigan was giving too many of the "right" answers.

As the meeting ended, Carrigan was asked to take with him the whole pack of cigarettes and candy the Vietnamese had carefully laid out on the table between us.

"The whole pack?" he replied, chuckling. "I know what you guys are trying to do to me."

Immediately we held a tense meeting with Oanh and the commander in charge of the POWs. I stumbled through a trans-lator trying to say that we could not evaluate the truthfulness of the claims of good treatment and would prefer not to make a public statement about their situation when we returned to the United States. The truth was that we were certain that Carrigan was lying in front of the Vietnamese. Why else would he make the crack about "what you guys are trying to do to me"? Yet if we accused him of deception in front of our hosts, he presumably would suffer. If we went home and said he opposed the war, we would be perpetuating a phony story. I asked my-self, did the Vietnamese really think these POWs were changing their minds on the war by reading the Geneva Agreements?

I was surprised by the unhappiness of the Vietnamese com-mander, Major Bai, in response to my less than enthusiastic remarks. "The whole thing became a tremendous misunder-standing," Vivian recorded in her notes.

Major Bai replied angrily that other American visitors who saw prisoners believed that they were treated well and were grateful to the Vietnamese. Then he added, like a person with arbitrary power, that they would have to "reevaluate whether anyone should visit with POWs again."

At this point, our friend Oanh interrupted:

Personally, I can't stand these meetings and sitting and looking at the pilots. These meetings were arranged against my will. I think they create more problems between the prisoners and ourselves.

A month ago, my brother-in-law was killed, five days after his marriage to my sister. I received a card from my sister announcing the marriage, and her husband was already dead. I can't stand looking at these pilots.

That ended the most honest and painful dialogue of our visit. In our hotel rooms later, we continued to explore the incongruities we had experienced. Vivian wrote:

It was rather awful. We all fell into a closeness with pilots on the basis of being Americans. Not until the middle of Carrigan's talk did I realize not to trust what he said at all. We are clearly "communists" to those guys.

Afterward, Rennie said he felt close to Carrigan, that he felt he understood him and trusted him. I didn't. I felt he was baiting and bullshitting us, because he wants to please the Vietnamese to get good treatment.

We returned to the hotel, very upset. We argued among ourselves into the night, to no conclusion, and Vivian remembers thinking that later we all went to our rooms and threw up. It was the one experience that marred our trip, because it brought competing agendas to the surface of an otherwise moving experience. The Vietnamese wanted us to meet the POWs, think well of their treatment, and become a nonofficial channel for correspondence with their families. The POWs seemed to want communication with their families, but who could tell what games they were playing with their captors? It was clear we couldn't go home saying that they were converted to the Geneva Agreements. We could achieve greater legitimacy in the States by having met with the POWs, but how were we being used, and by whom? It was crazy: We were Americans opposed to everything our government was doing, and yet, as Vivian said, we started bonding with the POWs, which made the Vietnamese distinctly uncomfortable; were we using the POWs to feel more like Americans in this communist country? These questions aside, it was clear that the Vietnamese were prepared to start a new policy toward captured Americans, with American peace activists as a channel. For the first time, they were willing to pass hundreds of letters from POWs to their families, carried back by peace movement representatives. There also was the likelihood, as the Vietnamese had indicated, that they would actually release some prisoners as a goodwill gesture. I strongly favored going ahead with the opening, not knowing quite where it would lead.

At the end of this Hanoi trip, it was decided that there would indeed be a POW release at last. I was asked to wait in Phnom Penh.

Phnom Penh, a city of 600,000, was beautiful in November. Rural Cambodia seemed lush and tropical, the palm trees and rice paddies encircling the city's outskirts, so that it appeared that the capital emerged from the plush countryside itself. A blend of Khmer and French, Eastern and Western architecture gave the city its distinct quality, a mingling of French-style boulevards and Buddhist pagodas. Like Hanoi's, the streets were filled with bicycles, though there seemed to be more cars. The taxi service was provided by cyclo drivers, their legs powerfully muscled from constantly pedaling and pulling two or three passengers behind them. There was an air of relaxation I had not seen in Hanoi. Cambodia was an oasis in the war, even though the border with South Vietnam was only sixty miles away.

I was exhausted from all my travel and checked in for a long sleep at the modest Hotel Khemara on the Boulevard Preah Bat Monivong near the center of the city.

It was an unusual moment for Cambodia. Prince Sihanouk, the neutralist monarch who almost single-handedly maintained political stability and a sense of national pride in the country, had opened the previously closed gates to the American and Western press corps stationed in Saigon, in order to let them investigate for themselves whether there were North Vietnamese and NLF "sanctuaries" or base camps along the Cambodian border with Vietnam. Additionally, Jacqueline Kennedy Onassis and her party had been given permission to visit the ancient Khmer ruins at Angkor Wat in northern Cambodia, and some of the press corps was following her. When they were not bouncing around dirt roads looking for communists or Kennedys, the correspondents were gathered around the swimming pool and bar of the historic Hotel Royale. Because of my mission, I tried to stay away from the press, but that was impossible in the small-town atmosphere of central Phnom Penh. I made mysterious explanations for my presence when a few of them asked and continued my wait.

Since I could not use the telephones in either French or Khmer, the only languages spoken, I would hire a cyclo-driver every morning to take me to the NLF Embassy for word about the POWs. According to Western rumors, the cyclo-drivers were collecting intelligence for the underground Khmer Rouge, which was planning to carry out an insurrection if Sihanouk's neutralism failed. I tried my best to explain that I wanted them to take me to "the Vietcong," a request rarely if ever made. I wrote down *National Liberation Front of South Vietnam*, then tried saying "VC! VC!" I received only a bemused response from the drivers. Finally I drew a blue, red, and gold-starred flag on a piece of paper, and their eyes lit up with surprise. "Yes, yes!" said one driver with skin the color of walnut from the daily sun, and I climbed into the seat behind him.

The NLF Embassy was a walled-in compound with a large, two-story building within. I believe it had once belonged to the Americans, who were withholding diplomatic relations from Sihanouk for his perceived pro-NLF tilt. The NLF ambassador was Nguyen Van Hieu, who would play a key role in the Paris peace talks in the years ahead. He was a professional diplomat, courteous and remote, friendly and formal, squinting behind his glasses to communicate in an elementary French that I could only half understand. I still had little notion of what his people had in mind, though by cable to the United States I had already created a committee to announce the prisoner release that included Dr. Benjamin Spock, Dave Dellinger, and SNCC founder Julian Bond. At last, Hieu offered more details. The POW release had been delayed because of recent American bombings, but was now going ahead, largely because of the urging of antiwar activists. The American POWs would be taken by sampan and jeep from the jungles of South Vietnam to the embassy where we were sitting, rest one day, hold a press conference, and, Hieu proposed, leave with me on a commercial airliner back to the States. Hieu emphatically stressed that he wanted no Pentagon intervention, especially seizure of the men. Any such act would jeopardize future releases, he said, indicating for the first time that this might be the beginning of a longer process of POW repatriation.

"Please come back tomorrow at exactly twelve noon," Hieu said. The embassy yard, I noticed, was filled with perhaps twenty very alert NLF soldiers, and I wondered (correctly, it turned out) if the POWs were not already somewhere inside the compound. I returned to the hotel, where I had been wired some quickly raised funds from New York, and checked the international plane schedules carefully. There was a Czech flight through Bombay to Beirut, with connections on Pan American to Paris and New York, the day after tomorrow. I ordered four tickets in my name, and counted on the NLF to work with the Cambodian authorities to facilitate our departure. I finally went over to the Hotel Royale to tell a couple of American reporters what was in the works, then went back to the Khemara to try to sleep. The U.S. government certainly knew of the imminent release and my presence by now, and I wondered how they would react to this amateur diplomacy.

The next morning was Armistice Day in America. The press were all over the Hotel Khemara, but I had left early for the sanctuary of the NLF compound. Just after noon, I was ushered into a small waiting room with a long, low table full of fruits, cigarettes, and tea. Hieu ushered me to a chair. Just then a swinging door opened, and three Americans, one white and two black, walked into the room warily. One of them was very gaunt and walked with a limp; the other two seemed to be in reasonable physical condition. All three stared at me with eyes that seemed to gauge and calculate everything instantly. Behind them was a tall Vietnamese soldier, urging them into the room, smiling politely.

I tried to make the most of this strange situation, going forward to shake hands, introduce myself, and ask about their health. They, of course, had no idea who I was and were trying to assess their new circumstances.

The most at ease was James Jackson, a twenty-seven-year-old black Green Beret from West Virginia, who had been captured in the Mekong Delta after a battle eighteen months before. Powerfully built and reflective in manner, he seemed to lead the threesome and quizzed me in detail about my background. He knew something about the pre-1965 SDS, seemed sympathetic when I told him of my experience in the South, and appeared to become more comfortable as we talked.

While Jackson and I conferred, the white POW, Dan Pitzer, was easing their exhausted third comrade into a leather chair. Under the grinning, watchful guard, Pitzer then began helping himself to the fruit and cigarettes, his gestures quick and furtive, almost animal-like. Pitzer had been a captive for over five years, a miracle in itself. Historically guerrilla movements rarely took prisoners because their clandestine and constant movement would be hampered by having to guard a group of bound-up foreigners. Life under such circumstances would be unbearably harsh for an American. The average GI only went on short missions into the jungle and was rotated out of Vietnam in a year. But Pitzer had survived this long, and I could see the tension and suspicion in his eyes as he started asking me questions.

"What are you, some kind of communist?" he asked sharply, with an edge of anger.

No, I replied. But I said I was opposed to the war and had visited North Vietnam, encouraged them to release American prisoners, and was here on a strictly humanitarian mission. I said their captors would not release prisoners to the U.S. government directly, only to antiwar Americans like myself.

"Trust me, it'll be all right," I went on, not fully believing myself. "I've got no quarrel with you guys, only with our government's policy. This is the only way your release can happen. It's all worked out. I've got the plane tickets. We can be out of here tomorrow. You'll be fine. You're going home."

Pitzer sat back, thinking rapidly about every angle of his new situation. Meanwhile, the third POW, Edward Johnson, was lying back in his chair exhausted, trusting his buddies to get him the rest of the way. "Malnutrition and dysentery," Jackson said of him. "He gave up eating the rice."

The next hurdle was the press conference that Hieu had insisted upon. The embassy had already allowed the foreign press into a large room in another part of the building, and we had little time to decide what to do. Fortunately, Hieu made no special demands about what we should say.

"Just tell the truth." He smiled. "We have a policy of humane treatment of captured prisoners." I could tell the Americans thought this was diplomatic bullshit, and that beneath their politeness, they despised their guard, who, it turned out, had been in charge of them in the South. They called him Mr. Mafia. Seemingly unaware of their hostility, he volunteered to go shopping and buy them some clothes and presents as farewell gifts. Unlike most Vietnamese I had met, Mr. Mafia projected an air of self-importance. This was plainly some kind of career peak for him, and he wanted the POWs to be grateful for his role as their master over the years.

"When they released the three of us, we left behind another American, Jim Rowe, who was held with us. They still have him, and we have to try to get him out," Jackson said in a rapid low-keyed burst that our Vietnamese hosts couldn't quite translate and understand. He stood up and was ready to meet the media.

The journalists were clamoring for photographs and throwing questions as we carefully walked into the brightly lit room and sat behind a long table with a podium. For virtually all of them, this was their first contact with the NLF—not to mention with released POWs.

"How did they treat you?" "Where were you held?" "What do you think of the war now?" "What do you think of the antiwar movement?" "Will you reenlist?" "Where are you staying tonight?" "What plane are you on?" "Have you asked to see the American military?" The questions came rapid-fire from all directions. After their years in jungle captivity, I wondered how my countrymen could possibly take this.

As it turned out, they knew exactly what they wanted to say. Each introduced himself, stated the place and date of his capture, and thanked the NLF for his release. I explained who I was but refused to provide details of our departure plans, though any competent reporter could figure out our options.

"This is a humanitarian gesture, nothing more. I want to stress that it is very important for future developments that our U.S. government not intercept or interfere with our departure on civilian aircraft," I emphasized. That said, the POWs rose to leave without answering further questions, to the disappointment of the noisy contingent of journalists.

Jackson looked me in the eye with assurance. "See you tomorrow," he said and was hustled off with his associates to their last night under guard. The NLF soldiers, with Cambodian police assisting, escorted them into a gray military vehicle with Mr. Mafia and nearly killed a couple of camera crews driving out of the embassy toward their unknown destination.

Drained by the session, I paid a visit to the home of Wilfred Burchett, one of the most unusual experts on the Indochina conflict. An Australian journalist by background, an independent Marxist by preference, Burchett had written for the West-ern press from inside the communist world for decades. Whether he was defined as a communist apologist or intrepid adventurer, his advice and company were sought by a wide range of journalists and even diplomats trying to comprehend the mysteries of the "other side." Banned from Australia, he had married a vibrant and opinionated Bulgarian woman, Vessa, with whom he had three children, who were born, amazingly, in Moscow, Hanoi, and Peking during Burchett's travels. The family was now living in a charming villa in Phnom Penh due to the generosity of Burchett's close friend Prince Sihanouk. Their young children were playing amid the banyan trees and cages of pet monkeys, birds, and a new baby bear as I entered their yard to tell Burchett of the POW release and ask his assist-ance in getting me to the airport without the press following me everywhere. Wilfred agreed to pick me up at the hotel early the next morning, take me to his house for breakfast, and drive me hidden in his jeep to the small airport.

Sleep never came that night, and in the morning I waited nervously for Burchett's arrival. He finally drove up thirty min-utes late, with one of his hands and lower arms completely bandaged; the new pet bear had playfully bitten through his hand that morning, and he had rushed to the hospital to check for infection. Great, I laughed, now I have a one-handed driver taking me on mission impossible. Somehow we got to the air-port in time to purchase the tickets and obtain the necessary travel documents. The little, open-aired terminal was crawling with reporters, cameramen, and a large number of observers I took to be spies of one kind or another. There still was time for plenty to go wrong, and I had no idea when or how the POWs would arrive.

A tall, dignified man approached me and introduced himself as the Cuban ambassador to both Vietnam and Cambodia. In excellent English, he pleasantly informed me that if there was any "trouble" on the way home, our party would be welcome to fly from Prague to take asylum in Cuba. I thanked him po-litely and wondered where he got the idea that these men might desert. Someone was out of touch with reality, and I hoped it wasn't me.

A second diplomat, however, made me even more nervous. He was the Australian ambassador, who introduced himself as "representing the affairs of the United States in Cambodia."

Lowering his voice, he confided that a nearby plane was available to fly the three men to waiting American officials at an air force base one hour away in Thailand. "Is this an offer or an order you are transmitting?" I wanted to know; after receiving an ambiguous reply, I responded, "You know, I don't think the Vietnamese would appreciate these men, who have been released to civilians like myself, being returned to the U.S. military an hour from now. The guys left some prisoners back there in the jungle, and there's a chance we can get them out, but not if the Pentagon intervenes. Thank you for your offer, but it's not accepted." I had the unnerving feeling that the Australian would make the same statement to the three POWs if given the chance, putting them in a very serious spot.

There was one way to avoid this, I thought. I scanned the airport crowd for the face of longtime American correspondent Robert Shaplen, whose books and stories on Indochina had been appearing for years. I motioned to see him privately. From the "insider" expertise that his writings revealed, I guessed that he was very close on a personal level to many American officials and could be trusted as a private channel to them. Completely bluffing, I said in a low, forceful whisper, "Get hold of Harriman in Washington and tell him that if these men are even touched by the Pentagon, or taken away from me before they get home, that means the end of prisoner releases for a long time." Though slightly taken aback by the frenzy in my manner, he nodded as if he knew exactly what I meant, and went off to a telephone.

Finally, Ambassador Hieu arrived to see me off. He called me into a corner.

"The three men will be taken directly to the plane. Everything is arranged. You need to have their tickets, nothing more." He seemed satisfied with our conspiratorial plan.

I had to ask him a question: "Mr. Hieu, I would like to know if you expect these three men to be antiwar in their feelings or statements, because you should know that they are not." I told him of the sudden Cuban offer, and how it shook me. Hieu maintained his permanent smile and said in French, "I know, I know."

"This fellow Pitzer in particular," I went on, "may say loud and angry things about you, and I worry whether it will affect the prospect of future prisoner releases."

"Okay, okay," he said, switching to his very limited English.

"The truth is the truth." Then he rubbed and shook his hands, to show the affair was over. "They may say anything." I wanted to know if he was disappointed, but I couldn't tell.

The plane was ready to depart. I walked out of the terminal across the tarmac, through the throng of reporters, still uncertain where my traveling companions were. Then I noticed a fleet of three or four military vehicles driving across the airfield about a quarter of a mile away, heading in a direct line for the ramp of the airliner. Sure enough, as I left the press behind and came closer to the plane, the vehicles swerved to a halt, and a dozen or so soldiers and police disembarked. In their midst were the three Americans. I caught up with them at the first step of the plane.

"All aboard," said Jackson, and up the steps we climbed, perhaps the first prisoners ever released to an opponent of a war, flying home first class.

Unknown to us, an Associated Press story out of Saigon was reporting that unnamed sources believed the three POWs had been "brainwashed." I never discovered who was attempting to discredit us, but the three men were furious.

As we crossed the world, the men's suspicion started to ease ever so slowly. Pitzer, I later learned, was considering an escape when we stopped in Bombay for fuel but decided not to try. I liked him despite his nastiness. Jackson joked that the only reason Pitzer was still alive was his "mean and ornery nature." Pitzer had fought in Korea and was among the earliest U.S. military "advisers" to enter Vietnam. He had lost about 40 pounds from his 180-pound frame in captivity. He complained to me of rickets, weakened eyesight, and bouts of dysentery, but as the flight progressed, his mood improved. When I asked why he joined the army in the first place, he said, "The army's a good life because you always know where your next check is coming from." He reminisced about running a bar for soldiers in West Germany and accused the Czech stewardess of being a worse cook than he was. When she served him a plate with rice, I thought he would throw it at her. Instead, he swore at the rice and said he never wanted to see any again.

Johnson remained quiet all the way home, sleeping wrapped under two blankets. I learned from the others that he was forced to drop out of college for lack of money in 1945, was drafted, and spent twenty years in the military until being captured on pa-

trol with Saigon troops three years earlier. He had gone to
Vietnam, he said, because the work offered decent pay. He was
frail and exhausted and weighed only about a hundred pounds.
He said he couldn't explain his illness, but the other two believed it was due to psychological exhaustion. Jackson, a medic
among other things, said that when Johnson stopped eating rice,
it was a sign of surrender they all went through.

"You have to live with rice, tropical diseases, and the Vietcong, and you can't let any of them get to you. If you do, you
give up the will to live, and that's about eighty percent of the
problem," Jackson observed.

Jackson continued to impress me. As a young southern black,
he had the strongest social conscience among the three. Having
been held for less than two years, he also had the closest connection with the realities of the outside world and had followed the
"news" provided by his captors with keen interest. He knew of
the uprising among blacks in American cities and devoured all
the information I gave him about Newark. But he was a committed military professional and was prepared to return to combat.
He respected the Vietnamese enormously, but as adversaries,
wishing only that the Saigon side had men of the NLF's caliber.
In Special Forces school, he became something of a black belt
in his mastery of the martial arts. In Vietnam, he often performed the terrifying job of slipping into dark tunnels to engage
the enemy in hand-to-hand combat. He had learned to speak
Vietnamese and penetrated the Ho Chi Minh Trail near Laos,
where, clad in black pajamas and floppy hat, he trotted alongside
the thin column of NLF soldiers bringing supplies and guiding
personnel from the North. He was an expert on every bug,
branch, and berry that could be eaten for nourishment in the U
Minh forest. We talked intensely as the hours passed, feeling a
closeness despite our different lives. He didn't know it at the
time, but he was suffering from a strained heart, the result of
malnutrition, that would keep him on careful medication for the
rest of his life.

Jackson and Pitzer's curiosity about events in the United
States was keen, even exaggerated, since they refused to believe
anything their captors told them. Pitzer had even refused to
believe President Kennedy was dead for two years, until another American prisoner confirmed it for him. They were skeptical about the size of the antiwar movement until I handed

them an issue of *Time* magazine with a cover photo of demonstrators besieging the Pentagon the month before. They wanted to know the World Series scores, the latest movie hits, and what American women were wearing.

As Pitzer opened up about his prisoner experience, he began talking more respectfully of his captors. Prisoners liked some of their guards, he said, and intensely disliked others. He said he spent time teaching English to Vietcong cadre and translating for them. It was the way to survive, he shrugged.

As we flew over the Middle East toward Lebanon, Pitzer opened a bottle of Johnny Walker Red Label that I bought him as a present. He drank three or four glasses and promptly passed out. An hour later, I tried to give him a couple of aspirin, and he muttered to Jackson, "Watch that guy, he might be trying to knock me out." When we touched down at the Beirut airport, Pitzer was still sleeping, and I noticed that he looked pallid, even green. I knew that we would be met at this stop by American officials, so I shook Pitzer awake and told him where we were. He jumped up like a wild man and staggered to the bathroom. I followed, and could hear him throwing up. The plane doors opened, and I looked down to see that our private little journey was over. At the bottom of the steps were a great many official-looking Americans. I climbed down the steps while the POWs waited and was introduced to several Americans from the embassy who politely asked to see my three companions.

"We want to welcome them back and provide you gentlemen with a shower and an American meal and a night's sleep. There are reservations for you to continue your flight home tomorrow," one of the State Department representatives said firmly. I would have preferred to keep flying on straight to New York, but I knew there was no choice but to accept the offer and went inside the plane to convey the news. The United States had agreed to allow our private flight home as the Vietnamese had demanded, I told them, but was insisting on an overnight checkup and debriefing. Jackson agreed with the suggested plan, and went down the steps with Johnson to meet the American officials while I rushed to the bathroom to sober up Pitzer.

I stuck my head in the bathroom door to tell him what was happening. He threw water on his face repeatedly and straightened up. Fully erect, drawing on his invisible survivor resources, he literally marched down the steps to the waiting delegation of officials.

At the U.S. Embassy on the edge of the Mediterranean, the three prisoners were finally back in the "territory" of the United States. After being greeted and congratulated by the ambassador and staff, they were given the chance to make their first calls home. While the others were short and sweet, I will never forget Pitzer's call to his wife in North Carolina. "Yeah, I'm fine, honey, don't worry, I'm fine," he began, then launched into a tirade against his captors. "The goddamned communists are trying to take over that country, and we've got to keep fighting over there. Yeah, I feel the same way as ever. I hate those red bastards. They tried to brainwash me, but they couldn't. If I was stronger, I'd want to enlist and go back. America is the greatest country in the world, and we've got to stop the communists from taking over."

As he went on, I realized he was not talking for the benefit of his wife, but for the American officials who were listening. No, sir, *he* hadn't been brainwashed. Dan Pitzer was still a red-blooded John Wayne American. I wondered if he would tell the officials about the translations and the English classes he did for the red enemy. This survivor would make it. A few months later, he would throw out the first baseball of the 1968 season with another patriotic American, Richard Nixon, at his side. Then he would plunge into speaking out about the POW experience at military bases, involve himself in right-wing veterans' groups, and gradually retire in North Carolina. The last time I talked with Pitzer, in 1986, he said that while he still hated my politics, he wanted to "live and let live."

DEPARTMENT OF STATE   TELEGRAM   CONFIDENTIAL

NOVEMBER 12, 1967

YOU MAY INFORM HAYDEN HE MAY TRAVEL WITH THREE MEN . . . AS STATE 68070 MADE CLEAR, WE STRONGLY RECOMMEND MILITARY MEDICAL EVACUATION, ESPECIALLY IN LIGHT JOHNSON'S MEDICAL CONDITION. STATE AND DEFENSE CONCUR THAT HAYDEN MAY ACCOMPANY MEN ON MILITARY TRANSPORTATION IF HE SO DESIRES.

SUGGEST YOU AVOID PUBLIC COMMENT ON HAYDEN ROLE AND STICK TO LINE THAT US GRATIFIED AT RELEASE THESE MEN, WHO BEING RETURNED TO THEIR FAMILIES IN US. YOU SHOULD THANK HAYDEN PRIVATELY FOR HIS ROLE IN FACILITATING EVACUATION FROM CAMBODIA.

RUSK

DEPARTMENT OF STATE   **TELEGRAM**   **CONFIDENTIAL**

NOVEMBER 12, 1967

FROM AMEMBASSY BEIRUT TO SECSTATE WASHDC FLASH 3742

I JUST HAD A LONG POST-MIDNIGHT CHAT WITH THOMAS HAYDEN. IT WAS BASICALLY CONSISTENT WITH REPORT OF KARNOW'S CONVERSATION CONTAINED BANGOK'S 5883. HAYDEN VERY TIRED, BUT APPEARED LUCID, AND DETERMINED AS EVER CARRY ON HIS CRUSADE.

GIST OF HIS COMMENTS WAS HE HOPED NO ACTIONS OF PRESS OR USG WOULD BE TAKEN WHICH MIGHT JEOPARDIZE POSSIBILITY FUTURE POW RELEASES. THERE NO ASSURANCE THAT NLF WILL MAKE FUTURE RELEASES BUT HE THINKS THERE IS HOPE. ANY GLOATING OVER POWS CHANGE OF TRAVEL PLANS IN BEIRUT OR INDICATION THIS REPRESENTED A US "VICTORY" WOULD ALMOST CERTAINLY REDUCE FUTURE CHANCES FOR OTHER POWS. SO ALSO WOULD INDICATIONS THAT JACKSON, JOHNSON OR PITZER WERE BEING PUT UNDER RESTRAINT OR OTHERWISE PENALIZED FOR HAVING SOMEHOW "DEALT WITH NLF."

HE WAS ELOQUENT IN DEFENSE THREE MEN. HE SAID THERE WAS NO QUESTION THEIR LOYALTY TO US AND DESIRE TO RETURN.

I EXPLAINED TO HIM AND HE AGREED THAT OUR ACTIONS IN BEIRUT WERE IN NO WAY A PRESSURE PLAY. MEN CONCERNED WERE QUITE FREE TO MAKE THEIR OWN DECISION ON THEIR RETURN TRAVEL. HE SAID HE WAS GRATEFUL (AND SO WERE THE MEN) THAT THEY WERE BEING SENT BACK BY COMMERCIAL AIRCRAFT.

HE ADDED THAT OUR BEHAVIOR IN BEIRUT LET HIM HOPE THAT USG WAS UNDERSTANDING OF DELICACY OF SITUATION.

I spent the night at the embassy, eating a huge meal and arguing about Vietnam with the marine who was assigned as our security. Again, I couldn't sleep and tried to wake myself up with a shower before heading the next morning back to the airport. There everyone looked rested, and we were joined by a silver-haired gentleman carrying a briefcase, who introduced himself as A. W. Beeton, a Federal Aviation Administration official, who had been asked by the State Department to accompany us home. Oh, sure, I thought, assuming that he was from the CIA and wondering what the briefcase actually contained.

The Hayden home in Royal Oak, Michigan, where I grew up, 1946–57.

On the beach with my mother, Gene Hayden, Detroit, 1942.

Below left: My father, Jack Hayden, 1944.

Below right: My first communion, 1950.

Little League, Royal Oak, 1951. I am fourth from left in the front row.

Casey Hayden.

Editor of the Michigan *Daily*, 1960.

Being attacked by Carl Hayes in McComb, Mississippi, 1961.

Paul Potter, SDS president 1964–65, who died of cancer in 1986.

With Casey at a SNCC meeting, 1962.

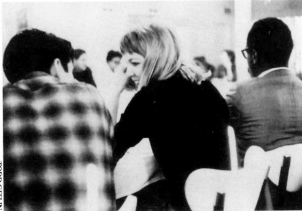

Dick and Mickey Flacks with their son, C. Wright Flacks, and Mickey's mother in Chicago in the late sixties.

Sharon Jeffrey, circa 1962.

Left to right: SDS National Secretary Lee Webb, Richie Rothstein, and Andrea Cousins, 1963.

SDS National Council meeting, Bloomington, Indiana, 1963. I am at the far left, Carl Wittman is fifth from left in the back row, Rennie Davis is at the far right, and next to him from left to right are Robb Burlage, Mickey and Dick Flacks, and Todd Gitlin.

Below left: Knocking on doors, Newark, 1964.

Right (from left to right): Bob Zellner, James Foreman, and Bob Moses at a SNCC meeting, 1964.

Demonstrating for a traffic light with Junius Williams (center, with dark glasses) and the Sampson brothers (right), Newark, 1965.

Jessie Allen, Jerry Jefferson, and Carl Wittman in the NCUP office, 1966.

Interviewing peasants, North Vietnam, December 1965.

Examining U.S. antipersonnel bombs with Vivian Rothstein, Rennie Davis, and Do Xuan Oanh, Hanoi, October 1967.

Unexploded U.S. bombs, Hanoi, October 1967. Left to right: Rennie Davis, Norman Fruchter, Do Xuan Oanh, and Carol McEldowney.

Leaving Cambodia with American POWs, November 1967. I'm helping Edward Johnson aboard the plane. Jim Jackson is center, Dan Pitzer on lower steps.

Democratic National Convention: Chicago police lieutenant spraying Mace at photographer and woman, September 28, 1968.

Helping Professor Frances Fox Piven into the Mathematics Building, Columbia University strike, 1968.

Rally in Lincoln Park, Chicago, 1969.

Last day of the Chicago convention, 1968. Dick Gregory is behind me at the tree.

National Guardsmen confront demonstrators at People's Park, Berkeley, 1969.

Above left: The defendant, 1969.

Above right: Rennie Davis, 1969.

With Leonard Weinglass and Anne Weills.

With Jane, Troy, and Vanessa, late 1974.

Judge Julius Hoffman, 1971.

The eight defendants in the conspiracy trial, Chicago, 1969. Top, left to right: Jerry Rubin, Abbie Hoffman, Tom Hayden, Rennie Davis. Bottom, left to right: Bobby Seale, Lee Weiner, John Froines, David Dellinger.

Campaigning with Cesar Chavez, Los Angeles, 1976.

First meeting with Hubert Humphrey, Democratic National Convention, New York City, 1976

With Governor Edmund G. Brown, Jr., 1978.

Meeting with President Carter, White House 1978.

Primary election, Santa Monica, June 6, 1982, the night of my father's burial in Detroit.

Filming television spot for 1982 Assembly race. Paul Potter and Leni Zeiger's son, Jesse, at far left; my son, Troy, second from left.

Dodger Manager Tommy Lasorda, Troy's self-proclaimed uncle, with us in Dodgertown, 1983.

Fishing with Troy, 1983.

The conspiracy revisited, 1987. Left to right: Abbie Hoffman, Rennie Davis, Bobby Seale, Jerry Rubin, me, Lee Weiner.

With Casey at former SNCC freedom house, Mississippi, 1987.

With Mayor Unita Blackwell in a Mayersville, Mississippi, cotton field, 1987.

At the Vietnam War Memorial with Vietnam Veterans of America leader Bobby Mueller, 1986.

On the floor of the Californi[a] legislature, 1986.

Coaching Troy in the Babe Ruth League, Culver City, 1987.

"Holiday Greetings, 1986."

"Just an old pilot going to visit his sick father," Beeton said of himself. I once again explained to embassy officials that it was very important to future releases, and perhaps to the larger peace process, that we be allowed to travel home together and privately. They merely indicated that they understood.

But having Beeton aboard turned out to be useful. He never bothered us, but in Rome we needed his services. At least ten reporters had purchased tickets for the flight from Rome to Paris, several hiding cameras under their coats until we were airborne. Suddenly they pulled out cameras and notebooks, and started advancing down the aisle toward the rear of the plane, where we had been seated for privacy. "Uh, oh," I thought, but before I could react, Beeton was leaping up from his seat a few rows ahead of us and throwing a pretty good stiff arm for an "old pilot" into the face of the first reporter. With two stewardesses' screaming encouragement, he managed to get everyone seated.

In Paris we were joined by Connie Brown, who had flown from New York with news of the planned reception at Kennedy Airport. Soon we were departing Paris and speeding over the Atlantic. Jackson and I sat in the darkened plane talking almost the whole way while the others slept. I told him that Che Guevara was captured and killed in Bolivia two weeks earlier. He was surprised, impressed, a little upset. "A worthy adversary," he said. "There were a lot of Che Guevaras where I was." He became very silent, and then the lights of America, like a string of pearls in the sky, became visible. Jackson started to softly cry; maybe, I thought for the first time in many years.

While I felt overwhelmed by his feeling of being home, I kept looking for my own meaning in the lights. There below was Newark, where Connie and I lived, and where I watched so many Jimmy Jacksons drafted out of the ghetto to fight and die in Vietnam. And there was New York, where millions of Americans were sitting down to dinner. Were they talking to each other, or to their sons, about this war? I resented their comfort and ignorance. I resented their sending the Jimmy Jacksons to fight this war they knew nothing about. I felt closer to Jimmy Jackson, killer of communists, than to those people down there watching television with their slippers on.

The plane taxied to a halt in a remote corner of Kennedy, and all the other passengers got off ahead of us. Then, more quickly than I expected, a small phalanx of officials boarded and marched toward us. One introduced himself as CIA, another from the Department of Defense, and one was Frank Sieverts from the State Department, an old National Student Association friend, who thanked me and invited me to Washington for a meeting with Averell Harriman the next day. Then, before we could say a proper good-bye, the three former prisoners were whisked away. They looked over their shoulders at me and said, "Thanks," and they were gone. At planeside, they waved quickly to the crowd of photographers, reporters, and well-wishers including Benjamin Spock.

DEPARTMENT OF STATE   TELEGRAM   CONFIDENTIAL

SUBJECT: THREE PRISONERS OF WAR RELEASED BY VIET CONG

THREE MEN ARRIVED NEW YORK IN GOOD SPIRITS AT 1900 EST NOVEMBER 13. THEY SAW PRESS BRIEFLY AT AIRPORT BEFORE PROCEEDING BY MILITARY AIRCRAFT TO WASHINGTON AND FORT BRAGG. JOHNSON WITHSTOOD FLIGHT WELL DESPITE OBVIOUS WEAKNESS FROM DYSENTERY AND MALNUTRITION AND IS NOW IN WALTER REED, WHERE HIS WIFE WILL MEET HIM TOMORROW. JACKSON AND PITZER REMARKABLY WELL IN LIGHT LONG ORDEAL AND ARE EN ROUTE TO BRAGG, WHERE FAMILIES AWAIT THEM. ALL THREE MEN APPEAR FINE MENTALLY, AND DEEPLY RESENT "BRAINWASHING" IMPLICATION STEMMING FROM SAIGON AP STORY.

HAYDEN DISEMBARKED IN NEW YORK, AND, FOLLOWING NORMAL CLEARANCE THROUGH IMMIGRATION AND CUSTOMS, HELD SHORT PRESS CONFERENCE SEPARATE FROM THREE MEN. HE PRIVATELY INDICATED INTEREST IN ATTEMPTING ACHIEVE FURTHER RELEASE. WE PLAN TALK WITH HIM FURTHER SOON.

APPRECIATE GOOD WORK BY BEIRUT AND OTHERS IN HELPING ARRANGE SAFE TRANSIT THESE THREE MEN, WHO GRATEFUL TO ALL CONCERNED.

RUSK

The next day I took the shuttle to Washington, having been away from America for a month. The historic march on the Pentagon had come and gone, but its impact continued. The U.S. government had been forced to call out the army—ten thousand troops altogether, at a cost of over one million dollars—to defend the Pentagon from antiwar protestors. If democracy was becoming a sham, how long could its image be protected by bayonets? According to the secret Pentagon Papers, the October protest was a "serious problem" for the administration:

> While the "politics of confrontation" may be distasteful to the majority of Americans, the sight of thousands of peaceful demonstrators being confronted by troops in battle gear cannot have been reassuring to the country as a whole, nor to the president in particular.

Rennie had been among the major speakers there, holding up his fragmentation bomb and describing it to the throng. His conversion to the antiwar movement leadership was complete, and the idea of repeating the Pentagon scene at the Democratic convention was given new momentum. The Yippies had failed in their announced plans to "levitate" the Pentagon, but in the engaging analysis of Allen Ginsberg, they had lifted its authority and returned it to the people. In the meantime, the Dump Johnson movement headed by Allard Lowenstein was gathering speed in its search for a candidate. A gathering of "new politics" forces had failed to agree on a common presidential strategy at a national meeting during my absence, and Dr. King had rejected launching a symbolic candidacy, but rumors were rife of a potential announcement by an unnamed Democratic senator. Eugene McCarthy announced on November 30.

I quietly had coffee that mid-November morning with Ambassador-at-Large Averell Harriman and thanked him for the government's cooperation in allowing us to make the journey home privately. There was now a way to pass letters between POWs and their families, and a channel had been opened, I suggested, for the possible release of other prisoners in the future. I also noted the importance of trying to secure the release of Jim Rowe, the POW left behind. (He, in fact, escaped two years later and was picked up in a rice paddy by an American helicopter crew.) I later went over my notes with interested State Department experts, indicating the urgency of a new effort at negotiations before the war worsened even further. I detected no change in the official position, however, and went back to Newark dejected.

It was time to think about the next step of protest.

· · ·

I didn't know it at the time, but on his return Jim Jackson had a private conversation with the president of the United States at a reception. After the formalities of thanks and congratulations, Jim told Lyndon Johnson that while coming out of captivity via the Mekong River, he had noticed enormous numbers of enemy barges carrying large-scale military equipment toward the Mekong Delta he was leaving. In his years before and during captivity with the guerrillas, Jim told the president, he had never seen preparations for battle on a scale like this. He believed our government ought to be prepared for something big. Lyndon Johnson told him not to worry; he wasn't going to cut and run; there would be a change for the better in 1968, on the battlefield and at the ballot box. The president put his arm around Jackson's shoulder. Not to worry; good to have you home.

Two decades later, Pitzer remained in the Fort Bragg area. I lost track of Ed Johnson, who, some say, married a German woman and moved to Europe. But Jimmy Jackson and I became fast friends over the years. After Vietnam, he saw clandestine service on another continent, then retired. Occasionally, his buddies from the clandestine soldier-of-fortune world would call to propose lucrative "contracts," but his interest had waned. He married, had two children, settled near Kansas City, and went into the nursing-home business. My family went to a Royals baseball game with the Jacksons in 1986 on his POW's lifetime pass, and we stayed in close touch. Troy loved to hear Jim's survival stories.

During the same period, Jim Jackson traveled to Sacramento in my behalf when Republican legislators tried to oust me from the Assembly for "treason." The emotion that day was intense. Jim and Troy sat behind me on the Assembly floor, as did a group of supportive combat veterans. When a Republican spokesman named Gil Ferguson called Jimmy a "monkey," I thought the next Vietnam War was going to erupt on the Capitol floor. His racial attack on Jimmy's patriotism seemed even more bizarre when I discovered that the most militant Republican superpatriots were fighting a war in Sacramento they had missed in Vietnam. Ferguson, portrayed in some papers as having served two or three tours in Vietnam, was actually there for a few weeks as a "public information officer." Republican leader Pat Nolan was introduced as a "highly decorated combat veteran" to a gathering of medal of honor winners, but in fact he spent only ten days in basic training. Congressman Robert K. Dornan similarly implied that he was a combat pilot in both Korea and Vietnam; in fact, he was a journalist whose most accurate declaration was that "he was fighting this war on television."

Against their charges, I declared, "I am a patriotic American, and no narrow-minded bigot can take that away from me."

Jimmy and I embraced and laughed afterward. It was twenty years since we left Cambodia. The war might never end for some, but we at least had achieved our personal peace with honor.

11. | *Vietnam Reconsidered*

Two decades later, it is still difficult for me to untangle my feelings about Vietnam and how they affected me then. Certain of my beliefs remain as they were before. For instance, I have no doubt today that the Vietnam policy, far from the "noble cause" described by President Reagan, was an American tragedy—moral, political, economic, and military. The rationale for the war—to stop Chinese communist expansion—was mistaken at the time, became absurd when Nixon shook hands with Mao Tse-tung, and turned grotesque as the American government eventually sided with China and the genocidal Khmer Rouge against Hanoi. I also continue to believe that the Vietnamese conducted one of the most remarkable and heroic resistances to foreign intervention in the annals of history. To salute their tenacity and skill is no more "un-American" than recognizing the greatness of Sitting Bull and the Sioux after the tragic battle of Little Big Horn.

I also believe it is crucial to deflate the Rambo mentality of the mid-eighties, which assumed a mythical American invincibility, as well as the many revisionist histories that claim America was defeated at home rather than on the battlefield. When the world's leading industrial power commits 500,000 troops and drops more bomb tonnage than that used by all sides in World War II, and still fails after a decade to crush the soldiers of an undeveloped peasant nation, the result is—in plain English—a defeat. I believe that as a nation we have to develop wisdom from the experience of losing, instead of indulging in romantic escapism about how things might have been. Since it is difficult to accept that 58,000 Americans died for false pride or, worse, for nothing, it is understandable that those responsible have searched for scapegoats. But the blame cannot and should not be shifted; otherwise the folly will be repeated.

I also remain aware of the hypocritical double standards that tend to tarnish American judgments of revolution in other countries. We fought our own American Revolution not only for independence, after all, but also as a nation that permitted slavery, denied rights to women, and overwhelmed its native inhabitants with false promises and brute force. Down through history and to this day, America has—for "strategic" purposes—befriended regimes, from white South Africa to Communist China, with worse human rights records than the Vietnamese regime we still shun.

But I was also very wrong in certain of my judgments: Time has proved me overly romantic about the Vietnamese revolution. I think Paul Berman's 1987 observation in *The New Republic* was correct in saying that my writings at the time "misinterpreted the egalitarian selflessness that arises in any popular war, and in the first moments of any revolution, as an essential quality of Vietnamese communism." The other side of that romanticism was a numbed sensitivity to any anguish or confusion I was causing to U.S. soldiers or to their families—the very people I was trying to save from death and deception. And I displayed a minimal concern over NLF-inflicted atrocities on Vietnamese civilians, as at Hué during the Tet offensive.

As I consulted my old notebooks and tried to re-create the way I saw Vietnam in 1965–67, I was struck by the flatness of the panorama I painted. My tendency was to see everyone as gentle, as lacking hate, and as having insight. In my admiration, I turned the Vietnamese into caricatures of revolutionaries, a people who provided me with an alternative to cynicism. I failed to consider that the people I befriended were those most like myself: Western-educated, liberal, understanding of American society—exceptional bridges between our cultures. So identified was I with their people's suffering and struggle that I lost objectivity; like an intoxicating spell, their mythical stature served to heighten my apocalyptic intuition of the American future.

It was hard not to mythologize them, for they challenged the most fundamental of our conventional assumptions. Lyndon Johnson once called them a "raggedy-ass, little fourth-rate country." Henry Kissinger refused to believe that a "little fourth-rate power like North Vietnam doesn't have a breaking point." I delighted in the Vietnamese frustration of American arrogance and came to view them as representing the human spirit struggling against the most advanced technology ever used in war. Further, they exhibited a reverence for ancestors, for land, for the environment, against a machinery that uprooted, poisoned, and defoliated the natural world on an unprecedented scale. They embodied all the poor and ignored people throughout history who seemed always to lose. Most of all, they represented a revolt against the managerial way of life and the cost-effective mentality that dominated the horizons of our lives. They were a romantic triumph over the modern age itself, over the mind of a Robert McNamara whose "genius for statistics," according to Barbara Tuchman, "left little respect for human variables and no room for the unpredictables."

The Vietnamese were able to inspire and organize an extraordinary resistance. They created a massive human wall that survived bombing, search-and-destroy operations, repression, and torture. But they also were human beings. After forty years of fighting, they were not as capable of coping with peace, economic development, and tolerance of political pluralism. I was blind to the core of authoritarianism that, while crucial to military operations, led to the forced degradation of "re-education" camps, the horrifying exodus of the boat people, and the subordination of "third-force" southerners and even former NLF cadres to the power and ideological interests of Hanoi after the war.

There are mitigating explanations, I know, for each of these sad outcomes. It is no doubt true that the American government bears responsibility for continuing to bleed and besiege Vietnam today. Keeping postwar Hanoi isolated and threatened only hardens their hierarchy's siege mentality and cements further their alliance with the Soviet Union. But I do not accept the familiar axiom of the Left that the flaws of Vietnam, or any such revolution, are principally caused by external pressure.

I think many of Vietnam's postwar problems originated in the nature of Marxism-Leninism itself. It was inevitable that the rigid structure of Hanoi's military apparatus, the rigid visions of its aging leadership, and above all the rigid categories of its Marxism-Leninist thought would be imposed on the South harshly and inefficiently. A theory that promotes a particular class as "revolutionary" (as Marxism does) and invests power in the centralized "vanguard" of that class (as Leninism does) may serve the interests of a clandestine revolutionary movement, but it is bound to promote a self-perpetuating bureaucracy with little enthusiasm for economic and political pluralism, ruled by a permanent elite with interests of its own. That is what happened, I believe, when the Hanoi-based Lao Dong (Communist) party suddenly captured power throughout South Vietnam. The northerners were puritanical, isolated, disciplined revolutionaries accustomed to using their state power for military and economic ends. The southerners, from French colonial times on, were more individualistic, richer in rice, more urban, cosmopolitan, and Westernized. If there had been a negotiated political settlement much earlier—anytime from Geneva in 1954 until perhaps Tet in 1968 when so many NLF cadres were killed—there might have been a neutral South Vietnam without a U.S. military presence, with protections for Saigon's urban middle class and delta farmers, one that would have taken gradual steps toward reunification. But in the brutal course of the war, the fabric of the South was decimated. When the Saigon army collapsed, the North marched into the southern vacuum, and its own leadership and agenda took command.

Nothing is permanent, however, and there were signs in the mid-eighties that the postwar grip of the North may be relaxing. A southern desire for greater self-determination and identity was aggressively reasserting itself. Official attitudes toward returning "boat people" were relaxed. Limited forms of entrepreneurial activity have reappeared, according to longtime observers like Robert Shaplen and reporters for *The Washington Post* and *The New York Times*. The *Post*'s reporter may have overstated the trend in claiming that the "southern part of Vietnam appears poised to 'liberate' the North from economic decline and rigid, doctrinaire thinking." But the *Times* was almost certainly right in portraying the conflict as between "Hanoi's orthodox Marxists" and a "group of more pragmatic and flexible leaders." According to the *Times* report from Ho Chi Minh City, "Communism is not being challenged here. But Vietnamese say openly that the party has lost the public's confidence. If it fails to regain this, 'Who knows what will happen?' an editor said." Even the Communist party leadership has acknowledged "mistakes" in the attempt to impose its blueprint in the 1975–79 period.

In this ongoing struggle for Vietnam's soul, our government has been strangely on the sidelines. After decades of claiming to defend freedom and anticommunism in Vietnam, U.S. policymakers seemed petulant while the most recent drama unfolded. Citing Hanoi's occupation of Cambodia and foot dragging on the question of Americans missing in action, Washington continued rigidly in 1987 to impose a punitive diplomatic and economic embargo. Though the war was over, our government seemed to believe its leverage was stronger than before. A "leading," but unnamed, American official was quoted in *The Washington Post* as expressing a "widespread sentiment among American policymakers and other Vietnam specialists" when he declared that "if the Vietnamese think we're going to rush in there with aid, they're out of touch with reality. Vietnam's intrinsic importance to the United States is zilch, zero."

This was a case of wounded pride taking the place of policy. Vietnam remained one of the poorest, most traumatized nations on earth, and those who did so much to destroy it had, it seems to me, an obligation to help rebuild it.

Whether we do so or not, I hope that with the healing of time, with proper incentives and aid, the resourceful people of Vietnam will successfully insist upon making theirs a more open society.

My retrospective feelings about Cambodia are far more anguished. My lingering image of Phnom Penh is of a charmed oasis in a sea of violence, where one could hear the bombing and shelling of war only sixty miles away over the tinkling of glasses at outdoor restaurants. Now when I can make myself remember at all, the tinkling reminds me of wind chimes in a graveyard.

Elizabeth Becker's *When the War Was Over*, William Shawcross's *Sideshow*, Nayan Chanda's *Brother Enemy*, and the film *The Killing Fields* have revealed the history of the Khmer Rouge holocaust. The U.S. rejection of Prince Sihanouk, the B-52 bombing of the Cambodian borders, the U.S.-ARVN invasion of 1970, and the U.S. support of General Lon Nol (described in a 1972 Pentagon memo as a "vague and unstructured individual" whose "mental facilities deteriorated rapidly after a recent stroke") created the feverish setting in which the Khmer Rouge grew from a small guerrilla faction into a massive, malevolent tumor. I want to believe that if the United States had recognized and supported Prince Sihanouk's neutralism in the sixties, there would have been no such genocide in the seventies. But I was wrong in my analysis of what would happen at the time.

I remember in April 1975 arguing in Washington with Congressman Pete McCloskey, who had just returned from Phnom Penh, about whether military aid to Lon Nol should be terminated. It was similar to a discussion over whether a life-support system should be pulled for a dying patient. Etienne Manac'h, then the French representative in Peking, was trying desperately to arrange for Prince Sihanouk to arrive in Phnom Penh before the Khmer Rouge armed forces took control, but his efforts were too late. In response to an urgent request, Sihanouk sent my office a long cable from Peking listing peace conditions, which I immediately transmitted to dovish U.S. senators and congressmen. In addition, the seemingly gentle, well-educated Ok Sakun, the Khmer Rouge representative I knew in Paris, told friends of mine, "We are ready to welcome everyone but the Lon Nol clique into our front. We are prepared to forget the past." Most important, Sokhom Hing, the leader of Cambodian exile groups in America and a faculty member at the State University of New York at Stony Brook, whom I knew well and respected, was similarly adamant that U.S. military aid should be cut off. But McCloskey, known as an outspoken dove, heatedly insisted that supplemental aid should be sent to help Lon Nol survive the dry-season offensive of the Khmer Rouge, who were by then at the outskirts of Phnom Penh. It would be an ineffectual gesture, I thought, simply an expedient way for Congress (or McCloskey) to avoid blame for the coming debacle. I agreed with *New York Times* columnist Anthony Lewis, who asked, "What future possibility could be more terrible than the reality of what is happening to Cambodia now?"

At the time, I could not imagine that a slaughter even more terrible than B-52 bombing was coming to Cambodia. When the Khmer Rouge troops entered Phnom Penh, they immediately forced the population to march into the rural areas for "purifying" labor. In short order, they put Sihanouk under virtual house arrest and abolished private property, the monarchy, and Buddhism as a "reactionary religion." More U.S. military aid would not have prevented their ultimate savagery. "The Nixon Doctrine in its purest form," as President Nixon called his Cambodia policy, had unleashed the whirlwind.

What continues to batter my sense of morality and judgment is that I could not even imagine that the worst stereotype of revolutionary madness was becoming reality. At the hands of the Khmer Rouge, a systematic genocide took place in Cambodia during the next three years in behalf of the megalomaniac Pol Pot's twisted theory of revolutionary purification. It is too easy to classify what happened as some sort of Oriental "despotism." Although the violence had cultural sources no one understood, what the Khmer Rouge tried to accomplish also had its roots in Stalin's "forced collectivization" and Mao Tse-tung's "Great Leap Forward" of 1968.

The top leadership of the Khmer Rouge was educated at fine French universities in the fifties by members of the French Communist party and later by the Chinese communists. Their Stalinist doctrine was an echo of Frantz Fanon's philosophy of the cleansing function of violence. In practice, it was like *Lord of the Flies*, William Golding's allegorical novel in which a group of young boys become a savage tribe and break the glasses—and soul—of one boy who symbolizes the intellectual. The Khmer Rouge's most-trusted spies and executioners were young people who had been separated from their parents and raised in revolutionary cells since childhood.

Pol Pot and the Khmer Rouge became the Stalins and Hitlers of my lifetime, killing hundreds of thousands of people for being "educated" or "urban," for attracting the paranoid attention of a secret police who saw conspiracies behind every failure of the grand plan to be achieved. Most Western estimates settle on 1.5 million killed between 1975 and 1979 until the Vietnamese invaded and began establishing a new government. Hanoi, motivated by its own power interests, became an occupier itself, but at least the genocide was halted.

Among the apparent survivors was Ok Sakun, rumored dead but produced in 1978 by the Khmer Rouge to impress the journalist Elizabeth Becker. She described him as a "skeleton, if not a ghost" who aimlessly commented on the beauty of flowers, and "was not allowed to talk with us without an interpreter." Later she surmised he had been in a labor camp, under suspicion but a protected protégé of Ieng Sary, the regime's number two man, and permitted to return to diplomatic service outside the country.

Countless Cambodians who flocked back to their country from overseas at the invitation of the Khmer Rouge suffered in labor camps, died, or were executed. My friend Sokhom Hing from Stony Brook, for example, was among the elated ones to return. I had last seen him, I believe, at a huge Kent State rally where Daniel Ellsberg and Jane Fonda spoke in 1972. When he returned to "rebuild" his homeland in 1975, he was sent to a labor camp—to eradicate his "bourgeois" and "intellectual" characteristics. According to fragmentary stories, one day while working in the fields, he took an unauthorized break to reach for a coconut. For this, he was accused of "individualism," and subjected to "criticism, self-criticism." Finally, he was taken to Tuol Sleng, a detention and torture center near Phnom Penh, where he was eventually killed. When the Vietnamese troops liberated Tuol Sleng in 1979, they found thousands of purported "confessions" by those who were killed there. Sokhom Hing's order of execution claimed that he was a spy for both the CIA and the KGB, recruited by American antiwar activists.

None of this persuades me that Nixon and Kissinger were right: to this day I am shocked by the U.S. government's continued diplomatic recognition of and assistance to the Khmer Rouge.

As a result of these experiences, revolution has lost much of its romantic quality for me. I still oppose U.S. military policies in places like Central America, and I believe that violent revolution is inevitable where peaceful reform is blocked. But I feel a numb cynicism at most of the romantic exhortations of Third World revolutionaries. I understand their pain and rage, but my former innocence has yielded to a foreboding that I can do nothing about.

What, then, did anyone gain from the Vietnam experience? It is too early to know. Like myself, many people have difficulty reconsidering former opinions. Certain things, of course, we do know:

- The Vietnamese achieved their inestimable national independence after forty years of war, but they lost over one million of their bravest sons and daughters and inherited a wasteland.

- Laos has disappeared from American consciousness into the peaceful status of a Hanoi protectorate.
- The Cambodians lost perhaps one third of their people and remain occupied by the Vietnamese and threatened by the Khmer Rouge.
- Those responsible for America's Vietnam policies, with few exceptions, carry on their duties in Washington as ever.

If anything truly begins to justify the Vietnam experience, it is that U.S. foreign policy has been altered. The antiwar critique shattered the entrenched Cold War consensus that somehow it was in our interest to support anticommunist dictators, that it was our duty to oppose all such revolutions with force. The post–Vietnam War questioning of that consensus has probably prevented direct American intervention in the quagmires of Central America, Angola, and the Philippines in the past decade. Foreign policy in America has been opened to public review and challenge—in a word, *democratized*—as never before.

However, a new foreign policy consensus remains to be formulated. "No more Vietnams" is a healthy reaction to the past, but not a clear policy blueprint for the future. Perhaps we are coming to a time when a new U.S. consensus can be projected in foreign affairs; if so, it will have to be a democratic consensus, not an elite one.

That is perhaps the key legacy of Vietnam: the new and hard-won potential of Americans to think twice before accepting our leaders' words.

CHICAGO

Part Five

12. The Violence of Spring: 1968

As 1968 began, I felt I was living on the knife edge of history. It did, of course, turn out to be a year of extraordinary turmoil, a climax to events that had begun five years earlier with the assassination of President Kennedy, when for the first time, someone central to our national life was brutally and publicly eliminated. The killing of leaders became legitimized. A nation turned numb to violence, whether in Mississippi or Vietnam. The places I lived in those times—Atlanta, Newark, then Chicago—cemented the status quo with coercion and violence. The American immune system was breaking down: The nation had been immune to presidential death for a century; the government had been immune to disruption; the armed forces to defeat. But now, in 1968, a massive and continuous system malfunction occurred. The power elite, which C. Wright Mills had portrayed as invincible, was under siege on all sides. The Tet offensive, student uprisings, Lyndon Johnson's resignation, and the killings of Martin Luther King and Robert Kennedy led to a meltdown of the system's core. The breakdown happened not only in Chicago, not only in America; in some mysterious way, it was a global phenomenon.

Perhaps history is random and the search for logical meaning a fruitless illusion. But why did so many forces flow toward a climax in this one particular year, the watershed year for a generation? Surely there has been no other year quite like it in American history. Like a Greek drama, it started with legendary events, then raised hopes, only to end by immersing innocence in tragedy—an experience, for those who went through it all, felt to this day in failed dreams, enduring hurts, unmet yearnings.

FBI MEMORANDUM

FROM: DIRECTOR

THOMAS EMMETT HAYDEN

The Bureau feels that to insure full and effective coverage of Hayden and other Key Activists such as Dellinger and the activities they are engaged in, consideration should be given to placing a technical surveillance on ███████.* New York is therefore authorized to conduct a survey to determine the feasibility for such a surveillance, provided full security is assured.

I began that year still living in Newark but planning to move to Chicago, where, with Rennie Davis, I would serve as co-director of the projected protests at the Democratic National Convention.

Not only was Chicago the tough heartland of America, it was, incidentally, the national headquarters of SDS. The organization had moved there to be in Middle America. SDS leaders like Rennie, Todd Gitlin, Nanci Hollander, Leni Zeiger, and Casey (who had left SNCC in 1966) had worked in the ERAP project among poor whites on Chicago's Northside. Sharon Jeffrey was directing the Woodlawn Organization, a powerful neighborhood organization, and Richie and Vivian Rothstein had migrated to a middle-class suburb, where they were organizing around school issues. Paul Booth, as ever, was working to reform the Democratic party. Dick Flacks and Bob Ross were budding sociologists at the University of Chicago, while actively building the New University Conference (NUC), which they saw as an academic wing of the movement.

Chicago under Mayor Richard Daley was a difficult city to reform in any way. Backed by rabidly conservative editorials in the *Chicago Tribune,* the Daley machine treated critics as mortal enemies and employed all forms of harassment against them. Martin Luther King's 1966 struggle to break down the city's

---

*Material deleted by the FBI.

rigid segregation, including the march through Cicero and rallies of fifty thousand at Soldier's Field, had failed, and the black leader was denounced by Daley for "creating trouble in every city he visited." The ERAP project was raided and disrupted by the police's "Red Squad," who planted drugs and hypodermic needles on the premises.

In response to the riots after King's murder, the *Chicago Tribune* declared, "Here in Chicago we are not dealing with the colored population but with a minority of criminal scum" and urged Daley not to behave like the "spineless and indecisive mayors who muffed early riot control" in Newark and Los Angeles. Three days later, on April 10, the *Tribune* accused Rennie of being the conspiratorial instigator of a plan to turn a King peace memorial service into a violent uprising, stating, "It is an outrage that this country has to deal with a second front at home against rioters and beatniks when the fighting men are risking death overseas." It was later established that *Tribune* writers cooperated with the FBI in preparing their coverage of SDS.

Nevertheless, activists in Chicago and around the country were expectantly discussing a mass action in Daley's town. The previous year's escalating protests against the draft in Oakland, at the Pentagon, and at New York's Whitehall Induction Center had triggered a magnetic interest in the process of confrontation, in which flower children faced soldiers, shadowy street people threw back tear-gas canisters at police, and bayonets were used to guard democracy. For these militants, the force of logic having failed, the logic of force was fast becoming the only alternative. As Mario Savio, a 1964 Mississippi veteran and the articulate leader of the free-speech movement at Berkeley, had declared two years before:

> There is a time when the operation of the machine becomes so odious, makes you so sick at heart, that you can't take part: you can't even tacitly take part, and you've got to put your bodies upon the gears and upon the wheels, upon the levers, upon all the apparatus and you've got to make it stop. And you've got to indicate to the people who run it, to the people who own it, that unless you're free, the machines will be prevented from working at all.

There was also the view that this was the stuff of fantasy, that the only result of such romantic militance would be the further alienation of Middle America and, quite possibly, repression. This reaction came not only from the older leftist peace groups, but more potently from those committing themselves to working within the political system to dump Johnson. Senator Eugene McCarthy had announced his antiwar presidential campaign on November 30, 1967, and already thousands of liberal young people were signing on. A frequently bitter debate was triggered among radicals and antiwar activists over whether to be "clean for Gene." After the experiences of Mississippi in 1964 and the massive escalation of Vietnam under a Democratic administration, liberalism itself had become suspicious, if not the enemy itself. Therefore, when this "new" liberalism arose in reaction to the crisis of the times, it was difficult for many of us in the New Left to embrace it as our salvation.

Rennie and I decided to make the most of all these dissident forces. Those with a more radical reading of the American system would "confront the warmakers" in Chicago with a huge demonstration, forcing the Democrats to choose between ending the war and alienating key electoral constituencies. This very confrontation would enhance the arguments of reformers within the party, I predicted, while also keeping the antiwar movement independent and in the streets. I could identify with the idealism and commitment of the McCarthy workers who slept on floors across the country, although I thought Robert Kennedy would be a better candidate. I was impressed with the seriousness of their planning. However, if they succeeded against the top-down delegate selection rules, it would shock me. I drove up to a Yale seminar given by an old friend, Geoff Cowan, who had been active in McComb in 1964 and during the Mississippi FDP summer challenge at the Democratic convention. Geoff was angered at the Democratic party rules that allowed convention delegates to be controlled by party bosses—many of them even before the 1968 primaries began. He was prepared to carry a challenge all the way to the Chicago convention, demanding a share of delegates in proportion to a candidate's vote in primaries. If they failed, as I expected, they would still be a formidable factor in the antiwar movement and at least would have forged a power base for dissent within the Democratic party.

I felt that our movement's long debate over the nature of American power, started by C. Wright Mills and continued at

Port Huron, might be resolved in this election year. Was there a stable power elite above even the president? Could an incumbent president be defeated by an electoral movement? Could the United States be forced to leave Vietnam? Would the elite suspend the democratic process in favor of repression if their interests were too deeply threatened? Or could democracy—not just democracy at the ballot box but democracy in the streets—be an effective antidote to the conspiracies of the state? We would see, through the events of history rather than academic speculation.

At the start of the year, the Vietnamese launched their Tet offensive and began imprinting a new legend on our consciousness. When the fires of Tet subsided two months later, the defenders of U.S. policy climbed out of their public relations bunkers to make the Orwellian claim that the real result was a military defeat for North Vietnam and the NLF, but a psychological setback for the United States because of demoralizing media coverage.

Against these Pentagon spokesmen, who seemed like morticians with their body-count mentality, the Vietnamese seemed to me like supermen. They were ruthless, as in the Tet killings of civilians in Hué, but I was awed by their fearless survival under the American military pounding. Their Tet offensive did not overthrow the Saigon government, but it destroyed the U.S. pacification program and shattered any Pentagon illusions about a "light at the end of the tunnel." As the U.S. military turned into a wounded Cyclops stumbling through the rice paddies, fighting to retain beseiged outposts like Khe Sanh, the war was becoming what one historian called the "peak folly of an older generation." The weekly American death toll rose to 542, an intolerable high; the generals requested 206,000 more troops, an unacceptable burden; the White House proposed a $32 billion Vietnam budget for 1968–69, an unacceptable cost. The turning point had been reached. Change was in the air.

I spoke to Rennie in Chicago daily during the Tet offensive. He was planning to set up an office for the convention actions which were six months away.

"Hey, man, is the war over?"

"I don't think so, but this doesn't help Johnson a whole lot, does it? Do you think Kennedy will get in now?"

"I don't know, but I bet he wishes he had. Anyway, what the hell can we plan on? If there's an escalation by Johnson, forget permits and get ready to die in riots at the convention. If there is a de-escalation and peace talks, maybe we lose steam and should reconsider the whole thing."

"You ready out there?"

"Yeah, I'm gettin' my Ho Chi Minh sandals on."

"I'm coming by sampan over Lake Michigan."

"Did you hear the papers said the Yippies will put LSD in the water supply?"

"Oh, great."

"You got it, man. Let's meet. I think we can still convince them that we can control it. I'm talking to the Justice Department about mediating with Daley and getting the permits for us."

After what they considered the Pentagon humiliation of the previous October, the administration was in no mood to accommodate still another demonstration at the convention. In fact, they appeared to be moving in the other direction, toward rigidity and even repression. Shortly after the Pentagon confrontation, the government indicted the symbol of our "permissive" generation, Dr. Benjamin Spock, along with Yale Chaplain William Sloan Coffin and others, on charges of conspiracy to promote draft resistance. Also indicted were the Oakland Seven, who led Stop the Draft Week. And unknown to us, a "domestic war room" was created in the Pentagon, coordinating the efforts of one thousand military intelligence agents gathering data and photographs on eighteen thousand citizens. Additionally, the FBI already had some seven thousand operatives at work on the perceived threat of the New Left.

Rennie and I met in New York with lawyers in late January to plan our effort to obtain Chicago permits for both a giant antiwar march and the Festival of Life visualized by the Yippies. We needed a group of legal volunteers on the streets in Chicago to obtain bail for those arrested. One of the law students who attended the meeting was Bernardine Dohrn, a bright, stunning, aggressive representative of the new forces flowing into SDS. Exhilarated by the Pentagon demonstration, she and other new SDS leaders had decided on a springtime offensive called

Ten Days That Shook the World, after John Reed's book on the Russian Revolution. While details were vague, the ambitious notion was that "actions" against the war and racism would take place on campuses across the country, attempting to resist and disrupt all ties to the military. But we were having a difficult time convincing SDS that our intentions for Chicago should be supported. Rennie and I were becoming seen as old guard, or perhaps older sibling rivals, of the new leadership, who classified us as politically "reformist," if not already "bourgeois."

It is true that we were not comfortable with the development of abstract rhetoric and fierce factionalism in the organization, which once had been like a family. Having abandoned Port Huron, the official SDS leaders now made such pronouncements as "To respect and operate within the realm of bourgeois civil liberties is to remain enslaved," or "The problem with participatory democracy is its basic inadequacy as a style of work for a serious radical organization." I was losing credibility with the organization, as was Rennie, although he remained far more in the pragmatic mainstream than I did. I will never forget one particularly arrogant SDS national secretary, Michael Klonsky, the brash and unreconstructed son of a doctrinaire Marxist, condemning Rennie and me for being "New Left," by which he meant that the entire period 1960–68 had been a wasted middle-class detour for SDS. Now, he asserted, the organization was on track, embracing doctrinaire Marxism. As it turned out, the Klonskys, deluded into imagining themselves the next Lenins, were preparing the graveyard not of capitalism but of SDS. Klonsky subsequently formed something called the Revolutionary Communist Party, which sang the praises and organized tours of Khmer Rouge Cambodia.

We thought there still was a margin of opportunity for reforming America. Since late 1967, for example, Martin Luther King and SCLC had been trying to fashion a massive, nonviolent alternative to impending violent confrontations in black communities like Chicago. While rejecting the use of rocks, bottles, and guns from a moral and practical standpoint, King was struggling also to define another choice aside from the Black Power cry that was sweeping the ghettos. To save the worsening situation and prevent his personal irrelevance, King was talking of a "revolution of values," a "redistribution of power," and a last, desperate form of nonviolent civil disobedience. His idea, announced on December 4, 1967, drawn from the common experience of civil rights and ERAP projects, was for a Poor People's Campaign in the nation's capitol, starting in the late spring.

"I am personally the victim of deferred dreams, of blasted hopes," he said in an anguished Christmas sermon at his Eben-ezer Baptist Church. Later biographies portray him in this pe-riod as struggling with a melancholy fatalism. "Maybe we just have to admit," he confided privately to his close friend Ralph Abernathy, "that the day of violence is here. . . . The nation won't listen to our voice; maybe it'll heed the voice of violence. Maybe we just have to give up and let violence take its course." On a personal level, rather than believing any longer in saints, he subscribed to the notion of "a schizophrenic in all of us . . . a Dr. Jekyll and Mr. Hyde." In public he never gave in to his secret despair. Instead he seemed to respond with calls for a heightened but steadfastly nonviolent response. Now there had to be a response to the "international emergency which involves the poor, the dispossessed, and the exploited of the whole world."

In the legal tyranny of the South, marches had been forms of rebellion in themselves; but after his bitter Chicago experience of 1966, King felt that marches couldn't solve the crisis of the northern cities.

King's plan, like that of the Bonus Marchers who brought their unemployment crisis to Washington in 1932, was to gradu-ally besiege the nation's capital with an irresistible moral and political force of poor people: black, white, Hispanic, native American. A mule train would lead a long march of the poor to Washington, where they would camp in parks and confront decision makers with demands for ending their miseries. Among the most creative of the desperation protests suggested by King's aide Andrew Young was flooding Walter Reed Hospi-tal, where elected officials were entitled to free health care, with hundreds of sick Americans demanding similar care for them-selves.

Although King's advisers were as divided over the Poor Peo-ple's Campaign as antiwar activists were over our Chicago plans, Rennie and I both were excited about a potential meshing of the protests. The Kerner Report on Civil Disorders, commis-sioned by President Johnson immediately after Newark, had described the United States as "moving towards two societies, one black, one white—separate and unequal." The commission was recommending a thirty-billion-dollar program to create two million jobs, better schools, and more housing—exactly the annual cost of the Vietnam War. Perhaps we could work with Dr. King's campaign in the summer, with the mule train heading for Chicago at the time of the convention. Rennie called Abernathy and received an immediate favorable response. We were elated; it was all coming together now.

TO: SAC, Albany   3/4/68

FROM: Director, FBI   PERSONAL ATTENTION

GOALS:

1. Prevent the coalition of black nationalist groups . . . An effective coalition of black nationalist groups might be the first step toward a real "Mau Mau" in America, the beginning of a true black revolution.
2. Prevent the rise of a "messiah" who could unify, and electrify, the militant black nationalist movement. ▇▇▇▇* might have been such a messiah; he is the martyr of the movement today . . . ▇▇▇▇ could be a very real contender for this position should he abandon his "obedience" to "white, liberal doctrines" (nonviolence) and embrace black nationalism. ▇▇▇▇ has the necessary charisma to be a real threat in this way.
3. Prevent violence on the part of black nationalist groups. . . . Through counter-intelligence, it should be possible to pinpoint potential troublemakers and neutralize them before they exercise their potential for violence.
4. Prevent militant black nationalist groups and leaders from gaining respectability, by discrediting them . . .

The next uplifting news came from the McCarthy presidential effort. Fueled by post-Tet public discontent, the once-quixotic crusade caught on in New Hampshire, where an unheard-of ten thousand students were going door to door in the heavy snows. Before Tet, the president dominated McCarthy in national polls by 63 to 18 percent. In March, they were virtually even, and on primary day, March 12, McCarthy received a stunning 42.2 percent of the votes from conservative and traditional New Hampshirites.

With some excitement now, Rennie and I put the finishing

*Material deleted by the FBI.

touches on an outline of our plans for Chicago, presenting it to a cross section of about two hundred peace, civil rights, and radical activists who assembled outside of Chicago for the weekend of March 22–24. We were still facing an uphill effort in getting an endorsement for our project. We envisioned three days of decentralized protests across Chicago leading to a vast "funeral march" to the International Amphitheater on the last night of the convention, which we expected to end in Johnson's renomination. But because of our sympathies with the confrontation at the Pentagon, many traditional pacifists worried that we wanted to initiate violence. Our answer was that we *expected* violence, from the police and federal authorities, but we would not initiate it ourselves. Committing ourselves more formally to nonviolence, we wrote that while the demonstration would be "clogging the streets of Chicago with people demanding peace, justice, and self-determination for all people," the protest campaign "should not plan violence and disruption against the Democratic National Convention. It should be nonviolent and legal."

This assurance, however, did not speak to the larger criticism hurled at the project from everyone suspicious of electoral politics. With McCarthy's upset showing in New Hampshire, it was widely assumed that any demonstrations in Chicago would turn into rallies for the Minnesota senator. Though Geoff Cowan, the planner of the challenge to the Humphrey delegates, was there to describe his "open-convention" strategy, most of the people present were distinctly uninterested in electoral politics. They feared that instead of being on the cutting edge of change, the movement would be co-opted into liberal politics. Even worse, those in SDS and many others argued that lurking just behind Eugene McCarthy was the far more serious possibility of a Robert Kennedy candidacy. Wasn't the Chicago protest plan just a "stalking horse" for the Kennedy interests, they wanted to know? A widely quoted *Ramparts* article by Robert Scheer warned that Kennedy "could easily co-opt prevailing dissent without delivering to it . . . providing the illusion of dissent without its substance."

"Look," I argued, "whatever happens in the primaries, there will be a need for the peace movement to be at the convention to pressure the Democrats." I angrily announced at another point that we were not going to let this consultative meeting exercise a veto power over the idea of going to Chicago. Many people were enraged by this declaration. Staughton Lynd, who was now active in an ERAP-type project among industrial workers, thought I was risking the movement's resources on a "one-shot" national fantasy. "You're leading this movement either into co-option by the Kennedy forces or into repression and violence," another SDS leader charged. With that tone, the meeting ground to its inconclusive end.

Few could understand how I could seem at the same time to support North Vietnam, plot disruptive confrontations, and work cooperatively with such figures as Averell Harriman and Robert Kennedy. In many minds I was some kind of wandering adventurer, a more radical version of Allard Lowenstein, showing up at scenes of the crisis with a personal solution for everything. In fact, I later learned that the FBI actively planted rumors that I was on the U.S. government payroll.

A feature writer [should] be given the task of writing up a story pointing out the coincidences of Hayden's visits to certain cities and news stories emanating from Washington, DC, pointing to Hayden as the source. The connection may be spotlighted including certain sidelights of confidential bits of information which may only be known to Hayden or a Bureau source. It is realized that the above will take time, but in order for the plan to be effective, it must have a solid basis and a continued investment.

In fact, I had come to a simple, though high-risk, theory of ending the war: The Vietnamese would have to frustrate the U.S. military effort at a painful cost of lives on all sides; the antiwar movement would have to impose a serious cost, a breakdown between the generations, on those intent on continuing the war. The resulting polarization would gradually bring a more rational alternative leadership into being on the national level. The antiwar movement would continue applying pressure, even on this more rational leadership, until the war ended. If that was not possible, I saw an unending spread of malignant strife. The "rational alternative" to the war and tumult, in the back of my mind, was Robert Kennedy.

My feelings about Robert Kennedy are difficult to re-create. In more recent years, I have become personal friends with his wife and children, which only intensifies the importance of his loss to me. Though I knew him rather briefly, I was perhaps the one New Left leader who knew him at all. My feelings were guarded, for our relationship was a cause of intense suspicion in my circles. And yet, in that year of turmoil, I found that the only intriguing politician in America was the younger brother of John F. Kennedy. Perhaps it was the qualities we happened to share: Irish, Catholic, competitive, athletic, and radical and existential temperaments. Perhaps I thought that he alone, from personal experience, could understand the vertigo and pain that followed the hope of the early sixties.

During that long winter, Robert Kennedy, like Martin Luther King, had been wondering if history was passing him by. Since the mid-sixties, he had turned to reading Camus for philosophical answers, traveled to South Africa to stir the students there, and increasingly adopted an ERAP-like identification with the poor on the fringes of society. In a 1967 book, he wrote of youth's disenchantment with liberal institutions and praised our attachment to the poor of Appalachia, the farm workers of California, and the sharecroppers of the Mississippi Delta. He told my friend Jack Newfield, who wrote a moving book about him, that in another life he would have been a "juvenile delinquent or a revolutionary." He invoked the phrase "participatory democracy" and, in perhaps his most remarkable speech, one which startles me now in its resemblance to Port Huron, he declared:

> We will find neither national purpose nor personal satisfaction in a mere continuation of economic progress, in an endless amassing of worldly goods. We cannot measure national spirit by the Dow-Jones Average, nor national achievement by the gross national product. For the gross national product includes air pollution and advertising for cigarettes, and ambulances to clear our highways of carnage. It counts special locks for our doors, and jails for the people who break them. The gross national product includes the destruction of the redwoods, and the death of Lake Superior. It grows with the production of napalm and missiles and nuclear warheads. . . . It includes Whitman's rifle and Speck's knife, and the broadcasting of television programs which glorify violence to sell goods to our children.
>
> And if the gross national product includes all this, there is much that it does not comprehend. It does not allow for the health of

our families, the quality of their education or the joy of their play. It is indifferent to the decency of our factories and the safety of our streets alike. It does not include the beauty of our poetry or the strength of our marriages, the intelligence of our public debate or the integrity of public officials . . . the gross national product measures neither our wit nor our courage, neither our wisdom nor our learning, neither our compassion or our devotion to our country. It measures everything, in short, except that which makes life worthwhile; and it can tell us everything about America—except whether we are proud to be Americans.

Robert Kennedy remained deeply, almost inexplicably unresolved about Vietnam and the presidency as the plague years of Lyndon Johnson wore on and the public sought a progressive national leader. Not until after the SDS march in 1965 did he speak out on the war as a senator, calling for negotiations between Saigon and the NLF, but voting for the war appropriation. Several months later, on November 5, he revealed the more unconventional side of his character, approving of students who were preparing to send blood to North Vietnamese victims of American bombing, an endorsement which Barry Goldwater labeled treasonous. The following February, after the Fulbright hearings surfaced new criticism of the war, he called for "power sharing" in South Vietnam and was met with a storm of criticism from administration officials, led by Vice President Humphrey. He did not speak out again for over a year, until well into 1967.

Robert Kennedy's reticence in reappraising Vietnam stemmed from his early, enthusiastic support of the policy of the Kennedy administration. Now he would have to repudiate his brother's policy and his past role in making it. Moreover, he was surrounded by many friends and advisers from that era, including Averell Harriman, Theodore Sorenson, Robert McNamara, and his brother Teddy Kennedy, who, according to Newfield's account, pleaded with him not to oppose the policy. When Staughton Lynd and I met with Robert Kennedy in mid-February 1967, it was evident that he was rethinking his Vietnam policy, but still cautiously.

We did not even try to convince him of immediate withdrawal, which we considered morally right but politically unthinkable. Instead, while I listened, Staughton made an almost lawyerly, historical presentation of the history of the conflict, how the Vietminh were denied the 1956 national elections promised by Geneva, how a diplomatic process could start with a bombing halt, and how a new coalition could be formed in South Vietnam.

Kennedy didn't disagree, but added about Geneva, "You know, communists don't hold free elections, they rig them."

"Let's talk about Mississippi or Chicago elections, or Johnson's rigging of next year's primaries," I interjected, challenging him. With a laugh, Kennedy nodded.

"Our own histories show that Ho Chi Minh would have won overwhelmingly," I added. "That was the problem."

Kennedy reiterated his feeling that it was more complicated, and his worry that Thailand could be the next domino. He didn't use the term *domino*, as I recall, but he seemed to believe in the Eisenhower-era theory.

The long conversation ended amicably, with our urging him to take more of a leadership role against the war. As twilight came, he asked us to dinner with Arthur Schlesinger and John Kenneth Galbraith. We politely declined and descended the elevator from his Riverside Drive apartment, wondering what he would finally decide to do.

On March 2, and after many more consultations, he gave a six-thousand-word speech on the floor of the Senate opposing the war and taking responsibility for his part in it. It was still relatively cautious, but as Newfield wrote, "It emancipated Kennedy psychologically and intellectually about Vietnam. Having confessed guilt for his past, and having heeded not the cautious counsel of his friends but the prompting of his passions, he was a freer man."

A similar Hamlet-like vacillation was apparent in Kennedy's approach to running for the presidency, allowing many people like myself, especially antiwar activists, to assume that he was showing timidity, expediency, and opportunism as 1967 went on. I remained a qualified Kennedy defender, however, drawing mistrust from friends and antiwar activists, mistrust so deep-seated at times that it was fruitless to speak my mind. Critics said I had been seduced by personal access to Kennedy and his aides. It is difficult to recall who was more hostile, the SDS radicals who hated anything to do with electoral politics or the Dump Johnson activists who became McCarthy supporters and who perceived in Kennedy the ambition that was the antithesis of their presumed purity. My choice was complex: to waste energy fighting everybody—the McCarthy people for their double standards and the SDS people for reducing everyone to meaningless opportunists—or, with Rennie, to continue focusing on Chicago and trying to get along with all the forces heading there.

Kennedy, listening to his more pragmatic advisers rather than the Jack Newfields of the world, made a final decision not to run, ironically, just as the Tet offensive was about to sweep away all conventional assumptions. At about the same time, he received an impassioned letter from a friend of Newfield's and mine, Pete Hamill, another *Village Voice* writer, protesting Kennedy's decision in terms that would haunt Bobby for weeks. Hamill went to the Kennedy gut, writing that his hope for the presidential campaign was

> gone, along with other [hopes] that have vanished in the last four years. . . . I suspect that all nations have their historical moment, some moment when it all seems to have been put together . . . our moment was 1960–63. I don't think it's nostalgia working or romanticism. I think most Americans feel that way now . . .
>
> I wanted to say that the fight you might make would be the fight of honor. . . . I wanted to say that you should run because if you won, the country might be saved. . . . I say that if you don't run [the Democratic party] will end up nationally, the way it has in New York, a party filled with decrepit old bastards like Abe Beame, and young hustlers with blue hair, trying to get their hands on highway contracts.
>
> I wanted to remind you that in Watts I didn't see pictures of Malcolm X or Ron Karenga on the walls. I saw pictures of JFK. . . . I don't think we can afford five summers of blood. I do know this: if a 15 year old kid is given a choice between Rap Brown and RFK, he *might* choose the way of sanity. . . . Give that same kid a choice between Rap Brown and LBJ, and he'll probably reach for his revolver.

According to Newfield, Kennedy carried the Hamill letter around with him as he continued to ponder his fate. As McCarthy's prospects in New Hampshire started to improve dramatically, Kennedy reopened once again the internal discussion among aides about running, and when McCarthy did well in New Hampshire, it was decided. Three days later, Robert Kennedy announced for the presidency. It was determined at that moment that the anti-Johnson challenge among Democrats would be both widened, since Kennedy brought many regular Democrats to his side, and bitterly divided, since most of the McCarthy workers resented the decision openly and angrily. And the dire fear of the SDS radicals was coming true: The system might work.

Now the pace of history would not abate. As in a chapter from Mills's *Power Elite*, the president summoned an advisory group, loosely known as the "wise men," to the White House. Most of them were members of the Council on Foreign Relations, major corporate attorneys who had served in high government positions over many years: Dean Acheson, George Ball, McGeorge Bundy, Arthur Dean, Douglas Dillon, Abe Fortas, Arthur Goldberg, Henry Cabot Lodge, John Jay McCloy, Robert Murphy, Cyrus Vance, and two generals, Omar Bradley and Matthew Ridgway. The wise men, at the direction of Secretary of Defense Clark Clifford, were asked to make a several-day private review of the Vietnam crisis and give the president their counsel. This they did and, according to the Pentagon Papers, convinced themselves that the U.S. policy had become completely counterproductive, that the war was a military failure, and that divisions in American society had become dangerously deep. Said Cyrus Vance, "We were weighing not only what was happening in Vietnam, but the social and political effects in the United States, the impact on the U.S. economy, the attitude of other nations. The divisiveness in the country was growing with such acuteness that it was threatening to tear the United States apart." Interestingly, they did not discuss the morality of the policies, only their overall cost-benefit ratios. On March 19, they had an elegant social luncheon with Lyndon Johnson, and when it was over, delivered their verdict: Forget about seeking a battlefield solution to the problem and instead intensify efforts to seek a political solution at the negotiating table. The president was "greatly surprised at their conclusions."

Eleven days later, on Sunday, March 31, President Johnson went on television to offer a partial bombing halt over North Vietnam, appoint Averell Harriman to seek talks with the enemy, and withdraw himself from the 1968 presidential campaign.

I was sitting on a rug in a friend's living room in Newark.

When Johnson read his withdrawal statement, I did a backward somersault from a sitting position.

On April 3, the first steps toward diplomatic talks between the United States and North Vietnam were announced. I sent a long telegram to Hanoi supporting their decision to come to the conference table and encouraging another release of POWs as a gesture of goodwill. (In February, Dave Dellinger and I had coordinated a second POW release, sending Father Daniel Berrigan and historian Howard Zinn to Hanoi to return with three U.S. pilots.) I made an appointment to see Harriman in Washington, as well as Sargent Shriver, former Peace Corps director, who was appointed ambassador to France, where the talks would take place.

The following day in Memphis, a 30.06 bullet killed Martin Luther King while he was preparing to go to dinner with friends during an intense period of demonstrations for the city's striking garbage collectors.

I traveled early the next morning to Nashville, where I was to speak at Fisk University on a stage whose backdrop was a gigantic American flag. All I remember afterward was getting drunk with Julian Bond, an old friend from what now seemed to be a previous life. An Atlanta SNCC founder in 1960, Bond was now a Georgia state senator. We listened to the sirens and watched the military vehicles that patrolled angry Nashville. Stokely Carmichael, friends later told me, went berserk in those hours on the streets of Washington, waving a pistol and telling blacks to arm themselves. Bernardine Dohrn, weeping openly, joined other New York City activists in trashing store windows aimlessly in Times Square. I talked on the phone with Rennie in Chicago, where fires were being set across the city. Mayor Daley shortly issued an infamous order that his police officers should "shoot to kill" arsonists and "shoot to maim" looters.

Everything was without precedent as urban America blew up. There were outbreaks of black violence in over seventy-five cities and more than seventy thousand troops were called in to reimpose order. Forty-six people were killed, nearly all of them black, twenty-five hundred were injured, twenty-eight thousand were jailed, and fifty million dollars' worth of property damage occurred. In response to King's death, Congress finally passed a fair housing law as a tribute. Attached to it was a little-noticed "anti-riot" amendment by Senator Strom Thurmond, making it a felony to travel between states with the "intent" of causing a "riot."

The first and only persons to be indicted under this amendment would be the Chicago Eight, of which I was to be one.

As I did after John Kennedy's death, for two days after King's murder, I did little or nothing but stare at television, watching repeated footage of King's 1963 "I have a dream" oration and his "I may not see the Promised Land" speech of only a few nights before. They were interspersed with the scene of Bobby Kennedy breaking the terrible news to poor blacks during an Indiana campaign stop, quoting them the haunting passage from Aeschylus that he said consoled him after his brother's death:

> "In our sleep, pain which cannot forget falls drop by drop upon the heart until, in our own despair, against our will, comes wisdom through the awful grace of God." . . . Let us dedicate ourselves to what the Greeks wrote so many years ago: "To tame the savageness of man and make gentle the life of this world."

I was torn apart with a grief which has not healed to this day. I went to Washington, while the city still burned, to keep my appointment with Harriman. Outside the windows of Harriman's office, one could see flames and smoke shooting up over the nation's capital and fire trucks and squad cars rushing everywhere. The secretaries were extremely tense, talking on the phones to their husbands and children about routes out of the city. Harriman, some seventy-seven years old, was about to leave for Paris, and the exploratory peace talks were on his mind. I briefed him as clearly as I could with the drama of urban rage flaring up behind his silver hair, describing my understanding of what the other side would be demanding at the talks, arguing that it was not yet too late for a political solution in South Vietnam, even with Johnson sitting as a lame-duck president. I also indicated that I would urge the North Vietnamese to release more American POWs. All I got from Harriman was a sense of optimism because talks were opening, as well as an interest in any possibilities of another prisoner release.

My time with Sargent Shriver was more productive, although rushed. He was leaving by limousine for his large home in the capital's suburbs and took me along so that we could discuss his Paris role. Sitting on the small seat across from him in the back of the limo, I was able to tell him in detail what Etienne Manac'h in the French foreign ministry had told me of the Vietnamese approach to settlement and give him the names of some French journalists and historians he might see privately in Paris. He seemed actively interested in playing whatever role he might while in Paris during the talks, I presumed as an intermediary for his brother-in-law, Robert Kennedy. I was pleased with his frankness, though I felt distinctly uncomfortable riding in a limousine while out the back window I could continue to watch the blaze above the skyline. "The last people who did this to us were the British," Shriver said with a laugh, referring to the city's burning during the War of 1812. When we finally reached his home, he thanked me and dispatched his driver to take me to the airport.

Dr. King's funeral was April 9, about the time I began ending my four years in Newark and started getting ready for Chicago. Still traumatized by the upheaval of the previous July and now stunned by the death of King, progressive momentum in Newark was at a standstill. Blacks would regroup, on their own, in the quest for political power. The work of NCUP still would continue through the actions of many stalwart people, but it was clearly understood that an era was over, that the crisis of war (whether abroad or at home, it was hard to distinguish) would have to be resolved before the possibility of effective community organizing could begin again. Several of my closest friends in Newark committed themselves to going to Chicago later in the summer.

I was disconnecting from my personal life. Connie and I had come together at a particular moment; now the moment was over. The sixties were like that, relationships existing in parentheses, floating without a past or future. Now adrift personally, I wanted to end the relationship with Connie, but I couldn't speak the words. She knew well what I could not say and was hurt; still, we planned to move to Chicago together for the convention period. After that, who could tell? However desirable, a stable, rooted connection to anyone seemed beyond reach. Our few married friends with children, like the Flackses, were living in a context as different as land is from the sea. I could not imagine a future for myself, certainly not one with family responsibilities. I had not heard from my father for over three years. I knew he was raising my sister Mary without the knowledge that she had a brother, and I began to wonder if I would—or should—ever know her; in my gloom, I even contemplated the possibility that my father had done the right thing.

Perhaps my life, precarious as it seemed, *should* be empty of family. As for romance, which I considered very different from committed love, another woman had entered my emotions, but she was thousands of miles away, a convenient dream, a way perhaps for me to love the idea of love but not its responsibilities. Perhaps I was beginning to seek Destiny more. Years later, Connie remembered my telling her that I had "an odyssey to go on," and that I didn't know where it would lead.

COLUMBIA AND STUDENT REVOLUTION

In late April, students at Columbia University initiated the most widely watched campus rebellion of the sixties, amid the largest national student strike in American history. SDS and its militant vision were suddenly catapulted into a national and international prominence. To activists and authorities, it seemed to be a rehearsal for a coming apocalypse in Chicago.

I was in New York at the SNCC office on Tuesday, April 23, when an anxious phone call came from some black students at Columbia University. There was a sit-in on campus, and a Columbia dean was being held hostage in his own office. They asked for advice and support. I decided to take the subway to the Upper West Side campus and observe the situation firsthand, hardly expecting that I would be enveloped for one week under police siege.

Like most universities at the time, Columbia was administered in an autocratic way that vested virtually all power in its president, sixty-seven-year-old Grayson Kirk, and its board of trustees, a group of white males averaging sixty years in age with ties to such prestigious institutions as *The New York Times,* Lockheed, Consolidated Edison, IBM, and CBS. No power was shared with the faculty and student body. Kirk himself compared the students to "transitory birds" in explaining why they should have no voice in the university community's affairs. Student identification cards declared that "the University is free to cancel this registration at any time, on any grounds it deems advisable." Under a regulation unchanged since 1754, all disciplinary power over students was exercised unilaterally by the university president, with no legal proceedings or due process provided the students.

Further, Columbia was a textbook example of what SDS described as "complicity" in war and racism: It enjoyed close and secretive ties to the Institute for Defense Analysis (IDA), a consortium of twelve universities doing weapons research for the Department of Defense, including evaluations of counterinsurgency techniques in South Vietnam and their possible applications in American cities.

On the Harlem border of the campus, Columbia was displacing several thousand blacks as a result of its expansion plans, which included construction of a gymnasium. This project, which involved the unusual leasing of public park land to a private institution, was sharply criticized by many city officials and Harlem residents.

Five days after Martin Luther King's death, the university convened a memorial service in St. Paul's Chapel on campus. It was disrupted by Mark Rudd, a young SDS leader who simply walked on stage, took the microphone, and denounced the university elders for the hypocrisy of honoring King while disrespecting Harlem. With about fifty others, he marched out. The service proceeded, but the act upset the campus community and set a new tone within what became known as the "action faction" of SDS. Tired of intellectualizing, cynical about rational appeals to university authorities, and instilled with the impatience of the time, Rudd's action faction believed that disruptive, confrontational deeds were necessary to force people, especially students and intellectuals, into real choices about themselves and society. On March 27, they had carried out a chanting, unruly demonstration in Low Library, where Kirk's office was located; as a result, on April 22, they were disciplined and placed on probation, which meant that their educational future was at risk if they participated in any further political activity.

Angered at what they considered political repression, the SDS activists called a rally at noon on April 23 on the Sundial at the center of campus, followed by a march of several hundred to the gym construction site in Morningside Heights. There was a blocked attempt to tear down part of the fence at the site, a scuffle with police, a rough arrest of a black student leader, and a march back to campus, where the students soon began a sit-in at nearby Hamilton Hall. Spontaneously, they decided to shut Dean Henry Coleman in his Hamilton office while they announced several demands, including amnesty for the students placed on probation, dropping of any charges against the black student just arrested, cessation of the gym construction, and severing of Columbia's ties with IDA.

I had never seen anything quite like this. Students, at last, had taken power in their own hands, but they were still very much students. Polite, neatly attired, holding their notebooks and texts, gathered in intense knots of discussion, here and there doubting their morality, then recommitting themselves to remain, wondering if their academic and personal careers might be ruined, ashamed of the thought of holding an administrator in his office but wanting a productive dialogue with him, they expressed in every way the torment of their campus generation. Utterly disregarded themselves, they struggled with whether they had the right to treat their administrators with a similarly cold indifference. I stood and watched, fascinated. Various faculty and, as I recall, administrators intermingled with these "revolutionary" students, perpetuating the traditional and casual mode of campus life just at the moment of its dissolution. There in the midst of this revolutionary disorder, for example, was Roger Hilsman, one of the architects of President Kennedy's "counterinsurgency" doctrine and now a professor. What, I wondered, did he think of the insurgency coming home?

I could not resist the intense curiosity that drew me back to Columbia the following day. The black students, as part of the black-power orientation of the time, had asked the white students to leave Hamilton Hall as tensions with the university rose during the night. The blacks were rumored to include some individuals with weapons who entertained visions of an apocalyptic shoot-out. Still rebellious, a number of white students decided at dawn to enter Low Library and occupy the offices of Kirk himself. The overwhelming majority of the old SDS chapter were against this "provocative" action, but Rudd's action faction stormed out and did it anyway. Later that day, the Columbia faculty began to meet and play a mediating role, and Dean Coleman was released from a twenty-four-hour ordeal in his office, walking out through a sea of tense but peaceful students. Shortly after, another campus building, Avery Hall, was seized by student rebels as they realized that their demands, and therefore their futures at Columbia, would not be achieved without forcing the university's hand.

Mark Rudd was a new type of campus leader. At age twenty, he was only nine years younger than I was, but already there was a world of difference. While I had experienced the religious and reformist South at his age, he had already visited revolutionary and socialist Cuba as part of an SDS contingent. While I had gone through an intense intellectual development in formulating *The Port Huron Statement*, he considered "SDS intellectuals" impediments to action. He was absolutely committed to an impossible yet galvanizing dream: that of transforming the entire student movement, through this particular student revolt, into a successful effort to bring down the system. A nice, somewhat inarticulate, suburban New Jersey kid with blue eyes, sandy hair, and an easygoing manner, nondescript in appearance, apparently having no time for changing clothes or engaging in sterile debate, Mark was hard to take seriously as a satanic figure threatening the Columbia system. But in fact, he was committed to revolutionary destruction, sarcastic and smugly dogmatic. I sensed in Mark an embryo of fanaticism that made me feel slightly irrelevant in his presence. But he could also be disarmingly personal, a young boy.

Two days after the revolt began, I had spent enough time at Columbia to know that I couldn't walk away. I offered my help to Mark and other SDS leaders, knowing of course that I couldn't lead them but wanting to participate in this new stage of student struggle, and they accepted. What could be more fitting, perhaps they thought, than to involve Tom Hayden, the (twenty-nine-year-old) old man of the student movement, in this turning point of history?

And so, just after midnight on Thursday, April 26, I found myself joining a silhouetted wave of students surging across Columbia's grounds and entering, with a key volunteered by a graduate student, the darkened shell of Mathematics Hall. The next five days were an experience resembling the Paris Commune of the nineteenth century. While five buildings were occupied, a Strike Committee was formed to negotiate day and night with the university administration and faculty. The theory of democratic participation held firmly in the occupied buildings, requiring that the thousand or more strikers be given a voice in the fateful decisions ahead, not to mention immediate ones like the obtaining of food and basic supplies. Aside from these procedural necessities, however, those of us in the five buildings now were on our own, almost never to be in contact with the world outside until a showdown was reached.

I was chosen to chair the commune in Mathematics Hall, which consisted of over 150 students and an occasional smattering of outsiders from the immediate community surrounding the campus, including Abbie Hoffman. For me, it was like a large SNCC or ERAP meeting, with countless people wanting to be heard, disparate viewpoints needing to be explored, and an internal consensus having to be built. What was unique was the context. Having often been accused of living in a world of our own, now we actually were in one, a world with finite boundaries, which would probably come crashing down in arrests and violence.

In the first hours of the occupation, all of us were overtaken by the fear that an attack on us was imminent. Perhaps it was the sense that we were wrong in trespassing into this academic sanctuary. But there was also the reality of counterdemonstrators outside, many of them campus athletes and fraternity leaders, who were loudly threatening violence. The Kirk administration had shown a blind indifference to our demands and might at any moment request the assistance of the city police. We were outlaws, and feeling it.

We held a mass meeting on how to conduct ourselves in the event of a police order to leave the building. Everyone referred to a "bust" as inevitable, only a matter of time. There seemed to be only a few in favor of surrendering and walking out to be arrested. On the other hand, there was virtually no support for property destruction or militant physical resistance to the police. (There was one fellow in green fatigues who claimed to be with the National Liberation Front and declared that he would fight to the end alone. "That's fine, man," I said to him, nodding.) We arrived at a consensus after about an hour that when and if the police came, we would block the entrances to the building but sit nonviolently when they entered and allow ourselves to be carried out. There would be no violence, but we would prolong the university's torment if they chose to send the police against their own students. This consensus would be rediscussed on a frequent basis, but for now there was a more urgent task: We proceeded to organize a building defense squad to make the police assault as slow and difficult as possible.

We carefully barricaded the doors on the first floor and searched for ways to close off the underground tunnels that we thought the police might use to enter the building at any moment. One woman, inspecting a supply closet, found a liquid soap that could be applied to the stone stairwells to impede a surprise charge by jocks or police. The same coed, an English major from Long Island, located all the fire extinguishers and hoses. Meanwhile, every chair and desk from the Math building's library was loaded on an elevator and sent down to the first floor, where an enormous barricade continued to be constructed across the main entrance to the building.

After several hours, the Math building was as secure as it could be against the expected forces of the military-industrial complex. We could now turn from defending our immediate safety to building a community among ourselves for the hours or days ahead. Fortunately, there was a large, carpeted room that could be used for meetings and a lounge that permitted coffee making and food preparation. A secret committee was swiftly appointed to slip in and out of the building to procure orange juice, bags of coffee, peanut butter and jelly, and if possible, salami and *The New York Times*. A stereo as well was imported, and soon the sounds of Dylan and the Beatles were floating around us. Dope smoking was banned, but not romance. Sentries were chosen to watch the barricades and communicate with strike headquarters so that we could sleep a few hours at night without worrying about waking up with police flashlights in our faces.

Two opposed viewpoints were expressed constantly in the mass meetings, mirroring the very dilemmas of those seeking social change in the outside world. Despite the fact that we had seized property and, to some extent, power over the university's functioning, a significant number of the students, probably a majority, really wanted the university only to recognize that they mattered, that their demands were legitimate and reasonable. They favored what came to be known as "restructuring," the serious acceptance of students and faculty in the decision-making process, not unlike the early vision of Port Huron. From there, they would take their chances in a fair fight to reorder

Columbia's priorities. It was quite remarkable, I thought, that they were driven to employ such risky and revolutionary means to such essentially moderate ends.

The other, "revolutionary," viewpoint was that any such involvement of students in campus decision making was an opportunistic compromise, enfranchising students who were already privileged enough to gain university admittance at the expense of the minority communities that the university helped to oppress. Fervent activists of the Progressive Labor party, the rigid sectarian group bent on taking over SDS, pushed their doctrine of a "student-worker alliance" as opposed to "student power." Rudd, and the new core of revolutionary SDS leaders, stood for goals that simply could not be achieved within the context of the university. Partly driven by the ideological pressure of the Progressive Labor faction, they proposed that students essentially forsake their privileged status and align themselves not with passive workers but on the side of Fanon's "wretched of the earth."

Instead of aspiring to a reformed university as a potential base for social change (the Port Huron notion), Rudd's goals were "creating a human society" by "destroying racism and imperialism." An "intermediate" step, which Rudd proposed to Columbia's vice president during a meeting where he took off his boots because, in his words, they "made his feet sweat," was the immediate creation of a "provisional government" of the university run by students, employees, and Harlem citizens.

I disagreed with both the viewpoints dividing the strikers. Such were the times. The advocates of restructuring, I thought, were in danger of winding up with only a greater advisory role in what would essentially be the same Columbia, constructing its Harlem gym and conducting secret research; but at least they could achieve recognition, tangible gains, and a modest redistribution of power at Columbia. Rudd's perspective, on the other hand, captured the frustration and anger of the times; but in addition to being ideologically to the left of most of the students' (who were not, for example, socialist), it dismissed any reform and sought the impossible: the university's surrender. Admittedly, Rudd wanted the probation orders rescinded, the gym shelved, and ties with IDA ended. But these were "organizing tools," not demands that would appease him if they were achieved. What animated Rudd and his colleagues was revolutionary action itself.

Between these sharply polarized views, I thought, there was the possibility of achieving meaningful reform on the issues of student rights, the gym, and IDA, leaving students with a greater role in the university and a more radical consciousness of themselves in society. My non-Columbia identity, however, limited the advice I might give. After all, the slogan I believed in was "Let the people decide." I was not here to lecture anyone on *The Port Huron Statement*. And besides, these divisions, which loomed larger in the months ahead, were minor ones at the moment compared to the strikers' unity toward the impending bust.

As recently as April 12, President Kirk had declared: "Our young people, in disturbing numbers, appear to reject all forms of authority, from whatever source derived, and they have taken refuge in a turbulent and inchoate nihilism whose sole objectives are destruction. I know of no time in our history when the gap between generations has been wider or more potentially dangerous." Columbia faculty member Zbigniew Brzezinski, later national security adviser, proclaimed that student protest was a "death rattle of the historical irrelevants" in a technocratic society.

What was the most interesting to me about the striking students, however, was not their "nihilism" but their acute moral sensitivity. Apart from the politicized and, some would say, hardened SDS leaders, I encountered students who were almost regretful about the upheaval they had to cause and deeply idealistic about university education, even as they violated its hallowed institutional customs. Since I kept no notes, I can only rely on the images of memory, but none are negative. There was an angelic young Asian woman who chastely and serenely slept next to me on the floor at night; by day, she read for her history classes when she was not politely building barricades and smuggling supplies through the windows. I remember certain radiant faces like hers, intense relationships, the joy of singing, an atmosphere of caring for each other's feelings during the debates. The spirit was symbolized in a magical moment one night when all the strikers briefly gathered at one place for a wedding in this war, between two strikers named Richard and Andrea. About five hundred of us formed a circle to receive and applaud the two lovers, each dressed in borrowed white garments, he in a Nehru jacket, she in sweater and jeans. They were a couple before the strike, but its intensity made them want to be married in the movement's circle of love. The "congregation" was ecstatic for them and for the hopeful promise they represented. My tears welled up as a candlelit procession of strikers brought the couple to the center of our circle, where a minister waited.

I, who had not found marriage possible, was overwhelmed at this shining pair as the minister pronounced them "children of the new age."

"The line has to be drawn somewhere if an orderly society is to survive," *The New York Times* editorialized as the strike wore on. The *Times* neglected to mention that its chairman of the board, Arthur Hays Sulzberger, was a Columbia trustee. Such was the justification of the largest police arrest in the history of American campuses. It began in the early-morning hours of April 30, after the Columbia administration asked the New York Police Department to accomplish by force what they could not negotiate.

Inside Mathematics Hall, the night of April 29 was a night like any of the others, communal life proceeding normally amid rumors and alarms. If anything, there was increased hope, since large numbers of faculty were now pressuring the administration for a resolution of the crisis without violence. The longer we occupied the buildings—this was the fifth night—the more it seemed that fruitful negotiations were a possibility.

At two A.M., however, the water and phone lines to the building were cut; police had entered the campus and were preparing for mass arrests. Outside, it was bedlam: Floodlights beamed over the campus, illuminating thousands of students and supporters who, hearing by radio of the impending bust, were rushing to the grounds. Long lines of police filed across the Sundial, while scores of undercover officers dispersed into the shadows of the campus. We watched it all from the upper floors of the Math building, then quickly prepared to accept our fate. The faithful core of students had remained all week. (We were joined by a few of the SDS leaders and an anarchist street group of artists and intellectuals who called themselves Up Against the Wall, Motherfucker, or "Motherfuckers" for short, adopting their name from a LeRoi Jones poem.) Our huddled masses lit candles, which had been saved for the occasion. Everyone made sure that they had handkerchiefs to protect their eyes and faces against tear gas. The barricades were checked. It would take the police some time to break through any entryway. Finally, there remained just one task: to find partners, link arms closely, sit down en masse atop the building's staircases, and wait.

Time passed. I kept visualizing the brute anger of the police, whipped up by the forces of authority behind them, gathering at the outside of our fragile sanctuary, until they would finally pull, push, and burst their way through the barricaded doors, their furies rising as they towered over us. I didn't believe anyone would be shot, but like every individual sitting there I was expecting to be clubbed, punched, and kicked while being carried out. Not wanting to be alone with our thoughts, we sang and laughed and chanted, and waited again.

Ours was the last building to fall. Backed by a phalanx of police under the outside trees, surreally lit by the roving cameras of the media, a university official formally requested over a bullhorn that we surrender and leave the building. "Up against the wall, motherfucker!" people began chanting back. We resumed our positions on the staircase, arms around each other for the last time. You could hear the police shaking and pulling the big outer doors. *Crunch. Crunch. Crunch.* They were open.

Now we could see a mass of dark blue masked men thrashing at the pile of chairs and desks we had lashed together with fire hoses. We started chanting; it would be only a minute or two before they were upon us. We linked and hugged more tightly.

Now they had cleared every obstacle and stood triumphantly, panting, in front of their quarry. I wondered what they thought at the sight of the "enemy," the mass of middle-class kids seated in front of them. A later police memorandum criticized the university administration for having "grossly underestimated the numbers of students inside the buildings and the extent of the involvement of the faculty in sympathy with the students," implying that the police thought they would make short work of a small handful of bizarre troublemakers.

Whatever their surprise, however, the police performed their job with ruthless efficiency. Just as we expected, they struck and kicked virtually every striker as they dragged us away from our communal family, one by one, and jostled us to the waiting paddy wagons. I was pushed along in the middle of a line of students, my right arm pinned behind my back. The students were holding V-signs aloft. It was almost dawn.

In all, over seven hundred arrests had been made. Some students were hurt badly, their scalps bleeding from brass knuckles used by police undercover agents. There were 120 charges of police brutality made against the police, the largest number in department history.

I took leave of my new friends the following day and tried to resume my focus on preparing for Chicago. The Columbia strike went on through another month, yet another mass arrest on May 21, and a "counter graduation" at which Erich Fromm praised the students for their "revolution of life" amid a "society of zombies." Eventually, the advocates of restructuring the campus prevailed over those who struggled in futility to define a more radical direction. But Rudd and his allies in the new SDS leadership (including Bernardine Dohrn, who was actively involved in the legal defense) were the winners of a larger battle to create the image of a revolutionary student movement threatening the priorities of the larger society. In those months at Columbia, the seeds of the Weatherman faction of SDS, which would embark on revolutionary violence in 1969, were planted. Eventually, their emphasis on sparking confrontation through disruption and violence would envelop them in an isolated and self-destructive world. For now, however, they were simply the extreme form of a larger consciousness that was spreading through American campuses. It is not usually remembered that Columbia was only the most publicized outbreak of that April's Days of Resistance, which involved a one-day strike by at least one million students, the largest ever. A Yankelovich survey taken in the fall of 1968 confirmed the scale of student radicalism: 19 percent of all American students, or just over one million, agreed on the need for a "mass revolutionary party." Between 1967 and 1969, the number of students considering themselves "doves" jumped from 35 to 69 percent in Gallup polls.

The spring of 1968 saw an astonishing uprising of students across the world. France was immobilized, West Germany and Mexico were shaken, and a massive civil rights movement developed in Northern Ireland. Prague and Warsaw saw massive upheavals as well. Tanks and bullets were used by bureaucrats against youth everywhere. I know of no historian who has adequately explained the simultaneous nature of these intercontinental developments. Perhaps it was the global effect of Vietnam, perhaps the unifying influence of television, perhaps (as I believe) a generational fissure across national boundaries.

FBI MEMORANDUM   **5/14/68**

FROM: Director

TO: SAC (Special Agent in Charge-Albany)
Counter Intelligence Program: Internal Security: Disruption of the New Left.

... The purpose of this program is to expose, disrupt, and otherwise neutralize the activities of the various new left organizations, their leadership and their adherents. It is imperative that activities of those groups be followed on a continuous basis so we may take advantage of all opportunities for counter intelligence and also inspire action where circumstances warrant. The devious maneuver, the duplicity of these activists must be exposed to public scrutiny through cooperation of reliable news media sources, both locally and at the seat of government. We must frustrate every effort of these groups and individuals to consolidate their forces or to recruit new or youthful adherents. In every instance, consideration should be given to disrupting organized activity of these groups and no opportunity should be missed to capitalize on organizational or personal conflicts of their leadership.

Offices which have investigative responsibility for KEY ACTIVISTS should specifically comment in the initial letter to the bureau regarding these individuals. These offices are aware [that] these individuals have been identified as the moving forces behind the new left.

No counter-intelligence action may be initiated by the field without specific bureau authorization.

The bureau has been very closely following the activities of the new left and the Key Activists and is highly concerned that the anarchistic activities of a few could paralyze institutions of learning, induction centers, cripple traffic, and tie the arms of law enforcement officials. All to the detriment of our society. The organizations and activists who spout revolution and unlawfully challenge society to obtain their demands must not only be contained, but must be neutralized. Law and order is

mandatory for any civilized society to survive. Therefore, you must approach this new endeavor with a forward look, enthusiasm, and interest in order to
accomplish our responsibilities. The importance of this
new endeavor, cannot and will not be overlooked.

TO: SAC, Newark (100-48095)   5/17/68

FROM: Director, FBI (100-438281)

THOMAS EMMETT HAYDEN

SM-C
(KEY ACTIVIST)

Reference Buairtel [Bureau air telegram] captioned "Investigation of the New Left, Key Activists," dated 1/30/68.

. . . It will be incumbent upon the Bureau to intensify its investigations of those individuals who have assumed leadership in the
new left. Hayden was designated a key activist in referenced
Bureau airtel as a result of this leadership activity. Instructions
as to the handling of this investigation were promulgated at that
time.

It is to be noted that a recent edition of Life magazine carried
a photograph of Hayden participating in the Columbia University
demonstrations which effectively shut down that institution. No
information in this regards was furnished by your office. This
points out the apparent inadequacy of your day-to-day coverage.
It should not be necessary for the Bureau to rely on news media
for this type of information. Since Hayden has no connection
whatever with Columbia University, it is obvious that what his
expressed purpose for being on campus was to furnish leadership
and assistance to the student revolt.

. . . The subject's travel both nationally and abroad should be
closely followed. As office of origin you will be expected to develop advance information in this regard and to issue sufficient
instructions to offices in whose territory he is traveling to insure
that his activities are fully covered while is in a travel status. This
phase of your investigation must be given close attention to insure that the Bureau is aware of his movements at all times.

No information is located in Bufiles [Bureau files] to indicate
that you have conducted any investigation into Hayden's financial activities. You should promptly pursue this line of inquiry to
develop his financial status, the source of his income, and the
source of funds which enables him to travel. This should be a
continuing project.

In evaluating this case, you should bear in mind that one of your
prime objectives should be to neutralize him in the new left movement. The Bureau will entertain recommendations of a counterintelligence nature in order to accomplish this objective. You

should, therefore, furnish the Bureau with your suggestions along this line. Take no positive action however in this regard until you have received specific Bureau instructions.

    The investigation of Hayden, as one of the key leaders of the new left movement, is of <u>prime importance</u> to the Bureau. You will be expected to pursue it <u>aggressively and with imagination.</u> Inadequate and delayed reporting of important developments will not be tolerated.

As I traveled through the country securing commitments from activists to come to Chicago, the question of the Democratic primary battle between McCarthy and Kennedy kept growing in importance. My close friend Jack Newfield was deeply involved with Kennedy, covering the campaign for *The Village Voice* and keeping notes for a book. Other friends like Geoff Cowan were now in charge of McCarthy's strategy of persuading delegates to support an "open convention." Yet in mid-May, a *Newsweek* poll gave Hubert Humphrey, who was campaigning only through proxies in the primaries while he lined up backroom Democratic support, a total of 1,279 delegates, to Kennedy's 713 and McCarthy's 280. It was becoming clear to me that if anyone could break open the tightly controlled convention, it was Kennedy with his greater ties to regular Democratic politicians, including Mayor Daley himself. The McCarthy camp remained bitterly opposed to Kennedy, however; sometimes, in fact, they seemed to prefer Humphrey to Kennedy.

The Kennedy campaign successfully prevailed in the conservative climates of both Indiana and Nebraska in May and took the District of Columbia. In Oregon on May 29, however, McCarthy made a comeback, leaving California as the last and decisive prize between the two challengers. The Humphrey slates, meanwhile, were receiving only a bare 20 percent of the primary votes, leading Robert Kennedy to mention on his arrival in California, that if Humphrey were nominated "there will be no candidate who has opposed the course of escalation of the war in Vietnam. There will be no candidate committed to the kinds of programs which can remedy the conditions which are turning our cities into armed camps."

I came to California during the last frantic days of the primary. Most of the state's middle-class, left-to-liberal reformers, grouped under the umbrella of the California Democratic Coun-

cil (CDC), were crusading for McCarthy. Their anti-Kennedy
rancor was so great that they booed San Francisco Assemblyman Phillip Burton, who spoke in behalf of Kennedy at CDC's
statewide convention. Kennedy had an odd coalition of machine
Democrats, represented by Assembly Leader Jesse Unruh, combined with movement leaders like Cesar Chavez, with whom he
had taken Mass during a farm-worker fast in March. John
Lewis, the former chairman of SNCC, and Charles Evers of
Mississippi were campaigning hard for Kennedy in the ghettos,
along with athletes Rafer Johnson and Roosevelt Grier. The
Johnson-Humphrey element of the party was led by former
Governor Edmund G. "Pat" Brown, San Francisco Mayor Joseph Alioto, and party chairman Charles Warren. They were
not doing well, losing the reformers to McCarthy and the
minorities to Kennedy, leaving only the skeleton of their former
power.

As Kennedy explained to Newfield, and Newfield to me, a
"new coalition" was needed for the Democratic party and the
country to hold together. Soured by organized labor's staunch
support of Hubert Humphrey and the Vietnam War, Kennedy
increasingly looked to racial minorities and the poor, along
with students, as new forces that could be harnessed toward
political change. But he could also reach the white ethnics,
Newfield insisted, recalling for me a night in Gary, Indiana,
when Bobby rode in the backseat of a car with former boxing
champion Tony Zale, the saint of the white ethnics, and Richard Hatcher, the young black mayor of the city. Jack quoted
Kennedy as saying, "We have to convince Negroes and blue-
collar whites that they have common interests. If we can reconcile those two hostile groups, and then add the kids, you can
really turn this country around." In short, Jack argued to me,
Kennedy "agrees with you, but because of who he is, he can be
elected president."

Newfield showed me a napkin bearing Kennedy's scribbled
signature. Late one night at a restaurant, the candidate had
mischievously asked Jack what he wanted from an RFK presidency. "Only two things," Jack immediately replied, "get out of
Vietnam and make 'This Land Is Your Land' the national anthem." Kennedy, laughing, signed his agreement on the wrin-
kled napkin.

FBI WASHINGTON DC

FBI CHICAGO

5:22 PM URGENT 5/31/68

TO DIRECTOR (100-438281), NEWARK (100-48095), NEW YORK (100-48904) AND SAN FRANCISCO

FROM CHICAGO (100-39500) (P) 2P

THOMAS EMMETT HAYDEN, SM-SDS, KEY ACTIVIST, 00 NEWARK

SOURCE ADVISED TODAY HAYDEN BELIEVED TO HAVE SCHEDULED SPEAKING ENGAGEMENT AT UNKNOWN LOCATION SAN FRANCISCO AREA. HE IS ACCOMPANIED BY ONE CONNIE BROWN.

HAYDEN APRIL THIRTY LAST ARRESTED BY NEW YORK CITY COLUMBIA UNIVERSITY FOR CRIMINAL TRESPASS. SUBJECT REPORTEDLY IN NEW YORK CITY MAY TWENTY SEVEN LAST, POSSIBLY FOR TRIAL IN CONNECTION WITH ABOVE ARREST. HAYDEN'S NAME APPEARED IN PARTICIPANTS LIST AS CONVOCATION SPONSORED BY FOREIGN POLICY ASSN. HELD AT NEW YORK HILTON HOTEL, MAY TWENTY SEVEN-NINE LAST.

HAYDEN DESCRIBED AS WHITE MALE, FIVE FEET TEN, ONE FOUR FIVE POUNDS, BORN DEC. ELEVEN NINETEEN THIRTY NINE, BLACK HAIR, BROWN EYES. CONNIE BROWN DESCRIBED AS WHITE FEMALE, AGE TWENTY-THREE, FIVE FEET FOUR, ONE THREE FIVE POUNDS, CHUNKY BUILD, BROWN HAIR (BOYS STYLE), BROWN EYES.

NEWARK FURNISH SAN FRANCISCO BEST CURRENT PHOTO AND COMPLETE DESCRIPTION OF HAYDEN. REVIEW INDICES RE BROWN AND IF NEWARK SUBJECT PROVIDE PHOTO AND COMPLETE DESCRIPTION TO SAN FRANCISCO AND CHICAGO.

END

In San Francisco, I met with Kennedy adviser Richard Goodwin to explain the upcoming Chicago plans and ask the campaign's help in lobbying Mayor Daley for permits. Then I went to the Kennedy-McCarthy debate on June 1. It was held at the KGO television studios on Golden Gate Avenue, and I sat among the three hundred or more reporters covering the event. McCarthy was supposed to be a superior television personality, because of his distinguished white hair and well-educated manner, but I thought Kennedy did quite well. They disagreed somewhat on Vietnam, with McCarthy favoring a coalition government in the South and Kennedy wanting one only after negotiations. On the racial issue, I found Kennedy to be accurately devastating. He supported both political empowerment and improvements in jobs, housing, and schools within the ghetto, a conclusion I had drawn in Newark. But McCarthy, a traditional liberal advocate of racial integration, suggested that this amounted to "apartheid." In turn, Kennedy was demagogic in calling McCarthy's suggestion of "sending ten thousand blacks [through public housing] into Orange County" a catastrophic idea. McCarthy seemed aloof, more a college professor (or the senator that he was) than a president. Kennedy seemed real. At one point, asked why so many people thought him ruthless, Kennedy smiled impishly and said, "I don't know," implying that the charge might be true but conveying a sense that he could make fun of his flaws. A *Los Angeles Times* poll indicated that television viewers, by a 2–1 margin, favored Kennedy in the debate.

Late that night as I walked through the lobby of the Fairmont Hotel with Connie Brown, we came upon Robert Kennedy heading toward the elevator. He introduced me to astronaut John Glenn and others in his party, and we entered the elevator together. Though his expression had been fresh in the earlier debate, and his attitude clearly buoyant, he now appeared as tired as Newfield had described him. His eyes were withdrawn, his face lined and gaunt, his nose burned from the California sun. What struck me most, though, were his hands. Strong, athletic hands whose palms were nicked, scraped, and sore from thousands of outreaching hands of supporters in his motorcades. They reminded me of stigmata, of hands crucified.

"Are you helping? How's it look?" he asked quietly inside the elevator.

"You won the debate tonight," I replied, "and I think it looks good. I want to work with your people on demonstrations in Chicago against the war."

"Good," was all he said, then his eyes drifted off to another thought. We reached his floor, and I shook the hand again. "Good luck," I said. "Thanks. Good night," he replied and patted his hand across Connie's back. The elevator door closed, and I watched him, almost limping down the hall, for the last time.

I saw the California election returns in a New York apartment with Len Weinglass, Connie, and several others. Newfield was on the fifth floor of the Ambassador Hotel in Los Angeles, and I expected to see him the following day. The next primary was in New York. If Kennedy won, Newfield said, it would possibly start an earthquake under the regular party delegates. If Kennedy lost California, on the other hand, Jack would title his book *The Late Senator Robert Kennedy.*

It was nearly two A.M. in New York when the returns showed Kennedy winning. I watched with a stirring of excitement as he introduced and thanked farm workers, along with black and labor activists who had labored to turn out their votes that day. He finished, exclaiming, "On to Chicago!"

In Los Angeles, Newfield and *Ramparts* editor Bob Scheer took the elevator down to the ballroom expecting to follow Kennedy to a party. Suddenly there came crackling, almost popping noises over the television, a cry in the confused crowd, a call for a doctor, and I knew it was over.

On yet another haunted night, I stayed up watching the constant reruns: the words *On to Chicago,* followed by the human wailing and the eerie kitchen scenes. I listened without hope to the periodic hospital reports, and without much credence to the early information on Kennedy's assassin. Sometime in the night, Jerry Rubin called in hysteria, saying he believed Sirhan did it "because he's an Arab." I called a few close friends as if I might never talk to them again. "I love you," I told one, thinking I might never have the chance to tell her. I was behaving, without quite recognizing it, as one does before one's own death.

The next day Newfield called. He caught the early-morning plane to escape Los Angeles and wanted to have dinner somewhere. Jack and his wife, *Voice* photographer Janie Eisenberg, showed up, stricken. Geoff Cowan and several other friends from McCarthy's campaign—Paul Gorman and Harold Ickes, Jr.—linked up with us somehow. In our emptiness, we decided to go to St. Patrick's Cathedral, where Bobby Kennedy's body awaited final ceremonies the next morning. When we arrived at the dark and massive cathedral, hundreds of New Yorkers were lining up outside. They were from various walks of life, but mainly they were poor and marginal people who had come to pay their respects as close to the funeral service as they could be. We walked through the silence to an entrance where we encountered a Kennedy aide who invited us in. It must have been well after midnight, only a few hours before the opening of the cathedral for the service.

I sat down in a pew toward the back of the cavernous chamber. Police and carpenters were hard at work setting up wooden platforms for television crews. Priests hovered near the altar. Some Kennedy family and staff stood together trying to concentrate on arrangements. It was a while before I noticed the coffin of Bobby Kennedy. It was sitting by the altar rail, containing all that remained of last night's hopes of the poor. Nothing left of that hope now, gone in a coffin while crews hammered away and police awaited the crowd. I started to cry hard. After another while, the Kennedy aides motioned to me, asking that I come forward to the coffin. I walked slowly forward and, next to Geoff, stood in silent vigil.

When morning came, I went home, *On to Chicago* repeating itself in my head.

FBI MEMORANDUM   **7/20/68**

. . . Source went on to relate, that it was rumored prior to the assassination of Senator Robert F. Kennedy, that substantial sums of "Kennedy money" were given to Tom Hayden and Rennie Davis, both affiliated with the National Mobilization Committee to End the War in Vietnam, to create demonstrations at the National Democratic Convention, August 1968.

According to source these demonstrations, funded by "Kennedy money" were to be directed against President Lyndon B. Johnson, and for Senator Kennedy. Tom Hayden, according to source, was supposedly confronted with this rumor and vehemently denied it; however, during the late winter of 1968 a large meeting was called at an unknown lake outside Chicago, Illinois for the purpose of planning these demonstrations.

Source related one ████████ * coordinated the invitations to this conference, and made free airline tickets available to various groups, through Hayden and Davis.

---

*Material deleted by the FBI.

13. The Streets of Chicago: 1968

The stunning events of the spring—LBJ's withdrawal, the Paris peace talks, the sudden deaths, and the riots—left people depleted and plans for the convention protest in doubt. If the Paris talks signaled the beginning of peace, the war would no longer be a cause for marching; if the talks were a sham, what was the leverage on a president who already had withdrawn from the race? The big question was, What could we hope to achieve with RFK dead and McCarthy no longer viable? What was the point?

I felt the plans for protest should go forward, if only to continue opposing a war which the president was trying to wipe off the front page during the election year. It appeared to me that the war was escalating in a new way. In late May, the American media reported the existence of a secret U.S. directive calling for an "all-out offensive against the enemy" over the summer. Though U.S. bombing had been halted in most of North Vietnam, bombing missions sharply increased over the "panhandle," the narrow strip of the North stretching down to the seventeenth parallel. The overall tonnage of bombs dropped on North Vietnam now was greater than before the president's March 31 limitations. In July, the number of U.S. troops in South Vietnam increased by 19,000 to 535,000, and the *Times* reported that the "Pentagon's estimate of enemy troop strength has remained unchanged between 207,000 and 222,000 despite repeated charges of heavy enemy escalation." These reports increased my paranoia about what Johnson's "peace plan" actually meant.

In July, the Vietnamese decided to release several POWs as a conciliatory gesture. I couldn't go to Hanoi because of the preparations for Chicago. But I decided to fly for forty-eight hours to Paris to set up the release and learn for myself how far apart the two sides were.

Three Americans were with me in Paris, en route to Hanoi: Vernon Grizzard of ERAP; Stewart Meacham, a Quaker leader; and Ann Weills Scheer, a Berkeley radical and feminist. We met with Harriman about the POWs. He argued that they be returned aboard U.S. military aircraft; we sharply disagreed, demanding that they return by commercial aircraft with the peace activists, which is what eventually happened. But one remark of Harriman's stayed with me. "The Vietnamese, you know, have a lower standard of morality than we do," he said, out of nowhere. I thought Anne was going to explode, but she controlled herself, and we let the comment pass. In fact, none of us could believe that we heard Harriman correctly until we compared notes later. So much for a thaw in U.S.-Vietnamese relationships, I concluded.

The vast differences between the two sides were not simply diplomatic, but were best symbolized in their living situations. Harriman's party was staying at the finest suite of the elegant Hôtel Crillon, while the NLF-PRG delegation was in a small compound outside Paris where they could care for their own chickens and gardens. After two days, I flew back to Chicago convinced that the war would continue.

Years later, I asked historian Doris Kearns about Lyndon Johnson's 1968 intentions. She was a White House intern in the sixties, a dove, and a symbol to Johnson of the younger generation that he was losing. The president became obsessed with Kearns, often arguing with her while also confessing his inner thinking. These conversations became a book on the Johnson years, *Lyndon Johnson and the American Dream,* and made Kearns one of the few experts on the president's personal view of the times.

After Robert Kennedy's death, according to Kearns, Johnson briefly and ambivalently considered getting back into the presidential race. Stopping Robert Kennedy had been paramount for him. After RFK's death, he worried about a "draft Teddy" movement. "The way he would talk about it was by saying that all sorts of politicians were asking him to run, telling him that with the war on a better footing, he was the only one who could win," Kearns said. While these were largely fantasies, Johnson at least wanted to be present at the convention for his sixtieth birthday, on August 27. "He wanted them to fête his accomplishments and, if the convention fell apart, crazy as it seems, he would be there, available."

In any event, after Kennedy's death, the possibility of antiwar forces defeating Hubert Humphrey, Johnson's handpicked successor, slumped to zero. Humphrey's effort was denounced by Jack Newfield as "undemocratic and illegitimate"; in retrospect, it is difficult to believe how closed the Democratic party was. Of the 7.5 million Democrats who voted in the 1968 primaries, 80 percent voted for either Kennedy or McCarthy. Only 20 percent voted for Humphrey "stand-ins" in New York and California; RFK received 50 percent of the vote in South Dakota, Humphrey's home state. Yet according to the rules, most of the Democratic convention delegates were selected almost two years before the convention. They were already pledged to Lyndon Johnson's ticket and platform. Therefore the McCarthy campaign, viewed realistically, became little more than a protest within a closed system, although its idealistic stalwarts still believed in miracles.

On the Chicago activist front, nothing was going very well either. SDS had moved unrecognizably to the left: Bernardine Dohrn was elected to the national leadership at their June convention, declaring, "I consider myself a revolutionary communist," which meant a supporter of the NLF, the Cubans, and Third World revolutionaries in general. They continued to worry over the twin perils of repression and liberal reformism during Convention Week. The Yippies were having their troubles too; their local meetings and fund-raising concerts were disrupted by Chicago police. Entertainers like Judy Collins began saying they could not perform in Chicago unless permits and sound systems were guaranteed. In New York, Jerry Rubin and Abbie Hoffman were privately debating a cancellation. The National Mobilization itself was internally divided and still had not issued an official call to Chicago by the summer, although Dave Dellinger was personally committed. In the official corri-

dors of Washington and Chicago, there was hope that the protests could be squelched; in fact, a White House memo indicated
that Democratic party chairman John Bailey was "optimistic,
and expects none of the major groups that originally planned
demonstrations to go through with them. But precautions will
be taken [and] those attending the convention will leave Chicago
remembering it as a friendly city." To discount such rumors,
Rennie, Dave and I held unilateral press conferences on June 29
declaring that the demonstrations *would* happen—even though
the cumbersome National "Mobe" still had not acted.

Rennie was getting nowhere in trying to meet with city officials about securing permits. Having negotiated with government officials for permits before, however, he was convinced
that the city would wait until the last few days before the convention, in order to keep the numbers of protestors down, and
then grant the permits.

According to one exhaustive history, the city decided as early
as April not to issue permits or to cooperate in any way. The
mayor's longtime press secretary said, "Our idea was to discourage the hippies from coming." The city was "not to give a
staging ground" to the protestors by providing permits. Why
should permits be given, he asked, for outside agitators "to plop
on the ground" and "be taken care of?"

Unaware that such attitudes were already determined, Rennie tried a new approach, involving the U.S. Department of
Justice. The department contained a little-known branch called
the Community Relations Service, headed by Roger Wilkins,
Roy Wilkins's nephew and a talented negotiator whose assignments were usually to deal with mulish officials in southern
cities. At Rennie's invitation, Wilkins flew to Chicago for a
discussion of our plans and was asked to act as an intermediary
with the mayor. Rennie told me after the meeting how much he
liked Wilkins, as I did when I met him later.

After meeting with Rennie, Wilkins sent a private memo to
Attorney General Ramsey Clark that described Rennie as "an
honest, intelligent man who was being candid with me" and
recommended that

> the President and Vice President be apprised of the plans of the
> Mobilization, as we now know them, at the earliest possible time
> [and] one of them or someone clearly acting in their behalf call

Mayor Daley to apprise him of that point of view and that the Mayor be advised that I will be coming to Chicago next week to inform him of the Mobilization's plans and . . . to set up a continuing working relationship between the city officials and the Mobilization.

Ramsey Clark, as far as I know, did not talk to Johnson or Humphrey, but refused FBI Director Hoover's request for wiretaps on several of us. It was arranged that in the following week Mayor Daley would talk with Roger Wilkins. But, according to Wilkins's account, the mayor was not interested in hearing our plans and seemed offended that federal officials would try to intervene in his city's affairs. Daley ended the meeting after about ten minutes.

Not long after, Wilkins again met with Rennie, this time bringing several Justice Department officials. One of them was Thomas Foran, a former political appointee of the mayor and the U.S. attorney for Chicago who would later be the chief prosecutor in the Chicago Eight trial. Hearing from Wilkins that the mayor was opposed to any permits, Rennie made a direct appeal to Foran, the only official close to Daley, for help. Foran was noncommittal. But the very next day, Deputy Mayor Stahl (whom we jokingly called "Stall") called the Mobe office. He complained about our going to the Justice Department but agreed to meet informally with Rennie. Rennie's stratagem had worked; we were ecstatic and believed the city would now be forced to grant us permits. It already was August 2, just over three weeks from the opening ceremonies of the convention. Time was of the essence.

Our hopes were quickly subdued. Meeting at a downtown coffee shop, Stahl told us that public parks couldn't be used as campsites, and the long-proposed march to the amphitheater was impossible for "security" reasons. In addition to these capricious views, Stahl's most telling comment, because of its clear dishonesty, was that all decisions regarding permits would be made by the Parks and Sanitation Department along with the police. In fact, as both sides at the coffee table knew, all such decisions in Chicago were made by one individual, Mayor Daley, not by lower bureaucrats. There was one last attempt at a City Hall meeting with Stahl, on August 12; it too ended in fiasco. On the same day, Senator McCarthy, after a personal appeal from Mayor Daley, made a public call for demonstrators to stay away from Chicago because of the "possibility of unintended violence or disorder." Shortly after, the open-convention advocates, including Alland Lowenstein and Geoff Cowan, were denied a permit for a Soldiers Field rally and called off their activities for Convention Week.

On August 7, Vice President Humphrey's executive aide, William Connell, telephoned the FBI to ask for political intelligence on the upcoming Convention, as was provided President Johnson on the Mississippi Freedom Democrats in 1964. Hoover assistant Carla De Loach assured Connell that the FBI's "Chicago office is well prepared to gather intelligence and pass such intelligence on to appropriate authorities during the convention," and that "full preparations have been made by the Chicago Office to handle the matter of passing intelligence to the Vice President and his aides."

Our hopes not only for permits but for large numbers of demonstrators were beginning to collapse. How many people were going to spend four or five days in Chicago with no assurance that they could participate in a rally, attend a concert, march to the convention, or unroll a sleeping bag in Lincoln Park? Meeting continually now, some Mobe leaders—Dave Dellinger in particular—held out their belief that a lawsuit combined with public pressure would bring permits at the last hour, as happened the previous October on the eve of the Pentagon demonstration.

My mood darkened. "They're just fucking around with us, stalling for time, and they have no intention of giving us permits," I argued in a late-night meeting. "They gave no permits to Rennie and Maced these people in April during a nonviolent peace march, and they're going to do the same thing now. They want to keep most people out of town and drive the rest of us off the streets. We can't back down. We're not just protesting the war. We have to fight for the streets. We have to fight just for our right to be here." The city's strategy was working effectively to reduce our numbers, but it would backfire, I thought, in another way, by building an American iron curtain around the convention and creating a police state in the streets.

I went out later for a beer with John Froines. John and his wife, Ann, had been through ERAP with me, and we shared a passion about Vietnam. Like many people, John wanted to devote himself to an academic career but felt pulled into the vortex of Chicago. John recalls my saying that night that twenty or twenty-five people could die in the convention protests. If I did, I have blanked it out, but I do remember thinking that it was time to prepare for the worst scenario. The experimental questioning of American society that began at Port Huron was yielding bitter evidence; America was turning out to be more like Mississippi than not. How much difference was there, after all, between Jackson, Mississippi, and Mayor Daley's Chicago? In the South, we could at least appeal to a higher, and arguably more tolerant, level of government; in this case, that higher level in Washington was fully aligned with Chicago City Hall. At Port Huron, we believed that apathetic individuals could be transformed into active, thinking citizens who could influence government by building local organizations. Here in Chicago, every organization we had tried to build—the JOIN Community Union, the April Twenty-seventh Peace Coalition, and many others—had been routinely harassed, raided, sprayed with Mace, and attacked by police and denied even the smallest victories of the kind we were able to achieve in Newark. There was the shoot-to-kill, shoot-to-maim rhetoric. And now, by denying permits, the mayor—and the White House behind him—was smugly denying that the First Amendment should protect the rights of hippies to sleep in a park, or McCarthy workers to rally at Soldiers Field, or the Mobilization to assemble at the amphitheater. I was convinced we had to lay aside whatever hopes we harbored for respectability, for career, for step-by-step reform. It was a time to risk our necks to take democracy back, a time no longer for visionary platforms but for suffering and physical courage. I told a New York audience that they should come to Chicago prepared to shed their blood.

Camus had warned against the politics of resentment I was beginning to embody, calling it an "evil secretion, in a sealed vessel, of prolonged impotence." But I believed that I was still acting in the spirit of Camus's rebel, and partly I was. His rebel was never realistic, nor was I then. Rebellion, for Camus, was "apparently negative, since it creates nothing," but it turned out to be "profoundly positive, in that it reveals the part of man which must always be defended," the human dignity shared by all. We had to resist police and political oppression in Chicago,

I felt, not because it was realistic but because it was important to act, if only because not acting meant succumbing.

The protest plan for the convention, now only twelve days away, was being refashioned constantly. We repeatedly tried to explain its outline to city officials:

> August 24: a decentralized "people's assembly" at over a score of "movement centers," where individuals would receive a briefing about the week's schedule, and meet together for the first time;
>
> August 25: opening day of the convention: nonviolent and legal picketing on sidewalks outside delegates' hotels in the Loop;
>
> August 26: rallies and meetings in Lincoln, Grant and Hyde Parks;
>
> August 27: concert and rally at Coliseum, Yippie Festival;
>
> August 28, day of Humphrey's nomination: rally in Grant Park, march 10 miles to International Amphitheater;
>
> August 29: decentralized actions at institutions representing war and racism.

Despite the uncertainty, we planned to go ahead with the schedule. If the city gave us a last-minute permit, so much the better. If not, we would have to become very creative. One of the key factors in our survival now was the training of about a hundred Mobilization marshals, who in a situation without rules would have to play an important leadership role on the streets. In past demonstrations, marshals were used mostly as "traffic directors," guiding people toward a rally site, keeping marchers in orderly lines, shouting instructions or chants over bullhorns. But Chicago had to be approached differently. Instead of a "vertical" organization with leaders in front and followers marching obediently behind, we would need a "horizontal" structure of small groups as the vital base of the Mobilization. There was too clearly a danger that leaders like ourselves would be arrested or hurt, cut off from the mass of activists. Further, as we wrote in the instructions to the marshals, the police were expected to "operate from a strategy of containment and mass arrest rather than indiscriminate brutality." This meant a danger of hundreds or thousands of people being encircled and removed from the streets before the convention came to its climax on the twenty-eighth. We wanted to fill the streets as much as possible, not be held in jails on exorbitant bail.

Therefore, it was necessary to improvise what we called mobile tactics. During parts of Convention Week, small groups of fifty to a hundred demonstrators would picket at a decentralized site, for example, a draft board office. That way, if they were rounded up, thousands of others would remain at large. On the other hand, for situations when large assemblies would come together, the marshals were being trained to lead people out of the danger of mass arrest. The marshals awkwardly tried to mimic the "snake dances" used by Japanese students as a way to break out of police lines while avoiding either attacks by demonstrators on police or leaving isolated individuals behind. A few practiced karate self-defense moves, teaching techniques for protecting vital organs from clubs and boots. But it was amateur theater compared to the riot-control techniques that were efficiently being practiced against simulated long-haired demonstrators by the National Guard over the summer. What was deadly serious, however, was the training of our marshals in makeshift first-aid techniques against head wounds, serious bleeding, and tear-gas or Mace attacks. Marshals also studied by map and on foot most of the throughways, bridges, and alleys from Lincoln Park to Grant Park, and to the amphitheater.

On August 22, the police shot and killed a seventeen-year-old Indian named Jerome Johnson in Lincoln Park. Johnson, an early arrival for the Festival of Life, was said to have "threatened" the officers who killed him. The next day, Judge Lynch (another aptly named friend of the mayor's) rejected our appeal for permits; the National Guard was provided fifteen sites for sleeping and assembling. There was nothing further to negotiate. The sides were now assembled, as in a medieval battle.

In their camp were eleven thousand Chicago police on full alert; six thousand National Guardsmen with M-1 rifles, shotguns, and gas canisters; seventy-five hundred U.S. Army troops; one thousand federal agents from the FBI, CIA, and army and navy intelligence services (one of every six demonstrators was an undercover agent, they would claim later). Electronic surveillance was conducted against the Mobilization, the Yippies, McCarthy headquarters, and the broadcast media. The amphitheater was secured with a two-thousand-foot barbed wire

fence, roadblocks in every direction, a ban on low-flying aircraft, and electronic equipment to certify the identity of delegates. The convention police command was centralized in a
secure headquarters at the amphitheater, complete with giant
electronic maps of Chicago, video and radio links to every security unit, and hot lines to the White House and Pentagon.

On our side were approximately a thousand people, mainly in
their early twenties, waiting nervously in a park, looking for
places to sleep.

It was Saturday morning, August 24, one day before the official opening of the convention. I was sleeping late. The bedroom
door opened. Drowsily, I saw a naked woman, who had risen
earlier. Maybe she'll come back to bed, I was thinking, when she
said quietly:

"There's a man outside with a gun."

Well. No need for coffee now. She went back to observe him
through the front-room curtains while I dressed and composed
a plan. Grabbing an apple, I jumped out the kitchen window of
the apartment building in Hyde Park, ran several blocks, and
hopped the El train to Chicago's Loop. There I made my way
through thick crowds of shoppers to our Mobilization offices,
high in an office building on South Dearborn.

FBI MEMORANDUM   **9/27/68**

████████,* assigned to Area 5, Chicago Police Department, advised that he and ████████ at 2 a.m. on August 24, 1968, were
assigned to conduct a physical surveillance on Tom Hayden at
6027 South Kimbark Avenue, Chicago. ████████ stated his shift
commenced at 2 a.m., and lasts until 2 p.m. each day during the
Democratic National Convention.

████████ stated that he had very little visual contact with Hayden
during the weekend of August 24–25, 1968 while he stayed in
the apartment.

When I left the elevator at the floor of our office, there was a
beefy, casually dressed man with crossed arms, menacing eyes,
and greased hair standing against the wall. A hit man, I thought,
and quickly entered the office. Rennie was there already and

*Material deleted by the FBI.

asked, smiling, "Have you met yours yet?" He had first encountered the man now outside the office door on his apartment steps
that morning.

Our two plainclothes tails were Chicago police officers named
Ralph Bell and Frank Riggio, although they never introduced
themselves formally. They were assigned to follow us at the
fairly claustrophobic distance of about ten feet wherever we
went. We went to the bathroom; they followed. We went to
lunch; they sat glowering at the next table. We drove to a meeting; they lurched behind in their car. When close enough, they
made remarks about "getting" us, or "arresting you every time
you're in the streets." The larger of them, Bell, had a real habit
of losing his temper, getting wild-eyed, moving close, and
threatening to do away with me on the spot. A phone call notified us that Jerry and Abbie were being followed too.

If this is a preview, I thought, we are not going to be free to
meet or plan, and we will be lucky to survive. The week's events
were grim already; now we were being followed by characters
usually found in cheap movies about the Soviet Union.

By the afternoon, more and more demonstrators were arriving, filling Lincoln Park, getting to know each other, looking
over maps of the city, taking down the phone number for legal
aid, mainly waiting apprehensively for some direction. As night
fell, the Yippies, who had nominated a live pig for president the
day before on a platform of "garbage," were urging compliance
with the eleven P.M. curfew. Allen Ginsberg, chanting *om*, believed he could calm the tension with the police. At eleven P.M.
promptly, the police surged through the park on motorcycle and
foot, removing a few hundred people but with minimal arrests.

As the delegates arrived in their hotels the following day, the
twenty-fifth, we felt that the curtain of uncertainty caused by
the lack of permits had to be pulled back and tested in daylight.
With Rennie carrying a bullhorn and taking the lead, we
marched from Lincoln Park all the way to the Loop's hotels—
without incident. However, uniformed and plainclothes officers, including Bell and Riggio, strode beside us all the way,
quarreling over the details of the route, until we reached Grant
Park, across from the Conrad Hilton Hotel, where we dispersed.
We were pleased, but no more certain of where the police would
draw the line.

Lincoln Park is always dark, but it was absolutely eerie, filled with the silhouettes of young dropouts, militant protestors, McCarthy volunteers, voyeurs, and undercover agents. This would be the night, I sensed, that the battle for Lincoln Park could get out of hand. The convention was beginning the next morning, most of the protestors had arrived, and the police would try to establish dominance. An anticipation of police harassment held the people together, allowing them to forget the relatively low turnout of a thousand or more. If the police had done nothing, the protest might have fizzled, directionless. But it wasn't to be.

Off and on during the past two days I had lost my police tails, only to have them show up at the next place or event where they expected me. Tonight they found me in the park and began glaring from behind trees as I wandered through the crowd. If there was going to be a confrontation at eleven, I knew that Rennie and I would not survive it one minute if we were closely tailed. I also knew that I would get little sleep unless I could get away from these pursuers to a safe and quiet apartment for the rest of the night.

A plan took shape: Bell and Riggio had driven their unmarked car into the park before following us on foot. If a tire was deflated, they could be stopped cold. With mingled friends providing protection, I stepped out of sight, circled the park, and approached the darkened car. An accomplice named Wolfe Lowenthal took most of the air out of one tire when Bell and Riggio suddenly appeared out of the trees, saw Wolfe at work, and quickly grabbed him. I ran up, and they turned on me, holding me against the vehicle, trying to shove me inside. What saved me from taking a very rough ride in that unmarked car was a crowd that quickly gathered around the officers, chanting, "Let him go, let him go!" Bell and Riggio, sensing their loss of control, backed away. When I last looked back, they were stooped over fixing their rear tire.

The police waited until an hour past eleven to enforce the curfew that night, then swept Lincoln Park with clouds of tear gas. Our precautions for the gas attack were minor; people were instructed to cover their faces with Vaseline and soaking handkerchiefs or towels, even the sleeves of their shirts if necessary. But the gas canisters did their job, turning the balmy night air into a jolting, choking, inescapable darkness. It was as if someone held me down and stuffed pepper in my mouth, nose, and eyes. The impact made everyone gradually give way, screaming at the police or throwing rocks at their shotguns, then running blindly in whatever direction promised relief from the clouds of gas. The streets around the park were jammed for hours, as the citizens of Chicago began to feel the presence of confrontation for the first time. Some motorists shouted their sympathy, but most were enraged at the tie-up or immobilized at the sight of police weaving on foot between cars, clubbing longhairs into the pavements. The police also unleashed a volley of hate toward the press, beating many reporters and photographers who were wearing their press badges and attempting to cover the melee.

Temporarily free of Bell and Riggio, I slept a few hours on the couch of Vivian and Richie Rothstein's apartment. The next day, Monday, the twenty-sixth, the convention began formally. McCarthy supporters and dissident Democrats now held out no hope for derailing Humphrey, who, in addition to restating his allegiance to Johnson's policies, was making obsequious statements of support for the Chicago police. The only hope remaining to the progressive delegates calling for an open convention was a Vietnam peace plank they sought to add to the Democratic platform. The platform committee's draft endorsed Johnson's policies, however, despite the fact that a 53 percent majority of Americans in the Gallup poll now thought the war was a "mistake," up from 25 percent two years before. The alternative peace plank, calling for cessation of the bombing of North Vietnam, a mutual troop withdrawal from South Vietnam, and a coalition government in Saigon, would have a lot of delegate appeal, I thought. It would also bring Lyndon Johnson all the way from the Pedernales River if necessary to crush it. "He called me at the convention, where I was with my antiwar friends," Doris Kearns remembered. "He wanted to come, was planning to come. He went on for fifteen minutes about how the country was rejecting him."

I went to Lincoln Park for a meeting of our marshals early that afternoon. Since it appeared that the police would continue their gassing, clubbing, and arrests to drive us away from the convention areas, we needed an emergency response plan. Our exhausted medical volunteers were working on the injured and supplying crucial advice on coping with tear gas. How could we keep the police from arresting them? Our legal teams were similarly swamped, between bailing people out of jail all night and taking down endless affidavits against police brutality. They were frustrated on many levels, for example, by the police practice of covering their identifying badges with tape before the clubbing began. Virtually all communication with city officials, police commanders, and Justice Department liaisons was over.

As we contemplated what to do, I noticed a police wagon and a second vehicle bouncing straight over the grass, coming our way, pulling to a stop less than a hundred feet from us. After a moment, Bell and Riggio, backed by several uniformed and club-wielding officers, jumped out. There was no escape, so I simply said to the marshals, "I'm going to be arrested right now." The officers grabbed me by the arms and marched me into the wagon along with Wolfe Lowenthal, and we took off on a bumpy and rapid ride downtown while a surprised and angry crowd gathered in our way on the grass.

"I oughta kill you right now," Riggio said as we rode in the cramped back compartment of the van. He was nervously dragging on a cigarette and staring at me as if I were an animal. I concentrated on what to do if he started carrying out his threat. "But you're gonna get it. You're gonna get federal charges and go away for a long time." There it is, I thought. He's already been given the big picture by someone. And this is only day one of Convention Week. They jailed me downtown. Several stories below me I could hear marchers shouting, "Free Hayden!" Another demonstration had been permitted, I happily thought. The rules were changing by the moment. I rested quietly in my cell, trying to plan how I was going to make it through this week on the streets outside. My thinking was interrupted by a jailer who unlocked the cell door, informing me that I was bailed out.

Relieved that it was not yet dark, I quickly left the station— only to discover a new man with a gun leaning against the wall of the precinct. As I groaned to myself, he said, "Well, I've finally caught up with you." He was the original tail, who had waited outside my apartment Saturday morning. I didn't catch his name, but he was indistinguishable from the others, a nastiness seething from and marring his ethnic working-class face. He sauntered close behind me as I looked for Rennie to get a report on the day's events and the night's expected chaos. We reconnected, were surprisingly able to lose my newest tail in the Chicago traffic, and decided to cruise by Lincoln Park as curfew neared.

FBI MEMORANDUM   **9/20/68**

██████* advised that he was one of the officers assigned to a surveillance team on Thomas Hayden during the daytime hours. During that four day period, ██████ and his partner, ██████, spent most of their time trying to locate Hayden, who actively made every effort to lose his police escort through that period. Due to the crowds, Convention, and demonstration-type activities, Hayden was successful in these efforts.

The second night was worse than the first. In addition to the heavy gas, the police fired salvos of blanks from shotguns at the crowd in Lincoln Park. Allen Ginsberg and his friends seemed to think they could blissfully vibrate the violence away, and I'm sure he was disappointed that so many of us were consumed with what he considered negative energy. At the time I thought, however, that Ginsberg was crazy, sitting lotuslike in the grass, eyes closed, chanting *om* over and over while the police lines tightened. I didn't think our bad karma was particularly responsible for what was happening. In retrospect, I can see now that my own hostility was partly self-fulfilling, but it was also an honest response to being choked by the gas, to doubling up with pain, to crawling or running for safety, and to rubbing blood, dirt, and tear gas into one's eyes.

The scene was totally surreal, a cultural war between thousands of police and protestors just blocks, even doors, away from the exclusive Gold Coast section of Chicago, where the affluent citizens went about their "normal" lives, trusting the police to keep their existence sanitized. It was crazier still in the Loop, where convention delegates wearing straw Humphrey hats, festooned with candidate buttons, were partying in the lounges just a sidewalk away from the police lines and the ominous darkness of Grant Park.

I was watching the delegates return from the amphitheater to the Conrad Hilton about midnight, when I encountered Jack Newfield, Geoff Cowan, and Paul Gorman, the McCarthy speech writer. They described how Hubert Humphrey that night had cemented his pact with the southern Democrats against the antiwar liberals in pushing for the status quo plat-

*Material deleted by the FBI.

form plank on Vietnam. I tried to explain how insane it was in the streets, but it was as if we were in two worlds, invisible to each other. They invited me into the Hilton, where they had rooms. I got as far as the revolving door, where a hotel officer held out his arm. "We don't want this man in here," he said. Bemused, my friends started arguing that I was their guest. I became jittery. Just across Michigan Avenue a line of police was confronting a new crowd of demonstrators. Suddenly, Riggio appeared at the edge of our circle, smoking a cigarette, staring at me, his boots pawing the ground. "Forget it," I said and started to cross the street, careful to move away from the confrontation brewing in the park.

Suddenly, I felt the hint of a tornado over my right shoulder. Out of nowhere came Bell, charging like a linebacker, crashing both of us to the street, beating my head, dragging me through the kicking boots of other police, twisting my arm in a karate hold, and slamming me into a police car.

It was just after midnight, and I was going back to jail for a second time.

TO: FBI WASHINGTON

FROM: FBI CHICAGO

2:48 AM URGENT 8/27/68 PAK

TO DIRECTOR (157-8489)

FROM CHICAGO (100-44963) IP

DEMCON

ADVISED THOMAS HAYDEN, COFOUNDER, STUDENTS FOR A DEMOCRATIC SOCIETY (SDS), WAS ARRESTED AT ZERO ZERO FIVE ZERO HOURS, AUGUST TWENTY SEVEN INSTANT AT NORTHEAST CORNER BALBOA AND MICHIGAN AVENUES, CHICAGO. CHARGED WITH SIMPLE BATTERY AND RESISTING ARREST (SPITTING ON POLICE OFFICERS). HAYDEN TRANSPORTED TO CHICAGO PD HEADQUARTERS, ELEVENTH AND STATE. ATTORNEY (FNU) SPELLMAN COUNSELED HAYDEN ALMOST IMMEDIATELY ON ARRIVAL. SPELLMAN WITH HAYDEN TWENTY MINUTES, THEN DEPARTED AND HAYDEN PROCESSED BY CHICAGO PD.

ADMINISTRATIVE

SECRET SERVICE AND MILITARY FURNISHED TELETYPES. US ADVISED. CHICAGO WILL FOLLOW.

The atmosphere in the detention room was ugly. I noticed among the thirty or so prisoners the faces of many younger SDS members—Bill Ayers of Ann Arbor, Terry Robbins of Cleveland, Jeff Jones from the Columbia strike—who had worked in civil rights and community projects. Whereas my first taste of violence in the South allowed me to *hope* for a response from the national government, their introduction to mindless sadism was coming at the convention of the Democratic party and Johnson administration. In two years, several of them would decide to form the Weatherman Underground and engage in offensive violence. Tonight they were sprawled on the floor, nursing cuts and bruises, listening to raging officers call them scum and threaten to beat them to death. Fortunately, Newfield, Geoff's brother, Paul Cowan, and Jim Ridgeway, all writers for *The Village Voice*, followed me to police headquarters and, after two hours, bailed me out. When I left the jail, it was three or four in the morning, and with my friends I walked the streets trying to get my bearings. It was no time to be arrested again, and I wondered where I could be safe. As Newfield later recalled that night, "Almost every noise was martial: fire sirens, the squawking of two-way radios, cop cars racing from place to place, the idle chatter of police on duty." I felt naked. I could not be me, not on the streets of Chicago.

As we wandered down the street, several prostitutes approached us, asking if we wanted sex. They were black, well dressed, and wore pink sunglasses and large McCarthy-for-president buttons. "No thanks," I said politely. "I just got out of jail."

"You did?" the lady replied. "So did we."

I grabbed a taxi to the *Ramparts* magazine office, where they published a daily "wall poster" on the convention. They would be up all night, and I could find sanctuary, coffee, a couch, and contemplate a solution to my problem.

Late the next afternoon, Tuesday the twenty-seventh, a new Tom Hayden appeared on the streets. Behind the fake beard, sunglasses, neckbeads, and yellow-brimmed hat which I alternated with a football helmet, no one knew me. A friend procured a variety of disguise materials from a stagecrafts store, and by dusk I was ready to rejoin people in the streets. My friends didn't know me until they heard my voice. To others, I looked like an undercover cop or random weirdo. I strolled right by the police. Bell and Riggio were hopelessly lost.

That night, the Unbirthday Party for LBJ was held in the coliseum, a peaceful sanctuary for bringing together the whole coalition. There were bruised faces and bandaged heads, diehard McCarthy volunteers, the tattered and tired and tenacious listening to Phil Ochs singing "I Ain't a'Marchin' Anymore" and "The War Is Over." At the chorus, somebody lit and raised a match in the darkened theater. Somebody else. And another. Ten. Fifty. Five hundred. A candlelight chorus, everyone singing, crying, standing, raising fists, reaching delirium at the words, "Even treason might be worth a try / The country is too young to die."

The reformist spirit of the civil rights movement, withered and repressed, had turned into the hardened rhetoric of the Black Panther party, whose chairman, Bobby Seale, flew in from Oakland to address the crowd in Lincoln Park the next day. The Panthers were the living incarnation of Frantz Fanon's "revolutionary native" for whom the acceptance of violence was a purifying step toward self-respect. Formed in late 1966, they carried out the call of Malcolm X for armed self-defense. Like Malcolm, they were street people, "brothers off the block," channeling the chaotic rage into armed street patrols, a newspaper that reached 200,000 people weekly, a children's breakfast program, and a support network that enjoyed massive backing in black communities, especially among young people. Their founder, Huey P. Newton, was a mythic figure on the streets of Oakland; he was imprisoned for a gun battle in late October 1967 that left one Oakland policeman dead, another seriously wounded, and Huey shot in the stomach. Yet because of the Panther presence, Oakland was one of the few black ghettos that never erupted in spontaneous violence in the late sixties. Even two days after the murder of Martin Luther King, when a Panther named "Little Bobby" Hutton was shot and killed while surrendering to Oakland police along with Eldridge Cleaver, the community remained still. Because of this focus on an almost military discipline, the Panthers initially considered the Yippies foolish anarchists and urged their members to stay away from Chicago during the convention. But under the lyrical spell of Eldridge Cleaver, a convicted rapist whose *Soul on Ice* was a nationwide best seller, the Panthers began to reconsider their stand on Chicago, embracing the notion that a cultural rebelliousness among young white people was a necessary prelude to their becoming real revolutionaries.

Seale flew in to endorse the Chicago demonstrations in the middle of the week. While only there a few hours, he gave a speech rich enough in violent metaphors to lead to his indictment a year later. Cleaver was launching a symbolic presidential campaign with the help of the white members of the Peace and Freedom Party, appealing to the Yippie constituency for his white support. Jerry Rubin eagerly endorsed Seale's remarks about "roasting pigs."

It must have been a truly disorienting sight for the undercover agents: a stern Black Panther in beret and black leather jacket boasting of the necessity of "picking up the gun," together with a hairy Yippie dressed, I recall, in love beads and plastic bandolier. It is a measure of the alienation of the times that what seem now to be caricatures of rebellion could have been taken seriously, but they were. The black underclass was connecting with overprivileged whites in a strange and explosive alliance of resentment and guilt. It was deadly serious, especially to Rubin's personal bodyguard, one of several undercover agents posing as Panthers and the Yippies in the crowd.

Though nothing happened after Seale's appearance, it was only a matter of several hours before the nightly ritual of battle resumed. This time a group of ministers held a vigil around a large wooden cross they carried into Lincoln Park. Over a thousand people sang the "Battle Hymm of the Republic," "Onward, Christian Soldiers," and "America the Beautiful" before a huge city truck began gassing them more heavily than the previous night. In addition, our medical stations were overrun and smashed, and numerous reporters were again beaten badly. Again the nearby streets were choked with running figures, with rocks, bottles, and police batons everywhere in the air. From Lincoln Park, we began trotting in twos and threes southward, over the several bridges on the way to the Loop and Grant Park, where the delegates were returning from the convention. I remember running the several miles fearing that the police would order the drawbridges lifted to cut us off.

Once outside the Hilton Hotel, we took a dual approach to the returning Democratic delegates. For the most part, we tried chanting "Join us, join us." A number of them actually did, especially as the week went on. But for the LBJ-Humphrey delegates, drinking nightly in the bars, filled with alcoholic disgust for hippies, we had another approach. They became the targets of our secret guerrilla-theater unit, a small group with the goal of exposing, surprising, and confronting delegates with the need to take sides. Mainly women, they dressed smartly and strolled through security lines without incident. Kathy Boudin and Cathy Wilkerson used lipstick to scrawl VIETNAMESE ARE DYING on the mirrors in ladies' rooms, and spray painted CIA in huge red letters outside an office we believed to be the agency's local headquarters. Connie Brown and Corrina Fales, another former NCUP staffer, along with Kathy, dropped stink bombs in the Go-Go Lounge of the Palmer House, by dipping facial tissues into butyric acid, a chemical that smelled like rotten eggs. Connie, not a very good criminal, was caught red-handed by a security guard. "I don't know what you're talking about," she protested to the guard. But she couldn't explain the foul-smelling odor coming from her purse. She was hustled away; feeling sorry for her, Corinna and Kathy turned themselves in as well. The three were thrown into cells filled with black lesbians and told by furious Chicago police that they would be jailed for twenty years. Kathy was particularly worried because she was planning to enter law school. Months after, on the advice of her father, noted attorney Leonard Boudin, the three pled guilty to malicious destruction of property and served no time. They became "unindicted co-conspirators" in the Chicago conspiracy trial one year later. Kathy never attended law school; two years later she joined the Weather underground, and in 1984, she pleaded guilty to second-degree murder and armed robbery and was sentenced to twenty years to life.

FBI MEMORANDUM   **9/20/68**

████████* stated in connection with the apartment where Hayden was staying at 6027 South Kimbark, he noticed photographs in the Chicago newspapers of three young girls who were arrested by the Chicago Police Department for throwing a "stink bomb" in the Conrad Hilton Hotel. He identified these three girls, one he recalled named Brown, prior to her arrest as previously visiting the apartment at 6027 South Kimbark.

████████ stated he was informed by the janitor of the building that the girl named Brown was a sub-lessee on the apartment at 6027 South Kimbark where Hayden was staying.

---

*Material deleted by the FBI.

There were far worse ideas circulating spontaneously. For a friend of mine from the New York Motherfuckers, who threw a sharp-edged ashtray at the faces of the police, yelling, "Here goes a provocateur action," this was the apocalypse. Another proclaimed to anyone listening, "You're not a free person until the pig has taken your honkie blood!" At one point I even prepared a tape to be played and amplified from inside the Hilton to embarrass the police into thinking I had penetrated their thick lines. The tape ended by calling on the protestors to "join me." Wiser and more cautious heads decided to throw the tape away before anyone tried to follow me. It was difficult not to be immersed in a frenzy.

About two A.M., the police commander curiously announced on a bullhorn that we could stay in Grant Park overnight, provided we were peaceful. A triumphant cheer of relief went up, and the tension was transformed into a more idyllic collective experience. People were lying on the comfortable grass singing protest songs with Peter, Paul, and Mary, the floodlit Hilton in the background. At moments like these, it was perfectly clear how peacefully the protests of Convention Week might have gone.

But suddenly at three A.M., the reason for the relaxed police behavior became stunningly apparent. Down Michigan Avenue in complete battle preparedness came the first units of the National Guard. Not only did they bear M-1 rifles, mounted machine guns, and gas masks, but they were accompanied by vehicles we'd never seen before, jeeps with giant screens of barbed wire attached to their front bumpers, which we came to call "Daley dozers." They abruptly took positions in front of us, menacing but making no move. A few protestors starting shouting, "Chicago is Prague!"

While the extreme tension continued, many of our people could take it no more and began lying down on the grass or in sleeping bags to rest before the sun came up. I became worried, as did our marshals, that a preemptive mass street arrest might be launched by the Guard, sweeping us off these streets as the very day of Humphrey's nomination dawned. I took a bullhorn and told everybody to go home. Then I left quickly to get a few hours' sleep myself before the most critical day of the convention.

That night the police carried their vendetta against the media onto the convention floor, where a security officer slugged Dan Rather. On national television, Rather said, "This is the kind of thing going on outside the hall. This is the first time we've had it happen inside the hall. I'm sorry to be out of breath, but somebody belted me in the stomach." Walter Cronkite added, "I think we've got a bunch of thugs here, Dan."

I was exhausted. I asked Bob Ross, who also lived in the Kimbark building, if he would stay with me in the streets the next night. After being arrested and hunted, I told him that I was worried about what the police might do if they caught me again.

FBI MEMORANDUM   **9/20/68**

████* learned from other individuals, primarily Rubin and his fellow Yippie Abbie Hoffman, that Hayden had been an active participant in the street disturbances . . . Rubin and Hoffman together with assorted associates were in the habit of discussing events of the previous evening over their morning meals, and it was during these conversations that remarks were made indicative of the fact that Hayden had been one of the few demonstration leaders who actually had taken part in the street action on the occasions previously referred to . . .

In this connection, ████ volunteered the opinion, based on ████ and his observations of Hayden, that Hayden was one of the most likely among their number to deliberately start or create an incident of violence, since Hayden appeared to be one of the few in this leadership who does not mind, or fear, actual participation in disorder . . . it was extremely difficult to remember specific or isolated remarks and incidents . . . Hayden made remarks at various times to the effect that the strength and future of the movement lay in the young people in this country who must be induced to follow the lead of himself and his associates. There was no question that their goal is generally the radical remaking of the structure and form of the United States Government, including its overthrow if necessary. He qualified this comment to the effect, however, that he could furnish no specific quote or remark which in itself would be illustrative of this goal.

With little or no rest, our leadership met the next morning—Wednesday, August 28, the day of Hubert Humphrey's ascen-

*Material deleted by the FBI.

sion to the presidential nomination and the day long anticipated as the showdown between the protestors and official powers.

Dave, Rennie, and I led a meeting in the empty, gray, paper-littered Mobe office. John Froines attended, as did Irv Bock, an undercover agent from the Chicago Police Department posing as the representative of the Chicago Peace Council. Irv was one of the week's marshals, a big, strong fellow who claimed to have time off from his job with American Airlines. He was suspicious since he didn't fit the stereotype of a protestor, but at this point his presence didn't bother us; we had nothing to hide now. Though weary and strained, we had to decide the most crucial questions of the week. Even if the demonstrations were mainly spontaneous, we had the heavy duty of calling the actions, setting the time and place, communicating with the police and press, and making sure that medical and legal help was available.

The dilemmas before us that morning arose from the physical impossibility of achieving our long-standing goal of reaching the amphitheater, about ten miles south of the Loop, at the moment of Humphrey's nomination. We were bottled up in the parks, yet we could not stand by in silence. We did not relish more violence, certainly not after the previous night, but we did want direct moral engagement with the delegates and politicians who we felt were selling out the country.

What, we asked ourselves, were our options? The police were offering the Grant Park Bandshell, near Lake Michigan, about a half mile from the Hilton, for a strictly contrived afternoon rally where we would be allowed to voice our grievances, then be ordered to disperse. This was completely unacceptable from our standpoint. The police wanted our rally to end in the afternoon, while we wanted to demonstrate *during* the nomination proceedings at night. And I suspected that the police were planning to surround us at the bandshell to prevent another night of protest in Grant Park across from the Hilton—the closest thing to demonstrating at the convention site.

We agreed that there should be a rally at the bandshell at noon, to take advantage of the temporary police permit and try to involve those thousands of Chicago citizens who were simply afraid to join us at night. We agreed on music, poetry, and speeches by a cross section of movement leaders and victims of violence. But there were only two choices for those who intended to remain after the "legal" rally. The first, preferred by Dave, was to organize a nonviolent march toward the faraway amphitheater. This, of course, would be blocked promptly by the police and probably end in mass arrests without even getting out of the bandshell area. The second notion was to get out of the park by mobile tactics after the rally and regroup in front of the Hilton by the time Humphrey was being nominated. This would avoid the snare of everyone being arrested in the afternoon. If they were going to make a mass arrest anyway, we could try to delay it to the time of the nomination and make them crush us visibly in front of the Hilton rather than in a remote park.

Feeling honest about the alternatives we would lay before the assembled crowd, we made our way to the bandshell about noon. Irv Bock went to a phone booth to inform his superiors of our intentions.

When we arrived, there were about ten thousand people at the bandshell, mostly an outpouring of Chicago citizens. I remember embracing Mickey Flacks, who came with her newborn baby, Mark, trusting, with so many others, that the rally would be a peaceful one. Vivian Rothstein told her she was crazy, but she wanted to be there. We began at 2:25, with people still filing into the park. Phil Ochs started singing. Dave was chairing. A few speakers from draft-resistance organizations and Vietnam Veterans Against the War were heard. I sat toward the rear with a few savvy marshals, trying to assess the large contingent of police who had arrived and stationed themselves in the corner of the bandshell area that was on the most direct route to the Hilton.

They were handing out a leaflet announcing that "in the interests of free speech and assembly, this portion of Grant Park has been set aside for a rally," then going on to warn that "any attempts to conduct or participate in a parade or march will subject each and every participant to arrest." Meanwhile, Vivian and others were distributing a leaflet appealing to the police. While I fully expected the police to continue their brutal behavior, there was nothing wrong with reaching out to their better judgment. Forty-three U.S. Army soldiers at Fort Hood has just been court-martialed for refusing "riot-control" duty in Chicago; why not some of Chicago's finest? The leaflet was poignant in its entreaty to the police:

Our argument in Chicago is not with you.

We have come to confront the rich men of power who led America into a war she voted against. . . . The men who have brought our country to the point where the police can no longer serve and protect the people—only themselves.

We know you're underpaid.

We know you have to buy your own uniforms.

You often get the blame and rarely get the credit.

Now you're on 12-hour shifts and not being paid overtime.

You should realize we aren't the ones who created the terrible conditions in which you work. This nightmare week was arranged by Richard Daley and Lyndon Johnson, who decided we should not have the right to express ourselves as free people.

As we march, as we stand before the Amphitheater, we will be looking forward to the day when your job is easier, when you can perform your traditional tasks, and no one orders you to deprive your fellow Americans of their rights of free speech and assembly.

By now the convention itself was unraveling from the strain of the week's events. Many of the delegates were joining our nightly protests as they returned to the hotels. Idealistic McCarthy workers, who turned "clean for Gene" from New Hampshire to Chicago, were heartbroken, alienated, radicalized. The effort to nominate their hero was only a matter of going through the motions. On this night, Hubert Humphrey would inevitably be nominated, the wheels of the party machine relentlessly turning regardless of the political consequences. However, a spirited fight would be taking place over the Vietnam platform plank in the afternoon. The Johnson-Humphrey position would prevail numerically, but the size of the peace bloc would measure how far the antiwar movement had reached into the Democratic mainstream.

Suddenly there began a commotion by a flagpole situated between the bandshell and the police line. A shirtless longhair was climbing the pole toward the flag. Nothing seemed to madden the police more than affronts to the American flag, although their hearts never seemed to melt when we sang "America the Beautiful" or "This Land Is Your Land." On this occasion, the teenager on the flagpole intended to turn the Stars and Stripes upside down, an international distress signal, though no one knew his intention at the time. People at the foot of the flagpole were yelling their approval or disapproval. Led by Rennie, our marshals headed over to keep order. A column of police waded in with clubs to make a forcible arrest. A few people threw stones and chunks of dirt at a police car. Dave urged calm over the microphone. The vast majority remained in their seats as Carl Oglesby, the SDS president, was introduced. Carl was an extraordinary orator, and was saying that while we tried to give birth to a new world there were "undertakers in the delivery room" when thick lines of police, clubs in position, began forming in front of the flagpole, facing off against our marshals, who had largely succeeded in calming people down. Rennie later remembered taking the megaphone and telling the police it was under control, we had a permit, and they should pull back to avoid further provocation. "On that last word," Rennie said, "they charged."

The police started forward in unison, then broke ranks, running and clubbing their way through the marshals and into the shocked people sitting on their benches. Human bodies flipped over backward. Others staggered into the benches and fell. Some police stopped to beat again and again on their helpless forms, then moved forward into the screaming, fleeing, stumbling crowd. Tear gas was wafting into the air, and I saw Mickey Flacks running off with her baby's face covered. The police were the Gestapo to her. She approached several of them, screaming, "Here, do you want the baby? Take him, take my baby!" Gaining her control, she began shuttling injured demonstrators to the university hospital on the south side, with the baby asleep in a backseat carrier.

Somebody yelled to me that Rennie was hit and lay bleeding, trampled, and unconscious. Oglesby kept speaking, describing the police state unfolding even as he tried to exercise his freedom of speech and assembly. I was not disguised, so I took my shirt off to change my appearance for the moment. Then I turned over and piled up several park benches to slow the charge of the rioting police. Next I circled around the melee toward the flagpole area to check on Rennie. He was being attended to by our medics and readied for an ambulance. His head was split open and blood was flowing over his face and down his shirt. The man standing over him with a microphone and tape recorder, I later learned, was from Naval Intelligence. Rennie was taken to the hospital by our own medics. Within a short while, the police arrived at the hospital to arrest Rennie, who was beginning to recover from a concussion and abrasions. The hospital staff hid him under a sheet, rolled him on a gurney through the police lines, and placed him in a cab. He was driven to South Kimbark, where he watched the rest of the night's events from the Flackses' couch, his aching head heavily bandaged.

Somehow the insanity subsided after half an hour. The police pulled back to their original position, but now they were reinforced by new units and helicopters from every direction. National Guardsmen were moved into place by the bandshell as well, also taking up visible positions on nearby bridges and the roof of the Chicago Museum. Bleeding, gassed, and disoriented, we were now surrounded on all sides. A full force of twelve thousand police, six thousand army troops with bazookas and flamethrowers, and five thousand National Guardsmen with Daley dozers stretched from the bandshell back to the Hilton and the Loop.

Surprisingly, the rally went on, with Allen Ginsberg, Dick Gregory, and several other speakers. But eventually it came to a final focus. Dave Dellinger announced that there were options for people: first, joining himself in a nonviolent parade attempting to go to the amphitheater; second, staying in the bandshell area; and third, moving out of the park for "actions in the streets." He then introduced someone from the Peace and Freedom Party who made the out-of-place proposal that we go picket with the striking Chicago transit workers. Next came a bizarre Jerry Rubin, with a live pig, which he wanted to enter in nomination for the presidency. A little flustered by these suggestions, Dave reiterated that his proposed nonviolent march would begin in the far corner of the park, and then he introduced me. I was reaching a climax of anger and, curiously, freedom. It didn't matter what happened now. "Rennie has been taken to the hospital, and we have to avenge him," I began, repeating it twice to get people's attention. I pointed out the police, guardsmen, and droning helicopters, and warned that we were now surrounded as twilight approached. I urged people not to get trapped in the park, to find their way out and back toward the Hilton: "This city and the military machine it aims at us won't allow us to protest in an organized fashion. So we must move out of this park in groups throughout the city and turn this overheated military machine against itself. Let us make sure that if our blood flows, it flows all over the city, and if we are gassed that they gas themselves. See you in the streets."

Seconds later, I disappeared from the park with Bob Ross, heading for my Kimbark apartment and a new disguise. A *New York Times* reporter drove with us. I heard on the car radio that the Vietnam peace plank was rejected by the convention by a 1,500–1,000 margin and that a protest rally had begun on the convention floor. In about an hour, I was back at the bandshell with a fake beard and helmet to cover my face. It was late in the day, perhaps five o'clock. Dave's march of over a thousand people was half sitting, half standing, blocked by a line of police who would not let them out of the park. Meanwhile, individuals and small groups of demonstrators were headed north along the lakeshore chain of parks looking for a bridge to cross onto Michigan Avenue and access routes to the central downtown area. Each of the crossings was occupied by troops employing mounted machine guns and the Daley dozers.

By some miracle, our trotting, winding crowd finally came to an open bridge at Jackson Boulevard, north of the Loop, and with a great cry of liberation ran over the short space and into Michigan Avenue, turning left to head the mile back toward the Hilton. There were over five thousand people cheering, running, shaking fists or making V-signs, flowing like a peasants' army toward the castle of the emperors. Seemingly from nowhere, the mule-drawn Poor People's Caravan, which Dr. King had intended to lead before his death, materialized in our ranks with Ralph Albernathy leading it as we headed down Michigan Avenue. It was seven-thirty, nearly time for Humphrey's nomination. The streets were open, as the police were forced to regroup into the face of our surprising initiative. The Dellinger march disintegrated, and everyone found their way toward the Hilton.

It was nearly dark, the city lights turning on, as we reached the corner of Michigan and Balboa, where all the swirling forces were destined to meet. Lines of blueshirts were in front of us, clubs at the ready. The protest column filled the street and swelled with unity as we moved straight ahead now. The first lines sat down.

As if by magic, hands were suddenly in the evening air, and we began chanting, "The whole world is watching, the world is watching, the whole world is watching."

We saw smoke and heard popping noises a split second before tear gas hit our front lines and began wafting upward into the Hilton and nearby hotels. We stopped, choking, trying to bite into our shirts. Then the blueshirts charged, chopping short strokes into the heads of people, trying to push us back. They knocked down and isolated several people, leaping on them for terrible revenge. One very young longhair was caught in the gutter, four or five police cutting his head open with their clubs. A reporter took a famous picture of him, face bleeding, holding up the V-sign, before he passed out. Medics wearing Red Cross armbands, who tried to get to him and others, were clubbed, choked, and kicked down in the street. Mace was squirted in the face of any others who approached, including the photographers. The mass of people fell back, stunned but orderly, helping the injured, to regroup for another march forward.

Bob and I got through the front lines and around the police to the very wall of the Hilton, where a mixed group of fifty or so McCarthy workers, reporters, protestors, and—for all I knew—plain ordinary citizens, were standing frozen against the wall, between the hotel and the police, who were facing the oncoming marchers. When the marchers fell back, the police turned on our trapped crowd, moving in with a vengeance, clubs and Mace pointed at our faces. We instinctively joined arms. They started pulling off one person at a time, spraying Mace in their eyes, striking their kidneys or ribs with clubs, and tripping them. Their eyes were bulging with hate, and they were screaming with a sound that I had never heard from a human being. Someone started shouting that a woman was having a heart attack. We were so besieged that I couldn't turn around to see what was happening. Then, as people started staggering backward, someone kicked in the window behind us, and we fell through the shattered street-level opening to the Hilton's Haymarket Lounge (named, strangely enough, in memory of Chicago police killed by an anarchist's bomb during a violent confrontation between police and protestors in 1886). The police leaped through the windows, going right by me, turning over tables in the swank lounge, scattering the drinkers, breaking glasses and tables.

Now, the *inside* of the Hilton was a battleground. Trapped demonstrators were trying to sit inconspicuously—in Levi's and ripped shirts—in chairs in the lobby until it was possible to get out safely. Bloody victims were walking about dazed, looking for help, as bellboys and clerks stared in shock. Reporters were rubbing their heads and trying to take notes. The McCarthy forces started bringing the injured to a makeshift "hospital" on the fifteenth floor, where they had headquarters. It had been a very bad night for them. The candidate's wife, Abigail, and children were warned by the Secret Service not to attend the convention; she assumed this was because they could not be protected from the Chicago police.

Upstairs now, the staff members of the defeated presidential candidate were ripping up bed sheets to serve as bandages. Many of the wounded were their own. Some flipped-out political aides were throwing hotel ashtrays at the police down in the street; others were trying to pull them away. Lights all over the McCarthy floors of the Hilton were blinking on and off in solidarity with the protestors in the streets below. Soon, the police cut the phone lines to the McCarthy suites and, in a final orgy of vengeance, stormed the fifteenth floor, dragging sleeping volunteers out of bed and beating them up as well.

At the convention, Humphrey was being nominated, but not without resistance. Senator Abraham Ribicoff, in nominating Senator George McGovern, stated that "with George McGovern, we wouldn't have Gestapo tactics on the streets of Chicago." Mayor Daley, in the first row, was interpreted as screaming, "Fuck you, you Jew son of a bitch, you lousy motherfucker, go home."

After Humphrey's nomination, which took until midnight, the McCarthy contingent vowed to march back to their hotels. About three in the morning, we welcomed them, a funeral column of tie-wearing delegates, each somehow holding a candle against the foul night air. Robert Kennedy had been fond of quoting a Quaker saying in his brief presidential campaign: "Better to light a candle than curse the darkness." Now it had come to this: While I welcomed these candles in the park, I *wanted* to curse the darkness.

I had reached exhaustion; so had the protest. So too had the hopeful movement I had hoped to build only a few years before. Over the course of the next day, the defiance wound down. Dick

Gregory led a march halfway to the amphitheater before it was stopped by more arrests, this time of many convention delegates themselves. We heard Eugene McCarthy, with gentle dignity, urge us to "work within the system" to take control of the Democratic party by 1972. He was harangued embarrassingly by SDS leader Mike Klonsky as a "pig opportunist." Ralph Abernathy spoke from an impromptu stage, an upside-down garbage can, calling it a symbol of Martin Luther King's last cause.

I lay on the grass, pondering the alternatives. Reform seemed bankrupt, revolution far away. We had taught the pro-war Democrats the lesson that business as usual was a formula for political defeat and moral self-destruction. But was anybody listening?

I felt drawn into a tunnel of our own, with no light at its end.

FBI MEMORANDUM

FROM: THE DIRECTOR

Once again, the liberal press and the bleeding hearts and the forces on the left are taking advantage of the situation in Chicago surrounding the Democratic National Convention to attack the police and organized law enforcement agencies. When actual evidence of police brutality is not available, it can be expected that these elements will stretch the truth and even manufacture incidents to indict law enforcement agencies. We should be mindful of this situation and develop all possible evidence to expose this activity and to refute these allegations.

The National Commission on the Causes and Prevention of Violence, appointed by President Johnson, concluded that a "police riot" was to blame for the disaster. In his introduction to the report, *Los Angeles Times* reporter Robert J. Donovan described the Chicago police behavior as nothing less than a "prescription for fascism."

Drawing on twenty thousand pages of witness statements, most of them from the FBI and the U.S. Attorney's offices, and 180 hours of film, Walker's team came to conclusions at great variance from Daley's accounts. There were 668 arrests during Convention Week, most of them involving individuals under twenty-six years of age, the vast majority being young men from Chicago with no previous arrest records.

About 425 persons were treated at the movement's makeshift

medical facilities. Another two hundred were treated on the spot by movement medics, and over four hundred received first aid for tear gas. A total of 101 required treatment in Chicago hospitals, forty-five of those on the climactic night of the twenty-eighth.

There were twenty-four police windshields broken, and seventeen police cars dented (by whomever). In addition, 192 of eleven thousand officers checked themselves into hospitals. Of this number, 80 percent were injured in the spontaneous events at Michigan and Balboa on the twenty-eighth. Only ten police, according to their own affidavits, said they were kicked, six said they were struck, and four said they were assaulted by crowds.

In contrast, of three hundred press people assigned to cover the street actions, sixty-three (over 20 percent) were injured or arrested. Fifty (including Dan Rather) were struck, sprayed with Mace, or arrested "apparently without reason," in the words of the Walker Report. The Daley machine had tried to sharply limit television access to the convention and streets; when that failed, the whole world was watching their tactics.

When the convention was over, Richard Daley offered his personal explanation for the violence in an interview with Walter Cronkite. Rennie, Dave, and I were communists, he darkly hinted, and that somehow explained it all. The mayor's words recall the blind mendacity of those times:

DALEY: Well, there really isn't any doubt about it. You know who they are.

CRONKITE: No, I really don't actually.

DALEY: Well, you know Hayden, don't you, and what he stands for?

CRONKITE: I don't know that he's a communist.

DALEY: . . . You sure know Dellinger, who went to Hanoi. Why don't, why isn't anything said about these people? They're the people who—go over now, see if your cameras will pick them up in Grant Park. Rennie Davis. What's Rennie Davis?

CRONKITE: Well, I don't know that they're communists.

DALEY: Well, neither do I, but . . .

I suppose it was fitting that such a bad year would end with the election of Richard Nixon to the presidency. The Democrats never recovered from the convention cataclysm and, more fundamentally, from Vice President Humphrey's continued allegiance to Lyndon Johnson. In retrospect, it is almost inexplicable that Humphrey did not distance himself from the president until late in the campaign, and then ever so timidly. The president's long-standing position was that there could be no American bombing halt without a "reciprocal" North Vietnamese military response. On September 30, Humphrey proposed an unconditional halt of bombing to clear the way for diplomatic progress, though he reserved the right to resume the air war. Immediately, there was a subtle shift of new support toward Humphrey. As Theodore White's history noted, there were no antiwar hecklers after that. A newspaper photo showed a student with a sign reading IF YOU MEAN IT, WE'RE WITH YOU. The McCarthy forces began supporting Humphrey actively. At the same time, support for third-party candidate George Wallace was eroding.

The Gallup poll of October 21 showed the depth of Humphrey's problem. Richard Nixon, pledging both law and order and a "secret plan for Vietnam peace," was leading by a 44–36 margin. In late October, Hanoi agreed to sit at the same table with the Saigon regime if the bombing stopped. On October 31, with the election less than a week away, Johnson played his trump card, announcing the bombing halt. On November 2, both the Gallup and Harris surveys shaved Nixon's lead to a perilous 42–40. According to White, "had peace become quite clear, in the last three days of the election of 1968, Hubert Humphrey probably would have won the election."

There has been much political conjecture that Hanoi wanted a victory at the American ballot box. Yet if any Vietnamese party meddled in American politics in 1968, it was the Saigon regime. By all accounts, they hoped for a Nixon victory to improve their bargaining position. As several histories of the 1968 election have indicated, staunch Republicans, such as Mrs. Anna Chennault, intervened to persuade General Thieu, on behalf of candidate Richard Nixon, not to join the new Paris talks. Hold out for a Nixon presidency, they implied, and a better strategic position. Thieu agreed, and Johnson's peace initiative fell through at the last minute.

Nixon's victory was by 0.7 percent: 43.4–42.7.

· · ·

This was the concrete explanation for Humphrey's defeat, but the broader question lingers: Did the radicalism of Chicago elect Richard Nixon? Having struggled with this question for twenty years, I find there is no "neat" answer. For years afterward, I tried to deny it, not wanting to take any blame for Nixon's victory. It would have been easier for me to accept blame if I truly believed the differences between Nixon and Humphrey were meaningless, or if I subscribed to the view that electing Nixon would "sharpen the contradictions" and accelerate the process of change. But I did not. I do not know if Humphrey would have ended the war sooner or differently than Nixon. I would like to think so, but it would have required Humphrey to break with the basic liberal anxiety of two decades about "losing" countries to communism. However, I am certain that a Humphrey administration would have avoided the scandalous Watergate conspiracies of the Nixon years, directed as they were against so many mainstream Democrats, and I doubt that Humphrey would have indicted the Chicago conspirators.

But it is too simple to place the primary blame for Humphrey's defeat on the New Left or the demonstrators in Chicago. I still believe that Humphrey would have won the November election if he had separated himself from Johnson's policies and spoken out for a negotiated Vietnam settlement earlier. To blame the protestors in Chicago, and student radicals in general, unfairly absolves the Johnson White House and the Democratic leadership from primary blame for their own self-destruction. Our cause was both just and rational, even if all our methods were not. Our values were decent ones, even if we could not always live up to them. We were not responsible for the killing in Vietnam or the segregation in Chicago. We arrived at a confrontational stance not out of political preference but only as a last resort. In repudiating our demands, the national Democratic leadership was cementing an alliance of expediency with its conservative and militarist southern wing against the more progressive ideals of its student, black, and peace constituencies.

The movement that had begun on the back roads of Mississippi saw its dreams napalmed by Vietnam; similarly, we who proposed political realignment found ourselves after 1964 and 1968 still excluded from a Democratic party that meanwhile upheld such affronts to peace and justice as allowing segregationist Mississippi senators to remain entrenched as chairmen of the Judiciary and Armed Services committees in America's highest legislative body. Mississippi blacks had been excluded in 1964; now the entire reform wing of the party was out in the streets. Emotionally scarred by eight years of battle, politically convinced that the party was beyond reform, I found it unimaginable that in just four years there would be a triumph of reform, that George McGovern would be nominated or that Richard Daley would lose his status as a convention delegate. My belief in the system was in critical condition.

I believe that, had he lived, Robert Kennedy would have been elected president in 1968. I interviewed several people in 1987 to determine whether this conclusion was wishful. I asked former U.S. attorneys Tom Foran and Richard Shultz, allies of Mayor Daley, who prosecuted the Chicago conspiracy trial; and Mike Royko and Studs Terkel, two famed Chicago journalists who were critical of the police and Mayor Daley. They all felt, with myself, that Robert Kennedy would have persuaded Mayor Daley to defuse the convention confrontation and would have been nominated in August.

Seeking the opinion of someone with a truly inside perspective, I went to Steve Smith, a Kennedy in-law and top campaign adviser to all three Kennedy brothers. Smith had kept his knowledge to himself for two decades. "Who can say with certainty?" he replied to my question. "But we were full of confidence. I don't know that Daley agreed with Bobby. There may have been some concern. But the relationship was left full of promise. 'Stay at it,' Daley told us. New York was next. I think we'd have won it. We were of a mind that if we won New York, Daley'd have been there."

Assuming Kennedy had won the nomination, I believe he would have been elected in November. He could have retained Humphrey's basic vote, cut into Wallace, and turned out large numbers of disaffected voters that Humphrey could never rouse.

But it was not meant to be. Instead, 1968 ended as a Greek tragedy. I understand why Robert Kennedy found meaning in the ancient Greeks. Tragedy involved folly, and every mistaken folly of politicians was recorded by Thucydides twenty-five hundred years earlier. "Love of power, operating through greed and through personal ambition, was the cause of all these evils,"

Thucydides wrote in his *History of the Peloponnesian War.* "Revenge was more important than self-preservation" among the rulers of the time. The doomed policy of Pericles could have consoled U.S. leaders: "All who have taken it on themselves to rule over others have incurred hatred and unpopularity for a time; but if one has a great aim to pursue, this burden of envy must be accepted." Blind arrogance made Chicago and the disaster of Vietnam seem inevitable.

But tragedy has another dimension, a noble one. Edith Hamilton described the "suffering of a soul that can suffer greatly" and the experience of loss for an entire generation that began with its soul fired with great hope. The two great periods of tragedy in Western culture, she pointed out, were Periclean Athens and Elizabethan England. Both were times, like the sixties, "when life was seen as exalted, a time of thrilling and unfathomable possibilities." Tragedy takes place only amid such possibilities of greatness.

Rarely, if ever, in American history has a generation begun with higher ideals and experienced greater trauma than those who lived fully the short time from 1960 to 1968. Our world was going to be transformed for the good, we let ourselves believe not once but twice, only to learn that violence can slay not only individuals, but dreams. After 1968, living on as a ruptured and dislocated generation became our fate, having lost our best possibilities at an early age, wanting to hope but fearing the pain that seemed its consequence.

As Jack Newfield wrote, after 1968, "The stone was at the bottom of the hill and we were alone."

14. | The Indictment Begins: Berkeley, 1969

With the election of Richard Nixon, a new period of political repression began in America, the first since the McCarthy era, during which Nixon served as vice president and learned the usefulness of questioning others' patriotism. Under Nixon, a variety of surreptitious and illegal "counterintelligence" actions were authorized, leading finally to the 1972 Watergate break-ins and the subsequent impeachment scandal. One of the Nixon administration's first moves to restore "law and order" was the indictment in March 1969 of the Chicago conspiracy defendants. In less than a decade since being inspired by John Kennedy, I was indicted by the same federal government—or was it the same? The cold chill of indictment now fell not only on myself but on the whole protest movement.

I emphatically did not want to be on trial in Chicago. Six months earlier, the day after the Chicago battle, I had driven to a nearby farm for a one-day respite. I took a walk with Joan Andersson, an old friend from the Newark project. It was the first time I had experienced soothing peace and quiet in months. I was tired, not simply from the street battles, but from the rootless and faction-filled organizing within lifeless bureaucratic structures like the National Mobilization. Farewell, old Mobe; I was leaving the national scene. I felt bad only in abandoning Rennie, who was determined to continue resisting the war at the national level. I now wanted to be in a community again, where both politics and life could be carried out on a human scale. I caught a plane to the Bay Area.

At twenty-eight years of age, I had not lived in a college town since Ann Arbor five years before. I had missed the flowering of alternative politics and life-styles that had swept the youth communities of the sixties. I wanted to settle in, reinvigorate myself with different friends, an infusion of energy, a fresh base. Living on a book contract and occasional speaking fees, I rented an apartment on the top floor of a building in north Oakland near the Berkeley border, with a magnificent view of the sunsets over San Francisco Bay.

There was no escaping the rush of continued post-Chicago conflict, however. The first night I arrived in Berkeley I found myself strolling, without notice, along Telegraph Avenue, the colorful Main Street of youth culture, amid a crowd of ten thousand people who were demonstrating their solidarity with Chicago, with the French students, and with the suppressed people of Prague.

That fall marked yet another upsurge of militant protests on campuses across America, with Berkeley very much in the forefront. University and city authorities were deeply threatened by the rising wave of change that had begun with the free-speech movement and now threatened to engulf all local institutions. In addition to being the campus focal point, the Black Panther party, whose national headquarters were near the Berkeley city line, was engaged in seemingly endless confrontations with the Oakland police. The swirling violence I left behind in Chicago was reappearing with full force in this idyllic community known as the "Athens of the West."

Governor Ronald Reagan and many Sacramento legislators were overstating the crisis for political gain and placing intense pressures on the university's board of regents. "Preservation of free speech does not justify letting beatniks and advocates of sexual orgies, drug usage, and 'filthy' speech disrupt the academic community," Reagan declared on the campaign trail. Reagan appointed Edwin Meese III, a hard-line, anti-student prosecutor from Berkeley's Alameda County, as his chief of staff, and the pair jointly pursued a war against campus radicalism. (According to a later review of the Reagan years by *The Sacramento Bee*, the Reagan-Meese team only "aggravated" the campus climate, causing "unrest to escalate under the Reagan Administration.")

The triggering issue in September 1968 was a decision by the regents of the university, under pressure from Reagan and the legislature, to deny academic credit to students taking a lecture course by Panther leader and author Eldridge Cleaver. The popular Cleaver series, which had been initiated by students and approved by a faculty board, was terminated three weeks into the semester. Demonstrations involving up to four thousand students immediately erupted, calling on the regents to reverse their Cleaver decision and add more minorities to the university faculty. In late October, hundreds of protestors occupied several buildings. I joined one group of 250 in Moses Hall, a classroom building. Inside, many of the students reminded me of the Columbia strikers, with their middle-class backgrounds and earnest radicalism. Two of those I met barricading the building were Bruce Gilbert and Carol Kurtz, recently graduated from Beverly Hills High School, now swept up in the revolutionary ferment. (Fifteen years later, Bruce produced several of Jane Fonda's most successful films, and Carol was chief of staff in my Assembly office.) That night ended with the police arresting 121 young people in a scene reminiscent of Columbia. Worried about another arrest only two months after Chicago, I decided not to give myself up voluntarily. Instead, I climbed over the rooftop to the ledge of an upper window, and waited. Below, two thousand demonstrators set fires in trash cans, chanted, and taunted the heavily armed police. I half expected the police to find me, and I worried how to get off the ledge when they did. But when dawn came and the confrontation ebbed, I jumped to the limb of a nearby tree, climbed down, and wandered away.

A few weeks later, Eldridge Cleaver, facing almost certain return to prison, left San Francisco and went underground, destination Cuba. The Berkeley students asked me to teach a new version of his lecture course. To circumvent the regents, they cleverly arranged for students to receive academic credit for independent study, supervised by individual faculty members. My task was to give lectures on social change; they attended, did outside reading, and wrote term papers for their professors. The lectures got under way in January with three hundred students in attendance and Reagan declaring his opposition. "We're checking out whether you can study revolution for credit," I joked. In hindsight, it would have been far better for the university to accredit such studies than to declare them illegitimate—especially with college sports, fraternities and sororities, and ROTC accorded respectability within academia.

But the Berkeley campus, like San Francisco State across the bay, was soon swept by a massive strike, led by Chicano and black students demanding a college of ethnic studies. My lecture class came to a halt. Reagan declared a "state of extreme emergency" on February 5 and asked for legislation that would, among other measures, ban unauthorized loudspeakers from campuses and make faculty members convicted in campus demonstrations ineligible for future employment. As the demonstrations continued, Reagan gave the regents a "tongue lashing," in which, according to *The New York Times*, he demanded an immediate program to "end guerrilla war." Campuses should be protected, he declared, "at the point of bayonet if necessary. . . . I don't care what force it takes. That force has to be applied." One regent, former Kennedy adviser Fred Dutton, complained that the administration was "not getting to the basis of the problem," but the regents overwhelmingly imposed a minimum two-week "interim suspension" when there was a cause to believe that a student had engaged in "disruptive" activities. With that decision, thousands of students were threatened with de facto suspension from the university on the arbitrary judgment of police and campus administrators. Their anger grew. Later that month, police made repeated charges into student picket lines, finally clubbing and arresting two Chicano student leaders.

The campuses were now slipping out of control, not simply in the Bay Area, but across America. All kinds of demonstrations were happening in every part of the country, about every issue, on any day of the week, as never before. Glancing back at United Press wire stories for that single day when the clubs fell in Berkeley—February 27, 1969—one finds the following items:

- At the University of Wisconsin, Madison, hundreds of students rampaged through nine campus buildings, demanding increased black enrollments.
- At the University of Chicago, the law school building was locked in the face of a student march. Stink bombs were set off in six buildings. (The student demands were not reported on the national wires.)

- At Wiley College in Marshall, Texas, the administration decided to reopen the school March 12. It was closed because of student demonstrations, the purpose of which was not reported.
- At Notre Dame, two students were indicted by a campus board for showing "pornographic" films on campus.
- At all-black Stillman College in Tuscaloosa, Alabama, a five-day sit-in was ended.
- At American University in the nation's capital, five hundred students occupied a building to protest the campus administration's refusal to allow an appearance by Dick Gregory.
- At the University of Tennessee, 250 students attended a noon rally demanding the end of dormitory curfews for coeds.

From fall 1968 through spring 1969 in Berkeley, there were six major confrontations involving twenty-two days of fighting in the streets; over two thousand arrests; 150 suspensions or expulsions from the University; forty days of occupation by police forces from surrounding cities; twenty-two days of National Guard occupation; four months of locally declared state-of-disaster conditions and five months of "extreme emergency" declared by Reagan. In the worried calculations of the establishment, Berkeley occupied the same sinister, conspirational, and central role which, in their view, Havana played in the Third World. "There is substantial reason to believe that the rampant current philosophy of student revolt [at Berkeley] has been developed, tested and subcontracted to other institutions throughout the country," a Reagan spokesman told a congressional investigating committee. The truth was more that Berkeley, from the free-speech movement forward, continually set an example for movements across the country. To be in Berkeley was to feel yourself at the center of history being made.

The bloodiest 1969 confrontation, a precursor of Kent State and Jackson State one year later, took place over "People's Park," an acre of neglected vacant land belonging to the university just south of campus and one block from Telegraph. The university, it was believed, was quietly planning to transform the lot into a colorless mall, hoping to pressure away the legions of hippies, teenage runaways, sidewalk jewelers, and tarot readers, not to mention revolutionary leafleteers who dominated the once-respectable south-campus area. Instead one day, a group of quite gentle street people took up shovels and began making a community park out of the littered and unused lot. Their act caught on, and over several weekends a growing number labored, hammered, and planted grass until a charming, green, little gathering place came into existence, with plenty of benches for relaxing, and swings and building blocks for kids. Tambourines and flutes played into the night as the builders took pride in their creation. Stew Albert and Judy Clavir, two of the most political Yippies, drew me into this creation of "turf." I helped a little with the manual labor, enjoying this refreshing respite from the usual wars with the system. Many political radicals viewed the park project as a hippie cop-out from serious revolutionary work, and a lively debate developed over where the life-style component fit into one's agenda. This inquiry was cut short rather quickly, however, since the university looked with growing distress at this unauthorized urban beautification project. They would not tolerate it, and we would not abandon the gardens and saplings just planted. To head off an irrational confrontation, several city officials and faculty leaders proposed negotiations with the university for a change of ownership of the $1.3 million property. The debate over the park drew such national figures as General William Dean, a Korean War commander who pushed a hard line, and Thomas Hoving, director of New York's Metropolitan Museum of Art, who urged creation of the new park. Meanwhile, a handful of local activists posted themselves in the park every night, sensing possible trouble.

With no warning, hard-line elements decided to move against the park, on the night of May 14. Captain Charles Plummer pulled his battle-ready Berkeley police together for a pep talk, declaring that they were "the last stronghold against the Commies, and today we are going to crush them." Just before dawn, Berkeley police officers, backed by a helicopter and 250 highway patrolman, marched into the park, forcing out the young people maintaining the watch. At five A.M., about fifty construction workers, protected by the police, erected an eight-foot-high chain link fence all the way around the block containing the park. Like many Berkeley activists, I was awakened early in the morning with phone calls recounting what happened. By eight A.M., many were standing in cold disbelief around the fence being spiked into the park they had built. Inside the fence, heavily protected Berkeley police lounged and laughed on the children's swings. According to the press, the university ex-

plained that the fence was installed "to make sure that the land
was recognized as University property."

By noon, at least five thousand people were massed in nearby
Sproul Plaza to protest the destruction of the park. Though an
exact plan was never discussed, it was clear that the angered
crowd would tear the fence down if they reached it. I was
scheduled to speak on the steps of Sproul Hall and was wondering what to advise while I listened to student body president
Dan Siegel. Dan called out something about the need to "take
back the park"—and was drowned out by the impatient throng,
who turned his phrase into a chant, and before our eyes began
moving in a giant sea toward Telegraph Avenue and the three
short blocks to the location of the park. Ahead of them, we could
see thick lines of police with gas masks already on. They also
held tear-gas launchers and shotguns. As the crowd walked and
trotted toward their positions, the police began wafting canisters of gas, trailing a wisp of white smoke, at the front line. The
marchers held, covering their eyes, and a few ran forward to
pick up the hot canisters and hurl them back toward the police.

From this initial stand-off, there began seventeen consecutive
days of street fighting, the longest such battle in American history, finally ending in a solemn and nonviolent march to the
park fence by almost thirty thousand people. During those days,
scenes of the Vietnam War were replayed on a college campus
for the first time. The Alameda County sheriffs carried shotguns
loaded, not only with birdshot but with deadly double-O buck-
shot, never before used against students. About 150 demonstrators were shot and wounded, many in the back. Seventy people
were treated for gunshot wounds at local hospitals.

On May 15, the day the fence went up and we marched down
Telegraph Avenue, a Berkeley freshman named Steve Carr
climbed on the roof of an apartment building overlooking the
skirmishes. Now a loan officer at Citibank in San Francisco, he
remembered being a Naval ROTC student who was "curious
about what was going on." He wanted to get above the tear gas,
so he sat on a rooftop and watched. The sheriffs' response to the
march had been immediate; they started opening fire on people.
But then there was a lull, Carr recalled. A car was burning, but
the avenue had quieted down. I was on the avenue, where debris, rocks, and overturned trash cans reflected a growing war
zone. I was choking from the gas and yelling that people should

move off the avenue, where they were easy targets. The police looked like armed and swaggering astronauts, slowly swiveling in the avenue with weapons pointed only a few feet away. Then Carr saw someone who'd thrown a brick from the rooftrop twenty minutes earlier. "I turned and told him not to do it again. Then I felt a tremendous concussion, like a tear-gas canister." The sheriffs had spun and fired across four rooftops. Carr was hit with 125 pieces of birdshot; one pellet was less than a millimeter from his eye; another was lodged against his carotid artery. The individual sitting next to him, Alan Blanchard, was not lucky enough to have turned his head and was instantly blinded. Two roofs over, a twenty-five-year-old carpenter named James Rector was wounded and bleeding. All three waited over forty-five minutes in an apartment before being taken to the hospital, where Rector died twenty-four hours later.

On the day following Rector's death, a funeral march and vigil was met by a National Guard helicopter, which dropped white clouds of misty CS gas over Sproul Plaza. Several hundred faculty members started to boycott the university the next day, calling for the chancellor's resignation and charging that the campus was becoming an "experimental laboratory for the National Guard." The student paper demanded the closing of the university as "not safe for human beings."

On the other hand, Major General Glenn Ames, commander of the state National Guard, defended the helicopter drop of CS gas as "perfectly logical." Ronald Reagan had not yet made his famous statement—"If the students want a bloodbath, let's get it over with"—but the murderous precedent was established. (Reagan's bloodbath comment was made to the Council of California Growers on April 7, 1970—one month before Kent State.)

Steve Carr, whose father was a military officer, spent three days in an intensive care unit at Oak Knoll Naval Hospital, where an American soldier wounded in Vietnam slowly died next to him. He watched the rest of the Berkeley events on television among the war-wounded in the hospital and was released ten days later. He testified at a coroner's inquest and trial that he thought the policies of Ed Meese and the county sheriffs were an "extreme reaction." I went to visit Alan Blanchard shortly after he was shot, fighting off feelings of responsibility for what had happened to him. He was a blond, long-haired young man in his mid-twenties, an aspiring artist. But now he was uncomfortably rotating his head to locate me, trying to adjust to his sudden deprivation. Though still in shock at the sudden and random nature of his loss, he moved me by his acceptance of the life he now faced. I went away still feeling guilty.

I was in a particularly morbid mood during the entire People's Park confrontation. On May 5, in Chicago, Dick Flacks was almost killed. He had gone to the university office to see someone who identified himself as a reporter. There his skull was fractured in two places and his wrist slashed, his right hand almost severed. He was unconscious and bleeding profusely when someone found him a few minutes later. The news reached me immediately, and I called Mickey at the emergency room of a Chicago hospital. She was in a state of controlled hysteria.

"He could be like a vegetable" was the most optimistic prognosis she could give.

After four hours of surgery, in which a piece of bone was removed from his skull, Dick was temporarily out of danger. He stayed in the hospital for a month. At first unable to walk or use his right hand, he slowly showed signs of recovery. In six weeks he was better. The Flackses decided to leave Chicago.

The assailant or assailants were never apprehended. Chicago authorities speculated that the attempted murder had political overtones. Flacks was outspoken and visible on the campus as an "SDS founder," leading to right-wing groups writing letters to the university calling for his removal. In March, a right-wing group called the Legion of Justice had physically attacked a Vietnam sit-in on the campus with which Flacks had been associated. The legion had grown out of the anti–Martin Luther King forces of 1966 and had cooperated with the police Red Squad and an army intelligence unit in Evanston, from whom the legion obtained tear gas, Mace, and bugging equipment. Later, they stole records from the defense office of the Chicago conspiracy trial.

Aside from the depression Dick's suffering caused me, there was a further lesson I could not escape from drawing: There seemed to be no refuge from the coiled spring of personal violence. Of the original SDS leadership, the Flackses were the two who most consciously chose to lead professional lives within the system and raise a family. They wanted "normalcy." Dick was speaking out, but he was not leading any confrontations in the streets. But the system was no protection against the stereotyping and vengeance-seeking hatred that assaulted him at his university desk.

TO: DIRECTOR, FBI   **7-26-68**

FROM: SAC, CHICAGO

SUBJECT: COINTELPRO-NEW LEFT

Enclosed for the Bureau is one copy of a letter prepared by Special Agents of the Chicago office with the thought in mind of sending it to members of the Board of Trustees of the University of Chicago and to the Chicago Tribune . . .

The Chicago office recognizes that the administrative officers of the University of Chicago are probably aware of the existence of the New University Conference and its program. The Board of Trustees, however, is composed of individuals such as John D. Rockefeller whose wide interests might preclude any knowledge on their part . . . *The letter is intended to stimulate an interest in the proposed activities of the New University Conference and to prod the Board of Trustees into some action against Flacks* [emphasis added].

Bureau authority is requested . . .

TO: SAC, CHICAGO   **8/2/68**

FROM: DIRECTOR, FBI

REURLET [re: your letter] 7/26/68

Authority is granted to make the anonymous mailing of the letter . . . The letter is to be prepared on locally purchased stationery which cannot be traced to the Bureau or to the Government. Assure that all of the necessary steps are taken to protect the Bureau as the originator of the letter.

Any positive results obtained should be promptly furnished the Bureau.

. . . *This proposal has merit as it may discourage Flacks or even result in his ultimate removal from the University of Chicago* [emphasis added].

At this same time I was indicted with seven others by the Nixon Justice Department for conspiracy to incite violence at the Chicago convention. This meant going back to Chicago for a long trial starting in September and, I expected, the probability of five or ten years in jail. There seemed to be no exit from the state of permanent siege I was under, no future without walls.

In my early months in Berkeley, I had glimpsed briefly the possibilities of a real family relationship with a woman. I had known Anne Weills Scheer only at a distance. A Berkeley native from a comfortable background, she was a tall, striking, and intensely serious activist who was recently separated from her husband of several years, *Ramparts* editor Bob Scheer, with whom she shared an infant son, Christopher. One of Berkeley's most capable radicals, Scheer authored some of the earliest and widely read pamphlets against the Vietnam War, received 45 percent of the vote running as an antiwar challenger for Congress in the 1966 Democratic primary, and made *Ramparts* into the first successful "alternative" magazine. Scheer himself became the first New Left leader to be a commercial success. The perception was that he lived at a glamorous, high-spending, coast-to-coast pace, going through *Ramparts*'s money on unheard-of indulgences such as suites at New York's fashionable Algonquin Hotel. His high-roller status generated a mixture of envy and awe. His marriage deteriorated, partly due to his long separations from home, but also from the anti-institutional pressures of the time. Anne and I began seeing each other, enjoying a personal and political relationship. Through her life, I could see the joy of being a parent, something I had long dismissed.

I took responsibility for Christopher half time, the new ethic for fathers. It was a wonderful surprise to be around a child, and I discovered I was good at taking care of him. I actually liked smearing on pungent gobs of Desitin to prevent diaper rash, shampooing a screaming youngster in a bathtub, watching him slobber over yogurt at breakfast, rubbing his back at nap time, babysitting, and reading Dr. Seuss stories at night. But these were only peripheral pleasures compared to the breathtaking experience of unconditional love, in which I had to put the infant's immediate needs ahead of my own. It was not the way I had learned to understand the workings of the world.

But Anne felt, with some reason, that it was impossible for her to enter a stable relationship so close to her own separation, and she struggled with guilt as a mother leaving a marriage. At a time when women's consciousness-raising groups were appearing across the country, Anne helped form one of the first. Above all, she wanted to be free, no one's extension. It was not easy. She dazzled men with her attractiveness, but her evident brains and boldness were threatening. Wanting independence, she was seen more often as either a desired ornament or an intimidator. Her view of love, not surprisingly, was modeled on Simone de Beauvoir's, as she once wrote me:

> I don't take at all seriously the apparatus of living together, in fact I'm beginning to think that's one way to kill love. . . . You get bogged down in the super-structure and you forget why you're there. . . . It's hard to keep track of the essence, with the demands of politics, the denial of physical confrontation because of the kid, the frustrations of being a woman in this Shit Society, the need to be financially independent . . . to me, responsibility is taking care of those core emotions and not living each other's lives.

Nevertheless, through Anne and her son, I discovered an instinct I had not known before, a desire for family, for children. The more illogical it seemed, the more the desire rose. I was adrift from my own family and headed for a future without cozy hearthsides where parents read bedtime stories to snuggled children. Yet what was this desire telling me that my life was too narrow, too meager emotionally? Was it a repressed part of my human nature protesting that it would never have a chance to come to life in the future I was choosing? Was it a cry for lost possibilities just as I hardened myself for prison? I couldn't make it go away. All I could do was take this new vulnerability with me to the Chicago courtroom.

15. The Trial: 1969-70

There can be no doubt that behind all the actions of this court of justice, that is to say in my case, behind my arrest and today's organization, there is a great organization at work. An interrogation which not only employs corrupt wardens, oafish inspectors, and Examining Magistrates of whom the best that can be said is that they recognize their own limitations, but also had at its disposal a judicial hierarchy of high, indeed of the highest rank, with an indispensable and numerous retinue of servants, clerks, police and other assistants, perhaps even hangmen, I do not shrink from that word. And the significance of this great organization, gentlemen? It consists in this, that innocent persons are accused of guilt, and senseless proceedings are put in motion against them . . . considering the senselessness of the whole, how is it possible for the high ranks to prevent gross corruption in their agents? It is impossible.

—Joseph K., in *The Trial* by Franz Kafka

A successful prosecution of this type would be a unique achievement of the Bureau and should seriously disrupt and curtail the activities of the New Left.

—J. Edgar Hoover, October 23, 1968

CHICAGO POLICE DEPARTMENT   Intelligence Division
March 27, 1969

Captain Kinney (Newark police intelligence) called to relate that a meeting was held in New York City . . . by attorneys who will

represent the eight demonstrators indicted by the Federal Grand Jury.... The following information was obtained at this meeting:

1. Attorneys are taking the attitude that the demonstrators will be convicted and will work to force error on the part of the judge in order to get an appeal.
2. An attorney from New York named Weinglass will attempt to discredit the judge sometime during the trial.
3. The defendants will attempt to turn the proceeding into a circus and will wear false faces during at least one day of the trial. . . .

This information was telephonically forwarded to Assistant U.S. Attorney Richard Schultz.

THE SCENE: the twenty-third floor of the Chicago Federal Building, a black steel tower shielded from natural light and air by its green tinted windows, described by the Chicago Art Institute as a building in which "the commitment to order everywhere present is translated into an authoritarian and heroic presence." It is September, a brisk, gray season in Chicago that turns soon into the bitter cold winter on the Lake Michigan windy shores.

Leaving the elevator on the twenty-third floor, one is confronted by federal marshals, about a dozen of them keeping order in the hallway. Spectators trying to get into court will have to start arriving at five A.M. and wait outside in the cold. Then they will have to leave their coats and belongings on the hallway floor, pass the inspection of the marshals, and hope they will be among the few who get in. Otherwise, they must begin again another day. Once successful in getting into the courtroom, they risk losing their seat if they need to go to the bathroom, if they read, if they talk to someone, and absolutely if they groan or laugh.

The courtroom is a square chamber with mahogany walls, carpeted floor, an entire ceiling of fluorescent lights. At the sides are doors leading off to the jury room, the judge's private chambers, and next to the defendants' table, a corridor of gray stone cells. In the front is a giant seal of the United States, and just beneath it is the tiny, bespectacled, hairless head of Judge Julius J. Hoffman. The head moves in a regular bobbing motion, perhaps from a nervous tic, perhaps because of the judge's years, then being seventy-three. The head, which is all we could see of the judge, is elevated about ten feet above the floor. Behind it are several framed portraits of America's Founding Fathers.

Judge Hoffman is known to his friends as "strict," and to most observers as a "hanging judge." (Years after the trial, in 1976, Hoffman was rated as "unqualified" by 78 percent of the lawyers polled by the Chicago Council of Lawyers. But in 1969, his Chicago critics confided that they could never openly protest what they called his imperious behavior for fear of losing future cases before him. Protected thus from lawyers' criticism, the judge was further insulated from the ferment of the sixties by a conservative life-style. A Republican, he was a resident of the exclusive Gold Coast area of Chicago overlooking Lincoln Park. Through marriage, he was the millionaire beneficiary of stock in a defense firm, the Brunswick Corporation, which had been the target of antiwar pickets in 1968.)

Below and slightly to the right of Judge Hoffman is the neat table of the prosecution. There sits the main prosecutor, U.S. Attorney Thomas Foran, whom Rennie had approached unsuccessfully in 1968, asking that Foran appeal to Mayor Daley for permits. Foran was in a unique position to know the mayor, having once been his appointee at City Hall for land acquisition (known to irate community groups as the "urban removal" program). Foran is a former Golden Gloves boxing champion and a veteran who flew over a hundred bombing missions in World War II. Short and muscular, his curly hair turning gray, he has a rasping tone of voice, which develops an edge of disgust in referring to us. He expresses little emotion, though he endlessly clicks the end of his ball-point pen. Foran's assistant DA, Richard Schultz is a younger man, a year older than I am, a driven legal professional. While Foran is a man of political leanings and ambitions, Schultz is computerlike, fascinated with details, collecting and sorting alleged facts into the grand design of conspiracy. (He would study FBI transcripts of my speeches, for example, until two or three in the morning. "I would get absorbed in it because it was beautifully written and argued," he told me many years later. "Then I would snap out of it.")

Both Foran and Schultz were themselves on the streets of Chicago in 1968, in liaison roles between the federal authorities and the Chicago police. Schultz was on the very spot where demonstrators including myself fell through the windows of the Hilton's lounge on August 28. Both were aware that Attorney General Ramsey Clark opposed convening a grand jury to seek criminal conspiracy charges. After Nixon's election, Foran and Schultz visited the new attorney general, John Mitchell, and in Foran's words, "really liked his legal mind." They gave serious thought to not indicting us, they claimed, only because of the platform we would be provided. But in the last analysis they pursued the indictments because otherwise it would appear that we "got away with it." In Foran's theory, keeping us "sitting on a needle" would bring the movement to an end. To this day, they deny any "conspiracy" of their own with the judge or FBI to control the trial to their benefit, and they remain convinced of our absolute guilt.

Perhaps with this goal of "ending the movement" in mind, they selected as defendants eight individuals from Chicago 1968 who represented the varieties of radical dissent: Rennie and I were the New Left, Abbie and Jerry the counterculture, Dave Dellinger the conspiratorial antiwar network, and Bobby Seale the Black Panthers. John Froines and Lee Weiner, the only two defendants who were not symbols of larger movements, were indicted for their alleged lawbreaking as Mobe marshals and were the only defendants completely acquitted by the jury. In addition, it appeared that women sui generis were not considered dangerous or subversive, since none were indicted—an omission that actually angered several women who thought they were as qualified for prosecution as any of the male defendants.

FBI MEMORANDUM   **4/16/69**

TO: DIRECTOR
FROM: SAC, CHICAGO

The United States Attorney, Chicago, has requested a continuous flow of information concerning public statements made by the defendants, including their press releases, newspaper clippings, and verbatim transcriptions if available. . . .

The United States Attorney, Chicago, anticipates possible use of such statements to show possible admissions, to thwart a possible attempt to seek a change of venue due to publicity, and to show possible contempt of court before, during, and after the trials by the defendants and their lawyers.

The United States Attorney, Chicago, will furnish the Chicago Division with all itineraries as soon as they are received. . . .

We were charged technically with a conspiracy to travel interstate for the purpose of "fomenting a public disturbance" involving three or more people in "actual or threatened" violence. For each defendant, there was one count of conspiracy and one count of inciting violence, each carrying five-year penalties. The charge of conspiracy is well known as a "prosecutor's dream" because it requires no evidence of actual meetings, actual decisions, or actual implementation of a plan of violence. Thus, it didn't matter that several of us in this conspiracy had never met each other before being in Chicago, or in the case of Bobby Seale, before being indicted. All that was necessary was providing a *pattern* in our actions implying a collective "intent." The charges erased the traditional meaning and protection of the First Amendment. The well-defined freedoms of speech and assembly, as we understood them, allowed a citizen to *advocate* any doctrine, no matter how offensive or revolutionary. Such advocacy could not be considered criminal unless connected directly and tangibly with the *carrying out* of the idea in violation of personal or property rights. The classic formula of the courts was that freedom of speech ended when one cried "Fire!" in a crowded theater.

But according to the law under which we were prosecuted, a new limit on freedom of speech would be introduced. If any of us had justified "violence" or "confrontation" or "militant action" in a speech long before Convention Week, and there was indeed violence during Convention Week, our *prior* speech was to blame for that *later* violence—even if we were not present at the violence itself, and even if it happened without our knowledge or will.

For instance, one item of evidence introduced against Dave Dellinger was a speech given on July 12, 1968, one month before the convention, in San Diego. Present was a paid FBI informer, Carl Gilman, who took notes on Dellinger's one-hour talk. His notes were inexplicably destroyed, but Gilman testified that Dellinger said: "Burn your draft cards. Resist the draft. Violate the laws. Go to jail. Disrupt the United States government in any way you can to stop this insane war." Assuming these were Dave's exact words, they were perfectly legal, however shrill, by usual understandings of the First Amendment. His speech was not followed by any illegal action; it was pure advocacy. The only statement about Chicago, according to the FBI agent, was a comment at the end of the speech in which Dellinger allegedly stated, "I am going to Chicago to the Democratic National Convention, where there may be problems." The speech ended with applause, then Dellinger said, "I'll see you in Chicago." The "problems" in Chicago which Dellinger referred to in his speech, the agent testified, were related to the anxieties demonstrators felt over the nature of their welcome to the city. On such a thin thread of evidence was the giant web of violent conspiracy woven.

Another example was a speech by Rennie in Cleveland on August 17, 1968. This talk, tape-recorded by another FBI informer, made no mention of violence or disruption aimed at the convention, the government, or any other institution. In fact, Rennie was quoted as saying:

> "We want to say here in Cleveland that our fight is not with the policemen, not with the National Guard troops, our fight is not with the young men who are being ordered in Fort Hood in Texas to come to the convention for the protection of that convention from its own citizens. Our fight is with the *policies* of the United States government that have created this situation. . . ."

Even though Rennie described in some detail the agenda and program of entirely legal activities for the week, the prosecutors singled out one phrase: "the anger and militancy will be strongly expressed to the governing party and the world."

There were three speeches on which the prosecution depended to prove my guilt. The first and second were given in New York City, in March and July respectively. At the first one, notes were kept by Louis Salzberg, a photographer of twenty years with full press credentials, who had been receiving seven to eight thousand dollars yearly from the FBI for photographing demonstrators. Salzberg's testimony was that I had said we would "fuck up" the convention. But he confessed to have burned his own notes and claimed the words *fuck up* were not included in the typewritten version of his report to the FBI because the agency had "young girls as stenographers, and they will not print them that way." In addition, he acknowledged that I expressed hope that there would be no riots in Chicago and that a Yippie speaker accompanying me had stressed that our purpose was not to incite violence at the convention.

The second New York speech, in July, was on the subject of the Vietnam War and the Paris peace talks. Listening this time for the FBI was Frank Sweeney, a New York advertising man who had been approached to become an informer by an FBI neighbor at a Little League game. Sweeney made no notes until an hour and a half later, when he paraphrased the speech while waiting for a bus. He remembered that I had called for "shedding blood" and "breaking the rules." What I in fact said was that we had to be "prepared for shedding *our own* blood" and that the "rules of the game" of politics were rigged and ought to be broken.

The third speech was the spontaneous one from the Grant Park stage on August 28 after Rennie had been beaten, the crowd clubbed and gassed, and the park surrounded. This speech, the prosecution claimed, led to the mass demonstrations in front of the Hilton some four hours later. In one sense, they were right. But I had hardly crossed state lines intending to give such a speech. The key question was, Who provoked the violence that night? On this point, the Walker Commission was clear: The police themselves had rioted.

The thought of finding the complex truth about Chicago by selecting eight individuals as scapegoats was absurd from any investigative point of view. Conspiracy theories, after all, are self-fulfilling. They ignore as irrelevant the underlying cause that lead individuals to rebel. They deny that riotous behavior can occur spontaneously. Using informers for evidence virtually guarantees that phrases or sentences will be taken out of context and blame focused on single individuals. From Mississippi to Chicago, the establishment had always externalized its own responsibility by claiming "outside agitators." Lyndon Johnson had been cited in several histories as believing that international communist conspiracies lurked behind the American antiwar movement. As Leonard Weinglass tried to point out, an informant looking for evidence of conspiracy might have found Jesus guilty of urging young people to kill their parents, based on Matthew 10:34-36:

Think not that I am come to send peace on earth: I came not to send peace, but a sword.

For I am come to set a man at variance against his father, and the daughter against her mother, and the daughter in law against her mother in law.

And a man's foes shall be they of his own household.

"The substance of the crime," Judge Hoffman said one day, was a "state of mind." The phrase was close to that of Deputy Attorney General Richard Kleindienst, who labeled people like us as "ideological criminals" who should be placed in detention camps. Going further, Attorney General John Mitchell boasted in those years, "We are going to take this country so far to the right you won't even recognize it." By this, I assumed that the meaning of the First Amendment would be narrowed in the way suggested by the conspiracy charges against us and applied to other war resisters as well. Moreover, I believed, there would be expanded wiretapping and other forms of intrusion into civilian, democratic life by the FBI, CIA, and military intelligence, perhaps even preventive detention, denial of bail, and roundups, as happened to radicals in 1920 and to Japanese-Americans during World War II. Certainly, I expected Nixon's appointees to the higher courts to be staunch conservatives, dimming our prospects of successfully appealing a verdict in Chicago. Leonard Weinglass told me before the trial to expect a legal railroading and a ten-year sentence. If I drew "good time" as a model prisoner, he said, I could be out in seven years. In my anxiety, I imagined prison riots behind bars, even death, as did happen later at Attica State Prison in New York.

We had to make an immediate decision about our legal counsel and defense strategy. Our choice for defense attorney was Charles Garry, the Panthers' general counsel. We accepted Garry primarily because he was the incarcerated Bobby Seale's personal lawyer, but also because of his general reputation for brilliance in defending unpopular clients. An Armenian by birth, Garry was a silver-haired San Franciscan who put himself through law school at night in the thirties and also a wise man in the up-and-down history of the Left—perhaps too much so. When we first met with him soon after the indictments, he said he was sure one of us was an agent. I don't know if it was said simply for effect or to indicate how coldly and carefully he would handle the case if he entered. The second thing he said was that he would only enter if he could be chief counsel and make all the final decisions. He also lectured us against any outbursts or disrespectful behavior in the conduct of the trial. If there was, Garry said, we could all "go to hell." In the light of the later history, it might seem amazing, but we all agreed.

But we also wanted a hand in picking the other lawyers who would be part of the defense team. My personal choice was Leonard Weinglass; even though he'd never handled a federal case, I thought he had the sensitivity and courtroom skills to win any jury. The Yippies were worried that Len was too "straight" and inexperienced and was only a friend of mine (although they later turned to him for aid during every major crisis of the trial). They wanted, and we all gladly agreed, to have William Kunstler, a civil rights attorney who had argued many cases in the South. Then in his late forties, Kunstler was located at the Center for Constitutional Rights in New York, and he was a close associate of my Newark friend Morton Stavis. If Garry was the king of skillful cross-examination and novel defenses, Kunstler got by less on technical skills than on righteous oratory. Len was slated to be the key technician of the three, preparing witnesses, organizing the order of the defense case, researching points of law, and constructing appeals on the judge's rulings.

Then on September 9, two weeks before the trial began, there came a hearing that changed everything. Charles Garry was in a San Francisco hospital, recovering from an emergency gall-bladder operation. He sought a six-week postponement in the trial, and submitted a doctor's affidavit indicating precisely how long recovery would take. For some reason, the judge adamantly refused, setting the stage for the crisis which was to come. "We don't characterize anybody as chief lawyer or just plain Indian lawyer," he declared, in clear violation of any defendant's right to be represented by counsel of his choice. This was particularly true in the case of Bobby Seale, facing not only Chicago charges but a Connecticut murder trial, locked in jail every night without contact with the outside world. Bobby had been driven to the trial by marshals, in chains, all the way across the country despite a court order in San Francisco against his removal. He had every reason to want Garry's guidance for his daily defense.

Bobby was fundamentally different from his image as an American Mau Mau. The real Bobby was an angry and inflammatory person, to be sure, but he also exuded a humanity, keen powers of observation, a sense of humor, and a desire for simple decency behind his mask. Not all the Panthers were as responsible as Bobby. I remember one meeting at the Oakland Panther headquarters where a minor political disagreement led to a Panther security guard strangling me until Bobby stopped him. This was not a party of gentlemen. Bobby was three years older than I was, came from a rough home life, was discharged from the air force for a "bad attitude," attended Merritt Community College in Oakland, worked as a draftsman and mechanic, and most enjoyed being a stand-up comedian. When Malcolm X was killed in 1965, Bobby went berserk and threw bricks at police cars; but the same Bobby worked on community relations and federal antipoverty programs in north Oakland for the next year. He became the right-hand man of Huey Newton, whom he called the "baddest nigger ever," and when Huey went to jail, Bobby was left to represent and run the whole party himself, which by that time was growing by leaps and bounds. One month before the Chicago trial began, while leaving an Oakland wedding he was arrested on conspiracy charges involving the murder of a suspected black informant in New Haven, charges that were eventually dropped. Slapped in handcuffs that night in Oakland, he was driven all the way to Chicago by federal marshals to stand trial with ourselves while the Connecticut charges were pending. He was awakened at Cook County jail each day at five A.M. and brought to the courtroom. Local Panther leader Fred Hampton, a twenty-one-year-old, hardworking organizer, built like a halfback and wearing a broad smile, brought messages to Bobby faithfully every morning in court and made calls in his behalf during the day. In addition, a black law student named "Mickie" Leaner kept the Panther leader supplied with legal citations regarding the constitutional rights of black Americans, which Bobby carefully wrote into his yellow pads. In refusing to grant the six-week postponement, the judge tried to claim that Bobby was amply represented by Kunstler, Weinglass, and several other attorneys who had only appeared to argue pretrial motions.

At the time, I thought, rivalries between the Garry and Kunstler camps were contributing to a failure to solve the problem. Garry didn't want Kunstler to represent Bobby or other Panthers and was insisting that Bobby go to trial without a lawyer. I could understand Bobby's need for Garry, but I feared it would make matters worse if he had no lawyer at all. The cunning Garry was hoping for a declaration of mistrial to separate Bobby from the rest of us, thinking he could vindicate Bobby more easily in a later trial without the seven of us involved. He could show that the Panther leader was in Chicago for less than one day and knew virtually none of the defendants at the time. But that, I thought, would be dividing the defendants along race lines and against ourselves. A lesser evil would have been to let Kunstler go ahead and defend Bobby with the rest of us. But there was no persuading the Garry office. They gave strict instructions for Bobby simply to stand on his right to counsel of his choice.

And so on opening day, after each of the lawyers for the prosecution had made opening statements, Bobby rose and walked to the lectern in front of the judge. Asked who his lawyer was, Bobby said, "Charles R. Garry." Foran jumped up, demanding the jury be removed from the room, which it was, and then a profound argument between Bobby Seale and Julius Hoffman began. Seale politely but firmly insisted he had constitutional rights, under the nineteenth-century Reconstruction amendments, to the legal defense of his choice. The judge pointed out that Bobby had a "very competent" attorney in Bill Kunstler. Then Bobby drew the lines clearly: "If I am consistently denied this right of legal defense counsel of my choice by the judge of this court, then I can only see the judge as a blatant racist of the United States court."

"What's that, what's that?" the Judge replied, startled. Then he launched into the first of many nostalgic remarks about past newspaper editorials praising him for his liberal decisions on desegregation in the fifties. They were at loggerheads, Bobby having a protected right he could not compromise, the judge unwilling to be flexible about a starting date for the trial.

When the trial finally opened, Hoffman escalated his attack on the lawyers. As we began, Kunstler stated for the record once again that not all the defendants were fully represented because of Charlie Garry's absence. Prosecutor Foran claimed that not only were we represented by Kunstler and Weinglass, but that our several pretrial lawyers should be brought in. We, of course, refused, and so the judge promptly issued bench warrants for Gerald Lefcourt in New York and Michael Tigar and Michael Kennedy in California. They were picked up by marshals or turned themselves in, arrested for not agreeing to defend us in court. The judge again tried to bargain the defense into accepting Kunstler instead of Charles Garry, even telling Kunstler, "You can give them the key to the county jail." The threat was refused, and so the pretrial lawyers were thrown in jail and given contempt citations. According to Tigar, in whose empty room I had stayed when I hitchhiked to Berkeley in 1960, Foran said, "If you don't convince Bobby Seale to drop his right-to-counsel claim, we're gonna hold you in Cook County jail all weekend, where you can get your white asses raped." Instead, the pretrial lawyers were granted bail by a higher court, and when hundreds of lawyers poured into Chicago to protest from around the country, the four pretrial lawyers were released from the judge's order.

The jury-selection process gave other ominous signs of things to come. When we first saw the roomful of hundreds of people from whom our jury of twelve "peers" would be drawn, I felt as if I were at a convention of the silent majority. There were virtually no young people, no nonwhites, no one not registered to vote (since the names were drawn from voter lists). Weinglass made a motion, to no avail, that a true "jury of peers" would have to include a broader cross section of people than these. Then we got down to the rough task of choosing the best people possible from this unrepresentative assemblage. To make matters worse, the judge would allow no questions of the prospective jurors except concerning their job and family status. We could ask nothing about whether they harbored feelings about Convention Week, the Vietnam War, blacks, long hair, or anything that would indicate an ability to be objective.

The judge began by reading the indictment to the room of jurors, relishing and emphasizing every phrase about "rioting" and "incendiary devices," until Kunstler stood and objected to his reading the charges "like Orson Welles reading the Declaration of Independence." When our turn came, we tried a different sort of appeal to the jury, having Weinglass declare that we regarded the eventual twelve people selected as the "highest authority" in the courtroom, a legal principle that is well grounded if little used. The judge, furious at the implied challenge to his own authority, stopped Len short. But we weren't indulging in a gesture; from the beginning, we knew the jury was our only hope. We scarcely entertained the possibility of an acquittal; there were too many charges and too many defendants for everyone to be found innocent. What we really feared was that the government had created the ingredients for a jury to reach a "compromise" verdict sending us to jail for five-year, rather than ten-year sentences. Our courtroom strategy was to achieve a "hung jury," persuade a hard-core minority to hold out for total acquittal on the permissible grounds that they had reasonable doubt about our guilt. Then, we were convinced, the government might not want to go through the negative publicity and cost of trying us a second time. The key was to select some jurors capable of maintaining their own principles to the end.

In the game of jury selection, twelve people are chosen by lottery to take their seats in the jury box. Then the prosecution and defense are allowed seventeen peremptory challenges, by which they can throw a juror out of the box without a stated reason. Next a new juror from the large panel is chosen to fill the seat, and the guessing game goes on until one side has exhausted its peremptory challenges or both sides are happy with the twelve in the box. The government expected us to use up all of our peremptory challenges on the grounds that the whole jury panel was unacceptable to us. But we decided on a different path: to protest that the game was rigged, but then play the percentages. We would wait until a moment that Foran indicated the jurors were acceptable to him, then in a surprise move accept the same panel. We didn't need a perfect jury. We just had to be reasonably sure a handful were winnable to our point of view.

Jury selection was a guessing game. Our side was limited to staring at the faces and appearances of the prospective jurors and listening to a few of their words. We whispered, passed notes, tried to get the jurors to look at our eyes. The prosecutor removed two we thought were potentially good: a young chemist and an unemployed black electrician. But we took hope from Kristi King, a young woman with a decent face who had a sister in VISTA, the domestic Peace Corps. Then our eyes bulged at the sight of a book under the arm of the next juror: It was by James Baldwin, unusual reading material for a white Chicagoan.

Mrs. Jean Fritz was a woman of about forty with a kind face. Had Foran seen that book? Was this Fritz lady trying to signal her sympathy? Or was it a trick to get the support of the defense? We asked for a break so that we could meet. It was granted, and we found ourselves arguing in a jail cell that the judge kindly made available. There were nine women and two men on the current panel, including Kristi King, Jean Fritz, and a few other possibles. But next in line was a young, sincere-looking woman named Kay Richards, whom several of us believed was on our side. If we accepted the jury as it was, we would keep King and Fritz, but Richards would only remain an alternate who would join the jury if someone got sick during the trial. If we continued the guessing game, we would get Richards into the jury box but might have Fritz or King bumped. We took a collective gamble and instructed Kunstler and Weinglass to accept the jury the way it was. When we returned to the courtroom and announced our satisfaction with the jury, Foran looked surprised and disturbed. It was a conservative, middle-American jury, but we believed we had at least two good jurors and a very good alternate in Kay Richards.

We were in for some real surprises, however.

In 1987, I talked with Jean Fritz and one of her daughters at length about her impressions of the trial. She was still living in Des Plaines, a Chicago suburb, with her husband of fifty years, Marvin, a tire-store owner. Her three girls, Nancy, Margie, and Janice, were all grown up, and she and Marv were spending their new leisure time fishing and generally enjoying life. It had taken her a long while, however, to get over the Chicago trial, and she shared with me what it was like, week to week, for a Middle American like herself.

When she took the elevated train to Chicago for jury duty that morning, she carried the Baldwin novel simply to keep her mind stimulated. She had followed the riots of 1968 through the media and felt the accused conspirators were a "bunch of jerks." Little changed her opinion as she sat for hours through the jury-selection process that day and the next. She remembered getting on an elevator with Abbie Hoffman and thinking, "God, why doesn't he take a bath?" Those were the times, as she recalls, "when even soap was out." Her opinions were shared by the other jurors. "No one was sympathetic to the defendants. We were just a bunch of middle-class people who only knew what we read in the papers."

A few days later, as the trial's second week began, the judge announced that "threatening letters" had been sent to two of the jurors, including Kristi King. The letters, both written in the same hand and mailed from the same place, simply said, "You are being watched" and were signed "The Black Panthers." Bobby and the rest of us immediately suspected a right-wing plot to discredit the Panthers and knock one of our best jurors out of the box.

The incident allowed the Judge to make two serious decisions. First, he sequestered the jury, putting them under permanent supervision of federal marshals for the rest of the trial at the Palmer House Hotel, instead of at home with their families, where they could feel free, read and hear the news, and, we thought, be more able to understand our case. "We couldn't even know about the moon landing!" Jean Fritz remembered. "When they walked us from the Palmer House to the Federal Building, we couldn't even look in the windows. I almost had a fight with one of the woman sergeants." At night, the jurors watched endless James Bond movies, courtesy of the marshals.

Second, the judge used the alleged Panther letters to remove Kristi King from the jury. It was totally unnecessary, because she had never seen the notes herself. They were received by her parents, who turned them over to the FBI. The judge brought her alone into the jury box and asked her to read one of them. She said she had never seen it before. Then the judge announced that it had been sent to her and demanded to know if she could still be impartial. Her face reddened, she looked in shock over at Bobby Seale, paused in confusion, and said, "No." She was immediately removed. Our intuition that she was on our side was later confirmed by Jean Fritz. The other juror who received a letter, Mrs. Ruth Peterson, said she had already read and discussed the letter with another juror (which was improper in itself) and could remain impartial. The young alternate, Kay Richards, was now added to the jury. We felt that was a plus, but we questioned the bogus letter and demanded that the court order a full investigation. The judge agreed to our request. However, I was more convinced than ever that the real conspiracy was not among the defendants but on the government's side. It was very difficult to believe they were following their duty *not* to communicate among themselves. I didn't know how they were conspiring, but I believed that the judge of the district, William J. Campbell, a former law partner of Mayor Daley, was linked to Judge Hoffman and perhaps to Foran himself. Later FBI documents strongly hinted that this was so.

FBI MEMORANDUM

[Assistant U.S. Attorney] requested letter sent to Peterson family and King family be examined for latent fingerprints. He desired absolutely no other investigation or outside contacts at this time. No investigation should be undertaken without contacting him or the USA. Judge Hoffman concurs.

Kay Richards "was for Foran one hundred percent from the beginning," Jean Fritz said later. "She kept questioning all the other jurors about their opinions, because she said she was writing a book. Her boyfriend was Tom Stevens, who worked somehow for Mayor Daley. She was always talking about him, and after the trial, she married the guy."

FBI MEMORANDUM   **10/7/69**

TO: DIRECTOR
FROM: SAC, CHICAGO

As the Bureau is aware, with appropriate Bureau authority and with security guaranteed by the SAC, SAs have monitored and where possible recorded speeches at public gatherings by the defendants, as well as some of their supporters.

The United States Attorney (USA) Thomas A. Foran and the presiding judge at the captioned trial, the Honorable Julius Hoffman, are concerned that the defendants will claim on appeal of any conviction in captioned case that defendants could not receive a fair trial due to the publicity surrounding the trial. Judge Hoffman and USA Foran must be in a position to prove that the publicity was caused by the defendants, their lawyers, and their associates rather than the government. In addition, Judge Hoffman has indicated to USA Foran, and USA Foran is in full agreement, that many of the statements made by the defendants, their lawyers and possibly others such as the unindicted co-conspirators, may well be in contempt of court. *Judge Hoffman has indicated in strictest confidence that following the trial he*

definitely plans to reconsider various individuals for possible con-
tempt of court [emphasis added].

Our state of mind and behavior cannot be understood apart
from the serious events that were taking place *outside* the courtroom. Nixon's pledge of a "secret plan" to end the Vietnam War
looked more and more like a deceitful escalation. The president's goal was to reduce American casualties while increasing
the number of Indochinese deaths, on the cynical assumption
that most Americans would not care about nonwhite "body
counts." Under the "Vietnamization" policy, about sixty thousand American troops were being withdrawn by the start of the
Chicago trial. American combat deaths for 1969 were down by
one third, from a high of 14,592 in 1968 to an eventual 9,414 in
1969. Recorded Vietnamese deaths were ratcheting upward, not
winding down; between 1969 and the end of 1973, Saigon army
losses increased by 50 percent, to 250,000, and civilian casualties
in the South alone by 50 percent, claiming another 1.5 million
people. United States figures for enemy deaths in South Vietnam in 1969 were 157,000. Later U.S. Senate investigations estimated that four million people in Indochina were turned into
refugees between 1969 and the summer of 1971. The masterpiece
of Nixon's doctrine was the secret B-52 bombing of Cambodia,
begun in March 1969. It was called *Operation Menu*, since the
United States bombed a specific area designated as *Breakfast*,
then waited for a North Vietnamese response before proceeding
with raids identified as *Lunch, Dinner, Dessert,* and *Snack*. In those
raids alone, 3,650 B-52 sorties dropped four times the tonnage of
bombs dropped on Japan in all of World War II.

Nixon, it is now known, was also planning a severe further
escalation of the war if Hanoi did not enter productive negotiations by late 1969. Labeled *Operation Duck Hook*, the proposed
options included destruction of Hanoi and Haiphong, the mining of North Vietnam's rivers and harbors, attacks on the dike
system to provoke massive flooding, and—if necessary—use of
nuclear devices on the Ho Chi Minh Trail.

During the trial, we read the first published reports of the 1968
My Lai massacre after the Pentagon had suppressed the evidence for a year. The slaughter of anywhere from two hundred
to five hundred unarmed Vietnamese villagers, depending on
whose numbers were believed, injected yet a new sense of hor-

ror for many who thought themselves numbed to the war. The scene of women, children, and babies mutilated and dumped in a long ditch would become the Guérnica for my generation. "I sent them a good boy, and they made him a murderer," cried the mother of one of the soldiers at My Lai. Apart from this single hideous incident, there was a systematic repression campaign, labeled *Operation Phoenix* and supported by U.S. advisers, computers, and funding, which targeted the "Vietcong infrastructure" in South Vietnam—an estimated 2 percent of the population or well over 350,000 organizers, farmers, teachers, unionists, students, and women suspected of being "national security threats." Massive jailings, interrogations, torture, and outright killing took place through the Phoenix program.

The war was becoming macabre and absurd to many American soldiers. The same breakdown of discipline that could lead to My Lai also meant the rise of cynical antiwar, anti-officer sentiments among the American troops. American soldiers were going through an evolution parallel to that of our generation at home: From an expectation that the government was telling the truth, they now assumed deceit; from a belief that the war had a valid purpose, there was headshaking cynicism; from a willingness to follow leaders, there grew hatred of them; from innocence and dedication grew alienation and even nihilism.

Starting in 1969 the desertion and AWOL rates increased fourfold over the 1965–68 figures. In the same year, fragging (grenade assaults) against officers began, averaging 240 incidents per year, 11 percent of them fatal. Between 1969 and 1972, there were 86 officers killed and 700 injured. The U.S. Navy conducted 488 investigations of sabotage in its own ranks in a single year. Marijuana use doubled from 30 to 60 percent of all GIs in the Nixon phase of the war; more gravely, heroin addiction jumped from 2 to 22 percent. By 1971, while 5,000 American GIs would need hospitalization for combat wounds, over four times as many—20,000—were treated in military hospitals for drug abuse. In the end, 500,000 Vietnam-era veterans would receive "less than honorable" discharge papers.

The Vietnam War, in short, was destroying the American idealism of an entire generation, whether in Chicago or Saigon.

In the meantime, the protest movement at home was exploding dramatically. Suddenly, it was no longer deviant but legitimate—patriotic even—to express an alternative. Just before the Chicago trial began, Abbie and Jerry attended the vast gathering of Woodstock, in upstate New York, the coming of age of the youth culture. Then in mid-October, the Vietnam Moratorium—organized primarily by former McCarthy workers Sam Brown and David Mixner—became perhaps the largest public protest in American history. Precisely because it lacked militance and a clear set of demands—"give peace a chance"—the Moratorium provided a safe channel in turbulent times for Middle Americans to step forward into the ranks of dissent. As many as ten million Americans gathered in town squares and college campuses to speak out against the war. For our part, on October 15, Dave tried reading the names of American and Vietnamese war dead and we placed American and Vietcong flags on our defense table before Judge Hoffman's proceedings commenced. But the judge and the prosecution flew into a rage, ordered us silenced and the flags removed. Outside, during the lunch break, several of us spoke to one of the largest crowds I have ever seen at a Chicago rally. The two events together—Woodstock and the Moratorium—reflected exactly the spirit of a generation we had dreamed of expressing in the original planning for Chicago 1968. Now, one year later, the time had come.

There was another, more sobering, flare-up of radical anger that October: the Days of Rage. SDS had splintered into two warring factions: Bernardine Dohrn's group, which included many like Mark Rudd from the Columbia uprising, wanted to create a disruptive and revolutionary youth movement to weaken the American state. They took their name from Bob Dylan's lyric, "You don't need a weatherman to know which way the wind blows." The Progressive Labor faction tended to cite the sayings of Mao Tse-tung or Stalin on every question. The Weathermen, however, adopted yet another communist doctrine, that of China's Lin Piao, who believed that liberation wars *outside* the centers of Western imperialism would bring about global revolution.

Unlike the utterly mechanical Progressive Labor, most of the Weathermen were friends of mine or people I'd known for years. Besides Bernardine and the Columbia radicals, there were Billy Ayers and Diana Oughton from Ann Arbor, Terry Robbins and Kathy Boudin from Cleveland ERAP, and Cathy Wilkerson from Swarthmore SDS. Most of them, though not Bernardine, were beaten up and jailed in Chicago. In experience, they lacked the image of the hopeful, loving community rooted in the earliest years of SDS and SNCC, and had no patience for the complicated moral and political philosophizing of the Port Huron generation.

The Weathermen knew that it was not possible to build a progressive America. What was needed was not a Vietnam moratorium, but an extension of the war itself "behind enemy lines." It was past time to "realign" the Democratic party, it was time to smash it. They scoffed at those who spoke of "long-term organizing" or "building stable families and lives." It was time for Vandals and Visigoths, the loveless barbarians who undermined the Roman Empire. Another Dylan lyric summarized the strategy: "The pump don't work 'cause the vandals stole the handle."

Terry Robbins exemplified the amazing transformation that had taken place in one generation of SDS. A native of New York who had attended Kenyon College in Ohio, Terry joined SDS in the mid-sixties, spent some time in an ERAP project, and seemed to be an earnest, idealistic organizer. He was short and wiry, a friendly follower. As SDS was radicalized, he became a regional organizer in the Midwest, making a close team with Billy Ayers, the son of a wealthy Chicago executive who, like Rudd at Columbia, was tired of the "intellectual bullshit" of the SDS chapter in Ann Arbor. Ayers, along with his girlfriend, Diana Oughton, who had recently returned from the Peace Corps in Guatemala, formed a Jesse James Gang in Ann Arbor similar to Rudd's Action Faction at Columbia. Ayers and troupe swiftly disrupted and purged the "intellectual" elements of the Ann Arbor SDS chapter, the one I had started in 1961, still called VOICE at the time of its savaging. Soon the Jesse James Gang added Terry and became a network throughout the Midwest dedicated to "revolutionizing" SDS chapters and young people generally. The impatience was palpable. Why should the Vietnam War stop at the borders of the country we were invading? they asked. Why shouldn't we bring it home, here and now?

This was more than politics, however; it was also a transformation of personalities into "instruments of revolution." To become a Vandal, after all, required a Nietzschean will to power, an understanding of the dark side of things. So people like Terry threw off layers of their personality that might interfere with their becoming a "tool of necessity." They tried to alter their consciousness with drugs, with free sex, with shattering self-criticism sessions, with anything that would erase the sentimental "hang-ups" of individualism. Where I emotionally remained involved with Anne, they scorned monogamy as a "male power trip" and tried to recruit her to their ranks.

Strange as it might seem now, there was an attraction about them, a sinister one, for many radicals. The mystery of what was out there, beyond normal experience, was magnetic to some from bourgeois backgrounds. Terry was changing from a shy introvert to a devilish charmer exuding a charisma of violence. He was seriously planning for the Armageddon many of us agreed was around the corner. It was coming, they said, and it would have to be met with attacks on property, disruption of the repressive government, formation of an underground, and finally armed conflict. Eldridge Cleaver was already in Cuba or Algeria; many other Panthers were underground, mostly as fugitives from arrest. In New Mexico, Chicano leaders like Reyes Lopes Tyerina, claiming that the United States was illegally occupying their land, were staging armed confrontations and hiding in the mountainous north. In a nonviolent way, such an underground was being considered by Catholic radicals like Daniel and Philip Berrigan and was already in effect for thousands of draft evaders in the United States, Canada, and Sweden.

A similar but often more violent process was happening around the globe, from West Germany and Italy to Uruguay and Brazil, with middle-class students hurling themselves into the liberated despair of armed struggle. Between January 1969 and April 1970—roughly the period of the Chicago trial—according to the Treasury Department figures, there were over five thousand bombings in the United States, a phenomenon that had never occurred before.

The difference between a Bernardine or Terry and myself was one of perspective colored by age and time. While they thought the direction of America toward fascism was inevitable and therefore that an underground was necessary, I thought it was only one possibility to prepare for. After all, my own liberty was staked on a belief in persuading cautious middle-American jurors that our wild and irreverent behavior was somehow justifiable. Failing that, I had to hope that higher courts would throw out the case or find the conspiracy law unconstitutional. Disruption, I thought, could be justified as a *tactic* for waking people up and exposing the powers that be, as part of a strategy for "making the system work." As a strategy in itself, however, it would mean regarding a majority of Americans as hopeless, an enemy. Revolutionaries like the Weathermen, having given up on changing American society, thought of themselves as a "fifth column" or, in Malraux's phrase, "doomed executioners." There would be no social revolution in America, just wreckage, possibly a new Dark Ages. While I was still very much a child of Port Huron, they were war orphans. As I said in a bitter argument with Terry, they were not the conscience of a generation, but its id, finally surfacing.

The Weathermen marked the end of SDS. An organization that at its birth believed in thinking and acting in new ways to change the world, that thought itself immune to the historical factional fighting and ancestor worship of the Left, that worried not at all about its free-floating structure being subverted, had in just seven short years fallen victim to every dire and cynical prediction ever made about revolutionary movements. It all came crashing home to me one day during the trial when an excited Weatherman announced, "Well, we offed the pig." He meant that they had closed down the SDS national office.

The Weathermen shadowed and intersected the experience of the Chicago conspiracy in strange ways. They prepared a Days of Rage for early October that would result in almost everything the prosecutors were accusing the Chicago Eight of doing the year before at the Democratic convention. There were supposed to be thousands of hard-core revolutionaries descending on Chicago for the Days of Rage, but the event failed beyond anyone's wildest fears. Only a few hundred showed up after months of "actions" around the country (attempting to arouse youth by rampaging through a Pittsburgh high school and starting a fight at Detroit's Metro Beach by carrying a red flag through a crowd) that were supposed to attract rootless young people to the city. When a relative handful showed up, failure was simply redefined as success: These were the only people "ready" enough, brave enough, to push on through to the other side.

On October 6, the Weathermen blew up the statue commemorating the police victims of the Haymarket bombings a century before. On October 8, the official beginning of the Days of Rage, a "rally" was called in Lincoln Park. Anne Weills had come to town, fascinated to see what the Weathermen were doing. I sat in the courtroom all day, aware that the conspiracy defendants were invited to drop by the evening's "rally." I had no idea what would occur, but I worried that my bail would be revoked if I went there. I also worried that I would be accused of cowardice if I didn't. My ego won, and she and I drove up to the park after darkness fell, accompanied by John Froines and Abbie.

The scene was otherworldly, like a tribal cult gathering in anticipation of a powerful, life-altering, and traumatic ritual. They were standing around a blazing bonfire, wearing loose-fitting shirts and pants, faces covered with Vaseline and masks, helmets on their heads, and boots or running shoes on their pacing feet. Besides adrenaline, they must have been fueled by drugs. Some carried Vietcong flags, others just two-by-fours. I didn't recognize anyone, and none introduced themselves to me. I felt the nausea of fear. Had I helped bring this on? It was clear there was no "rally," just an anxious milling, as if all were awaiting a specific hour.

Finally, someone handed me a bullhorn and asked me to say a few words. I took the bullhorn and hesitated. No one appeared to be looking at me. I said something ambiguous and largely inaudible like, "The conspiracy defendants send their greetings; we welcome any efforts to intensify the struggle" and handed the microphone back. Photographer lights were flashing. I quickly drifted into the shadows with John; I don't remember where Abbie went. We waited, and then, on some signal that eluded me, the group assembled itself quickly in formation and started half-trotting away from the fire through the darkness, toward the streets of the Gold Coast. I went back to the car and drove off.

Soon reports of a wild rampage started coming over the car radio. The Weathermen were running through the Gold Coast, smashing expensive cars and shop windows. It was the beginning of three days of steady rampages, which would shock the city. Even Black Panther leader Fred Hampton condemned the actions as "Custeristic." On the first night alone, three Weathermen were shot. By the end, three hundred were arrested, dozens were badly injured, and one Chicago official was paralyzed from the neck down trying to tackle a running Weatherman. During this time, I attended the trial by day and heard reports from Anne at night. She called the Weathermen "crazed" and managed to talk Bernardine and Kathy Boudin out of certain actions which Anne thought "suicidal." But there was admiration in her tone of voice, especially when she described an "action" by about seventy women—women alone—kicking, tackling, and wrestling with police trying to arrest them on a march to the Chicago draft board. Her wrist was scraped and cut and wrapped tightly in a bandage, contrasting sharply with her fashionable clothes. It was displayed prominently that night as we posed for pictures by the famed photographer Richard Avedon, in town to take portraits of the Conspiracy defendants.

I lay down that night in a state of such complete tension that I thought all my muscles would lock forever into spasm. Where was this going? Between Judge Hoffman's courtroom and the Weathermen, where was sanity? A paranoid thought flashed that Anne was having an affair with Terry. Then I remembered that Weatherpeople didn't have affairs; they slept collectively together on living-room floors. I visualized them writhing on a floor in the midst of others. No, it was not true, I told myself. I couldn't ask her. I was becoming impotent, hysterical.

Meanwhile, as this real and acknowledged conspiracy to incite violence was occurring in the streets, back in the dreary oppressiveness of the courtroom, the government was busy grinding out its case against the Conspiracy defendants.

Juror Jean Fritz's initial dislike of the conspirators was deepened by the Yippies' defense of drugs. A friend of hers had "lost her mind" because of drugs, and she worried about her daughters. But as the weeks passed, she began having doubts about the government's case. It was not the details of testimony that affected her; it was Judge Hoffman's eccentric and arbitrary behavior. "The judge changed me a lot in the beginning," she said.

One night that winter, Rennie spoke at Northern Illinois University, just outside the city. His statements sparked a lively debate among the student audience, prompting Margie Fritz, Jean's daughter, to stand up suddenly. Her words were critical of the prosecution. When she announced that her mother was a member of the jury, the FBI agents surveilling Rennie turned their tape recorders and notebooks toward her. The following morning, Jean Fritz was called before Judge Hoffman in his chambers. She was asked if she had communicated with her daughter. An affirmative answer would have resulted in her removal from the jury. Telling the truth, she said no. In the prosecutors' imagination, the daughter was having an affair with Rennie. "Margie used to come to the trial when she could, and we would look at each other across the room," Jean said. "One day a marshal came up and told her that I could go to jail for six months because of what she said at the college. She became a total wreck and quit school for six months." Jean Fritz was allowed to remain on the jury.

The prosecutors brought to the witness stand a cross section of the very city bureaucrats who had denied us permits in 1968, as well as various undercover agents who swore to tell the truth. One official testified that he took seriously an offer of Abbie's to leave town in exchange for $100,000. Foran and Schultz fought to have us referred to by our last names: "Objection, Your Honor, to the familiar child terms for mentally grown men." A police agent testified that the chief act of violence he saw Jerry Rubin commit was throwing a sweater at an officer during the gassing of Lincoln Park. Another described how he joined a motorcycle gang headed by two men named "Banana" and "Gorilla" in order to penetrate the Yippies. This police agent, who became Jerry Rubin's "bodyguard," said he witnessed Rubin throwing paint at a police car. While that was the only act of violence he recalled Rubin committing, the agent testified that he himself had taunted police as "pigs," thrown objects at them, helped rock a surrounded police car, taken drugs, picked up a gang girlfriend, and sold his memoirs to *Official Detective* magazine for one hundred dollars.

As this shady testimony droned on, we became restless and more worried. The judge was ruling in behalf of the prosecution on virtually every motion and objection. He allowed Foran to make unusually disparaging remarks about our lawyers. Foran told Kunstler, "Instead of watching yourself on TV tonight, you can study evidence." But the real edge of ugly conflict continued to be the treatment of Bobby Seale.

By October 20, three weeks into the trial, Bobby was actually permitted to argue a motion that he be allowed to defend himself. Using the research supplied him, Bobby argued not only on the grounds that citizens may represent themselves in court, but also on the specific grounds that arose after the Civil War in response to false representation of southern blacks by white lawyers, guaranteeing black people the right of legal self-defense. It was clear and well argued, but summarily denounced by Schultz as a "ploy." The government claim was that Bobby would make so many mistakes that he could appeal for a new trial. The judge even declared that the "complexity of the case" was too much for Bobby to follow, which enraged Bobby into responding: "You denied me my right to defend myself. You think black people don't have a mind. Well, we got big minds, good minds, and we know how to come forth with constitutional rights."

Being acted out was a symbolic conflict of particular importance to the Panthers, which Eldridge Cleaver had described as that in which the Supermasculine Menial is feared by the Omnipotent Administrator, not for violence or sexual power but for attempting to assert his own equal intelligence in exposing discrimination as irrational. The more the Menial asserts his own ideas, Eldridge wrote, "the more emphatically will they be rejected and scorned by society, and treated as upstart invasions of the realm of the Omnipotent Administrator. . . . The struggle of the Menial's life is the emancipation of his mind, to achieve recognition for the products of his mind, and official recognition that he has a mind."

Bobby now embodied this struggle in the courtroom. He confined his statements to those moments when evidence specifically against him was introduced by prosecutors or witnesses. He would then object that he was without counsel and denied the right of defending himself by cross-examination of the witness. The conflict became tense on October 28, when a police agent named William Frappolly mentioned Bobby in his testimony. Bobby strode to the lectern, stating: "I object to this testimony because my lawyer is not here. I have been denied my right to defend myself in this courtroom." The judge cut him off, suggesting that Bobby was in contempt of court for making his remarks. Bobby bitterly replied that it was the judge who was "in contempt of the constitutional rights of the mass of people of the United States. . . . I am not in contempt of nothing. The people of America need to admonish you and the whole Nixon administration." At the end of that afternoon, the judge had a chilling surprise. Obviously well prepared, he flatly informed Bobby that "under the law you may be gagged and chained in your chair."

MR. SEALE: Gagged? I am being railroaded already.

THE COURT: The Court has that right and I—

MR. SEALE: The Court has no right to stop me from speaking out on behalf of my constitutional rights.

THE COURT: The Court will recess until ten o'clock tomorrow morning.

THE MARSHAL: Everyone will please rise.

MR. SEALE: I am not rising. I am not rising until he recognizes my constitutional rights. Why should I rise for him? He is not recognizing—

THE COURT: Mr. Marshal—

MR. SEALE: I am not rising.

THE COURT: Mr. Marshal, see that he rises.

THE MARSHAL: Mr. Seale—

THE COURT: And the other one, too. Get all the defendants to rise.

THE MARSHAL: Mr. Hayden, will you please rise?

THE COURT: Let the record show that Mr. Hayden has not risen.

THE MARSHAL: I would request Counsel to tell their clients—Mr. Kunstler, would you advise your clients to rise?

MR. WEINGLASS: If the Court please, it is my understanding that there is no constitutional or legal obligation on the part of the defendants to rise so long as his failure to rise is not disruptive.

THE COURT: You advise your clients not to rise, do you?

MR. WEINGLASS: I have no obligation to advise my clients to rise. He is doing nothing disruptive in this courtroom.

THE COURT: We will determine that later.

MR. KUNSTLER: I might add that the clients are in protest of what you have done in their opinion to Bobby Seale's right to defend himself.

MR. WEINGLASS: They are sitting silently.

THE COURT: Will you advise your clients to rise, Mr. Kunstler?

MR. KUNSTLER: Your honor, if you direct me to, I will advise them.

THE COURT: I direct you to.

MR. KUNSTLER: Then I will pass on the direction. . . . They have heard you direct me but I cannot in good conscience do more than that. They are free and independent and have to do what they please.

THE COURT: Let the record show that none of the defendants has risen.

Chains? On a black person one hundred years after slavery? Gagging? For a person who could so easily be granted the right to represent himself? We went away dazed. We checked the law; such stern measures were warranted in the few exceptional cases in which a defendant had thrown chairs at the judge or witnesses, but never when one simply spoke out in court. What were we going to do? Sit there? Pretend we were going through a normal trial, making motions, examining witnesses, chatting with the press, going home after the day was done—ignoring a black defendant, bound and gagged, sitting in our midst as in a living nightmare out of the American past?

FEDERAL BUREAU OF INVESTIGATION   **10-29-69**

TO: DIRECTOR
FROM: SAC, CHICAGO

BUAGENTS AT SEVEN TEN A.M. TODAY OBSERVED EIGHT MEMBERS OF BPP OUTSIDE OF FEDERAL BUILDING, CHICAGO, TO SHOW SUPPORT FOR DEFEND-ANT BOBBY SEALE. AS OF SEVEN THIRTY A.M. NUMBER OF GROUP HAD EN-LARGED TO TWENTY AND SEVERAL INDIVIDUALS CARRIED SHOPPING BAGS BELIEVED TO CONTAIN PAMPHLETS AND LITERATURE. SEVERAL OF GROUP THEN WENT TO NEARBY SUBWAY STATION WHERE THEY JOINED ABOVE GROUP. AS OF EIGHT THIRTY A.M. TODAY GROUP OUTSIDE OF FEDERAL BUILDING TOTALED FIFTY ONE, SIXTEEN OF WHOM ARE WHITE. AS OF EIGHT FORTY FIVE A.M. TODAY, THIRTY FIVE NEGROES AND TEN WHITES OF ABOVE GROUP WERE ADMITTED TO FEDERAL BUILDING AND SEARCHED BY USMS. THESE INDIVIDUALS WILL BE ALLOWED TO ATTEND TRIAL AS SPECTATORS IF SEATS ARE AVAILABLE.

CHIEF JUDGE WILLIAM J. CAMPBELL ADVISED SAC EIGHT FORTY FIVE A.M. TODAY IN STRICTEST CONFIDENCE THAT JUDGE HOFFMAN BASED ON AC-TIONS OF THE DEFENDANTS AND ATTORNEYS IN THE COURTROOM MAY CALL A MISTRIAL AND SEND ALL DEFENDANTS AND THEIR ATTORNEYS TO JAIL FOR CONTEMPT FOR SIX MONTHS. TRIAL WOULD BE STARTED AGAIN IM-MEDIATELY UPON DEFENDANTS' RELEASE FROM JAIL. BUREAU WILL BE KEPT ADVISED.

When we arrived the next morning, October 29, there were at least twenty-five armed marshals lining the walls. A few anxious Panthers and young whites sat on the edge of their seats waiting for what was to come. When Bobby was led into court, carrying his familiar yellow notepad, he smiled and returned a clenched-fist salute from his supporters. Still standing at the defense table, he made an unmistakably clear appeal for his supporters to keep order. "Brothers and sisters," he said very personally to them, "we have the right of self-defense if pigs attack us, but today let's be cool, let's be cool, whatever happens. I'm going to defend my constitutional rights and, whatever happens, be cool, and if the marshals ask us to leave, just leave." The small group replied, "Right on, Bobby," and sat down.

Minutes later, the judge entered from his chambers and before he could begin speaking, Schultz was on his feet at the lectern, almost whining. "Your Honor, Your Honor," he said, "minutes before this court was in session, the defendant Seale was addressing his followers back there about an attack by them on this court."

Bobby jumped up, yelling that Schultz was a liar, that he had urged people to "be cool," that Schultz was a "racist and a fascist" for his remarks. The judge started pounding his gavel as defendants, spectators, and even reporters shook their heads and complained about Schultz's twisting of Bobby's remarks. Meanwhile, Bobby was still demanding that Schultz apologize. Bobby then pointed to the portraits of the Founding Fathers behind the judge and asked, "What can happen to me more than what happened to the slaves under George Washington and Benjamin Franklin?" The judge reddened and told the marshals, "Take that defendant into the room in there and deal with him as he should be dealt with in this circumstance." Five or ten of them did, gouging and dragging Bobby into his chair. All of us jumped up. Dave Dellinger tried to put himself between the marshals and Bobby, getting knocked aside. Jerry Rubin got punched in the face as he yelled, "They're kicking him in the balls." I tried to get the judge's attention: "Your Honor all he wants is to be legally represented, not be a slave here." As each of us would speak or move, the prosecutors would excitedly declare, "Let the record show . . ." and then describe our behavior for future contempt citations. They finally got the struggling

Bobby down. We continued storming around, cursing, asking each other what was going to come next.

It was a repeat in the courtroom of what had occurred in the streets of Chicago the year before. We had been accused by the prosecutor of provoking violence, triggering a cycle of outraged resistance that gave the pretext for an act of repression. The chains and gags were probably waiting in the next room for just this occasion. Now we were threatened with revocation of bail: "Since all the defendants support this man in what he is doing," the judge intoned, "I, over the noon hour, will reflect on whether they are good risks for bail, and I shall give serious consideration to the termination of their bail." We froze, refusing to rise again.

THE COURT: I direct you to ask your clients to rise and I tell you that I will not retain on bail in this court men who defy the United States District Court and I will give them the noon recess to think about it.

MR. KUNSTLER: They are protesting your Honor, and I think that it is protective of the First Amendment.

THE COURT: They will have to obey the law in the process of protesting, sir. Now if they prefer to sleep in the county jail, let them reflect on it.

We didn't have much to "reflect on" over the lunch hour. We weren't going to stand in respect for a judge who was about to crush the rights of Bobby Seale. We didn't know what to expect when we returned to court, but we instructed Bill Kunstler to give the following reply to the judge:

MR. KUNSTLER: The defendants want me to say that under no circumstances will they let their liberty stand in the way of the assertion of the constitutional rights of Bobby Seale to defend himself, and if the price of those rights is that they must remain in jail, then that will have to be the price that is paid. Many have paid much greater prices in the past for the defense and assertion of constitutional rights.

No one in court that day will ever forget the loathsome sight of Bobby Seale being carried back into the room. Surrounded by marshals, he was sitting in a high chair with his wrists and ankles strapped under clanking chains. Wrapped around his mouth and back of his head was a thick white cloth. His eyes and the veins in his neck and temples were bulging with the strain of maintaining his breath.

As shocking as the chains and gag were, even more unbelievable was the attempt to return the courtroom to normalcy. The judge ordered the cross-examination of the witness on the stand to resume. The jury returned from lunch and sat down; one member, Jean Fritz, was visibly quaking. The press reopened their notebooks. And the judge and prosecutor became suddenly solicitous and polite to Bobby. Foran proposed that if Bobby expressed a willingness to be quiet, the court would consider ungagging and unchaining. The judge leaned over Bobby and lamented that he had "tried, with all my heart, to get him to sit in this court and be tried fairly and impartially." He told Bobby to indicate "by raising your head up and down or shaking your head, meaning no, whether or not I have your assurance that you will not do anything that will disrupt this trial. . . ."

To everyone's surprise, Bobby's voice pierced through the gag, forcefully though if somewhat muffled: "I can't speak. I have a right to speak. I have a right to speak and be heard for myself and my constitutional rights." The judge leaned farther over, shaking his head politely as if he were at a loud cocktail party. "I can't understand you, sir." I started to laugh in relief and admiration; they can't gag Bobby, no way. Bobby even criticized Kunstler through the gag. Bill had tried to describe the metal chair, handcuffs, and gag for the court record, and Bobby muttered through the gag, "You don't represent me. Sit down, Kunstler."

Now there was real trouble for the government. Their "quick fix" to this human problem had broken down. Embarrassed but stubborn, the judge blamed the problem on the marshals: "I don't think you have accomplished your purpose by that kind of contrivance. We will have to take another recess." They carried Bobby into the side room and this time pushed a pluglike device into his mouth before tying the cloth gag around his face. When Bobby returned, the judge again tried to resume the normalcy of the trial. We interrupted with motions for a mistrial, which were denied, and Foran went back to taking routine testimony from the witness.

By now this process had proved deeply unsettling to four of

the jurors; besides Jean Fritz, they were Shirley Seaholm, Frieda Robbins, and a black woman, Mary Butler, who Jean thought was very compassionate. Mary was ill at the time and died a few years later. Each of the four women had teenage children. They became a subgroup, taking many of their meals together. "What set us off was when they did all that to Bobby Seale," Jean said later. "I'd never seen anything like that in my life, and never will again. The marshals came in the back room where we were waiting to go out, and all they told us was, something was going to be different when we went back out in the courtroom. I was shocked when I saw him."

That night, after seeing Bobby's chains and gag on national television, Bernardine and Terry wanted to see me. I met them in a Hyde Park restaurant, and after dinner, we took a long walk. They were angry that the other defendants didn't react to Bobby's chaining by trashing the courtroom and joining him in jail. By what right, she asked, were we continuing the trial with a black defendant chained and gagged? Weren't we displaying the very skin privilege that meant the black community couldn't count on white radicals?

The questioning of my guts, as usual, was effective. I felt a certain guilt over my restraint in the courtroom. But I also knew, through a third party, that Charles Garry wanted Bobby to take his punishment alone. Anything shifting the spotlight would be confusing, Garry thought, and could weaken Bobby's case ultimately.

"Look," I finally said, "I'm committed to a trial, not a riot in the courtroom. I think they have to take the gag off Bobby. They *want* us to tear the room up and go to jail. I think we should put on a defense, speak on campuses, get our message out, and win with the public."

Bernardine shifted her tack, replying slowly and carefully. "Don't you listen to Nixon and Agnew? Don't you understand what this judge is doing? You are going to jail at the end of this trial. What I really think is that you should split before it's over. Fascism is what's happening. I think you should go underground before they take you out."

During the People's Park street fighting that spring, Bernardine and a few other SDS leaders had quietly slipped into Berkeley to observe events firsthand. She and I had felt an attraction to each other in the intensity of that crisis and spent one night together. She had changed radically from the earnest law student I'd met three years before, into a free-spirited SDS communist, pulsating with a sense of her own power. As the poets said of revolutionary Ireland, a "terrible beauty" was born in Bernardine.

The fatalist in me sensed that she was right. It was illusion to rely on the courts in the age of Nixon. It was not my belief in the system, but my fear of the unknown, that kept me going through the motions each day. The rationalist (or was it the dreamer?) in me, on the other hand, could not accept the inevitability of domestic fascism.

"I think we can convince some of the jury to hang with us. I think through the media, we can build public pressure on the system to give us bail if we're convicted, and even throw the case out. I believe that because that's me, that's how I'm made up."

The argument was over. I wasn't sure if I was right or if I could think clearly anymore. My emotions—paranoia, hate, fear, guilt—were spinning, confusing me. I needed to sleep. When I got home, there were two women sleeping together in my bed, thinking I wouldn't be back. I lay down on the edge of the bed, but I couldn't shut by eyes without seeing courtroom images. Instead of legal process I was seeing a fistfight. I left the bedroom and listened to Rolling Stones albums the rest of the night. "Sympathy for the Devil" kept repeating in my head. At dawn, I turned up "Street Fighting Man" and drank some coffee.

That morning, Len was directed to go ahead with cross-examination. But there was a scraping and clanking sound from Bobby's chair. Len stated to the court: "The buckle on the leather strap holding Mr. Seale's hand is digging into his hand, and he appears to be trying to free his hand from that pressure. Could he be helped?" The jury was excused, and barely out of the room, when a group of marshals got into a pushing conflict with Bobby and knocked his chair over.

At once, everyone was up, and marshals were slugging and elbowing the other defendants, spectators, and even members of the press. The emotion simply exploded without any focus. Bobby was yelling through the gag that his blood circulation was being stopped. Jerry Rubin protested, "This guy is putting his elbow in Bobby's mouth," and got kneed and knocked over himself. Kunstler took the lectern tightly between his hands, and asked, "Your Honor, are we going to stop this medieval torture chamber that is going on in this courtroom?"

Everything became unreal. Now I knew how wars started.

MR. KUNSTLER: Your Honor, this is an unholy disgrace to the law that is going on in this courtroom and as an American lawyer I feel it is a disgrace.

MR. FORAN: A disgrace created by Mr. Kunstler.

MR. KUNSTLER: Created by nothing other than what you have done to this man.

MR. ABBIE HOFFMAN: You come down here and watch it, Judge.

MR. SEALE: You fascist dogs, you rotten low life son of a bitch. I am glad I said it about Washington used to have slaves . . .

MR. DELLINGER: Somebody go to protect him.

MR. FORAN: Your Honor, may the record show that it is Mr. Dellinger saying somebody go to protect him—and the other comments were by Mr. Rubin.

THE COURT: Everything you say will be taken down.

MR. KUNSTLER: Your Honor, we would like the names of the marshals. We are going to ask for a judicial investigation of the entire condition and the entire treatment of Bobby Seale.

THE COURT: Don't point at me in that manner.

MR. KUNSTLER: I just feel so utterly ashamed to be an American lawyer at this time.

THE COURT: You should be ashamed of your conduct in this court, sir.

MR. KUNSTLER: What conduct, when a client is treated in this manner?

THE COURT: We will take a brief recess.

MR. KUNSTLER: Can we have somebody with Mr. Seale? We don't trust—

THE COURT: He is not your client, you said.

MR. KUNSTLER: We are speaking for the other several defendants.

THE COURT: The marshals will take care of him.

MR. RUBIN: Take care of him?

THE COURT: Take that remark down. The Court will be in recess.

When court resumed, the judge instructed Len to continue a cross-examination, but he couldn't. The crisis was now too unbearable. Len moved that the jury be asked if it could continue to deliberate fairly while one defendant was chained and gagged. That began another eruption of objections from Foran, and at once nearly everyone was rising and arguing. Several of the defendants decided that we would tell the puzzled jury what was happening as soon as they reappeared. When they came back in the room, Rennie stood and gazed at the jury and declared, "Ladies and gentlemen of the jury, he was being tortured while you were out of this room by these marshals. It is terrible what is happening. It is terrible what is happening." The judge ordered the jury out again, and some almost ran while others moved slowly, trying to listen over their shoulders. Bobby tried to appeal to them, through his gag, and was knocked down by the marshals. I shouted, "Now they're going to beat him." Abbie snarled, "You may as well kill him if you are going to gag him. It seems that way, doesn't it?" To which the judge replied, "You are not permitted to address the court, Mr. Hoffman, you have a lawyer." "This, man, isn't a court," Abbie declared, "*this is a neon oven.* This disruption started when these guys got into overkill. It is the same thing as last year in Chicago, the same exact thing."

Somehow, "order" was restored again, and the judge commanded another witness to the stand. But the testimony was meaningless since all the attention was on the strapped and seething figure of Bobby. Finally, on the third day of the ordeal, Len, Jerry Rubin, and I asked permission to fly out to meet Charles Garry over the weekend. We badly needed a break for a strategic discussion. Surprisingly, the judge granted the request as long as we promised not to "vilify" him on television. I said that was not the purpose of the trip, but that I would not be gagged by such an order. On Friday night we found ourselves flying to San Francisco.

As soon as we landed, rented a car, and started for Garry's house, state police pulled us over. They wanted to know if any of us intended to make statements for television or public appearances during the weekend. Slightly startled by the long arm of the Chicago law, we indicated there were no such plans and continued on. Garry and his legal team were waiting for us at his comfortable hillside house in Daly City, just south of the San Francisco city line. After we described for them what they had been reading and watching in the media, it was apparent that there wasn't anything Garry himself could do at this point. He drafted a strong statement condemning the denial of Bobby's right to self-defense, called for a dismissal of the case as "irretrievably prejudiced" against all the defendants, and concluded that "even if I were physically and medically able to take part in a major trial, which I am not according to my physicians, my participation could in no way cure the fundamental constitutional infirmity with which it is already plagued."

On Monday morning, yet another surprise awaited: There sat Bobby Seale in his chair, without chains or gag, his yellow notepad in front of him. Over the weekend, someone decided that the nationally televised spectacle of the brutalized Black Panther had to end. But it made no sense simply to take off the shackles without resolving the central issue of his representation. Before the jury came in, the judge and Schultz once again tried to get Bobby to waive his legal claims. After Bobby emotionally objected to his cruel and unusual punishment and reasserted his determination to defend himself, Len leaned over and whispered to me, "They've decided to get rid of him. It'll be a mistrial."

He was right, but the ripe moment for the government did not come for two days. On November 4, the prosecution chose to call to the stand one Bill H. Ray, a deputy sheriff from California who had observed Bobby boarding a plan for the Chicago demonstrations in 1968. He was the only witness the government called to prove the "interstate travel" part of the indictment against any of the eight defendants. If there had been an informant at the airport, I realized, they must have been planning to indict Bobby even before he flew to Chicago to speak. As soon as the witness identified him, Bobby tried to assert his right of cross-examination. By now I felt I was watching a play with predictable characters; the only question was who had written the script and what the last act was. When the judge dismissed the jury, I sensed the climax would come right after the lunch break. Sure enough, about two-thirty the judge entered the courtroom holding up a thick sheaf of papers, which he began to read aloud:

> "As we all know, the defendant Bobby G. Seale has been guilty of a conduct in the presence of the court during this trial which is not only contumacious in character but of so grave a character as to continually disrupt the orderly administration of justice. . . . Accordingly I adjudge the defendant Bobby G. Seale guilty of 16 criminal contempts. . . . There will be an order declaring a mistrial as to the defendant Bobby G. Seale and not as to any other defendants."

He looked up over his spectacles with finality. The marshals were taking up positions all around the room, several of them removing their badges, waiting for us to explode. The full weight of the judge's act took a minute to absorb. All our legal research indicated that a judge could never sentence someone to more than six months for contempt of court without a jury trial on each count. What Judge Hoffman had done to avoid the embarrassing possibility of sixteen separate new trials for Bobby was to sentence him to three months in prison for each contempt "to run consecutively." That would avoid the jury-trial requirement and result in a total sentence of more than four years.

Then came a most surreal moment. After ten weeks of silencing Bobby's attempts to defend himself, the judge leaned down to the sentenced Panther and said in a kindly and paternal voice, "You may speak now, sir."

Bobby, startled, responded, "I can speak now, but I can't speak to defend myself?" As the judge's mistrial order was read, Bobby looked around and asked, "Wait a minute, I got a right—what's the cat trying to pull now? I can't stay?" As the marshals moved toward Bobby, the judge ordered everyone to rise and recess for the day. To scattered calls of "Free Bobby," the marshals took him by the arms as he spoke his last words: "I have a right to go through this trial. I'm put in jail for four years for nothing? . . . Hey, I want my coat." Then they marched him rapidly through the side door to prison.

. . .

The trial within a trial, that of Bobby Seale versus American justice, was over. The trial of the Chicago Seven was just beginning. For hours, for days, we felt a hollowness, as if the life of the trial had ended with the punishment and severance of Bobby. But the government went on, relentlessly introducing its witnesses, targeting the seven of us as its next victims. We realized we had a job to do, speaking to and educating a confused country about what happened to Bobby.

And somehow, we had to prepare a defense of our own to take to the jury.

16.   The Verdict

We became known as the Conspiracy. The seven remaining defendants camped in apartments in the Hyde Park area near the university, about forty-five minutes from the Federal Building. If Chicago meant living under siege, these were the barracks. Leonard Weinglass and I rented a railroad apartment; besides ourselves, a few staff members moved in during the trial. The place was barren. At night it became the central headquarters of the legal defense team. It quickly became known that Kunstler was better at giving seat-of-the-pants speeches and partying at night than at the drudgery of preparing the legal defense. Therefore, after court each day, we would spill into a local bar, drink and eat, then return to our apartment to prepare for the next day. We would often be preparing witnesses, writing memos, and arguing the case until well after midnight. We lived on junk food, coffee, wine, and bourbon. The Yippies stayed mostly to themselves in an apartment nearby, preferring marijuana and plotting their adventures late into the night as well. At our apartment, a kind of camaraderie of the damned continued until we dropped in exhaustion, people often crashing on the floor in sleeping bags. Sometimes we were joined by sympathetic celebrities like Dustin Hoffman, my hero from *The Graduate*, who was interested in learning to mimic both his namesakes, Julius and Abbie. Very few friendships could blossom in these stark conditions, and many were strained and abandoned. Women in our ranks—whether they were lovers and/or Conspiracy staff—were especially frustrated, since all of them were forced into the classic secondary, supportive roles that their feminist consciousness was rejecting.

Abbie, Jerry, and to a lesser extent, Rennie, were aroused by their roles as defendants, and actually dreamed of forming a permanent national organization if we survived the trial, which was developing a national television audience several times a week. I thought it was a crazy idea for several reasons: We were not likely to be vindicated; we couldn't agree among ourselves politically; our egos were blindly competitive; we were all men; and none of us had real constituencies to be accountable to. I felt that organizations like the Mobe and the Yippies were beginning to outlive any useful purposes, and we would be perpetuating little more than our own image and notoriety.

What I really wanted was a home. Almost every Friday afternoon, I caught a five P.M. plane to Berkeley, adding to my distance from the other defendants. But coming from the harsh, and usually freezing, reality of Chicago made forty-eight hours in Berkeley seem even more unreal. I could see Anne and Christopher and a few friends, but before I could feel relaxed and close to anyone, it was time to catch the Sunday night red-eye back to O'Hare Field. I would take a cab to the apartment, shut my eyes for an hour, shower, and leave for the courtroom again.

One weekend was a particular nightmare. The Rolling Stones were performing at nearby Altamont. I wanted to stay home with Anne and Christopher, but most of our friends went. They were full of anticipation that this would be another Woodstock, a time of good vibes and the music of revolution, but they returned a day later, shaken. Bad drugs, probably cut with speed, were being passed out free, causing people to flip out and get sick. Mick Jagger's lyrics, oozing with violence toward women ("Under My Thumb"), made one of my friends flash for twelve hours on being raped; around her women *were* being raped. And around the prancing Jagger were hulking Hell's Angels, one of them wearing a wolf's head, serving as bodyguards. At the climax of the concert they beat up and stabbed to death a black man. My scared friends were throwing up and taking Thorazine.

During the same few days, the Charles Manson "family" was

indicted for the sadistic murders of actress Sharon Tate and others in Los Angeles. Anne and I were nauseated by the report of Tate's stomach cut open with a fork; Tate was pregnant at the time. It was the ultimate in barbarism. But many people, including several underground papers, fell into the illusion that Manson was a persecuted and misunderstood hippie. Jerry Rubin was one. He and Phil Ochs went to see Manson in prison. Manson told them that he wanted to conduct himself defiantly like the Chicago Seven in his upcoming trial. Jerry was fascinated. Looking back twenty years later, Jerry told me, "In my frame of mind I wanted to believe that the charges against Manson were an FBI frame-up. I was so into romanticizing outlaw behavior that I looked for any possible explanation to find something good in the outlaw. If society had made Manson mad, then I thought that society was to blame for Manson's crimes, not Manson. And that attitude was part of the madness of the times."

Far more unbelievable was the attitude of Bernardine Dohrn, who called Manson's act "far out." At the last Weathermen meeting before they went underground, Bernardine stood on a stage in a miniskirt and high leather boots, raising her hand in the air, her fingers making the sign of Manson's fork, a symbol of the brutality that the Weathermen had decided to inflict on bourgeois society. The Weathermen had concluded that white babies were "pigs." The presence of Christopher in my life made me even more shaken over these emerging depravities. What did it mean? The face of evil—of fascism—had appeared in the youth culture. What had started with love and peace, pushed too far, seemed dialectically to become its opposite. Before I could absorb the stories from Altamont and the coverage of Manson, I had to return to Chicago.

That same week was the worst of the trial. On the evening of December 4, as Leonard Weinglass recalls it, the two of us were visited by Fred Hampton at our apartment. The Panther leader was jokingly known in the community as the "ice-cream bandit," because of a conviction and sentencing to a two- to five-year term for helping black children steal seventy-one dollars' worth of ice cream from a vendor during the hot summer of 1968. For this, the Chicago police and media described him as a "known felon." There was an aura about Fred, who had been an NAACP youth leader and a top student and athlete at a suburban high school, that made everyone smile, and he was especially supportive to Bobby in the courtroom.

Fred's ice-cream conviction had been upheld by an appeals court, which is what brought him to our door for advice. Accompanied by a Panther security guard we didn't recognize, Fred wanted to know how much time the appeal would take. He was clearly calculating whether to jump bail and go underground. If imprisoned, he expected to be killed. We held a short, whispered meeting in the hallway outside our apartment, after which Fred and his guard departed. My impression was that he was leaning toward vanishing. Though their security operation seemed fragile, a number of Panthers had already managed to go underground successfully.

Following the meeting, I rushed off to join the other defendants for a prescheduled filming of an absurdist version of the trial by Nicholas Ray, the director of *Rebel Without a Cause*. I played the role of Judge Hoffman, sitting on a platform elevated twenty-five feet in the air. Afterward, we stayed out drinking and clowning around. I ended the lost night sitting in a bathtub with a woman from the production company and did not go to sleep until after three A.M.

At five A.M. the phone rang in our apartment. I was completely dazed when I heard a staccato of startled voices: Fred Hampton and another Chicago Panther were dead at the hands of the Chicago police. I rolled onto the floor, head in my hands. Some of the staff members living in the apartment were already weeping. I showered and came to a stony acceptance, an unemotional sense that this was reality. Driving to court, there was no feeling left in me at all.

The details of the deaths were still coming over the radio as we arrived in court. Chicago police fired eighty rounds of ammunition into the Panther apartment, killing two and wounding four. Fred was shot four times, twice in the head, and was found lying unclothed in his bed. The morning paper carried a picture of several police officers, strangely grinning, as they carried Fred's covered body out of the apartment. The official who planned the raid, Cook County State's Attorney Edward Hanrahan, announced that the police had shown "good judgment, considerable restraint, [and] professional discipline."

Over five thousand people attended the services. It was later revealed that William O'Neal, the Chicago Panthers security chief, stationed inside Fred's apartment that night, was a long-time FBI informant. He later admitted that the assorted guns inside the Panthers' apartment, which he controlled, were "just gathering dust."

With the weight of the Panther killings around us, we had to begin mounting our legal defense against these same Chicago police. The prosecution had finished its case, calling fifty-four witnesses, all but one of them from law enforcement.

By this time, our four sympathizers on the jury were beginning to feel isolated in their sequestered world. "The rest of them hated the four of us," Jean Fritz recalled. Kay Richards continued her proselytizing against us. Jean Fritz started developing phlebitis in one leg and needed the marshals to provide her a prop on which to rest that leg in the jury box. She began going to bed early every night, sometimes without dinner.

The defense was our chance to tell the jurors and, through the media, the public our version of what happened in Chicago and why. In addition, a protracted defense would make it possible to do more speaking on campuses around the country. The genuine jury of our peers was out there, we felt, and if they found us not guilty when the judge threw us in jail, we hoped it would set off massive demonstrations to free us around the country. The court of public opinion was our only hope.

We were not interested simply in denying that Jerry Rubin threw paint, that Dave Dellinger meant something else in a speech, that undercover agents were distorting and lying; we wanted to go beyond the narrow terms of the prosecution to the larger picture of what was going on in America that motivated us to take a stand in Chicago and, in turn, what was behind the government's indictment of us. We wanted to argue that our intentions were protected by the First Amendment, that Washington and Chicago authorities conspired to deny our rights in order to prevent embarrassment during their plan for a ritualistic endorsement of Johnson's policies through Humphrey's nomination, that we were made into symbolic scapegoats to draw attention away from the real violence of Vietnam abroad and repression at home, and that we had a certain "right of resistance" to the precise extent that our constitutional rights were denied.

Within this consensus, there were sharp differences. I was the most cautious of the defendants, wanting to reach the jury by pursuing a thorough, rational defense, combined with a public-education campaign, stressing that a prolongation of "Nixon's war" would inevitably lead to widening political repression. John Froines seemed to take a similar view. The Yippies were advocates of disruptive courtroom theater, including deliberate contempt of court (as the judge defined it), because they felt the media image would both desanctify the judicial system and win more identification with our cause. Dave Dellinger was more inclined to courtroom defiance as well, stemming from his background of nonviolent civil disobedience and "moral witness." Rennie, in his usual role, was mediating and trying to hold all the currents together. I think Lee believed everyone was right; he kept reading the *I Ching*.

We allowed a good deal of latitude for each defendant to maintain his own style inside and outside the courtroom. We also decided that the defense would stress the antiwar and the youth-culture emphasis of our politics equally, calling both Mobilization and Yippie witnesses. I virtually became a third lawyer, working with Ann Froines. With help from others, she would labor on the phones by day and, with me, by night, identifying and flying in a parade of witnesses and preparing them to testify. It was exhausting, but it was the only way I could hold on to my rationality.

Among the 104 witnesses we called, Staughton Lynd, as a historian, explained most articulately the basis of our actions in Chicago. We identified Staughton as an expert witness on the American Revolution to draw historic parallels with the 1968 demonstrations. The judge refused to let the jury hear Staughton on the grounds of "irrelevance," and so he could only summarize for the record what he would have told the jury. Staughton said that the First Amendment "right of petition" was based on the revolutionary Declaration of Independence and therefore protected far more militant forms of expression than usually realized.

Staughton compared our actions in Chicago with the "kind of intermediate resistance which the makers of the American Revolution carried out from 1765 to 1775," such as the boycotts of imported English goods. There was a "peculiar resemblance," he noted, between Chicago 1968 and aspects of the Boston Massacre of March 1770. In 1767, in an "unheard-of event," four regiments of British troops were landed in Boston to maintain "order." The soldiers angered the townspeople and the dock-workers as a potential "threat to democracy" and provoked a series of "minor scuffles and incidents." One night three years later, a group of townspeople surrounded a particular British sentry; according to Staughton, "They called him 'lobsterback,' because of his red coat, a kind of eighteenth-century equivalent of 'pig.' They threw oyster shells and hunks of ice at him, and at a certain point, he called out the Guard." The Guard indeed came out, the people kept up the name-calling, and finally an order to shoot was given, and five colonists were killed. Staughton continued:

> The British said that the soldiers had been provoked because oyster shells and lumps of ice were thrown at them. But the colonists, Sam Adams and Paul Revere, took the position that the provocation consisted in the presence of the British soldiers having turned the city of Boston into an armed camp. That's why acts of resistance, even though certainly far more than the customary speech and assembly, seemed appropriate to people like Sam Adams and Thomas Jefferson because they were responses to an oppressive situation which had gone far beyond those normal circumstances in which speech and assembly and free press and petition were adequate responses. . . .
>
> It seems to me that the jury might wish to consider the entire process of the [1968] demonstration as a kind of petitioning process in which people who felt that their elected government was no longer responsible to them, who felt themselves to be in the same position as the colonists before the American Revolution, came to Chicago to make one last direct appeal to the men of power who were assembled in the Democratic convention.

By introducing over one hundred witnesses from all backgrounds, we tried to show that the events in Chicago were not a conspiracy of a few but a shocking encounter for many people with a police state.

For testimony about permit negotiations, we had Chicago lawyers, McCarthy campaign representatives, and even U.S. Justice Department officials on the stand. On the subject of the "police riot," we had a British member of Parliament who was sprayed with Mace, several ministers who were called "fucking fakes" by the police, a black police officer who heard his own colleagues chanting "kill, kill, kill" in preconvention drills, and a woman medical volunteer who heard the same chant from police at the Conrad Hilton on the bloody night of August 28. We even found the young man who pulled down the flag on the afternoon of the twenty-eighth, giving the police their pretext for charging the crowd. Angus Mackenzie testified that he was pulling the flag to half-mast because "they killed democracy." In addition to all these unknown eyewitnesses, we called authors and artists like Norman Mailer, Allen Ginsberg, Judy Collins, Country Joe MacDonald, Phil Ochs, and Arlo Guthrie; and political representatives like Richard Goodwin from the Kennedy campaign, Sam Brown from the McCarthy coalition, Congressman John Conyers, and Georgia Representative Julian Bond. The trial defense became a reenactment of the history of the sixties.

We chose to put only Rennie and Abbie on the stand as representatives for all of us. The beginnings and conclusions of their testimonies, which lasted a week in each case, convey the way they tried to speak in more than their own narrow defense:

MR. WEINGLASS: Will you please identify yourself for the record?

THE WITNESS: My name is Abbie. I am an orphan of America.

MR. SCHULTZ: Your Honor, may the record show it is the defendant Hoffman.

THE COURT: Oh yes, it may so indicate.

THE WITNESS: Well, it is not really my last name.

MR. WEINGLASS: Abbie, what is your last name?

THE WITNESS: Well, there is some confusion about it because my grandfather was a Russian Jew, and he decided to protest the anti-Semitism in the Russian army.

MR. SCHULTZ: Objection. If the defendant has a last name let him state it, but not—

THE COURT: All we want to know, sir, is your last name.

THE WITNESS: My slave name, sir, is Hoffman. My real name is Sheboysnikow, but I can't spell it.

MR. WEINGLASS: Where do you reside?

THE WITNESS: I live in the Woodstock Nation.

MR. WEINGLASS: Will you tell the court and jury where it is.

THE WITNESS: Yes, it is a nation of alienated young people. We carry it around with us as a state of mind in the same way as the Sioux Indians carried the Sioux Nation around with them. It is a nation dedicated to cooperation versus competition, to the idea that people should have better means of exchange than property or money, there should be some other basis for human interaction . . .

THE COURT: No, we want the place of residence, if he has one, place of doing business, if you have a business. Nothing about philosophy or Indians, sir. Just where you live, if you have a place to live. Now you said Woodstock. In what state is Woodstock?

THE WITNESS: It is in the state of mind, in the mind of myself and my brothers and sisters. It is a conspiracy. Presently the nation is held captive in the penitentiaries of the institutions of a decaying system.

MR. WEINGLASS: Can you tell the Court and jury your present age?

THE WITNESS: My age is 33, I am a child of the sixties.

MR. WEINGLASS: When were you born?

THE WITNESS: Psychologically, 1960.

MR. SCHULTZ: Objection if the court please, I move to strike the answer.

MR. WEINGLASS: What is the actual date of your birth?

THE WITNESS: November 30, 1936.

MR. WEINGLASS: Between the date of your birth November 30, 1936, and May 1, 1960, what if anything occurred in your life?

THE WITNESS: Nothing. I believe it is called an American education.

And from the end of Abbie's testimony:

MR. WEINGLASS: Could you explain to the jury and to the Court what you understand by the term "Yippie myth."

THE WITNESS: The term "myth" refers to an attitude, a subjective historical view of what is going on in society . . . It is a subjective reality; the alliance between what actually happened and between thoughts and wonders and dreams about projections . . . For example, people's prejudices about what they see, since it is subjective, play a great role.

There is a famous experiment in psychology in which a man, a white man in a business suit, stabs a young black man in a film and it is flashed very rapidly. White people, because they have a tendency to be racists, will invariably switch it around so that the young black man has the knife and the one with the business suit on is getting stabbed; that is, the victim in a sense becomes the criminal.

The events in Chicago would be a type of myth, a kind of subjective analysis. If there was a conspiracy on the part of the Government and city officials, you see, to form violence, they would have to project that on someone else. They would have to call the victims the conspiracy that fostered the violence.

Rennie attempted to trace his development:

THE WITNESS: The first time I came to the City of Chicago was to visit the International Amphitheater in a poultry judging contest in 1956. It was the international contest and I had just won the Eastern United States Poultry Judging Contest in 4-H and I came to Chicago to participate in the contest here.

MR. WEINGLASS: What is your occupation?

THE WITNESS: Since 1967 my primary work and concern has been ending the war in Vietnam. Until the time of this trial I was the national coordinator of the Mobilization to End the War in Vietnam.

MR. WEINGLASS: Now, directing your attention to the evening of November 20, 1967, do you recall where you were on that night?

THE WITNESS: I was at the University of Chicago. It was a meeting of a group called The Resistance. I was a speaker with Bob Ross and David Harris, who is the husband of Joan Baez.

MR. WEINGLASS: Could you relate now to the Court and Jury the words that you spoke, as best you recall, on that particular night?

THE WITNESS: I began by holding up a small steel ball that was green, about the size of a tennis ball, and I said, "This bomb was dropped on a city of 100,000 people, a city called Nam Dinh which is about 65 miles south of Hanoi."

I said, "It was dropped by an American fighter jet, an F-105," and that when this bomb exploded over Nam Dinh, about 640 of these round steel balls were spewed into the sky. And I said, "When this ball strikes a building or the ground or slows up in any way, these hammers are released, an explosion occurs which sends out about 300 steel pellets.

"Now, one of these balls," I explained, "was roughly three times the power of an old-fashioned hand grenade and with 640 of these bombs going off, you can throw steel pellets over an area about a thousand yards long, and about 250 yards wide.

"Every living thing exposed in that thousand-yard area from this single bomb, ninety percent of every living thing in that area will die," I said, "whether it's a water buffalo or a water buffalo boy."

I said that if this bomb were to go off in this room tonight, everyone in the room here would die but as quickly as we could remove the bodies from the room, we could have another discussion about Vietnam.

I said, this bomb would not destroy this lecture podium, it would not damage walls, the ceiling, the floor. I said, "If it is dropped on a city it takes life but leaves institutions. It is the ideal weapon, you see, for the mentality that reasons that life is less precious than property."

I said that in 1967, one out of every two bombs dropped on North Vietnam was this weapon. One out of every two. And in 1967 the American government told the American public that in North Vietnam it was only bombing steel and concrete.

Then I said, "I went to Vietnam not as a representative of the government, and not as a member of the military, but as an American citizen who was deeply perturbed that we lived in a country where our own government was lying to American people about this war. The American government claimed to be hitting only military targets. Yet what I saw was that pagodas had been gutted, schoolhouses had been razed, population centers had been leveled".

Then I said that I am going to the Democratic National Convention because I want the world to know that there are thousands of young people in this country who do not want to see a rigged convention rubber stamp another four years of Lyndon Johnson's war.

MR. WEINGLASS: I show you an object marked D-325 for identification and ask, can you identify that object?

THE WITNESS: This was the bomb that I brought back from Vietnam.

MR. FORAN: Your Honor, the Government objects to this exhibit for the following reasons. The Vietnamese war, your honor, has nothing whatsoever to do with the charges in this indictment.

Rennie ended his testimony, describing what happened after the flag-lowering incident:

MR. WEINGLASS: What were you saying, if anything, on the microphone?

THE WITNESS: I kept directing the marshals to form a line, link arms, and then I constantly urged the people in the crowd to stop throwing things. I said, "You're throwing things at our own people. Move back." As our marshal line grew, I urged our marshal line to now begin to move back and move the demonstrators away from the police.

MR. WEINGLASS: What were you doing as the police were advancing?

THE WITNESS: Well, as the police advanced, I continued to have my back to the police line, basically concerned that the marshal line not break or move. Then the police formation broke and began to run, and at that time I heard several of the men in the line yell, quite distinctly, "Kill Davis, Kill Davis," and they were screaming that and the police moved in on top of me, and I was trapped ... The first thing that occurred to me was a very powerful blow to the head that drove me face first down into the dirt, and then, as I attempted to crawl on my hands and knees, the policemen continued to yell "Kill Davis, Kill Davis," and continued to strike me across the neck and ears and back.

I guess I must have been hit 30 or 40 times in the back and I crawled for maybe—I don't know how many feet, ten feet maybe, and I came to a chain fence, and a policeman fell over the fence, trying to get me, and another police hit the fence with his nightstick, but I had about a second or two in which I could stand and I leaped over a bench and over some people and into the park, and then I proceeded to walk toward the center of the park.

MR. WEINGLASS: And as you walked to the center of the park, what if anything happened?

THE WITNESS: Well, I guess the first thing I was conscious of, I looked down and my tie was just solid blood, and I realized that my shirt was just becoming blood, and someone took my arm and took me to the east side of the Bandshell, and I lay down, and there was a man with a white coat who was bent over me.

We were prevented from testifying about the central question of the trial, that of "intent." For instance, Rennie and I had written a twenty-one-page strategy paper on the proposed Chicago demonstrations for a movement conference in February 1968. This paper sketched out the alternative scenarios for Chicago and bluntly ruled out the use of violence. If the paper had advocated violence, of course, it would have been the prosecution's centerpiece. But because it advocated nonviolence, the judge ruled it "self-serving" and refused to let the jury examine or even hear about it.

The judge and prosecutor eliminated key documents or testimony again and again. None of our expert witnesses—on American history, on the youth culture, on racism in the Democratic party, or on war crimes in Vietnam—were allowed. Abbie's two books, *Revolution for the Hell of It* and *Woodstock Nation*, were blocked from the jury. A policeman who knew of the Chicago preparations for repression was excused as a witness without telling his story, as was a National Guardsman who knew of similar plans and of live ammunition being used. The Roosevelt University president who chaired the official commission on the April 1968 police suppression of a peaceful march—widely thought to be a tactical rehearsal for the August convention—was kept silent about what he knew. So was the archivist who kept all the interview data that went into the official Walker Commission report, *Rights in Conflict*, including the interviews with Foran and Schultz.

Mayor Daley made his entrance into the courtroom, complete with his own bodyguards, on January 6. It was Jean Fritz's "biggest kick." In the back hallways where the jurors waited, she recalled, "there were guys everywhere with guns." The court itself was ringed with additional marshals as if to emphasize that the mayor's attitudes toward "security" had not changed since 1968. None of us had ever seen him before that moment. A legendary figure, this round, red-faced, sixty-year-old Irish Buddha was not without a certain charm. We respected his unpolished platitudes, his protection of working-class people, and his awareness of being one of a kind, a museum piece. While the mayor sat in the witness stand waiting to begin, Abbie rose with a big grin and challenged him to fight it out with fists; everyone in the room, including the marshals and the mayor, burst into laughter. We called Mayor Daly as a witness, and we sought a technical ruling by the judge that the mayor be considered a "hostile witness," a step which would have allowed us to do the same sort of probing cross-examination we would to a prosecution witness. No one could have been considered more hostile than the mayor, yet virtually all of Kunstler's questions were ruled out of order and the motion to have the mayor declared a hostile witness was denied, according to the judge, because the mayor's "manner had been that of a gentleman."

If that were not absurd enough, a melee broke out when someone in the spectators' section smirked at the mayor's statement that Foran was "one of the greatest attorneys in this country and the finest man I have met in public and private life." It was Frank Joyce, a defense staff member who had gone to high school with me. One of the mayor's personal bodyguards jumped into the spectator's section and the transcript recorded the rest:

VOICE: Ouch! Ow, don't step on me, please!

VOICES: He isn't doing anything. She isn't doing anything!

MR. KUNSTLER: Your Honor, that is one of our staff people. I don't understand. I would like the Court to inquire.

THE COURT: Regardless of who the person is, if the person has been disorderly, the marshal must ask the person to leave.

VOICES: What's going on?
Leave him alone.
Hey, leave him alone.
Leave him alone.
Ouch!
Leave her alone.

(shouts and screams)

VOICES: Hey, stop that.
Hey, stop that.
Leave them alone.

(shouts and screams)

VOICES: You're hitting Frank in the face.
Leave him alone. Leave him alone.

MR. KUNSTLER: The defendants request to know what happened.

THE COURT: The Marshals will explain at an appropriate time.

Two of our trial staff people were arrested for "assaulting marshals," charges which were later dropped. The mayor's attitude
and entourage had provoked another replica of the cycle of
events that began in 1968. Still, we could ask him no questions.

Not long after, on January 28, former Attorney General Ramsey Clark was called to the stand. He was in some ways our key
witness, since his testimony could go to the heart of the 1968
permit negotiations and subsequent handling of the demonstrations. We had tried, and failed, earlier in January, to get testimony before the jury from two of his assistants, Roger Wilkins,
who met with Rennie in 1968, and Wesley Pomeroy, who was
Clark's special liaison to the convention. Both would have testified that they found Rennie a flexible negotiator and the city
administration, including its ally, Tom Foran, rigid and
unyielding by comparison. They had written reports conveying
this message to their chief, the attorney general. Pomeroy was
particularly important because he had supervised security at
events as diverse as the 1964 Republican convention and the 1969
Woodstock festival. He was prepared to testify that the entire
convention disaster could have been prevented by different police conduct and that he called the attorney general on the night
of August 28, 1968, to say he was "ashamed to be a law enforcement officer" after seeing the police brutality in the streets. All
this potential testimony was stricken by Judge Hoffman, on
grounds that it was "hearsay." We argued that the government
could bring in the mayor or the relevant Justice Department
officials to verify or refute Pomeroy's testimony. But our arguments were pointless.

So we embarked on the delicate mission of getting Ramsey
Clark to the witness stand. Leonard Weinglass, John Froines,
and I flew to the suburban Virginia home of Clark and his wife,
Georgia, one weekend to ask if he would testify. The former
attorney general received us very correctly and warmly.
Dressed in casual clothes, he offered us a snack and apologized
that he had to leave shortly to visit a sick child. We sat down to
interview him immediately. What surprised me was the presence of two note-taking officials from the current Nixon Justice
Department. Clark, as a courtesy, had notified the department
that we were coming and invited them to observe. We knew the
two officials would report immediately to Foran and Schultz on
whatever transpired, but we were happy, however, that Clark

was willing to testify without "favoring any party but the truth," about his conversations with Mayor Daley, Tom Foran, President Johnson, and other cabinet officials, and with his own representatives, Wilkins and Pomeroy. It was dynamite: The former head of the Justice Department, who had declined to seek indictments against us, explaining why he disagreed with the approach of the new department in Washington.

After this efficient and useful discussion, we left the room briefly to wash up and confer on whether anything remained to be asked. When I returned to Clark's study, the two Justice Department officials were intently talking to him by the fireplace, urging him not to be a witness for the defense. I was shocked, but I stepped back to let the encounter unfold. Clark held his ground, saying he didn't know if his testimony would be accepted, or whether it would help the prosecution or defense, but he intended to go ahead in the interests of the whole truth being available. I sensed an unbreakable commitment under his seemingly neutral and cautious phrasing.

When Ramsey Clark arrived in Chicago to testify, he was kept entirely out of the jury's sight while Schultz got up to argue that he should not even be sworn in. We again had underestimated the extreme lengths to which the prosecution would go in order to protect its case. Never to my knowledge in the history of American jurisprudence had defendants been denied the right of bringing a witness to the stand—not to mention a witness who was a former attorney general. Schultz nearly leaped to the podium, his hands full of notes made by the Justice Department officials at Clark's home. "Nothing he could say would possibly be admissible," Schultz declared with a rising tension in his voice. According to the Code of Federal Regulations, Schultz said, disclosure of Justice Department material was prohibited without "prior approval of the attorney general"—John Mitchell. The rule referred to the control of certain kinds of documents, not to the muzzling of former attorney generals. As Kunstler pointed out to Judge Hoffman, "If the regulation were interpreted as Mr. Schultz obviously would like it interpreted, this would mean that nobody in the federal government could ever testify after having left the federal government."

The judge faced this dilemma: How could the accused in a trial be prevented from calling whomever they wanted to the witness stand? He claimed discretion on the grounds that we had previously attempted to "inject irrelevant and extraneous evidence," citing the example of Mayor Daley, who "was called with much fanfare but was able to give virtually no evidence that was material to this case." Of course, the judge could protect Mayor Daley from questions, but it would be bad form indeed to "protect" Ramsey Clark from our questioning. Finally, the judge agreed to have Ramsey Clark take the stand, outside the jury's presence, to determine what Clark would say—an unprecedented "screening" of a witness's testimony.

Clark entered the courtroom more than puzzled about what was occurring and took the stand. Although his subsequent testimony was all but completely objected to by the prosecution, he still penetrated the screen with some small bits of information. On the assessment by Roger Wilkins of the prospects for negotiations, Clark testified that Wilkins "didn't feel that we were likely to get the cooperation that we hoped for and that the attitude from the mayor's office didn't seem conciliatory." By contrast, Clark said, Wilkins had been "favorably impressed" with Rennie Davis "as being a sincere young person." He related that a meeting was held shortly before the convention in the Oval Office of the White House to discuss the prepositioning of troops, but the prosecution successfully objected to Clark's sharing what he advised the president. Finally, Clark was able to testify that on August 30, 1968, two days after the convention, he spoke by phone with Foran and instructed him that only a factual investigation would be made of the convention events, rather than a grand jury investigation—implying that he had no intention of prosecuting.

It wasn't even close to all Clark could say, but it was significant. Yet upon hearing the proposed testimony, the judge flatly ruled out bringing Clark before the jury. It would be a "needless delay of this trial," the judge announced. The former attorney general, dismissed from the court, melted tight-lipped through the reporters and puzzled spectators. We were instructed not to mention anything about the incident in front of the jury. It was as if the highest law-enforcement official of the previous administration was not only a nonwitness but a nonperson. *The New York Times* editorialized that this was "the ultimate outrage in a trial which has become the shame of American justice."

We definitely weren't going to accept this suppression quietly, no matter what the judge had instructed. The only question was which defendant was going to take the contempt to let the jury know. For a change, I was more than glad to do it. I sat quietly, secretly enjoying the search for the proper moment. A few days later, Foran made one of his many remarks about the irrelevance of the defense testimony, and I blurted out as the jury was leaving the room, "*You* should talk. You wouldn't even let Ramsey Clark testify for us." For that the judge sentenced me to six months, the maximum for a single count of contempt.

We also attempted to subpoena one of the most shadowy figures in the Chicago case, FBI Director J. Edgar Hoover, who, we were convinced, was actively and illegally involved in harassing protestors throughout the sixties and during the Chicago events of 1968. We wanted to compel by subpoena any information about illegal surveillance, informers, provocateurs, or wiretaps used during Convention Week. We also wanted to reveal, however difficult it was, that Hoover's agency was behind a widespread pattern of political repression against all sorts of citizen groups in America. Not surprisingly, Judge Hoffman ordered our subpoena quashed. What we didn't know was how closely the court and the FBI were collaborating.

FBI MEMORANDUM   **12/7/68**

TO: MR. DE LOACH
FROM: A. ROSEN

As a result of our discussions with the Department [of Justice], the Department has instructed the US Attorney in Chicago to immediately file a motion to quash the subpoena that has been served for the Director in this matter and William Campbell, Chief US District Judge in Chicago, has advised the Special Agent in Charge (SAC) that he will insure that the subpoena is quashed.

A copy of the subpoena was immediately brought to the attention of the Director ... The Director's statement 9/18/69 before the National Commission on the Causes and Prevention of Violence has been reviewed ... No reference is made to any of the defendants or co-conspirators of the Chicago trial or to any type of electronic or physical surveillance. SDS is described as being composed of radicals, anarchists, communists and malcontents with an almost passionate desire to destroy the traditional values of our democratic society and the existing social order ... the protest activity of the New Left and SDS, under the guise of legitimate expression of dissent, was described as creating an

insurrecting climate which has conditioned a number of young Americans to resort to civil disobedience and violence. The above comments in no way relate to the subpoena . . .

Page 27, last paragraph of the statement expressed agreement . . . that the media will highlight "police brutality" and ignore or minimize premeditated and provocative acts of demonstrators. Paragraph two, Page 2, states it is a tribute to the authorities that the Convention was not disrupted, the city was not paralyzed, not one shot was fired by police at demonstrators and not one life was lost. It is conceivable that the defense might attempt to utilize these statements during direct examination . . . and to provide a basis for probing the sources of information disseminated by the Bureau to local authorities.

With regard to the request in the subpoena for data relating to surveillances . . . it would be physically impossible . . . To comply would require the most extensive file search throughout the field . . . Since the Chief US District Judge in Chicago has given his assurance the subpoena will be quashed, it does not appear to be justified to instigate such a gigantic project at this time.

The winter days blurred into each other; the judge ordered us to continue the case on Saturdays, and our frustration grew as February and the end of the trial approached. There was one more vindictive insult to withstand before the final day: the revocation of Dave Dellinger's bail. As the trial unfolded, Dave had gradually lost his patience. Either from despair or a Quaker sense of direct action, he began reacting vocally, often eloquently, at outrages in the courtroom. Sometimes the situation was absurd, as when the judge ordered us to go to the bathroom in an adjoining cell instead of the public facility in the hall. Jerry Rubin and Schultz got into a heated argument with each other, and the marshals moved in. Dave said, "Don't touch him," and was ordered by the marshals to "shut up." Dave replied, hurt, "You don't have to say 'shut up.'" At other times it grew out of frustration. On January 14, for example, the judge erroneously accused Dave of saying something, to which Dave replied, "That's a lie." The judge, aroused, declared that he had "never sat in fifty years through a trial where a party to a lawsuit called a judge a liar." That stirred Dave's deepest philosophical convictions, and he rose up: "Maybe they were afraid to go to jail rather than tell the truth, but I would rather go to jail for however long you send me than to let you get away with that kind of thing." (Neither judge nor prosecutor knew the intensity of Dave's feelings. A lifelong pacifist, he went to jail for his beliefs in World War II; when released, he was asked to sign a new document making him eligible for the draft again. He refused, turned around, and served another year until the war was finally over.)

Close to the end of our defense, on January 30, the judge stopped the proceedings to announce that "one of the defendants" had given a speech in Milwaukee criticizing the judge's handling of the trial. It was Dave. The judge warned that another such speech would result in termination of bail. Once again we were threatened with jail for exercising freedom of speech. Since we were nearing the end of the trial, and public support for the defense was building, especially on the campuses, the judge may have wanted to curb a final round of mass rallies. We spent the next week speaking as often as possible, wondering how much time we had left.

A week later, on February 4, Dave lost his composure entirely. Chicago's deputy police chief, James Riordan, was testifying about Dave's role on August 28, the day that Dave stood at the front of the blocked nonviolent march near the bandshell. Riordan claimed an "unidentified speaker" told the marchers to break into small groups and disrupt the Loop and that Dave went off with a group carrying Vietcong flags, falsely suggesting that Dave had engaged in the later violence.

"Oh, bullshit," Dave blurted out from the defense table. Was that Dave? I asked myself. Now he was angrily appealing to the witness, "Let's argue about what you stand for and what I stand for, but let's not make up things like that." It was the pretext the judge needed. He excused the jury and terminated Dave's bail without hearing arguments from our attorneys. Dave walked out the door, the oldest of us, suffering from all sorts of stomach ailments, to live out the rest of the trial in Cook County Jail, waking up at five o'clock each morning to arrive in court on time.

We figured he was only about a week ahead of ourselves.

That night the remaining defendants had the bitterest argument of the trial. Abbie and Jerry wanted to force the judge into revoking all our bail the following morning. Solidarity with Dave would be the declared reason, but they also wanted to end the trial with us already in jail. They were not just arguing, they were ranting and raving around the table at the Chicago ACLU office where we had many of our meetings. We were fast unraveling as a group. I felt that deliberately acting to have ourselves thrown in jail would only persuade people that we were intentionally trying to stop the trial through disruption and would shift a crucial degree of support back to the judge. I wanted the trial to climax around the final summations to the jury and a nationwide series of rallies or militant actions organized from our Chicago office while the jury was out deliberating its verdict. We were unable to resolve the issue, finally breaking up and going off in the grimy cold Chicago night to decide individually how to act the following day.

The next morning, Abbie and Jerry appeared in court wearing black judge's robes covering blue Chicago police department shirts. Even I had to applaud their sense of theater. They were definitely intent on going to jail, but by one of the paradoxes of the trial, the judge proved unwilling to exploit their loud, defiant tactics. Abbie even started needling the judge in Yiddish: "You *schtunk. Schande vor de goyim,* huh? [Fronting for the gentiles, huh?]" He told Hoffman, "Stick it up your bowling ball," and asked, "How is your war stock doing, Julie?" Jerry Rubin screamed at him, "You are the laughingstock of the world, Julius Hoffman, the laughingstock of the world. Every kid in the world hates you, knows what you represent." The judge acted as if they were not there and instructed the lawyers to finish their case.

His ultimate vengeance was coming.

On February 10, the summations began. All the testimony was over, all our words were spoken, all our energy was now concentrated on the appeals to the jury. Our lawyers would try to frame the case in historical perspective.

It was a duel for the souls of the presumed minority of jurors favoring our case. The prosecutors would be happy with convictions of most, if not all, of us. The indictment was structured to promote just such an outcome, with two charges against each of seven defendants. The government needed to persuade our potentially sympathetic jurors that a compromise verdict was the best they could hope for. That would still mean five-year (instead of ten-year) sentences for most of us.

It was now exactly a decade since four black students began the sit-in movement in Greensboro, North Carolina, trying to awaken and challenge their own parents' generation and the conscience of America. My decade of struggle had had the same purpose: to end the apathy of the fifties, to make the Constitution and the Bill of Rights mean something, to put ideals into practice, to reach my parents. As I looked into the unexpressive faces across the courtroom, I realized that the jury was a microcosm of the same America that taught me to think and speak out and then broke my heart. If only a minority of the jury, even one of them, believed in our innocence and would take an absolute stand on that belief, the government would be thwarted. A hung jury would free us, and the government would be faced with the decision of trying a very unpopular case all over again. Not only would we prevail, but the government might be deterred from bringing future conspiracy cases against other dissenters.

The approach of Foran and Schultz was to combine themes that would solidify their hard core on the jury while wooing our sympathizers as well. Schultz's job was to weave together the fragments of evidence into the cloth of conspiracy. He tried at length to restore the credibility of the government's main witnesses, all undercover agents, while reciting the charges against us in one compressed outpouring. With all these accusations, he was implying that we must have done something. It was Foran's task to focus on the greater themes of the case. Opening on a note of populism, he called us "intellectuals" and "sophisticated men" and "well educated." And "you know," he flattered the jurors, "many men will be highly intellectual and yet they will have absolutely terrible judgment." Then he tried to seal us off from legitimate protestors and from leaders like Martin Luther King or Robert Kennedy. We were "liars" and "obscene haters" and, above all, "as evil as they can be." We were trying to prey on lofty causes and the innocence of young people to legitimize violence and destroy America. "There are millions of kids," he continued,

> who, naturally, resent authority, are impatient for change . . . They feel that John Kennedy went, Bobby Kennedy went, Martin Luther King went—they were all killed—and the kids do feel that the lights have gone out in Camelot, the banners are furled, and the parade is over. . . .
>
> And there is another thing about a kid, if we all remember, that you have an attraction to evil. Evil is exciting and evil is interesting, and plenty of kids have a fascination for it. It is knowledge

of kids that these sophisticated educated psychology majors know about. These guys take advantage of them. They take advantage of it personally, intentionally, evilly, and to corrupt those kids, and they use them . . .

The lights in that Camelot kids believe in needn't go out. The banners can snap in the spring breeze. The parade will never be over if people will remember, and I go back to this quote, what Thomas Jefferson said, "Obedience to the law is the major part of the patriotism." . . . Do your duty.

"Foran was speaking to *me*, looking at *me*," Jean Fritz said. "I was scared of them. Of what they were going to do to me. To Margie."

Leonard Weinglass began our summation by trying to puncture the factual case presented by Schultz, by quoting an old legal maxim: "You can create in a courtroom anything that you have witnesses for." He then tried to reinforce the jury's likely suspicion of police agents and government informers:

> Doesn't the Government have the obligation to present before you the whole truth? Why only city officials? Why only policemen, undercover agents, youth officers and paid informers? In all of this time, couldn't they find in this entire series of events that span more than a week one good, human, decent person to come in here to support the theory Mr. Schultz has given you?

By contrast, he reminded the jurors, we brought in a variety of citizens, McCarthy people, pacifists and revolutionaries, authors, performers, religious people, medical workers. He asked the jurors if those people "could all be fooled, could all be tricked, could all be duped as the government is suggesting they were." He then pointed out that though we had been tracked and trailed for a week, nothing more violent than throwing a sweater had been reported against any of us by the government's witnesses.

Having tried to persuade the jurors that their own government might lie, Len then confronted the social prejudice that lay at the heart of the indictment. He blamed the government's behavior on an overall failure to understand the new generation's sensitivities. For an example, Len pointed to the government's cross-examination of Allen Ginsberg, when Foran only asked if Ginsberg wrote poems about homosexuality, as if that were enough to discredit his whole testimony.

These men are attempting to first get us to confront the reality of what life is about and then attempt to get us to do something about it. It is not something that is scribbled on the walls of a bathroom like the way Mr. Foran reads it. To take it out of context and to make it sound dirty and bad is just reaching too far to gain a conviction.

My throat was dry as Len spoke; his argument was very personal and very challenging to the jurors' attitudes about themselves and the younger generation. By now my own former ignorance had given way to an awareness of the gay issue, but I sensed that Foran had been effective. Outside the courtroom, Foran had told his audiences that they were losing their children to the "freaking fag revolution."

Then Len shifted to a no less emotional ground, trying to reverse the conservative interpretation of patriotism. The government's case, he said, tried to picture us as "men who bear hatred for their country, who are clearly unpatriotic, men not worthy of your consideration." He reminded the jury that Abraham Lincoln of Illinois once did "what no other congressman has done since or before: He introduced a resolution condemning the Mexican War as immoral and illegal." For that action Lincoln met such public scorn that he was defeated in his bid for reelection. "It seems to me that if the lesson of the country teaches anything, it is that the true patriots are the people who take a position on principle and hold to it." The basic issue of the case, Weinglass concluded, was

> whether or not those who stand up to dare can do so without grave personal risk, and I think it will be judged in that light and, while you deliberate this case, history will hold its breath until you determine whether or not this wrong that we have been living with will be righted by a verdict of acquittal for the several men on trial here.

Bill Kunstler, asserted that because we were right, we were being martyred. But, he asked, could the jurors connect all the martyrs of the past, once scorned but now respectable, with the disheveled, disrespectful, angry group sitting across from them today? Or would the jump involve too much reexamination of American history, too much reexamination of their own daily assumptions about the rightness of "law and order"? Kunstler quoted the Chicago attorney Clarence Darrow, defending radical dissenters fifty years before:

> "When a new truth comes upon the earth, or a great idea necessary for mankind is born, where does it come from? Not from the police force, or the prosecuting attorneys, or the judges, or the lawyers. Not here. It comes from the despised and the outcasts, and it comes perhaps from jails and prisons. It comes from men who have dared to be rebels and think their thoughts. And what do you suppose would have happened to working men except for these rebels all the way down through history?"

In conclusion, he laid the responsibilities of history before this jury of twelve people, who, as far as we knew, were never before faced with decisions affecting history and politics. I watched their impassive faces as he made the final appeal:

> You can crucify a Jesus, you can poison a Socrates, you can hang a John Brown or a Nathan Hale, you can kill a Che Guevara, you can jail a Eugene Debs or a Bobby Seale. You can assassinate a John Kennedy or a Martin Luther King. But the problems remain. . . . The hangman's rope never solved a single problem. . . . And perhaps if you do what is right, perhaps Allen Ginsberg will never have to write again as he did in the poem "Howl," "I saw the best minds of my generation destroyed by madness,' and perhaps Judy Collins will never have to stand in any courtroom again and say as she did here, "When will they ever learn? When will they ever learn?"

And so it ended. "We're gonna win every day until the last," Abbie had joked with reporters. Now with the jury gone to deliberate, the juggernaut of punishment went into gear. To the surprise of many, the judge announced that he would immediately begin sentencing the defendants for their contempts of court. We were going to jail even before the verdict was in! There was little time to prepare, but an electric excitement went through everyone in the courtroom as the judge proceeded to read from an enormous memo already outlined for him. He started with Dave Dellinger, finding him in contempt thirty-two times, a sentence of two years, five months, and sixteen days. "Mr. Dellinger, do you care to say anything? I will hear you only in respect to punishment."

Dave rose slowly, already tired from two weeks in the county jail. He tried to reply to the specific findings of the judge, but was stopped once more by the command to speak only "to mitigate his punishment." Dave reacted sharply, suddenly gaining the eloquence he desired for a final statement:

> You want us to be like good Germans supporting the evils of our decade and then when we refused to be good Germans and came to Chicago, now you want us to be like good Jews, going quietly and politely to the concentration camps while you and this court suppress freedom and the truth. And the fact is that I am not prepared to do that—

The marshals started moving in on Dave, at the judge's instructions.

> You want us to stay in our place like black people were supposed to stay in their place, like poor people were supposed to stay in their place, like women are supposed to stay in their place, like people without formal education are supposed to stay in their place, and children are supposed to stay in their place and lawyers are supposed to stay in their place. . . .

The marshals came closer, grabbing Dave's arms.

> People will no longer be quiet. People are going to speak up. I am an old man and I am speaking feebly and not too well, but I reflect the spirit that will echo throughout the world . . .

"Take him out," the judge commanded. There was an uproar in the spectators' section, and I saw Dave's fifteen-year-old daughter, Michelle, red-faced, screaming, a crying tiger being held around the throat by a marshal. Her father tried to move toward her. Both were held from each other by a dozen marshals. Everybody in the courtroom was standing. Reporters were crying. Bill Kunstler collapsed over the lectern, weeping and asking to be punished next:

> My life has come to nothing, I am not anything anymore. You destroyed me and everybody else. Put me in jail now, for God's sake, and get me out of this place. Come to mine [my sentencing]

now, Judge, please. I beg you, come to mine. Do me, too. I don't want to be out.

The judge indicated Kunstler would have to wait; when the jail door closed on Dave, it was Rennie's turn. Twenty-three contempts, for a sentence of two years, one month, nineteen days. Rennie too tried to speak in defense of his actions. "You may not believe this, but we came here to have a trial with a law that we regarded as unconstitutional and unfair, and a jury that was inadequately selected. We came here, nevertheless, to represent our full case to this jury . . ."

The judge silenced him also for not speaking to the subject of his punishment. Rennie tried to explain the circumstances that led to those acts which were being judged as "contempt." The judge would not let him talk about the chaining and gagging of Bobby Seale. Rennie finally blurted out all his anger: "Judge, you represent all that is old, ugly, bigoted, and repressive in this country, and the spirit at this defense table will devour you and your sickness in the next generation." Then he too was gone, behind the door.

Strangely, we then recessed for lunch. Those of us not already sentenced were free to do as we liked. Then we would return, of our own free will, to be placed in jail. Safe citizens at lunch, convicted criminals by the afternoon. As I walked out of the Federal Building for possibly the last time, I had no sense of gravity. I hugged the supporters outside and looked for Anne. She had traveled from Berkeley for the ending. We walked off to an obscure, basement-level delicatessen and bar frequented by poor people and skid-row denizens, where we avoided the press and other spectators.

I ordered a beer and a sandwich, but neither of us could eat or drink. We sat across the table, touching hands, with silent thoughts. I missed Christopher. Time was running out, I imagined. The government was persecuting love. I was a fool to hope for any permanence. Fuck it. Anne wrote later, "We had never really talked about the pain of separating. We were running so fast and fighting so hard we didn't have time to think of losing and going to jail. Especially for a long time. He started to cry openly, I started crying too." We walked back to the courthouse. Anne debated whether she could refuse to break down in front of the government she hated; she decided to return to the courtroom. We hugged good-bye on the sidewalk. I walked into the building to the elevator, alone, pushed a button, and drifted up the shaft.

When court resumed, I was next to be sentenced. I waited for court to begin. "Every time our eyes met we would cry—silently this time," Anne wrote. The judge delivered my sentence: Eleven counts, it would be, one year, two months, thirteen days. Did I have anything to say with respect to this punishment? I did, and I stood up at the defense table.

> The problem for those who want to punish us is that the punishment does not seem to have effect. Even as Dave Dellinger was taken away for two years this morning, a younger Dellinger fights back. Your threat of punishment has not silenced our protest, and will not stop people from demonstrating or speaking their minds. It only fuels the protest. So, your Honor, you have been seeing before your eyes the most vital ingredient of your system—punishment—collapsing. The system does not hold together.

Offered this intellectual challenge, the judge could not resist interrupting: "Oh, don't be so pessimistic. Our system isn't collapsing. Fellows as smart as you could do awfully well under this system. I am not trying to convert you, mind you." He was playing with me even as he prepared to send me to jail.

"The point I was trying to make, your Honor, is that I was thinking about what I regretted about being punished. The only thing that affected my feelings," I stumbled, "that affected my own feelings, was that someday I would like to have a child." I bit my lip.

The judge leaned forward, smiling cruelly. "Well, there is where the federal prison system can do you no good."

"But the federal prison system will do you no good in trying to prevent the birth of a new world, Judge." I picked up my notebooks full of defense testimony, patted my fellow defendants, felt my eyes welling up, and marched unescorted through the door to jail.

While I sat in a holding cell, Jerry Rubin was sentenced to two years, twenty-three days; John Froines to six months, fifteen days; Lee Weiner to two months, eighteen days; and Abbie Hoffman, for reasons no one could explain, to only eight months. Our lawyers were judged severely, although they were allowed to remain out of jail to continue their work on the case.

Kunstler received twenty-four citations and a sentence of four years, thirteen days; and Weinglass, whose manner was continually polite and correct, was nonetheless cited fourteen times for a sentence of one year, eight months.

As soon as we arrived at the Cook County Jail, the officials cut off our hair, particularly relishing Abbie's long locks. It was a scalping of hippies. The hair was triumphantly displayed at a press conference by Sheriff Joseph Woods—the brother of President Nixon's personal secretary, Rosemary, later to become famous for eighteen minutes of missing presidential tapes during the Watergate hearings.

The jury was still deliberating, totally unaware that we already were in jail. According to Jean Fritz, our sympathetic jurors would never have found any of us guilty if they knew the judge had already put us in jail. While we waited for the verdict we were paired up and placed in small six-by-twelve-foot cells among the other prisoners. We were the only whites in the jail, as far as I could see. We were minor celebrities among the prisoners, but there was a moderating recognition that we were special, privileged, that with all the publicity we would surely get out of jail. Most of these men were in jail simply because they could not afford pretrial bail; many would serve as much time in jail before trial as they would serve if found guilty and sentenced. One night as I was lying on the floor to keep cool, a prisoner's voice from the next cell started asking me questions about our case. "Are you those white boys who burned their draft cards?" the voice asked. I said, no, not exactly, but that we knew and supported some young men who did that. "Man, I'd like to burn my birth certificate," my neighbor responded.

The jury deliberations dragged on. There were a couple of false alarms when the jury returned to court to ask further questions about the indictment. "We asked for more information," Jean Fritz said. "Two or three times, we told them we could not agree on a verdict. But the marshal kept coming back in, saying, 'You have to keep deliberating.' "

We spent hours arguing what the delays meant, hoping for a hung jury. Then suddenly we were assembled for the drive back to the courtroom early on the morning of the fifth day of jury deliberations.

Almost as soon as we sat down, the judge and marshal announced that a verdict was ready. Schultz moved that all wives and family be removed from the court before the verdict was read, and the judge concurred. The marshals swept the court, and for a final time, we sat in our chairs while our friends and family were banged, shoved, and pulled off their benches and through the doors. Schultz smugly pointed out "for the record" that "we have in the hallway now the same kind of screaming we had in the courtroom." Then the jury entered.

From the moment we saw their faces we knew the verdict would not be good. Jean Fritz was ashen, her face lined. The jury foreman, Edward Kratske, a streetcar conductor who looked something like Mayor Daley, handed the verdicts to the marshal, who in turn passed them to the clerk for reading. Dave, Rennie, Jerry, Abbie, and myself were found not guilty of conspiracy, but guilty of incitement. John Froines and Lee Weiner were acquitted on all counts. They were free, but they cried at the separation.

We were hustled back to jail to await sentencing. That day's press carried stories that alternately cheered and depressed us in our cells. It seemed as if demonstrations and riots were breaking out all over the country in protest against the verdict. The first interviews of the jurors showed that four members felt we were totally innocent. Why, we wondered, had they voted for the compromise verdict instead of sticking with their consciences? Foran said the verdict proved that "the system works." Vice President Spiro Agnew called it "an American verdict."

The foreman of the jury, Kratske, was welcomed home by his wife and poodle, presented with a new color television and a bowl of oxtail soup. He declared, "I've seen guys, real bums with no soul, just a body—but when they went in front of a judge, they had their hats off. These defendants wouldn't even stand up when the judge walked in. When there's no more respect, we might as well give up on the United States." What had that to do with whether we were guilty of crossing state lines to incite a riot in 1968? Nothing, I realized, and everything.

On two occasions the jury sent a message to Judge Hoffman that they were hopelessly deadlocked. "But," according to Jean Fritz, "the marshal came back in, saying, 'You have to keep deliberating.'" Jean thought the judge would keep them locked in the jury room indefinitely. The judge never answered the jury's notes. This improper pressure from a marshal apparently had its effect, and the jurors went back convinced that they had to arrive at a verdict.

By the third and fourth day of jury deliberations, Jean Fritz and the other three jurors favoring acquittal could not sleep. They felt a severe, hostile pressure to concur in a guilty finding. Fritz said later that had she understood that we wanted a hung jury or that we were sentenced on contempt charges while the jury was out, she would be "still in that deliberating room to this day." But she was certain then that a hung jury would result in the government's calling a new trial with possibly an even worse jury. And she believed that Judge Hoffman's continuous threats about contempt of court would result only in a "bawling out," not in jail sentences. She and her three allies finally became hysterical and collapsed under the pressure. Upon returning to the jury room after the reading of the verdicts, the four began weeping. "I went to pieces," Fritz recalled later. "I started to cry, and I couldn't stop. I kept saying over and over again, 'I just voted five men guilty on speeches I don't even remember.' "

It took Jean Fritz a month to recover physically. She also received bomb threats and hate mail for two years. "We're going to burn your house down if you don't move in a month" is the way she recalls a typical threat. Slowly she recovered. "It's just lucky I had a good family," she said. "My husband was wonderful."

The next day, February 20, we were brought back for sentencing and our final say. Dave reiterated that he would "sleep better and happier and with a greater sense of fulfillment in whatever jail I am in for the next however many years than if I had compromised, if I had sat here passively in the courthouse while justice was being throttled and the truth being denied." Rennie spoke ironically of his boy-next-door image, warning Foran that when he was released from prison he would move next door to him and convert his children. Abbie spoke of the portraits behind the judge. "I know those guys on the wall. I know them better than you. I played with Sam Adams on the Concord bridge. It was right near my home in Massachusetts. I was there when Paul Revere rode right up on his motorcycle and said, 'The pigs are coming, the pigs are coming.' " Then Abbie turned more emotional than I'd ever seen him:

> I don't even know what a riot is. I thought a riot was fun. I didn't want to be that serious. I was supposed to be funny. I tried to be, but it was sad last night in jail. I am not made out to be a martyr. I tried to sign up for a few years, but when I went down there they

ran out of nails. So what was I going to do? So I ended up being funny. But it wasn't funny last night sitting in a prison cell, a five-by-eight room, with no light and bedbugs all over. And it's fitting that if you went to the South and fought for voter registration and got arrested and beaten eleven or twelve times on those dusty roads for no bread, it's only fitting that you be arrested and tried under a "civil rights" act. That's the way it works.

Jerry Rubin held up a copy of his new book, published opportunely in time for the trial's end. Inside there was a picture of him as a clean young Cincinnati reporter. "I used to look like this, Judge, see," he said, holding up the volume.

Most everyone around this table once looked like this, and we all believed in the American system. . . . I'm being sentenced to five years not for what I did in Chicago but because some of us don't want to have a piece of the pie. . . . You are sentencing us for being ourselves. Because we don't look like this anymore. That's our crime.

Jerry then gave a copy of the book to the judge, with the inscription "Julius, you radicalized more young people than we ever could. You're the country's top Yippie."

For my last words I chose to speak as rationally as possible to Foran and the press, to underscore the futility of what the government was doing. Foran had commented that the verdict showed that "the system worked." I invited him to bring television cameras into Cook County Jail to have the prisoners there comment on how the system was working. I tried to analyze the verdict as a perfect example of how a seemingly "democratic" system could actually be repressive. Foran had structured the indictment, I claimed, so that the jury could find some of the defendants innocent (Froines and Weiner) and find the rest of us guilty of one charge but not the other, thus achieving a "fair" conclusion. I asked Foran directly, "If you didn't want to make us martyrs, why did you do it? If you wanted to keep it cool, why didn't you give us a permit?" Finally I spoke of the jury, now departed:

I feel sorry for the jury. I have a lot of sympathy for the jury that is similar to the sympathy I have for the older people of America who try their best to see through a network of lies . . . and go home

each night with good consciences feeling they have done everything they could to help everybody all around. . . .

The older people of America have tried their best to end the war
in Vietnam. They have gone on record many times against the
war in presidential primaries, in Gallup polls. And that should be
enough in a democracy to prevent a war of massive aggression
from going on. People try through the system to register their
feelings, and then they go home to watch color TV, have oxtail
soup and see their poodle, hoping that nobody blames them. Well,
I don't blame them. I feel it is a tragedy, and in a tragedy you don't
blame a person.

In fact I feel that if a group of people the jury's age from this
Chicago area could hear everything from the police and prosecutors they've told about us, and if four of them still believe we are
innocent, I believe that is testimony of the ability of people to
wake up, to wake up from the nightmare of American life. The
tragedy is that people of that older generation do not yet know
how to hold out, and probably never will, do not know how to
fight to the end . . .

I have no doubt—that if we had a jury of our peers, by any
definition of the term peers, we would have walked out of this
place, or we would have had an absolutely hung jury because
younger people in the country today know what principles are
. . . and know how to stand up. . . . They are expressing their
convictions now in the streets; our real jury is acquitting us now.
But they do not have power yet.

They will have power. They will have power very soon. They
will have the power to right the wrong that Len Weinglass spoke
about. They will have the power to let us out of jail. They will
have the power to see that this never happens again. . . . They are
proclaiming an imperative from the streets. Someday—we are
going to proclaim that imperative from the statehouse and from
the courthouse. It's only a matter of time. You can give us time,
and you are going to. But's only a matter of time.

We went back to jail for another week, denied bail. While our
lawyers appealed the judge's bail denial, we watched on prison
television reruns of young people burning down the Bank of
America in Santa Barbara. The media reported that half a million people went into the streets protesting the verdict. We said
nothing. In prison everyone wears masks. We wondered if the
burning and rioting would influence the higher courts to grant
us bail, or whether it ensured our imprisonment as "dangerous

men," the term Judge Hoffman used in denying our bail. We had a few visits from lawyers and friends, who could speak to us only through tiny screened partitions on the other side of thick glass walls.

On February 28, the decision came from the Seventh Circuit Court of Appeals: We were granted bail. We were free again. We whooped and packed our books and clothing, then waited for the bail money to be raised, twenty-five thousand dollars per man. Somehow the amount that came spilling in to free us ran over the level needed by seventeen thousand dollars. We immediately and joyously turned it over to our fellow prisoners, bailing out nearly twenty of them with us.

In the days and weeks ahead, we learned significantly more about the jury that convicted us. The information was contained in copyrighted articles in the Chicago *Sun-Times* published by our early hope, juror Kay Richards, articles which were arranged, we learned, by her husband, Tom Stevens, whom Jean Fritz had correctly identified as a Daley man. Kay believed that "the trial had to come to some kind of conclusion just to prove that it works. *It hurts people but it works.*" To fail to come to a verdict, in other words, would not be a triumph of individual conscience but further proof that the system was falling apart. Therefore, Kay described her attempts to put together a "compromise on punishment" between the eight jurors who favored conviction (including, she said, two who thought we should be shot) and the four who favored acquittal. The individual juror's judgment of whether the facts justified a guilty or not-guilty verdict were beside the point in this effort to arrange a trade-off. "We couldn't understand the indictment. We didn't really know what the charges were," Kay wrote. Instead they tended to divide into one faction of those that believed in stern punishment for rebellious kids and another, more permissive bloc.

"I think we just gave in," Jean Fritz said. "We were scared, and we had just given in." When she finally returned home, she said, "the whole street was filled with cameras."

When it was over, I called my mother in Oconomowoc, trying to cheer her up. "I think we'll win on appeal, Mom. Don't worry about it. The appeal takes a long time." She was hiding from reporters, having her mail forwarded from Michigan to where she was staying. In Wisconsin, she could get daily news coverage of the trial from the Chicago media. During the trial she called Anne in Berkeley a few times—a woman she didn't know in a place she'd never been—to get reports on my doings and interpretations of the trial's progress. She would close by making Anne promise to make me brush my teeth. Now that the verdict was in, I don't think she believed my breezy assurances.

In Detroit, my father closed the drapes in his house. He told his wife, Esther, an emotional and forgiving woman, of his fear that little Mary, my six-year-old sister, might be kidnapped. No one should know who her brother is, he warned. I continued to write him, not expecting an answer. He would read the letters at the dining-room table, and say nothing.

"Why don't you write to Tom, you bullheaded Irishman?" Esther would yell at him. "You know Tom and his friends are young. This is not our world anymore, and you've got to let them do what they want to do."

He never answered. Every night he watched the television news of the trial and pored over the Detroit papers. Once he turned to Esther and muttered about a "goddamned lie," advising her "don't believe what you read in the papers." Another time, speaking directly to the television set, he said, "My son is not a communist." When the trial ended, and the news coverage was over, he rose, as he did every night, and went into their bedroom without saying a word.

It was winter in America. The sixties were over.

URGENT

TO: DIRECTOR   MARCH 6, 1970

FROM: NEWARK

SENT BY CODED TELETYPE

IN ATTENDANCE AT LEONARD WEINGLASS' OFFICE TEN A.M. THURSDAY MARCH FIVE, LAST, WERE WEINGLASS, KUNSTLER, "MICKEY" LEANER, AR- THUR KINOY, AND STUART BALL, JR., ALL OF WHOM ARE ATTORNEYS.

FOLLOWING DECISIONS MADE AT CONFERENCE: WEINGLASS WILL BE IN CHARGE OF THE APPEALS FOR THE CHICAGO DEFENDANTS AIDED BY LEANER AND BALL. EXPENSES FOR APPEAL SUPPOSED TO BE FROM THIRTY TO FIFTY THOUSAND DOLLARS. IT WAS STATED THERE IS PLENTY OF MONEY....

APPEAL FOR CHICAGO DEFENDANTS IS GOING TO BE BASED UPON FOLLOW- ING: (ONE) PSYCHIATRIC REPORT ON JUDGE HOFFMAN. (TWO) INFORMATION ABOUT THE JURORS BOTH PRINTED OR OTHERWISE. (THREE) ENDEAVORING TO GET TRANSCRIPT OF US ATTORNEY FORAN'S SPEECH, WHICH HE DELIV-

ERED AFTER VERDICT CALLING DEFENDANTS' NAMES. . . . THEY EXPECT TO USE LAW STUDENTS FOR RESEARCH, PAYING THEM TWENTY DOLLARS A WEEK.

KINOY WARNED THAT THE ABOVE MUST NOT BE MADE PUBLIC UNTIL THEY SUBMIT THE PAPERS FOR THE APPEAL OR IT WOULD IN HIS WORDS "LOSE ITS PUNCH."

SOURCE HAS LEARNED THAT DEFENDANTS HAVE INFORMANT IN USA OFFICE, CHICAGO. BELIEVED TO HAVE IRISH NAME.

END

REUNION

Part Six

We cannot revive old factions
We cannot restore old policies
Or follow an antique drum.

. . . .

We shall not cease from exploration
And the end of all our exploring
Will be to arrive where we started
And know the place for the first time.

—T.S. ELIOT, "Little Gidding"

17.   At Decade's End

After the Chicago trial ended in 1970, everything around me continued to decay, our lives spiraling toward some personal and political abyss. I felt something akin to what the psychiatrist Robert J. Lifton terms *death immersion*, in which one's life "remains an existence with a large shadow cast over it, [a] life which in a powerful symbolic sense, the survivor does not feel to be his own."

The war in Indochina was steadily becoming invisible to Americans as U.S. troops continued to withdraw. But the agony continued, dramatically punctuated by the invasions of Cambodia (1970) and Laos (1971), the mining of Haiphong (1972), the carpet bombing of Hanoi (Christmas 1972), the failed Paris Peace Agreement (1973), and the fall of Phnom Penh and Saigon (1975). From the first killing of an American in Vietnam to the last, it was a contemporary Thirty Years' War.

During its military effort to "protect our image as a guarantor," as a Pentagon memo explained the purpose of Vietnam, the Nixon administration extended the tentacles of the executive state at home. The Chicago case was only one of at least sixty-five indictments that attempted to isolate and harass radical critics, from the Berrigan brothers to Daniel Ellsberg. The counterintelligence programs of the sixties became standard operating procedures for "plumbers" in the Nixon White House.

The brutal climax of the Nixon doctrine came on April 30,

1970, when Saigon troops, backed by American forces, invaded Cambodia. It happened, by coincidence, during a weekend of protests in New Haven over the pending trial of Bobby Seale and Ericka Higgins.

New Haven, on the eve of that event, was more frightening in some ways than Chicago had been in 1968. Over ten thousand demonstrators were expected. Many of the stores were boarded up and the city deserted as we drove into town. The apartment where we stopped to check in was bristling with weapons; the Panthers feared an attack on their office and houses. However, Yale officials, led by President Kingman Brewster, had separated themselves sharply from the Nixon-Agnew world view and built a wide base of sympathy among students, even among radical activists. In addition to opposing the war, Brewster had openly questioned whether black revolutionaries could have a fair trial anywhere in America. Vice President Agnew in turn had criticized the liberal Yale president. The tension was incendiary.

There was a key meeting at Brewster's home that night between myself, Dave Dellinger, and John and Ann Froines on one side and Brewster, Yale Chaplain William Sloane Coffin, and Yale trustee Cyrus Vance on the other. At first, everyone graciously tiptoed around the issue of what would happen in the streets. With the Cambodia invasion unfolding, we sensed the beginning of one of the worst moments of recent history. After the diplomatic niceties had gone on for half an hour, I interjected: "Look, let's be very clear. We are not necessarily your friends and allies. But we—the Chicago defendants—agree with the Panthers that there should be no violence here this weekend. We agree with you on means and need to work together."

That seemed to break the ice, and the conversation became more focused. Our proposed plan was to hold rallies by day and "seminars" inside Yale's college buildings at night. But that would not satisfy the anger of everyone outside, where word of the Cambodia events was creating a growing fury. Froines went out trying to calm down one group of angry demonstrators on the Yale green and was hit in the groin by a tear-gas canister fired at long range by the New Haven police. He was taken to the hospital briefly and released.

By Sunday, May 2, the crowd had swollen to twenty thousand, and the Cambodian crisis was overshadowing the Panther trial. I had gone to New Haven out of an obligation to Bobby, but at the same time I was becoming tired of the government ignoring mass rallies. I was indicating as much in a speech that afternoon when suddenly Froines handed me a note to read to the gathering. It said that a group of student-government leaders, meeting in a nearby building, had just called for a national student strike. As I came to the closing words, the crowd began to chant "strike, strike, strike" for what seemed like five minutes.

On May 4, four students were killed and nine wounded at Kent State University in Ohio. Ten days later two more students were killed at Jackson State University in Mississippi. During those few weeks, students carried out the most massive strike in American history, far greater than the waves of protest in 1968. By May 10, a Brandeis student strike center announced that 448 campuses were either striking or shut down. In California, Ronald Reagan didn't wait; he closed the whole university system for a week. A Harris poll of students found that 80 percent reported a May 1970 protest on their own campus. Moreover, 58 percent said that they had participated, and 75 percent said they agreed with the protest goals. A similar 75 percent favored "basic changes in the system," while 11 percent described themselves as radical or "far left." Forty-four percent agreed that social progress was most likely to come through "radical pressures from outside the system."

Thus the Port Huron vision of a reconstituted university had come true, at least in this singular moment. The President's Commission on Campus Unrest noted that in May 1970, the students "did not strike against the universities, they succeeded in making their universities strike against national policy." For example, amid the fifty thousand demonstrators who gathered in Washington May 9–11, there were one thousand Yale students led by Kingman Brewster lobbying their congressional representatives.

The Kent State deaths finally began to turn Main Street Americans away from the war. The photograph of the teenager at Kent State kneeling over a dying student, raising her arms to the sky, crying in disbelief, was a powerful turning point, comparable in impact to such images of the era as the Saigon police chief executing a political prisoner, and the unforgettable Vietnamese girl, napalmed and naked, running along a road in South

Vietnam. This was the American government "driven to the use of weapons of war upon its youth," in the biting words of the presidential commission. The sacrifices of young people were softening the hearts of many of our parents. Vivian Rothstein, in her Hanoi diary, had written movingly and anxiously of the "haste of youth," the kind of impatience that could divide generations into uncomprehending friction. Here it was the loss of their own children with which American parents were faced. For those with sons in Vietnam, loss meant a death without clear purpose; for those with sons and daughters in the "war at home," there was a fear that college campuses were becoming free-fire zones. Most American parents did not want their children killed for purposes of state. The war was becoming less a matter of national interest, and more an affair of the heart.

Henry Kissinger once described the students of 1970 as children of "skeptics, relativists, and psychiatrists." Apparently, he meant that they were reluctant to believe American government spokesmen at face value or to impose American values on other peoples by all necessary force. But Kissinger missed the basic point, that whatever parents originally believed about stopping Vietnamese communism, they became skeptical enough to refuse to impose their views on their own offspring. By no means was this an inevitable process. Each generation of parents eventually decides whether it lives to perpetuate its past or free its children. Many have decided to sacrifice their offspring for lost but glorious causes. Perhaps this was the only issue that finally mattered for the divided generations of 1970.

Still, I never heard from my father.

After Kent State there came massive antiwar protests by Vietnam veterans, the first time in American history that large numbers of returning combat veterans had demonstrated against a war in progress. They carried with them a credibility that could perhaps be ignored—as indeed it was—but never refuted. It began to reunite the torn fragments of a generation around a common plight. There was a glimmer of realization that both poles of the sixties generation had acted from a sense of duty, both had been manipulated by their own government, and both had suffered the scorn of their elders for a pointless war.

This thaw in American attitudes was soon reflected in the political process. A day before demonstrators converged on Washington that May, Nixon fired the infamous General Lewis

Hershey as director of the Selective Service and agreed to withdraw all United States troops from Cambodia within thirty days. Shortly after, the Senate repealed the Gulf of Tonkin resolution and passed the Cooper-Church amendment by a 58–37 margin, barring future aid to Lon Nol without congressional approval. In the Democratic party, meanwhile, reform of delegate-selection rules, which began at Atlantic City in 1964 and became urgent after Chicago in 1968, was taking on a new momentum under a party commission chaired by Senator George McGovern. The Democrats, at last liberated from responsibility for the war, could forthrightly oppose it. (Even Averell Harriman, for example, endorsed the October 1969 Moratorium.) The eighteen-year-old vote became a reality in 1971; combined with the 1965 Voting Rights Act, that meant that the two major constituencies of the sixties—students and southern blacks—were enfranchised in the greatest widening of the electorate in fifty years.

In sum, the system was beginning to respond.

But just as the silent majority was beginning to change, many in the radical movement became engulfed in bitterness, committing themselves to believing that it was reform which was fantasy and revolutionary rhetoric that was somehow real. Much of the movement had disintegrated from the "beloved community" of the early SNCC to a Dostoyevskian nightmare. Blacks and whites had little in common. Women warred against the dominance of men. Declining structures like the Mobilization were filled with inbred quarrels over slogans and logistics; the newer radical structures were either small, communal groups or invisible underground networks. There was no longer an open, pragmatic, radical grass-roots organization like the early SDS.

The final aftershock from the destruction of SDS came in February 1970, when Terry Robbins, working with manic urgency to begin armed struggle against human targets, instead crossed two wires and blew himself, Diana Oughton, and Ted Gold to shreds in a New York townhouse. Ironically, Terry was making a homemade version of the fragmentation bombs used by the United States in Vietnam. Two others, Cathy Wilkerson and Kathy Boudin, stumbled, half naked, away from the ruins. They went just down the street to a townhouse that had been lived in by Henry Fonda when he was married to Susan Blanchard, a dealer in women's art. Saying that there had been an accident, Cathy and Kathy borrowed coats from Susan and left. Next, Kathy called her friend Connie Brown, then working at Random House, and in a controlled voice asked if she could borrow an apartment. Connie couldn't help her and hung up, thinking the call strange.

The townhouse destruction and the dynamiting of University of Wisconsin building a few months later, resulting in the death of a researcher, spread a pall over what remained of the movement. There dawned a shocked sense that the times were driving people on toward madness. The broad and creative energies once directed toward civil rights and peace were, for some, channeled into hardened "cadre organizations," cults whose members increasingly sought purity, fixed answers, and reinforcement. In addition to the Weathermen, the death throes of SDS gave birth to several tiny Marxist and Maoist organizations, which named and renamed themselves as they splintered into the future. The Progressive Labor Party, which had lived like a fungus on the SDS body for several years, shriveled up as the body itself died.

In Berkeley, one response to the pressures of constant street demonstrations and police harassment was the formation of small collectives, or communes, to meet the needs for close-knit communication and mutual support that were missing in an impersonal mass movement. Collectives usually created an atmosphere in which it was easier for women to assert themselves, unlike the speakers' platforms at mass rallies where macho rhetoric filled the air. Typically, they practiced the "free relationships" between men and women advocated by Simone de Beauvoir. Some collectives held classes in karate and self-defense, taught medical aid for injured demonstrators, and developed methods for harboring underground fugitives. Usually, there was a vast distance between their reality and their names, which were chosen to be as provocative (and psychedelic) as those of rock groups. The one that Bruce Gilbert and Carol Kurtz belonged to in Berkeley, for example, was called the Committee on Public Safety (the COPS commune), after Robespierre's committees in the French Revolution. The COPS commune led a drive for community control of police after twenty of its members were arrested for smoking marijuana during a Passover Seder.

Anne and I, along with several COPS members and a few

other friends, joined in a commune we called the Red Family. It even included her former husband, Bob, with whom she and I were on improving terms after a short period of painful distance. Bob and I obtained a loan from Stanley Sheinbaum, a *Ramparts* contributor and a wealthy Democratic antiwar activist, which paid for three adjoining properties in a neighborhood south of the campus. There we constituted ourselves as a "vanguard" of all the revolutionary trends then converging around us: women's liberation, anti-imperialism, pro–Black Panther, self-defense. Of these, the struggle to shed male chauvinism, in both personal relationships and movement work, was the most consuming. Women met in their own consciousness-raising groups, which were rather exhilarating, while the men went to morbid meetings in which we explored why males were oppressive and given to the appalling "ego trips" that seemed to account for everything from Abbie Hoffman and Jerry Rubin's self-promotion to Terry Robbins's violent self-destruction. We discussed why it was difficult for men to become genuine, open, noncompetitive friends. The women were tired of dealing with male power plays, self-centered jealousies, and wounded egos; it was up to the males, they argued, to reform themselves. The discussions took the form of self-criticism, a group psychotherapy in which it was assumed that anything said in one's own defense—whether about washing dishes, exhibiting macho attitudes, or being attracted to a woman—was probably a self-serving and defensive alibi. I found these meetings to be torture sessions, though I knew from long experience that I could be closer to women than men (and sometimes, as in the case of Carl Wittmann, not even able to communicate when I reached an impasse). More enjoyable was the community child-care center we started, named by the children the Blue Fairyland, where it was thought that men on staff could get in touch with the nurturing side of themselves.

It was also at this point—just after the trial, while the convictions were on appeal—that I began worrying more intensively about the probability of a police state and the question of forming an underground in response. I preferred and wagered on the continuation of democratic liberties, but I increasingly felt that an open society no longer was guaranteed. The trial experience had scarred me with an indelible paranoia. If Nixon was planning greater persecution, I decided to explore the shrouded world beyond everyday life and law. The pivotal question was whether going underground—to avoid roundups or long jail terms—was even a possibility in America and, if so, how. There were techniques to learn: how to obtain false identification, disguise an appearance, establish safe houses, and so on. Through trial and error, it became clear that such tasks could be accomplished, and one could become a hidden outlaw, but much more difficult was the change of consciousness required. I soon realized that I could never survive underground because of my extrovert's need for individual expression. Underground life, by definition, required anonymity, blending in, ego denial, extreme caution—all traits that I lacked. So while I was pulled toward the romanticism of, and tried to make myself expert in, the intricacies of underground organization, a growing part of me simply realized that I had a deep personal stake in the preservation of civil liberties and the very political system I outwardly opposed. I blocked thinking about what I would do if the higher courts rejected our appeals and ordered me to seven years' imprisonment.

There was a deeper implication of going underground, one that I retreated from: the likelihood, sometime, somewhere, of being killed or perhaps having to kill. Whether you engaged in "armed struggle" or not, the chances were good that you would not be treated politely if caught; more likely, you would be shot in your bed like Fred Hampton. The lure of violence and martyrdom were powerful subterranean forces in my makeup. But deeper still was the lure of life, family, a future, made real and immediate with Christopher. It was why I loved the Blue Fairyland nursery. I had seen the personality changes in Weathermen and Panthers as they struggled to become "tools of necessity." They became drained of human feelings, in readiness to die or perhaps kill, to accept personal oblivion for an ideology. The closer I came to this choice, the more I recoiled. Was it fear, cowardice, or opportunism? I thought it was sanity, my survivor's instinct. The possibility of a police state was real; but the belief that we already lived under fascism was a self-fulfilling hallucination.

I believed the ultimate purpose of the collective was not internal therapy but the forging of a more effective political action unit. After the People's Park bloodshed, I favored channeling the confrontation into the political arena by supporting an initiative for community control of police. The specific proposal was to end the occupying role the police played by creating elected oversight boards and requiring that police live in the community they serve (virtually none did). The strategy was to break out of radical isolation and appeal to the larger public through conventional processes. At the same time, some Berkeley radicals, naming themselves the April Coalition, decided for the first time to run a slate for City Council.

These notions split the radical community, which largely shunned or detested the electoral process. For them, politics meant such heresies as putting forward charismatic leaders, brokering diverse interest groups, and becoming respectable in the eyes of middle-class voters. After inconclusive internal debate, the collective endorsed the idea that I, along with Carol Kurtz, would take on the project. I quickly buried myself in the history of police science and soon produced with Carol a well-designed pamphlet describing the need for the community-control proposal. Next we fixed a flatbed truck with a circuslike platform on the back and carried on a block-by-block mobilization, banging drums and cymbals as we arrived on each residential corner, with teams of volunteers distributing literature and registering voters at the door as the makeshift band played marching music.

If this was an odd new presence in politics, so were the people we tried to enlist as new voters. I remember one woman whose door I knocked on and befriended, whose entire building was engaged in primal therapy, the latest approach to purgative self-realization. While the primal screaming could be heard through the windows, I kept dropping by occasional reminders to vote.

On election day, we lost community control, but the April Coalition won several seats on the city council. The middle class voted; the radicals and hippies did not. The big winner for the April Coalition was Loni Hancock, whose quite radical politics were tempered by her "bourgeois" appearance as a neatly tailored professor's wife (by 1988 she was mayor of Berkeley, married to my seatmate in the state Assembly, Tom Bates). I was enthused at the campaign experience despite the defeat, for we had a wide impact. But it left a sour taste for some members of the collective who not only questioned electoral politics but were suspicious that I was reverting to my old power-seeking ways.

These tensions accelerated in the intimate life of a collective where people were constantly together. The inequalities of power clashed with the egalitarianism practiced within. Even if I did the dishes, took phone duty, and worked in the Blue Fairyland like all the rest, I received most of the credit and status on the outside, where the group was widely known as "Hayden's collective."

I was particularly ill suited for becoming a "new man." My notoriety in the media, my extensive national contacts, my habits of using power, my attraction to speaking, writing, and organizing, and my ambition to be in the center of things were all features of my personality that I certainly wanted to reevaluate in the wake of the sixties. I felt uncomfortable in becoming a movement "superstar" or "heavy." I remembered Bob Moses in SNCC changing his name, moving out of Mississippi, then leaving the country altogether in an effort to escape such a status. I felt drawn to the Berkeley collective as a possible place to change my behavior to be more cooperative and less alienating to others, but I was not ready to abandon my basic nature as a "counterrevolutionary."

There was a basic incompatibility: My aggressive qualities were seen as oppressive burdens by other members of the collective, who often felt themselves defined as appendages of Tom Hayden and manipulated. Perhaps most significantly, my relationship with Anne deteriorated. In a drive to establish her own forceful identity, after having been defined first as a wife and then as a girlfriend of two well-known radical men, it almost was inevitable that I would become an obstacle to her independence. I was threatened and could not stop acting possessively toward her. Since she was a central figure in the group, I had to leave.

It happened in a frightening way. Returning to the Oakland airport from an East Coast speech, I was met on motorcycle by Dick Fein, a member of the collective and a doctor at San Francisco General Hospital. I thought it was unusual to be picked up in this way, but I was tired and appreciative as we rode back to Berkeley. I entered our house expecting to take a shower; instead I encountered a tense meeting of the other members. They sat in a prearranged circle, pointing me toward a chair. I was filled with apprehension; had I committed a particular transgression? slept with someone? taken the wrong line in a public speech?

Sitting solemnly in their circle, they announced that they wanted me to leave. In my absence, they had made the decision that I was an oppressive male chauvinist and that the group's potential would best be realized without having someone of my character in its midst. One of them derisively called me a "politician." She had worked on the community control of police election and accused me of being "into manipulating people," the mortal sin of the times. I looked into their faces and saw glazed unanimity. I reacted angrily and defensively. How could they do this without my participation, without my having a chance to answer their criticisms, without a trial period to give reform a chance? No argument worked. Each one sounded like more manipulation on my part. There were no open minds, only a collective will. What about Christopher? I looked at Anne. Was I supposed to leave without explanation and never see him again? What would she tell him, that I was "counter-revolutionary"? She just stared at me. Finally, as the tension became unbearable, I got up and left. My chest was on fire. I felt stunned that the collective, so recently a circle of friends, had drifted into a cult, away from what I considered reality. It was attempting to purge and purify itself of all that was wrong with the world: racism, sexism, male chauvinism, and now, macho leadership. Beyond studying Mao's *Little Red Book*, they were discovering a new object of idol worship, North Korea's Kim Il Sung, whose obscure theory of *juche* (self-reliance) called for struggle from the bottom up. In retrospect, it is hard to believe that a group of literate, middle-class people became so shrouded in this exotica. The Polish writer Adam Michnik has given perhaps the best explanation: "Every conspiracy demoralizes," he once wrote, because its participants "feed on their own traumas and emotions, which, in turn, strangle their reason and their ability to see reality. . . . In its depths flourishes the spirit of a sect that uses a language all its own." I was humiliated, and my grief at the sudden, arbitrary separation from Christopher was impossible to handle. But I knew that I had to leave Berkeley's radical claustrophobia. I drove away in my beat-up Volkswagen convertible to Los Angeles, the notorious New Left leader and national security threat alone in a world of hurt.

Within a few months, it turned out, the Berkeley collective self-destructed, its members scattering everywhere. The appetite for splits and purges was uncontrollable. Eventually, Anne started living with Dan Siegel; she married him, had a child, joined a tiny Marxist splinter group, worked in a factory, and plowed through more internal purges. Bob Scheer, dethroned at *Ramparts* for alleged elitism by women connected with the Red Family, eventually became a respected *Los Angeles Times* writer, carrying the *Ramperts* tradition of investigative journalism into the mainstream. Carol Kurtz left Bruce Gilbert for Jack Nicholl, split from Berkeley with a new baby, and returned in time to antiwar activity. Bruce did the same until he became a film producer. Another member, Andy Truskier, died of leukemia; I was with him at the end. I lost track of all the rest. The bitterness between us took years to subside fully. I never saw Christopher again until 1984 when, at the Democratic National Convention in San Francisco, a blue-uniformed security guard surprised me, saying, "Why don't you say hello to me? You used to take care of me when I was a baby." It was Christopher, now a student at UC Santa Barbara, taking classes from Dick Flacks and doing well.

Los Angeles was the end of the road for me that night in 1970, as it has been for many people escaping unsolved problems and hard times. I moved into an apartment building in Venice, a coastal neighborhood of L.A. created in the 1920s out of the dreams of a visionary who intended to duplicate the canals of the ancient Italian city. In the fifties, Venice became home for the beat generation, in the sixties a counterculture community opposing rampant commercial development; now, like my dreams, Venice was beginning to decay. The artists and bohemians remained, joined by increasing numbers of schizophrenics, burglars, and/or heroin addicts—a community of liberated lifestyles whose streets were unsafe for women and the elderly. I rented a single-room apartment on a particularly seedy corner dominated by drug dealers. For $110 per month, I could view the ocean sunsets.

I rented the room under the name of my grandfather, Emmett Garity, killed in the 1920 industrial accident that left my mother and eleven sisters behind. I didn't want the FBI bothering me (although my friendly landlord told me they did, questioning him about activities about one month after I moved in). Someone was certainly aware of my local presence, because my VW's tires were slashed and windshield shattered on four separate occasions. Nevertheless, I was relieved at the level of privacy. I wasn't in a hurry for new projects, waiting for my pains to subside and my feelings to sort out. I didn't want to be bothered with being Tom Hayden to my neighbors. I didn't want their curiosity, and I wanted to remember what it was like being anonymous again, to see what it felt like to live without fame. I took up reading history on the beach, changed my diet to vegetables and brown rice, studied martial arts and acupuncture, and pondered what to do.

A woman named Joan Andersson helped me survive my exile. She had attended UCLA, graduated from Yale Law School in 1968, spent time in Newark, and worked on the legal issues arising from the Chicago conspiracy trial. After Chicago, at age twenty-six, she replaced Bernardine as the national organizer for the lawyer's guild. At any other time, she might have worked on relatively rational civil liberties issues, but at decade's end her arena looked more like a war zone than a courtroom. She was the attorney, for example, who informed Black Panther Ericka Huggins, in jail, of the slaying of her husband, John Huggins, in a shoot-out with a rival black group on the staid UCLA campus. I remember her telling me of prison visits where she sat in lawyer-client interview rooms with Huey Newton's Panther faction in one corner and Charles Manson chatting with this attorney in another. On another night, after seeing Stanley Kubrick's *A Clockwork Orange*, we were stunned at headlines that another Yale Law graduate, attorney Stephen Bingham, was indicted as an accomplice in killing three prison guards during yet another shoot-out that left Panther leader George Jackson and two other inmates dead as well. (Bingham went underground fearing for his life, returned to stand trial thirteen years later, and won a jury acquittal.)

Joan was attractive and athletic, bright and political, qualities that had always drawn me to her, and now we began a tentative relationship in Venice. She was in some ways an ideal friend in my period of retreat. She was a healing force, able to help me see my flaws without reacting defensively. We liked to read, play with her dogs, wander the Venice beach at night, practice hopkido. Above all, we could talk endlessly about the crisis infecting the movement (though we didn't call it that anymore). She too was swept up in internal struggles within a "people's law collective" called the Bar Sinister after the heraldic symbol of a bar pointing toward left, thought to indicate descent from bastards;

the members of the Bar Sinister considered themselves the bastard children of the legal profession. They too were involved in male-female struggles over leadership, pointed at a man that Joan had long loved, a replay of the struggles that drove me from Berkeley. She needed a retreat of her own and temporarily found it in our relationship. How we got along at all in the supercharged tensions between political men and women at the time is not clear to me. Every physical attraction or impulse of the heart was subject to merciless radical analysis: Was my infatuation with her a way of shoring up my wounded ego after Berkeley? On the other hand, was Joan backsliding from a feminist commitment to autonomy by having this affair? Members of the Bar Sinister thought so, telling her that I was not only a disagreeable chauvinist but not even a Marxist. If I stayed at her house on Third Street in Santa Monica was it "laying a trip" on the other Bar Sinister members living there? If she stayed with me in Venice, was it a sign of higher loyalty to a personal relationship? We both felt obligated, in the overheated vernacular of the time, to "struggle" to become liberated men and women. In this politicized climate of struggle, it was difficult sometimes to understand love as anything but a delusion covering the raw drives of sex and lust, power and possession, competition and advantage—the burning themes of widely read poetry and novels by Marge Piercy, a former SDS activist turned radical feminist. A typical dilemma of the time, expressed by Joan in a "love letter," was whether her occasional desire to settle down into a monogamous relationship with me was counterrevolutionary. We never solved the issue. I was still shaken by my Berkeley period, and I pondered whether it was possible to re-create the special core of that experience by having a child with Joan. But I was indecisive, and she was hardly ready for motherhood and questioned whether I really knew what I wanted. She was right to doubt. Never able to resolve what we wanted, we drifted away from each other, though our friendship would reemerge.

I spent a few days visiting Rennie. I drove out to his parents' old home in northwest Virginia and found him in a small cabin without electricity in a thick woods. He had lost his local moorings after the trial and become enveloped in increasingly militant antiwar actions. The most apocalyptic of those, Mayday, was just ended. After the massive disobedience of that spring, about forty of the Mayday Tribe, a collective of sorts, went on a weekend retreat; after separate women's and men's meetings, they took mescaline at a party together. John Froines, who was there, recalled that the men in Rennie's group went through a shattering crisis. John went downstairs into a room of fluorescent lights where a strange woman wanted him to help her boyfriend go underground. He didn't know the woman and told her it was impossible. But when Froines told several of his friends of the request, it triggered a panic. They became obsessed with discussing the lack of personal trust among men, trying to nurture each other. When Rennie told John that he wanted to build closeness and trust, John inexplicably walked away. Another friend of ours stormed back and forth, proclaiming that he couldn't love or be loved; when he heard that someone was requesting help in going underground, he was overcome with paranoia and ran off.

I wondered how Rennie was doing now. He was living with Susan Gregory, who had a young son named Joshua. The relationship had slowly become a suffocating one for Susan, who had worked invisibly throughout the long trial. She was experiencing a surging desire for independence, not unlike Anne Weills's. It was like looking into a mirror of my Berkeley episode. Like me, Rennie understood how the generalized hostility to powerful leaders, which had been alive in SNCC and SDS from the very beginning, coupled with the new need of women for a sharp break from past dependency, was causing a volcano to erupt within traditional structures, from the personal to the political. We sat for hours in the candlelit cabin and took walks in the pitch-dark woods, whispering of what we knew about the Weathermen, who had scattered underground after the townhouse explosion. We assessed the never-ending war. We talked of fearing death, of estranged parents, of our surprise at loving to take care of little children, and of our failures in so many relationships. We drank some whiskey and cried.

Rennie proposed that we return to Washington and form a new collective, working as a team again. I told him it was too late; it would be literally combining our powerful personalities in a single unit, which was sure to be attacked as yet another "male elite." Besides the hostility that would come from activists, it would increase the surveillance and harassment programs by the FBI and local police. It would only be consolidating power in a disintegrating movement. I headed back to the West Coast, more alone knowing how alone Rennie was.

In the Port Huron period, which now seemed so long ago, there had been an easy assumption that the white, middle-class American was open to idealism, to caring about others, to participation in a democratic society. We were those people ourselves, or at least their sons and daughters. By decade's end, this assumption had become strained and, finally, shattered by the public's support for the status quo. That was why women, blacks, and Chicanos were asserting new identities of their own, becoming separatist in response to the icy indifference of America to their quests for recognition. Reading volume after volume of history in my Venice apartment, I became gripped by how Vietnam was more like our early history than an aberration. There were countless My Lais at forgotten places like Wounded Knee. "The only good Indian is a dead Indian" was a comment easily adapted to the "gooks" of Vietnam. Like the occupants of the strategic hamlets of South Vietnam, countless Indian villagers were uprooted and forced on reservations. Like the stalled Geneva Accords, there was a trail of broken treaties.

Living in the Southwest for the first time I started to learn about the Chicano community by attending the trial of the Biltmore Seven, whom Joan was defending as an apprentice to Oscar "Brown Buffalo" Acosta, who was made famous in *Rolling Stone* by Hunter Thompson before he mysteriously disappeared in 1974. I found that the Chicanos had gone through an experience not unlike the black civil rights and antiwar movements, with attempts at reform and nonviolence rebuffed, bringing militant violence to the surface. The Biltmore Seven were acquitted of attempting to set fire to a hotel where Governor Reagan was proposing to eliminate bilingual education programs.

This trial led me to an interest in the original inhabitants of the country, the Native Americans, as well as the Mexicans who had historical claims to California. Slowly I realized I was searching, in the aftermath of Berkeley, for my own identity, my own roots in history. Every group with which I identified was struggling for its own identity; now I needed to better understand mine.

A passage from Carl Jung's diary seemed to set American

culture, from the Indian wars through Vietnam, in a larger and more appealing perspective. An Indian had said to Jung:

> "See how cruel the whites look. Their lips are thin, their noses sharp, their faces furrowed, and distorted by folds. Their eyes have a staring expression; they are always seeking something. What are they seeking? The whites always want something, they are always uneasy and restless. We do not know what they want. We do not understand them. We think they are mad."

When this Indian told Jung that whites "think with their heads" the psychiatrist asked what Indians think with. The Indian touched his heart and provoked in Jung a dark vision:

> This Indian had struck our vulnerable spot, unveiled a truth to which we are blind. I felt rising within my life a shapeless mist, something unknown but deeply familiar. And out of this mist, image upon image detached itself.
>
> First, Roman legions smashing into the cities of Gaul, and the keenly excised features of Julius Caesar, Scipio Africanus and Pompey. I saw the Roman Eagle on the North Sea and on the banks of the Nile. Then I saw St. Augustine transmitting the Christian creed to the Britons on the tips of Roman lances, and Charlemagne's most glorious forced conversions of the heathen. Then the pillaging and murdering bands of the Crusading armies . . . Then followed Columbus, Cortez and other conquistadores who, with fire, sword and Christianity, came down upon even these remote pueblos, dreaming peacefully in the sun, their Father. I saw too the peoples of the Pacific Islands decimated by firewater, syphilis and scarlet fever carried in the clothes the missionaries forced on them.
>
> It was enough. What we from our point of view call colonization, missions to the heathen, the spread of civilization, etc., has another face—the face of a bird of prey seeking with cruel intentness for distant quarry—a face worthy of a race of pirates and highwaymen. All the eagles and other predatory creatures that adorn our coats of arms seem to me apt psychological representatives of our true nature.

I sat there, struck by the passage, pondering whether my original democratic hopes were really a historical illusion, whether Fanon and Sartre were right that the conservative and limited vision of my parents' generation was an infirmity with

deeper historical roots, the flawed essence of the American character. If so, if I was the descendent of well-meaning Indian-
killers, then there really was little choice but to accept a marginal and alienated status, become an isolated ally of other struggles, or drop out altogether. But these had never been choices
for me. No matter how hard and honest I tried to be toward
myself, I felt no loathing of who I was. No matter how much
Anne criticized my male chauvinism, I felt no guilt about gender. I wished to correct my faults, but more basically, I wanted
to continue making a mark on my times. No matter how bitter
I was toward my parents' generation or the Chicago jurors, I felt
no lasting hate toward them either.

My problem, then, was how to reconcile and make sense of
these warring images: the genocide and slavery that suggested
an American character damaged beyond repair and the survivor's impulse I retained, which believed in everyone's human
possibilities. I began making notes on the parallels between
Vietnam and the Indian wars. Even without further reflection,
I realized there was one fundamental difference between the
past and present: Ho Chi Minh was no Sitting Bull, but John
Wayne *was* General Custer. The United States would lose the
Vietnam War, and Americans would have to face the meaning
of failure, perhaps for the first time. As individuals or as a
culture, we could either retreat into rigid escapism or, possibly,
receive maturity and strength from loss.

I continued my struggle to understand identity by turning
toward Ireland, the land of my roots but a place which had never
before attracted my curiosity. I was trying to understand how
the various Haydens, Garitys, Foleys, and Duceys were driven
by a combination of desperation and hope to seek *their* identities
as Americans, how their Irish ethnicity had been dissolved over
a century and replaced by the bland, middle-class American
identity of my parents. Not only was this new identity lacking
in cultural richness, but I realized that its attainment involved
an erasure of a historical consciousness of having once been
oppressed. The "famine Irish," after all, were forced out of
Ireland by the dynamics of hardhearted British rule, not simply
by natural calamities. Their Irish-Catholic faith and their Gaelic
language were the focus of persecution for centuries. And yet,
within two generations of being forcefully stripped of their
cultural dignity, they were gladly joining a middle class forget-

ful of those roots which, if remembered, might forge a link with the modern poor.

The qualities I most liked in my parents—my father's irony, my mother's warmth, their resentment of elites, their gut populism—might well be the remnants of their ethnic heritage, while the qualities that disturbed me—their desire for acceptance, their civil obedience, their difficulty in embracing a radical son—represented the lures of assimilation. Here, I realized, was part of the answer to the identity quest. The melting pot, the idealized notion of total assimilation, though obviously important in a fragmented society, went too far—it erased the memories that could link Americans with the struggles and sufferings of other people. Now I grasped, for example, why in my experience Jews were the most liberal "whites" in American society; it was because they remained the least assimilated, the most sensitive to the experience of oppression. And I began to realize that what young Americans, and perhaps increasingly Americans of all ages, were looking for was a new, richer identity in life than just "making it."

Down the alley in Venice lived a burnt-out Bobby Kennedy worker named Larry Levin. Bald at twenty-five, Jewish, and a student dropout, he seemed an unlikely person to have discussions of Ireland over bottles of Guinness. But after the RFK slaying, Larry swore never to get involved in politics again and drifted off to Europe. There, by accident, he fell into the drama and romance of the massive Northern Ireland civil rights movement of 1969, which partly was inspired by the black and student movements in America. Larry stayed for months, steeping himself in the lore of Irish martyrs. I listened to his tapes, records, and stories for hours, spellbound. The Irish heritage of romantic fatalism spoke exactly to my experience in the sixties. The fact the Irish Catholics were inspired by the American civil rights example, however, interested me more, indicating again that there was something hopeful at the core of the American experience. I became so taken that by 1971 I decided to fly to Ireland, to explore my roots in county Monaghan, where the Irish Republic borders Ulster, and to experience a Catholic version of the American civil rights movement. I read everything obtainable on the country and took a night flight out of New York's Kennedy International.

FEDERAL BUREAU OF INVESTIGATION   **DECEMBER 15, 1971**

URGENT

TO: DIRECTOR
FROM: LOS ANGELES

THOMAS EMMETT HAYDEN

SOURCE ADVISED DECEMBER FIFTEEN INSTANT, THOMAS EMMETT HAYDEN
DEPARTED LOS ANGELES EVENING OF DECEMBER FOURTEEN LAST, FOR NEW
YORK CITY, ULTIMATE DESTINATION, IRELAND. SOURCE STATED HAYDEN
PLANS ON GOING TO NORTHERN IRELAND THROUGH SOUTHERN IRELAND
AND ANTICIPATES TAKING PART IN PRESENT REVOLUTION. ROUTE OF
TRAVEL FROM LOS ANGELES TO NEW YORK UNKNOWN BY SOURCE. SOURCE
STATED HAYDEN MAY BE UTILIZING THE NAME EMMETT GARITY, MAIDEN
NAME OF MOTHER.

When we landed for refueling at Shannon Airport, my excitement was cut short immediately. I was told to deboard the plane,
taken to a glass-enclosed office inside the terminal, and held for
over twelve hours by security forces. The U.S. intelligence community had informed the Dublin government of my coming,
and they in turn believed that I was going north with the Irish
Republican Army to create unknown "disturbances." I couldn't
believe it. The "outside agitator" theory even extended here.
Larry, who was already in Dublin, arranged calls to the authorities from members of the Dáil (parliament) and the Irish *Times.*
Additionally, I was able to generate calls from Senator Ted
Kennedy and New York City Council President Paul O'Dwyer,
but it was to no avail. After one full day in the terminal, I was
escorted back aboard a flight to New York City, first class, my
visa stamped REJECTED by an Interior official in Dublin. As I sat
on the long flight home, I knew decisively that there was no
going back in search of lost threads of identity. I was who I was,
a third-generation American, "looking uncomfortably at the
world we inherit," as I had written in *The Port Huron Statement.*
If my soul was somehow Irish, it was in equal measure, or more,
suburban, which meant very American. If I had been radicalized in the sixties, it was *that* experience that was the real key
to my identity.

At this point an extremely important person rolled his wheelchair into my life. His name was Ron Kovic, he was from a
suburb in Long Island like mine in Michigan, he talked with a

familiar middle-American dialect, and he loved baseball. Kovic had won thirteen medals in combat in Vietnam before taking the bullet that made him a paraplegic. He lived not far from me in Venice and could often be seen sitting in the front-yard sunshine with a bunch of buddies. At first glance, they appeared to be typical Venice bohemians, the men with longish hair, the women in tank tops, Levi's, and Earth shoes. Looking more closely, I saw all of the men wore faded U.S. military jackets, and several leaned back in wheelchairs. They represented a subculture of angry and outspoken Vietnam veterans with whom I became heavily involved. Kovic contained a barely suppressed fury at the government, which he felt deceived him into a disastrous mischanneling of his courage and loyalty. He was writing a stream-of-consciousness memoir, which was finally published as *Born on the Fourth of July* and became a best seller. He was the model for the character played by Jon Voight in *Coming Home*, and he inspired Bruce Springsteen's "Born in the USA" anthem. Ron met Joan Andersson when both were thrown to the pavement by Los Angeles police during an anti-war protest; they began an intense relationship when Joan and I broke up. When I met him, Kovic was in that state of raw intensity that swells beyond all control when no one seems to be listening. He and I immediately connected on a personal level and discovered that we had come to common conclusions. Ron's story contained all the evidence I needed about the infinite possibility of Americans to change and grow, an American that Jung's dark vision could not have seen. To anyone who timidly asked him about the lessons of his experience, his ready answer was "I lost my body, but at least I gained my mind."

I began realizing in a rush how far many of us had strayed from the original disposition of the sixties. We had become isolated, self-enclosed in a universe of political rather than human life. In this sealed universe, social relationships were contained within organizations, language turned to jargon, disputes were elevated to doctrinal heights, paranoia replaced openness, and the struggle to change each other became a substitute for changing the world.

I decided to recharge my commitment to ending the endless war, "reborn" in the form of the early sixties, reviving my roots. Like Camus's Rieux in *The Plague,* I would focus on the pestilence of spiritual depression. I would assume that the average

American still didn't know or feel what the plague of Vietnam was all about. I would organize "teams" of volunteers to educate and organize the public against the threat in their midst. I would be a teacher. I would form an "information project" on the war; my renewed faith was that if the public knew what was being done in their name, they would withdraw support.

Larry Levin pointed me toward Immaculate Heart College in downtown Los Angeles and suggested that I try obtaining a teaching job there. Immaculate Heart, despite its pious name, was a controversial institution within the conservative Catholic firmament. Run by the Sisters of the Immaculate Heart, an order of five hundred nuns who were gently demanding greater democracy in the Church, it reflected a sixties spirit of independence within the context of a venerable institution. They struggled with the archconservative Cardinal James Francis McIntire over such issues as flexible hours for prayer, the wearing of habits, the right to provide graduate study to their own members, and the larger issues of social justice. Father Daniel Berrigan spoke at an Immaculate Heart retreat in 1965, the college began offering classes about the United Nations, and a spirit of freedom and inquiry flowered at the college. The tension became so great that in 1970, the order became a lay community, with its own vows and promises, no longer formally recognized by Rome.

The IHC dean, Mary Jean Pew, had left the order formally in 1968, no longer sure of her religious loyalties. Unlike the forbidding nuns I recalled from Royal Oak, Mary Jean had a positive, cheerful moral energy which I immediately liked. In addition to teaching political science, Mary Jean was the volunteer coordinator in the campaign of a former Jesuit seminarian, Jerry Brown, for secretary of state, whom she wanted me to meet. She also introduced me to the college's art department, which was widely known for the poster works of the well-loved Sister Corita Kent. Among Sister Corita's works, the one that touched my heart was a handwritten quote from Camus, "I would like to love Justice, and my Country too."

I felt buoyed and energetic in their midst and explained the proposal Larry and I had worked out. I wanted to teach a course on the history of Indochina which, I said, would actively involve the students in learning about the Vietnamese as people rather than as objects, experimenting in ways to communicate the truth of human suffering to a numbed and apathetic public. I would require reading, offer lectures and discussions, and give tests, but mainly I would motivate the students toward reasoned involvement. I envisioned a specific result: a series of informational pamphlets, slide shows, poster art, and perhaps documentary films that could be exhibited graphically anywhere in America with a compelling human impact. The facts of the war had become dehydrated through rhetorical abuse, I felt, and needed to be reattached to life.

To my pleasant surprise, the proposal was met with enthusiasm. The sisters had no problem with my clearly antiwar viewpoint, as long as I made my students do their own thinking. Excited at this opportunity, I began to explore the possibilities of offering the same seminar simultaneously on other campuses. By September 1971, I was teaching similar classes at Pitzer College, part of the Claremont Colleges, and at UCLA Adult Extension.

In 1971, the Nixon strategy to keep Indochina invisible failed. The Berrigans and several others were indicted in January for a wide-ranging and spectacular conspiracy, including alleged plans to kidnap Henry Kissinger; the prosecution eventually failed. That same month Senator George McGovern announced his quest for the presidency; the new party rules, engineered by a commission McGovern had chaired, now made an insurgent, antiwar campaign plausible. In February, the Saigon army, with massive U.S. air support, invaded Laos and suffered heavy losses. Hundreds of thousands of protestors rallied once again in Washington and San Francisco. Then came the audacious Mayday effort designed to "stop the war or stop the government," modeled after Dr. King's last desperate vision for a 1968 encampment in the capital. Military helicopters, tear gas, ten thousand paratroopers from Fort Bragg, and twenty thousand National Guard and police were called in to contain thousands of people committing nonviolent but disruptive civil disobedience. Rennie, Abbie, and John Froines were indicted once again on federal conspiracy-to-riot charges; the government later dropped the charges because it did not want to divulge who its infiltrators were.

The most important event of 1971 was probably the July publication of the Pentagon Papers in *The New York Times*. These documents, a history of U.S. policies through the summer of

1968, complete with classified memos, were copied and stolen from the Rand Corporation in Santa Monica by Daniel Ellsberg and Anthony Russo. Ellsberg was a former counterinsurgency adviser in Vietnam; Russo interviewed Vietcong prisoners and did studies of chemical spraying on rice crops. The antiwar movement affected their consciences and led them to disclose the papers, causing a daily scandal as the *Times* continued to publish them. In effect, this was the first case of key professionals and a major newspaper deciding on a course of action denounced as "treasonous" by the administration. Ellsberg and Russo were indicted and eventually freed on a mistrial that arose because of government intrusion in the case; the *Times* won the Pulitzer Prize.

I was enthusiastic that former government officials and policy analysts were turning against the war and that the *Times* was willing to risk a legal confrontation with Washington. I came to know Ellsberg and Russo quite well, persuaded Leonard Weinglass to join their legal defense in Los Angeles, and testified as an "expert witness" on peace diplomacy in their trial. I remember taking a long walk in the Santa Monica mountains before the trial with Ellsberg, who told me in detail how he came to his decision. He seemed haunted by his experience, by shadows out of the past who, he said, "know what I know." I thought him understandably paranoid, but he was actually quite uncanny; at just that time the Nixon Watergate teams were drawing up plans targeting him for break-ins, burglaries, and physical attacks.

I read the papers cover to cover, thousands of pages, with a growing sense of fascination. In neat, formal prose, here were the inner thoughts of the Vietnam decision makers, surprisingly explicit. The key revelations of the papers confirmed much of what the antiwar movement had been trying to say for years:

1. The United States was in Vietnam mainly to preserve an image of strength.
2. The United States knowingly violated the Geneva Accords.
3. The U.S. government was planning military action in 1964, even while Lyndon Johnson was pledging "no wider war."
4. The United States was fighting against a popular-based nationalist movement.
5. U.S. planning was indifferent to human factors. The docu-

ments included any number of Orwellian observations like
this 1966 one: "By shallow-flooding the rice, it leads after time
to widespread starvation (more than a million?) unless food is
provided—which we could offer to do at the conference
table."

The Pentagon Papers confirmed my desire to believe that the
American people would oppose the war if they knew the
truth—and that was precisely why administration after administration had hidden the truth. By August, one month after
the papers were released, a majority of Americans in a Harris
poll said the war was "immoral," and in a Gallup poll 61 percent
favored complete withdrawal.

I began a project to reduce the papers to a readable pamphlet
for the public. Eventually 100,000 copies were circulated free
across the country during the 1972 elections. I had come full
circle, scarred but surviving, back to what I did best. I could lead
by writing, teaching, and local organizing in the mainstream—
instead of distilling myself into a hardened revolutionary. I
could work on being more human myself—and try to outgrow
or avoid male power rivalries. I could feel better about America—instead of resigning myself to an alientated war against the
system.

And then I met a woman who changed my life again.

18. Jane

She came from the orbits of fame, power, and success. A popular actress and the daughter of Henry Fonda, she burst like a dislocated star onto the movement scene in 1970 but came only slowly and haltingly into my life. In February 1971, I was in Ann Arbor, speaking about Vietnam at an event promoting Mayday, when I met Jane on the stage. Beginning with visits to the Indians occupying Alcatraz, and accelerating after Kent State, she was constantly crisscrossing the country at the time, followed by cameramen and FBI agents, as she supported students, feminists, Black Panthers, Indians, and especially, GIs being prepared for assignment to Vietnam. For several months she had been encouraging and recruiting veterans who had told her of atrocities in Vietnam to testify at the Winter Soldier investigation being organized in Detroit (which was founded on Tom Paine's distinction between phony sunshine patriots and truly committed winter soldiers). On the stage in Ann Arbor that night, she showed the tensions of the constant motion. She was skinny and taut, her long fingers playing nervously with the purple shirt that was pulled over her jeans. There was something shrill and perhaps memorized in her brief, impassioned call to "stop the government unless it stops the war," but her urgency was real and the audience was moved.

FBI MEMORANDUM   **6-25-70**

TO: SAC, LOS ANGELES

FROM: DIRECTOR, FBI

You are authorized to prepare a letter and mail to Army Archerd, the Hollywood "gossip" columnist. Insure that mailing cannot be traced to the Bureau.

NOTE: Los Angeles proposed that a letter from a fictitious person be sent to Hollywood "gossip" columnist of the "Daily Variety" in connection with the column on 6/11/70 indicating Jane Fonda, noted film actress, would attend a Black Panther Party fundraising function on 6/13/70. The proposed letter states the writer attended the function and was searched upon entering, urged to contribute funds for jailed Panther leaders, and to buy guns for the "coming revolution." Also, that Jane and one of the Panthers led a refrain, "We will kill Richard Nixon, and any other M.....F..... who stands in our way." It can be expected that Fonda's involvement with the BPP cause could distract from her status with the general public if reported in a Hollywood "gossip" column.

I called her at a Howard Johnson's in Detroit the next morning. We met in the coffee shop, where Jane was sitting alongside a Frenchwoman, a writer who wanted to talk about American radicals. I was disappointed that she wasn't alone.

It wasn't love at first sight; in fact, to this day, Jane cannot remember what we talked about. She admired my writing and thinking, and she does remember my letting her know that I was "in a relationship" with someone; she was "in a relationship" herself, with Donald Sutherland. She remembers that when she couldn't understand what I was talking about, she would nod her head, or say, "That's interesting." We discussed the trend in the movement toward collective groups, and she spoke of possibly giving up her movie-star status to find a new role in some sort of political film collective. She had already spent months living in a Detroit household filled with veterans, attorney Mark Lane, and some of the staff of the Winter Soldier investigation. I remember cautioning her against giving up acting, knowing from experience how collectives could confuse professionalism with privilege. I could imagine the Red Family demanding that she work underground to shed her bourgeois leanings. All in all, however, it was a casual conversation. Nothing clicked.

The next day, however, in a carload of people dropping me at Detroit Metro Airport for my flight to the Coast, we had a better time. I was sitting in the backseat, and Jane was in the front. Suddenly I put my Irish cap on Jane's head. She turned, and our eyes locked. Both of us finally noticing each other as human beings, we found ourselves laughing absurdly in the middle of a war crimes discussion.

I didn't see or call Jane for a year. We seemed destined not to connect. A few months after the uneventful Howard Johnson tryst, she came to Berkeley to film *Steelyard Blues*. Asking my whereabouts, she was told that I had left the commune; no reason was given by the tight-lipped cadre. Mystified but trusting, Jane moved into the neighborhood and left her two-year-old daughter, Vanessa, at the Blue Fairyland day-care center, under the care of Bruce Gilbert, a twenty-one-year-old Beverly Hills High School graduate who had occasionally dreamed of being a Hollywood producer before joining the revolution.

FBI MEMORANDUM   **8/18/71**

TO: SAC, SAN FRANCISCO

FROM: ▮▮▮▮▮▮▮*

▮▮▮▮▮▮ stated that this nursery school seems to be operated by various radicals who reside on Bateman Street. She further advised that Jane Fonda has been observed by her on Bateman Street during the past week when Fonda was filming some kind of a picture with the residents of Bateman Street. ▮▮▮▮▮ stated that it is her understanding that Vanessa Fonda is attending the Blue Fairyland Nursery school and that her mother, Jane Fonda, will return for her in the near future.

FBI MEMORANDUM   **12/28/71**

▮▮▮▮▮▮ advised on 11/21/71 that he recently was made aware of the fact that a child care center being operated at 3031 Bateman Street, Berkeley, California, was operating without having previously obtained a state or local license. ▮▮▮▮▮ has noted approximately one dozen children on the premises and paraphernalia indicating that a school of some sort was being conducted.

I had seen *Barbarella* in Berkeley with Anne, and both of us were properly critical of its political shortcomings. In those

*Material deleted by the FBI.

times, there was a "correct line" even on movies, especially regarding sexism. To be entertained (which I was) was not a valid reason for seeing a film. Sexual arousal (which I experienced) was to be sublimated and, if possible, denied. Earlier, I had been very moved by *They Shoot Horses, Don't They?*, which Jane shot in 1968. About the Depression, it could as well have been about the spiritual exhaustion induced by Vietnam.

It was with intense curiosity that I went to watch this suddenly serious woman in *Klute* in 1971. I did not expect to be as affected as I was. Jane brought tremendous life to Bree Daniels, an independent, aspiring actress whose unashamed ethics justified making a living as a high-class call girl and becoming the "invalidation of all the official virtues," as Simone de Beauvoir once described the prostitute. The movie was about the sexual exploitation of women, following Bree down a slope of loneliness that, on the one hand, avoided genuine love as too threatening to personal freedom, but also left her vulnerable to sadistic violence in the unregulated shadow world beyond the law.

There were several improvised scenes in which Bree talked with a therapist about her emotional dilemmas; in these I felt it was really Jane talking to a camera about herself. I could see nothing but her face and hands, and I felt unavoidably pierced by the sense that she was having an intimate conversation with me. Describing her life alone, before she fell in love with the detective who protected and saved her (Donald Sutherland, as John Klute), she says, "I don't really give a damn. What I would really like to do is be faceless and bodiless and be left alone." At a later point, after becoming aware of unexpected intimacy and the beginnings of love toward Klute, she reacts by saying,

> I just wish I could let things happen and enjoy it for what it is . . . and while it lasts, and . . . relax about it. But all the time, all the time I keep feeling the need to destroy it, to break it off, to go back to the *comfort of being numb* again. . . . I keep hoping it's going to end because, I mean, *I had more control* before when I was with tricks . . . I set everything up.
>
> Now I . . . that's what's so strange, I'm not setting anything up . . . It's a new thing and it's so strange, the sensation that *something that is flowing from me naturally to someone else without its being all prettied up* . . . he's seen me horrible, he's seen me ugly, he's seen me mean . . . and it doesn't seem to matter and he seems to accept me . . . I guess having sex with somebody and feeling those sorts

of feelings toward them is very new to me and *I wish I didn't keep wanting to destroy it* [emphasis added].

Jane Fonda as Bree Daniels (or was it Bree Daniels as Jane Fonda?) touched me sharply at a moment when I was painfully open. I too seemed to prefer the "comfort of being numb," if that meant I could "set everything up" and keep a self-protective control over my relationships; the choice of intimacy, or losing control to another, had always seemed in my life to fail and transform itself into anguished loss. Such intimacy had been fleeting at best with my parents, my friends, my lovers. My history was one of broken connections. However, despite my powerful feelings of attraction toward the Bree/Jane character, or perhaps because of them, I had no conscious thought of seeing Jane Fonda again. How the conscious self deceives.

By the beginning of 1972, my Indochina classes involved nearly one hundred students in busy workshops producing pamphlets, slides, and most impressively, a portable poster display that could transform an entire room into a museum of Indochina. It was not the conventional political art with peace doves, clenched fists, and slogans, but instead an art designed to upset assumptions and leave individuals to reorder reality for themselves. There were floor-to-ceiling panels of repeated photo-silkscreen images of land, people, and war. Flanking these images would be panels of cryptic quotations by U.S. officials or poetry by eighteenth-century Vietnamese writers. The whole exhibit could be folded into a large suitcase. With these tools, it was possible to bring the human reality of the war anywhere in the country, as a multimedia teach-in. I began taking the program on the road, enjoying the experience of teaching again. I started writing a book on the same subject and creating a version for public television.

On the distant horizon, the barricades began to beckon. The Republicans planned their 1972 national convention in San Diego, and I joined a group of southern Californians considering a massive demonstration. This was a time, still unknown to the public, of intense counterintelligence activity by the White House plumbers unit. Illegal operations were intensified against the antiwar movement after Kent State. On July 23, 1970, Nixon approved what *Newsweek* called a "blueprint for a super secret police," under the direction of such individuals as Tom Charles

Huston, Charles Colson, and E. Howard Hunt, whose hatred
for the New Left went back to their roles as leaders of Young
Americans for Freedom in the early sixties. After targeting and
burglarizing Daniel Ellsberg in 1971, one of their next major
projects was to counter any demonstrations at the upcoming
San Diego convention. They had some contact with a paramili-
tary extremist group in San Diego, the Secret Army Organization (SAO). According to later Watergate testimony, G. Gordon
Liddy proposed the kidnapping of myself and other demonstration leaders and our abduction to Mexico during the convention. On January 6, 1972, a bullet was fired through the window
of the San Diego house where Bruce Gilbert participated in a
meeting about the convention plans. The bullet missed Bruce's
head by less than a foot and shattered the wrist of an activist
named Paula Tharp. The shot was fired by an SAO member
from a parked car; an FBI informant was sitting next to him.
Fortunately, in the end, the Republican convention site was
shifted to Miami, without the administration's admitting the
embarrassing fact that they had been "forced out by the threat
of antiwar demonstrators," as White House official Jeb Magruder later wrote. The subsequent arrests of White House
operatives in June 1972 at the Watergate complex in Washington
subdued the repressive visions in the White House basement.

During this period, Jane was engaged in an effort of consciousness-raising among GIs, called the FTA show (leaving the
audience to guess whether the initials meant Free the Army or
Fuck the Army). With a troupe of talented people including
Donald Sutherland, she was providing antiwar theater for GIs
at bases in the United States, Okinawa, and the Philippines
(they were denied permission to perform in South Vietnam). An
alternative to the usual Bob Hope fare, the FTA was drawing
large crowds and making the Pentagon extremely nervous. So,
early in 1972, when I heard Jane was making a speech and slide
presentation at the Embassy Theater in Los Angeles, it was
natural for me to attend.

There we met for keeps.

By now she was an accomplished speaker, effectively sub-
limating the nerves that showed the year before and making a
persuasive presentation to a sympathetic audience. I noticed
that her approach was more "political" than mine, using slides
primarily to show the results of U.S. bombings, heroic NLF

guerrillas dashing forward, and the Seven-Point Peace Plan being offered by the other side. It was effective, but primarily for the well informed or converted. I went backstage to say hello and ask if we might cooperate somehow in creating these educational resources. I must have been a strange sight. Deeply immersed in researching native American parallels to Vietnam, I had let my hair grow long, pulled back by a headband. We spoke for only a minute and agreed to meet soon. Jane claims that I touched her knee, and at that moment she *knew* we were going to fall in love. All I sensed was a gleam of friendliness from her; I was still self-absorbed in my inquiry into identity. Besides, I was also with Joan, although she was going to Cuba for a few weeks. Jane had separated from Donald Sutherland and was "seeing" (in the technical phrase of the time) any number of men, including Bob Scheer, whom she met while Vanessa was in the Blue Fairyland. Complicated relationships would not go away.

Something was happening to me, because, not long afterward, I went to Jane's Laurel Canyon house to show her my Indochina materials. We sat on her living-room floor in front of the fireplace, and I flashed slide after slide on the opposite wall. Reflecting my emphasis on culture and people, the slides went through the unknown history of Vietnam, the village culture, the importance of land, their cultural modesty. Then it switched to the "Honda culture" of Saigon, the impoverished refugees, the brothels and bars full of teenage prostitutes.

Jane was starting to cry. I kept flipping slides of grotesque young Saigon women, talking about the breast and eye operations performed to turn them into round-eyed, round-bodied Westernized women, transforming them body and soul into creatures of our culture. Suddenly I understood why she was weeping: I was talking about the image of superficial sexiness she once promoted and was now trying to shake. I looked at her in a new way. Maybe I could love someone like this.

Jane was right. We did fall in love soon after. I was thirty-two, she thirty-four; both of us were starting over.

The passion of our common involvement no doubt caused our involvement in passion for each other. Being able to fight the same hazardous battles daily, and to do so *together* rather than in loneliness, was a powerful basis for this love. Work now took on a sheer enjoyment for the first time in years. Inner sources of love between two people cannot be fully analyzed; they are private and full of mystery. But it was important that Jane was a woman who could not be eclipsed or diminished in my shadow, and I was a man who was not threatened by her greater fame and power. She was fatigued by men who either pursued her as a notch on their belt or were rattled by being in her shadow. In addition, each of us reassured the other in fundamental ways: She wondered if she could be taken seriously, genuinely, as a committed person or whether she was a shallow latecomer to a decade-long movement; I wondered if there was any way to assert a public leadership role without damaging my personal relationships. We helped each other overcome these doubts.

Of course, there were differences too. She had missed the early years of the sixties, which were so important to my vision, patience, and organizing approach. She had entered the movement at its most overheated state, when everyone and everything had hardened. In a very deep way I was still participating in the experience of youth, an outsider with no possessions or responsibilities, living by wits and ideals on the economic margin. She had dropped out of Vassar, gone straight into a successful career, become a mother, and amassed significant income, which was spent on her material desires. I could keep my clothes in one large drawer; she needed extensive closets and domestic help. I was a famous radical who was morally and politically skeptical about fame; she was an actress whose career itself depended on public acclaim. We must have appeared like a remake of *Beauty and the Beast,* but these differences were more amusing than stressful as we happily came to know each other that summer. Not least of the pleasures was getting to know Vanessa, then three, who was born at the time of Chicago 1968 and had lived in the Blue Fairyland just after I left Berkeley; we had been just missing each other at these key moments in our lives. The first night that Jane and I made love, Vanessa marched out of her bedroom, a three-year-old inspector, and stared at me. I stared back, smiling; here I was starting over in yet another relationship with a young child not my own. Her father, Roger Vadim, seemed to be a loving and supportive parent, with children from several marriages scattered from Los Angeles to Paris, so I didn't worry much about Vanessa finding her own way in life. Besides, after the shattered relationship with Chris-

topher, I was very tentative about committing myself to someone else's child.

Then, on a spring day in a New York hotel room, fresh from
Vietnam, where she had seen women having children in the face
of death, Jane was moved to create life as her answer to numb
alienation. With a slight sigh, she stood behind me, naked, and
whispered, "I want to have a child with you." With a tearful
smile, I said yes.

My answer was immediate, even though my feelings toward
having a family had oscillated between extremes. The breakup
of my parents after my father returned from the marines had
been an utter shock. When I married Casey, the threat of war
became my excuse to forswear having children. For several
years the concept of children had simply been erased, or repressed, from my desires; in the same way, I had separated
myself from all conventions of society. At one point in the
mid-sixties, when an important woman in my life became pregnant, we immediately decided on an abortion, without emotion
or debate, as if there were no other real choice. Then, as the
polarization of society deepened, only survival seemed to matter. What I didn't realize until living with Christopher in Berkeley brought it home, was that I had smothered a longing that
was volcanic. Jane's simple words caused it to erupt.

This new infatuation with life seemed to embolden us toward
a new commitment to ending the incessant war. In fact, rather
than withdrawing into personal happiness, or sharply dividing
private from public life, we decided that the only meaningful
course was to hurl our personal relationship into the center of
public life and resume antiwar work as a team, pregnant and all.

In a few months, we created an ambitious plan to barnstorm
America against the war. We decided to organize an educational
speaking tour of vast proportions, a campaign against the numb-
ness that had set into people's thinking after a decade of Vietnam body counts, with three goals in mind: First and foremost,
it was to revive public attention to Nixon's war at a time when
the media interest was waning; to urge people, especially young
people, to register to vote against Nixon in November; and to
move the antiwar forces out of their growing isolation and into
the mainstream. It was an effort to repair the painful gap between generations, between radicals and Middle Americans. We
rapidly assembled a national network which we called the Indo-

china Peace Campaign (IPC), mostly composed of sixties veterans like myself who yearned to work again in the mainstream. In fact, the personal dimension of the project was akin to a rebirth for many, a return of exiles.

I remember the excitement, for instance, of Shari Whitehead Lawson, the middle-class daughter of a military family who had become a typical Berkeley revolutionary. IPC offered many like her a path out of the mounting debris of the movement. As a sign of our return to the mainstream, I gave her an American flag pin to wear on her jacket, which she happily did, as she orchestrated the first IPC tour event at, of all places, the Ohio State Fair.

We were worried at what the reception would be in the American heartland, and we were delighted at what we found. On a rainy September night, we spoke to three hundred people gathered under a tent. We watched a high school theater group perform a program about the generation gap, which was called *They're Killing Us with Words.* That same night we were welcomed at another state fair in Dayton, ending with a midnight presentation in a downtown theater. We called the experience the Ohio miracle. We were "coming home."

FBI MEMORANDUM 9/13/72

RE: INDOCHINA PEACE CAMPAIGN

On September 4, 1972, a first confidential source, who has furnished reliable information in the past, advised that an organizational meeting was held at the Wesley Foundation, 82 East 16th Avenue, Columbus, Ohio. The purpose of the meeting was to organize the programs of the Indochina Peace Campaign for Ohio and the Midwest region. Among those present and representing the National Headquarters of the IPC were Jane Fonda, movie actress, Tom Hayden, Holly Near and Ruby Ellyn.

The sheer magnitude of the speaking tour was unique. Jane and I, along with singer Holly Near and former POW George Smith, spoke several times a day in ninety cities that fall, a more grueling schedule in many respects than a presidential campaign. Immaculate Heart's multimedia exhibition was shown all over the country, from city halls to art museums. The Indochina slide show was reproduced in two hundred sets and sent to local organizers across the country, who showed it two thousand times in those two months. We hawked 100,000 copies of the Pentagon Papers digest. But the centerpiece of our educational kit was a four-page leaflet designed by Fred Branfman, a pioneering researcher on casualties in Indochina. On the front page was a photo of Richard Nixon's smiling face lifted from the Committee to Re-Elect the President (CREEP). It was entitled *Six Million Victims: The Human Cost of the Indochina War Under President Nixon.* Inside, the human costs were documented in credible and detailed statistics and charts. Newspapers reprinted much of the material, and George McGovern began referring to "six million victims" in his antiwar speeches. We distributed two and a half million copies.

There was some hostility, especially to Jane over her recent trip to North Vietnam. I was amazed, and still am, at the hatred and controversy her trip generated. She was accused, but never charged, with having made seditious broadcasts to American GIs. She met several POWs and believed them when they indicated that they were not tortured. She was photographed wearing a helmet and looking at an antiaircraft gun. Unlike her critics, I listened to her interviews on Hanoi radio and heard her talk of bombed villages in the same way she talked at home. If anything, these were acts of naïveté, not acts of treason. More important, the international publicity surrounding her trip may have helped prevent U.S. plans for bombing the dikes of North Vietnam. She was deeply troubled by the Pentagon Papers memo recommending shallow flooding of the rice to threaten widespread starvation and traveled to Hanoi principally to protest any such American plan. But the hostility she triggered was shocking. Forgotten were her years of work with American GIs; now she was attacked as the enemy. Was it because she was a woman? a sex symbol turned into an accuser of macho men? a successful American rejecting the system that rewarded her? Why the hate? I wondered. What if a famous American actress had visited the Indians fighting the U.S. Cavalry a century before? Would history still define her act as scandalous today? What were these groups of narrow-minded patriots showing up at our rallies really angry about?

We had some minor violence in Morristown, New Jersey, at a Methodist church, where a right-wing group cut the electrical wires and threw cherry bombs into the audience. There were hostile pickets in many places, and frequent bomb threats. But what was most amazing was the open interest of most of the people we met around the country. In Muskegon, Michigan, where George Wallace won the Democratic presidential primary and the local press was merciless toward us, two thousand citizens turned out at the local auditorium and stayed late. We were proudly introduced there by an eighty-year-old man who said he opposed the Vietnam War in the 1950s. He made Holly Near cry as she sang that night. In Detroit, we spoke at the State Fair, with my mother in the audience, and at a community college where my old high school coach was the president. We saw many people change before our eyes. In Philadelphia, as a Vietnamese student friend of ours spoke movingly about her homeland, I saw a young Nixon campaign worker remove his button. In Chicago, we met a veteran who said he was the security guard who kept Jane off an air force base the previous year; he handed her his badge this time.

Holly was a wonderful, rapid writer, and one day I asked if she could put these transforming experiences into a song. She said she would try, starting with her memory of the eighty-year-old man in Muskegon. In a few days, she did it. The song was called "Oh, America," and its chorus was always interrupted by applause and often brought hopeful tears to longtime antiwar activists.

> *Oh, America,*
> *I now can say your name,*
> *Without feeling bitter,*
> *Without feeling shame.*
> *Because I've traveled 'cross the country,*
> *To your cities and your towns,*
> *And I've seen some friendly people*
> *Who turned my head around.*

Jane was a tremendous trouper and almost always won over skeptical members of the audience. If people expected to hear how she intended to change society, they left with more of an understanding of how people like themselves, "ordinary Americans," had changed her. She described an empty life in the sixties ("I didn't think women could change anything, except sheets"). Then she told of meeting Vietnam veterans when she lived in Paris, men who recounted stories of war crimes she didn't want to believe. Then she saw the Chicago demonstrations in America over television, amazed at their scale and intensity. So she stopped being Barbarella, floating in space, and came home. After telling her story to the audience, Jane usually ended by raging against the forces that had made people like herself feel helpless and numb for so many years. Far from being a glitzy and remote movie star, she connected on a personal level.

On November 1, the Seventh Circuit U.S. Court of Appeals reversed the Chicago conspiracy convictions. The appellate decision cited the "demeanor of the judge and prosecutors," as well as numerous judicial errors, in a lengthy and historic opinion. The government prosecutors announced they would not retry the case. A few months earlier, the same federal court had reversed Judge Hoffman on the contempt-of-court charges and ordered a new hearing, before a new judge. (It was remarkable that during those several years of political trials on conspiracy charges, the federal government failed to win against *any* of the sixty-five conspiracy defendants. Such defendants as the Harrisburg Seven, the Camden Seventeen, and the Gainesville Eight always managed to win, either before juries or appeals courts, a dramatic difference from the McCarthy era, only fifteen years before.)

I was delighted to have my paranoia proven wrong, and the long burden of a five-year sentence at last lifted. There was something miraculous as well. Not only was the threat of imprisonment removed, but I was going to have the child that prison would have denied me. At about the same time as the court reversal of the Chicago convictions, Jane became pregnant. We think it happened in an upper berth of a van between speeches in Upstate New York.

Back in Santa Monica, I bought my first house for forty-five thousand dollars. I was finally settling down. It was a two-story, wood-shingle dwelling in a small, charming, unconventional neighborhood one block from the ocean. To say the least, Jane was accustomed to more luxurious surroundings than I was. My tastes had not changed much since college; I liked old, sagging, wood-frame houses. She yielded, and found ways (like sandblasting the walls) to give it at least a rustic elegance.

I called my mother with the news that she was going to be a grandmother. At first she hadn't believed that her son's relationship with a movie star would last. Now the thought of having a grandchild caught her completely by surprise. Instead of being delighted, I could tell she was worried by something. "What's the matter, Mom?" I wanted to know.

"You're not getting married?"

"So?" The thought of marriage hadn't much occurred to me, and Jane didn't bring it up either.

"Don't you understand what people are going to think? Don't you have enough causes already?"

Despite my happy embrace of the mainstream, I had all but forgotten that people out there still got married and still wagged their heads at those with children out of wedlock. Under the influence of Simone de Beauvoir, the sixties culture suspected marriage of being a hoax that killed natural love and eroticism and created a form of servitude for most women. In addition, our own experience was negative: Our parents were divorced, we had gone through failed marriages, and I only knew two or three couples whose marriages had survived the sixties.

I talked it over with Jane. Did we want to fight the war, fight Nixon, and fight marriage? A good question, she agreed. That's how our consideration of marriage began. But as we talked, over and over, we realized there was a deeper problem we were starting to face: commitment.

To have a child meant wanting to have a future together. That commitment seemed so profound that, like a pair of walking wounded, we took it one day at a time. But the more we talked, the more we understood that a future was what we missed and wanted in our lives. So with Jane three months pregnant, we were married at her home on January 19, 1973. About forty friends, from Vietnamese students to Vietnam veterans, Irish priests, and balladeers, gathered 'round to see us through the vows. Henry and Shirlee Fonda, who were always supportive, sat by the fireplace with Vanessa on their laps. Peter Fonda sang sweet songs with Holly Near. My mother watched with a smile and pride from a corner. The only one missing was my father. We invited him, but heard nothing back.

It wasn't exactly Norman Rockwell, but we made a family.

FEDERAL BUREAU OF INVESTIGATION 2/21/73

RE: THOMAS EMMETT HAYDEN

Marriage Security Matter

Los Angeles Times (1/20/73)

An article appeared in the above newspaper which contained a picture of Jane Fonda, noted actress and peace activist, and Thomas Hayden. The article stated that Hayden and Fonda celebrated their marriage at her Los Angeles home on Friday, January 19, 1973. The article stated that Hayden and Fonda were wed in a free form ceremony that included poetry, Vietnamese music and a vow to keep their sense of humor.

In the larger world, however, division and war remained handmaidens. The Watergate scandal had unfolded too slowly to undercut Nixon's reelection campaign. And though the hope for peace was tantalizing, there was to be none. Kissinger's cryptic election-eve promise that "peace is at hand" finished George McGovern's faltering presidential campaign. Shortly after Nixon's reelection, Kissinger indicated that the peace agreement draft was "ninety-nine-percent complete." But evidently feeling the intoxication of his landslide victory, Nixon decided on a last, massive show of force: He launched the saturation bombing of Hanoi and Haiphong for eighteen days during the 1972 holiday period. I was in Norway briefly visiting Jane, who was on location filming Ibsen's *A Doll's House,* and both of us had gone to Paris for Christmas. We were watching *Last Tango in Paris* when the bombing of Hanoi began. Both of us went straight to the North Vietnamese mission, where we found Nguyen Minh Vy, a longtime negotiator we had met previously. Normally polite and cheerful, Vy was in a state of frenzied anger like I'd never seen. He recounted details of the secret peace talks for us, insisted that Hanoi would make no further compromises to help the United States withdraw, and predicted that the B-52 bombing of Hanoi would be a military and moral "suicide" for Nixon's government.

He was proved correct. World condemnation was total. A Washington demonstration planned for Nixon's inauguration was growing toward explosive proportions. The bombing of Hanoi was a brutal fiasco. At least fifteen giant B-52s—costing seven million dollars each—were shot down over Hanoi as well as a dozen other U.S. planes. Sixty-two pilots were killed and thirty-one captured; one was court-martialed for refusing duty. The bombing then ended as suddenly as it began.

A few weeks later, having failed to budge Hanoi significantly with the B-52s, the United States signed virtually the same peace agreement that had been ready in draft form in October. The agreement recognized at long last the unity of Vietnam, the temporary nature of the division at the seventeenth parallel, accepted the presence of North Vietnamese troops in the South, and recognized the NLF as one of the "two parties, two administrations" which had to negotiate their future in the South. Kissinger's signature appeared next to that of Madame Nguyen Thi Binh, representing the Provisional Revolutionary Government of South Vietnam. The United States agreed to withdraw all its remaining forces within sixty days and retained the right to resupply the Saigon administration with military and economic aid. Hanoi would release the American POWs in the same time frame. The agreement was signed in Paris, with Rennie Davis watching, the week of our wedding.

Instead of trying to heal the wounds of war, Nixon chose the POWs as his true heroes, making no comparable reference to the three million American enlisted men or the fifty-five thousand dead. He touted his Christmas bombing as having achieved "peace with honor." He demanded that the media "quit making national heroes out of those who steal state secrets and publish them in the newspapers."

Nixon resurrected an old rage still close to my surface. Asked for a reaction by reporters, I recall snapping back that the POWs were "liars, hypocrites, and pawns in Nixon's effort to rewrite history." Jane remembers that it was actually she who made the comment. In any case, Jane and I were immediately quoted everywhere. Temper had carried me away. The statement was inaccurate, exaggerated, and insensitive toward the POWs, but there was nothing I could do to retrieve the words. I was as capable of "Vietnam flashbacks" as any veteran trying to return to normal American life.

FBI MEMORANDUM   **3-22-73**
LOS ANGELES, CALIFORNIA

COMMUNIST—REVOLUTIONARY ACTIVITY—EXTREMIST IN-FILTRATION OF MOTION PICTURE—TELEVISION—RADIO—ENTERTAINMENT INDUSTRIES.

When it was certain that the peace agreement was bringing neither peace nor honor, the Indochina Peace Campaign opened an office in Santa Monica and launched a national campaign to implement the agreement and cut off further military aid. Bruce Gilbert, Jack Nicholl, and Carol Kurtz, former members of the collective in Berkeley with whom I reconciled, got involved, as did Sam Hurst and Paul Ryder, a pair of bright ex-students who had worked hard on the Ellsberg-Russo defense. In addition to California, we fostered organizations in the large electoral states of New York, Massachusetts, Pennsylvania, Ohio, Michigan, and Illinois, where Jane and I had traveled exhaustively in 1972. We linked up with other peace groups in Washington to lobby and barrage Congress with constituent mail. The growing Watergate scandal gave us a rising sense of vindication. It also provided what we called the Watergate opportunity, a strategic chance to end the war by awakening Congress to assert its foreign-policy perogatives against the besieged administration.

When we weren't working against the war, we sat around our little house in Santa Monica imagining a film that Jane could make about the Vietnam experience. With Ron Kovic as an inspiration, the story became *Coming Home,* produced by IPC Films, a production company formed by Jane and Bruce, whose seemingly absurd dream of becoming a Hollywood producer was coming true in the most unorthodox way. At the time, Jane's career was in jeopardy because of her ceaseless involvement in controversial stands, and it troubled her more than I knew. The McCarthy period and the House Un-American Activities Committee hearings had chilled Hollywood just at the time her film career began, and it was only in the sixties that serious political movies became thinkable again. In ways she did not realize at the time, her early career was limited by a lack of such challenging roles; then, by the late sixties, she became the

*Material deleted by the FBI.

most visible Hollywood celebrity since the beginning of the Cold War to project a rebellious and controversial political profile. In the process, she provoked animosity and made many in her industry nervous. But she kept on her political track, slowing down only slightly as she grew heavier with the baby.

FBI MEMORANDUM   **7/10/87**

TO: ACTING DIRECTOR, FBI
FROM: SAC, LOS ANGELES
SUBJECT: INDOCHINA PEACE CAMPAIGN REVOLUTIONARY ACTIVITIES

The Los Angeles office has assumed office of origin in this matter, based upon information contained in referenced New York letter dated 4/27/73 to the effect that one of the National Resource Centers is in the Los Angeles area and that two main spokemen for the Indochina Peace Campaign (IPC) are Thomas Emmett Hayden and Jane Fonda, both key activists of the Los Angeles office.

Our son Troy was born July 7 (we were hoping for July 4), 1973, and Jane, Vanessa, and I drove home with the new baby two days later. I only remember lying next to him, rubbing his back, staring at this little creature for what seemed like days. Jane was blissful and tired. We had created life. Lying next to him, I felt like a wild animal. My hair was long and natural; the house was my cave; I resented having to dress for the outside world. I only wanted this baby to open his brown eyes toward mine, to lie with him on my stomach, and to whisper words of love to him. At times I found myself crying unexpectedly, and one night I made a list of what in recent years had brought me to tears: having this child, the end of my trial, and the death of Robert Kennedy. Then and there, however, I made a pledge: I would build my life around this little boy until he became a man. He would not go through the family separation I went through, and Jane and Vanessa went through, no matter what.

I sent photos of the baby to my father, with a short note providing the important details. His wife, Esther, told me later that when he received them in Detroit, he said nothing but began to cry. Still, I never heard from him.

TO: SAC, LOS ANGELEES　　　　　　　　　　　　　**3/27/75**
FROM: DIRECTOR, FBI

Jane Fonda
Subversive Matter

Tom Hayden
Subversive Matter

Los Angeles is requested to promptly prepare a letterhead memorandum (LHar), under the Hayden caption only, incorporating specific data relative to Fonda's and Hayden's son and also,
succinctly set forth information concerning Hayden's recent subversive activities.

In late October 1973, I went back to Chicago for a new trial on
the contempt charges. The atmosphere in the courtroom (and in
the country) was totally changed. Many of those at the federal
level who had tried to jail us were now being driven from office
themselves. The new judge, Edward Gignoux of Maine, was a
patient, rational, flexible presence, and the case went smoothly
forward for several weeks.

I was looking forward to the new contempt trial, because I felt
that the original contempt charges were widely misunderstood.
The Chicago prosecutors tried to claim that we intended to
disrupt the trial from the beginning, an impression that gained
credence through the televised images of the courtroom confrontations. The truth was otherwise. After the trial, a Chicago
law professor, Harry Kalven, who had openly criticized our
tactics, took the time to study the twenty-two thousand pages of
transcript for himself. To his surprise, he found that most of the
contempt charges occurred within only sixteen days of the
five-month-long trial. He concluded with an apology:

> I am impressed, contrary to the impressions I had gotten from the
> press coverage, by the sense that the interruptions were in no
> sense random events, and that two or three triggering events, such
> as the handling of Seale and the revoking of Dellinger's bond,
> account for the major part of the troubles. . . . The incidence of
> unrest seems not easily compatible with the notion that the de-
> fendants and counsel relentlessly and steadily pursued a single-
> minded strategy of disturbing the trial process.

After a five-week trial, Judge Gignoux arrived at a similar
conclusion to Kalven's. He upheld as valid only thirteen of

Judge Hoffman's original 159 judgments for contempt. The rest he declared, "can, in each instance, reasonably be said to have been in response, albeit an excessive response, to peremptory action of the Judge."

I was cleared of all charges and carried Troy on my shoulders out of the Federal Building, free at last, over five years since the Chicago convention and four years since the original trial.

Jane and I went on the road against the war again that fall, traveling to ten states. We carried Troy with us. The quiet throbbing of airplanes always made him sleep serenely. At other times, he napped in dresser drawers. He became very familiar with the immense variety of ceilings, since he lay on his back in a portable carrier much of the time. Jane was breast-feeding him and sometimes had to cut her speeches short when her natural duties called.

In spring 1974, we went out for another month, this time adding swings through Georgia and Texas. Then in mid-1974, we moved to Washington for six weeks to intensify the lobbying effort for an end of military funding. We met with forty or fifty members of Congress. I taught my Indochina seminar to about seventy congressional staffers in a hearing room of the House of Representatives with the assistance of Congressmen Ronald Dellums and Don Edwards and Senator Alan Cranston. We were creating an impressive operation on Capitol Hill, coordinated primarily by Larry Levin, who had moved from Los Angeles to direct what we called the Coalition to Stop Funding the War.

That year, antiwar lobbying efforts brought the first defeat of a Vietnam military appropriation in the decade since the 1964 Tonkin Gulf Resolution. But it was an intense struggle, and a turning point for me in working through the system. Antiwar efforts over the previous year succeeded in shaving nearly $500 million from the Pentagon's request for Saigon military aid, but $1.1 billion for the 1974 fiscal year was still substantial. Then in March, the Pentagon requested an additional $474 million, exactly the amount cut the year before. This was the moment to mobilize all the lobbying contacts we had been making across the country for two years. Larry's forces went to work. The coalition secured the official opposition of seven major religious denominations, the U.S. Conference of Mayors, the United Auto Workers, Common Cause, and even the moderate-Republican Ripon Society. On the streets, IPC organizers set up tables and encouraged citizens to sign petitions and send telegrams to their representatives. They also organized delegations to visit their local media, most of whom editorialized against the supplemental aid. In the end, the Vietnam military-aid provision was deleted by a 177–154 vote, after a bitter debate, to a tremendous cheer from the House balcony. We walked out into a starry Washington night, thanking the heavens for our trust in the process.

That November of 1974, the congressional elections produced an independent, post-Watergate freshman class with a critical interest in wresting power back from the executive branch. From that moment, the future of greater military assistance to Nguyen Van Thieu or Lon Nol was thrown in terminal doubt. But instead of looking for a last-minute settlement, the administration continued to fuel the deepening crisis in Southeast Asia. In March 1975, I testified before Senator Humphrey's Foreign Relations subcommittee that the administration should try to negotiate a power transition between Sihanouk and the Khmer Rouge to contain a possible disaster when they inevitably arrived in Phnom Penh. On this issue, at long last, Humphrey and I agreed, and took humorous note of the irony. House Democrats, led by Ronald Dellums, Bella Abzug, Toby Moffett, and Bob Carr, decided to oppose further supplemental aid. The U.S. subsidy of war came to an end. Then the Khmer Rouge marched into Phnom Penh, the returning Sihanouk was placed under informal house arrest, and their unexpected revolutionary madness was unleashed. Shortly after, the North Vietnamese military offensive burst through the sagging defense of the Saigon army and rolled toward Saigon. After twenty years of rejecting a coalition government in the South, the American fear of a North Vietnamese takeover became self-fulfilling.

It was hard to believe the war was over. I had spent over ten years opposing it, since before my twenty-fifth birthday. So many possibilities were gone, so many had perished. Anyone who even made it through the decade with senses intact, I felt, was lucky. The sixties were, in Carl Oglesby's phrase, a "decade ready for the dustbin." The New Left had served its major purposes and faded away, leaving only sectarian ashes. The Black Panthers were disintegrated by a combination of internal rivalries and costly police and legal pressures. The Weathermen had steadily lost their purpose and their bearings. The Yippies were a poster on the wall. The post-SDS Marxist factions continued to fragment into smaller and smaller cells.

Allen Ginsberg's 1950s poem "Howl" began with the line "I have seen the best minds of my generation destroyed by madness." Many of the bravest people of the sixties lost their way. The closest to me was Rennie. I must say of Rennie that he persevered like no other. He will always be the true hero of the antiwar movement for me. He stayed as point man for several more Chicagos after Chicago: in May 1970, when sixty thousand came to Washington; in May 1971, when thirteen thousand were arrested trying to "stop the government"; in August 1972, at the Miami Republican Convention, when a tear-gas canister hit him while he led a march of ten thousand; and in January 1973, when one hundred thousand protested Nixon's second inaugural. I admired his standing in the dead center of these cyclones and his seemingly endless capacity to suffer personal unhappiness and attack.

What I understood less was that his capacity was not infinite. Perhaps to justify his extraordinary sacrifice, Rennie believed that ending the war would usher in a New Age. After Mayday, while stoned, Rennie told John Froines that he expected an ecological holocaust, from which only those labeled "freaks" would survive and achieve power. Once during an IPC tour, he told Jane and me joyfully that the Vietcong were Jesus Christ; that was all he said, and I didn't ask what he meant.

After the 1972 Republican convention, where he was surrounded by countless undercover agents on the one hand and the unrecognizable remnants of the sixties movement on the other, he was totally exhausted and feeling betrayed: The Yippies had degenerated into "zippies," who considered Abbie and Jerry to be sellouts whose idea of a media event was dropping their pants in front of cameras. The tear-gassing had occurred just as he was ending a forty-day fast, and it temporarily poisoned him. At that moment, with Nixon renominated, he could think of nothing more he personally could do to end the war. A few months later, he attended the signing of the Paris peace agreement, came home convinced the war was finally over—and was more disoriented than ever.

Then, he told me, a former roommate from Washington offered him a plane ticket to India. The roommate, Larry Canada, was one of a number of American followers of an Indian guru, the fifteen-year-old, Maharaj Ji. Rennie accepted the trip as a vacation, professing no interest in the guru. But when he came back, he showed up at my apartment in Venice a changed person. Rennie asked me to take an evening walk, where he proceeded to pour out a personal tale so unexpected that it stunned me.

"I know you'll think this is crazy, that I've gone out of my mind," he began, "but I have to tell you what I've experienced because you are my closest friend in the world and I need you to understand this."

When he went to India, Rennie recounted, he met several "former movement people" who had turned into followers of the guru. They spoke to him of meditation, of experiencing something called "light," of having the same transcendental visions as Whitman, Dante, and Blake.

"At first, it turned me off. Here was this fat kid with a lot of brothers and sisters, wearing expensive clothes and driving expensive cars, surrounded by rich Americans at an ashram. I said it was absurd, and they would say that's just the point, try it.

"So I went through this initiation ritual. It blew out every socket in my head. I saw light. I could only see light for two whole weeks. It scared the shit out of me, because I lost my identity in it. It was so total and ecstatic, though, I couldn't believe it.

"Then one day I was at this little stream washing my clothes. All of a sudden this giant black bird, with huge wings, is hovering right above me, coming closer and closer. He was beating the air with his wings, and I just knelt there. I couldn't move or get away.

"It was like he was entering me, opening me up, and all of a sudden I felt helpless, prostrate. I saw myself from outside myself, and all I saw was ego. That's why I was hung up, because of ego. And that's why I dismissed the guru, because I looked only at his appearance. He was wearing all the symbols of ego to throw me off. I felt that I was in the presence of a larger force than myself. I was blissed out, man."

Listening to Rennie, I thought I was going to be ill. Here was my best friend in front of me, present in form only, his mind gone somewhere else. I believed in mystical experiences and a religious dimension of life, but not prostration in front of a fifteen-year-old with a taste for Rolls-Royces. From the way I stared at him, Rennie knew that he hadn't reached me. He also was ready with a soothing logic to rebut whatever counter explanations I attempted. Rennie always knew how to make the wildest ideas seem plausible. He explained that he was part of the guru's Divine Light Mission, which was to convert our generation. Rennie was starting with me, but intended to visit all his old friends, make public his new identity, and organize a massive religious event at the Houston Astrodome with John Lennon, Bob Dylan, one hundred thousand converts, and live coverage by Walter Cronkite.

We said good-bye that night and didn't see each other again until the Chicago contempt retrial that October, when there was a last, wild, and tumultuous meeting of the Conspiracy defendants. We tried political argument, hard denunciation, and emotional pleading to stop Rennie's new direction. We failed. For several years after that I couldn't spend time with him because I was too upset. Once the most stable and dependable of leaders, the person I relied on as my own anchor, he was lost to the mystery of altered consciousness. Eventually Rennie's dream fizzled. The Astrodome event was not the Second Coming and his loyalty to the guru waned, but not before Rennie tried and failed at converting the whole movement. I never found an adequate explanation for what happened.

Ten years later, Rennie had left the guru's operation, feeling bad about his involvement, but he was still convinced that his light experience had been real. He was living in Colorado, seeking investment capital to support research on "New Age" ventures, while still exploring the mysteries of the universe.

Rennie might have fizzled as a promoter, but he was not alone in developing an apocalyptic religious temperament. Al Haber followed a strange and mystical path as well. At the end of the seventies he was constructing a cherry-wood conference table for a global peace summit he envisioned being held at Megiddo, the site in Israel where the biblical Armageddon is prophesied to occur. He seemed to me blissfully without an anchor.

Also among many early leaders of the movement who chose an Eastern religious path was Bob Moses of SNCC. After leaving the South, he disappeared into African villages for several years, then reemerged at Harvard in the field of philosophy, built a family, and quietly pursued the mastery of Zen Buddhism. Another to take a spiritual path was Casey. After the demise of SNCC and ERAP, and a brief stint of welfare work in New York, she organized a commune in Vermont (where she lived in a tepee), then met a self-styled yogi, and helped create something with him called the Integral Yoga Institute in San Francisco. They had two children together, but the relationship was disastrous, and after its end she turned to more serious study of Buddhism in Colorado. She left that community and by 1983, she returned to Atlanta in the administration of Mayor Andrew Young, still loyal to Buddhist teachings and now a believer in a Mayan view of "harmonic convergence."

I have long searched for an understanding of these religious transformations. Of course, my old friends were very different from each other: Al a floating mystic, Casey a poet full of pain, Bob an existentialist in action, Rennie a traveling pitchman. But each of them was an originator of the sixties movement and each had moved to a spiritual plane at decade's end. What they and many others shared was a desire not simply for results but for ultimate meaning in life. They first sought it through immersion in a total community—the early movement circle—that provided love, friendship, adequate income, and a sense of useful, indeed historic, purpose. They gave a key decade of their lives, the decade when young men and women typically position themselves for career success, to these intense communities. Paul Potter likened the movement in those years not to a political party, but a church. Then, beginning in the mid-sixties, their communities disbanded. In place of them came a chamber of horrors. Rennie, I remember, complained of the movement becoming surreal, "weird." Casey felt "ripped off" by Stokely Carmichael, who denounced the early integrated SNCC and moved to Africa. As a reaction, instead of making history, there came a new consciousness, an immersion of the self in a larger "flow" of the universe. The failure of secular reform led to consoling explanations from Eastern thought: that reality is illusion, power struggles are vanity, an ego a shadow on the inner and universal Light. From a political stance, many turned (or returned) to the world of *Siddhartha*. In simple terms, the odysseys of the era had worn many people out. One friend of mine, Leni Zeiger, spent years as an ERAP organizer, renamed herself Leni Wildflower, married Paul Potter, had one child with him, adopted another who belonged to a woman in the underground, and became tired of peanut butter, brown rice, and free love. "In the end," she wrote me later, "we couldn't be each other's church and religion and home. People needed ways to find inner peace, to heal from the intensity and anger and pressure."

Though my first reaction was to distance myself from someone like Rennie after his conversion, I later realized that my own experiences in Berkeley had not been so superior. The latter-day SDS and similar revolutionary collectives were closed enclaves with leadership worship, thought control, collective devouring of individual autonomy—totalist cells awaiting an apocalypse that never came. Such groups seemed to proliferate as refugee centers for those unable to live amid the moral and spiritual deficits of society. Though I initially encouraged and was fascinated by them, they were ultimately as alienating as the governing institutions I had abandoned years earlier. Nor could I fully accept the key premise that American society was becoming fascistic. After the Chicago trial experience, I had to acknowledge that the system was beginning to work. It had gone to the brink of breakdown, to the preliminary stages of civil strife, but now there were signs that working within the fabric of society was producing change. Now it was time, I thought, to make an adjustment to reality. But were those who went through trauma and trial capable of returning to reform? The difference between my "religious conversion" and Rennie's was that I was a "born-again" Middle American, emotionally charged by my reacceptance in the political mainstream.

The slow ending of the war ended a period of my life—an extended youth—and offered an opportunity for a fresh start. I had committed myself to working within the political system since the 1972 McGovern campaign. I had lobbied Congress sufficiently to know how the system works. Then I had become an interested follower of California's new governor, Jerry Brown, who was first introduced to me at Immaculate Heart in 1971 when he was California secretary of state. We became very close. I wrote for *Rolling Stone* about Brown's successful 1974 governor's race and found myself attracted to his new-generation theme. Millions of Americans had been changed by the decade, and I felt energized by the new possibilities of the mainstream. All that I needed was a plan of action.

Jane wanted to rebuild her acting career. Though not "blacklisted," she had been shunned by studio executives who believed that controversy made her less "bankable." She wanted to try making movies that were both successful and meaningful. She plunged into scripts. I wanted to be part of a positive, post-Vietnam politics in America. In 1973, I had speculated about the postwar future in an IPC pamphlet. "Will we be even more of an isolated remnant of the New Left by then," I wrote, referring to the war's end,

> or will we have a legitimate place, based on our work, in the debate about American identity and priorities that is surely ahead? The future of our whole generation of radicalism since 1960 could be settled in the next two or three years. Either we will go down as one more "healthy" wave of protest that was absorbed and then fragmented, or we will go forward from the antiwar movement to a fuller movement trying to reflect the needs and aspirations of most Americans in the postwar years.

My friends in IPC went their separate ways, all bound by a common experience of successful organizing, and the same hopeful analysis of post-Vietnam America. We agreed that, after Vietnam, America's unchallenged dominance in the world was ending. The affluence of the fifties was no more; the American middle class was threatened by inflation and stagnation. In response, we anticipated a period of domestic populism. On the right, there would be a conservative backlash against all those perceived as having weakened the country against its enemies, a new McCarthyism fueled by sudden and legitimate economic and security anxieties. In the political center, we anticipated the "outsider" populism that came to be reflected in the Jimmy Carter campaign. On the Left, we believed that a "progressive populism" was a real possibility, applying the original SDS notion of participatory democracy to winning grass-roots power within the system.

Some of my longtime friends decided to organize women office workers—the new work force—for decent pay and dignity, as a way to bridge the interests of feminists and organized labor. They eventually formed 9 to 5, the National Association of Working Women, which became famous in a comedy of the same name, starring Jane, Dolly Parton, and Lily Tomlin, and produced by Bruce and Jane. Eventually, 9 to 5 affiliated with the Service Employees International Union and the AFL-CIO.

Others chose to organize citizen action organizations at the grass-roots level. These groups would canvass communities door to door on economic issues like utility rates and property taxes, building local and state coalitions to pressure lawmakers for reform, appearing in Ohio, Massachusetts, and Illinois and eventually fifteen states. In time, they formed an umbrella organization, Citizen Action, the most effective nationwide grass-roots organization of its kind in the eighties.

I chose the path of electoral politics, trying to galvanize the new generation of candidates and voters in the Democratic party.

It began one night in Washington in January 1975. I was sitting around with Larry Levin and a few others discussing how to keep the underlying issues of Vietnam alive after the war. John Holum, an aide to George McGovern, suddenly said, "Why don't you run against Tunney for Senate? You'll lose, but maybe you'll win the next time." The idea germinated for six months, and then I decided to do it. After all, Judge Hoffman had said I could "go far under this system"; why not give it a try?

FBI MEMORANDUM   **6/6/75**

TO: SAC, LOS ANGELES
FROM: DIRECTOR

THOMAS EMMETT HAYDEN

Recent newspaper articles have indicated Hayden announced on 6/2/75 that he would enter the 1976 Democratic Party primary for the US Senate seat in California now held by John V. Tunney.

You are referred to SAC memorandum 49-74, line (D), dated 10/15/74 which refers to action to be taken by a field office regarding subjects of subversive investigations who are candidates for public office . . . you should continue to submit 90-day communications to the Bureau setting forth synopsis of subversive activities on his part and your recommendation as to whether or not he continues to qualify for ADEX [agitator index]. You are reminded that no active investigation is to be conducted of Hayden during the period he is a candidate for public office.

It was a quixotic choice, to say the least, but three reasons persuaded me: Such a race would create a visible platform for debate over post-Vietnam directions like no other; it would allow me to change my status and, by implication, that of the sixties activists, from outsiders to mainstream participants in national politics; and it would provide a way to build a statewide grass-roots organization after the war. The only question was whether I could do well enough to be taken seriously; was there a chance of actually winning?

In seeking advice from many people, the most important suggestions came from farm workers leader Cesar Chavez. A thoughtful, utterly dedicated organizer whom I much admired, he was bemused at first. But after a long conversation, he said, "We've seen many candidates come and go. It would be a waste of time and money unless you build something lasting, like a machine. Not like Mayor Daley has, but a machine for people. That would interest us."

John Tunney was not a reactionary senator, but an orthodox liberal. There were some serious issue differences between us: He favored building the B-1 bomber and deregulating natural gas prices and claimed that national health insurance was "too expensive." He had been a Vietnam hawk in the mid-sixties, a Humphrey delegate in 1968, an opponent of the farm workers' grape boycott, and was elected to the Senate in 1970 after a negative campaign against a more liberal congressman, George Brown. The biggest question was whether after Vietnam, after the sixties, the voters wanted a new alternative to politics as usual.

I held my first serious organizational meeting at the International House of Pancakes in Santa Monica. There I asked Bill Zimmerman, a longtime antiwar activist, to manage the campaign. Bill's formal academic training was years of psychological research on dolphins and human-brain behavior, which he eagerly wanted to apply to politics. He had a fine imagination, a sense of administrative detail, and a curiosity—rare for movement activists in those days—about the possibilities of mass direct-mail and media advertising. He was also an adventurer; with Larry Levin, he flew an emergency relief mission into Wounded Knee, South Dakota, where Sioux leaders were under siege by state troopers in 1972. Coincidentally I introduced him to Joan Andersson, with whom he fell in love and later raised a family. Sam Hurst, a former student leader, IPC activist, and legal researcher on the Ellsberg-Russo case, became issues coordinator and press secretary. Jane agreed to throw in whatever money she could and help contact performers who might do concerts or appearances; Henry Fonda was one of the first to sign on. The list grew rapidly and diversely, until it included Arlo Guthrie and Groucho Marx, Linda Ronstadt and Red Buttons.

Instead of a conventional campaign platform, we felt, there had to be a new "manifesto." I called in Dick and Mickey Flacks, Paul Potter, and Fred Branfman to begin a draft. I envisioned an update of *The Port Huron Statement,* reflecting the transition from protest to power, from arguing political realignment to making it happen. When we finally finished writing, the document was 278 pages long. It was called *Make the Future Ours.* Leaving aside its voluminous detail, its broad theme was generational and future-oriented. "The radicalism of the sixties has become the new common sense of the seventies," it dramatically proclaimed, implying that those who protested in the streets were entitled to replace the officials who had so discredited and ruined the country during the Vietnam and Watergate years.

The paper defined a fundamental choice between "Government of the Corporations" and "Government of the People." It included, however, the assertion that "I am not running for the U.S. Senate simply to replace Big Business with Big Government." We proposed, starting with the campaign itself, the creation of a citizens' movement for real control over everyday issues, a decentralized, nonbureaucratic alternative to purely governmental or corporate solutions. Drawing from Thomas Jefferson, we proposed an "economic democracy" in which accountability would be expected of large corporations through greater involvement in decision-making processes by their employees, as well as the consumers and communities they impacted. Many of the themes echoed those of Jerry Brown, who remained neutral in the primary between Tunney and myself, and who leaped into the Democratic presidential primaries himself.

We were neophytes down to the most elementary campaign details. When one Democratic politician asked me about plans for GOTV (get-out-the-vote), I thought he was talking about cable-television franchises. Yet, it was our audacity and naïveté, a combination I had drawn on before, that made the campaign possible at all. We drew together hundreds of people like ourselves, from Vietnam veterans to advocates of disabled rights, who shared in common, during that twilight of the sixties era, a burning desire for a new rebirth. Even after I lost, I kept receiving letters like this one:

> Writing this at 5:30 A.M., on the grey overcast morning following the election, my mood matches the tone of the sky. But despite the clouds, you—and all of us—have reason to see something other than defeat this day . . . You have proven undeniably that sixties political activism does indeed have a place near the mainstream politics in the seventies (God knows how far you would have gotten in 1968 or '72, probably an extended jail term and about eighteen votes). On a more personal level, I wish to thank you for stirring me from my self-imposed political exile . . .

For most of a year, Tunney sailed along in the polls with a comfortable 55–15 percent lead; nothing I did produced any change. But everywhere, apparently, we planted seeds that began to sprout in the last month. As a sign of dedication to the grass roots, I began a thousand-mile walk through the state. In each stop, small or large, a contingent of activists would leaflet local business districts and elected neighborhoods while I shook hands, held press conferences, and continued putting one foot ahead of the other. Privately, I was extremely worried that the campaign had failed, that I would end with only 20 percent of the vote—a rejection of myself, all I stood for, and the thousands of people whose hopes had been resurrected.

I crossed over the Golden Gate Bridge carrying Troy on my shoulders on the morning of May 17, three weeks before the primary election. A small crowd of fifty were there, and to cheer themselves up, a local orator compared me to George Washington starting out with a "ridiculous handful" on his side. As I began trudging into San Francisco, the rhetoric was not enough to hide the tension in the campaign, however. We knew that a Mervin Field California poll would come out the following day. It could doom our campaign.

Miraculously, the Field poll showed Tunney at 50 percent while I had risen to 33 percent. Field called the twenty-seven-point shift a "significant surge which could foreshadow the beginnings of a tide."

Tunney, who had ignored my candidacy for months, suddenly began a powerful counterattack on television and radio, wildly and inaccurately accusing me of being a radical "big spender" who was "soft on Russia." He flew in high-powered media consultants David Garth and Jeff Greenfield and attacked me in a televised debate for wanting to "roll over and play dead in front of the Russians" and create a "gray Czechoslovakia-type system." Nevertheless, I continued to rise in the polls. In the final days, a Los Angeles headline proclaimed SENATE PRIMARIES AT THE WIRE; TUNNEY FIGHTING FOR POLITICAL LIFE.

But my surge was too little, too late. Tunney's counteroffensive stopped my momentum at the end. The final percentages were Tunney 54, Hayden 36.7, and other candidates 8.

Because of who I was, however, the defeat was interpreted as a victory, and it felt like one. It may have been the largest vote in the nation's history for a candidate so clearly defined as a "radical." We carried the eighteen- to thirty-five-year-old voters and those who defined themselves as "independent," an early appearance of the sixties-generation baby-boomers in the political process. I announced on election night that I would try to act as a political representative of the 1.2 million Californians who voted for me. In November, the voters indicated their apparent disillusionment with Tunney by choosing S. I. Hayakawa, the little-known, charming, and hard-line former president of San Francisco State as their U.S. senator.

After the campaign, I felt obligated to carry through on my promise that a vehicle be created to promote progressive causes and candidates for offices around the state. In 1976, the Hayden-for-Senate network formed the Campaign for Economic Democracy (CED), which ultimately became Campaign California. In this brief, almost-forgotten era, with Brown in Sacramento and Jimmy Carter in the White House, the times were ripe once again for new initiatives for the first time in my experience since 1960–63. In the face of skyrocketing inflation, we sponsored successful rent-control initiatives in Santa Monica and elsewhere. CED elected a majority to the Santa Monica City Council and helped elect more than fifty local candidates throughout the state. We threw ourselves into the no-nuke crusade of the late seventies. We proposed, and Jerry Brown accepted, proposals to develop a solar-energy program and reinvest pension funds out of South Africa and into affordable housing. But conservatives counterattacked, and we suffered some defeats. For instance, the State Senate refused to confirm Jane as a Brown nominee to the

California Arts Council, condemning her for her Vietnam activities. But I became a member of the governor's political inner circle, chairman of the state's solar program, the governor's representative on U.S.-Mexican border issues, and generally a symbolic bridge for Jerry Brown to the sixties generation.

As part of this novel acceptance, I visited the White House for the first time since 1962, when I had sounded off to Arthur Schlesinger, and was welcomed by Jimmy Carter as a "patriotic American." To my surprise, he had read *The Port Huron Statement,* and we discussed the role played by dissenting radicals like Norman Thomas in American history. Having known Thomas, I offered my opinion that too many American radicals ended up honored but irrelevant. The president noted that many of Thomas's proposals were ultimately carried out by the Democratic party. But, I said, when Thomas was asked how *he* felt about the fate of his message, he replied, "They carried it out all right, in a coffin." The discussion was unexpectedly informal, and as it was breaking up, I decided to take the opportunity to raise with the president my current concern, that multinational corporations with unelected leaders seemed to have more power in our democracy than elected officials, including himself. "Yes, I agree," he answered evenly, "I learned that my first year in office."

As the seventies came to an end, many veterans of the sixties were making successful transitions to useful work on community levels throughout America. They were invisibly entering professions, making up for lost time in their personal lives and careers, but retaining most of their underlying values. They would reappear with new labels, from *yuppie* to *baby-boomer.* Some were in elective office or joined the Carter administration, like Andrew Young, Sam Brown, and John Lewis; others were lesser known. Whether in politics or professions, or simply in their lives, they were eager for the long haul. After the apocalypse of youth, a belief in the future had finally returned. As one example of this commitment, Jane and I purchased a 160-acre ranch, called Laurel Springs, in August 1977, high in the mountains above Santa Barbara, and turned it into a children's summer camp stressing environmental education and performing arts. Local conservatives opposed our permit on the grounds that we planned to "brainwash" these small children, but we eventually won approval. Our simple belief was that kids should have a moment to glimpse life's potential through belonging to a hopeful community of all races and backgrounds, to share a better society in the here and now that it might inspire their future.

Jane made an amazing return as an actress, with *Coming Home, Julia, 9 to 5,* and *The China Syndrome*—all triumphs. Like myself, she was definitely healing from the sixties. One sign was a new closeness with her father, as she prepared for production of their first film together, *On Golden Pond.* I was fortunate to spend several weeks in New Hampshire during the filming, done in an intimate location on a private lake, and to watch the interaction between art and life. The script was about a difficult and distant father-daughter relationship that mirrored that of Jane and Henry. During most of the sixties, their relationship was marked by Henry's disapprovals, misunderstandings, cool distance, and long silences. Jane fought his authority in often irreverent ways. He was a shy, repressed, withdrawn man who expressed himself best through the characters he played. He was Mr. Roberts to the World War II generation, and he believed his government when it said that communism should be stopped with force in Vietnam. When his daughter became the antithesis of all respectability, it was hard on him.

But part of Henry Fonda was also Tom Joad, the SNCC-style organizer in John Steinbeck's *The Grapes of Wrath.* He was a liberal Democrat who opposed blacklisting and detested Richard Nixon. He understood courage, taking a stand for principle, and being unpopular with the establishment. I always wished that, if an actor was going to be president, it would be Henry Fonda rather than Ronald Reagan. I don't know what he thought upon first hearing that his daughter, already separated and with a young daughter of her own, was pregnant and planning to marry a "revolutionary." But when we first went out for a hamburger in Santa Monica with Henry and Shirlee, we got along very well. Henry surprised me with his constant support—appearances, television spots, and contributions of his incredible paintings and drawings to our campaigns.

Like my father, he was a passionate fisherman. During the time in New Hampshire, when he and Jane were obviously overjoyed to be living and working with each other, I used to go fishing for bass with Henry and Troy in the evenings after work. I even caught a record twenty-three-inch smallmouth bass. It was just like in the script and, more poignantly, reminded me of fishing trips with my own father long ago.

19. *Reunion*

One day in August 1978, I received a letter from Detroit. I recognized the careful handwriting on the envelope, although I hadn't seen it in over a decade. Standing in my driveway by the mailbox, I tore it open. The message was terse, I guess as much as he could express:

> Tom,
> In case you don't have my number, it's (313) 555-4493.
> Give me a call.
>
> Dad

I had continued to write and send him pictures of Troy, Vanessa, and Jane, and there was always a void on the other end of the mailbox. I showed the note to Jane and, feeling very agitated, dialed the number.

"Hello?" a girl's voice answered. She was almost sixteen.

"Hi," I said, hesitating. "Is Jack Hayden there, please?"

"Just a minute." Pause. "Who's calling?"

"This is your brother, Tom."

"I know. Wait a second." She left the phone and went into the living room. "There's a man on the phone," she told my dad, then sat down with her arms folded.

A few moments later I was listening to his voice. The conversation was brief, restrained. "Tom? Good to hear you. I thought it was time we got together. I'd like to come out."

"Great, Dad," I answered, and the conversation quickly turned to the trivia of airline and hotel reservations.

He went back to the living room and asked Mary, "Do you know who that was?"

"Yes," she began evenly, "that was my brother. You deprived me all these years of my brother. I hate you."

She ran into her room. My father sat down and cried. Then, after a few minutes, he went into her room and apologized, saying over and over, "Kid, I'll make it up to you, I'll make it up to you."

He had aged deeply since I'd last seen him in 1965. He was seventy years old, thinner in the arms and stoop-shouldered, but lively and alert in his mind. I introduced him to his five-year-old grandson, who walked up, took his hand and said, "Hello, Grandpa." I looked at my sister for the first time since she was a baby. "Hi, sister." "Hi, brother." We hugged silently.

From there, we steadily became closer. My dad read countless books to Troy, was bothered when Troy wanted to be with someone else, and wrote him funny short stories from Detroit. He made sure that he didn't neglect Vanessa, either. Jane was a wonderful daughter-in-law, acting as if some long-lost relatives had been found. Henry and Shirlee Fonda were delighted; in my dad, Henry found someone who talked even less than he did. I took my dad fishing for bass and crappie at Lake Cachuma, near Laurel Springs Ranch. We went to Northern California, where on my sister's sixteenth birthday, I took them to an event for Jerry Brown, then running for reelection. They met Cesar Chavez and stayed overnight at Delancey Street, a halfway house for drug addicts that some friends of mine had started. I took them into my life fully, in short, without worry of rejection. We couldn't say much at first, but just enjoyed the new experience of each other's company.

One morning, when we were standing alone on a sidewalk, my father said, out of nowhere, "Son, I'm proud of you." Those simple words, so hard to say, were all I needed to hear. "Thanks, Dad. I love you. I'm sorry it's been so long."

After that, he came out frequently. Mary visited for several weeks, and Troy was entertained by Grandpa in Detroit a couple of times. I let my mother in Wisconsin know what had happened, and she too was pleased.

At the time, Jane was preparing to film *The China Syndrome,* about the hypothetical meltdown of a nuclear power plant. My father said it couldn't happen, although he enjoyed it as a thriller. Then, in an odd case of synchronicity, the Three Mile Island nuclear accident occurred just after the movie's release. Jane and I went on another national tour in late 1979, promoting the antinuclear cause. We visited the crippled nuclear reactor at Three Mile Island, spoke to a Washington rally of 100,000 people, and indirectly explored presidential possibilities for Jerry Brown.

The promise of those few years ended with the demise of Jimmy Carter as president and Jerry Brown as governor. The political thaw of the mid-seventies was over, and by 1980 a reaction against inflation, OPEC, and Iran was settling over America. Ronald Reagan became president, and conservative George Deukmejian governor of California. With the short period of effective alliances with future-oriented incumbent Democrats at an end, I decided to run for the state legislature from my home district in 1982. This would not be a symbolic effort, an organizing drive, like the U.S. Senate race of five years before. This would be for real, to win or lose, to determine whether I was electable and effective inside the political system. I had concluded that my protests and policy proposals would always be categorized as "utopian" or "too radical" as long as the messenger, myself, was perceived as an outsider. On some deeper level, I wanted the democratic process to confirm my legitimacy as nothing else could. Trying to represent my own backyard, rather than running for Washington office, was compatible with the family life I was committed to, and it reconnected me with the most enjoyable chapters of my political past. The chances of winning in a 57-percent-Democratic district, while not guaranteed, were good.

But there were still considerable risks. I didn't know how much my "specter" still preceded me, causing reactions from discomfort to paranoia in the political establishment. Some Democrats in the legislature, at the urging of Republicans, considered abolishing the Forty-fourth Assembly District during reapportionment. Instead, they redesigned it, replacing left-liberal Venice voters with more conservative voters from Malibu and the Pacific Palisades. One Orange County Democrat, a conservative former Marine named Richard Robinson, bragged that the district was "Hayden-proofed." Many other Democrats opposed me in the primary. John Tunney endorsed my leading Democratic opponent. The building trades seized on the fact that Jane and I were remodeling a new house with non-union labor. (She had prevailed in our differences over taste and was supervising the creation of a much larger home in Santa Monica.) Union picket lines appeared outside our yard. Theirs was a political act; no one in Southern California used union labor in remodeling. Nevertheless, we switched to an all-union crew.

On the Republican side, meanwhile, it seemed that the party faithful regarded my candidacy as the Second Coming of Lucifer and the place to really draw the line against the sixties. When I reminded them that I was simply taking their advice to work within the system, they were not sympathetic. They sent mail to tens of thousands of Republican donors nationwide, warning that I was a communist, a traitor, and a diabolical revolutionary who had lowered rents in Santa Monica and was bent on using a State Assembly seat as a stepping-stone to the presidency. Young Americans for Freedom picketed and disrupted my events. Former President Ford, Governor Deukmejian, and actor Charlton Heston campaigned against me.

Meanwhile, I tried to run on the issues, promising to promote new technologies in the state's economy, incentives for genuine entrepreneurs, more employee involvement in decision making, an energy conservation program, more investment in the schools, and neighborhood-based crime prevention programs. My overall message was that compassion was being repressed in the Reagan era and that we needed to practice a "politics as if human beings mattered."

I soon realized that the election was nothing less than a referendum on Tom Hayden. Every inflammatory remark I ever made, usually distorted for heightened effect, was mailed out to the voters several times, and for weeks many of these alleged quotes—like "abolish private property"—appeared on giant billboards throughout the Westside of Los Angeles. Walter Mondale told me with humor that every time he campaigned in West Los Angeles that year, the billboards made him feel he was on a ticket with Lenin.

I was opposed in the Democratic primary by an assistant to the very popular Mayor Tom Bradley, a Jewish candidate who insinuated that I was pro-PLO and anti-Israel throughout the Jewish community, which constituted over 25 percent of the Democratic primary vote. There was no evidence for the charge; I had become closely involved with the Israelis in 1978 on joint solar-energy projects with California, and when asked by reporters during the campaign, Israeli officials themselves always described me as a friend. I struggled to ensure that local, even liberal Democratic officeholders, who worried that association with me might tarnish them, stayed neutral instead of backing my opponent. All the ghosts of the past, real or imagined, were resurrected and made fiercely alive among the 200,000 voters in the district. Violence and hate were in the air. Campaign spending went to historic highs; when the election was over, more than $1 million was spent on each side—over $300,000 of it by Jane.

Realizing that *I* was the issue, I campaigned accordingly. Sid Galanty and his partner, Bill Zimmerman, produced a television commercial in which Troy and I kissed Jane good-bye and drove downtown, where we were confronted by angry demonstrators shouting that I was a traitor. Though performed for the camera, it was a scene from the real world. With my arm wrapped around Troy, who was then nine years old, my voice said, "I'm not the same angry young man I used to be, but I still believe in change, in improving my community." The commercial ended with about twenty-five of Troy's school friends surprising me with HAYDEN FOR ASSEMBLY spelled out on individual placards they had painted (the *Y* in *assembly* was upside down).

Mostly, however, I campaigned the hard way. I knocked on about five thousand individual doors, introducing myself to voters and giving them my platform. I talked at about five hundred "house meetings," small gatherings of twenty-five or so neighbors where I could be questioned and tested on any subject. Jane walked precincts, too, shocking many voters at their doorstep. We created a volunteer network that could distribute ten thousand leaflets at doorsteps on a weekend and bring back a count of supporters (labeled #1s), waverers (#2s), and hostile voters (#3s). Thus identified, we would plan our strategy around turning out the #1s and #2s on election day.

About three weeks before the hotly contested primary, my sister Mary called to tell me that dad was in the hospital. He fell down at home, dislocating his hip. There were "complications." She didn't know what was wrong, but she thought I should come immediately.

He was strapped under a maze of tubes in the intensive care unit, but he was conscious and clear of mind. Esther was crying uncontrollably and couldn't go into the room. Mary, in training to be a nurse, sat near him watching the dials and graphs.

"Get me outa here," my father said. He was sure the hospital was making him worse. A good attitude, I thought. "Are you winning the election?"

"I think so, Dad."

"I want you to win, Tom."

"Thanks, Dad. It's a fight, but I'm doing my best."

"I want you to win, son." His eyes were clear and deep, his body thin and weak. I held his tired hand, noticing that his grip was like a small child's.

The medical staff couldn't give a prognosis. A lifetime of smoking, drinking, and no exercise was taking a deadly toll. They tried to stabilize him. He continued to complain that he wanted to sue the hospital.

Days passed with not much change in his condition. It looked as if nothing would happen for a while. I kissed him, asked him to hang on, and returned to Los Angeles for the last week of the primary. On the Friday before election day, my sister called. "He's dead." I flew back with Jane and Troy.

We buried him in Detroit on the morning of election day. In an emotional fog, we flew back to Los Angeles with my sister and one of her closest friends. Mary would represent my father on election night.

About midnight, the returns showed that I had won the primary by a six-point margin, solid but not impressive.

As a victory speech, I decided on a eulogy for my father:

> "Tonight marks the passing of generations in my family. . . . My father, who lived seventy-six years, gave me a commitment to learning, a love of children, a stubborn Irish will, a sense that things usually go wrong for the honest person, and an uncanny ability to wait in patience for largemouth bass.
>
> "I grew up in my father's image but in a new and very different America from the thirties. Where my father dropped out of college to work, I went to a university with middle-class security and

a hunger for new frontiers. Where the enemies of democracy had been Japanese militarism or German fascism, my generation saw democracy unfulfilled at home. . . . There was little authority to respect. The few who could inspire us were assassinated, and with their deaths came the death of hope itself. Millions of families were divided across a generation gap of noncommunicating—my father and I could not speak for over a decade.

"Then came a thaw in the political ice age, a democratic springtime in America. The Vietnam War ended. Repression was turned back. Watergate dirty tricks were exposed and defeated. The rebels and radicals of the sixties were vindicated on most counts. But years of confrontation had taken a toll on us, creating negativity, burn-out, the excesses of self-destructive extremism.

"I survived. In time, I won the inner peace that comes from realizing that patience and commitment, love and struggle are not opposites but are the foundation of balance. I learned to be a better human being through love, marriage, fatherhood.

"But a bleeding hole remained in my life—I needed to finally end the ruptures of the sixties by restoring my relationship with my father. It was not easy, because he was even more stubborn than I am. But I am happy to say that we succeeded in becoming a loving father and son again. . . . And we extended the generational cycle into the future, as he became a proud and happy grandfather. He remained a Republican—but a Republican populist who raged against the media image of his son. He wanted me to win tonight. . . .

"So I come here tonight from my father's funeral with a heavy heart, but a full one, with a greater sense of family responsibility than before, humbly mindful that there are more important things in life than political power, and knowing that this victory will only be meaningful if it helps improve the quality of existence of human beings as they pass through the briefness of their lives. . . . As the Bible admonishes, 'The day of our years are threescore and ten; and if by reason of strength they be fourscore years, yet is their strength labor and sorrow; for it is soon cut off, and we fly away. . . . So teach us to number our days, that we may apply our hearts unto wisdom [Psalm 90:10–12].'

"My father's spirit is with me and my family here tonight. Death is the parent of birth, birth is the parent of death. My father wanted to live for this night, but he had to die a proud supporter. Dad, may you rest in peace."

The general election in November was similar to the primary in its ugliness and tension. But I defeated my Republican opponent, an insurance salesman named William Hawkins, by nine points, 53–44 percent.

After the election, I visited the Sacramento State Capitol with the other new members of the legislature. It is a beautiful building with a gleaming white dome like the U.S. Congress, carefully restored to its original nineteenth-century façade. The speaker of the Assembly then (and now) was Willie Brown, a ten-term San Francisco veteran who himself had gone through the Bay Area sit-ins, the antiwar movement, the Panthers, and the McGovern campaign before winning the highest position of legislative leadership in Sacramento. He smiled broadly at me, extended his hand, and loudly said, "Welcome home."

That night, as we drove away from the brilliantly lit Capitol, Troy, who was staring out the window, exclaimed, "Just think—*we're* in there now."

I plunged into being an assemblyman. The California legislature is a full-time body which passes a forty-one-billion-dollar budget and over one thousand laws yearly. It is in session in Sacramento four days a week, eight months every year. A member has two offices, one in the district and another in the capital. A staff has averages about fifteen full-time dedicated personnel.

When I arrived at the Capitol, no one knew what to expect. A bevy of ultra-right Republicans demanded my ouster on charges of "treason." They instigated what became a three-million-dollar mail campaign nationally to force my ouster from the chamber. On the other hand, I received high marks for being a team player, doing my homework, defending my district, dressing appropriately, and not banging my shoe on the desk. One reporter even noted that I wore a wristwatch. I felt as if I were in a time warp, with most people looking at me through their own subconscious image of the sixties. From 1975 through 1982, newspaper headlines kept recycling the story that I was "moving into the mainstream." No matter my election margins, I apparently still wasn't there.

I found, however, that the legislature was open and businesslike, a place where even a freshman could speak and introduce meaningful legislation affecting people's lives. My first exciting moment came when I obtained two million dollars to restore a pier in Santa Monica damaged by winter storms. It was amazing how easy it was to accomplish something real.

With a conservative Republican governor like Deukmejian

holding the veto power, however, there were definite limits on what any Democrat could accomplish. Nevertheless, in my first term I was able to get fifteen bills signed into law, including a tax credit for solar energy and computer donations to public schools, a statewide "neighborhood watch" program, and an Agent Orange counseling program for Vietnam veterans.

I was selected as chairman of the policy committee overseeing higher education and began tackling the very issues of higher education that had obsessed me in Ann Arbor twenty-five years earlier. Three years later, I became chairman of the Labor and Employment Committee, where I could launch strategies for working women, child care, workplace safety, and greater workplace participation in economic decision making. On the environmental front, where the governor's veto was a roadblock, I turned to grass-roots ballot initiatives, for example, chairing the hard-fought but successful Proposition 65 campaign to keep toxic chemicals out of drinking-water supplies in 1986 and initiatives to close a nuclear power plant, stop pollution of Santa Monica Bay, build affordable housing and shelters for the homeless in 1988. Throughout, I was reelected to my Assembly seat, each time by increasing margins. And I commuted home virtually every night.

At the same time, my family life took an important new turn. In the summer of 1983, a friend called from Wisconsin extremely worried about my mother. Normally a private and secluded person, now she wasn't going out at all, the friend said, and in phone calls her voice sounded slurred, like that of a person who was drinking. It was possibly a stroke, she said. I picked up the phone in fear, wondering how my mother could keep her condition a secret from the thirty or more sisters, nieces, nephews, and friends she had in Oconomowoc. I reached her, and she said, in a distant and wobbly voice, not to worry. She never wanted anyone to worry about her and would retreat into a shell of pride if they tried. I asked her, however, to see her doctor immediately and to give me his phone number.

Soon it was clear that something was seriously wrong. She was occasionally disoriented, dangerously losing weight, and the doctor confirmed that she might have suffered a slight stroke in addition to her emphysema. I told her I was coming to take her out of Wisconsin and rented a plane to fly me immediately to Oconomowoc. There, with the help of a sister and a friend,

I picked her up, carried her straight to the plane, and raced back to Los Angeles. A tiny person to begin with, she was losing weight to diarrhea, drifting into delirium, behaving like a baby in my arms.

Back in Los Angeles, we began a three-year rest and treatment program. Her heart was gradually weakening, but doctors told us she could still live a quality life. A proud and independent woman all her life, she bridled emotionally at the prospect of dependency. After my parents' divorce, she had worked in the Royal Oak film library without missing a day for twenty-five years. Her Social Security benefits were meager, but she was a penny pincher. Mindful of the Depression, she kept a few thousand dollars in three separate Oconomowoc banks, the funds wrapped in tinfoil for protection against fire. She proudly drove her own car and did her own shopping. She didn't want anyone taking care of her. But in the face of reality, she slowly relented. Her condition improved to the point where she could take walks outside, read the papers, listen to twenty-four-hour radio news (she had never quite accepted television), and hold forth over coffee with Shirlee Fonda and other visitors. She lived with us for three years, with the help of caring nurses, in a little bedroom off the kitchen.

There were now three generations of my family under one roof. Occasional tensions would arise, for example, if my mother disapproved of one of Vanessa's friends, or if she felt Troy wasn't dressed warmly enough. But we learned to live together as a family. My mother never turned her all-news radio station off, and she would inform me morning and night of the latest political news and, more frequently, reports of the death of celebrities. She adored Troy and Vanessa and asked for frequent confidential reports on how they were doing in school. She watched Troy in Little League, and when I started playing baseball again after some thirty years, she was the only member of the family who thought it normal. She would smile from the kitchen table and say in her eccentric way, "Bye-bye, Tom-Tom," when I left in my uniform on Saturday mornings. I was becoming her "parent" in terms of responsibilities, but her presence constantly and vividly brought up images my own childhood. God, I realized I missed my father's voice in the stands.

She died in 1986 of heart failure in the midst of yet another political campaign. We returned to bury her in Wisconsin, on a pretty hillside in Oconomowoc, the town little changed since my teenage summers there, amid a funeral gathering of friends and relatives, descendants of Duceys and Garitys who had lived there for generations, undisturbed, and would continue to do so, I suppose, for generations to come. After her name on the marble tombstone, next to that of her brother, who died in World War II, near her father, who died in the 1920 cannery explosion, I had inscribed MAY HER PROUD SPIRIT LIVE.

Even in grief, I knew I was a lucky man. We all want to make our parents proud, to make loving peace with them, but how hard it was in the sixties. As marriage and family brought a completeness to my life, my parents and I were blessed in a completeness at death. There is little worse than separation and death without a last look, a last embrace, a last word. So many suffered without that final connectedness through the violent divides of our time. After a long torment, I was blessed by reunion.

As I wandered across that Wisconsin hillside where my mother lay buried, I felt a form of personal relief. I saw the fields where I played as a boy, the railroad tracks I walked along, the blue lakes and tiny dams where I caught bass, the green yards where I threw the ball. It was all still there, beckoning me. The harmonies of my early life, disrupted by the civil wars of the sixties, were healing and reappearing, like blades of grass after a fire, in my middle years.

Perhaps there comes a time for all people when they feel the end of being young and the definite onset of those middle years. So it was for me after my parents died. I experienced the very real sense of being unfettered from a past, looking back instead of feeling part of it. It was not that I wanted to escape from the past; far from it. I could see it, accept it, reconnect with it for the first time as an older, more mature human being. Wandering through that Wisconsin town, having seen my mother's family, I felt a quickening interest in revisiting certain people and places—from Chicago to Mississippi and Port Huron—that were crucial to my journey through the sixties—before it became too late. From that point on, my ability and commitment to write about my life and times were created. It was no longer an intellectual project, but a personal need.

The forces of circumstance were cooperative. One day soon

after, Jeremy Kagan, a film director acquaintance of mine, called to say that Home Box Office (HBO) had agreed to finance a feature-length reenactment of the Chicago trial. Jeremy, a bearded, energetic, compassionate director, had been carrying the script around unsuccessfully for seven years. Now, he said excitedly, there was renewed interest in the sixties, and he wanted to see me about his project.

When we met in my office a few weeks later, I was eager to cooperate. But Jeremy seemed anxious about something, and I asked him what was on his mind.

"Frankly," he said, "I wondered if you would want all this past stuff brought up or whether you felt it could hurt you politically."

I laughed. "Jeremy, the past is always with me whether I like it or not. I hope you'll give people a chance for an honest and deeper understanding than the images they have in their heads. Besides, I thought you told me there's a new interest in the sixties, so why not?"

The HBO production was filmed over a two-week period at a studio in Glendale. I found it hard to stay away. Jeremy sent me the script, which was mainly based on the courtroom proceedings, and I found myself reliving the late sixties as I reviewed it. Because it condensed a six-month trial into a two-hour drama, I felt there was a tendency to mythologize the intense courtroom disruptions at the expense of the slower but significant clash of argument, but it had the ring of truth. Equally interesting, Jeremy wanted to interview each of the conspiracy defendants in order to splice a past and present commentary into the film. This provided the occasion for the first reunion of the defendants in fifteen years. Not only did Jeremy want us for separate interviews, but to come together for the final day of filming.

I took Troy to the filming on two occasions. It was an unexpected shock to enter the studio with him and to find myself thrust back in time, to an occasion in 1970 when I told Judge Hoffman that I regretted not being able to have a child. "Dad, Dad, there *you* are," Troy exclaimed. Coming toward us was thirty-year-old actor Brian Benben, who played me. With his longish hair and green fatigue jacket, I was told that he bore an exact resemblance to the Tom Hayden of 1969. He said he was delighted to meet the person he was portraying, and we discussed the feel of the courtroom. The other actors playing the defendants, attorneys, spectators, and Judge Hoffman were equally authentic in their appearance, creating in me a sense that I was a dead person revisiting his past, strangely able to reappear to discuss his retrospective feelings. It was moving, but not all fun. With a knot in my stomach, I watched over ten rehearsals of the chaining and gagging of Bobby Seale. Troy, who is a conventional teenager despite his quite unconventional parents, made only two remarks that day, both of which stuck with me. "You guys were really crazy," he said, shaking his head at Jerry and Abbie's antics. And a little later: "That judge is really an asshole." It seemed a fair summary of the Chicago trial.

Finally, the day came when the other defendants would arrive en masse. I was expectant, but quite tense. I had not seen any of them, except John Froines, for several years, and we had not parted the closest of friends. Now we were middle-aged men, no longer the notorious targets of the Justice Department but the subjects of an HBO movie. America has a funny way of turning even its outlaws into minor celebrities, I mused, as I entered the studio. And there they were, my old co-defendents, mingled in a cafeteria with their actor counterparts, offering a striking image of then and now. There were broad smiles and hugs offered by one and all, and I knew at once that our past tensions would be suspended during this collective reminder of what we had stood for and what we had endured. Only Dave Dellinger was missing among the defendants; fittingly, he was on trial in Washington for demonstrating against United States aid to the Nicaraguan *contras*. Both Kunstler and Weinglass were away making courtroom appearances.

The defendants posed happily for photos with our counterparts, watched a few hours of shooting, and sat around informally catching up with each other's lives. It interested me that at this point in our lives there was less testing of each other's political principles—perhaps because there was little at stake—and more inquiring into each other's well-being. Bobby Seale seemed to be happily busy as a doctoral student at Temple University in Philadelphia, where he was building a historical archive on the Black Panthers and still speaking at local schools. Lee Weiner was a political consultant in Washington, and John Froines was a public health professor at UCLA. Jerry Rubin, after a decade of personal therapies, was now a New York yuppie and ran a "networking salon" for young businesspeople. Abbie Hoffman, after a long spell as a fugitive from drug charges, published a manifesto against urine testing and was recently acquitted with Amy Carter and others on charges of obstructing campus recruiting by the CIA. His trial attorney had been Leonard Weinglass. Even Rennie, whom I felt the most anxiety at seeing again, seemed to have achieved a new balance in his life. He was no longer with the guru, he told me, and was trying to "forgive" himself for that period of his life. Yet, he still believed in miracles and was looking forward to another "special time" like the sixties.

As I listened to everyone talking animatedly around the table, I sensed that no one wanted to be particularly judgmental or competitive, although the old tensions were not completely gone. We had traveled our separate ways. It would be easy enough to question if some had departed too much from our radical past or if others were frozen in time, but what would be the point? We had been chosen not for our consistency but almost by accident, to stand up for our beliefs at a certain moment of history. For all our imperfections, we had met the challenge honorably enough and prevailed over the massive power of the government. Richard Nixon and John Mitchell were gone. Julius Hoffman was deceased. Thomas Foran, having failed in an Illinois gubernatorial bid, was practicing law with Richard Schultz in Chicago; both men refused to consult with Home Box Office. Those who tried to imprison us had gone to jail themselves.

I laughed. "After all we've been through, it may seem like a small blessing, but I'm glad we're still alive and well," I blurted out. "Right on," said Bobby. "And maybe what began then is not over," Rennie chimed in. Jerry eagerly wrote his home phone number for me on a stock offering in his new company. Abbie started talking about how strange it was to be a "Jewish road warrior," trying to build a new student movement at age fifty. We all applauded Dave and worried whether he was taking care of himself. Abbie's teenage son, named america, watched the old Conspiracy with what seemed like fascination and amusement.

I was getting a headache from the day's experience. It was time to go before creeping nostalgia or former tensions took over. I was both elated and sad over what we had done together

and what had eluded us. Neither martyred nor fully triumphant, we were what we were: participants in a television special at middle age, a political version of *The Big Chill*. We
promised to stay in touch.

After reliving Chicago, I turned next toward the place and
person that evoked my earliest inspirations of the sixties. I called
Casey and asked if she would meet me in Mississippi. She was
living in Atlanta and, when I phoned, said she had been thinking about me. "It's time to become friends again," she said, "and
sort out what happened to us all." She had written a poem which
she promptly sent me, called "Re-integration." It recalled and
compared our lives:

> *I am carrying the baby*
> *while Chicago burns*
> *I am saying my mantra*
> *while Vietnam explodes*
> *I'm making an altar instead of a book,*
> *a poem instead of a law*
> *No point to make, trying for one-pointedness,*
> *colorless, crystalline, honoring the lucidity*
> *of the recent past.*
> *I'm remembering beds in Atlanta,*
> *New York, Wisconsin, Tennessee,*
> *Motels, apartments*
> *Pillows and sheets and blankets*
> *The snow through white curtains in the early*
> *morning light,*
> *Colors just beginning, emerging from the*
> *night.*

I met her in the Jackson, Mississippi, airport. Casey looked
like Annie Hall, wearing a designer safari jacket over a long
white shirt, flowing skirt, and the brown shoes of an elf. "I'm
still beautiful, just a little older," she said mirthfully. We rented
a car and kept filling each other in with information about our
lives as we drove; it had been almost five years since we'd seen
each other. Her life was more together than it had been in a long
time, she said, though she missed her two kids—both in their
late teens—in New York. Restless for new challenges, she had
written an excellent introduction to a recent SNCC memoir by

Mary King, her old roommate, then some poems, and now she pondered writing a novel. We talked gently about our breakup. I admitted how unprepared for responsibility I was at the time; she recalled that we couldn't even decide on our wedding vows. She spoke of many unfortunate involvements with men who threatened her independence. One broke her ribs when she was meditating because she told him she needed her own space and another time burned all of her writings. Several men took her camera equipment, tools of a budding profession. She talked of how children from families with histories of alcoholism, like her own, were conditioned to give way to someone else's need. Having chosen a very private life, she admitted missing a public, and still looked for ways to link the spiritual and the political as sides of a single coin.

We talked of our interior journeys until we became caught up in the darkening land along the interstate outside of Jackson. We were heading toward the Delta as a flat sun descended over the still-vast fields of cotton. All the old eerie feelings returned.

Our first destination was Mayersville, a community of 350 people about a hundred miles northwest of Jackson, a former port on the Mississippi River where African slaves were unloaded in the New World. As we drove, we noticed mechanical cotton harvesters, large vehicles with metal limbs and lights for the night that looked like science-fiction creations. They had displaced black field workers who, finding no other jobs, migrated from the Delta northward. The black population of the region had dropped from 550,000 in 1960 to perhaps 400,000. Sixty percent of the Delta's blacks remained poor by official definitions. Mayersville, the county seat of Issaquena County, where blacks have always been a majority, was no exception to the pattern of economic depression.

The bright spot of Mayersville was its mayor, Unita Blackwell, one of the first local people to join the SNCC workers in the early sixties. People like Mrs. Blackwell persevered, through violence and isolation, after Atlantic City, after SNCC was gone. Once the 1965 Voting Rights Act was passed, they registered up to 80 percent of all blacks in the Delta. Several hamlets like Mayersville were soon incorporated, thus becoming able to levy local taxes, build sewers, and set up utility districts. In the process, Mrs. Blackwell was elected mayor, the first black woman mayor in the state's history.

We found her in a modest single-story brick home at the end

of a narrow road across from a cotton field. She was living alone, surrounded by friends. Her son Jeremiah was in the navy in Long Beach. "We all went through divorce in the civil rights movement." She smiled at Casey. Behind this house was another one, a fading, unpainted wooden structure overgrown with bushes on all sides. It was all that remained of the freedom house of the sixties, where Mrs. Blackwell and untold SNCC workers lived, worked, and slept in fear. Across the way were two impressive single-story buildings under construction with federal funds—housing units for twenty-six elderly poor people. The bricks of all these houses were a matter of great pride; for decades, federal housing agencies had been unwilling to finance brick units for Mississippi blacks. Mrs. Blackwell also wanted to restore the freedom house, perhaps declare it a historical site.

Mrs. Blackwell was delighted to see us. She had aged little, though she complained about gaining weight. A dark commanding woman with a radiant smile, she seemed pleased with her accomplishments and still enthused over organizing. One difference we noticed at once was that the former climate of terror under a one-party state was dissipated. Political life was normalized. Not only was Mrs. Blackwell a local mayor, but her phone was ringing with calls from political allies—black and white—when we took our leave.

We drove north from Mayersville to Greenville, a Delta city of a few thousand residents on the Mississippi River Road. We checked into a motel on the river, asking for two separate rooms under the name Hayden, to the puzzlement of the receptionist. The next morning I took a run along the Mississippi while Casey photographed the young black hostess in the restaurant. As I jogged along the river's muddy and swirling bank, I was suddenly overwhelmed by phobias from the past. Where I came upon dead fish bobbing in the shallow water, I kept seeing images of mutilated blacks. Back at the motel, over a breakfast of eggs and grits, when we asked what the young hostess remembered of the civil rights movement, she said, "Nothing." She had been too young. I wanted to tell her of my nightmare vision, but it would have made no sense to her. I had not adjusted to the changes in the South, while she took for granted the routine of her job. She even seemed puzzled that Casey was taking pictures of her. Like many others we met, she had no memory of what had transpired in her city twenty-five years before.

Then we talked with the leaders of the two Delta-wide organizations located nearby, Mississippi Action for Community Education (MACE) and the Delta Foundation, both of which grew out of the SNCC period. These two agencies had struggled in the post-sixties era to train a network of local black leaders and attract economic investments to the forsaken region. MACE, in fact, grew out of meetings and urgings by Bob Moses, Unita Blackwell, and Fannie Lou Hamer, who worried that the early movement would leave nothing behind.

In a large, sparse storefront office we talked with thirty-eight-year-old Larry Farmer, who was a teenager during the "old days." A big, easygoing man who was a professional baseball prospect before deciding to stay in the Delta, Farmer wistfully told of his "grandma coming back from SNCC meetings, saying, 'Those people are saying crazy things like blacks folks can vote.' " Without the civil rights movement, he added, "I don't know what kind of guy I'd have been." His father migrated to Milwaukee and worked two jobs for twenty years to support his large family. Now all of that generation born in the North, he said, were on public assistance. "When we started, we were trying to get them on, now we're trying to get them off," he lamented. He worried that the "new South is like the old North," with problems of drugs and teenage pregnancy emerging in places like Greenville. Nor was segregation really over. "Now we live under a democratized version of apartheid," he said, with most whites retreating from the public sector into private business and residential enclaves.

Yet I found a strong trace of the buoyant energy in Larry Farmer and Unita Blackwell that always seemed more alive to me in the rural areas of the South than anywhere else. Farmer laughingly recounted a MACE slogan: "We have done so much with so little that we are now qualified to do anything with nothing." Indeed there was a profound change in the Mississippi political order at the beginning of the eighties, an aftershock of the civil rights movement. The lily-white Democratic party did not last for long after the 1964 FDP challenge; its demise began in 1968 and was completed by 1976. Within five years, a bright young group of white moderates had been brought into office replacing the old diehards. And most significantly, by the mid-eighties, 20 blacks had been elected to the state legislature out of 172 members, 52 of 410 county supervisors were black, and no politician, we were told, could be elected to statewide office without the black vote.

"Now everybody on the street talks politics, that's the simplest way to explain the change," said Bennie Thompson, a 1968 Tougaloo College graduate who now serves as a supervisor in Hinds County, covering eight thousand voters in the Jackson area in addition to being a Democratic National Committee member. We visited Bennie in a Muslim restaurant, Ummi's, on Farish Street in Jackson, near the site of the old SNCC headquarters. Signs of urban decay and hopelessness, northern-style, abounded on the dark street, but Bennie too was far from war-weary. While considering himself more radical than most politicians in the state, he took a long view of progress and was hopeful about the future of black-white statewide coalitions. He felt that Jesse Jackson was a powerfully positive asset in mobilizing the black community; on the negative side, he too worried about a "loss of memory" of the sixties in the state.

We also interviewed thirty-nine-year-old Secretary of State Richard Molpus, one of the circle of emerging statewide leaders. It was the first time I'd ever been in a white person's home or driven casually through a white neighborhood in Mississippi. Molpus is a native of Neshoba County, where the three civil rights workers were killed in 1964, and he recalled for us his teenage memories of seeing an elderly black man beaten before his eyes. Instead of leaving Mississippi for more tolerant vistas, Molpus remained to try to claim modern, moderate leadership from the older generations of racists. He spoke movingly of the massive effort in 1981–82 to enact new laws finally establishing kindergarten, compulsory public schools, and better teacher's pay in the state, a genuine public crusade by blacks as well as whites. It not only succeeded, but in the process, it overthrew the legislative speaker of three decades, an iron-fisted good old boy from Mrs. Blackwell's home county.

Finally, we drove ninety minutes south down the interstate to McComb, as I had twenty-five years before with Bob Moses and Paul Potter. Here my emotion and memory became so overwhelmed with images of the past that it was difficult to recognize the contemporary city as we arrived. My twenty-five-year-old image had been filled with the eighties Americana of fast-food franchises and video parlors; the population had almost doubled to fourteen thousand but the white, residential parts of the city still bespoke a soothing timeless charm. At first, I had a difficult time finding the viaduct that one passed through, and the railroad tracks one crossed over, to enter the black community. But suddenly I was there, feeling an old vulnerability as I slowly passed through its still-narrow streets.

At 222 De Soto Street, on a short block of a few residences and stores, was Noble's Cleaners, where the SNCC workers found their first protection in McComb twenty-six years earlier. Ernest Noble, still strong but slightly stooped after so many years, was inside where I expected him, since Saturday was always his busy day. We fell into conversation immediately, while his daughter took care of the steady trickle of surprised customers dropping off their clothes.

While Casey snapped photos, Noble showed us the clothing rack where Bob Moses hid twenty-five years before. When Bob first came here, Noble recalled vividly, no one would give him a place to meet. Noble remembered Bob with his shirt ripped and his scalp covered with blood. "It was strange. He came down from New York. He didn't have to be here. He would have died for us. But you couldn't give Bob five dollars for a steak sandwich. He wouldn't take anything from us."

Noble drove with us to two of the homes that were bombed, one of which remains in disrepair, and to Mrs. Quinn's South of the Border restaurant, which had also been bombed, leaving one of her children deaf. Then, at my urging, he directed us a few blocks to the high school where Paul Potter and I were beaten up in 1961. To my surprise, the pleasant-looking facility was now a junior high school for black and white students from all over McComb.

Having seen all this, I asked if anything really had improved in McComb. Mr. Noble drew in his breath and replied, "Yes and no." The schools were somewhat integrated. There was no police brutality or fear of violence. Registering to vote was easy. Two of the five county supervisors were black. But jobs were on the decline overall, he said, and young people were moving away. In short, dignity was recognized, but development was down.

After thanking him, I decided to drop by the police station before leaving town. An orange brick building, it sits on a slight rise in the white community, overlooking the blacks. I asked for the watch commander, and was shortly introducing myself to Robert Dunaway, a tall, slender, moustached officer whose pitch-black uniform and dangling weapons kept reminding me of a dreaded past.

Describing myself as the Tom Hayden who was "arrested and had the shit kicked out of him" twenty-five years earlier, I asked after Chief George Guy and learned that he had died a few years previously. Dunaway spoke in a deep, clipped drawl and looked away from me as we chatted. He said he had "heard about the times they were blowing up churches and such," but those were over. He insisted there was no more of "what they used to call police brutality." Then out of nowhere, he raised both arms and said angrily, "If you ask me, it was those damn Yankees who created all that trouble."

"Wait a minute," I replied amusedly, "you're talking to one of them now." He looked away, smiling slightly.

"Here's all I want to know—is it fairer with blacks having a vote?" I asked.

"Yes," he said, nodding. "It is."

"And is it therefore more peaceful?" Yes, he agreed again.

"Thank you for your time," I said, extending my hand. Then we were out the door.

Before leaving town, I looked up Carl Hayes, my assailant of 1961, in the phone book, presuming he would still be in town, and dialed his number. I wanted to invite him for coffee and ask if he remained proud of beating up myself and Paul. After three rings, a woman's voice answered and informed me that Carl would not be back for a few hours. Who shall I say called? she wanted to know.

"Tell him Tom Hayden was passing through McComb and wanted to see him about the old days," I said. Then I drove with Casey back to the Jackson airport.

Casey stopped to see what remained of another old freedom house where she, Mary King, and other SNCC workers stayed near Tougaloo College. She found a dilapidated structure with barred windows and a yard full of rusted car bodies. When she knocked on the door, it was answered by an ancient, toothless man with his pants unzipped and a key chain hanging out of his fly with a Coca-Cola medallion on it.

The homeless of the eighties were living in the freedom houses of the sixties.

I left Casey and Mississippi an hour later. "It has been a trip," she said, laughing. We embraced, promising to stay in touch. Casey's fiftieth birthday was coming soon, and I asked how she felt. "Great," she responded, saying the number fifty had a solid feel. "It gives you a kind of license to say you know some things about life." She said she wanted to be known as a person recovering.

The highs and lows of the day churned inside me as I boarded the plane. Looking at the newspaper headlines, I discovered that President Reagan was encountering difficulty in winning U.S. Senate approval of his Supreme Court nominee, Robert Bork, who was widely viewed as a defender of "states' rights" in the days when that label protected southern segregation. Bork's problem, the media noted, was with the senators from the South who were elected by the black vote. There was a straight historical line between the registration drives of long ago and the rejection of a judicial nominee who appeared to favor turning back the clock. I smiled gratefully and fell immediately asleep during the flight north.

Around the same time, I was drawn back to Port Huron, to visit the spot where we gave voice to our dreams. Not wanting to go alone, I called Mildred Jeffrey, Sharon's mother, the UAW leader who had secured the site for the SDS conference in 1962. The conference center at Port Huron had belonged to the AFL-CIO, built by union women in the thirties. It was a favorite spot of Millie's, I knew, even before its use by her daughter's generation. Millie was delighted by my call. We had stayed in occasional contact over the years. She remained a leading figure in the UAW, women's organizations, and the national Democratic party, and she loved to be working on common issues with Jane and myself. She was ecstatic that Jane had filmed *The Dollmaker*, an epic novel of Detroit in the thirties by Michigan writer Harriet Arnow. A spry and aggressive seventy-year-old, Millie asked me to pick her up on the steps of the Detroit Museum of Arts at Wayne State University, where she served as a trustee and lived in a condominium. When I arrived, she was already sitting on the steps, a floppy sun hat covering her white hair. She eagerly pulled me out of the car and led me into the museum. "You have to see the Diego Rivera murals," she exclaimed, bouncing along. "They are fantastic, the jewel of the campus."

I was quickly surrounded by a panoramic mural filled with scenes and shapes, grotesque and uplifting, of working people in the fiery cauldron of the thirties. The murals also recalled labor's greatest era, the time when Millie had started toward a life of social activism. Her generation built the UAW and the Michigan Democratic party and saw their children begin a new wave of change in the sixties.

Alongside the achievements, however, Millie had suffered. Her leader and close friend, Walter Reuther, died in a plane crash in 1970. Her other national leaders—the Kennedys and King—were gone as well. The labor movement had weakened in membership and clout. The auto economy had slackened, and Detroit was reeling from unemployment, racism, and crime. Her daughter's generation had the same hopeful beginning and ambiguous legacy, a return of history's wheel. Sharon had continued in her mother's footsteps as an immensely skilled organizer through most of the sixties, then had joined the "human potential" movement in a reaction to what she felt was the neglect of her internal life. Now, Millie told me, Sharon was married to a highly successful crystal jeweler in Marin County, California, and running local seminars on leadership and group process. One of their cut crystals was going into the *Guinness Book of World Records*. It wasn't how Millie once imagined the future, I supposed, but there was a tone of loving pride and acceptance as she talked about her daughter. I also marveled at how Millie's social commitment was virtually effervescent; on this day, for example, we took with us Ann Arbor State Senator Lana Pollock, whose upcoming campaign for U.S. Congress was the most current focus of Millie's political enthusiasm.

The roads north to Port Huron were wide open, and we arrived in less than two hours. Twenty-five years before, it had been dark when I arrived for the Port Huron convention, so I had never seen the town by light of day. This time we stopped in town to stroll around. I went into a sporting goods store and purchased high school athletic shirts emblazoned with the logo *Port Huron Big Reds*. At Millie's direction, we proceeded about ten miles north of the town, looking for the old camp where the Port Huron convention was held. Millie, getting more excited, was sure it was just ahead, but I kept pulling into gas stations and fast-food franchises to ask if there was a "labor camp" somewhere ahead. Finally we found the site, now redesignated as a state park, and we turned off a newly constructed ramp. After parking, we crossed over a bridge toward the site.

At first I recognized nothing. There were neat cement sidewalks, brick rest rooms, and a small sandy beach overlooking the

still-majestic coastline of Lake Huron. On a hunch, I turned left
at the beach, and walked up the shoreline through the trees. In
two minutes I came to what felt like familiar territory, a sandy
path shaded by overhanging trees, with small circular groves on
both sides, like a natural chapel. No one was there. I stood alone,
drawing in the memories, then walked a few yards on. To my
left in a small clearing was a park ranger vehicle, with the ranger
reading behind the wheel. I approached him.

"Hello, officer. I wonder if you might help me. My name is
Tom Hayden, and about twenty-five years ago somewhere
around here we founded an organization named Students for a
Democratic Society, and we held a convention here to write a
statement. . . ."

His eyes lifted from a notepad, looked carefully at me, and
then he smiled.

"You're at the spot," he confirmed, introducing himself as a
history teacher at Port Huron's Northern High (the Big Reds).

"Where are the conference buildings?" I asked.

"Oh, they came down years ago. All that's left are the pipes,"
he said, pointing to a rusted brown pipe running along the
beach until it disappeared into the lake waters.

"Does anyone know what happened here?" I asked curiously.

"For a while, some of my students at Northern were interested, and they visited here to feel part of what happened. But
not much lately. Students are more reactionary these days, I
think," he answered.

I stayed a few minutes more in the glade, walked along the
water's edge, and for a souvenir picked up a smooth rock with
a shell protruding from it. I was moved by being back; but when
I asked Millie, strolling through the softly lapping waves, how
she felt, she replied only, "Sad." Lana too said she felt a sense
of loss.

That night I visited my sister, and her new husband, Doug
Frey, who were starting a life in Grosse Pointe Woods. The
month before, I had stood as best man at their wedding, in place
of my father. She was twenty-five now, a talented nurse, and he
was an accountant whiz like my father. I needed to borrow some
socks, and they were understanding. I was heading for the thirti-
eth reunion of my senior class in Royal Oak, and I needed some
dress socks. Properly attired, I drove along Woodward Avenue,
through the ravaged ghetto of Detroit, past my place of birth,

images of Newark flickering through my head. Twelve miles out of Detroit, I reached the boundaries of Royal Oak and took a right onto Main Street. In a few minutes, I was passing my old high school. The baseball field was grown over, uncared for in the summer, but otherwise it looked unchanged from thirty years before. Three blocks farther away, I came to my old house, which looked much smaller than my childhood memory. I thought of knocking on the door, but decided against it. I wheeled the car toward my mother's old office at the school board and just behind it to the old Red Run Country Club, where the reunion was under way.

As I entered, someone was leading some two hundred people in a prayerful silence "for our classmates who have gone to their graves before us." My God, I thought, how old are we? I was relieved in a few minutes to learn that only six of our class of five hundred had passed on. I stared at a disorienting scene from the fifties, a pleasant banquet room filled with hundreds of people, at once intimate and foreign to me. In a few moments, however, I found a table full of my oldest friends, looking not much different than they had in 1957, carrying on as if it were lunchtime in our senior year. There was Jim Lau, my best friend and coeditor of *The Daily Smirker*, with his wife, Val. He was running a television studio on the Michigan State campus. There was Roberta, the subject of my first short story, still mysteriously appealing, a substitute teacher in town ("What else can you do if you don't know what to do?" she asked). There was Hal, a writer and counseling teacher at the University of Iowa. There was Shirley, who went from high school to Ann Arbor with me, raising a family on a farm, a radical ecologist, worrying whether I'd become too conservative in political office. There was Dave McKercher, my old tennis partner turned local businessman, giving me a welcome-back hug. There was Bobby Inman, the hero of the baseball team, flown in from Oregon because his father had a stroke ("You never know at this point in life," he said). There was Lynne, the only fundamentalist Christian of all my friends, who had once taken me to a Billy Graham revival meeting, now a writer in cosmopolitan Boston. There was Dick Sisler, remembering Royal Oak as a place with little anti-Semitism, exchanging baseball cards with me. My old girlfriend, Anne Grimm, was president of the chamber of commerce and Royal Oak's "citizen of the year." There were my former coaches, my teachers, the big men on campus, and it all came down to this: No one checked hairlines or income levels or divorces or partisan labels as much as they asked about family and health and happiness. There was real caring, real values, each for the other, as we moved toward and beyond our maturity in life. Partisan labels and stereotypes didn't seem to matter as much as caring about the quality of each other's lives. For me it felt like a return, not of everyone's favorite son, but not a prodigal one either, just a native son. I hadn't expected it, and I left several hours later exhilarated and satisfied.

I drove to Ann Arbor late that night, as I had many times before on humid and stormy summer nights. I thought about the day, my sister, my hometown, Port Huron.

This life was organic. The buildings at Port Huron had disappeared, but the yearnings of youth recorded there still remained alive, like spirits in Irish legends. I could feel them in the trees, in the paths, waiting for renewal. They were in the imaginations of my high school classmates who spoke the language of understanding, acceptance, reconciliation. The change was slow but secure, gradual but real. I felt at home again and waited expectantly for a new generation.

20. Epilogue

Looking back from life's mid-passage, what did the generation of the sixties achieve? What does it mean today?

By the most measurable standards, we accomplished more than we expected, more than most generations ever accomplish. Consider the most obvious:

- Students led the civil rights movement, which destroyed a century-old segregation system and which politically enfranchised twenty million blacks.
- Students were the backbone of the antiwar movement, which forced our government to abandon its policies in Vietnam and the nation to reconsider the Cold War.
- Because of student criticism, most universities retreated from their traditional paternalism toward an acceptance of active student participation in decision making.
- Movement activists were the key factor in making Lyndon Johnson withdraw from the presidency in 1968 and in transforming the political rules that permitted reformers to prevail in the Democratic party, which then endorsed "participatory democracy" in its 1972 platform.
- The same movement was conceded the eighteen-year-old vote by the 1970s.
- These movements were direct catalysts for the reemergence of the women's movement, the birth of environmentalism, and other diverse causes.

In short, we opened up closed systems. From Georgia and Mississippi to the South as a whole, from Newark and Chicago to the cities of the North, from the 1965 Vietnam teach-ins to the 1973 War Powers Act, from the Democratic convention of 1968 to that of 1972, there was a steady evolution from patterns of exclusion toward greater citizen participation in basic decisions.

More generally, the New Left fostered a vision that gradually took hold throughout much of society. At the center of that vision was a moral view of human beings, "ordinary people" in the process of history, a view which held that systems should be designed for human beings and not the other way around. The dignity of the individual in this perspective could only be realized through active citizenship. That in turn required a society of citizens, or a democracy of participation, where individuals had a direct voice in the making of decisions about their own lives. We were expressing a rising dissatisfaction with all institutions, even liberal and expressly humane ones, that absorbed power into their hierarchies. Instead of "taking power," we imagined creating the new power out of the raw material of apathy. At the same time, new measurements of excellence, such as the quality of life and personal relationships, were to take on greater significance than external status symbols and material monuments, in both our lives and the existence of our country.

These perceptions and values are an ongoing legacy of our generation. They do not always prevail in our culture or politics today, nor are they always recognized as arising from the sixties. Yet their enduring and widening impact can be seen in a variety of ways. Enlightened business and labor viewpoints now concur that humane treatment of the worker, including participation in decision making, is not only an ethical good, but a plus for productivity as well. More broadly, the survey researcher Daniel Yankelovich, in his book, *New Rules* concluded that

> the campus upheavals of the sixties gave us the first premonitory sign that the plates of American culture, after decades of stability, had begun to shift. . . . Then in the seventies the public as a whole began to experience them and the mass reappraisal of American life values was launched.

The Yankelovich study concluded that the mainstream American goal is "to build a more productive economy and at the same time a society in which the cravings of the spirit as well as material well-being can be satisfied."

These findings were also reflected in an extraordinary work of social science, *Habits of the Heart*, published by a UC Berkeley team of researchers in 1985. One of their purposes was to review and revive the nineteenth-century French writer, Alexis de Toqueville, whose observations in *Democracy in America* in some ways foreshadowed the theme of participatory democracy. De Toqueville celebrated the town meetings and voluntary associations that constituted the rich political core of early nineteenth-century American society and warned of the dangers of rampant individualism, under which participation could atrophy and be replaced by imperial forms of rule. The authors of *Habits of the Heart*, responding to the resurgent individualism of the religious right of the eighties, cited local chapters of the Campaign for Economic Democracy among the many representative efforts at restoring an emphasis on democracy at the community level, noting that "the morally concerned social movement, informed by republican and biblical sentiments, has stood us in good stead in the past and may still do so again."

These conclusions and many others like them represent nothing less than the maturing of the awkward formulations of *The Port Huron Statement* into the cultural vocabulary of the mainstream of American life.

The logical question then is why the New Left did not succeed in building an organized and permanent leftist presence on the American political spectrum? Why did we produce so few political leaders? Why did we, who were so able to shake existing institutions, leave so little behind? Part of me inclines to the view of the New Left's better administrative leaders, like Paul Booth and Richie Rothstein, that our profound distrust of leadership and structure doomed us to failure on the level of political organization.

But the American political system is inhospitable to third parties, isolating them before gradually absorbing their ideas and activists into the two-party system. The most that could have been organized out of the New Left might have been an "adult" SDS, a kind of American Civil Liberties Union for social justice. Of course, without the Kennedy assassinations the history of our generation would have been different, and I believe most of the New Left would have found itself politically involved as part of a new governing coalition by the end of the sixties, just as Millie Jeffrey's generation became linked with the politics of the New Deal. But it was not to be. Instead, in Jack Newfield's summary phrase, we became "might have beens."

In the end, most of the sixties generation was not narrowly political. Most were not interested in attaining office but in changing life-styles. They were not so interested in being opinion makers as in changing the climate of opinion. Most felt personally ambiguous or distrustful of ambition and power and lacked the qualities that carried others into political careers. They were more likely to become professors (Todd Gitlin, Bill Ayers, Dick Flacks, John Froines, Bob Ross), labor leaders (Karen Nussbaum, Richie Rothstein, Paul Booth), social service advocates (Vivian Rothstein, Mary Varela, Casey Hayden), lawyers (Dan Siegel, Anne Weills, Bernardine Dohrn and six other former members of the Weather Underground), filmmakers (Bruce Gilbert, Paula Weinstein, Mark Rosenberg, Thom Mount), or therapists and counselors (Connie Brown, Andrea Cousins), than politicians. But if few of us went from protest marching to political office, the changes that the sixties generation made in public attitudes nevertheless became a factor that all politicians had to take seriously, including Ronald Reagan, who spent most of his presidency trying to reverse the legacy of the sixties.

There are such strong feelings of nostalgia on the one hand and loss on the other among so many who went through those times because the sixties were about more than practical reforms. It was a decade not focused simply on specific goals, like the organization of American workers in the thirties or the issue agendas of the Populist and Socialist parties at the century's beginning. The goal of the sixties was a larger transformation. Perhaps the only parallels might have been during the times of the American Revolution and Civil War, when individuals became caught up in remaking America itself. The goal of the sixties was, in a sense, the completion of the vision of the early revolutionaries and the abolitionists, for Tom Paine and Frederick Douglass wanted even more than the Bill of Rights or Emancipation Proclamation. True democrats, they wanted the fulfillment of the American promise through a different quality of relations between people, between government and governed, a participatory democracy within a genuinely human community. The sixties movements were inspired toward that loftier goal and were blocked in the quest by the intervention of fate.

Like the American revolutionary period, the awakening of the early sixties was a unique ingathering of young people— many of them potential leaders—to proclaim and then try to carry out a total redemptive vision. This visionary quest is what bound each of us together in a community, from Gandhian Freedom Riders to disillusioned Marxists. The gods of our parents had failed or become idols. Then a new spiritual force came in 1960, to move in the world. We felt ourselves to be the prophets of that force. When we first used the term *revolution,* it was not about overthrowing power but about overcoming hypocrisy, through a faithfulness to a democratic and spiritual heritage. Then came rejection and both physical and spiritual martyrdom, and later a discovery that we ourselves were not pure. We faltered, lost our way, became disoriented above all by death upon death. What began on a soaring spirit suddenly was over, perhaps to be finished permanently. We who claimed to be masters of our future discovered that we were not.

The sacrifices were many, and there were no distinguished service medals. In writing this book, I found it revealing that there is nowhere a factual summary of all the suffering that people went through—shootings, beatings, firings, expulsions, arrests, not to mention psychological pain—to achieve quite elementary goals in the sixties decade. It is as if the sacrifices were not worthy of record, but should be suppressed and forgotten. With the help of Eric Dey, a UCLA graduate student, I developed a minimal estimate of our untabulated sacrifices:

- During the southern civil rights movement (1960–68), at least 28 activists were killed, and 31,000 people were arrested. There is no calculating the numbers who were beaten, fired, or expelled from schools.
- In the black civil disorders of 1965–70, 188 people were killed, at least 7,612 were injured, and another 52,920 were arrested.
- In the campus and antiwar protests of 1965–71, for which data are woefully unrecorded, at least 14 were killed, thousands were injured or expelled from colleges, and at least 26,358 were arrested.
- It therefore would be safe to estimate that in a society priding

itself on its openness, 100,000 arrests of protestors occurred in the decade of the sixties. They were prophets without honor in their time.

For all these reasons, the sixties leave a sense of troubling incompleteness and shortcoming alongside that of proud achievement. But if the time has remained difficult to capture, it is also possible that the sixties are not over. The decade itself was perhaps only the beginning of a time of vast change that is not yet fulfilled. Our generation, after all, has only lived into its middle years. Why conclude that life's most powerful moments already are behind us? If the sixties are not over, it is up to the sixties generation to continue trying to heal our wounds, find our truth, and apply our ideals with a new maturity to our nation's future.

Since 1980, however, the official mood of the nation has been contrary to a spirit of reconciliation. Rather, the tone has been one of escape from bitter realities toward an immortalizing vision of nostalgia proposed by President Reagan. There has been a strong pressure to wipe out the "Vietnam syndrome," which allegedly left us prostrate before our enemies. Thanks to greater military spending, we are told that America is "back," is "standing tall," that the "naysayers" have been vanquished. I find this stance to be an armed reminder of the most rigid view of my parents' generation when they wanted to impose the lessons of their experience on their children and grandchildren. But my personal experience gives me faith that this official obsession with restoring a mythic past will give way to wiser consciousness in the era ahead:

- An emerging generation of voters—about eighty million born since 1945—will seek newer philosophies than those which led to constant government scandal these past two decades.
- Those who experienced the inner reality of Vietnam—from the end of police clubs or in jungle darkness—will unite around a more mature foreign policy, based on the strength of democracy.
- Americans will increasingly look to human merits, rather than color, class, or gender, in choosing those who represent them, even for the presidency.
- The quality of life will replace the quantity of possessions as American's standard of excellence in our lifetime.

- A new generation of entrepreneurs will come to learn that human and natural resources require cultivation rather than depletion.
- Democracy and human rights will grow more powerfully contagious in a world linked by satellites and television.
- The assassinations of the sixties left a bleeding and broken connection in our personal lives and political culture; that connection must and will be restored by a new cycle of leadership.

Times filled with tragedy are also times of greatness and wonder, times that really matter, and times truly worth living through. Whatever the future holds, and as satisfying as my life is today, I miss the sixties and always will.

Notes

Most of this book is autobiographical. There are statements throughout that are attributed to many individuals without citations. I have reconstructed these comments and dialogues from memory and notes. In many cases I called the individuals to corroborate who said what to whom. I am confident that I have captured the essential spirit, and nearly the letter, of what was said. Wherever such statements occur in the text without footnoting, I take full responsibility for their accuracy.

INTRODUCTION

p. xix   *And yet, tragedy . . . :* Rollo May, Carl Rogers, Abraham Maslow, *Politics and Innocence* (Dallas: Saybrook Publishers, 1968), p. 3.

I. "STAND BY ME"

p. 9   *Since this obvious . . . :* John Cooney, *The American Pope: The Life and Times of Cardinal Spellman* (New York: Times Books, 1984), pp. 19, 66; see also: Alan Brinkley, *Voices of Protest: Huey Long, Father Coughlin and the Great Depression* (New York: Vintage Books, 1983).

p. 11   *LEFTY GETS MIDGETS . . . : Royal Oak Tribune,* June 21, 1953.

p. 13   *These two boys . . . : Royal Oak Tribune,* October 24, 1956.

p. 17   *For Holden, school is . . . :* J. D. Salinger, *The Catcher in the Rye* (New York: Bantam Books, 1951), p. 88.

p. 19   *They were "nothing . . .":* Ann Charters, *Kerouac: A Biography* (New York: St. Martin's Press, 1987), p. 294.

2. THE CONVERSION

p. 26   *At the same time . . . :* Kirkpatrick Sale, *SDS* (New York, Random House, 1973), p. 20.

p. 26   *Setting a tone . . . :* Alexander Astin, *Achieving Academic Excellence* (San Francisco: Jossey Bass, 1986).

p. 26   *The shift was noted . . . :* Clark Kerr, *The Uses of the University* (Cambridge: Harvard University Press, 1963).

p. 26   *But he also saw . . . :* Landon Jones, *Great Expectations* (New York: Ballantine Books, 1980), p. 98.

p. 26   *Educational historian . . . :* Frederick Rudolph, *The American College and University: A History* (New York: Knopf, 1962), p. 450.

p. 39   *"A man can't cure . . .":* Albert Camus, *The Plague* (New York: Vintage Books, 1972), p. 195.

3. NEVER TURN BACK

p. 54   Voter registration data from *1961 Report to the U.S. Commission on Civil Rights* from the Mississippi State Advisory Committee, the Reverend Murray Cox, chairman. I utilized these data in *Revolution in Mississippi,* an SDS pamphlet published in December 1961 and in "Mission in McComb," published in *The Progressive,* January 1962.

p. 54   *One local movement . . . :* David J. Garrow, *Bearing the Cross* (New York: Morrow, 1986), p. 218.

p. 54   *One television commentator . . . : Ibid.,* p. 181.

p. 57   *Eventually, however . . . :* Jack Newfield, *Bread and Roses Too* (New York: Dutton, 1971), p. 196.

p. 58   *King's estimate . . . :* Stephen Oates, *Let the Trumpet Sound* (New York: Harper & Row, 1982), p. 201.

p. 59   *Another, from Mississippi . . . :* Howard Zinn, *SNCC: The New Abolitionists* (Boston: Beacon Press, 1964), pp. 198–204.

p. 66   *For a radius . . . :* W.E.B. DuBois, *The Souls of Black Folk* (New York: Library of America, 1986), p. 441.

p. 67   *A Negro was beaten . . . : The Washington Post,* June 8, 1959.

p. 69   *The Albany Movement . . . :* Zinn, *op. cit.,* p. 131.

p. 71   *Albany's mayor later . . . : The New York Times,* August 13, 1962; quoted in Garrow, *op. cit.,* p. 661.

p. 72   *"The white church . . .":* Garrow, *op. cit.,* p. 218.

p. 72   *Pat Watters . . . :* Pat Watters, *Down to Now: Reflections on the Southern Civil Rights Movement* (New York: Random House, 1971), p. 158.

4. PORT HURON

p. 74   *In the phrase of . . . :* Doris Lessing, *The Golden Notebook* (New York: Simon & Schuster, 1962), p. 189.

p. 76   *"Judging whether life . . .":* Albert Camus, *The Myth of Sisyphus* (New York: Knopf, 1950), p. 131.

p. 76   *"All I maintain . . .":* Albert Camus, *The Plague* (New York: Vintage Books, 1971), p. 238.

p. 76   *He wrote that . . . : Ibid.,* p. 120.

p. 77   *"I rebel—therefore . . .":* Albert Camus, *The Rebel* (New York: Vintage Books, 1956), p. 22.

p. 77   *If Auschwitz . . . :* Kenneth Kenniston, *Young Radicals* (New York: Vintage Books, 1960), p. 250.

p. 77   *"A single sentence . . .":* Albert Camus, *The Fall* (New York: Vintage, 1963), p. 6.

p. 77   *I understand why . . . :* Camus, *The Myth of Sisyphus, op. cit.,* p. 41.

p. 79   *Mills feared the emergence . . . :* C. Wright Mills, *The Sociological Imagination* (New York: Oxford, 1959), p. 171.

p. 80   *"Between the little man's . . . " :* C. Wright Mills, *White Collar* (New York: Oxford, 1951), p. xviii.

p. 81   *My fascination continued . . . :* Tom Hayden, *Radical Nomad: Essays on C. Wright Mills and His Times* (University of Michigan: Center for Research on Conflict Resolution, 1964).

p. 90   *In an insightful comment . . . :* James Miller, *Democracy Is in the Streets* (New York: Simon & Schuster, 1986), p. 114.

p. 91   *He went through an identity . . . :* Michael Harrington, *Fragment of the Century: A Social Autobiography* (New York: Saturday Review Press, 1973), p. 183.

p. 94   *Plato once wrote . . . :* Miller, *op. cit.,* p. 114.

p. 95   *"Man's capacity for justice . . .":* Richard Fix, *Reinhold*

Niebuhr: A Biography (New York: Harper & Row, 1985), pp. 219–20, 230.

p. 95   *Human greatness . . . :* Albert Camus, *Resistance, Rebellion and Death* (New York: Vintage Books, 1960), p. 39.

5. TRIUMPHS. TRANSITIONS. TRAGEDIES.

p. 106   *"None of you [men] . . .":* Doris Lessing, *The Golden Notebook* (New York: Simon & Schuster, 1962), p. 657.

p. 107   *At the time we were . . . :* Kirkpatrick Sale, *SDS* (New York: Random House, 1973), p. 18.

p. 108   *Like Camus's alienated . . . :* Albert Camus, *The Fall* (New York: Vintage, 1963), pp. 98–100.

p. 110   *We "practised love . . .":* Bertolt Brecht, *Poems, 1913–56* (London: Methuen, 1987), p. 319.

p. 111   *In June 1963 . . . :* David Halberstam, *The Best and the Brightest* (New York: Random House, 1969).

p. 111   *"If we cannot end our . . .":* Anthony Summers, *Conspiracy* (New York: McGraw Hill, 1980), pp. 344–45.

p. 112   *Over the next two months . . . :* Charles and Barbara Whalen, *The Longest Debate* (New York: Mentor, 1985), p. 191.

p. 112   *We face a moral crisis . . . : Ibid.,* p. xxi.

p. 113   *After the first death . . .:* Dylan Thomas, "A Refusal to Mourn the Death, by Fire, of a Child in London," *Collected Poems* (New York: New Directions, 1946).

p. 115   *Just two days after . . . :* Peter D. Scott et al., *The Assassinations: Dallas and Beyond* (New York: Vintage Books, 1976), p. 407.

p. 115   *Frederick Douglass's . . . :* Stephen Oates, *Let the Trumpet Sound* (New York: Harper & Row, 1982), p. 109.

p. 118   *This is the stuff . . . :* Mary King, *Freedom Song: A Personal Story of the 1960s Civil Rights Movement* (New York: Morrow, 1987), p. 342.

p. 119   *"It never occurred to us . . .": Ibid.,* p. 345.

6. NEWARK

p. 127   *In 1960, 32.5 percent . . . :* Ron Parambo, *No Cause for Indictment* (New York: Holt, Rinehart, 1971), pp. 5–8.

p. 149   *And so those very . . . :* William Julius Wilson, *The Truly*

Disadvantaged: *The Inner City, the Underclass, and Public Policy* (Chicago: University of Chicago Press, 1987), pp. 20–30.

7. THE FIRE NEXT TIME

p. 152 *In five days* . . . : These figures, and much of this account, are drawn from my earlier book: Tom Hayden, *Rebellion in Newark: Official Violence and Ghetto Response* (New York: Random House, 1967).

p. 152 *In May, a city* . . . : *Ibid.*, p. 8.

p. 153 *Under increasing* . . . : *Ibid.*, p. 15.

p. 154 *The patrolman questioned* . . . : Testimony of Captain Charles Kinney, Newark Police Department, Hearings, Committee on Un-American Activities, House of Representatives, Ninetieth Congress, April 23–24, 1968, p. 1853.

p. 154 *By the end of the weekend* . . . : Hayden, *Rebellion in Newark, op. cit.*, p. 37.

p. 155 *For instance* . . . : Accounts of these killings appear in my *Rebellion in Newark, op. cit.*, pp. 73–78; also in Ron Parambo, *No Cause for Indictment* (New York: Holt, Rinehart, 1971), pp. 131–32, 201, 248.

p. 155 *Though* Life *magazine* . . . : Parambo, *op. cit.*, p. 131.

p. 156 *Governor Hughes declared* . . . : *Newark Evening News,* July 15, 1967.

p. 156 *Perhaps carried away* . . . : Parambo, *op. cit.*, p. 122.

p. 160 *Zazzoli testified* . . . : *Ibid.*, pp. 131–32.

p. 160 *At the same Senate* . . . : Hearings, Committee on Un-American Activities, *op. cit.*, p. 1853–58.

p. 160 *A week later* . . . : Parambo, *op. cit.*, p. 248.

p. 160 *But a state fact-finding* . . . : *Ibid.*

p. 160 *You recommended* . . . : Richard Hughes/Tom Hayden personal correspondence, 1982.

p. 163 *I have hope for* . . . : *Thoughts of the Young Radicals* (New York: Harrison-Blaine, 1966), p. 34.

p. 164 *At the level* . . . : Frantz Fanon, *The Wretched of the Earth* (New York: Grove Press, 1963), p. 94.

p. 164 *"We are living at* . . . *": Ibid.*, p. 20.

p. 165 *The "irrepressible violence* . . . *": Ibid.*, p. 21.

p. 165 *Sartre condemned sympathetic* . . . : *Ibid.*, p. 25.

p. 165   *The new man . . . : Ibid.*, p. 23.

p. 166   *In an article for . . . in the United States:* Hayden, *Rebellion in Newark, op. cit.,* pp. 70–71.

p. 167   *He had a remarkable . . . :* Jack Newfield, *Robert F. Kennedy: A Memoir* (New York, Berkeley Books, 1969), pp. 87–112.

p. 169   *It means, at this . . . : Thoughts of the Young Radicals, op. cit.,* pp. 35–42.

8. THE OTHER SIDE

p. 178   *Our segregationist foe . . . :* Kirkpatrick Sale, *SDS* (New York: Random House, 1973), p. 229.

p. 178   *Vice President Humphrey . . . :* Michael Paul Rogin: *Ronald Reagan: The Movie and Other Episodes in Political Demonology* (Berkeley: University of California Press, 1987), p. 76.

p. 178   *Senators who would . . . :* Sale, *op. cit.,* p. 231.

p. 178   *James Reston of the . . . : Ibid.*

p. 178   *Attorney General Nicholas . . . : Ibid.,* p. 230.

p. 178   *Doris Kearns . . . :* Doris Kearns, *Lyndon Johnson and the American Dream* (New York: New American Library, 1977.

p. 178   *. . . "the battle against . . .":* Barbara Tuchman, *The March to Folly: From Troy to Vietnam* (New York: Knopf, 1984), p. 293.

p. 179   *"Indochina is critical . . .":* The New York Times, October 15, 1965.

p. 180   *. . . "bullied by any . . .": Congressional Record,* March 15, 1948, vol. 94, pt. 2, p. 2883.

p. 180   *"What do you call . . .":* Andre Malraux, *Man's Fate* (New York: Random House, 1984), p. xii.

p. 184   *"The Vietnamese revolution . . .":* Tom Hayden, Staughton Lynd, *The Other Side* (New York: New American Library, 1966), p. 191.

p. 186   *"It matters little . . .":* Nguyen Du, *The Tale of Kieu* (New York: Random House, 1973).

p. 186   There were those . . . : Nguyen Du, "Funeral Oratories to Ten Kinds of Souls," trans. by Le Hieu, *Vietnamese Studies,* Hanoi, No. 4, 1965.

p. 191   *Of Johnson's effort . . . : International Herald Tribune,* February 28, 1966.

p. 194   *"The father," the* Tribune . . . : *Royal Oak Tribune,* December 23, 1965.

9. THE WAR COMES HOME

p. 198   *In comparison the* . . . : U.S. Senate Committee on Foreign Relations, *Impact of the Vietnam War,* Congressional Research Service, Foreign Affairs Division, June 30, 1971.

p. 198   *Over one million* . . . : *Ibid.*

p. 202   *"These are not necessary* . . .": Thomas Powers, *The War at Home* (New York: Grossman, 1973), p. 31.

p. 203   *Indian tribes who turned* . . . : Derek Taylor, *It Was Twenty Years Ago Today* (New York: Simon & Schuster, 1987), p. 135.

p. 204   *The point, he argued* . . . : Powers, *op. cit.,* p. 250.

p. 207   . . . *illegitimate band* . . .": the Humphrey quote is cited in former Green Beret Donald Duncan's introduction to George Smith, *POW: Two Years with the Vietcong* (Berkeley: Ramparts Press, 1971), p. 15.

p. 215   *A total of 338,000* . . . : George Kahin: *Intervention: How America Became Involved in Vietnam* (New York: Knopf, 1986), p. 404.

p. 216   *Years later, Michael Krepon* . . . : *Ibid.,* pp. 404–5.

p. 218   *Faces all have an honest* . . . : Ho Chi Minh, *Prison Diary* (Hanoi: Foreign Languages Publishing House, 1972), p. 108.

10. PRISONERS

p. 239   *While the "politics of confrontation"* . . . : *The Pentagon Papers* (Boston: Beacon Press, 1971), Volume 4, p. 217.

p. 240   *Ferguson, portrayed in some papers* . . . : *Sacramento Union,* June 18, 1986.

p. 240   . . . *"highly decorated combat veteran":* *Los Angeles Times,* February 20, 1984.

p. 241   . . . *"he was fighting this war on television.":* Copley News Service, March 24, 1985.

11. VIETNAM RECONSIDERED

p. 243 ... "*misinterpreted the egalitarian* ...": *The New Republic*, August 10–17, 1987, p. 34.

p. 244 ... "*raggedy-ass, little* ...": Barbara Tuchman, *The March to Folly: From Troy to Vietnam* (New York: Knopf, 1984), p. 321.

p. 244 ... "*genius for statistics* ...": *Ibid.*, p. 285.

p. 245 The *Post's reporter* ... : *The Washington Post*, August 10, 1987.

p. 245 "*Communism is not* ...": *The New York Times*, August 20, 1987.

p. 246 *Even the Communist party leadership has acknowledged "mistakes"* ... : *Ibid.*

p. 246 ... "*widespread sentiment among* ...": *The Washington Post*, August 10, 1987.

p. 246 *The U.S. rejection* ... : William Shawcross, *Sideshow: Nixon, Kissinger and the Destruction of Cambodia* (New York: Simon & Schuster, 1987), p. 206; see also Elizabeth Becker, *When the War Was Over* (New York: Simon & Schuster, 1986) and Nayan Chanda, *Brother Enemy* (New York: Harcourt Brace Jovanovich, 1986).

p. 247 "*What future possibility* ...": Shawcross, *op. cit.*, p. 432.

p. 248 *In practice, it was like* ... : William Golding, *Lord of the Flies* (New York: Coward, 1954).

p. 248 *She described him as* ... : Becker, *op. cit.*, p. 416.

12. THE VIOLENCE OF SPRING

p. 255 ... "*creating trouble in every city* ...": David Farber, *Chicago 1968* (Chicago: University of Chicago Press, 1987, draft manuscript), p. 211.

p. 255 "*Here in Chicago* ...": *Chicago Tribune*, April 7, 1968.

p. 255 "*It is an outrage* ...": *Chicago Tribune*, April 10, 1968.

p. 255 *It was later established* ... : Frank Donner, *The Age of Surveillance* (New York: Knopf, 1980), p. 233.

p. 255 *There is a time* ... : Thomas Powers, *The War at Home* (New York: Grossman, 1973), p. 35.

p. 257 ... "*peak folly of an older generation.*": Michael Maclear, *The Ten Thousand Day War* (New York: St. Martin's, 1981), p. 199.

p. 258 *And unknown to us . . . :* Kirkpatrick Sale, *SDS* (New York: Random House, 1973), p. 406.

p. 259 *"To respect . . . radical organization.":* Ibid., p. 393.

p. 259 *To save the worsening . . . :* David J. Garrow, *Bearing the Cross* (New York: Morrow, 1986), p. 592.

p. 260 *On a personal level . . . :* Ibid., p. 612.

p. 260 *. . . "international emergency . . .":* Stephen B. Oates, *Let the Trumpet Sound* (New York: Harper & Row, 1982), p. 452.

p. 260 *. . . "moving towards two societies . . .":* Report of the National Advisory Commission on Civil Disorders (New York: Bantam, 1968), p. 1.

p. 261 *Before Tet . . . :* Maclear, *op. cit.,* p. 236.

p. 262 *A widely quoted* Ramparts . . . : Arthur Schlesinger, *Robert Kennedy and His Times* (New York: Ballantine, 1978), p. 865.

p. 263 *A feature writer . . . :* This FBI memo appeared in a 1973 article in the *Philadelphia Inquirer* by Aaron Epstein. The original article and memo have been destroyed. I confirmed the memo's existence in a phone call with Epstein in 1987.

p. 264 *In a 1967 book . . . :* Robert Kennedy, *To Seek a Newer World* (Garden City: Doubleday, 1967).

p. 264 *. . . "juvenile delinquent . . . Americans.":* Jack Newfield, *Robert F. Kennedy: A Memoir* (New York: Berkeley Medallion, 1969), pp. 5, 59–60.

p. 266 *"It emancipated Kennedy . . .":* Ibid. p. 147.

p. 267 *Hamill went to the . . . revolver.:* Ibid., pp. 224–25.

p. 268 *"We were weighing . . .":* Geoffrey Hodgson, *Foreign Policy,* 109, Spring 1973, pp. 3–40.

p. 268 *Forget about seeking . . . :* The Pentagon Papers (Boston: Beacon Press, 1971), Volume 4, p. 593.

p. 269 *There were outbreaks of . . . :* Oates, *op. cit.,* p. 494.

p. 272 *Kirk himself compared . . . :* Report of the Fact-Finding Commission Appointed to Investigate the Disturbances at Columbia University in April–May 1968 (New York: Random House, 1968), pp. 33–35; also see Jerry Avorn and the *Columbia Spectator* staff, *Up Against the Ivy Wall: A History of the Columbia Crisis* (New York: Atheneum, 1968), p. 119.

p. 272 *Student identification cards . . . :* Avorn, *op. cit.,* p. 14.

p. 273 *Under a regulation . . . :* Ibid., p. 22.

p. 273   *It enjoyed close and secretive* . . . : Avorn, *op. cit.*, p. 121.

p. 279   *"Our young people* . . .": The Kirk comment and Mark Rudd's "Up against the wall" reply are from Avorn, *op. cit.*, pp. 25–26.

p. 279   . . . *"death rattle of the historical irrelevants."*: *The New Republic*, June 1, 1968, p. 23.

p. 280   *"The line has to be drawn* . . .": Sale, *op. cit.*, p. 442.

p. 281   *A later police memorandum* . . . : Avorn, *op. cit.*, p. 146.

p. 282   *19 percent of all* . . . : Sale, *op. cit.*, p. 713.

p. 282   *Between 1967 and 1969* . . . : *Campus Life*, p. 233.

p. 285   . . . *"there will be no* . . .": Newfield, *op. cit.*, p. 303.

13. THE STREETS OF CHICAGO

p. 291   . . . *"an all-out offensive* . . .": *The New York Times*, May 25, 1968.

p. 291   *In July, the number* . . . : *The New York Times*, July 13, 1968.

p. 293   *"He wanted them to fête* . . .": Doris Kearns, conversation with the author.

p. 293   *Of the 7.5 million* . . . : *The New York Times*, September 15, 1968.

p. 294   . . . *"optimistic* . . . *city."*: David Farber, *Chicago 1968* (Chicago: University of Chicago Press, 1987, draft manuscript), p. 233.

p. 294   *"Our idea* . . . *taken care of?"*: *Ibid.*, p. 141.

p. 294   *The President and Vice President* . . . : *Ibid.*, p. 238.

p. 296   *On August 7* . . . : Athan Theoharis, *Spying on Americans* (Philadelphia: Temple University Press, 1978), pp. 182–83.

p. 297   *Camus had warned* . . . : Albert Camus, *The Rebel* (New York: Vintage Books, 1956), pp. 17–19.

p. 299   *In their camp* . . . : James Miller, *Democracy Is in Their Streets: From Port Huron to the Streets of Chicago* (New York: Simon & Schuster, 1987), p. 297.

p. 303   *"He called me at the convention* . . .": Doris Kearns, conversation with the author, 1987.

p. 307   *"Almost every noise* . . .": Jack Newfield, *Bread and Roses Too: Reporting About America* (New York: Dutton, 1971), p. 108.

p. 312   *On national television* . . . : *Rights in Conflict: Official Report of the National Commission on the Causes and Prevention of Violence (The Walker Report)* (New York: New American Library, 1968), p. 27.

p. 320 *The candidate's wife . . . :* Abigail McCarthy, *Private Faces, Public Places* (New York: Doubleday, 1972), p. 429.

p. 320 . . . *"with George McGovern . . .":* Nancy Zaroulis, Gerald Sullivan, *Who Spoke Up?: American Protest Against the War in Vietnam, 1963–75* (New York: Doubleday, 1984), p. 196.

p. 321 FBI MEMORANDUM . . . : Frank Donner, *The Age of Surveillance* (New York: Knopf, 1980), p. 234.

p. 321 *The National Commission . . . : Rights in Conflict, op. cit.,* pp. 314–320.

p. 323 *As Theodore White's . . . :* Theodore White, *The Making of the President 1968* (New York: Atheneum, 1968), pp. 356, 383.

p. 325 *"Who can say . . .":* Steve Smith, conversation with the author, 1987.

p. 325 *"Love of power . . .":* Thucydides, *A History of the Peloponnesian War* (New York: Penguin, 1954), p. 243.

p. 326 *Edith Hamilton described . . . :* Edith Hamilton, *The Greek Way* (New York: Norton, 1930), p. 140.

p. 326 *"The stone was at the bottom . . . ":* Jack Newfield, *Robert F. Kennedy: A Memoir* (New York: Berkeley Medallion, 1969), p. 337.

14. THE INDICTMENT BEGINS

p. 328 *"Preservation of free speech . . .": The Sacramento Bee,* October 1, 1970.

p. 328 *According to a later review . . . : Ibid.*

p. 330 *Reagan declared "a state . . .": The New York Times,* February 6, 1969.

p. 330 *As the demonstrations . . . : Ibid.,* February 21, 1969.

p. 330 . . . *"at the point of bayonet . . .": The Sacramento Bee,* January 10, 1969.

p. 330 *One regent . . . : The New York Times,* February 22, 1969.

p. 330 *Later that month . . . : Ibid.,* February 27, 1969.

p. 331 *"There is substantial reason . . .": The Berkeley Tribe,* August 22–29, 1969.

p. 332 *Captain Charles Plummer . . . :* Plummer's speech was described to me by a Berkeley officer who later resigned from the force.

p. 332 *According to the press . . . : The New York Times,* May 20, 1969.

p. 333 *About 150 demonstrators . . . :* These figures are approximate. *The New York Times* reported that some seventy young people were treated in hospitals for gunshot wounds. Tim Findlay, an on-site reporter for the *San Francisco Chronicle* with whom I spoke, remembers large numbers of students literally picking the birdshot out of their skin. Many were unwilling to go to hospitals for fear of arrest or expulsion.

p. 333   ... *"curious about what was going on ..."*: Steve Carr, interview with the author, 1987.

p. 334   ... *"experimental laboratory..."*: *The New York Times*, May 16, 1969.

p. 334   ... *"not safe for human beings."*: Ibid., May 16, 1969.

p. 334   ... *"perfectly logical."*: Ibid.

p. 335   *In March, a right-wing* ... : Donner, *The Age of Surveillance* (New York: Vintage Books, 1981), pp. 427–30.

15. THE TRIAL

All quotations from the Chicago trial cited in these chapters are based on the actual transcripts, as published in edited form in Judy Clavir and John Spitzer, *The Conspiracy Trial* (New York: Bobbs-Merrill, 1970). The original transcripts were twenty-two thousand pages long.

p. 341   *(Years after the trial ...)*: *American Bar Association Journal*, May 15, 1987, p. 33.

p. 341   *"I would get absorbed in it ..."*: Thomas Foran and Richard Schultz, interviews with the author, 1987.

p. 345   *Lyndon Johnson has been cited* ... : See particularly Doris Kearns, *Lyndon Johnson and the American Dream* (New York: New American Library, 1977. Doris Kearns confirmed Johnson's paranoia in an interview with the author, 1987.

p. 346   ... *"ideological criminals"* ...: Tom Hayden, *Trial* (New York: Holt, Rinehart, 1970), p. 22. The full statement by Kleindienst was "If people demonstrate in a manner to interfere with others, they should be rounded up and put in a detention camp."

p. 346   *"We are going to take this country ..."*: *The Washington Post*, July 10, 1973.

p. 350   *"If you don't convince ..."*: Michael Tigar told me that Foran made this statement to him. Foran denied it to a Chicago reporter.

p. 355   *American combat deaths . . . :* Michael Maclear, *The Ten Thousand Day War* (New York: St. Martin's, 1981), p. 253.

p. 355   *In those raids alone . . . : Ibid.,* p. 285.

p. 355   *Labeled* Operation Duck Hook . . . : Nancy Zaroulis, Gerald Sullivan, *Who Spoke Up?: American Protest Against the War in Vietnam, 1963–75* (New York: Doubleday, 1984), p. 259.

p. 356   *"I sent them a good boy . . ."*: *The New York Times,* November 30, 1969.

p. 356   *Massive jailings . . . :* Maclear, *op. cit.,* pp. 260–62.

p. 356   *Starting in 1969 . . . : Ibid.,* p. 280.

p. 356   *In the same year . . . : Ibid.;* see also Zaroulis, Sullivan, *op. cit.,* p. 386.

p. 356   *The U.S. Navy . . . :* Zaroulis, Sullivan, *op. cit.,* p. 367.

p. 356   *Marijuana use . . . :* Maclear, *op. cit.,* pp. 280–81.

p. 356   *In the end . . . : Ibid.,* p. 281.

p. 364   *Being acted out . . . :* Eldridge Cleaver, *Soul on Ice* (San Francisco: Ramparts, 1969), p. 138.

16. THE VERDICT

p. 380   . . . *"good judgment . . ."*: Roger Wilkins, Ramsey Clark, *Search and Destroy* (New York: Metropolitan Applied Research Center, 1973), p. 38.

p. 381   . . . *"just gathering dust."*: *The New York Times.*

p. 393   . . . *"the ultimate outrage . . ."*: *Ibid.,* February 1, 1970.

17. AT DECADE'S END

p. 415   . . . *death immersion* . . . : Jack Newfield, *Robert F. Kennedy: A Memoir* (New York: Berkeley Books, 1969), p. 20.

p. 417   *During those few weeks . . . : Report of the Presidential Commission on Campus Unrest* (New York: Avon, 1971), pp. 47–49.

p. 417   *the students "did not . . ."*: Nancy Zaroulis, Gerald Sullivan, *Who Spoke Up?: American Protest Against the War in Vietnam, 1963–75* (New York: Doubleday, 1984), p. 339.

p. 418   *Henry Kissinger once described . . . : Ibid.,* p. 329.

p. 439   *"By shallow-flooding . . ."*: *The Pentagon Papers (Gravel Edition)* (Boston: Beacon Press, 1971), Vol. IV, p. 43.

p. 439   *By August . . . :* Zaroulis, Sullivan, *op. cit.,* p. 369.

18. JANE

p. 443   ... the "invalidation of all ...": Simone de Beauvoir, *The Second Sex* (New York: Knopf, 1953), p. 219.

p. 444   *On July 23, 1970 ...* : *Newsweek*, June 4, 1973.

p. 445   *According to later Watergate ...* : *The New York Times*, June 14, 1973; see also Bill Ritter, Doug Porter, "Watergate: The San Diego Connection," *The Door*, June 1973.

p. 445   ... "forced out by the threat ...": Jeb Magruder, *An American Life: One Man's Road to Watergate* (New York: Atheneum, 1974), p. 200.

p. 455   *Sixty-two pilots ...* : Zaroulis, Sullivan, *op. cit.*, pp. 406–7.

p. 455   ... "quit making national heroes ...": *The New York Times*, January 30, 1973.

p. 458   *I am impressed ...* : quoted in Hayden, *The Trial* (New York: Holt, Rinehart, 1970), p. 65.

p. 459   ... "can, in each instance ...": Dellinger, 370 F Supp 1304, 1321, (N) (D), III, 1973.

p. 470   ... "significant surge ...": *Los Angeles Times*, May 18, 1976.

p. 471   *SENATE PRIMARIES ...* : *Los Angeles Times*, June 4, 1976, p. 1.

20. EPILOGUE

p. 502   *More broadly, the survey ...* : Daniel Yankelovich, *New Rules* (New York: Random House, 1981), pp. 46, 175.

p. 503   *The authors of ...* : Robert Bellah et al., *Habits of the Heart* (Berkeley: University of California Press, 1985), p. 295.

p. 505   *With the help of Eric Dey ...* : see A. Meier, E. Rudwick, *CORE: A Study in the Civil Rights Movement 1942–1968* (New York, Oxford, 1973); *Report of the Presidential Commission on Campus Unrest* (New York: Avon, 1971); U.S. Senate Government Operations Committee, *Staff Study of Major Riots and Civil Disorders—1965 Through July 31, 1968* (Washington: Government Printing Office, October 1968); *Staff Study of Campus Riots and Disorders, October 1967, October 1968, May 1969* (Washington: Government Printing Office, 1969); Howard Zinn, *SNCC: The New Abolitionists* (Boston: Beacon Press, 1964).

Index